W9-CBM-544

Financial Markets and Incomplete Information

Rowman & Littlefield Studies in Financial Economics
Jonathan E. Ingersoll, Jr., General Editor

Theory of Financial Decision Making
  Jonathan E. Ingersoll, Jr.

Theory of Valuation: Frontiers of Modern Financial Theory
  Edited by Sudipto Bhattacharya and George M. Constantinides

Financial Markets and Incomplete Information

Frontiers of Modern Financial Theory

edited by

Sudipto Bhattacharya

and

George M. Constantinides

Rowman & Littlefield Publishers, Inc.

ROWMAN & LITTLEFIELD PUBLISHERS, INC.

Published in the United States of America
by Rowman & Littlefield Publishers, Inc.
8705 Bollman Place, Savage, Maryland 20763

Copyright © 1989 by Rowman & Littlefield Publishers, Inc.

All rights reserved. No part of this publication may
be reproduced, stored in a retrieval system, or transmitted
in any form or by any means, electronic, mechanical,
photocopying, recording, or otherwise, without the prior
permission of the publisher.

Library of Congress Cataloging-in-Publication Data

Financial markets and incomplete information: frontiers of modern
   financial theory/edited by Sudipto Bhattacharya and George M. Constantinides.
(Rowman & Littlefield studies in financial economics)
   Includes Index.
ISBN 0–8476–7597–1
ISBN 0–8476–7598–X
   1. Finance.· I. Bhattacharya, Sudipto. II. Constantinides, George M.
   III. Series.
HG174.F523 1988   87–32124
332—dc19   CIP

Printed in the United States of America

to

Usha Bhattacharya and K.K. Anaskevic

Maria, Michalis, Stylianos, Olvia and Mikis

Contents

Acknowledgments

Major credit for the potential success of the two volumes is due to the contributors of original essays published in these volumes and to the authors and journal publishers who have given us permission to reprint earlier published articles. Several professional colleagues, particularly the series editor, Jonathan Ingersoll, have given us invaluable advice throughout this project. The staff of Rowman & Littlefield has provided the expert advice and has shown the patience that has made this project possible. Myrtle Sims and Stella Padmore have provided expert secretarial assistance. The first editor acknowledges financial and secretarial support from the Berkeley program in finance, the School of Business at Michigan University, and Bell Communications Research. The second editor acknowledges the financial support of his home institution, the Graduate School of Business, University of Chicago, and of the Marvin Bower fellowship program at the Harvard Business School.

Preface

The contemporary theory of financial economics is the beneficiary of major developments over the last 35 years in valuation theory and information economics. Developments in valuation theory over this period include the general equilibrium theory of Arrow and Debreu; the portfolio selection theory of Markowitz and the equilibrium valuation theory of Sharpe and Lintner; the no-arbitrage valuation theory of Modigliani and Miller and its application in corporate finance; the intertemporal no-arbitrage valuation theory of Black and Scholes; the intertemporal valuation theory of Merton; and the asymptotic no-arbitrage theory of Ross. Developments in information economics pertaining to the theory of finance include the role of prices in aggregating and communicating information; the signaling of asymmetrically known attributes through quantity-dependent, nonlinear prices; the revelation of information through contingent contracting; and the analysis of strategic coordination across multiple informed agents.

We have collected some important papers published from 1973 to 1986 and original essays contributed by eminent researchers with the goal of presenting a summary statement of recent research progress in theoretical financial economics to both specialist and nonspecialist financial economists. The second goal, and perhaps the most ambitious one, is to forecast, through the distillation of the opinions of these researchers, trends in the theory of financial economics. The third goal is to provide ready material for one Ph.D.-level course in financial economics or for a sequence of two courses covering valuation theory and information economics. Segments of these volumes may also be used for elective M.B.A., M.S., and advanced undergraduate courses.

In order to present a coherent picture within the confines of two volumes we focus exclusively on theoretical issues. Thus major strides in empirical research are, at best, noted in passing. A complementary book covering the empirical side is clearly warranted.

In selecting the eighteen articles reprinted in these volumes, we have applied the criteria of originality, coherence, comprehensiveness, and pedagogical clarity. This means that occasionally the earliest important, or landmark, article in an area has not been chosen. Furthermore, the task of spanning the entire field of theoretical finance with eighteen articles has proved awesome. In narrowing down the selection to the eighteen articles, we have been forced to make some arbitrary choices, and we offer our sincere apologies to authors whose worthy articles are not reprinted in these volumes.

An innovation of these volumes is the inclusion of original essays in addition to the reprinted articles. These essays provide comprehensive reviews of important topics in finance, update and extend the contribution of the reprinted articles, and offer directions for future research. Furthermore each of us has provided a detailed overview, one addressing the first volume on valuation theory and the other addressing the second volume on the application of information economics in finance.

We hope that the contributions collected in these volumes communicate the excitement of the field of financial economics to beginners and specialists alike and stimulate further research.

1 | Financial Markets and Incomplete Information: A Review of Some Recent Developments

Sudipto Bhattacharya

University of Michigan

I. INTRODUCTION

For more than a decade, there has been a great deal of research effort devoted to understanding the impact of incomplete information on the structure and functioning of financial markets and firms, whose role can be viewed as providing a "nexus of contracts" among users and providers of funds in intertemporal settings. The seminal papers in this literature, which overlapped in origination with the general development of information economics, include that of Rothschild and Stiglitz (1976) on insurance markets with asymmetric information about insurance risks and the work of Green (1973) on the aggregation and transmission of diverse information through prices in competitive financial (stock) markets. An important and early paper which suggested further developments along these lines was that of Stiglitz (1974).

The work of Rothschild and Stiglitz, as well as that of C. Wilson (1978), extended and drew its inspiration from the earlier work of Arrow (1973), Spence (1974), and Stiglitz (1975) on signaling and screening of asymmetrically known *mutually* payoff-relevant personalized attributes through non-linear pricing schedules linked to observable quantities. Green's work, on the other hand, extended the insights of Radner (1967) and Lucas (1972) on the role of prices in revealing information and modifying beliefs of agents, to incorporate heterogeneous information about commonly traded (not personalized) commodities. These models of Rational Expectations equilibrium extended purely competitive Walrasian (linear) price-taking analysis in a "natural" way.[1] Such an extension served to cement the links between the early partial equilibrium analysis of Hirshleifer (1971) and the rapidly evolving methodology of information economics (see P. Diamond and Rothschild 1978)

Papers referenced with an (*) are included in this or the companion volume. I thank Franklin Allen, Marshall Blume, George Constantinides, Douglas Diamond, and Joseph Stiglitz for discussions and comments. I assume responsibility for errors and omissions.

for a sample) and related ideas in decision and game theory (e.g., Harsanyi 1968).

Following these seminal analyses, many significant contributions were made that served to enrich our understanding of (a) specific financial markets (or the lack thereof), (b) corporate financial policies, and (c) the role of financial intermediation. In the process the rationale (if any) for governmental regulation of such entities was also elaborated on to some degree. Early contributions in category (a), using the rational expectations equilibrium concept, were made by Kihlstrom and Mirman (1975), Danthine (1978), Grossman (1976, 1977), and Grossman and Stiglitz (1980*), which enriched our understanding of classical issues such as hedging and speculation in futures markets, and the role of costly information in determining the degree of completeness and *"informational efficiency"* of financial markets.[2,3] The discussions by Admati and Kyle in this volume relate to developments along these lines.

Analyses and rationalization of observed corporate financial decisions on *capital structure and dividend policies* were developed by Ross (1977), Bhattacharya (1979*, 1980), and others, using and extending the signaling models pioneered by Arrow, Spence, and Stiglitz. The discussion by Williams elaborates on this literature. An early model of *financial intermediation* grounded in the same methodology, which sought to analyze rationales for diversification and multistage information signaling by firms in asymmetric information environments, was developed in Leland and Pyle (1977*) and notably extended by D. Diamond (1984) and others; see Diamond's discussion in this volume.

Another, somewhat distinct, line of attack on understanding corporate financial phenomena has been grounded in the evolving theory of asymmetrically observed endogenous noncooperative actions by parties in contractual relationships. The relevant analysis of "principal-agent models" and "moral hazard" was developed by Spence and Zeckhauser (1971), Ross (1973), Mirrlees (1979), and others. All but Ross were concerned with scenarios in which only one of two (or more) parties, bound together by the need for risk sharing, is able to observe and undertake an action involving nonpecuniary (and nontransferable) utility losses. Jensen and Meckling (1976) expanded the applications of these ideas and the resulting "agency costs" of second-best outcomes to the problems of conflicts of interest between insiders/managers and outside shareholders in firms. Myers (1977) considered related applications to shareholders' incentives for incremental investment with new equity issues or retention of earnings, given the postcontracting partial loss of cashflow benefits to creditors. The discussion by Kim elaborates and extends these themes. Analogous observations on some of these issues and trade-offs were also made by Fama and Miller (1972), Stiglitz (1974), and Grossman and Hart (1982). Tax trade-offs involved in the choice of capital structure are the focus of Miller (1977*) and the discussion by Scholes and Wolfson in this volume.

The work of Ross (1973) on principal-agent models, which drew on the pioneering analysis of R. Wilson (1968), considered a scenario in which nonpecuniary disutility of "effort" (or investment cost) is *not* inherent to the principal-agent conflict. Instead, although all payoffs are pecuniary and transferable, agreement on optimal actions is potentially impeded by the nature of the sharing rules required for optimal risk sharing. These works, as well as R. Wilson (1979), which considers private information regarding payoffs to actions as well, showed that optimal *linear* sharing rules result in unanimity regarding the first-best Pareto-efficient action. These results are related to those on the (constrained) *optimality of investment choices* in incomplete markets when optimal (feasible) sharing rules are linear. Conditions for optimality of such markets were developed by P. Diamond (1967), Hart (1977*), and Stiglitz (1982).[4] The discussion by Stiglitz in the companion volume deals with this literature, partly in the context of models of *mutual fund separation*—that is, preference or distributional assumptions that imply that optimal choices of agents' payoffs lie in a (lower-dimensional) subspace of the complete state-space.

The Ross-Wilson analysis of agency theory, discussed above, entailed the crucial assumption of no precontracting heterogeneity among agents that is mutually payoff relevant. When that assumption is relaxed and some agents have to be induced to reveal precontracting private information as well as undertake (jointly) optimal actions, a new set of issues is introduced. In recent work (e.g., Bhattacharya and Pfleiderer 1985*, Allen 1985, and Allen's discussion in this volume), such scenarios have been explored in the context of principal-agent and market *contracts for information producers* (regarding stock returns, for example). The resulting analyses, as well as related multiperiod work on management performance evaluation, promise to extend our understanding of contractual provisions and labor market reactions, and their roles in jointly giving rise to greater allocational and informational efficiency.

The literature on information economics in the late seventies and eighties has generally evolved to greater emphasis on game-theoretic methods (e.g., the analysis of interactions among multiple informed players, coordination problems across multiple Nash equilibria). Extensive literatures on "nonmarket" allocation procedures such as auctions (e.g., Myerson 1981) are examples of such progress. In an interesting application to corporate finance, Rock (1986*) has used the methodology of auction theory to analyze the *pricing of new equity issues*, given a precommitted upper bound on prices and some investors asymmetrically better informed than the issuing firms. The resulting model rationalizes a longstanding empirical anomaly regarding the "underpricing" of new equity issues (on average) in United States capital markets. Raviv's discussion elaborates on this set of issues further. The discussion by Kyle deals with other models of information revelation with asynchronous "real-time" trading.

In yet another set of applications of such explicitly game-theoretic analysis, Bryant (1980) and D. Diamond and Dybvig (1983*) have pioneered in analyzing coordination problems among depositors of banking intermediaries who are given nontraded contractual rights to payoffs at different time points.

The resulting analyses of *bank runs* and the role of government deposit insurance have been recently extended by several authors to scenarios involving additional private information about banks' asset qualities. A fully rigorous justification of the optimality of *nontraded deposit contracts* in environments with agents subject to intertemporal preference shocks was given by Jacklin (1987). The *regulatory implications* of these environments (e.g., reserve requirements and central bank rediscounting) were developed in Bhattacharya and Gale (1987). The discussion by Jacklin synthesizes this literature and also develops its connections with recent work on the macroeconomic implications of the behavior of financial intermediaries (e.g., credit rationing), surveyed by Weiss in this volume.

Strategic analysis with a "dominant player" has also been applied to the classic problem of *intertemporal speculation* in financial markets with multiperiod horizons and incompleteness. An early analysis with macroeconomic policy implications was contained in the pioneering study of Salant and Henderson (1978*). Other recent work, discussed here by Tirole, has analyzed conditions for lack of benefits to speculative strategies based on private information, the possibility of multiple intertemporal equilibrium dynamics and speculative "bubbles," the "stability" of speculative prices, and so on. All of this work has served to advance the integration of the work on static models of rational expectations equilibria with the classic issues posed in Samuelson (1958, 1972) and Grunberg and Modigliani (1954).

Much recent work on incomplete information models has also been directed at corporate financial phenomena that lie at the interface with the theory of industrial organization. A prime example is the developing literature on *corporate takeovers*, which received early attention in Stiglitz (1972), Hart (1977*), and Grossman and Hart (1980), which analyzed some implications of strategic behavior on the part of decentralized shareholders. More recently, there has been a veritable explosion of work analyzing the implications of models of (sequential) auctions with (possibly) multiple bidders for privately optimal behavior in takeover scenarios. Tentative analyses of regulatory provisions and restrictions have also taken place. Spatt surveys many of these recent developments, whereas Hart's paper provides a bridge with earlier work on the implementation of optimal investment decisions and the allocational role of takeover bids in that context.

Our goal in selecting papers for this volume was to highlight some of the most prominent and promising areas for applying information economics models to finance. The papers by Hart, Grossman and Stiglitz, Bhattacharya and Pfleiderer, Rock, Bhattacharya, Leland and Pyle, D. Diamond and Dybvig, and Salant and Henderson provide a wide-ranging "map" of such applications. Discussions of related topics by Kim, Spatt, Admati, Kyle, Allen, Raviv, Williams, D. Diamond, Jacklin, Weiss, and Tirole highlight alternative approaches to some of these problems and suggest promising lines of inquiry for further research. I shall not attempt to summarize further their excellent and helpful commentary.

Instead I would like to offer (with the help of unabashed borrowing from others) some thoughts on a couple of issues and areas of application that for reasons of space, choice criteria,[5] or "inadequate" progress to date have not been encompassed by the papers and discussions in this book. I would like to concentrate on the following two topics and provide brief glimpses of research progress and remaining issues: (a) *shareholder-bondholder conflicts* and their resolutions; (b) *disclosure regulation* in (financial) markets with asymmetric information. The first topic involves elaboration of our earlier discussion on applications of principal-agent models (of moral hazard) in a corporate finance context. The second topic encompasses the welfare economics of some of the extant models of information revelation through explicit disclosure as well as financial or managerial contracts. We compare and contrast several different genres of models of disclosure and its regulation in financial and product markets and suggest issues and directions for further research on this important topic.

II. MODELS OF SHAREHOLDER-BONDHOLDER CONFLICTS

Three major concerns have provided the cornerstones for much of the extant analyses in this area: (1) managerial incentives to consume perquisites or shirk at the expense of "outside" shareholders; (2) shareholders' incentives to underinvest or sell assets to pay dividends, given the sharing of future cash-flow benefits with (risky) debtholders; and (3) shareholder incentives to take on riskier projects than what is optimal for the firm as a whole, given the *convexification* of payoff structures produced by the "optionlike" feature of levered equity payoffs, given limited liability with respect to debt obligations. Early observations regarding these phenomena were contained in Fama and Miller (1972), Stiglitz (1974), and Jensen and Meckling (1976), and were further developed by Myers (1977) and others. Subsequent extensions, including the consideration of potential resolutions, are contained in (among others) Bhattacharya (1976), Grossman and Hart (1982), Stulz and Johnson (1985), Titman and Wessels (1985), and Smith and Warner (1979). Smith and Warner confine their focus largely to *explicit* prohibitions on the harmful distortionary behavior through the use of "bond covenant" restrictions on dividends and types of investments allowed.[6] More recent work (e.g., Brander and Lewis 1985) has begun to focus on the role of financial structure as a "commitment device" in oligopolistic product market interactions, as well as strategic issues in the resolution of claims in bankruptcy (Giammarino 1985).

The early analysis of Stiglitz (1974) and Jensen and Meckling (1976) suggested that there may be a trade-off between debt and equity in a firm's capital structure on these "agency-theoretic" grounds alone in a world without taxes or with irrelevance of taxes for valuation as in Miller (1977*). Essentially, higher levels of outside equity make for worse managerial incentives for perquisite consumption and shirking, given the lower "inside" stake in the firm, whereas higher debt levels create incentives for excessive risk taking and the attendant (opportunity) loss of net present value (NPV).

The implication of such trade-offs for optimal capital structure has been partially modeled by Grossman and Hart (1982), in which they assume that the event of bankruptcy, given risky debt, results in a process that "confiscates" managerial perquisites. Thus, a higher level of debt creates more (likelihood of) "discipline" for managers, but it also generates costs of greater undiversified shareholdings by insiders—other incentives problems created by risky debt are not considered.

The excessive risk-taking story associated with risky debt has been further analyzed by Merton (1978) and Bhattacharya (1982) in simple multiperiod models of depository intermediaries. Merton has shown that a differential between lending and borrowing rates for intermediaries reduces the shareholders' incentive to take on excessively risky projects, since they now also wish to protect future quasi rents. In Bhattacharya (1982) I have argued that, given the private equilibrium endogenization of this rate differential, *interest-rate controls* on bank liabilities are needed to bring about the Pareto optimal degree of risk taking. In a related model of credit markets with asymmetrically known differences in project risk (choices), Stiglitz and Weiss (1981) have argued that competitive market outcomes would result in (allocationally inefficient) "credit rationing" rather than market clearing through interest rates; the discussion by Weiss elaborates further on these issues.

Myers (1977) has explored in great detail the underinvestment incentives associated with risky debt in the capital structure. The essential issue here is the following. When shareholders finance a new project with issue (retention) of equity or with new debt whose claims are strictly junior (lower priority) to existing debt, then equity gains only part of the "gross present value" associated with the future cash flows from the new investment. Thus, the investment may not be undertaken even if its *net* present value to all claimants of the firm as a whole is strictly positive. Notice that asymmetric observability of the (realized) investment opportunity set by managers rules out obvious resolutions such as (a) insistence on a certain level of investment, or (b) renegotiating the contractual terms with the senior creditors so that their net gain from the new investment is sufficiently reduced to create a positive NPV for equity. Myers develops this view of investment opportunities as (suboptimally exercised) options to argue that high-growth firms should have lower debt levels, because of the greater importance of correct investment incentives, as well as higher riskiness, because of the greater "option component" to their overall firm value.

There are, however, some potential resolutions to this underinvestment problem through financial contracting. An obvious one, that of funding the new project as a separate corporate entity with a sufficiently high debt level (project financing), may not be always available (e.g., for maintenance projects in ongoing firms). A closely related, but distinct, alternative is to fund the project with *collateralized junior debt*. This is a new debt issue whose claims to cash flows from the old assets are subordinated to those of (senior) existing creditors but who have higher priority to the cash flows from the new project assets, which is an extrapolation of the terms of contracts such as leasing that is "realistic" when salvage values of assets are an important component of total value in bankrupt states.

In the remainder of this section, we follow Bhattacharya (1976) in providing sufficient conditions on cash-flow patterns under which the use of such collateralized debt *eliminates* the incentive problem with respect to investing in positive NPV projects. Note that senior creditors have little reason to prohibit the use of such debt in their loan covenants because, assuming nonnegative cash flows in all states, their stake in existing assets cannot be reduced by such debt, whereas they may still have some amelioration of their default risk from the residual cash flows of new projects, which may not otherwise be undertaken. (See Stulz and Johnson 1985 for evidence that such new debt is allowed by bond covenants, as well as for examples along explicitly option-theoretic lines.)

Let S be a finite set of states of nature, $s = 1, \ldots, S$, and let $C(s)$ and $G(s)$ be the future cash flows of the old assets and the (proposed) new project in state s, respectively. Let $P(s)$ be the state-contingent security price (valuation operator), and suppose that I is the amount of new investment required to launch the new project. Define

$$(1) \qquad\qquad C \equiv \sum_{s=1}^{S} C(s)P(s),$$

$$(2) \qquad\qquad G \equiv \sum_{s=1}^{S} G(s)P(s).$$

Now the value of the existing debt, with a single promised payment B and *absent* new investment, is

$$(3) \qquad\qquad V_0 = \sum_{S_1} BP(s) + \sum_{S_2} C(s)P(s),$$

where

$$(4) \qquad\qquad S_2 = [s|C(s) < B] \quad \text{and} \quad S_1 = [s|C(s) \geqslant B].$$

With the new project financed by collateralized junior debt with promised payment R, the value of senior debt would be

$$(5) \qquad V_1 = \sum_{S_1} BP(s) + \sum_{S_3} BP(s) + \sum_{S_4} [C(s) + G(s) - R]P(s)$$
$$+ \sum_{S_5} C(s)P(s),$$

where

$$(6a) \qquad\qquad S_3 = [s|s \in S_2 \text{ and } G(s) - R \geqslant B - C(s)],$$

$$(6b) \qquad\qquad S_4 = [s|s \in S_2 \text{ and } B - C(s) > G(s) - R > 0],$$

$$(6c) \qquad\qquad S_5 = [s|s \in S_2 \text{ and } G(s) - R \leqslant 0].$$

Clearly, $S_2 = S_3 \cup S_4 \cup S_5$.

Now, R itself must be sufficient to compensate junior debtholders for their financing of the investment I in the new project; that is,

(7)
$$I = V_j = \sum_{S_1} \min[R, \{C(s) + G(s) - B\}] P(s)$$
$$+ \sum_{S_3 \cup S_4} RP(s) + \sum_{S_5} G(s) P(s).$$

If $G - I \geqslant 0$, then the existence of an R satisfying (7) is obvious. We have the following result, proved in Bhattacharya (1976), detailing conditions under which equity obtains positive NPV from any project having positive NPV in the aggregate (i.e., with $G - I \geqslant 0$). Equivalently, we need to have $V_1 - V_0 \leqslant G - I$ while equations (3), (5), and (7) are satisfied.

Proposition: If for any $\{s_i, s_j\}, i \neq j$, $C(s_i) > C(s_j)$ implies $G(s_i) \geqslant G(s_j)$, then $V_1 - V_0 \leqslant G - I$.

Proof: Either $S_3 \cup S_4$ is empty, in which case $V_1 - V_0 = 0$, or $S_3 \cup S_4$ is nonempty. In the latter case we have, on using the weak ordering property of cash flows above, that $G(s) \geqslant R$ for $s \in S_1$. Thus, using equations (7) and (2), we obtain

(8)
$$G - I \geqslant \sum_{S_3 \cup S_4} [G(s) - R] P(s).$$

Hence, from equations (5) and (3) it follows that $V_1 - V_0 \leqslant G - I$. Q.E.D.

Remarks: The weak ordering property assumed in the Proposition applies to riskless new cash flows, so it is a (much) weaker condition than perfect positive correlation. Indeed, if the new project is a stochastic replica of old assets [i.e., $G(s) = (G/C)C(s)$ for all $s \in S$], and $(I/G) \geqslant (V_0/C)$, then $V_1 - V_0 = 0$ and *all* NPV gains from the new project accrue to equityholders, which may be easily verified (Bhattacharya 1976).

Thus, as in the model of Grossman and Hart (1982), sophisticated financial contracting may considerably ameliorate the disincentive effects associated with alternative financial structures. Hence, empirically robust assessments of the magnitude of these "agency costs" of second-best disincentives (relative to any net tax advantages to debt) are not easy to achieve. Not only may loan covenants and clever financial contracting have an impact on these costs, but arrangements such as privately negotiated debt contracts, which facilitate renegotiation, and well-designed managerial compensation schemes may also impact on the observability and incentives problems involved. The discussion by Kim in this volume sheds some further light on these issues.

III. DISCLOSURE AND ITS REGULATION

As noted in the Introduction, the literature on incomplete information models in finance has dealt with exogenous as well as endogenous action-induced informational asymmetries. The early work of Green (1973) and others modeled the transmission of agents' information about firms' future cash flows through a linear price mechanism. Green's notion of a rational expectations equilibrium has been extended to incorporate costly information gathering by decentralized *investors* (e.g., in Grossman and Stiglitz 1980*). In order to provide incentives for any costly information production, these models have assumed that the price channel for communicating/aggregating information is made noisy by the existence of "liquidity traders"; see Admati's discussion in this volume for further details. More recently, Allen (1984) and Laffont (1985) have considered the welfare implications of such equilibria in some detail. The broad lesson emerging from their studies suggests that, in the *absence* of strong productive effects from the information gathered (in determining the level of aggregate investment, for example), the production of costly information by investors is likely to be socially wasteful, in the sense that agents' ex ante expected utility levels are reduced relative to a situation with no information production. In essence, this happens because private incentives to "speculate" based on information diverge from social gains from collecting information; Hirshleifer (1971) pioneered this intuition.

Within the context of this type of noisy rational expectations modeling, D. Diamond (1985) and Verrecchia (1983) have considered disclosure policies of *firms*. Diamond analyzes a model in which firms can produce and disseminate information about their cash flows, and they can do so with endogenously determined precision of information. Verrecchia takes the precision of the information produced by firms as given, but he considers the additional strategic possibility of firms not disclosing their produced information. Both authors assume that misrepresentation of the information produced by the firm is *not* possible—that is, ruled out by prohibitively high potential penalties for "fraud." Verrecchia also assumes that there is a constant cost of disseminating any information, whereas Diamond takes this cost to be zero.

Working in the context of mean-variance models with normal distributions (of payoffs and signals) and negative exponential utility functions, Verrecchia shows that (a) sufficiently bad information will *not* be disclosed, and (b) more information (over a larger range) will be withheld as the cost of dissemination increases. Verrecchia does not analyze the welfare consequences of his equilibrium.[7] Diamond's model, in contrast, always has full disclosure of any information produced by the firm. However, he carries out a more complete welfare analysis, assuming that information of equal precision could also be privately produced by investors, at a cost not significantly lower than that of the firm. He then shows that the ex ante welfare-maximizing disclosure policy of the firm consists of producing and disseminating information of sufficient precision so that private investors perceive no (speculative) gains from producing information on their own account.[8] His results are consistent with the welfare analysis of Allen (1984).

Although the *no misrepresentation* postulates of the Diamond and Verrecchia papers are quite strong,[9] there are precedents for such assumptions in the earlier work of Milgrom (1981), Grossman (1982), and Jovanovic (1982) on disclosure of quality levels in goods markets. Milgrom, in particular, shows that, in the absence of costs of information dissemination, full disclosure is the *unique* perfect equilibrium (Selten 1975) in his "buyer-seller game." Jovanovic, in an analysis closely related to Verrecchia (1983), considers nonzero disclosure costs and shows that the resulting equilibrium has the feature that only quality levels above some cutoff level are (fully) disclosed; the rest are "pooled" at the bottom of the distribution of qualities. Jovanovic also provides welfare analyses for situations in which (a) the distribution of quality levels is exogenous, (b) the information disclosed does *not* improve buyer-seller "matching," and (c) buyers are risk neutral. Under these assumptions, he shows that disclosure is socially wasteful and that equilibrium without regulation can be improved upon by a subsidy to sell without disclosure!

Matthews and Postlewaite (1985) have recently extended the welfare analysis of quality disclosure by augmenting the sellers' choice set with the discretion to test or not test his quality level. Their welfare analysis implicitly assumes that the seller cannot only *not* misrepresent but also that his decision to test or not test is common knowledge. They show that when the quality of the good in question and other income are substitutes for consumers, then producers and consumers unanimously prefer to be informed, whereas if they are complements, then both unanimously prefer to be uninformed. These results are derived for quasi-linear utility functions of the form $V_s(x, y) = [Q_s V(x) + R_s y]$, where $V(x)$ is a concave utility function for the good x of quality Q_s in state s, and $R_s y$ is the utility for other income y; Q_s/R_s is increasing in quality (state s). Complementarity of quality and other income amounts to the assumption that R_s is also increasing in s. More generally, Matthews and Postlewaite show that unanimity regarding the disclosure policy (among sellers and buyers) need *not* hold. For example, in the "stock market" type of example—$V_s(x, y) = V(Q_s x + y)$, where $V(\cdot)$ is strictly concave—income and quality are substitutes, and yet consumers prefer the uninformed equilibrium, whereas firms prefer the informed one, both in an ex ante sense.

All of the above-mentioned papers on information production and disclosure take the probability distribution of the quality level to be an exogenously given datum rather than an endogenously determined variable, given incentives arising from informed pricing in the market. There are two significant exceptions to this trend in the literature on goods (atemporal) markets.[10] Stuart (1981) considers a model in which sellers can produce goods of two different qualities, and efficiency (maximization of producer plus consumer surplus) calls for production of the higher-quality good. In Stuart's model, sellers have *no* technology for credibly disclosing the quality of their goods to consumers. Consumers, on the other hand, can acquire costly information of varying precision about quality, where the cost is a convex function of the precision of information obtained. His results show that a pure-strategy equilibrium with only high-quality goods produced is *not* sustainable, since then no buyer has an incentive to "police" quality by testing; that is, the value of information is zero given priors consistent with this equilibrium. However, mixed-strategy equilibria in which the high-quality good is produced with some probability (fraction of sellers) do exist, and the expected/average quality level in the market does increase as buyers' cost of acquiring information declines. Based on this model, Stuart concludes in favor of regulations such as forced disclosure and/or mandated quality controls—that is, against caveat emptor.

Golding (1982) offers what is perhaps the most complete model of endogenous, but incomplete, disclosure as well as quality choice by sellers. He assumes that sellers know the realized quality level drawn from a distribution—which depends in a first-degree stochastic dominance sense on cost expended—only with some known probability less than unity. Consumers in Golding's model have utility functions that are (i) linear in income, (ii) increasing in the mean (conjectured) quality level, and (iii) decreasing in the variance of (conjectured) quality, as in Verrecchia (1983). In contrast to some other authors, some aspects of Golding's analysis focus on a welfare criterion that is conditioned on the realized quality level—that is, interim—rather than on ex ante expected utility levels. Subject to this difference in welfare analysis, Golding's conclusions are that (i) firms release too little information—that is, low revealed quality levels are *not* disclosed; (ii) firms' incentives for costly testing (increasing the probability of knowing quality) are too great; and (iii) firms' incentives to improve quality are too little at a given *imperfect* testing level, essentially because of effect (i). It would be interesting to extend Golding's analysis to incorporate all of these trade-offs simultaneously, using an ex ante welfare criterion and fairly general distributional assumptions about the quality random variable.

A second shortcoming in the above-mentioned papers has been the unmodeled nature of the assumption that (attempted) misrepresentation of quality levels is never feasible.[11] In effect, this is tantamount to assuming that the problem of signaling quality is resolved (a) without "deadweight" costs of costly signaling (Spence 1974), and (b) without explicit contracts such as warranties. Several other papers, in both the goods and financial markets literature, have sought to retain nondissipation (relative to first-best welfare levels) as a conclusion, but only by modeling the process of "contingent contracting" between buyers and sellers *explicitly*. Examples include Guasch and Weiss (1980) on labor markets, Bhattacharya (1980) and Ross (1979) on financial markets, and Palfrey and Romer (1983) on goods markets. The key idea in these models is that a worker, or financial asset, or a good produces a noisy ex post indicator that is commonly observable and exogenously correlated with the underlying ex ante attributes of the good in question. (This assumption may *not* be valid if employers can misstate test results, firms can manipulate earnings numbers, or unobservable consumer misuse can increase the probability of malfunctioning of goods.) Hence, under competition, one would expect to see contracts whose payoffs depend on the ex post observations, as well as signals or statements regarding the ex ante attributes, that are designed so that sellers are induced to reveal their ex ante attributes by their *choice among contracts*. Bhattacharya (1980) terms such an outcome a "non-dissipative signaling" equilibrium.

Given such possibilities for signaling through contingent contracts, Ross (1979) has argued that there is *no* need for governmental interventions such as mandated disclosure (of categories of information). In light of Bhattacharya

(1980), which shows that existence conditions for such separating signaling equilibria are somewhat delicate, I am not entirely persuaded by such an argument. In Ross's signaling model the contingent contracting is done between informed managers and shareholders. Given that the managers' human capital is significantly less diversified, the risk-neutrality (toward firm-specific risk) assumption required for nondissipative signaling is also less than compelling.[12]

In the model of Bhattacharya (1980) the contingent contract is an "implicit contract" between current shareholders and the market (or future share-holders) that reflects itself in price reactions to divergences between actual and expected earnings, which were predicated on forecasts or dividend announcements. However, I show that such nondissipative signaling equilibria may easily fail to be "perfect"; that is, given the information revealed by the menu of contracts and self-selection, it may *not* be in the ex post interest of a competitive market to enforce the terms of the contingent contract in market prices paid.[13] These difficulties with nondissipative resolutions are over and above those identified by Golding (1982) when informed agents are not *necessarily* better informed; that is, agents with bad information then have an incentive to lie and pretend to be uninformed, and some of them do so in equilibrium.

The work of Palfrey and Romer (1983) on issues of endogenized warranty choice and "buyer-seller disputes," given *exogenous* underlying average quality levels, pursues another set of difficulties with contingent-contracting resolutions. They analyze a setting in which both buyers and seller obtain noisy, conditionally independent signals about the (realized) quality of a particular item. Palfrey and Romer also assume that no strategic misrepresentation of the seller's signal is feasible. They then analyze situations where conflicts arise owing to discrepancies between the buyer's claim (of low quality) and the seller's signal, without considering the possibility of pooling the information of both parties in an explicit arbitration procedure. Given the nature of their equilibrium and the costs of obtaining informative signals, efficient (partial) warranties do *not* necessarily come about.

Much recent work on disclosure equilibria across product and financial markets has probably been motivated by the casual empiricism (e.g., based on insider trading profits) that full disclosure of all information available to subsets is *not* achieved in equilibrium. Aside from the dynamic "perfectness" issues introduced in Bhattacharya (1980), rationalizations for incomplete revelation in equilibrium have been based on either (a) the cost of *disseminating* information (Jovanovic, Verrecchia) or (b) imperfect testing and/or knowledge of realized quality on the part of the (potentially) informed agent (Golding, and Matthews and Postlewaite). Authors working along the former line, parti-cularly Verrecchia, have suggested that a nontrivial cost of disseminating information may (in part) be thought of in terms of the opportunity costs of disclosing proprietary information to competing firms, which may lead to a reduction in the private value of such information. For example, disclosure of internal accounting information on the profitability of different product lines may inform a firm's shareholders, but it may also lead to more informed entry or expansion decisions by competitors in these product markets.

Unfortunately, from a welfare-analytic point of view, it is completely inadequate to model such "proprietary cost" or *feedback effects* simply as private costs of disclosure. As Jovanovic's (1982) study well illustrates, such modeling leads to the somewhat hasty conclusion that there is too much disclosure in a private equilibrium, which ought to be discouraged by policy. When one models such feedback effects explicitly, as in Bhattacharya and Ritter (1983), no such conclusion is compelling.

In the model of Bhattacharya and Ritter, firms engaged in a "patent race" and needing to raise financing for research signal their prospects for winning the race by *partial* revelation of technological data regarding their capabilities. (The model is structured so that no other contingent contracts are feasible.) Such technological disclosure leads to a higher price for a firm's shares and, thus, lower "dilution" to raise financing, but it also improves the research capabilities of competing firms and thus reduces our firm's likelihood of winning the patent race. The conflicting welfare trade-offs in the model arise from (a) the societal benefit from improved research capability for all firms versus (b) the possibility of excessive entry into the "common property resource" of invention, and (c) the private disincentive to augment research capabilities, given its partial dissipation in the implementation/development phase, because of the need to communicate prospects to the capital market.

Given these trade-offs, which essentially have to do with the benefits and costs of knowledge *spillover*, it is difficult to ascertain if there is too much or too little disclosure in market equilibrium. Our model also suggests the potential superiority of alternative means of financing projects with potentially large spillover effects (e.g., through intermediaries that protect the privacy of proprietary information and are able to raise financing by diversifying their risks, or due to "reputation"). (The discussion by Diamond in this volume elaborates further on some of these issues with respect to intermediation.) In my view, it is clearly premature to carry out welfare analyses of such environments without a full and explicit elaboration of the underlying informational and institutional structures, which has only begun to be attempted in the literature.

In summary, I hope to have shown that the literature on disclosure and its regulation, which has taken some initial strides in using and extending recent developments in information economics, is still at an early stage of development.[14] Conclusions regarding nonoptimality of intervention by governmental institutions have only emerged in environments in which the (realistic) features of partial equilibrium disclosure, and endogenous choice of qualities and/or quantities, or detailed distinctions between private versus social costs of disclosure, have been drastically abstracted. However, we have learned about the properties of different classes of models in some detail, and the stage may have been prepared for a more complete and cogent attack on this important set of problems.

IV. CONCLUDING REMARKS

I have attempted to provide a partial overview of some of the most exciting developments in the application of models with asymmetric information to topics in financial economics. The views adopted above, with respect to historical importance and interconnection, as well as judgments regarding progress and promise of approaches along different lines, clearly reflect my biases (as well as that of friends). In any event, material progress in extending our understanding of the behavior patterns of investors, corporations, and intermediaries has clearly been achieved. In little more than a decade, explanations based on new premises and modeling techniques have vastly enriched our storehouse of knowledge in conceptualizing markets and institutions and in rationalizing empirical observations on financial structures and policies.

In many respects, research on financial markets under conditions of incomplete information has only begun to fulfill its full theoretical and, particularly, empirical potential.[15] New vistas and challenges, particularly in the areas of multiperiod credit market contracts (Stiglitz and Weiss 1983),[16] contracting among sovereign parties bound only by future incentives rather than enforceable contracts (Eaton and Gersovitz 1981), and more generally the incorporation and modification of models of *reputation* (Kreps and Wilson 1982, Klein and Leffler 1981, Dybvig and Spatt 1986) in a financial market context,[17] loom as exciting new frontiers.

NOTES

[1] The fact that the attributes (partially) revealed through prices relate to commonly traded as opposed to personalized commodities makes for very important differences in welfare analysis. Contrast, for example, Laffont (1985) and Prescott and Townsend (1984). See also Green (1977) and Arrow and Green (1974) for analyses of the behavioral postulates underlying (convergence to) rational expectations equilibria.

[2] Related contributions that show that commonly known (inferred) information does *not* result in dynamic revision of trades in "sufficiently complete" markets were made by Rubinstein (1975) and Milgrom and Stokey (1982).

[3] As in many areas of financial economics, empirical analysis developed alongside and sometimes preceded the relevant theoretical framework. Fama (1970) provides a lucid synthesis of early empirical work that sought to examine the notion of rapid incorporation of different types of (public and a priori private) information in prices, and suggests a classification scheme for the degree of "market efficiency" using different categories of (past, public, private) information.

[4] Related issues of unanimity regarding the implementation of optimal actions given privately known preferences also arise in the public goods literature; see Groves (1973) and D'Aspremont and Gerard-Varet (1979). A *thorough* investigation of the connections between the problems of public goods investments and that of efficiency and unanimity regarding investment decisions in share markets would be a welcome addition to this literature.

[5] Our overall policy on inclusion of papers has evolved in part from *not* wishing to duplicate papers contained in other collections of readings.

[6] The requisite observability assumptions do not make for a trivial problem in all circumstances. For example, a sufficiently rigid restriction on dividend payments may result in investment in negative NPV projects, given restrictions on the firm's flexibility in repurchasing its debt or (other firms') equity.

[7] Trueman (1984) has argued that managers in Verrecchia's model have an incompletely articulated objective function that does not fully reflect shareholders' intertemporal trade-offs. Trueman also shows that if early disclosure is informative about managerial abilities to predict and adjust production, then full disclosure may take place and yet there may be positive price reactions *on average* to such disclosure. His model thus provides an alternative explanation to Verrecchia's (partial disclosure) rationalization of the empirically observed price impact of earnings forecasts.

[8] Diamond's conclusion holds even if firms have some cost disadvantage in producing information, since disclosed information is perfectly perceived by investors rather than being "filtered" through a noisy price channel with its attendant speculative utility losses.

[9] Such a postulate assumes, in effect, that some governmental enforcement mechanism with prohibitively high penalties for detected lies exists, and also that lies can be perfectly distinguished from truth telling with nonzero probability (i.e., "moving support" monitoring).

[10] In the financial market context, an exception to this rule is the analysis of Allen (1984), who shows that when the *quantities* of different risky investments are endogenously sufficiently flexible in response to informed pricing, then information is more likely to be socially productive (i.e., increase ex ante expected utility levels).

[11] One is tempted to view this as a backhanded way of ascribing a role to governmental regulation that is impossibly perfect while simplifying the model sufficiently to eliminate other, more realistic, roles for policy. For further discussion related to this point, see Beales, Craswell, and Salop (1981).

[12] It might be argued, along the lines of Bhattacharya and Pfleiderer (1985), that large (syndicates of) diversified investors can easily compensate managers for the risk borne in their contingent contracts, which are small relative to overall firm cash flows. However, in that event, the same shareholders have an incentive to pay side payments to encourage managers to lie.

[13] Constantinides and Grundy (1986) show that the *possibility* of dissipative costs of inefficient investment out of equilibrium may considerably reduce the stringency of the conditions needed (on contingent contracts) to bring about a nondissipative signaling resolution. The *dynamic* (intertemporal) implications of their observation for the enforceability of contingent contracts is an important topic for further research.

[14] An interesting related literature, with important policy implications, deals with the rationales for regulating insider trading; see, for example, Grinblatt (1984). The work of Admati and Pfleiderer (1985) also deals with optimizing decisions by large strategic traders cum information producers.

[15] For a forceful and provocative advocacy of this point of view, see Stiglitz (1985).

[16] The work of Stiglitz and Weiss (1983) is part of a broader literature that argues that "involuntary" terminations and (associated) quantity constraints on credit, employment, and so on are essential components of market outcomes under conditions of (sufficiently) asymmetric information. This notion is clearly suggestive of macroeconomic policy implications of quantity "signals," such as money stock, although elaboration of such a role for policy has not been accomplished in existing work.

[17] The work of Dybvig and Spatt extends and applies the model of Klein and Leffler, with its infinite horizon and common-knowledge information partitions, to financial market contexts. Less compelling "financial" extensions of the finite-horizon, asymmetric-information model of Kreps and Wilson, developed in a goods market context of "predation," have also been attempted in recent work.

REFERENCES

Admati, Anat, and Pfleiderer, Paul. 1985. "A Monopolistic Market for Information." Stanford University (mimeo).

Allen, Franklin. 1984. "The Social Value of Asymmetric Information." University of Pennsylvania (mimeo).

———. 1985. "Contracts to Sell Information." University of Pennsylvania (mimeo).

Arrow, Kenneth J. 1973. "Higher Education as a Filter." *Journal of Public Economics* 2: 193–216.

Arrow, Kenneth J., and Green, Jerry. 1974. "Notes on Expectational Equilibria in a Bayesian Setting." Stanford University (mimeo).

Beales, Howard; Craswell, Richard; and Salop, Steven C. 1981. "The Efficient Regulation of Consumer Information." *Journal of Law and Economics* 24: 491–539.

Bhattacharya, Sudipto. 1976. "The Effects of Collateral on Incentives and Adverse Selection." Sloan School, M.I.T. (mimeo).

———. 1979. "Imperfect Information, Dividend Policy, and the 'Bird in the Hand' Fallacy." *Bell Journal of Economics* 10: 259–70.

———. 1980. "Nondissipative Signaling Structures and Dividend Policy." *Quarterly Journal of Economics* 95: 1–24.

———. 1982. "Aspects of Monetary and Banking Theory and Moral Hazard." *Journal of Finance* 37: 371–84.

Bhattacharya, Sudipto, and Gale, Douglas. 1987. "Preference Shocks, Liquidity, and Central Bank Policy." W. A. Barnett and K. J. Singleton (eds.), In *New Approaches to Monetary Economics*. Cambridge: Cambridge University Press.

Bhattacharya, Sudipto, and Pfleiderer, Paul. 1985. "Delegated Portfolio Management." *Journal of Economic Theory* 36: 1–25.

Bhattacharya, Sudipto, and Ritter, Jay. 1983. "Innovation and Communication: Signaling with Partial Disclosure." *Review of Economic Studies* 50: 331–46.

Brander, James A., and Lewis, Tracy R. 1985. "Oligopoly and Financial Structure: The Limited Liability Effect." University of British Columbia (mimeo).

Bryant, John. 1980. "A Model of Reserves, Bank Runs, and Deposit Insurance." *Journal of Banking and Finance* 4: 335–44.

Constantinides, George M., and Grundy, Bruce. 1986. "Optimal Investment with Stock Repurchase and Financing as Signals." Harvard Business School (mimeo).

Danthine, Jean Pierre. 1978. "Information, Futures Prices, and Stabilizing Speculation." *Journal of Economic Theory* 17: 79–98.

D'Aspremont, Claude, and Gerard-Varet, Louis-Andre. 1979. "Incentives and Incomplete Information." *Journal of Public Economics* 11: 25–46.

Diamond, Douglas W. 1984. "Financial Intermediation and Delegated Monitoring." *Review of Economic Studies* 51: 393–414.

———. 1985. "Optimal Release of Information by Firms." *Journal of Finance* 40: 1071–93.

Diamond, Douglas W., and Dybvig, Philip H. 1983. "Bank Runs, Deposit Insurance, and Liquidity." *Journal of Political Economy* 91: 401–19.

Diamond, Peter. 1967. "The Role of a Stock Market in a General Equilibrium Model with Technological Uncertainty." *American Economic Review* 57: 759–76.

Diamond, Peter, and Rothschild, Michael. Eds. 1978. *Uncertainty in Economics: Readings and Exercises.* New York: Academic Press.

Dybvig, Philip H., and Spatt, Chester. 1986. "Does It Pay to Maintain a Reputation? Quality Incentives in Financial Markets." Yale University (mimeo).

Eaton, Jonathan, and Gersovitz, Mark. 1981. "Debt with Potential Repudiation: Theoretical and Empirical Analysis." *Review of Economic Studies* 48: 289–309.

Fama, Eugene F. 1970. "Efficient Capital Markets: A Review of Theory and Empirical

Work." *Journal of Finance* 25: 383–417.

Fama, Eugene F., and Miller, Merton H. 1972. *The Theory of Finance*. New York: Holt, Rinehart and Winston.

Giammarino, Ronald M. 1985. "The Resolution of Financial Distress." University of British Columbia (mimeo).

Golding, Edward L. 1982. "Disclosure of Product Quality under Imperfect Information." Working paper No. 68, Federal Trade Commission, July.

Green, Jerry. 1973. "Information, Efficiency, and Equilibrium." Harvard Institute of Economic Research, March.

——. 1977. "On the Nonexistence of Rational Expectations Equilibrium." *Review of Economic Studies* 44: 451–65.

Grinblatt, Mark. 1984. "On the Regulation of Insider Trading." UCLA Graduate School of Management (mimeo).

Grossman, Sanford. 1976. "On the Efficiency of Competitive Stock Markets Where Traders Have Diverse Information." *Journal of Finance* 31: 573–85.

——. 1977. "The Existence of Futures Markets, Noisy Rational Expectations, and Informational Externalities." *Review of Economic Studies* 44: 431–50.

——. 1982. "The Role of Warranties and Private Disclosure about Quality." *Journal of Law and Economics* 24: 461–83.

Grossman, Sanford, and Hart, Oliver D. 1980. "Takeover Bids, the Free Rider Problem, and the Theory of the Corporation." *Bell Journal of Economics* 11: 42–64.

——. 1982. "Corporate Financial Structure and Managerial Incentives." In J. McCall (ed.), *The Economics of Information and Uncertainty*. Chicago: University of Chicago Press.

Grossman, Sanford, and Stiglitz, Joseph E. 1980. "On the Impossibility of Informationally Efficient Markets." *American Economic Review* 70: 393–408.

Groves, Theodore. 1973. "Incentives in Teams." *Econometrica* 41: 617–31.

Grunberg, Emile, and Modigliani, Franco. 1954. "The Predictability of Social Events." *Journal of Political Economy* 62: 465–72.

Guasch, Luis, and Weiss, Andrew. 1980. "Wages As a Sorting Mechanism in Competitive Markets with Asymmetric Information: A Theory of Tests." *Review of Economic Studies* 47: 653–64.

Harsanyi, John. 1968. "Games with Incomplete Information Played by 'Bayesian' Players, Parts I–III." *Management Science* 14: 158–82, 320–34, 486–502.

Hart, Oliver D. 1977. "Take-Over Bids and Stock Market Equilibrium." *Journal of Economic Theory* 16: 53–83.

Hirshleifer, Jack. 1971. "The Private and Social Value of Information and the Reward to Inventive Activity." *American Economic Review* 61: 561–73.

Jacklin, Charles J. 1983. "Demand Deposits, Trading Restrictions, and Risk-Sharing." In E. C. Prescott and N. Wallace (eds.), *Contractual Arrangements for Intertemporal Trade*. Minneapolis: University of Minnesota Press.

Jensen, Michael, and Meckling, William. 1976. "Theory of the Firm: Managerial Behavior, Agency Costs and Ownership Structure." *Journal of Financial Economics* 3: 305–60.

Jovanovic, Boyan. 1982. "Truthful Disclosure of Information." *Bell Journal of Economics* 13: 36–44.

Kihlstrom, Richard, and Mirman, Leonard. 1975. "Information and Market Equilibrium." *Bell Journal of Economics* 6: 357–76.

Klein, Benjamin, and Leffler, Kenneth. 1981. "The Role of Market Forces in Assuring Contractual Performance." *Journal of Political Economy* 89: 615–41.

Kreps, David M., and Wilson, Robert. 1982. "Reputation and Imperfect Information." *Journal of Economic Theory* 27: 253–79.

Laffont, Jean-Jacques. 1985. "On the Welfare Analysis of Rational Expectations

Equilibria with Asymmetric Information." *Econometrica* 53: 1–30.

Leland, Hayne, and Pyle, David H. 1977. "Informational Asymmetries, Financial Structure, and Financial Intermediation." *Journal of Finance* 32: 371–87. Reprinted Chapter 8, this volume.

Lucas, Robert E. 1972. "Expectations and the Neutrality of Money." *Journal of Economic Theory* 4: 103–24.

Matthews, Stephen, and Postlewaite, Andrew. 1985. "Quality Testing and Disclosure." *Rand Journal of Economics* 16: 328–40.

Merton, Robert C. 1978. "On the Costs of Deposit Insurance When There Are Surveillance Costs." *Journal of Business* 51: 439–52.

Milgrom, Paul. 1981. "Good News and Bad News: Representation Theorems and Applications." *Bell Journal of Economics* 12: 380–91.

Milgrom, Paul, and Stokey, Nancy. 1982. "Information, Trade, and Common Knowledge." *Journal of Economic Theory* 26: 17–27.

Miller, Merton H. 1977. "Debt and Taxes." *Journal of Finance* 32: 261–75.

Mirrlees, James. 1979. "The Implications of Moral Hazard for Optimal Insurance." Nuffield College, Oxford University (mimeo).

Myers, Stewart C. 1977. "Determinants of Corporate Borrowing." *Journal of Financial Economics* 9: 147–76.

Myerson, Roger. 1981. "Optimal Auction Design." *Mathematics of Operations Research* 6: 58–73.

Palfrey, Thomas, and Romer, Thomas. 1983. "Warranties, Performance, and the Resolution of Buyer-Seller Disputes." *Bell Journal of Economics* 14: 97–117.

Prescott, Edward C., and Townsend, Robert M. 1984. "Optima and Competitive Equilibria with Adverse Selection and Moral Hazard." *Econometrica* 52: 21–40.

Radner, Roy. 1967. "Equilibre des Marches a Terme et au Comptant en Cas d'Incertitude." *Cahiers d'Econometrie* 9: 30–47.

Rock, Kevin. 1986. "Why New Issues Are Underpriced." *Journal of Financial Economics* 15: 187–212. Reprinted Chapter 6, this volume.

Ross, Stephen A. 1973. "The Economic Theory of Agency: The Principal's Problem." *American Economic Review* 63: 134–39.

———. 1977. "The Determination of Financial Structure: The Incentive-Signalling Approach." *Bell Journal of Economics* 8: 23–40.

———. 1979. "Disclosure Regulation in Financial Markets: Some Implications of Modern Financial and Signaling Theory." In F. Edwards (ed.), *Issues in Financial Regulation.* New York: McGraw-Hill.

Rothschild, Michael, and Stiglitz, Joseph E. 1976. "Equilibrium in Competitive Insurance Markets." *Quarterly Journal of Economics* 90: 629–49.

Rubinstein, Mark. 1975. "Securities Market Efficiency in an Arrow-Debreu Economy." *American Economic Review* 65: 812–24.

Salant, Stephen, and Henderson, Dale. 1978. "Market Anticipation of Government Policies and the Price of Gold." *Journal of Political Economy* 86: 627–48.

Samuelson, Paul A. 1958. "An Exact Consumption-Loan Model of Interest, with or without the Social Contrivance of Money." *Journal of Political Economy* 66: 467–82.

———. 1972. "Mathematics of Speculative Price." In *Mathematical Topics in Economic Theory and Computation.* Philadelphia; Society for Industrial and Applied Mathematics.

Selten, Reinhart. 1975. "Reexamination of the Perfectness Concept for Equilibrium Points in Extensive Games." *International Journal of Game Theory* 4: 25–55.

Smith, Clifford, and Warner, Jerold. 1979. "On Financial Contracting: An Analysis of Bond Covenants." *Journal of Financial Economics* 7: 117–61.

Spence, Michael. 1974. "Competitive and Optimal Responses to Signals: Analysis of Efficiency and Distribution." *Journal of Economic Theory* 7: 296–332.

Spence, Michael, and Zeckhauser, Richard. 1971. "Insurance, Information, and Individual Action." *American Economic Review* 61: 380–87.

Stiglitz, Joseph E. 1972. "Some Aspects of the Pure Theory of Corporate Finance: Bankruptcies and Takeovers." *Bell Journal of Economics* 3: 458–82.

———. 1974. "Information and Capital Markets." Oxford University (mimeo). Reprinted in William F. Sharpe and Kathy Cootner, eds. 1982. *Financial Economics: Essays in Honor of Paul Cootner.* Englewood Cliffs, N.J.: Prentice-Hall.

———. 1975. "The Theory of Screening, Education and Distribution of Income." *American Economic Review* 65: 283–300.

———. 1982. "The Inefficiency of the Stock Market Equilibrium." *Review of Economic Studies* 49: 241–62.

———. 1985. "Credit Markets and the Control of Capital." *Journal of Money, Credit, and Banking* 17: 133–52.

Stiglitz, Joseph E., and Weiss, Andrew. 1981. "Credit Rationing in Markets with Imperfect Information." *American Economic Review* 71: 393–411.

———. 1983. "Incentive Effects of Terminations: Applications to Credit and Labor Markets." *American Economic Review* 73: 912–27.

Stuart, Charles. 1981. "Consumer Protection in Markets with Informationally Weak Buyers." *Bell Journal of Economics* 12: 562–73.

Stulz, Rene, and Johnson, Herbert. 1985. "An Analysis of Secured Debt." *Journal of Financial Economics* 14: 501–22.

Titman, Sheridan, and Wessels, Robert. 1985. "The Determinants of Capital Structure Choice." UCLA (mimeo).

Trueman, Brett. 1984. "Why Do Managers Voluntarily Release Earnings Forecasts?" UCLA (mimeo).

Verrecchia, Robert. 1983. "Discretionary Disclosure." *Journal of Accounting and Economics* 5: 179–94.

Wilson, Charles. 1978. "A Model of Insurance Markets with Incomplete Information." *Journal of Economic Theory* 6: 167–207.

Wilson, Robert. 1968. "On the Theory of Syndicates." *Econometrica* 36: 119–32.

———. 1979. "Incentive-Compatible Risk Sharing." Stanford University (mimeo).

Reprinted from
THE JOURNAL OF FINANCE · VOL. XXXII, NO. 2 · MAY 1977

The Journal of FINANCE

| VOL. XXXII | MAY 1977 | NO. 2 |

DEBT AND TAXES*

MERTON H. MILLER**

THE SOMEWHAT HETERODOX VIEWS about debt and taxes that will be presented here have evolved over the last few years in the course of countless discussions with several of my present and former colleagues in the Finance group at Chicago— Fischer Black, Robert Hamada, Roger Ibbotson, Myron Scholes and especially Eugene Fama. Charles Upton and Joseph Williams have also been particularly helpful to me recently in clarifying the main issues.[1] My long-time friend and collaborator, Franco Modigliani, is absolved from any blame for the views to follow not because I think he would reject them, but because he has been absorbed in preparing *his* Presidential Address to the American Economic Association at this same Convention.

This coincidence neatly symbolizes the contribution we tried to make in our first joint paper of nearly twenty years ago; namely to bring to bear on problems of corporate finance some of the standard tools of economics, especially the analysis of competitive market equilibrium. Prior to that time, the academic discussion in finance was focused primarily on the empirical issue of what the market *really* capitalized.[2] Did the market capitalize a firm's dividends or its earnings or some weighted combination of the two? Did it capitalize net earnings or net operating earnings or something in between? The answers to these questions and to related questions about the behavior of interest rates were supposed to provide a basis for choosing an optimal capital structure for the firm in a framework analogous to the economist's model of discriminating monopsony.

We came at the problem from the other direction by first trying to establish the propositions about valuation implied by the economist's basic working assumptions of rational behavior and perfect markets. And we were able to prove that when the full range of opportunities available to firms and investors under such conditions

* Presidential Address, Annual Meeting of the American Finance Association, Atlantic City, N.J., September 17, 1976.

** University of Chicago.

1. More than perfunctory thanks are also due to the many others who commented, sometimes with considerable heat, on the earlier versions of this talk: Ray Ball, Marshall Blume, George Foster, Nicholas Gonedes, David Green, E. Han Kim, Robert Krainer, Katherine Miller, Charles Nelson, Hans Stoll, Jerold Warner, William Wecker, Roman Weil, and J. Fred Weston. I am especially indebted (no pun intended) to Fischer Black.

2. To avoid reopening old wounds, no names will be mentioned here. References can be supplied on request, however.

are taken into account, the following simple principle would apply: in equilibrium, the market value of any firm must be independent of its capital structure.

The arbitrage proof of this proposition can now be found in virtually every textbook in finance, followed almost invariably, however, by a warning to the student against taking it seriously. Some dismiss it with the statement that firms and investors can't or don't behave that way. I'll return to that complaint later in this talk. Others object that the invariance proposition was derived for a world with no taxes, and that world, alas, is not ours. In our world, they point out, the value of the firm can be increased by the use of debt since interest payments can be deducted from taxable corporate income. To reap more of these gains, however, the stockholders must incur increasing risks of bankruptcy and the costs, direct and indirect, of falling into that unhappy state. They conclude that the balancing of these bankruptcy costs against the tax gains of debt finance gives rise to an optimal capital structure, just as the traditional view has always maintained, though for somewhat different reasons.

It is this new and currently fashionable version of the optimal capital structure that I propose to challenge here. I will argue that even in a world in which interest payments are fully deductible in computing corporate income taxes, the value of the firm, in equilibrium will still be independent of its capital structure.

I. Bankruptcy Costs in Perspective

Let me first explain where I think the new optimum capital structure model goes wrong. It is not that I believe there to be no deadweight costs attaching to the use of debt finance. Bankruptcy costs and agency costs do indeed exist as was dutifully noted at several points in the original 1958 article [28, see especially footnote 18 and p. 293]. It is just that these costs, by any sensible reckoning, seem disproportionately small relative to the tax savings they are supposedly balancing.

The tax savings, after all, are conventionally taken as being on the order of 50 cents for each dollar of permanent debt issued.[3] The figure one usually hears as an estimate of bankruptcy costs is 20 percent of the value of the estate; and if this were the true order of magnitude for such costs, they would have to be taken very seriously indeed as a possible counterweight. But when that figure is traced back to its source in the paper by Baxter [5] (and the subsequent and seemingly confirmatory studies of Stanley and Girth [36] and Van Horne [39]), it turns out to refer mainly to the bankruptcies of individuals, with a sprinkling of small businesses, mostly proprietorships and typically undergoing liquidation rather than reorganization. The only study I know that deals with the costs of bankruptcy and reorganization for large, publicly-held corporations is that of Jerold Warner [40]. Warner

---

3. See, among others, Modigliani and Miller [27]. The 50 percent figure—actually 48 percent under present Federal law plus some additional state income taxes for most firms—is an upper bound that assumes the firm always has enough income to utilize the tax shield on the interest. For reestimates of the tax savings under other assumptions with respect to availability of offsets and to length of borrowing, see Kim [21] and Brennan and Schwartz [12]. The estimate of the tax saving has been further complicated since 1962 by the Investment Tax Credit and especially by the limitation of the credit to fifty percent of the firm's tax liability. Some fuzziness about the size of the tax savings also arises in the case of multinational corporations.

tabulated the direct costs of bankruptcy and reorganization for a sample of 11 railroads that filed petitions in bankruptcy under Section 77 of the Bankruptcy Act between 1930 and 1955. He found that the eventual cumulated direct costs of bankruptcy—and keep in mind that most of these railroads were in bankruptcy and running up these expenses for over 10 years!—averaged 5.3 percent of the market value of the firm's securities as of the end of the month in which the railroad filed the petition. There was a strong inverse size effect, moreover. For the largest road, the costs were 1.7 percent.

And remember that these are the *ex post*, upper-bound cost ratios, whereas, of course, the *expected* costs of bankruptcy are the relevant ones when the firm's capital structure decisions are being made. On that score, Warner finds, for example, that the direct costs of bankruptcy averaged only about 1 percent of the value of the firm 7 years before the petition was filed; and when he makes a reasonable allowance for the probability of bankruptcy actually occurring, he comes up with an estimate of the expected cost of bankruptcy that is, of course, much smaller yet.

Warner's data cover only the *direct* costs of reorganization in bankruptcy. The deadweight costs of rescaling claims might perhaps loom larger if measures were available of the indirect costs, such as the diversion of the time and energies of management from tasks of greater productivity or the reluctance of customers and suppliers to enter into long-term commitments.[4] But why speculate about the size of these costs? Surely we can assume that if the direct and indirect deadweight costs of the ordinary loan contract began to eat up significant portions of the tax savings, other forms of debt contracts with lower deadweight costs would be used instead.[5]

An obvious case in point is the income bond. Interest payments on such bonds need be paid in any year only if earned; and if earned and paid are fully deductible in computing corporate income tax. But if not earned and not paid in any year, the bondholders have no right to foreclose. The interest payments typically cumulate for a short period of time—usually two to three years—and then are added to the principal. Income bonds, in sum, are securities that appear to have all the supposed tax advantages of debt, without the bankruptcy cost disadvantages.[6] Yet, except for a brief flurry in the early 1960's, such bonds are rarely issued.

The conventional wisdom attributes this dearth to the unsavory connotations that surround such bonds.[7] They were developed originally in the course of the railroad bankruptcies in the 19th century and they are presumed to be still associated with that dismal process in the minds of potential buyers. As an

4. For more on this theme see Jensen and Meckling [20].

5. A similar argument in a somewhat different, but related, context is made by Black [6, esp. pp. 330–31]. Note also that while the discussion has so far referred exclusively to "bankruptcy" costs fairly narrowly construed, much the same reasoning applies to the debt-related costs in the broader sense, as in the "agency" costs of Jensen and Meckling [20] or the "costs of lending" of Black, Miller and Posner [9].

6. Not quite, because failure to repay or refund the principal at maturity could trigger a bankruptcy. Also, a firm may have earnings, but no cash.

7. See Esp. Robbins [31], [27].

investment banker once put it to me: "They have the smell of death about them." Perhaps so. But the obvious retort is that bit of ancient Roman wisdom: *pecunia non olet* (money has no odor). If the stakes were as high as the conventional analysis of the tax subsidy to debt seems to suggest, then ingenious security salesmen, investment bankers or tax advisers would surely long since have found ways to overcome investor repugnance to income bonds.

In sum, the great emphasis on bankruptcy costs in recent discussions of optimal capital structure policy seems to me to have been misplaced. For big businesses, at least (and particularly for such conspicuously low-levered ones as I.B.M. or Kodak), the supposed trade-off between tax gains and bankruptcy costs looks suspiciously like the recipe for the fabled horse-and-rabbit stew—one horse and one rabbit.[8]

II. TAXES AND CAPITAL STRUCTURES: THE EMPIRICAL RECORD

Problems arise also on the other side of the trade-off. If the optimal capital structure were simply a matter of balancing tax advantages against bankruptcy costs, why have observed capital structures shown so little change over time?[9]

When I looked into the matter in 1960 under the auspices of the Commission on Money and Credit (Miller [24]), I found, among other things, that the debt/asset ratio of the typical nonfinancial corporation in the 1950's was little different from that of the 1920's despite the fact that tax rates had quintupled—from 10 and 11 percent in the 1920's to 52 percent in the 1950's.[10] Such rise as did occur, moreover, seemed to be mainly a substitution of debt for preferred stock, rather than of debt for common stock. The year-to-year variations in debt ratios reflected primarily the cyclical movements of the economy. During expansions debt ratios tended to fall, partly because the lag of dividends behind earnings built up internally generated equity; and partly because the ratio of equity to debt in new financings tended to rise when the stock market was booming.

My study for the CMC carried the story only through the 1950's. A hasty perusal of the volumes of Statistics of Income available for the years thereafter suggests that some upward drift in debt ratios did appear to be taking place in the 1960's, at least in book-value terms. Some substantial portion of this seeming rise, however, is a consequence of the liberalization of depreciation deductions in the early 1960's. An accounting change of that kind reduces reported taxable earnings and, barring an induced reduction in dividend policy, will tend to push accumulated retained earnings (and total assets) below the levels that would otherwise have been

8. In this connection, it is interesting to note that the optimal debt to value ratio in the hypothetical example presented in the recent paper by E. Han Kim [21] turns out to be 42 percent and, hence, very substantially higher than the debt ratio for the typical U.S. corporation, even though Kim's calculation assumes that bankruptcy costs would eat up no less than 40 percent of the firm's assets in the event of failure.

9. A related question is why there appears to be no systematic cross-sectional relation between debt ratios and corporate tax rates in the countries of the European Economic Community. See Coates and Wooley [13].

10. The remarkable stability of corporate debt ratios in the face of huge increases in tax rates was noted by many other writers in this period. See, e.g., Sametz [22, esp. pp. 462–3] and the references there cited.

recorded.[11] Thus, without considerable further adjustment, direct comparison of current and recent debt ratios to those of earlier eras is no longer possible. But suppose we were to make the extreme assumption that all the rise in debt ratios genuinely reflected policy decisions rather than changes in accounting rules. Then that would still have meant that the average nonfinancial corporation raised its ratio of long-term debt from about one-fifth to only about one-fourth of total assets during the decade.[12]

Whatever may have been the case in the 1960's, the impression was certainly widespread in the early 1970's that corporate debt ratios were rising rapidly and ominously. This was a period, after all, in which *Business Week* could devote an entire and very gloomy issue (October 12, 1974) to the theme "The Debt Economy."

Looking back now, however, with all the advantages of hindsight, the increases in debt of such concern in 1974 can be seen to be a transitory response to a peculiar configuration of events rather than a permanent shift in corporate capital structures.[13] A surge in inventory accumulation was taking place as firms sought to hedge against shortages occasioned by embargoes or price controls or crop failures. Much of this accumulation was financed by short-term borrowing—a combination that led to a sharp deterioration in such conventional measures of financial health as "quick ratios" and especially coverage ratios (since little of the return on the precautionary inventory buildup was showing up in current earnings and since inflation *per se* will automatically reduce the ratio of earnings to interest payments even with no change in the interest burden in real terms).

But this inventory bubble burst soon after the famous doomsday issue of *Business Week* hit the stands—providing one more confirmation of Allen Wallis' dictum that by the time journalists become interested in an economic problem, the worst is already over. In the ensuing months, inventories have been pared, bank loans have been repaid and conventional measures of corporate liquidity have been restored to something closer to their old-time vigor. New common stock issues have been coming briskly to market as always in the past when the stock market was bouyant. Thus, when the returns for the first half of the 1970's are finally in, we are likely to be facing the same paradox we did in the 1950's—corporate debt ratios only marginally higher than those of the 1920's despite enormously higher tax rates.[14]

11. Also acting in the same direction were the liberalized rules for expensing rather than capitalizing outlays for research and development. On the other hand, debt ratios would tend to be understated by the growth during the decade of off-balance-sheet debt financing, such as leasing and unfunded pension liability.

12. For manufacturing corporations, Federal Trade Commission reports indicate that long-term debt rose during the 1960's from 12.2 percent of reported total assets to 16.6 percent. Short-term debt rose from about 7 percent to 12 percent of reported total assets over the same period. The corresponding figures for the end of 1975 were 17.9 percent for long-term debt and 10.2 percent for short-term debt. The figures here and throughout refer of course, to gross debt without allowing for the substantial amounts of debt securities that are owned by manufacturing and other nonfinancial corporations.

13. For an independent reading of these events that is similar in most essential respects, see Gilbert [16].

14. The discussion in the text has focused mainly on debt/asset ratios at book value, in the hope that

Actually, the cognitive dissonance is worse now than it was then. In the 1950's it was still possible to entertain the notion that the seeming failure of corporations to reap the tax advantages of debt financing might simply be a lag in adjustment. As corporate finance officers and their investment bankers sharpened their pencils, the tax savings they discovered would eventually wear down aversions to debt on the part of any others in the Boardroom still in a state of shock from the Great Depression. But hope can no longer be expected from that quarter. A disequilibrium that has lasted 30 years and shows no signs of disappearing is too hard for any economist to accept.[15] And since failure to close the gap cannot convincingly be attributed to the bankruptcy costs or agency costs of debt financing, there would seem to be only one way left to turn: the tax advantages of debt financing must be substantially less than the conventional wisdom suggests.[16]

III. THE TAX ADVANTAGES OF DEBT FINANCING REEXAMINED

That the solution might lie in this direction was hinted at, but alas only hinted at, in the original 1958 MM paper. If I may invoke the Presidential priviledge of being allowed to quote (selectively) from my earlier work, we said there in the 57th footnote:

> It should also be pointed out that our tax system acts in other ways to reduce the gains from debt financing. Heavy reliance on debt in the capital structure, for example, commits a company to paying out a substantial proportion of its income in the form of interest payments taxable to the owners under the personal income tax. A debt free company, by contrast, can reinvest in the business all of its (smaller) net income and to this extent subject the owners only to the low capital gains rate (or possibly to no tax at all by virtue of the loophole at death).

We alluded to the same line of argument again briefly in the correction paper in 1963.[17] The point was developed in a more extensive and systematic way by Farrar and Selwyn [15]. Further extensions were made by Myers [30], Stapleton [37],

---

book value measures might give better insight to corporate capital structure objectives than would market value measures of leverage, which are highly sensitive to changes in the level of stock prices. As of the end of 1975, tabulations prepared by Salomon Brothers in their volume *The Supply and Demand for Credit, 1976*, indicate a ratio of long-term debt to market value for all U.S. corporations (including public utilities) of 27.1 percent. (Actually, even this is a bit on the high side since the debt is measured at face value and thus does not reflect the substantial fall in the value of outstanding debt in the 1st half of the 1970's.) In 1972, at the height of the boom, the long-term debt ratio at market value was only about 17 percent. The highest recent level reached in recent years was 30 percent at the end of 1974 after a two-year fall of $500 billion in the market value of common and preferred stock.

15. There are certainly few signs that firms were rushing to close the gap by methods as direct as exchanges of debt for their common shares. Masulis [22] was able to find only about 60 such cases involving listed corporations in the 1960's and 1970's. Most of these were concentrated during an 18-month period after the drop in the stock market in 1973; and some of these, in turn, appear more to be attempts to "go private" than to adjust the capital structure.

16. The resolution of the paradox offered in the CMC paper [24] was essentially one of agency costs and, in particular, that the costs of monitoring risky debt made such debt uneconomic as a market instrument.

17. In that paper, the major weight in resolving the paradox was placed on what might be called a "precautionary" motive. Corporations were presumed to want to maintain substantial reserves of high-grade borrowing power so as not to be forced to float common stocks when they believe their stock to be undevalued. Such motives are by no means inconsistent with the explanation to be offered here.

Stiglitz [38], and in two important papers by Fischer Black [7], [8]—papers still unpublished but whose contents were communicated to me, sometimes in very forceful fashion, in the course of many arguments and discussions.

When the personal income tax is taken into account along with the corporation income tax, the gain from leverage, G_L, for the stockholders in a firm holding real assets can be shown to be given by the following expression:

$$G_L = \left[1 - \frac{(1 - \tau_C)(1 - \tau_{PS})}{1 - \tau_{PB}} \right] B_L$$

where τ_C is the corporate tax rate, τ_{PS} is the personal income tax rate applicable to income from common stock, τ_{PB} is the personal income tax rate applicable to income from bonds and B_L is the market value of the levered firm's debt. For simplicity at this stage of the argument, all the taxes are assumed to be proportional; and to maintain continuity with the earlier MM papers, the expression is given in its "perpetuity" form.[18]

Note that when all tax rates are set equal to zero, the expression does indeed reduce to the standard MM no-tax result of $G_L = 0$. And when the personal income tax rate on income from bonds is the same as that on income from shares—a special case of which, of course, is when there is assumed to be no personal income tax at all—then the gain from leverage is the familiar $\tau_C B_L$. But when the tax rate on income from shares is less than the tax on income from bonds, then the gain from leverage will be less than $\tau_C B_L$. In fact, for a wide range of values for τ_C, τ_{PS} and τ_{PB}, the gain from leverage vanishes entirely or even turns negative!

Let me assure you that this result is no mere sleight-of-hand due to hidden trick assumptions. The gain evaporates or turns into a loss because investors hold securities for the "consumption possibilities" they generate and hence will evaluate them in terms of their yields net of all tax drains. If, therefore, the personal tax on income from common stocks is less than that on income from bonds, then the *before-tax* return on taxable bonds has to be high enough, other things equal, to offset this tax handicap. Otherwise, no taxable investor would want to hold bonds. Thus, while it is still true that the owners of a levered corporation have the advantage of deducting their interest payments to bondholders in computing their corporate income tax, these interest payments have already been "grossed up," so to speak, by any differential in the taxes that the bondholders will have to pay on their interest income. The advantage of deductibility at the one level thus merely

---

18. The expression can be derived in a number of ways of which the simplest is perhaps the following variant on the MM reply to Heins and Sprenkle [29]. Ownership of the fraction α of the levered corporation yields a return to the investor of $\alpha(\tilde{X} - rB_L)(1 - \tau_C)(1 - \tau_{PS})$ where $\tilde{X}$ is the uncertain return on firm's real (as opposed to financial) assets. This can be duplicated by the sum of (a) an investment of αS_U in the shares of the twin unlevered corporation, which yields $\alpha X(1 - \tau_C)(1 - \tau_{PS})$; plus (b), borrowing $\alpha B_L[(1 - \tau_C)(1 - \tau_{PS})/(1 - \tau_{PB})]$ on personal account. Since interest is deductible under the personal income tax, the net cost of the borrowing is $\alpha r B_L(1 - \tau_C)(1 - \tau_{PS})$ and thus the original levered stream has been matched.

Here and throughout, the tax authorities will be presumed to have taken the steps necessary to prevent taxable individuals or firms from eliminating their tax liabilities or converting them to negative taxes by "tax arbitrage" dodges (such as borrowing to hold tax-exempt securities) or by large-scale short-selling.

serves to offset the disadvantages of includability at the other.[19] When the rates happen to satisfy the equation $(1 - \tau_{PB}) = (1 - \tau_C)(1 - \tau_{PS})$, the offset is one-for-one and the owners of the corporation reap no gain whatever from their use of tax-deductible debt rather than equity capital.

But we can say more than this. Any situation in which the owners of corporations could increase their wealth by substituting debt for equity (or vice versa) would be incompatible with market equilibrium. Their attempts to exploit these opportunities would lead, in a world with progressive income taxes, to changes in the yields on stocks and bonds and in their ownership patterns. These changes, in turn, restore the equilibrium and remove the incentives to issue more debt, even without invoking bankruptcy costs or lending costs as a *deus ex machina*.

IV. TAXES AND MARKET EQUILIBRIUM

Like so many other propositions in financial economics this, too, is "obvious once you think of it." Let me belabor the obvious a bit, however, by a simple graphical example that will serve, I hope, both to illustrate the mechanism that brings the equilibrium about and to highlight some of the implications of that equilibrium.

Suppose, for simplicity that the personal tax rate on income from stock were zero (and we'll see later that this may be a less outrageous simplification than it looks). And suppose further, again strictly for simplicity of presentation, that all bonds are riskless and that there are no transaction costs, flotation costs or surveillance costs involved in their issuance. Then in such a world, the equilibrium of the market for bonds would be that pictured in Figure 1. The quantity of bonds outstanding is measured along the horizontal axis and the rate of interest along the vertical. The demand for bonds by the investing public is given by the upward sloping curve labeled $r_d(B)$. (Yes, it *is* a demand curve even though it slopes up.) Its intercept is at r_0 which measures the equilibrium rate of interest on fully tax-exempt bonds (such as those of state and local governments). The flat stretch of the curve immediately to the right represents the demand for fully taxable corporate bonds by fully tax-exempt individuals and organizations. Clearly, these investors would be the sole holders of corporate bonds if the market interest rate on corporate debts were only r_0. Any taxable investor who wanted to hold bonds in his or her portfolio would find it preferable to buy tax-exempt bonds.

To entice these taxable investors into the market for corporate bonds, the rate of interest on such bonds has to be high enough to compensate for the taxes on interest income under the personal income tax. More precisely, for an individual whose marginal rate of personal income tax on interest income is τ_{PB}^α, the "demand rate of interest" on taxable corporate bonds would be the rate on tax exempts grossed up by the marginal tax rate, i.e., $r_0(1/(1 - \tau_{PB}^\alpha))$. Since the personal income tax is progressive, the demand interest rate has to keep rising to pull in investors in

---

19. An analogous argument in the context of the lease-or-buy decision is given in Miller and Upton [26]. Reasoning of essentially this kind has also long been invoked to explain the otherwise puzzling survival of preferred stock (see, among many others, Miller [24, esp. note 40, p. 431]). The fact that 85 percent of any dividends received by a taxable corporation can be excluded in computing its taxable income, pushes down the yields on preferred stocks and thereby offsets the disadvantage of nondeductibility.

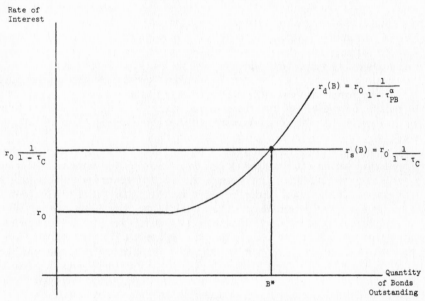

FIGURE 1. Equilibrium in the Market for Bonds

higher and higher tax brackets, thus giving the continuous, upward sloping curve pictured.

The intersection of this demand curve with the horizontal straight line through the point $r_0/1 - \tau_C$, i.e., the tax-exempt rate grossed up by the corporate tax rate, determines the market equilibrium. If corporations were to offer a quantity of bonds greater than B^*, interest rates would be driven above $r_0/1 - \tau_C$ and some levered firms would find leverage to be a losing proposition. If the volume were below B^*, interest rates would be lower than $r_0/1 - \tau_C$ and some unlevered firms would find it advantageous to resort to borrowing.

The market equilibrium defined by the intersection of the two curves will have the following property. There will be an equilibrium level of aggregate corporate debt, B^*, and hence an equilbrium debt-equity ratio for the corporate sector as a whole. *But there would be no optimum debt ratio for any individual firm.* Companies following a no-leverage or low leverage strategy (like I.B.M. or Kodak) would find a market among investors in the high tax brackets; those opting for a high leverage strategy (like the electric utilities) would find the natural clientele for their securities at the other end of the scale. But one clientele is as good as the other. And in this important sense it would still be true that the value of any firm, in equilibrium, would be independent of its capital structure, despite the deductibility of interest payments in computing corporate income taxes.[20]

One advantage of graphical illustration is that it makes it so easy to see the

20. The details of corporate strategy and investor valuation at the micro level implied by this model are interesting in their own right, but further analysis is best deferred to another occasion.

answer to the following inevitable question: If the stockholders of levered corporations don't reap the benefits of the tax gains from leverage, who does? Professors of finance, of course—though only indirectly and only after cutting in their colleagues in other departments. As Figure 1 shows, universities and other tax exempt organizations, as well as individuals in low tax brackets (widows and orphans?) benefit from what might be called a "bondholders' surplus." Market interest rates have to be grossed up to pay the taxes of the marginal bondholder, whose tax rate in equilibrium will be equal to the corporate rate.[21] Note that this can cut both ways, however. Low bracket individuals (and corporations) have to *pay* the corporate tax, in effect, when they want to borrow.

An equilibrium of the kind pictured in Figure 1 does not require, of course, that the effective personal tax rate on income from shares of the marginal holder be literally zero, but only that it be substantially less than his or her rate on income from bonds. As a practical matter, however, the assumption that the effective rate at the margin is close to zero may not be so wide of the mark. Keep in mind that a "clientele effect" is also at work in the market for shares. The high dividend paying stocks will be preferred by tax exempt organizations and low income investors; those stocks yielding more of their return in the form of capital gains will gravitate to the taxpayers in the upper brackets.[22] The tax rate on such gains is certainly greater than zero, in principle. But holders need pay no taxes on their gains until realized and only a small fraction of accumulated gains are, in fact, realized and taxed in any year (see, e.g., Bhatia [4, esp. note 12] and Bailey [2]). Taxes on capital gains can not only be deferred at the option of the holder—and remember that by conventional folk wisdom, 10 years of tax deferral is almost as good as exemption —but until the recent Tax Reform Act of 1976, could be avoided altogether if held until death, thanks to the rules permitting transfer of the decedent's tax basis to his or her heirs.

To the extent that the effective tax rate on income from shares is greater than zero, the horizontal line defining the equilibrium interest rate will be above that pictured in Figure 1. In the limiting case where the tax concessions (intended or unintended) made to income from shares were either nonexistent or so small that $(1 - \tau_C)(1 - \tau_{PS})$ implied a value for τ_{PB}^α greater than the top bracket of the personal

---

21. In point of fact, the spread between municipals and corporates has typically been within shouting distance of the corporate rate, though comparisons are difficult because of differences in risk (including, of course, the risk that the tax status of municipals will be changed) and though, admittedly, mechanisms of a different kind might also be producing that result. The recent study of the yield curve of U.S. Government securities by McCulloch [23] gives estimates of the marginal tax rate of holders of such bonds that are close to, but usually somewhat below the corporate rate.

22. The data presented in the study of stock ownership by Blume, Crockett and Friend [11, esp. Table G, p. 40] are consistent with this form of clientele effect, though its magnitude is perhaps somewhat smaller than might have been expected *a priori*. They estimate, for example, that in 1971, the ratio of dividends to the market value of holdings was about 2.8 percent for individual investors with adjusted gross income of less than $15,000 as compared to 2.1 percent for those with adjusted gross incomes of $100,000 or more.

By invoking this dividend clientele effect, an argument analogous to that in Figure 1 can be developed to show that the value of a firm could be invariant to its dividend policy despite the more favorable tax treatment of capital gains than of dividends. Some gropings in that direction were made in the MM dividend paper [25, esp. pp. 431–2]. A more explicit analysis along those lines was given by Black and Scholes [10]. For a related model dealing with tax shelters on real investment see Bailey [3].

income tax, then no interior market equilibrium would be possible. Common stock would indeed be a dominated security from the purely financial point of view, exactly as the standard micro model of the tax effect suggests. Common stock could continue to exist only by virtue of special attributes it might possess that could not be duplicated with bonds or with other forms of business organization, such as co-ops.

The analysis underlying Figure 1 can be extended to allow for risky borrowing, but there are complications. What makes things difficult is not simply a matter of risk *per se*.[23] Default risk can be accommodated in Figure 1 merely by reinterpreting all the before-tax interest rates as risk-adjusted or certainty-equivalent rates. The trouble is, rather, that bonds of companies in default will not, in general, yield the issuing stockholders their full tax shield (see MM [27, esp. note 5], Kim [21] and Brennan and Schwartz [12]). Unless the firm has past profits against which its current losses can be carried back, or unless it can escape the vigilance of the I.R.S. and unload the corporate corpse on a taxable firm, some of the interest deduction goes to waste. To entice firms to issue risky bonds, therefore, the risk-adjusted supply-rate would have to be less than $r_0(1/(1 - \tau_C))$, and presumably the more so the greater the likelihood of default.[24]

An essentially similar effect will be produced by the bankruptcy costs discussed earlier. And this will imply, among other things, that the full burden of the bankruptcy costs or lending costs is not necessarily borne by the debtors as is frequently supposed. Part of the costs are shifted to the bond buyers in the form of lower risk-adjusted rates of interest in equilibrium.

A model of the kind in Figure 1 could, in principle, clear up most of the puzzles and anomalies discussed in Sections I and II above—the seeming disparity between the tax gains of debt and the costs of bankruptcy particularly for large low-levered corporations; the lack of widespread market interest in income bonds; and especially the failure of the average corporate debt ratio to rise substantially in response 'o the enormous increase in tax rates since the 1920's (because these increases in rates in the late 1930's as well as subsequent decreases and reincreases have generally moved both the corporate and individual rate schedules in the same direction). The model could also account as well for other of the stylized facts of corporate finance such as the oft-remarked dramatic transition of the bond market from an individual to an institution-dominated market in the late 1930's and early 1940's.[25] On the other hand, many questions clearly still remain to be answered.

23. For the specialists in these matters, suffice it to say that in the equilibrium of Figure 1, the capital markets are, of course, assumed to be "complete." For a discussion of some of the implications of corporate taxes the deductibility of interest payments under conditions of "incomplete markets" see Hakansson [18].

24. These effects, however, do not imply the existence of "super-premiums" for riskless bonds of the kind visualized recently by Glenn [17] and earlier by Durand [14]. Those were presumed to arise from the segmentation of the bond market and especially from the strong preferences of the institutional sector for low-risk securities. In terms of Figure 1, any such increase in the demand for safe securities would show up in the first instance as a lower value for r_0 and, hence, a lower value for the equilibrium corporate borrowing rate, $r_0/1 - \tau_C$. (See the MM 1958 article [28, especially pp. 279–80]. See also Hamada's discussion of Glenn's paper [19].)

25. For an early account of that transition that stresses precisely the kind of tax effects that underlie Figure 1, see Shapiro [35].

What about cross-sectional variations in debt ratios, for example—a subject on which surprisingly little work has yet been done?[26] Can they be explained convincingly by the market equilibrium model presented here or some variant of it? Or do the variations observed reflect some systematic part of the equilibrating process that escapes the kind of aggregate market models discussed here? What about the distribution of stocks and bonds among investors? Does ownership sort out in terms of tax status as sharply as emphasized here? Or does the need for diversification swamp the tax differences and thereby throw the main burden of the equilibration onto other factors, such as agency costs?

The call for more research traditionally signals the approaching end of a Presidential Address; and it is a tradition that I know you will want to see preserved. Let me conclude, therefore, by trying to face up, as I promised in the beginning, to the kind of complaint so often raised against market equilibrium analysis of financial policy of the type here presented: "But firms and investors don't behave that way!"

V. Market Equilibrium and the Behavior of Firms and Individuals

If the phrase "don't behave that way" is taken to mean that firms and individuals don't literally perform the maximizing calculations that underlie the curves in Figure 1, then it is most certainly correct. No corporate treasurer's office, controller's staff, or investment banker's research team that I have ever encountered had, or could remotely be expected to have, enough reliable information about the future course of prices for a firm's securities to convince even a moderately skeptical outside academic observer that the firm's value had indeed been maximized by some specific financial decision or strategy. Given the complexities of the real-world setting, actual decision procedures are inevitably heuristic, judgmental, imitative and groping even where, as with so much of what passes for capital budgeting, they wear the superficial trappings of hard-nosed maximization. On this score, has there ever been any doubt that the Harvard cases (and the work of Herbert Simon and his followers) give a far more accurate picture of the way things really look and get done out on the firing line than any maximizing "model of the firm" that any economist ever drew?

Why then do economists keep trying to develop models that assume rational behavior by firms? They are not, I insist, merely hoping to con their business school deans into thinking they are working on problems of business management. Rather they have found from experience—not only in finance, but across the board —that the rational behavior models generally lead to better predictions and descriptions at the level of the industry, the market and the whole economy than any alternatives available to them. Their experience, at those levels, moreover, need involve no inconsistency with the heuristic, rule-of-thumb, intuitive kinds of decision making they actually observe in firms. It suggests rather that evolutionary mechanisms are at work to give survival value to those heuristics that are compat-

26. One of the few studies of cross-sectional differences in debt ratios is that of Schwartz and Aronson [34], but it really does little more than document the fact that utilities and railroads have substantially higher debt ratios than firms in manufacturing and mining.

ible with rational market equilibrium, however far from rational they may appear to be when examined up close and in isolation.[27]

But we must be wary of the reverse inference that merely because a given heuristic persists, it must have some survival value and, hence, must have a rational "explanation." The MM and related invariance propositions, for example, are often dismissed on grounds that corporate finance officers would surely not show so much concern over decisions that really "don't matter." The most, however, that we can safely assert about the evolutionary process underlying market equilibrium is that harmful heuristics, like harmful mutations in nature, will die out. Neutral mutations that serve no function, but do no harm, can persist indefinitely. Neither in nature nor in the economy can the enormous variation in forms we observe be convincingly explained in simple Darwinian terms.[28]

To say that many, perhaps even most, financial heuristics are neutral is not to suggest, however, that financial decision making is just a pointless charade or treat the resources devoted to financial innovations are wasted. A mutation or a heuristic that is neutral in one environment may suddenly acquire (or lose) survival value if the environment changes. The pool of existing neutral mutations and heuristics thus permits the adaptation to the new conditions to take place more quickly and more surely than if a new and original act of creation were required. Once these types and roles of heuristics in the equilibrating process are understood and appreciated, the differences between the institutionalist and theorist wings of our Association may be seen to be far less fundamental and irreconcilable than the sometimes ferocious polemics of the last 20 years might seem to suggest.

REFERENCES

1. Victor L. Andrews. "Captive Finance Companies," *Harvard Business Review*, Vol. 42 (July-August 1964), 80–92.
2. Martin J. Bailey. "Capital Gains and Income Taxation," In *The Taxation of Income From Capital*. Edited by A. Harberger and M. Bailey. (Washington, D.C.: The Brookings Distribution, 1969).
3. ———. "Progressivity and Investment Yields under U.S. Income Taxation," *Journal of Political Economy*, Vol. 82, No. 6 (Nov./Dec. 1974), 1157–75.
4. Ku B. Bhatia. "Capital Gains and Inequality of Personal Income: Some Results From Survey Data," *Journal of the American Statistical Association*, Vol. 71, No. 355 (September 1976), 575–580.
5. Nevins Baxter. "Leverage, Risk of Ruin and the Cost of Capital," *Journal of Finance*, Vol. 22, No. 3 (September 1967), 395–403.
6. Fischer Black. "Bank Funds Management in an Efficient Market," *Journal of Financial Economics*, Vol. 2, No. 4 (December 1975).
7. ———. "Taxes and Capital Market Equilibrium." Working Paper No. 21A, Associates in Finance, Belmont, Massachusetts, April 1971 (mimeo).
8. ———. "Taxes and Capital Market Equilibrium under Uncertainty," Working Paper No. 21B, Chicago, May 1973 (mimeo).

27. Has anyone a better explanation for the puzzle of why the pay-back criterion continues to thrive despite having been denounced as Neanderthal in virtually every textbook in finance and accounting over the last 30 years?

28. Any experienced teacher of corporate finance can surely supply numerous examples of such neutral variations. My own favorite is the captive finance company. See, e.g., the perceptive discussion in Andrews [1].

9. ———, Merton H. Miller and Richard A. Posner. "An Approach to the Regulation of Bank Holding Companies," University of Chicago, April 1976 (multilith).

10. ——— and Myron Scholes. "The Effects on Dividend Yield and Dividend Policy on Common Stock Prices and Returns," *Journal of Financial Economics*, Vol. 1, No. 1 (May 1974), 1–22.

11. Marshall E. Blume, Jean Crockett and Irwin Frend. "Stock Ownership in The United States: Characteristics and Trends," *Survey of Current Business* (November 1974), 16–40.

12. M. J. Brennan and E. S. Schwartz. "Corporate Income Taxes, Valuation and the Problem of Optimal Capital Structure," University of British Columbia, Vancouver, B.C., Canada, multilith, August 1976 (revised).

13. J. H. Coates and P. K. Wooley. "Corporate Gearing in the E.E.C.," *Journal of Business Finance and Accounting*, Vol. 2, No. 1 (Spring 1975), 1–18.

14. David Durand. "The Cost of Capital, Corporation Finance and the Investment: Comment," *American Economic Review*, Vol. 49, No. 4 (Sept. 1959), 39–55.

15. Donald Farrar and Lee L. Selwyn. "Taxes, Corporate Policy, and Returns to Investors," *National Tax Journal*, Vol. 20, No. 4 (December 1967), 444–54.

16. R. Alton Gilbert. "Bank Financing of the Recovery," *Federal Reserve Bank of St. Louis Review*, Vol. 58, No. 7, 2–9.

17. David W. Glenn. "Super Premium Security Prices and Optimal Corporate Financial Decisions," *Journal of Finance*, Vol. 31, No. 2 (May 1976), 507–24.

18. Nils Hakansson. "Ordering Markets and the Capital Structures of Firms, with Illustrations," Working Paper No. 24, Institute of Business and Economic Research, University of California, Berkeley, October 1974 (multilith).

19. Robert Hamada. "Discussion," *Journal of Finance*, Vol. 31, No. 2 (May 1976), 543–46.

20. Michael C. Jensen and William H. Meckling. "Theory of the Firm: Managerial Behavior, Agency Costs and Capital Structure," University of Rochester, August 1975 (multilith).

21. Han E. Kim. "A Mean-Variance Theory of Optimum Capital Structure and Corporate Debt Capacity," Ohio State University, undated (multilith).

22. Ronald W. Masulis. "The Effects of Capital Structure Change on Security Prices," Graduate School of Business, University of Chicago, May 1976 (multilith).

23. J. Huston McCulloch. "The Tax Adjusted Yield Curve," *Journal of Finance*, Vol. 30, No. 3 (June 1975), 811–30.

24. Merton H. Miller. "The Corporation Income Tax and Corporate Financial Policies," In *Stabilization Policies*, Commission on Money and Credit, Prentice Hall, 1963.

25. ——— and Franco Modigliani. "Dividend Policy, Growth and the Valuation of Shares," *Journal of Business*, Vol. 34, No. 4 (October 1961), 411–33.

26. ——— and Charles W. Upton. "Leasing, Buying and the Cost of Capital Services." *Journal of Finance* (June 1976).

27. Franco Modigliani and Merton H. Miller. "Corporate Income Taxes and the Cost of Capital: A Correction," *American Economic Review*, Vol. 53, No. 3 (June 1963), 433–43.

28. ——— and ———. "The Cost of Capital, Corporation Finance and the Theory of Investment," *American Economic Review*, Vol. 48, No. 3 (June 1958), 261–97.

29. ——— and ———. "Reply to Heins and Sprenkle," *American Economic Review*, Vol. 59, No. 4, Part I (September 1969).

30. Stewart C. Myers. "Taxes, Corporate Financial Policy and the Return to Investors: Comment," *National Tax Journal*, Vol. 20, No. 4 (Dec. 1967), 455–62.

31. Sidney M. Robbins. "A Bigger Role for Income Bonds," *Harvard Business Review* (November-December 1955).

32. ———. "An Objective Look at Income Bonds," *Harvard Business Review* (June 1974).

33. Arnold W. Sametz. "Trends in the Volume and Composition of Equity Finance," *Journal of Finance*, Vol. 19, No. 3 (September 1964), 450–469.

34. Eli Schwartz and J. Richard Aronson. "Some Surrogate Evidence in Support of the Concept of Optimal Financial Structure," *Journal of Finance*, Vol. 22, No. 1 (March 1963), 10–18.

35. Eli Shapiro. "The Postwar Market for Corporate Securities: 1946–55," *Journal of Finance*, Vol. 14, No. 2 (May 1959), 196–217.

36. D. T. Stanley and M. Girth. *Bankruptcy: Problem, Process, Reform.* (Washington, D.C.: The Brookings Institution, 1971).

37. R. C. Stapleton. "Taxes, the Cost of Capital and the Theory of Investment," *The Economic Journal*, Vol. 82 (December 1972), 1273–92.

38. Joseph Stiglitz. "Taxation, Corporate Financial Policy, and the Cost of Capital," *Journal of Public Economics*, Vol. 2, No. 1 (February 1973), 1–34.

39. James C. Van Horne. "Corporate Liquidity and Bankruptcy Costs," Stanford University, Graduate School of Business, Research Paper No. 205, undated (multilith).

40. Jerold Warner. "Bankruptcy Costs, Absolute Priority and the Pricing of Risky Debt Claims," University of Chicago, July 1976 (multilith).

discussion | # Optimal Capital Structure in Miller's Equilibrium

E. Han Kim

University of Michigan
Graduate School of Business Administration

I. INTRODUCTION

It has been over 10 years since Miller delivered his innovative presidential address at the 1976 American Finance Association annual meetings. The equilibrium analysis in "Debt and Taxes" is elegant, and the conclusion is surprising. Numerous studies have followed in learned academic journals, attempting to dissect and scrutinize various parts of "Debt and Taxes." Some have sought to find flaws in Miller's logic, and others have endeavored to build on the new foundation he laid out. (See the Bibliography for a partial list of these papers.) This burgeoning literature has led to a better understanding of the magnitude of the tax advantage associated with corporate borrowing and of the way taxes affect corporate financing behavior.

"Debt and Taxes" is a study of the way taxes affect capital market equilibrium. Its basic premise is that taxes are the driving force in corporate financing decisions, and its contribution lies with the lucid demonstration of how taxes affect corporate financing behavior through their impacts on the aggregate supply of and demand for corporate securities. The insightful characterization of the bond market equilibrium has not only made it possible for corporate financial theorists to develop a more refined theory of optimal capital structure, but has also provided the field of public finance an equilibrium framework with which to examine various issues concerning the impacts of taxes on the economy.

In this chapter an attempt will be made to provide some historical perspective by briefly reviewing the status of capital structure theory at the time of the publication of "Debt and Taxes." Given this perspective, extensions of Miller's equilibrium that have led to a more refined theory of optimal capital structure will be summarized, and related empirical evidence will be examined.

In reviewing the theory of optimal capital structure, I do not include studies based on asymmetric information between insiders and outsiders.[1] Some of these studies are reprinted in this volume, and the essays accompanying them

This paper was supported by summer research grants from the Michigan Business School.

review the theories of capital structure that are based on information economics paradigms.

II. THE BALANCING THEORY AND "DEBT AND TAXES"

The general academic view at the time of the publication of "Debt and Taxes," although not a consensus, was that the optimal capital structure involves balancing the tax advantage of debt against the various costs associated with financial distress. Earlier versions of the balancing theory (Baxter 1967, Kraus and Litzenberger 1973, Scott 1976, and Kim 1978a) considered the direct and indirect costs of bankruptcy as the costs of financial distress. By the time "Debt and Taxes" was published, the list of costs of financial distress had grown much longer: the loss of tax shields in bankruptcy (Brennan and Schwartz 1978 and Kim 1978a); the possibility of adopting negative (smaller) net present value (NPV) projects and the various contracting, bonding, and monitoring costs that are necessary to reduce incidences of leverage-induced suboptimal investments (Jensen and Meckling 1976); and the possible rejection of positive NPV projects and the costly recontracting process in resolving conflicts of interest between stockholders and bondholders (Myers 1977). In addition, Titman (1984) has shown recently that the capital structure choice affects the stockholder's incentive to liquidate, and he has identified the unfavorable terms of trade with customers, workers, and suppliers, which arise from a positive probability of liquidation, as yet another cost of financial distress. The present value of these various deadweight losses increases with greater levels of financial leverage; thus, I define them as the leverage-related deadweight costs.

The balancing theory posits that firms weigh the leverage-related dead-weight costs against the tax advantage of corporate borrowing, the present value of which is often defined as the corporate tax rate multiplied by the amount borrowed (Modigliani and Miller 1963).[2] Miller, however, showed that an important factor had been omitted from the traditional balancing theory: the tax disadvantage to individuals holding corporate bonds relative to equities. The possibility that this tax disadvantage at the personal level may offset the tax advantage at the corporate level was first noted by Farrar and Selwyn (1967) and was extended further by Stapleton (1972), Stiglitz (1973), and Black (1971, 1973). However, it was not until the insightful analysis of the bond market equilibrium in "Debt and Taxes" that it became clear how the personal tax disadvantage leads to a higher cost of corporate debt.

Using a bond market equilibrium analysis, Miller argued that the higher cost of borrowing negates the entire benefit of corporate interest tax shields. This conclusion had surprising implications. Not only did it imply that the debt and equity choice is a matter of indifference to individual firms, but it also removed the only positive incentive, according to the balancing theory, for corporations to borrow. With the zero tax advantage of corporate borrowing, but with all the leverage-related deadweight costs still intact, the question that arose immediately was, why do firms that seek to maximize shareholder wealth issue risky debt? It was not readily apparent that the balancing theory could answer this question. It appeared, instead, that an explanation for the existence of risky debt required a new theory. Two alternative scenarios were available when "Debt and Taxes" was published: Jensen and Meckling's (1976) agency costs of outside equity and Ross's (1977) signaling model.

In Jensen and Meckling's framework, internal equity and riskless debt dominate outside equity and risky debt as a source of capital. When firms have insufficient internal equity and are unable to issue riskless debt, the optimal capital structure involves trading off the agency costs of outside equity against the leverage-related deadweight costs. That is, firms issue risky debt because issuing outside equity can be more costly. Unfortunately, this explanation applies only to firms that are privately held or managed by owner-managers who are not replaceable. If managers hold an insignificant fraction of total outstanding shares, or if they are replaceable and markets for managers function relatively well, issuing outside equity is not likely to change managerial incentives (Fama 1980). Without changes in managerial incentives, there will be no increase in the agency costs. Thus, for diffusely held public corporations, outside equity dominates risky debt as a source of capital.

Ross's model is based on asymmetric information between insiders and outsiders and constructs the debt-equity ratio as a signaling mechanism to convey information to outsiders about the firm's business risk and profitability. To make the debt ratio a credible signal, Ross imposes a bankruptcy penalty on managers, which makes the value of the firm increase with leverage. However, the model does not impose any penalties on stockholders or bondholders; as a consequence, an increase in financial leverage means only an increase in shareholder wealth with no offsetting effects. This gives the stockholders an incentive to offer a "side payment" to managers to induce them to adopt a debt ratio that is higher than the one that would provide the correct market signal. The side payment is indistinguishable from the normal managerial compensation. Thus, there is no mechanism in Ross's model that would prevent firms from giving false signals to the market. This weakness in Ross's model was pointed out by Chen and Kim (1979) and Bhattacharya (1980).

In sum, there were no viable alternative theories at the time of the publication of "Debt and Taxes" that could explain the existence of risky debt in the absence of the tax advantage of corporate borrowing.[3]

III. THE MODIFIED BALANCING THEORY WITH PERSONAL TAXES

The answer to the puzzle of why firms issue risky debt was hinted at by Miller on p. 271 of "Debt and Taxes." There he states that

> bonds of companies in default will not, in general, yield the issuing stockholders their full tax shield (see MM [27, esp. note 5], Kim [21] and Brennan and Schwartz [21]). Unless the firm has past profits against which its current losses can be carried back, or unless it can escape the vigilance of

the I.R.S. and unload the corporate corpse on a taxable firm, some of the interest deduction goes to waste. To entice firms to issue risky bonds, therefore, the risk-adjusted supply rate would have to be less than $r_0(1/(1 - t_c))$, and presumably the more so the greater the likelihood of default.

An essentially similar effect will be produced by the bankruptcy costs discussed earlier. And this will imply, among other things, that the full burden of the bankruptcy costs or lending costs is not necessarily borne by the debtors as is frequently supposed. Part of the costs are shifted to the bond buyers in the form of lower risk-adjusted rates of interest in equilibrium.

These statements are quite brief, and yet they cover most of the essential ingredients in the new versions of the balancing theory of optimal capital structure developed by DeAngelo and Masulis (1980a), Kim (1982), and, most recently, Ross (1985).

In this section the intuition underlying these new balancing theories is developed.[4] The following section then examines the resulting testable implications and reviews the empirical evidence.

A. Underutilization of Tax Shields

When firms do not have sufficient earnings to fully utilize current tax shields, they may suffer a loss of value due to underutilization of tax shields. Tax shields will be underutilized if firms are unable to costlessly carry forward or backward unused tax shields and cannot sell them at the full utilization value through sale and leasebacks or mergers. The loss of value can occur either with or without bankruptcy.

To isolate the impact of underutilization of tax shields on capital structure decisions, assume that the firm has already made its investment decisions; that is, both the level of nondebt tax shields and the probability distribution of operating earnings are determined exogenously.[5] Then additional borrowing will increase the total amount of tax shields and hence will increase the probability that some tax shields will be underutilized due to insufficient operating earnings. Thus, the *incremental* value of interest tax shields will decrease as the firm increases its financial leverage. In terms of Miller's framework, the declining incremental value of interest tax shields implies a negative slope for the supply curve of taxable corporate bonds.

Following Miller's notations, let t_c, t_{ps}, t_{pb} be the tax rates on corporate income, personal income from stocks, and personal income from bonds, respectively, and let r and r_0 be the risk-adjusted (certainty equivalent) rates of return on taxable and tax-exempt bonds. Also, let t_c' be the risk-adjusted marginal corporate tax rate that explicitly accounts for the declining incremental value of interest tax shields ($t_c' \cdot r$), and assume that the present value of personal taxes on income from stocks is zero ($t_{ps} = 0$). Then, by equating the marginal value of interest tax shields ($t_c' \cdot r$) with the differential cost between issuing bonds and (tax-exempt) stock ($r - r_0$), we obtain a supply curve: $r = r_0/(1 - t_c')$.[6] Because the marginal value of interest tax shields declines with additional borrowing, t_c' decreases with leverage, and hence, the

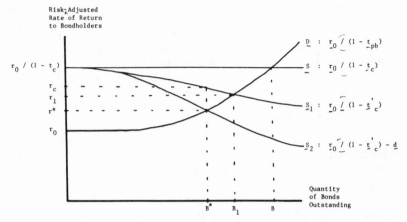

Figure 1. Equilibrium in the Market for Bonds with Underutilization of Tax Shields and Various Leverage-Related Deadweight Costs.

supply curve has a negative slope. This supply curve is depicted by S_1 in Fig. 1, along with Miller's supply and demand curves, S and D.

With a downward-sloping supply curve, the aggregate equilibrium borrowing (B_1) and the equilibrium taxable interest rate (r_1) are both less than those in Miller's equilibrium [B and $r_0/(1 - t_c)$, respectively]. This means that the marginal bondholder's tax rate, t_p^*, is less than t_c; hence, the personal tax premium demanded by the marginal bondholder, $r_1 - r_0 = t_p^* \cdot r_1$, is less than $t_c \cdot r_1$.[7]

Notice that $t_c \cdot r_1$ is the value of corporate interest tax shields only if a firm can fully utilize tax shields with certainty. Such a firm will find the marginal tax benefit exceeds the personal tax premium demanded by the marginal bondholder. Consequently, it will borrow more, making the probability of underutilizing tax shields positive and making the risk-adjusted marginal tax rate, t_c', smaller. The firm will stop borrowing when the marginal benefit of interest tax shields $(t_c' \cdot r_1)$ is equal to the difference between the costs of debt and equity $(r_1 - r_0)$. Because $r_1 - r_0 = t_p^* \cdot r_1$ from the demand equation, t_c' will be equal to t_p^*; that is, firms will maximize their market values when their risk-adjusted marginal corporate rate (t_c') is equal to the marginal bondholder's tax rate (t_p^*).

This is one version of the new balancing theory with personal taxes. Note that it does not even require a positive probability of bankruptcy. All that is needed to establish an interior optimum is the uncertainty regarding a firm's ability to fully utilize tax shields in low earnings states. However, this theoretical strength (generality) of the model can also be its empirical weakness. In this new balancing theory, the maximum possible net tax benefit is $(t_c - t_p^*)r_1$, which is substantially smaller than the traditional notion of the interest tax shields, $t_c \cdot r_1$. With only the possible underutilization of tax shields driving t_p^* below t_c, the difference between t_p^* and t_c may not be economically significant.

B. Leverage-Related Deadweight Costs

If the various leverage-related deadweight costs described in the previous section are included in the above framework, the difference between t_c and t_p^* will increase, and, as a consequence, the tax advantage of corporate borrowing will be more significant. The inclusion of deadweight costs will also provide more powerful empirical predictions. In this subsection a more general equilibrium condition is developed, with both underutilization of tax shields and leverage-related deadweight costs considered. For completeness, Miller's assumption that the present value of personal taxes on income from stocks (t_{ps}) is zero is also relaxed.

In the presence of deadweight costs, the cost of borrowing is different from the rate of return to bondholders. The marginal risk-adjusted before-tax cost of borrowing, r_c, consists of the equilibrium risk-adjusted rate of return to bondholders, r, and the marginal risk-adjusted ex ante leverage-related deadweight costs per dollar of borrowing, d; that is, $r_c = r + d$. The firm will be indifferent between issuing bonds and stocks if the marginal risk-adjusted after-tax cost of issuing bonds, $r_c(1 - t_c') = (r + d)(1 - t_c')$, is equal to the marginal risk-adjusted cost of issuing stocks, r_s:

(1) $$(r + d)(1 - t_c') = r_s.$$

Investors will be indifferent between holding stocks and bonds if the risk-adjusted after-tax rates of return are the same:

(2) $$r(1 - t_{pb}) = r_s(1 - t_{ps}).$$

Since, in equilibrium, demand must equal supply, substituting equation (2) into equation (1) yields the aggregate equilibrium condition

(3) $$r_s \left[1 - \frac{(1 - t_c')(1 - t_{ps})}{1 - t_p^*} \right] = d^*(1 - t_c'),$$

where d^* is the equilibrium level of the marginal ex ante deadweight costs borne by issuers of corporate bonds.

The left side of equation (3) is the net tax advantage per dollar of corporate borrowing, which should be strictly positive if the equilibrium level of deadweight cost is positive ($d^* > 0$). Thus, the equilibrium condition states that firms will issue risky debt to the point where the marginal tax advantage is equal to the marginal after-tax ex ante deadweight costs. At the margin the deadweight cost per dollar of borrowing, d^*, is the same for all firms.

To compare graphically this generalized balancing theory with the equilibrium conditions described earlier, we again assume for convenience that $t_{ps} = 0$. With this assumption, $r_s = r_0$, and hence the supply function in (1) becomes $r = r_0/(1 - t_c') - d$. This new supply curve is depicted by S_2 in Fig. 1, which has a more negative slope than S_1 because of the deadweight costs.[8] The vertical distance between S_1 and S_2 represents the marginal risk-adjusted leverage-related deadweight costs, d.

The steeper negative slope of S_2 reduces both the level of aggregate borrowing and the equilibrium risk-adjusted rate of return to bondholders (i.e., B_1 to B^* and r_1 to r^*). This results in a lower marginal bondholder's tax rate and hence a greater net tax advantage of corporate borrowing. In other words, leverage-related deadweight costs increase the marginal tax advantage of borrowing because they decrease the supply of bonds. A smaller supply of bonds translates to a lower equilibrium rate of return to bondholders and hence a lower cost of borrowing to the stockholders.[9]

To put it another way, the deadweight costs make it possible for stockholders to pay a lower rate of return to bondholders (r^*) and to eliminate a large portion of what Miller calls "bondholder surplus." In Miller's equilibrium, the entire area between the supply line S and the demand curve D in Fig. 1 represents the bondholder surplus; in this generalized equilibrium, only the area between the dotted line extending from r^* (through the intersection point of D and S_2) and the demand curve D is the bondholder surplus. This reduction in the bondholder surplus is the source of the positive net tax advantage of corporate borrowing.

IV. EMPIRICAL EVIDENCE

The upshot of these new balancing theories of optimal capital structure with personal taxes is the recognition that the existence of an optimal capital structure in Miller's equilibrium is essentially an empirical issue. If the underutilization of tax shields in low earnings states and leverage-related deadweight costs are economically significant, they will reduce the supply of corporate bonds and decrease the equilibrium rate of return to bondholders. A lower equilibrium return to bondholders, in turn, means a lower after-tax cost of borrowing relative to equity and hence a positive net tax advantage of corporate debt. Thus, to test the generalized balancing theory against Miller's irrelevance theorem, we must examine whether deadweight costs and underutilization of tax shields have significant impacts on the rate of return to bondholders.

To draw testable implications from the theory, we substitute equation (2) and $t_{pb} = t_p^*$ into equilibrium condition (3) to obtain

$$(4) \qquad 1 - t_p^* = \left(1 + \frac{d^*}{r}\right)(1 - t_c')(1 - t_{ps}).$$

Since $r = r_0/(1 - t_p^*)$, equation (4) can be written as

$$(5) \qquad \frac{r_0}{r} = \left(1 + \frac{d^*}{r}\right)(1 - t_c')(1 - t_{ps}),$$

which states that the ratio of the risk-adjusted tax-exempt rate to the risk-adjusted taxable rate (r_0/r) is positively related to d^* and is inversely related to t_c'. Note that both d^* and t_c' are economywide ex ante variables that are sensitive to general economic conditions. When the economy is sluggish, d^* will increase because of a higher expectation of default, and t_c' will decrease because of a lower expectation of corporate earnings; as a consequence, the ratio between the tax-exempt and the taxable rate (r_0/r) will increase. Conversely, the ratio will decrease during a period of vigorous economic activity. In other words, the theory predicts an inverse relation between the ratio of r_0/r and the level of economic activity.

This prediction is consistent with the evidence presented in a recent paper by Buser and Hess (1986). Using monthly yield data on newly issued one-year prime-grade municipal securities and one-year U.S. Treasury securities from 1959 through 1982 as measures of r_0 and r, respectively, they find that the ratio of r_0/r is significantly inversely related to changes in aggregate industrial production.

To provide more direct evidence, Buser and Hess also measure a marketwide default premium by the (normalized) yield spread for Baa corporate bonds and one-year U.S. Treasury securities. This default premium reflects the market's expectation of corporate default and hence is directly related to the market's valuation of the ex ante deadweight costs (d^*). Consistent with the theoretical [equation (5)], they find that r_0/r is positively related to the default premium at the 0.0001 significance level.

These findings by Buser and Hess are further supported in a recent study (1986) by Kamma and Trzcinka that reexamines Trzcinka's earlier study (1982). Trzcinka originally compared municipal bond rates to taxable corporate rates of comparable credit rating and maturity from 1970 through 1979 and found that the implied marginal bondholder's tax rate is equal to the corporate tax rate. However, when Kamma and Trzcinka perform similar tests on new data from 1979 through 1985, they reach a quite different conclusion.

In contrast to Trzcinka's finding, Kamma and Trzcinka produce an estimate for the marginal bondholder tax rate that is significantly less than the corporate rate. They attribute the difference in the results between the two studies to a dramatic decline in the marginal bondholder tax rate during the 1981–1982 recession. Because during recessions d^* increases and t'_c decreases, the balancing theory [equation (4)] predicts a fall in the marginal bondholder's tax rate.[10]

In sum, the most recent and most rigorous time-series analyses of the relation between tax-exempt and taxable interest rates provide strong evidence that deadweight costs and possible underutilization of tax shields are sufficiently significant to affect the pricing of bonds.[11] The evidence implies that the leverage-related costs reduce the supply of corporate bonds and lower the cost of borrowing, which in turn generates a positive net tax advantage of corporate debt. Firms will weigh the net tax advantage of borrowing against leverage-related costs in choosing their debt ratios.

This balancing theory also has a cross-sectional implication that some firms will borrow more than others. Recall that equilibrium condition (3) implies that the optimal level of the marginal ex ante deadweight costs, d^*, is the same for all firms. Thus, those firms that reach d^* relatively faster with additional borrowing will have less leverage, and those that reach d^* relatively slower will have more leverage. This means that firms that are more (less) likely to encounter financial distress for a given degree of leverage will be less (more) inclined to borrow.

Consistent with this prediction, Castanias (1983) finds that there is a significant negative relation between observed leverage measures and historical failure rates. He also documents that relative failure rates are rank stationary by business line while differing significantly across business lines. This justifies the use of historical failure rates as measures of expected failure rate. Thus, he argues that firms that are in businesses that are more likely to fail have less debt in their capital structures.

Finally, note that the probability of encountering financial distress for a given degree of financial leverage is positively related to the variability of operating earnings. Bradley, Jarrell, and Kim (BJK) (1984) demonstrate via simulation that the balancing theory implies an inverse relation between earning volatility and financial leverage.[12] The authors use the standard deviation of the first difference in annual earnings before interest, depreciation, and taxes, divided by the average value of total assets as a measure of earnings volatility. Using this variable, they find that long-run average debt ratios (as measured by 20-year averages) are significantly inversely related to earnings volatility. In addition, BJK show that industry classifications explain 54 percent of variation in firm leverage ratios. Furthermore, even when their regressions include dummy variables for industry categories, the inverse relation between earnings volatility and firm leverage remains highly significant.

In sum, the cross-sectional tests based on firm-specific data complement the time-series studies in providing results that are consistent with the predictions of the generalized balancing theory.[13]

V. CONCLUSION

We showed that both underutilization of tax shields and leverage-related deadweight costs reduce the supply of corporate bonds in Miller's equilibrium. A smaller supply of corporate bonds translates to a lower equilibrium rate of return to bondholders and hence a lower after-tax cost of debt relative to equity. This gives rise to the positive net tax advantage of corporate debt and necessitates the "balancing act" between the tax advantage of borrowing and leverage-related costs.

To test the generalized balancing theory against Miller's irrelevance theorem, we must empirically examine the economic importance of deadweight costs and underutilization of tax shields. The most recent and most rigorous time-series studies provide strong evidence that these costs have significant impact on rates of return to bondholders and, by implication, on the relative costs of debt and equity. Consistent with this conclusion, recent cross-sectional studies based on firm-specific data provide results that suggest that the leverage-related costs have important impacts on corporate financing behavior. Given this empirical support, it is difficult not to conclude that there exists an optimal capital structure in Miller's equilibrium.

NOTES

[1] This literature was instigated by Stiglitz (1972) when he attempted to model an optimal debt-equity ratio with a divergence in the estimation of the chances of bankruptcy between the lender and the borrower. Leland and Pyle (1977) and Ross (1977) later modeled the debt-equity choice as that of financial signaling. Since then, their models have been modified and extended by Talmor (1981), Heinkel (1982), Lee, Thakor, and Vora (1983), Myers and Majluf (1984), and Narayanan (1985).

[2] The above definition of the present value of interest tax shields requires the perpetuity assumption in the Modigliani and Miller tax correction model. With a finite maturity and an income tax, the present value of the interest tax shields is only a fraction of the amount defined above.

[3] Although it could have been argued that some firms issue risky debt in response to the demand arising from the financial leverage clientele phenomenon (Miller 1977 and Kim, Lewellen, and McConnell 1979), no one has derived the notion of financial leverage clientele in a setting that allows for risky debt.

[4] These theories are in essence analyses of the supply side of corporate securities in a modified Miller equilibrium. For extensive analyses of the demand side with risk aversion in Miller's equilibrium, see Modigliani (1982) and Kim (1982).

[5] See Cooper and Franks (1983) for an illustration of the possible impacts of underutilization of tax shields on firms' investment decisions.

[6] If income from stocks is untaxed, the risk-adjusted cost of equity must be the tax-exempt rate r_0.

[7] The personal tax premium comes from the demand equation that $r_1(1 - t_p^*) = r_0$.

[8] If t_{ps} is positive, the supply curves S_1 and S_2 in Fig. 1 become $r_0/(1 - t_c')(1 - t_{ps})$ and $r_0/(1 - t_c')(1 - t_{ps}) - d$, respectively, both with an intercept of $r_0/(1 - t_c)(1 - t_{ps})$.

[9] With the assumption of $t_{ps} = 0$, the optimal capital structure is reached when $(t_c' - t_p^*)r_0/(1 - t_p^*) = d^*(1 - t_c')$. Thus, unlike the earlier equilibrium described in Section III. A, the marginal corporate rate (t_c') remains above the marginal bondholder tax rate (t_p^*) at the optimal capital structure. The reason is that the deadweight costs drive a wedge between the risk-adjusted cost of borrowing and the risk-adjusted rate of return to bondholders.

[10] Kamma and Trzcinka also allow for the possibility that the effect of the 1981–1982 recession on the marginal bondholder tax rate may have been reinforced by the Economic Recovery Tax Act (ERTA) of 1981, which may have lowered marginal tax rates at every income level. They observe that decreases in personal tax rates increase the amount of taxable debt demanded at each taxable interest rate; that is, the slope of the demand curve in Fig. 1 becomes flatter when t_{pb} declines. A flatter demand curve will lower the marginal bondholder's tax rate below the corporate rate if and only if the supply curve is downward sloping. If, as Miller suggests, the leverage-related costs are trivial, the tax law changes should have no effect on the marginal bondholder tax rate.

[11] For previous empirical evidence on the relation between tax-exempt and taxable rates, see Skelton (1983) and Jordan and Pettway (1985).

[12] This intuitively appealing prediction on the relation between earnings volatility and leverage is not an unambiguous implication of the balancing theory. The ambiguity arises from the normality assumption on the distribution of firm value (see Scott 1976 and Castanias 1983). Simulations by Bradley, Jarrell, and Kim (1984), however, demonstrate that, if deadweight costs are economically significant, the debt ratio is inversely related to the variability of earnings.

[13] For other recent cross-sectional studies on issues related to optimal capital structure, see Chaplinski (1983), Cordes and Sheffrin (1983), Altman (1984), and Campbell (1986). The results provided in these studies are generally consistent with the existence of an optimal capital structure in Miller's equilibrium.

REFERENCES

Altman, E. I. 1984. "A Further Empirical Investigation of the Bankruptcy Cost Question." *Journal of Finance* 39: 1067–90.

Auerbach, A. J., and King, M. A. 1983. "Taxation, Portfolio Choice and Debt-Equity Ratios: A General Equilibrium Model." *Quarterly Journal of Economics* 98: 587–610.

Baxter, N. 1967. "Leverage, Risk of Ruin and the Cost of Capital." *Journal of Finance* 22: 395–403.

Bhattacharya, S. 1980. "Nondissipative Signalling Structures and Dividend Policy." *Quarterly Journal of Economics* 95: 1–24.

Black, F. 1971. "Taxes and Capital Market Equilibrium." Working paper No. 21A, Associates in Finance, Belmont, Mass., April.

––––––. 1973. "Taxes and Capital Market Equilibrium under Uncertainty." Working paper No. 21B, Chicago, May.

Bradley, M.; Jarrell, G. A.; and Kim, E. H. 1984. "On the Existence of an Optimal Capital Structure: Theory and Evidence." *Journal of Finance* 39: 857–78.

Brennan, M., and Schwartz, E. 1978. "Corporate Income Taxes, Valuation, and the Problem of Optimal Capital Structure." *Journal of Business* 51: 103–14.

Buser, S. A., and Hess, P. J. 1986. "Empirical Determinants of the Relative Yields on Taxable and Tax-Exempt Securities." *Journal of Financial Economics* 17: 335–56.

Campbell, C. J. 1986. "Industry Leverage Regularities: Optimal Capital Structures or Neutral Mutations?" Ph.D. Dissertation, University of Michigan.

Castanias, R. 1983. "Bankruptcy Risk and Optimal Capital Structure." *Journal of Finance* 38: 1617–36.

Chaplinsky, S. 1983. "The Economic Determinants of Leverage: Theories and Evidence." Ph.D. Dissertation, University of Chicago.

Chen, A. H., and Kim, E. H. 1979. "Theories of Corporate Debt Policy: A Synthesis." *Journal of Finance* 34: 371–84.

Constantinides, G. M. 1983. "Capital Market Equilibrium with Personal Tax." *Econometrica* 51: 611–36.

––––––. 1984. "Optimal Stock Trading with Personal Taxes: Implications for Prices and the Abnormal January Returns." *Journal of Financial Economics* 13: 65–89.

––––––. 1985. "Discussion." *Journal of Finance* 40: 657–58.

Constantinides, G. M., and Ingersoll, J. E., Jr. 1984. "Optimal Bond Trading with Personal Taxes." *Journal of Financial Economics* 13: 299–336. Reprinted Chapter 6, volume 1.

Cooper, I., and Franks, J. R. 1983. "The Interaction of Financial and Investment Decisions When the Firm Has Unused Tax Credits." *Journal of Finance* 38: 571–84.

Cordes, J. J., and Sheffrin, S. M. 1981. "Taxation and the Sectoral Allocation of Capital in the U.S." *National Tax Journal* 34: 419–32.

––––––. 1983. "Estimating the Tax Advantage of Corporate Debt." *Journal of Finance* 38: 95–106.

DeAngelo, H., and Masulis, R. 1980a. "Optimal Capital Structure under Corporate and Personal Taxation." *Journal of Financial Economics* 8: 3–30.

––––––. 1980b. "Leverage and Dividend Irrelevancy under Corporate and Personal Taxation." *Journal of Finance* 35: 453–67.

Dotan, A., and Ravid, S. A. 1985. "On the Interaction of Real and Financial Decisions of the Firm under Uncertainty." *Journal of Finance* 40: 501–18.

Fama, E. 1980. "Agency Problems and the Theory of the Firm." *Journal of Political Economy* 88: 288–307.

Farrar, D., and Selwyn, L. L. 1967. "Taxes, Corporate Policy, and Returns to Investors." *National Tax Journal* 20: 444–54.

Gordon, R. H., and Bradford, D. F. 1980. "Taxation and the Stock Market Valuation of Capital Gains and Dividends." *Journal of Public Economics* 14: 109–36.

———. 1981. "Corporation Finance." In H. J. Aaron and J. A. Pechman, eds., *How Taxes Affect Economic Behavior*. Washington, D.C.: The Brookings Institution.

Heinkel, R. 1982. "A Theory of Capital Structure Relevance under Imperfect Information." *Journal of Finance* 37: 1141–50.

Jensen, M. C., and Meckling, W. H. 1976. "Theory of the Firm: Managerial Behavior, Agency Costs and Ownership Structure." *Journal of Financial Economics* 3: 305–60.

Jordan, B. D., and Pettway, R. H. 1985. "The Pricing of Short-Term Debt and the Miller Hypothesis: A Note." *Journal of Finance* 40: 589–94.

Kamma, S., and Trczinka, C. 1986. "Marginal Taxes, Municipal Bond Risk and the Miller Equilibrium: New Evidence and Some Predictive Tests." Working paper, State University of New York at Buffalo.

Kim, E. H. 1978a. "A Mean-Variance Theory of Optimal Capital Structure and Corporate Debt Capacity." *Journal of Finance* 33: 45–64.

———. 1978b. "Discussion." *Journal of Finance* 33: 754–57.

———. 1982. "Miller's Equilibrium, Shareholder Leverage Clienteles and Optimal Capital Structure." *Journal of Finance* 37: 301–18.

Kim, E. H.; Lewellen, W. G.; and McConnell, J. J. 1979. "Financial Leverage Clienteles: Theory and Evidence." *Journal of Financial Economics* 7: 83–110.

Kraus, A., and Litzenberger, R. 1973. "A State-Preference Model of Optimal Financial Leverage." *Journal of Finance* 28: 911–22.

Lee, W. L.; Thakor, A. V.; and Vora, Gautam. 1983. "Screening, Market Signalling, and Capital Structure Theory." *Journal of Finance* 38: 1507–18.

Leland, H., and Pyle, D. 1977. "Information Asymmetries, Financial Structure and Financial Intermediation." *Journal of Finance* 32: 371–87. Reprinted Chapter 8, this volume.

Litzenberger, R. H. 1986. "Some Observations on Capital Structure and the Impact of Recent Recapitalizations on Share Prices." *Journal of Financial and Quantitative Analysis* 21: 59–72.

Litzenberger, R. H., and Van Horne, J. C. 1978. "Elimination of the Double Taxation of Dividends and Corporate Financial Policy." *Journal of Finance* 33: 737–49.

Masulis, R. W. 1980. "The Effects of Capital Structure Change on Security Prices: A Study of Exchange Offers." *Journal of Financial Economics* 8: 139–78.

Miller, M. 1977. "Debt and Taxes." *Journal of Finance* 32: 261–75. Reprinted Chapter 2, this volume.

Miller, M., and Scholes, M. 1978. "Dividends and Taxes." *Journal of Financial Economics* 6: 333–64.

Modigliani, F. 1982. "Debt, Dividend Policy, Taxes, Inflation and Market Valuation." *Journal of Finance* 37: 255–74.

Modigliani, F., and Miller, M. H. 1958. "The Cost of Capital, Corporation Finance and the Theory of Investment." *American Economic Review* 48: 267–97.

———. 1963. "Corporate Income Taxes and the Cost of Capital: A Correction." *American Economic Review* 53: 433–43.

Myers, S. 1977. "Determinants of Corporate Borrowing." *Journal of Financial Economics* 5: 147–75.

Myers, S., and Majluf, N. S. 1984. "Corporate Financing and Investment Decisions When Firms Have Information That Investors Do Not Have." *Journal of Financial Economics* 13: 187–221.

Narayanan, M. P. 1985. "Corporate Lemons and Capital Structure." Working paper, University of Florida, October.

Park, S. Y., and Williams, J. 1985. "Taxes, Capital Structure, and Bondholder Clienteles." *Journal of Business* 58: 203–24.

Ross, S. A. 1977. "The Determination of Financial Structure: The Incentive Signalling Approach." *Bell Journal of Economics* 8: 23–40.

———. 1985. "Debt and Taxes and Uncertainty." *Journal of Finance* 40: 637–56.

Scott, J. 1976. "A Theory of Optimal Capital Structure." *Bell Journal of Economics* 7: 33–54.

Skelton, J. L. 1983. "Banks, Firms and the Relative Pricing of Tax Exempt and Taxable Bonds." *Journal of Financial Economics* 12: 343–56.

Stapleton, R. C. 1972. "Taxes, the Cost of Capital and the Theory of Investment." *The Economic Journal* 82: 1273–92.

Stiglitz, J. E. 1972. "Some Aspects of the Pure Theory of Corporate Finance: Bankruptcies and Take-overs." *Bell Journal of Economics and Management Science* 3: 458–82.

———. 1973. "Taxation, Corporate Financial Policy, and the Cost of Capital." *Journal of Public Economics* 2: 1–34.

Taggart, R. A., Jr. 1980. "Taxes and Corporate Capital Structure in an Incomplete Market." *Journal of Finance* 35: 645–60.

Talmor, E. 1981. "Asymmetric Information, Signalling, and Optimal Corporate Financial Decisions." *Journal of Financial and Quantitative Analysis* 16: 413–36.

Titman, S. 1984. "The Effect of Capital Structure on a Firm's Liquidation Decision." *Journal of Financial Economics* 13: 137–52.

Trczinka, C. 1982. "The Pricing of Tax-Exempt Bonds and the Miller Hypothesis." *Journal of Finance* 37: 907–24.

discussion | **Issues in the Theory of Optimal Capital Structure**

Myron S. Scholes
Mark A. Wolfson

Graduate School of Business
Stanford University

I. INTRODUCTION

In 1976 in his presidential address to the American Finance Association, Merton Miller presented an equilibrium analysis of how taxes affect the optimal amount of debt in the firm's capital structure. In the published version of his address, "Debt and Taxes" (1977), Miller presented a clear and simple model demonstrating that when the tax positions of both the suppliers and demanders of debt are considered, the amount of debt in the capital structure of a firm may be a matter of indifference.

This conclusion was all the more striking because throughout the 10- to 15-year period following the Modigliani-Miller (1958) cost of capital paper and their tax correction paper (1963), researchers had been looking for the nontax costs associated with debt that balanced the benefits of the tax deductibility of interest.[1] Miller pointed out that an important cost of issuing debt that had been ignored was the premium required by bondholders in equilibrium to cover the tax penalty on interest income they earned on holding corporate bonds. To induce these individuals to hold bonds rather than tax-favored stock, issuers must pay a higher before-tax rate of interest. Miller showed that the resulting corporate after-tax cost of debt finance could be exactly the same as the risk-adjusted after-tax cost of equity finance. Although there would be an optimal aggregate amount of debt in the economy, there would be no tax advantage for any particular firm to issue either debt or equity.

In summarizing the debate that followed the publication of the Miller equilibrium, Kim (1988) points out that if there is no tax advantage to issuing debt rather than equity, firms would issue no risky debt, given its associated deadweight information costs. Such a statement becomes a non sequitur, however, once it is acknowledged that there are many circumstances in which the information costs of issuing equity exceed those of issuing debt, either

The suggestions of George Constantinides, Harvey Galper, John McConnell, James Patell, Joseph Stiglitz, and Sheridan Titman are gratefully acknowledged.

because of adverse-selection problems, such as those discussed by Leland and Pyle (1977) and Ross (1977), or because of moral-hazard problems associated with issuing outside equity, as discussed in Jensen and Meckling (1976).

On the other hand, if the corporate tax can be viewed as progressive (e.g., at low levels of taxable income, interest deductions cannot be fully utilized at the statutory corporate tax rate) and/or if the information-related costs of issuing debt less those of issuing equity are convex in the amount of debt issued (even if the difference is negative), then a unique interior optimum (in the amount of debt to be included in the capital structure of a corporation) can occur; that is, capital structure can matter. Indeed, as we will discuss later, the empirical evidence on how stock prices respond to exchange offers (e.g., debt-for-equity swaps), equity issuances and repurchases, and convertible debt issuances can be interpreted as evidence of a progressive corporate income tax in a setting in which managers are better informed about the prospects of their firms than are passive owners.

Even if we were to accept the premise that issuing equity entails no deadweight costs and that the deadweight costs associated with the issuance of risky debt are convex in the amount of debt issued, we would still have difficulty resolving one of the key puzzles that inspired Miller to produce a model in which the maximum possible tax advantage to issuing debt is small. And that puzzle is, how can we explain the modest amount of debt issued by the IBMs of the world, firms that not only have plenty of taxable income to shield, but also could issue essentially default-free debt (at negligible dead-weight costs)?

In the following sections we argue that such puzzles may be resolved if we consider a richer menu of capital structure components than simply debt and equity. There are many classes of claimants to the assets of the firm, including the firm's suppliers, employees, customers, bankers, limited partners, coventurers, lessors, various classes of bondholders, preferred stockholders, common stockholders, competitors, the public at large (to the extent they participate in litigation claims and redistributive claims brought about by legislation), and various government agencies, especially the taxing authority. The capital structure problem is but a small piece of a larger tax planning problem, which itself is a problem of the optimal design of organizations. The optimal tax planning strategy depends heavily on the tax rates of the firm and the tax rates of all of its claimants, both now and in the future. The optimal strategy also depends heavily on the costs, especially the idiosyncratic information costs related to problems of moral hazard and adverse selection, of issuing and retiring various types of securities. Adding to the problem are the costs of structuring and restructuring the asset side of the balance sheet to affect both the marginal tax rate and the information costs associated with issuing various classes of securities.

Optimal tax planning must also consider the taxation of the economic activities of the firm in all the tax jurisdictions wherein it faces liability, including states and localities, federal taxation in the United States, and a host of foreign country taxes. In addition, if cross-sectional differences in capital structure are to be understood, models must include the effects of the dynamic elements of the tax system [for example, the Tax Reform Act (TRA) of 1986 (and 1987 and 1997 and ...)] as well as cross-sectional differences in the ways various industries and economic activities are taxed. If we were to ignore the dynamic and uncertain elements of tax planning, as well as the costliness of reorganizing economic activity, the resulting theory of the effects of taxes on the investment and financing decisions of firms inevitably would become sterile and as hopelessly weak in predictive power as Myers (1984) suggested in his 1983 presidential address to the American Finance Association.

For example, the "IBM debt puzzle" might be explained, in part, by considering multinational tax planning problems. U.S. tax rules for the effective deductibility of interest (for income tax and foreign tax credit purposes) require that firms apportion interest deductions between the U.S. and foreign tax jurisdiction based on the book or market value of assets (unless the interest is on debt collateralized by assets concentrated in a specific tax jurisdiction). Even for corporations with plenty of taxable income, the marginal tax rate effectively applied to interest deductions may be insufficient to compensate for the risk-adjusted yield premium on debt (relative to equity) required by the marketplace. Alternatively, a firm that generates most of its income in a state without an income tax has less of a tax incentive to issue debt than one operating primarily in a high-state-tax jurisdiction. Similar considerations apply to a firm that generates enough "tax preferences" (such as accelerated depreciation) to be subject to the corporate add-on minimum tax, in which case its maximum marginal federal tax rate drops from 46 percent to only 39.1 percent, due to the interaction between the add-on minimum tax and the regular corporate tax.[2] Such a firm rationally could issue no debt despite generating considerable amounts of taxable income and despite being able to issue default-free debt without incurring any issuance costs.

The discussion above suggests that to build a rich model of capital structure planning requires that we abandon a neoclassical perspective where transactions can be effected costlessly and information is freely and equally available to all participants in the market.[3] It also requires that we consider the interactions between investments and capital structure. It is to these issues that we now turn, along with a discussion of the implications of the 1986 TRA for capital structure policy and the viability of the corporate organizational form.

II. TAXATION AND CORPORATE FINANCE

A. Substitutes for Debt to Produce Tax Shields

We certainly are not the first to point out the lack of independence between investment decisions and financing decisions. For example, DeAngelo and Masulis (1980) extended the Miller (1977) model by incorporating uncertainty and by introducing substitutes for interest deductions (notably depreciation) to serve as tax shields in tax planning. An important limitation of their work, however, is that production decisions are taken to be specified exogenously, and optimal debt-to-equity ratios are determined for a given level of depreciation shields and for a given distribution of corporate income. The dual of this problem would be to fix debt-to-equity ratios and to determine the optimal level of investment in depreciable equipment along with the optimal form of contracting for control of such assets (e.g., to buy or to lease). A more general approach, however, is to determine the most cost-effective means to organize the productive activities of the firm. This includes not only the information and transaction costs of contracting but also their interaction with the costs of producing tax shields. Taxes can be shielded not only by issuing debt and purchasing depreciable equipment but also by engaging in research and development activity, by accelerating compensation to employees, by entering into long-term construction contracts, and by selling products on an installment basis, among a broad list of other alternatives. In short, the tax planning problem is of considerably greater dimensionality than just the correct mix of debt and equity.

B. Effcient Tax Planning versus Tax Minimization

There are myriad institutional arrangements that are driven by a desire to mitigate the costs of taxation. In the presence of costly contracting, however, efficient tax planning often requires abandoning the goal of tax minimization. As discussed in Scholes and Wolfson (1986b), the goal of tax minimization often conflicts with such other goals as transaction cost minimization. This has important implications for organizational design in general and corporate financial policy in particular, as we intend to show.

To illustrate, let us consider the incentive of stockholders to increase the risk of investment and thereby make themselves wealthier at the expense of bondholders (e.g., Jensen and Meckling 1976, Myers 1977, Galai and Masulis 1976). Without taxes and other constraints, stockholders gain at the expense of bondholders by increasing the value of their right to put the firm to the bondholders. This can be accomplished by investing in projects that increase risks or by replacing equities with additional liabilities of equal or greater priority than those already outstanding. The presence of taxes, however, alters the incentive problem. In those states of nature wherein the put option would be exercised but for the tax considerations, the firm is most likely to have incurred net operating losses. If because of transaction costs, the firm cannot eliminate its net operating losses (NOLs) within its tax year (e.g., by cost effectively issuing equity and using the proceeds to buy fully taxable bonds), it faces a progressive tax schedule. In the extreme the stockholders could lose the value of their NOLs in the course of putting the firm to the bondholders. NOLs represent a potential claim against the government, and this asset reduces the value of the put option and influences the initial investment and financing decisions of the firm. A progressive schedule of corporate tax rates induces a degree of risk aversion, insofar as the selection of investments is concerned, that mitigates the preference for risk induced by the put option.[4,5]

C. Market Frictions and Tax Rule Restrictions Prevent Tax Arbitrage

In a world of no transaction or information costs, the corporate tax planning problem would be trivial. As long as there exist two assets whose returns are taxed differently, opportunities for tax arbitrage would be available if there were any cross-sectional differences in tax rates. It would be efficient to contract until all personal and corporate marginal tax rates were the same (possibly zero). Hamada and Scholes (1985) argue that one of the crucial assumptions of the Miller model is that entities in different tax brackets cannot engage in tax arbitrage: they cannot sell assets with returns that are taxed at one rate to profit from buying securities that are taxed at a different rate. Stiglitz (1985) presents similar arguments. Without costs, it is possible for tax planners to eliminate the differences between corporate and individual tax rates, and, depending on the particular configuration of rules and restrictions, the system could yield no tax revenue at all. Somehow this difficulty is finessed in many models in finance by imposing (implicitly or explicitly) exogenous restrictions such as no short sales, fixed supplies of securities, or infinite costs to implement certain tax planning strategies. But such restrictions are questionable in the frictionless perfectly competitive settings that are otherwise assumed.

Five important characteristics of tax codes encourage economic agents to expend resources in the tax planning process. One to which we have alluded already is statutory differences in tax rates as a function of income. The second is intertemporal differences in tax rates. The third characteristic is that alternative legal organizational forms used to produce the same goods and services or to hold the same assets are taxed differently. The fourth is that the returns from investing in different economic activities for a given taxpayer are taxed differently. And the fifth is that income may be taxed differently across different tax jurisdictions (e.g., multistate or multinational).

It is the tax rules themselves, however, complemented by the reality that contracting is costly, that constrain the elimination of all cross-sectional and intertemporal differences in marginal tax rates. This combination of market frictions and tax rule restrictions precludes tax arbitrage. Indeed, new tax rules often become necessary to prevent arbitrage as a change in technology (e.g., the creation of an active market in a new financial instrument) reduces the force of a friction.

D. Tax Clienteles and Implicit Taxes

To appreciate the role of taxes and transaction costs in the optimal capital structure decision, it is necessary to introduce the concepts of tax clienteles and implicit taxes. Tax clienteles arise because the ways in which taxpayers organize productive activities have different tax implications for the parties to a contract. Consider, for example, a buy-versus-lease decision in which the user of an asset compares two alternative ways to allocate the property rights to a particular asset. Company A plans to manufacture a product requiring machinery currently owned by Company B. Although Company A can use the investment tax credits and rapid depreciation deductions if it buys the machine, suppose that Company B places a higher value on these tax benefits. For example, suppose that Company B is flush with taxable income, but Company A is uncertain whether its taxable income will be sufficient to use all of the tax benefits of ownership (i.e., the anticipated costs of restructuring to generate taxable income are high). Company B has a tax incentive to lease the machinery to Company A. Company A will capture indirectly some of the tax benefits of using the machine through the terms of the rental contract (e.g., a reduced rental rate). Companies such as B that buy depreciable assets to use or to lease out and companies such as A that capture tax benefits indirectly by leasing are examples of tax clienteles.[6]

Related to the concept of clienteles is the concept of implicit taxes. Implicit taxes represent the *pre-tax* differences in cash flows from investments that are taxed differently.[7] The yield differential between municipal bonds and corporate bonds is an example. The lower pre-tax rate of return on an exempt bond (or on an investment that gives rise to generous investment tax credits and accelerated depreciation allowances) when compared to a taxable bond is an implicit tax. As pointed out earlier, the risk-adjusted required rate of return on shares in the Miller equilibrium could also be well below the rate on fully taxable bonds. Naturally, a taxpayer whose marginal explicit tax rate on taxable interest income is below the implicit tax rate on municipal bond income would prefer to hold taxable bonds; that is, the natural tax clientele for taxpayers that face relatively low explicit tax rates is to hold tax-disfavored assets, such as fully taxable bonds. It is in this sense that tax clienteles and implicit taxes are interrelated.

One could factor contracting (and recontracting) costs into the analysis by defining implicit taxes to include such costs. Clienteles then arise not only because of differences in tax treatment across organizational forms but also because of cross-sectional differences in transaction costs. Such costs are an additional source of cross-sectional differences in total (explicit plus implicit) marginal tax rates. Moreover, the presence of recontracting costs introduces a degree of intertemporal dependence in tax planning: history plays a role in the sense that the tax costs of landing in the "wrong" clientele (following a change in conditions or tax status) interact with the transaction costs of reorganizing corporate activities (mobility costs) to move the taxpayer into the "right" clientele.

E. Uncertain Future Tax Status and Changing Tax Clienteles

When the tax status of a firm changes, it generally will consider whether to alter its capital structure and/or its asset allocations. Low-taxed firms would want to buy tax disadvantageous assets (which bear high explicit taxes) and sell tax advantageous assets (which bear high implicit taxes). For example, a firm that purchases equipment (that is eligible for rapid depreciation for tax purposes) when its tax rate is high may find it efficient to sell the equipment, and perhaps lease it back, when its tax rate falls. In a setting wherein managers are better informed about the prospects for the firm than are outsiders, such restructuring might lead other market participants to infer that there is a change in the current or expected future taxpaying status of these firms. Since taxpaying status and real productivity surely are positively correlated, tax-induced changes in asset structure or capital structure could be accompanied by changes in the prices of publicly traded securities. Firms are "forced" to make the change in capital structure or asset makeup because of the implicit tax associated with being in the wrong tax clientele.

Empirical evidence to date is consistent with the valuation implications of this changing tax clientele hypothesis. For example, it has been documented that leverage-increasing exchange offers (e.g., debt exchanged for common stock) are associated with increases in stock price. The opposite is true of leverage-decreasing exchange offers. Moreover, equity issues and convertible debt issues are associated with reductions in stock prices, whereas equity repurchases are associated with increases in stock prices. (See Masulis 1983, Dann and Mikkelson 1984, especially Table 9 on p. 173, and Smith 1986.) This evidence increases our confidence in using capital structure data to make inferences about a firm's taxpaying status.[8]

There are many ways to restructure organizations that serve as substitutes for changes in debt or equity to respond to a change in tax status. For example, those firms emerging from low to high expected tax brackets might consider all of the following tax-motivated changes in strategy. (The opposite would be true for firms expecting a fall in marginal tax rates.)

1. Direct Changes in the Capital Structure. The firm could issue more straight debt rather than common stock, warrants, preferred stock, or convertible debt. Although the interest rate on straight debt will be higher, interest payments are tax deductible. The calculus required here is one of trading off the implicit subsidy received from issuing capital structure components that are tax favored in the hands of investors against the explicit subsidy from the tax deduction for interest on debt.

More specifically, the tax system encourages those firms with the highest expected marginal tax rates to issue "straight" debt with coupon interest fully deductible from taxable income. Among firms that issue straight debt, we would expect those with the highest expected marginal tax rates to issue the least secured debt, since risk premiums are deductible as paid even though they represent payments that compensate for expected future defaults.

The mobility costs associated with reorganizing the capital structure in the face of a change in tax status have implications for the optimal duration of debt. For example, when refinancing is costly, the issuance of noncallable long-term debt will be less expensive than rolling over short-term debt to the same term as long as the issuer remains inframarginal with respect to borrowing long term for the duration of the loan. Not all firms can "afford" the luxury of relatively cheap after-tax long-term debt. If the marginal tax rate becomes insufficient to use the tax shields of the long-term debt cost effectively, then the recapitalization costs associated with long-term debt may render short-term debt the more efficient financing strategy. Hence, issuers of long-term debt signal either that they expect to remain in high marginal tax brackets or that they expect reorganization costs to be low.[9]

Firms with expected marginal tax rates below those of the marginal holder of straight debt are induced by the tax rules to finance operations in ways that provide smaller explicit tax subsidies (the value of which is increasing in marginal explicit tax rates) to the borrower; for example, convertible debt, leases, warrants, preferred stock, common stock, limited partnerships, and joint ventures. The motivation for issuing each of these classes of debt or equity is the implicit subsidy paid to the firm by the suppliers of capital.

Firms with the lowest marginal explicit tax rates are encouraged to issue those instruments that offer the largest *implicit* tax subsidy. This means that the tax rules lead to financing with preferred stock and common stock for firms that expect marginal tax rates below those of firms making extensive use of convertible bonds, since convertible bonds provide both explicit and implicit tax subsidies to the issuer. On the other hand, when management is better informed about the prospects of their firm than are outside suppliers of capital, equity issues might entail "giving away too much of a bargain" to outside investors.

The popularity of convertible bonds is interesting, because they would appear to have some undesirable tax characteristics. Although low current deductions for interest (relative to straight debt) are consistent with a lower marginal tax rate for issuing firms (relative to firms issuing straight debt), conversion into common stock takes place in "good states" for the firm. Such a conversion would alter the capital structure in a way that is less sensible for the firm than before its good fortune. A more efficient tax policy would be for the bonds to be convertible into straight debt using the stock price as a conversion metric. Hence, it is unlikely that the issuance of convertible bonds is motivated primarily by tax considerations.

Another important class of firms that form a natural clientele for particular financial instruments includes those with significant uncertainty about their future tax status. These firms must plan for stochastic tax rates. Owing to the cost of changing the composition of capital structures, these firms must use relatively inefficient financing and investment policies to enable them to respond quickly to changes in their marginal tax rates. For example, as we discussed earlier, they would tend to use short-term debt when their tax rate is high. Alternatively, if marginal tax rates for these firms are highly correlated with reported income, income bonds would be a particularly tax-efficient form of financing. Tax-deductible payments are made to bondholders when income and tax rates are high. Although Miller (1977) lamented that few corporations issue such claims, many corporations do issue them indirectly. Common examples of indirect income bonds include (1) risky bonds with promised fixed coupon payments but payable only if the issuer is solvent; (2) operating leases where the lease payments are tied to revenue; (3) patent royalty agreements; (4) employee bonus plans where the bonus is tied to profitability; (5) pension plans where funding is timed to coincide with high tax rates; and (6) nonqualified stock option plans if there is a positive correlation between the stock price and the profitability of the firm. As with income bonds, many of these contracts involve payments that are contingent upon the realization of a random variable (e.g. revenue or "profit"), which is reported under conditions of moral hazard. In addition, the contracts differ in their degree of correlation between "interest payments" and tax rates. That we observe these substitutes for income bonds suggests that nontax costs of using direct income bonds might be greater than for these other instruments.[10]

2. Changes in Capital Structure Linked to Employee Compensation Contracts. Deferred compensation contracts (both those conditioned on the mere passage of time as well as those tied to future performance) become more attractive when the employer's tax rate is expected to be higher in the future (whether due to a reduced probability of not being able to use tax losses or for other reasons).[11] Similarly, nonqualified stock options become more attractive relative to incentive stock options.[12]

With more highly taxed income it becomes desirable to increase pension funding. Moreover, because of more generous funding opportunities, defined benefit pension plans become relatively more attractive than do defined contribution plans. Overfunded pension accounts earn, tax free, at the before-tax rate of interest.[13] The efficiency of overfunding pension plans depends on the extent of costs related to resolving any ambiguity of the property rights to such assets.

3. Changes in Capital Structure Linked to Customer/Supplier Contracting. Firms that expect their future tax rates to increase will find contracts that defer income to the future to be relatively undesirable. Hence, installment sales (wherein taxable income from the sale of goods is realized in proportion to principal payments received on a note issued by the seller to the buyer) become less attractive from a tax standpoint. Installment sales become more attractive, however, once the tax rate of the firm has increased and is expected to remain high.

Another way to shift income across periods is to sell or buy on credit, using credit terms that differ from market terms. The bargain or punishment element of the credit terms translates into a higher or lower "price" charged for the goods or services that are being financed. For example, cheap financing of a good results in a higher sale price, which in turn leads to higher current taxable income to the seller (lower taxable income to the buyer as the asset is expensed for tax purposes) and lower interest income to the seller in the future (and correspondingly higher income to the buyer due to reduced interest expense in the future).[14]

Note how careful one must be here in linking changes in capital structure to changes in tax status. A firm that generates NOLs may actually issue debt (at below market rates to finance the sale of assets) rather than issue equity to *reduce* its tax burden! A powerful empirical test of how taxes affect financing and investment decisions requires that we factor much more structure into our experimental designs than simply using first differences in debt-to-equity ratios.

4. Changes in Capital Structure Linked to Investment Policy. Lease obligations represent an important capital structure component. When the tax rate of a firm increases, it may be efficient to engage more heavily in buying rather than leasing long-lived assets. As we discussed earlier, it is tax efficient for low-tax firms to make extensive use of leasing (rather than buying) of its durable assets.[15] As with the issuance of equity, the pre-tax financing cost is reduced relative to that associated with the issuance of straight debt. The nature of the information problems, however, may be quite different with lease financing as compared to equity financing. It is not difficult to construct examples wherein leasing gives rise to no information-related costs of issuance at all, whereas such costs are quite high when equity is issued. On the other hand, owned property tends to be better maintained and hence more valuable than is leased property (see Jensen and Meckling 1976, Wolfson 1985, and Smith and Wakeman 1985). Hence, the optimal capital structure will depend not only on the firm's tax status but also on the nature of its information problems (that is, the contracting cost component of the implicit taxes associated with various elements of the capital structure).

Moreover, the firm need not stop at buying its own equipment. It could lease equipment to other companies that are inframarginal with respect to the tax benefits of ownership. General Electric Credit Corporation (GECC) and many commercial banks provide dramatic examples of this phenomenon. Stickney, Weil, and Wolfson (1983) estimate that GECC paid roughly 70 cents on the dollar for over $1.5 billion in tax benefits related to safe harbor leasing contracts in 1981.

The above discussion suggests that there are investment policy changes that represent substitutes for capital structure changes as a potential response to changes in tax status. Other examples are discussed below.

a. Purchase Other Companies. The expectation of an increase in taxes could trigger the purchase of other companies (in their same or other industries) that have NOLs. This strategy does not drive the firm's effective tax rate to zero, for it must pay an implicit tax on acquiring the tax shelter; that is, it must share the tax advantage with the shareholders of the acquired company. For example, if a purchase premium (including all costs of effecting the purchase) of 30 cents is paid for each dollar of tax loss carryforward of a target company, the acquiring company's implicit tax rate would be 30 percent. We mentioned companies in the same industry because of a firm's expertise in this field. An imperfectly competitive market for corporate combinations could leave a buyer with a larger share of the tax benefits and, therefore, a lower implicit rate of tax. Gilson, Scholes, and Wolfson (1987) describe various other ways in which taxes and information problems interact to determine the efficacy of a merger or other asset restructuring.

b. Research and Development (R and D). The firm that faces an increase in tax rates could increase the scale of its own internal R and D programs. Some firms contract out R and D programs (either directly or through limited partnerships) for the same tax reasons that they lease rather than buy durable goods. Internal R and D programs create their own tax credits and the immediate deductibility of the expenditures incurred in running them. As with ownership of durable assets, internal R and D also mitigates costly incentive problems that would otherwise naturally arise when the research is (1) conducted by outsiders or (2) conducted by insiders but financed with outsiders' funds through a partnership or joint venture.[16]

c. Other Tax-Favored Investments. The advertising policies and charitable contributions of firms should be affected by their tax rate. Firms facing tax rates that will be lower in the future because of reduced prospects for profitability might find it desirable to increase the budget for these items. This would reduce current taxable income (at a high marginal tax rate) in exchange for increased future income from, for example, sales generated by advertising campaigns that are designed to have a long-term impact on demand. Similar incentives exist to increase market research and personnel costs to lay the foundation for expansion of product offerings. In addition, the firm could replace nontaxable municipal bonds with high-yielding interest-bearing securities that are taxable. More generally, firms in low tax brackets avoid tax shelters such as real estate, advertising, and R and D (unless they sell the tax benefits to highly taxed entities), and high taxpaying firms naturally hold municipal bonds, high dividend-paying common and preferred stock, and a variety of other tax-sheltered investments.

d. Multinational Investments. The explicit marginal tax rate is lower, in present value, on foreign source income generated in certain countries (e.g., Ireland, Hong Kong) than it is on domestic income, because the United States tax on this income (other than so-called subpart F income) is deferred until it is repatriated to the United States. In addition, certain countries (e.g., Germany and some other European countries) impose higher tax rates than does the United States (even more so under the TRA of 1986). Limitations on the use of foreign tax credits depend, in part, on the distribution of worldwide income and tax rates.

When a firm's profitability increases, its demand for shelter may increase or decrease, depending on whether the increase comes primarily from low-tax-rate jurisdictions or high-tax-rate jurisdictions. A change in the firm's tax status can have dramatic implications for its multinational investment and financing decisions, especially with respect to its repatriation policies.

III. IMPLICATIONS OF TAX CLIENTELES AND TRANSACTION COSTS FOR THE EFFICIENT DESIGN OF EXPERIMENTS

In the preceding section we explored some of the ways in which the economic balance sheet of a firm might be reorganized in response to a change in tax status of the firm. These reorganization opportunities are only suggestive of a broad menu of possible strategies available to firms with changing prospects for profitability. One point should be kept clear: these firms have strong incentives to engage in (costly) tax planning that exploits cross-sectional and intertemporal differences in marginal tax rates, and, as argued above, though there are ample opportunities for them to do so, costs might preclude them from exploiting many of these opportunities. As such, the marginal tax rate could be quite different from the rate that a naive analysis would suggest, namely, either zero or the maximum statutory rate. To determine the "correct rate" requires consideration of many tax planning options, how tax benefits are shared among the various tax clienteles (i.e., implicit taxes), the cost of switching from one clientele to another, and the fundamental underlying uncertainty not only of prospects for future profitability but also of the tax rules themselves.

Myers (1984) points out that the empirical evidence collected to date, relating the form of financing and investment to the firm's tax status, is weak. He claims that no study exists that clearly demonstrates that a firm's tax status affects its debt policy (or asset allocation). He also claims that the prospects are bleak for documenting such relations in the future. Although we agree that the evidence to date has been weak, so have the experimental designs underlying the evidence. The studies do not exploit the rich set of substitutes in tax planning, the role that history and transactions costs play in "locking in" certain aspects of asset and capital structure (the tests are cross-sectional rather than longitudinal), or the importance of industry-specific or multi-national tax rules. Cross-sectional tests using seasoned firms in a variety of industries do not yield powerful results.

To illustrate some of the possibilities, we have conducted a pilot study on the relation between financing, asset allocation, and compensation policies of 60 firms that went public during 1979 and whose financial statements were available in the library of the Stanford Business School.[17] These firms are interesting because a majority of them start with tax loss carryforwards and tax credits, without any previous history of taxable income. This contrasts with companies that were once profitable, experienced financial distress, and changed components of their asset and capital structures without a complete reversal of policy because of the costs of restructuring operations or the costs of reorganizing specific elements of the capital structure.[18] By conducting cross-sectional tests on seasoned firms, we may well miss changes in policies that are related to changes in tax status. It is important to recognize that with costly restructuring, the most efficient response for some firms to a change in tax status will be to change leasing policy first; for others to change debt policy; for still others, to change asset allocations. Tests devised to account for changes among a set of policies could be more efficient than univariate or multivariate cross-sectional tests. There is a "downside" here as well. Since we argue that the dimensionality of the tax planning problem is so large relative to that reflected in the traditional experiments, improved specification of the problem might come at a cost of too many degrees of freedom being lost in estimating the many parameters of the system.

After the fact, it is obvious that from a tax planning standpoint, a firm with NOLs would prefer to have no debt in its capital structure. If there were no reorganization costs, it would prefer to use such strategies as exchanging its outstanding debt issues for equity. Such reorganization plans, however, really cannot be achieved costlessly, For example, some risky debt may be redeemable only at par, or negotiation costs to exchange public debt could easily be large enough to wipe out the tax advantage. An exchange of equity for some fraction of outstanding risky debt would increase the value of the remaining risky debt, which becomes less risky, at the expense of shareholders; again, the tax planning benefits may be vitiated. It is for reasons such as these that casual empirical observers might conclude that firms were not following optimal tax planning policies or that taxes appeared not to matter to the capital structure decision. They might observe debt in the capital structure of firms with NOLs. Such observations are by no means anomalous, however, in the presence of reorganization costs that are high enough such that apparent tax benefits rationally are left on the table.

It is for the reasons discussed above that we were motivated to consider the case of newly public companies. A high fraction of these firms begin public life with NOL carryforwards. History should pollute their decisions much less than it would for seasoned companies. And our evidence suggests that tax status *does* affect their decisions. For example, these firms use relatively little debt and rarely have pension plans. On the other hand, deferred compensation that is tied to future profitability (and hence tax status) is pervasive. Moreover, only 4 of the 60 firms in our pilot study used the last-in–first-out (LIFO) method to value inventories: when prices are rising, LIFO minimizes taxable income. None of these four firms had NOL, investment tax credit, research and development tax credit, or foreign tax credit carryforwards during the three years after going public, although 34 of the firms had such carryforwards, something that could occur by chance only 3.5 percent of the time.[19]

Summary Remarks

The upshot of the analysis is not only to exhort the researcher to look more broadly in search for evidence of the relation among tax status, capital structure, and asset structure, but also to argue that the marginal cost of capital will be idiosyncratic. This occurs for two sets of reasons: (1) entity-specific tax characteristics (e.g., accumulated capital gains and recapture taxes on long-lived assets that are a function of the date of purchase and purchase price of assets; industry-specific tax rules, including those that pertain both to tax rates as well as to special income and recognition rules; and multiple tax jurisdiction considerations); and (2) entity-specific transaction costs that affect the desirability of various tax plans and reorganizations.

When changes in tax regimes occur, these idiosyncrasies in tax status become even more pervasive, because many taxpayers find themselves situated in the wrong clientele under the new rules. We turn next to a consideration of the TRA of 1986 to illustrate how a change in tax rules both can affect the desirability of alternative organizational forms for new investment activities as well as the desirability of reorganizing ongoing economic activities.

IV. ORGANIZATIONAL FORM: THE IMPLICATIONS OF THE 1986 TRA

The 1986 TRA dramatically changed the tax rules for both individuals and corporations. The top marginal tax rate is scheduled to be reduced from 50 percent to 28 percent in 1988 for the highest-earning individuals (although there is a broad income range over which individuals face a 33 percent marginal tax rate before the rate once again becomes 28 percent). The top corporate rate is scheduled to be reduced from 46 percent to 34 percent, and the corporate add-on minimum tax, which resulted in a 39.1 percent marginal tax rate when binding, was replaced by an alternative minimum tax (AMT), which results in a 20 percent tax rate when binding.[20,21] The rates are phased in over a two-year period. In 1987, the top marginal rate for individuals is 38.5 percent; the top marginal rate for (calender year-end) corporations is 40 percent.[22]

When changes in tax rates occur over several tax years, it is desirable to time deductions to coincide with high tax rates and to time income to coincide with low tax rates. Tax planning becomes a bit more delicate when planning involves entering into contracts in which the tax rates of all of the contracting parties are changing in the same direction at the same time. In such a case it may not be possible to effect a tax arbitrage even without transaction costs. Moreover, it may become rational for a firm to *accelerate* the recognition of taxable income despite a falling tax rate if this results in a tax deduction being symmetrically accelerated for another party to the contract whose tax rate is falling even faster.[23]

Transition years such as 1986 through 1988 serve as a valuable laboratory to observe transacting among individuals and corporations with different fiscal year-ends and different marginal tax rates. Owing to the importance of transaction costs, many reorganization strategies that would be efficient in a frictionless setting will be too expensive to implement in the more realistic settings from which empirical observations will be drawn. For this reason, transition periods, such as 1986–1988 (or 1981–1984), provide the researcher with a golden opportunity to gather indirect measures of the costs of recontracting among entities and the effects of changes in tax rules on economic activity.

A. The Miller Equilibrium under the TRA of 1986

If it were not for information and transaction costs, the TRA of 1986 would cause massive restructuring of productive activities. Corporations would be replaced as an organizational form by partnerships for new ventures financed with equity; many existing firms would convert to partnership form, and without this conversion many corporations would add debt to their capital structures.

To see this, we begin with a comparison of the after-tax returns available to investment in corporate and partnership form. Let us denote the required rate of return on debt by r_b. For illustrative purposes let us assume that the rate is 9 percent. Further assume that the tax rate of the marginal investor setting prices in the market, t_{pb}, is 28 percent. The municipal bond rate, r_0, would then be 6.48 percent, as required by the relation

$$r_0 = r_b(1 - t_{pb}) = (0.09)(1 - 0.28) = 0.0648.$$

In equilibrium, the after-tax risk-adjusted rate of return to stockholders must also be equal to 6.48 percent. Similarly, those activities conducted in partnership (or sole proprietorship) form would also return 6.48 percent after all price adjustments in the market (including implicit taxes resulting from market frictions).

For the corporate organizational form to be competitive, the corporation must earn at a sufficiently high pre-tax rate such that it can pay corporate taxes, its stockholders can pay personal taxes, and stockholders will still be left with 6.48 percent after tax. Let us assume for the moment that the tax on income from holding shares, t_{ps}, is equal to zero and that the corporate tax rate, t_c, is equal to 34 percent. In equilibrium, the corporation, before paying corporate taxes, would have to earn at the following rate, r_c, per unit of capital investment:

$$r_b \frac{1 - t_{pb}}{1 - t_c} = 0.09 \frac{1 - 0.28}{1 - 0.34} = 0.09818.$$

Note that if the marginal tax bracket of investors in partnerships is 28 percent, then partnerships dominate corporations even if the tax on shares were equal to zero. The partnership would have to earn only 9 percent before tax to be competitive with passive investments. If, on the other hand, the marginal investor setting prices in the market were in a 33 percent bracket, and pre-tax bond returns remained at 9 percent, the required pre-tax returns for the alternative organizational forms would be much closer ($r_c = 9.136$ percent for the corporation versus $r_p = 9$ percent for the partnership).[24]

Let us now relax the assumption that the tax on holding capital assets such as bonds and stock is equal to zero. After all, the TRA of 1986 eliminated the exclusion for long-term capital gains at both the personal level and at the corporate level. Subsequent to 1987, capital gains (losses) will be taxed as ordinary income (loss); and losses will still be limited to $3,000 per year. These changes influence dramatically the explicit shareholder-level tax, t_{ps}. It is still possible to bequeath appreciated assets upon death to escape capital gains tax, or to donate appreciated stock to tax-exempt organizations (although the untaxed gain potentially is subject to the AMT for individuals, at a rate of up to 21 percent), or to make a gift of appreciated securities to low-income relatives, other than children under 14 years of age (to have the gain taxed at their lower rates). Those investors selling shares, however, will be subject to a marginal tax rate on the related gain that increases from a maximum of 20 percent (28 percent for corporate investors) under the rules in 1986 to 28 percent or 33 percent (34 percent for corporate investors) in 1987 and beyond. The TRA of 1986 also eliminates the opportunity to use installment sales to defer the gain on the sale of publicly traded shares. The rate of tax on shares is likely to be far greater post-TRA than it was pre-TRA. Moreover, corporate investors will be able to exclude only 80 percent of dividends received from these investments and may be subject to the 20 percent AMT on 60 percent of the dividend. [25,26]

Still, deferral of the tax on shares until sale helps to lower the present value of the explicit tax on shares to a rate that is below the maximum statutory rate. Holding non-dividend-paying shares post-TRA gives rise to (explicit) tax treatment similar to that from holding a single premium deferred annuity: taxation of the interim share appreciation is deferred until withdrawal. To illustrate this effect, asssume that the marginal investor setting prices in the stock market holds shares for n years. To find the equivalent annual rate of return on shares, r_s, that will make investors indifferent between paying the tax currently or at the end of n years, we must solve the relation

$$[(1 + r_s)^n(1 - t_{pb}) + t_{pb}]^{1/n} - 1 = r_b(1 - t_{pb}).$$

If we assume that n, the average holding period on shares (including the liquidation represented by dividends), is six years, then r_s is equal to 8.54 percent per year. That is, the required annual rate of return on shares before stockholder taxes is 8.54 percent, such that after stockholders pay personal taxes they earn a return of 6.48 percent. This translates into an equivalent annual explicit tax on shares, t_e, of 22.897 percent:[27] $(8.54 - 6.48)/9$ and an implicit tax on shares of only 5.11 percent: $(9 - 8.54)/9$. The total tax rate is 28 percent (i.e., 22.89 percent explicit plus 5.11 percent implicit), and this makes shares and bonds perfect substitutes for the 28 percent explicitly taxed taxpayer who would hold stock for six years.[28]

With an explicit tax on shares of 24.15 percent of the before-tax return, the required rate of return on equity-financed investments in corporate form must now increase from $r_c = 9.82$ percent pre-tax to 9.82 percent$/(1 - t_e) = 9.82/(1 - 0.24) = 12.95$ percent pre-tax![29] If the required before-tax risk-adjusted rate of return on new investments in corporate form is 12.95 percent, and only 9 percent in partnership form, corporations could not compete with partnerships to attract equity capital to be used in the production of goods and services. Growth of the corporate form of organization would require enormous nontax advantages of corporations over partnerships.

It is obvious from this exercise that under the new tax regime, it will be difficult to achieve a Miller equilibrium in which the corporate tax advantage to issuing debt is small. Although the tax shield on debt has been reduced because marginal statutory corporate tax rates have fallen from 46 percent to 34 percent, this does not imply that corporations will issue additional equity, as is naively claimed in the popular press. In our example the required rate of return on equity-financed corporate investments is 12.95 percent before tax and 8.55 percent after a 34 percent corporate tax; the cost to issue bonds is 9 percent before tax and 5.94 percent after a 34 percent corporate tax reduction. If a 34 percent taxpaying corporation could issue debt at an after-tax cost of 5.94 percent and invest the proceeds at an after-tax return of 8.53 percent, it would be quite eager to increase leverage.[30]

If reorganization costs are ignored, corporations facing this set of required rates of return under the new tax regime would prefer to reorganize as partnerships. With tax and other reorganization costs, however, an alternative is to substitute debt for equity to finance marginal investments.[31] As discussed earlier, the corporation will also have an increased demand for tax shelters. By converting its income from being explicitly taxed at the corporate level to being implicitly taxed at a rate determined by the price of tax shelters in the marketplace, the corporation may achieve a tax outcome closer to that of a partnership than its legal form might suggest. The new corporate AMT, however, represents a major constraint on this endeavor. If corporations invest sufficient amounts in tax-sheltered investments, the AMT will exceed the regular tax. When this occurs, the marginal explicit tax rate becomes 20 percent. At this low rate the corporation becomes inframarginal with respect to holding taxable bonds and other tax-disfavored investments. In addition, it would no longer be optimal to issue debt as long as t_{pb} is set by investors with marginal tax rates in excess of 20 percent. Instead, it would want to increase taxable income by buying tax-disadvantageous assets such as bonds until its next dollar of income was taxed at a rate above the AMT rate.[32,33] With uncertain taxable income, year-end tax planning becomes much more important for the corporation than in the pre-TRA era, and optimal strategies become much more heavily dependent on the transaction costs associated with year-end reorganization of economic balance sheets.

B. Dividend Policy under the 1986 TRA

Without an ability to reorganize at the corporate level to achieve tax treatment equivalent to that imposed on partnerships, a logical question arises as to whether the corporation should shrink its size by paying (liquidating) dividends. An important consideration here is that the required rate of return on retained earnings is less than that on new investment. To see this more clearly, consider the firm with one dollar of retained earnings. Assume that the marginal tax bracket of its stockholders is t_{p0} today and t_{pn} at time period n. Assume that on personal account stockholders can earn $r_{at,pn}$ per period after personal taxes, and that the firm can earn $r_{at,cn}$ per period after corporate taxes. Shareholders would wish the firm to retain the one dollar of earnings if and only if

$$(1 - t_{p0})(1 + r_{at,pn})^n < (1 + r_{at,cn})^n(1 - t_{pn}).$$

If the corporation can invest its retained earnings at the same after-tax rate as its shareholders, the advantage of the retention of earnings depends on whether the marginal tax rate of shareholders is greater currently or in the future. If the tax rate of any shareholders is expected to decline, retention at the corporate level is tax advantageous. Even if tax rates are expected to remain the same *on average*, but vary through time, retention provides each shareholder with a valuable timing option to realize a capital gain and pay a tax when their tax rate at some period s is such that $t_{ps} < t_{p0}$. This occurs, for example, when a shareholder is subject to the personal AMT rate of 21 percent; or when statutory tax rates change; or when a shareholder desires to make a charitable contribution, in which case $t_{ps} = 0$; or when a shareholder holds until death, in which case $t_{ps} = 0$; or when a shareholder makes a gift of stock to a lower-income relative, in which case $t_{ps} = t_{relative}$.* If there are nontax advantages to being in corporate form, such that $r_{at,cn} > r_{at,pn}$, there is further incentive to invest retained earnings in corporate form rather than pay dividends. Moreover, if the firm retains earnings, shareholders are less likely to realize capital losses on their shareholdings at the time of sale, which could otherwise prove costly due to the $3,000 capital loss limitation.

Still, dividends impose a smaller tax cost on investors under the TRA of 1986 than under the old tax rules wherein capital gains were subject to a maximum tax rate of 20 percent compared to a tax on dividends of up to 50 percent. This may have the very significant effect of reducing the "dissipative costs" of using dividends as a signaling mechanism; see Bhattacharya (1980) but also Miller and Scholes (1978). Whether dividends will be increased in the aggregate is an interesting empirical question that we would expect some research entrepreneurs to address.[34]

We are still left with the question of whether share repurchases dominate the payment of dividends to shareholders under the TRA of 1986. Taxable investors with a positive basis on their holdings of stock would prefer that the corporation repurchase part of their stock each period instead of paying them dividends of equal amount. This would further defer personal tax on that part of the payment that is considered to be a return of capital. Moreover, it enables shareholders to retain the timing option as to when they sell their shares to the corporation; they will step forward as sellers when it is in their interest to do so. On the other hand, share repurchases may not have the same signaling properties as do dividends. A precommitment to a policy of systematic share repurchases might duplicate the signaling and monitoring properties of a systematic dividend-payment policy, but it would also result in share repurchases being treated as dividends for tax purposes.

C. Corporate Restructuring under the 1986 TRA

As discussed above, the 1986 TRA contains many changes that collectively increase the costs of selling assets to restructure the balance sheet of the firm. Asset sales followed by liquidations no longer escape the corporate capital gains tax, shareholders can no longer use the installment sales method to defer their realizations of capital gains, and for many assets the depreciation deductions are much less generous than under pre-TRA 1986 rules. Although the corporation can still use the installment sales method to defer taxation on non-publicly-traded assets, the TRA of 1986 rules impose more restrictive provisions than existed previously. A clear prediction is that there will be fewer mergers and acquisitions that are motivated by tax considerations; indeed,

---

* Each alternative requires a consideration of implicit taxes.

there will be less of a tax incentive to turn over assets more generally.

There are also important implications of the increased cost of asset restructuring for capital structure changes. As we emphasized earlier, asset restructurings are in many ways substitutes for capital restructuring as a response to changes in tax status. The new bill increases the cost of employing such strategies as selling tax-favored depreciable assets and leasing them back. Since reducing debt and increasing equity is a substitute (albeit an imperfect one) for the sale-leaseback transaction insofar as tax planning is concerned, the new tax bill could make such debt-for-equity restructurings relatively more cost effective. On the other hand, the gross tax benefit of restructuring by repurchasing or issuing common shares or bonds is less in the post-TRA era. Stocks offer their corporate issuers a smaller implicit tax subsidy (relative to bonds) under the TRA of 1986, both because explicit tax rates on ordinary income have been reduced and because the capital gains tax rate has been increased. Moreover, if the pre-tax transaction cost of capital restructuring is as great after the new tax bill as before (as seems reasonable), the reduced level of tax rates will cause transaction costs to overwhelm the gross tax benefits in a larger number of cases.

V. CONCLUSION

We have argued that capital structure issues subsume a broad variety of financing and investment considerations. The optimal instruments (debt versus equity versus a rich menu of other asset and capital structure alternatives) cannot be chosen independent of information and tax consider-ations. An understanding of the dynamics of capital structure planning requires an understanding of the related problem of the dynamics of asset structure planning. These in turn require an analysis of the transaction costs associated with a reorganization of economic balance sheets in the face of changes in tax rates as well as analysis of the tax costs associated with *not* undertaking such reorganizations (i.e., the costs associated with being stuck in the "wrong" tax clientele).

If a reasonable predictive theory is to emerge, one that is designed to explain cross-sectional and intertemporal differences in observed capital structures, such a theory must recognize that the dimensionality of cross-sectional differences in tax status is vastly larger than whether a taxpayer has NOL carryforwards. In a world of costly contracting, the marginal tax rates of firms (including all implicit taxes) can vary dramatically, even if each firm faced the same statutory tax rate schedule. Moreover, each firm does *not* face the same statutory tax schedule. For example, thrift institutions, life insurance companies, and a host of tax-exempt corporations have faced significantly lower statutory marginal tax rates than have other corporations for many years. Firms operating in many (national, state, and local) tax jurisdictions may face very different explicit tax rates from those that operate in a single tax jurisdiction. Finally, as Miller (1977) has emphasized, efficient corporate tax

68 | Myron S. Scholes and Mark A. Wolfson

planning is inextricably linked to the idiosyncracies of noncorporate taxes (e.g., the personal tax).

NOTES

[1] These costs included deadweight bankruptcy costs (for example, Kraus and Litzenberger 1973, Scott 1976, and Kim 1978); loss of tax shields in bankruptcy (for example, Brennan and Schwartz 1978); and various agency costs associated with issues of moral hazard (for example, Jensen and Meckling 1976 and Myers 1977).

[2] Although the add-on tax is applied at a 15 percent rate on tax preferences, the amount of tax preference subject to the tax is reduced by any regular tax paid. Hence, when the add-on tax is binding, the marginal tax rate drops from 46 percent to 39.1 percent [or $0.46(1 - 0.15) = 0.391$].

[3] See Scholes and Wolfson (1986b) for an elaboration of this theme.

[4] The tax rules may reduce significantly the demand for explicit and costly debt covenants, since taxes can alter the very nature of the incentive problem. See Smith and Warner (1979) for an analysis of how bond covenants are used to mitigate conflicts of interest between bondholders and stockholders.

[5] Although a firm does not lose its NOLs in bankruptcy, there are explicit restrictions in the tax code against "selling" these losses to other firms. Under the 1986 TRA it will be even more difficult to sell such losses: following most changes in control of a company with net operating loss carryforwards, the NOLs will be restricted from offsetting other taxable income at a rate greater than the long-term after-tax rate on riskless bonds times the purchase price of the NOL firm. This rate of utilization is reduced even further if at least one third of the loss company's assets are nonbusiness assets (e.g., cash and marketable securities). Other changes that impair the ability to sell losses relate to new "continuity of business" requirements.

[6] In the absence of investment tax credits, whether low-tax-rate taxpayers form a natural clientele as lessees depends on the depreciation schedule permitted for tax purposes relative to economic depreciation. A generous depreciation allowance results in taxation of investment returns to the lessor that is more favorable than the taxation of returns to holding a taxable bond, and a competitive market would force the lessor to reduce the lease rate to below the taxable bond rate. In the special case of immediate expensing of the cost of the investment (and with no investment tax credits), the after-tax return to the investment is equal to the pre-tax return. In a competitive market this return, on a risk-adjusted basis, must be equal to the municipal bond rate. On the other hand, certain intangible assets (such as a trademark) that have finite economic lives but are nonamortizable for tax purposes are most efficiently owned by low-taxed entities. The equilibrium pre-tax return to such assets should exceed the taxable bond rate.

[7] See Galper and Toder (1983, 1984), Scholes and Wolfson (1984), and Mazur, Scholes, and Wolfson (1986). As an aside, empirical estimates of personal tax rates in the United States as a function of gross income do not factor in implicit taxes (and implicit subsidies). We are convinced that marginal tax rates have been far more progressive than, say, the estimates of Pechman (1985).

[8] More evidence remains to be collected, however, especially with respect to changes in asset structure and compensation policy. It will be important to show a direct association of taxpaying status with both financing policy and investment policy as well as with a change in share prices. Finally, the evidence to date suggests that when preferred stock is exchanged for common stock, stock prices increase, a result that would not be predicted by the tax hypothesis (i.e, such exchanges are tax neutral). See, for example, Pinegar and Lease (1986). On the other hand, it is not difficult to generate information-based models that imply such a result.

[9] Note that it is costly for a firm that does not expect to generate enough taxable income to use the interest deductions cost effectively to imitate the behavior of a firm that *does* expect to generate enough taxable income. The cost relates to being in the wrong tax clientele.

[10] Another possibility is that the taxing authority would reclassify direct income bonds as equity. See also McConnell and Schlarbaum (1981a, b) and Park and Williams (1985).

[11] There may be also a rather severe identification problem in sorting out whether the compensation packages that are observed are driven by tax considerations, incentive considerations, or both. See Miller and Scholes (1982a), Smith and Watts (1982, 1984), and Scholes and Wolfson (1984).

[12] Nonqualified options provide the employer with a tax deduction equal to the amount the employee includes in taxable income when the option is exercised. Incentive stock options provide deferred capital gains treatment to the employee, but the employer is denied any tax deductions. See Hite and Long (1982) for further discussion.

[13] See Scholes and Wolfson (1984) for further discussion of these tax planning issues.

[14] The TRA of 1984 introduced new original issue discount (OID) rules to reduce the use of *below*-market-rate loans to increase the reported sales price of an asset. Under the new rules a loan is viewed as being below the market rate when the rate on the loan is below the "applicable federal rate" (a riskless government bond rate matched to the term of the loan). Although firms that issue risky loans at this riskless rate clearly issue a loan with a below-market interest rate, it is not treated as such under the tax code. As discussed in Scholes and Wolfson (1985), even with the new OID rules, many tax planning opportunities still exist to use below-market-rate demand loans effectively in the compensation programs for employees.

[15] Shaw (1986) documents striking evidence of a propensity to engage in leasing as a means of exploiting firms' low marginal tax rates. In particular, 85 percent of the firms in his sample that sold tax benefits under "safe harbor lease" contracts during 1981 disclosed tax loss or credit carryforwards and at least $50 million in capital expenditures in their 1980 annual reports.

[16] Shevlin (1986) presents empirical evidence that is consistent with these arguments.

[17] We are grateful to Mark Mazur for assistance in collecting and in structuring the data.

[18] Leasing is a good example of the restructuring problem. Although changing from leasing to owning could reduce agency costs and other costs, it might not be possible for a firm to switch in the short run. Owing to the depreciation and investment tax credit recapture provisions of the tax laws, contracts might preclude a firm from terminating its lease. Similarly, a firm with a large portfolio of appreciated municipal bonds might find it too costly to sell such assets (due to the acceleration of the capital gains tax) despite a drop in its marginal tax rate that would render a *new* purchase of municipal bonds suboptimal.

[19] The 1983 balance sheet and income statement of Genetic Systems Corporation reveals that since its inception in 1980 it has suffered losses. It has established investment partnerships with profitable firms, committed to noncancelable operating leases, financed research and development through limited partnerships, issued incentive stock options for tax purposes to a far greater degree than nonqualified options, issued warrants and common stock, held interest-bearing marketable securities on corporate account, and issued little long-term debt. It has no pension plan. These are good examples of the expected associations of capital structure, asset structure, and compensation policy with the taxpaying status of the firm.

[20] The AMT is equal to 20 percent of the corporation's regular taxable income increased by tax preferences. For most corporations the main preferences include accelerated depreciation and, for a three-year period, one half of the excess of pre-tax

book income reported to stockholders over alternative minimum taxable income. This latter adjustment will affect those corporations that generate income that is exempt from the *regular* income tax, such as municipal bond interest and dividend income otherwise subject to 80 percent exclusion (down from 85 percent), both of which are included in book income. The adjustment also applies to the large number of accounting items that give rise to book income or book expenses at different times than does taxable income or tax deductions.

[21] Note that reduced federal tax rates effectively increase state and local income and property tax rates, and such taxes become a more important ingredient in planning for capital structures. In addition, United States tax rates are much lower now than are rates in many foreign countries. Unless these countries respond by reducing their rates, many corporations will restructure foreign operations and will repatriate profits earlier than would have been the case under pre-TRA rules.

[22] Noncalendar year-end companies face higher marginal tax rates early in 1987 and lower marginal rates later in 1987. For example, a June fiscal year corporation faces a 46 percent marginal rate throughout its fiscal year ending in June 1987, at which point its marginal rate drops to 34 percent.

[23] See Scholes and Wolfson (1986a) for further discussion.

[24] Prior to the TRA of 1986, corporations could be competitive with partnerships from a tax standpoint even with a moderate tax on shares at the stockholder level. For example, a 46 percent corporate-level tax and a 7.4 percent shareholder-level tax imply a before-tax required rate of return to corporate investments that is equal to that on partnership investments if the partners are taxed at a 50 percent rate.

[25] Hence, the marginal explicit tax rate on dividends to corporate holders is 6.8 percent when the AMT is not binding and up to 12 percent when the AMT is binding (although it is only 4 percent when the AMT is binding and dividends are not tax preference items).

[26] Although one might be tempted to argue that pension funds are the marginal investor in shares and, for this reason, t_{ps} can be assumed to be zero, this would further imply that the return on shares would be equal to the return on bonds, a relation that is inconsistent with the Miller equilibrium.

[27] This is a 24.15 percent tax on the reduced pre-tax yield of 8.54 percent.

[28] Assuming that before the TRA of 1986 the municipal bond rate was 6.48 percent, that the marginal holder of bonds was in a 50 percent tax bracket, and that the marginal holder of shares deferred gain recognition for only six years and paid tax at a 20 percent rate at that time (40 percent of the gain taxed at a rate of 50 percent), the required annual rate of return on shares would have been 7.829 percent, and the required before-tax bond rate (and return to partnership investments) would have been 12.96 percent. In this example, the equivalent annual explicit tax on shares would have been only 10.4 percent per year (the implicit tax on shares would have been 39.6 percent). By using an installment sale to defer the payment of the capital gains tax on the sale of the asset, the annual explicit tax on shares could have been reduced to substantially less than 10.4 percent (and as indicated, a 7.4 percent rate of tax on shares would equate the required pre-tax rates of return for investments in corporations and partnerships).

Since theoretical arguments and empirical evidence suggest that, pre-TRA of 1986, the equilibrium value of dividend income is little different, if different at all, from the equilibrium value of capital gains, it is unimportant to distinguish between dividend-paying stocks and non-dividend-paying stocks in these examples. See Miller and Scholes (1978, 1982a) and Litzenberger and Ramaswamy (1982).

[29] Alternatively, the required rate, r_c, must satisfy

$$\{[1 + r_c(1 - t_c)]^n(1 - t_{pb}) + t_{pb}\}^{1/n} = (1 + r_b)(1 - t_{pb}).$$

For $t_c = 0.34$, $t_{pb} = 0.28$, and $r_b = 0.09$, and $n = 6$, $r_c = 0.1295$. For $n = 20$, $r_c = 0.1181$, and for $n = 100$, $r_c = 0.1035$. For infinite holding periods, $r_c = 0.09818$, the same as if the explicit tax on shares were 0 percent.

[30] We still can think of situations in which the advantages of issuing debt would be small under the TRA of 1986, but such situations would seem to be perverse. For example, if the marginal holder of shares were an individual who avoided capital gains taxes by contributing shares to a charitable organization, the tax on shares would be zero for a non-dividend-paying stock. If, in addition, the marginal investors setting prices in the bond market were taxed at a rate of 33 percent rather than 28 percent, then the advantages of issuing debt would be significantly smaller. The after-tax required rate of return on shares in this special case becomes 6.03 percent [or $0.09(1 - 0.33)$], and the required before-tax rate of return on new corporate investment becomes 9.14 percent [or $0.0603/(1 - 0.34)$]. In this situation the advantage of issuing debt is 6.03 percent minus 5.94 percent for the 34 percent marginal-tax-rate corporation.

[31] The tax costs of converting to a partnership include the realization of a capital gain at the stockholder level. Subsequent to 1986, the corporation will also be subject to a capital gains tax on the sale of assets that have a market value in excess of tax basis; that is, it can no longer use the Section 337 or 338 liquidation rules that allow stockholders to escape the capital gains tax at the corporate level (the effect of the elimination of the so-called General Utilities doctrine). Conversion to a partnership also triggers recapture of depreciation as well as a loss of tax attributes such as NOLs and investment tax credit carryovers. (See Gilson, Scholes, and Wolfson 1987 for further discussion of these issues.) Moreover, if the conversion takes place after 1986, the partnership may inherit a less attractive depreciation schedule for its durable assets than the corporation would have enjoyed before the conversion. Finally, conversion effectively forces some tax-exempt investors to sell their shares (or to hold them indirectly in other organizational forms) since such investors must pay tax on "unrelated business income" earned through partnership interests.

[32] Note that it would be suboptimal for a firm to finance additional capital investments with debt and to forgo accelerated depreciation allowances to avoid generating tax preferences. Although such a strategy enables avoidance of not only the AMT but also all regular income tax, the pre-tax return available on such investments bears an implicit tax, because highly taxed investors compete for the right to take accelerated depreciation.

[33] Many leasing companies will cease to play the role of lessor once their level of leasing activities gives rise to tax preferences of sufficient magnitude to subject them to the AMT. Assuming such lessors have developed expertise in arranging leasing contracts, however, they will likely syndicate leasing deals with those corporations still paying tax at the marginal explicit rate of 34 percent. Such syndication deals will impose implicit taxes on the lessors through extra costs associated with such multiparty transactions. The propensity to syndicate leasing deals is also affected by the availability of an alternative minimum tax *credit* in years following the imposition of the AMT.

[34] For corporate holders of dividend-paying stocks, the 85 percent exclusion of dividends from corporate taxation pre-TRA resulted in a 6.9 percent tax rate (0.46 × 0.15), which might appear to compare favorably to an explicit capital gains tax of 28 percent. In a frictionless setting, however, the corporation could reduce the capital gains tax to its shareholders to zero by liquidating the firm to escape any corporate-level capital gains taxes (the General Utilities doctrine), and its individual and corporate shareholders, in turn, could use installment sales to reduce (or eliminate) the present value of the capital gains tax. As we noted above, however, under the new law, the tax rate on dividends for corporate holders will be approximately 6.8 percent, and the capital gains tax on realized gains at the corporate level will be 34 percent. With the repeal of the alternative corporate tax on long-term capital gains, with the repeal of the

General Utilities doctrine, and with the elimination of the opportunity to use installment sales for marketable securities, corporations are stuck with paying a high tax rate on capital gains. Hence, the *corporate* investor may have a strong preference for dividends under the TRA of 1986, which, in turn, provides an incentive for corporations to increase dividend payments.

REFERENCES

Bhattacharya, Sudipto. 1980. "An Exploration of Nondissipative Dividend-Signaling Structures." *Quarterly Journal of Economics* (January): 1–24.

Brennan, Michael, and Schwartz, Eduardo. 1978. "Corporate Income Taxes, Valuation, and the Problem of Optimal Capital Structure." *Journal of Business* (January): 103–14.

Dann, Larry Y., and Mikkelson, Wayne H. 1984. "Convertible Debt Issuance, Capital Structure Change and Financing-Related Information: Some New Evidence." *Journal of Financial Economics* (June): 157–86.

DeAngelo, Harry, and Masulis, Ronald W. 1980. "Optimal Capital Structure under Corporate and Personal Taxation." *Journal of Financial Economics* (March): 3–29.

Galai, Dan, and Masulis, Ronald W. 1976. "The Option Pricing Model and the Risk Factor of Stock." *Journal of Financial Economics* (January/March): 53–81.

Galper, Harvey, and Toder, Eric. 1983. "Measuring the Incidence of Taxation of Income from Capital." Brookings Technical Series T-026.

———. 1984. "Transfer Elements in the Taxation of Income from Capital." In Marilyn Moon, ed., *Economic Transfers in the United States.* The National Bureau of Economic Research and University of Chicago Press, pp. 87–138.

Gilson, Ronald J.; Scholes, Myron S.; and Wolfson, Mark A. 1987. "Taxation and the Dynamics of Corporate Control: The Uncertain Case for Tax Motivated Acquisitions." In John C. Coffee, Jr., Louis Lowenstein, and Susan Rose-Ackerman, eds., *Knights, Raiders, and Targets: The Impact of the Hostile Takeover.* Oxford University Press.

Hamada, Robert H., and Scholes, Myron S. 1985. "Taxes and Corporate Financial Management." In Ed Altman, ed., *Recent Advances in Corporate Finance.* Home-wood, Ill.: Irwin.

Hite, Gailen L., and Long, Michael S. 1982. "Taxes and Executive Stock Options." *Journal of Accounting and Economics* (July): 3–14.

Jensen, Michael, and Meckling, William. 1976. "Theory of the Firm: Managerial Behavior, Agency Costs and Ownership Structure." *Journal of Financial Economics* (October): 305–60.

Kim, E. Han. 1978. "A Mean-Variance Theory of Optimal Capital Structure and Corporate Debt Capacity." *Journal of Finance* (March): 45–64.

———. 1988. "Optimal Capital Structure in Miller's Equilibrium." Discussion, Chapter 2, this volume.

Kraus, Alan, and Litzenberger, Robert. 1973. "A State-Preference Model of Optimal Financial Leverage." *Journal of Finance* (September): 911–22.

Leland, Hayne, and Pyle, David H. 1977. "Informational Asymmetries, Financial Structure, and Financial Intermediation." *Journal of Finance* (May): 371–87. Reprinted Chapter 8, this volume.

Litzenberger, Robert, and Ramaswamy, Krishna. 1982. "The Effects of Dividends on Common Stock Prices: Tax Effects or Information Effects?" *Journal of Finance* (May): 429–43.

Masulis, Ronald W. 1983. "The Impact of Capital Structure Change on Firm Value: Some Estimates." *Journal of Finance* (March): 107–26.

Mazur, Mark J.; Scholes, Myron S.; and Wolfson, Mark A. 1986. "Implicit Taxes and Effective Tax Burdens." Working paper, Stanford University, August.

McConnell, John J., and Schlarbaum, Gary G. 1981a. "Return, Risks and Pricing of Income Bonds, 1956–76 (Does Money Have an Odor?)." *Journal of Business* (January): 33–63.

————. 1981b. "Evidence on the Impact of Exchange Offers on Security Prices: The Case of Income Bonds." *Journal of Business* (January): 65–85.

Miller, Merton H. 1977. "Debt and Taxes." *Journal of Finance* (May): 261–75. Reprinted Chapter 2, this volume.

Miller, Merton H., and Scholes, Myron S. 1978. "Dividends and Taxes." *Journal of Financial Economics* (December): 333–64.

————. 1982a. "Executive Compensation, Taxes and Incentives." In William F. Sharpe and Cathryn M. Cootner, eds., *Financial Economics: Essays in Honor of Paul Cootner*. Englewood Cliffs, N.J.: Prentice-Hall.

————. 1982b. "Dividends and Taxes: Some Empirical Evidence." *Journal of Political Economy* 90: 1182–1242.

Modigliani, Franco, and Miller, Merton H. 1958. "The Cost of Capital, Corporation Finance and the Theory of Investment." *American Economic Review* (June): 267–97.

————. 1963. "Corporate Income Taxes and the Cost of Capital: A Correction." *American Economic Review* (June): 433–43.

Myers, Stewart C. 1977. "Determinants of Corporate Borrowing." *Journal of Financial Economics* (November): 147–75.

————. 1984. "The Capital Structure Puzzle." *Journal of Finance* (July): 575–92.

Park, Sang Yong, and Williams, Joseph. 1985. "Taxes, Capital Structure, and Bondholder Clienteles." *Journal of Business* (April): 203–24.

Pechman, Joseph A. 1985. *Who Paid the Taxes, 1966–85?* Washington: Brookings Institution.

Pinegar, J. Michael, and Lease, Ronald C. 1986. "The Impact of Preferred-for-Common Exchange Offers on Firm Value." *Journal of Finance* (September): 795–814.

Ross, Stephen A. 1977. "The Determination of Financial Structure: The Incentive-Signalling Approach." *The Bell Journal of Economics* (Spring): 23–40.

Scholes, Myron S., and Wolfson, Mark A. 1984. "Employee Compensation and Taxes: Links with Incentives and with Investment and Financing Decisions." Working paper, Stanford University, October.

————. 1985. "Compensatory Loans to Executives Before and After the Tax Act of 1984." Working paper, Stanford University, September.

————. 1986a. "Taxes and Employee Compensation Planning." Working paper, Stanford University.

————. 1986b. "Taxes and Organization Theory." Working paper, Stanford University, September.

Scott, Jim. 1976. "A Theory of Optimal Capital Structure." *Bell Journal of Economics* (Spring): 33–54.

Shaw, Wayne H. 1986. "Measuring the Impact of the Safe Harbor Lease Law on Security Prices." Working paper, Cornell University, May.

Shevlin, Terrence J. 1986. "Research and Development Limited Partnerships: An Empirical Analysis of Taxes and Incentives." Ph.D. Dissertation, Stanford University.

Smith, Clifford W., Jr. 1986. "Investment Banking and the Capital Acquisition Process." *Journal of Financial Economics* (January/February): 3–29.

Smith, Clifford W., Jr., and Wakeman, L. MacDonald. 1985. "Determinants of Corporate Leasing Policy." *Journal of Finance* (July): 895–908.

Smith, Clifford W., Jr., and Warner, Jerold B. 1979. "On Financial Contracts and Optimal Capital Structure: An Analysis of Bond Covenants." *Journal of Financial*

Economics (June): 117–61.

Smith, Clifford W., Jr., and Watts, Ross L. 1982. "Incentive and Tax Effects of Executive Compensation Plans." *Australian Journal of Management* 7: 139–57.

———. 1984. "The Structure of Executive Compensation Contracts and the Control of Management." Working paper, University of Rochester.

Stickney, Clyde P.; Weil, Roman L.; and Wolfson, Mark A. 1983. "Income Taxes and Tax-Transfer Leases." *Accounting Review* (April): 439–59.

Stiglitz, Joseph E. 1985. "The General Theory of Tax Avoidance." *National Tax Journal* (September): 325–37.

Wolfson, Mark A. 1985. "Tax, Incentive, and Risk Sharing Issues in the Allocation of Property Rights: The Generalized Lease-or-Buy Problem." *The Journal of Business* (April): 158–71.

Reprinted from JOURNAL OF ECONOMIC THEORY   Vol. 16, No. 1, October 1977
All Rights Reserved by Academic Press, New York and London   *Printed in Belgium*

Take-Over Bids and Stock Market Equilibrium

OLIVER D. HART*

Churchill College, Cambridge

Received May 10, 1976; revised April 8, 1977

1. INTRODUCTION

The well-known general equilibrium model of Arrow and Debreu (see [2]) is based on the assumption that firms maximize profits. The usual justification for this assumption is that the higher firms' profits are, the wealthier firms' shareholders will be and hence the higher will be shareholders' utilities. As a result, the shareholders of a firm will unanimously favor a high profit production plan over a low profit one, and, if a firm wishes to act in its owners' interests, it should maximize profits.

The above argument relies implicitly on the assumption that either the future is certain or that firms can insure themselves against uncertainty by making contracts for contingent futures commodities. However, in a world of uncertainty where contingent contracts are not possible, the argument breaks down. In fact, under these conditions, profit maximization is not even well defined since profits are a random variable.[1]

Recently, a literature has developed on the objectives firms should pursue when they cannot insure themselves against uncertain events.[2] Most of this literature has assumed that markets for firms' shares exist as an imperfect substitute for contingent commodity markets. Various alternatives to profit maximization have been proposed such as expected profit maximization or the maximization of the market value of firms' shares. However, these objectives suffer from the disadvantage that they do not necessarily represent the interests of a firm's shareholders. In fact, in the absence of contingent

* I would like to thank Jacques Drèze, Douglas Gale, Sandy Grossman, Frank Hahn, Peter Hammond, Mervyn King, and Roger Witcomb for helpful discussions. I am also grateful to members of the S.S.R.C. stock market project and to an anonymous referee for useful suggestions. All errors are my own, however.

[1] The argument also breaks down if firms are not perfect competitors. Under these conditions, a profit-increasing change in production plan may cause a sufficiently large shift in relative prices to make some (or all) shareholders worse off.

[2] See, for example, [15] and the references therein.

Copyright © 1977 by Academic Press, Inc.
All rights of reproduction in any form reserved.   ISSN 0022–0531

commodity markets, there is in general *no* goal for a firm to pursue which represents the interests of all its shareholders.[3]

To see this, suppose that the economy contains a single firm which can produce either one unit of output in state of the world 1 or one unit of output in state of the world 2 (or convex combinations of these possibilities). Suppose that the firm has two shareholders, one of whom believes that state 1 occurs with certainty and the other of whom believes that state 2 occurs with certainty. Then, since the shareholders want the firm to produce output in different states, no production plan can satisfy both of them. In particular, there is certainly no numerical measure, like the market value of the firm, which shareholders will agree that the firm should maximize. (Of course, if there were two identical firms instead of one in this example, then one firm could produce output in state 1 and the other output in state 2 and the conflict between the shareholders would be eliminated. See Section 5 for a discussion of a model where the number of operating firms is determined endogenously.)

Since, as the above example shows, there will in general be disagreement about which production plan should be selected, it seems fruitful to analyze a firm's choice of production plan as the outcome of a cooperative game where the players are the shareholders. We adopt this approach in Section 3. (Section 2 is devoted to a discussion of the basic model.) We assume that a firm's production plan is determined by a vote at a meeting of shareholders. Following Drèze [4] we permit sidepayments so that shareholders who are made better off by a change in production plan can bribe those who are made worse off to vote for the change. In Drèze [4] it is assumed that a change in production plan can be made only if it has the support of all the shareholders. We show that, if the 100 % support requirement is relaxed even slightly, only trivial allocations can in general qualify as equilibria.

In practice it may be difficult for (possibly) large groups of people to get together at shareholders' meetings to organize changes in production. An alternative method of changing a firm's production plan is through a take-over bid; that is, an individual can purchase enough shares of a firm to gain control; change the firm's production plan; and then resell the shares at the new market price. In Section 4, we study take-over bids under the assumption that all of a firm's shares are required to gain control. It is often argued that the possibility of take-over bids will ensure the optimality of the stock market allocation. In general we will see that this is not the case. The reason is that take-over bids do not permit price discrimination: an individual who mounts a take-over bid must pay a uniform price for shares before the take-over bid and must charge a uniform price for shares after the take-over bid.

---

[3] One case where such a goal does exist is if the so-called spanning condition holds, that is, if every feasible production plan of every firm can be expressed as a linear combination of the existing production plans of firms in the economy (see [5]).

As a result it may be the case that an allocation is Pareto dominated and yet it pays nobody to carry out a take-over bid.

We will also find that take-over bids do not generally result in net market value maximizing behavior by firms. An exception to this is the case where firms' production functions exhibit multiplicative uncertainty—this case was first studied by Diamond [3]. Under the multiplicative uncertainty assumption we show that takeover bids do lead to net market value maximizing behavior by firms and also that take-over bid equilibria are (constrained) Pareto optimal.

In Section 5, we provide a further analysis of the reasons for the suboptimality of take-over bid equilibria. It turns out that the suboptimality can be traced to the fact that the economy is "small"—more precisely to the fact that individual firms are large relative to the aggregate economy. To show this, we make the economy large by replicating consumers. We assume that there is a fixed number of different technologies available in the economy and that there is free entry of firms with these technologies, subject to the payment of a set-up cost. As the economy becomes larger, more and more firms will choose to set up. We prove that, when the number of consumers is large, take-over bid equilibria are approximately (constrained) Pareto optimal. (In addition, firms will choose production plans which are approximately net market value maximizing.) The reason for this is that, in a large economy, the consumer surplus which a shareholder obtains from investing in any particular firm is close to zero. As a result, the impossibility of price discrimination, which is responsible for the suboptimality of a take-over bid equilibrium in small economies, becomes unimportant.

Section 6 contains our conclusions.

2. THE MODEL

We will use a variant of the model first introduced by Diamond and later extended by Drèze [4]. We consider an economy which extends for two periods 0 and 1 in an uncertain environment. There are I consumers, J firms, and T states of the world, indexed $i = 1,..., I, j = 1,..., J$, and $t = 1,...,$ T, respectively. When there is no ambiguity, we will use I, J, T to refer also to the sets of consumers, firms, and states. These sets are assumed to be finite.

We assume that the state of the world is known in period 1, but unknown in period 0. There are assumed to be a finite number of physical goods, M, available in period 0 and a single physical good available in period 1. The M goods in period 0 are used for consumption purposes and also as inputs in the production process; the single good produced in period 1 is used for consumption only. In period 0, there are markets for the M current physical goods and also for shares in firms. It is assumed that no contingent futures contracts are possible.[4] In period 1, consumers are allocated output according to the shares held in firms in period 0. In view of the fact that there is only one good in period 1 and the economy lasts for only two periods, there is no need for markets to reopen after period 0.[5]

Consumers

We represent consumer i's consumption plan by a vector $x_i = (x_i{}^0, x_i{}^1) \in R_+^{M+T}$, where $x_i{}^0 \in R_+^M$ is consumption in period 0 and $x_{it}^1 \in R_+$ is consumption in period 1 in state t.[6] Consumer i is assumed to have a complete preference preordering $\gtrsim_i$ over R_+^{M+T}. We assume:

(A.1)　$\gtrsim_i$ can be represented by a continuous, quasi-concave,[7] increasing,[8] utility function U_i $(i = 1,..., I)$;

(A.2)　U_i is strictly increasing in x_{i1}^0 and $U_i(x_i) = U_i(0)$ if $x_{i1}^0 = 0$ $(i = 1,..., I)$.

(A.3)　When $x_{i1}^0 > 0$, U_i is strictly quasi-concave and has continuous, finite strictly positive partial derivatives $(i = 1,..., I)$.[9]

Assumption (A.2) says, among other things, that consumers require positive consumption of good 1 in period 0 in order to obtain "positive" utility.

Firms

Firm j is assumed to have a production set $Y_j \subset R_+^{M+T}$. If $y_j \in Y_j$, we write $y_j = (y_j{}^0, y_j{}^1)$, where $y_j{}^0 \in R_+^M$ is a vector of inputs in period 0 and y_{jt}^1 is output in period 1 in state t. *Note that we treat inputs as nonnegative numbers.* We will usually assume:

(A.4)　Y_j is convex, closed, and contains the origin $(j = 1,..., J)$;

(A.5)　if $y_j \in Y_j$ and $y_j{}^0 = 0$, then $y_j{}^1 = 0$ $(j = 1,..., J)$.

---

[4] This might be because the costs of setting up contingent commodity markets are prohibitive.

[5] If the economy lasts for more than two periods or if there is more than one good in period 1, we would expect markets to reopen in period 1. This changes the analysis substantially. First, agents' expectations of the prices which will rule in period 1 must be specified. Secondly, agents' conjectures of the effect of a change in a firm's production plan in period 0 on the market value of the firm in period 1 must be modeled. Finally, it becomes much harder to arrive at a reasonable definition of constrained optimality. For a discussion of these issues, see [7].

[6] We use the notation $R_+^K = \{x \in R^K \mid x_k \geqslant 0 \text{ for } k = 1,..., K\}$ and $R_{++}^K = \{x \in R^K \mid x_k > 0 \text{ for } k = 1,..., K\}$. We also write $x^1 > x^2$ if $x_k^1 \geqslant x_k^2$ for all k; $x^1 > x^2$ if $x^1 \geqslant x^2$ and $x^1 \neq x^2$.

[7] That is, $U_i(x') > U_i(x) \Rightarrow U_i(\lambda x' + (1 - \lambda)x) > U_i(x)$ if $0 < \lambda < 1$.

[8] That is, $x' \geqslant x \Rightarrow U_i(x') \geqslant U_i(x)$.

[9] These partial derivatives are to be interpreted as right-hand derivatives when the relevant components of x_i are zero.

Initial Endowments

It is assumed that there is an aggregate initial endowment of goods in period 0, given by $\overline{X}^0 \in R^M_{++}$. For simplicity, we assume that there are no endowments in period 1.

We define a feasible allocation for the economy described above, relative to the institutional structure of the stock market.

DEFINITION. A stock market allocation is an array (x, y, S) such that:

(2.1) $x = (x_1, ..., x_I)$, where $x_i \in R^{M+T}_+$ for each i;

(2.2) $y = (y_1, ..., y_J)$, where $y_j \in Y_j$ for each j;

(2.3) S is an $(I \times J)$ matrix with nonnegative elements, s_{ij}, satisfying $\sum_i s_{ij} = 1$ for each j;

(2.4) $x_i^1 = \sum_j s_{ij} y_j^1$ for each i;

(2.5) $\sum_i x_i^0 + \sum_j y_j^0 = \overline{X}^0$.

Condition (2.5) states that the total endowment of goods in period 0 must be divided between consumption in period 0 and investment. Condition (2.4) says that the period 1 allocation of consumption can be achieved by some assignment of shares in firms in period 0, where s_{ij} is consumer i's shareholding in firm j. It replaces the usual condition in Arrow–Debreu economies that $\sum_i x_i^1 = \sum_j y_j^1$.[10,11]

We will denote the set of all stock market allocations by F. We will be particularly interested in those stock market allocations which are Pareto optimal relative to the set F; that is, which are Pareto optimal relative to the institutional structure of the stock market.

DEFINITION. Given the stock market allocations (x, y, S) and (x', y', S'), we will say that (x', y', S') Pareto dominates (x, y, S) if $x_i' \succsim_i x_i$ for all i and $x_i' \succ_i x_i$ for some i.

DEFINITION. The stock market allocation (x, y, S) is constrained Pareto optimal if there is no stock market allocation which Pareto dominates it.

Let P denote the set of constrained Pareto optimal stock market allocations.

---

[10] Note that we do not assume the existence of a bond. The analysis would be unaffected by the presence of a riskless bond. However, new issues are raised if firms are permitted to go bankrupt.

[11] Note that we rule out short sales. Short sales can easily be introduced into the analysis as long as we impose an exogenous lower bound on them and insist that consumers are solvent in every state in period 1. If no lower bound on short sales is imposed, however, the feasible set may exhibit pathological features: in particular, it may not be closed (see [8]).

PROPOSITION 2.1. *Assume* (A.1), (A.4), *and* (A.5). *Then* $P \neq \varnothing$.

Proof. See Drèze [4].

We follow Diamond [3] in using the term constrained Pareto optimum in order to distinguish Pareto optimality relative to the stock market from Pareto optimality in an Arrow–Debreu economy. Clearly, if one allows a full set of contingent futures commodity markets, the set of feasible allocations becomes much larger. For example, if $J = 1$, condition (2.4) says that consumer i should receive the same fraction of society's output in every state of the world, whereas, in an Arrow–Debreu economy, these fractions could vary with the states as long as their sum over consumers equaled one. Thus, there is no reason to expect a constrained Pareto optimal allocation to be fully Pareto optimal.

It turns out that the feasible set F, as well as being smaller than its Arrow–Debreu counterpart, also has a significantly different structure. In particular, as Drèze [4] has pointed out, it is nonconvex. This nonconvexity can lead also to a nonconvexity in the set of feasible consumption allocations, defined by $C = \{x \mid \text{there exist } y \text{ and } S \text{ such that } (x, y, S) \text{ is a stock market allocation}\}$, as the following example illustrates.

EXAMPLE 1. There are two consumers, one firm, two states of the world, and $M = 1$. Assume that the firm transforms y^0 units of input into λy^0 units of output in state 1 and $(1 - \lambda)y^0$ units of output in state 2, where $0 \leqslant \lambda \leqslant 1$ is a decision variable. Let $\bar{X}^0 = 1$. Consider the consumption allocation $x_1 = (0, (0, \frac{1}{3})), x_2 = (0, (0, \frac{2}{3}))$. This is clearly feasible since it can be achieved by putting $y^0 = 1$, $\lambda = 0$, $s_{11} = \frac{1}{3}$ and $s_{21} = \frac{2}{3}$. Similarly, the consumption allocation $x_1' = (0, (\frac{2}{3}, 0)), x_2' = (0, (\frac{1}{3}, 0))$ is feasible since it can be achieved by putting $y^0 = 1$, $\lambda = 1$, $s_{11} = \frac{2}{3}$, and $s_{21} = \frac{1}{3}$. However, it is easy to check that the consumption allocation $(x_1{}^*, x_2{}^*) = (\frac{1}{2}x_1 + \frac{1}{2}x_1', \frac{1}{2}x_2 + \frac{1}{2}x_2') = ((0, (\frac{1}{3}, \frac{1}{6})), (0, (\frac{1}{6}, \frac{1}{3})))$ is *not feasible*.

In mathematical terms, the reason for the nonconvexity is the presence of condition (2.4). The right-hand side of this condition is a sum of products of terms and thus is a bilinear form. A nonconvexity arises since bilinear forms are not concave functions.

There is an important case where this nonconvexity is inessential. This is when firms' production functions exhibit multiplicative uncertainty; that is, Y_j is given by $\{(y_j{}^0, f_j(y_j{}^0)a_j) \mid y_j{}^0 \in R_+^M\}$, where $a_j \in R_+^T$, $a_j \neq 0$, and f_j is a real-valued, increasing, continuous, concave function, with $f_j(0) = 0$. Under these conditions we may think of the stock market as being a market for the bundles of contingent commodities $a_1, \ldots, a_J$. Firms, through their choice of inputs, determine the aggregate supply of these bundles while consumers, through share purchases, determine aggregate demand. Since the stock market economy is now just an Arrow–Debreu economy with a transformed commodity space (see [14]), it follows that the set of feasible consumption allocations, C, is convex.

We will refer to the multiplicative uncertainty case as the Diamond model since it was first investigated by Diamond [3].

In general, the nonconvexity of F and C has serious consequences. For example, if we assume differentiability, the first order conditions for constrained Pareto optimality are necessary, but not sufficient (see [4]). In other words, the first order conditions may be satisfied at a local maximum, a minimum, or a saddle point. An implication of this is that any procedure for reaching a constrained Pareto optimum must permit not only local changes in the variables s_{ij}, y_j, but also simultaneous discrete changes in these variables (see [4]). This point will be important in motivating our definitions of stock market equilibrium in Sections 3–5.

3. COOPERATIVE EQUILIBRIA

Suppose that the economy reaches the allocation (x, y, S). Under what conditions would we expect the economy to remain at this allocation? First, it might be argued that, whatever production plans firms have chosen, trading in shares and period 0 goods (with or without the aid of markets) will bring about a Pareto optimum *relative to these production plans*.

DEFINITION. The stock market allocation (x, y, S) is an exchange equilibrium if there does not exist a stock market allocation (x', y, S') which Pareto dominates (x, y, S).

If the above argument is accepted, it seems reasonable to restrict our attention to exchange equilibria in our search for equilibrium concepts. Of course, given an arbitrary exchange equilibrium, there is no reason to expect that the production plans of firms will correspond to shareholders' wishes. We now ask under what conditions shareholders will find it in their interests to change firms' production plans.

Consider a meeting of the shareholders of firm j at which a change in production plan from y_j to y_j' is proposed, where we assume that any additional inputs required for the new production plan must be provided out of shareholders' period 0 consumption. In general, if shareholdings remain fixed at s_{ij}, some shareholders will be made better off and others worse off by such a change. Suppose now that the better-off shareholders can make sidepayments to the worse-off shareholders in the form of period 0 consumption goods (but assume that shareholdings remain fixed). Following Drèze [4] we assume that the change from y_j to y_j' will be carried out as long as, with the help of such sidepayments, a Pareto improvement in the position of all shareholders can be achieved. The economy is in equilibrium if no such change is possible.

DEFINITION. The stock market allocation (x, y, S) is a Drèze equilibrium if (1) it is an exchange equilibrium; (2) there does not exist $k \in J$ and a stock market allocation (x', y', S) which Pareto dominates (x, y, S), where $y_j' = y_j$ for all $j \neq k$ and $(y_k'^0 - y_k^0) + \sum_{\{i \in I | s_{ik} > 0\}} (x_i'^0 - x_i^0) = 0$.

Note that the above definition of equilibrium is based on the assumption that shareholders cannot change more than one firm's production plan at a time or make simultaneous changes in shareholdings and production plans. Also we are assuming that the final shareholders of a firm, i.e., those consumers who hold the firm's shares after the stock market closes, are free to change the production plan of the firm—in particular, they may reverse any decision made by the initial shareholders. (For an analysis of a model in which the initial shareholders are able to restrict the actions of the final shareholders, possibly by making a legally binding production plan, see Grossman and Hart (7)).

Let D be the set of Drèze equilibria. It is easy to show that D contains P, the set of constrained Pareto optima. To see this, consider an allocation (x, y, S) in P. Clearly, (x, y, S) is an exchange equilibrium. Suppose that (x, y, S) does not satisfy condition (2) of a Drèze equilibrium. Then, there is a change in some firm's production plan which is Pareto improving for the shareholders of that firm and which does not affect any other consumers. This contradicts the definition of constrained Pareto optimality. Hence, we have

PROPOSITION 3.1. $D \supset P$.

The converse of Proposition 3.1 does not hold, however; that is, in general there exist Drèze equilibria which are not constrained Pareto optimal (examples are given in Drèze [4]). The reason for this is that, as a result of the nonconvexity of the feasible set, it may be the case that a Pareto improvement can be achieved only by changing the shareholdings and production plans of several firms simultaneously. Such changes are ruled out in a Drèze equilibrium.

There are various ways in which the idea of a Drèze equilibrium can be strengthened. First we might assume that when shareholders meet to consider a change in firm j's production plan, sidepayments are made not only in period 0 consumption goods but also in the shares of firm j and of other firms. This can be shown to reduce the number of equilibria, but there will still remain equilibria which are not constrained Pareto optimal (see [8]). Secondly, we might assume that coalitions of consumers can form to change the shareholdings and production plans of several firms simultaneously.

If we insist that a coalition can control only those firms in which it has a 100 % shareholding, but allow sidepayments in the form of period 0 consumption and shareholdings, then the suboptimal equilibria are eliminated and the equilibrium set becomes equal to P.

A third possibility is to drop the assumption that a change in a firm's production plan can be made only if it has the backing of all the shareholders. For example, one might suppose that a group of shareholders needs to own only a majority of shares to change a firm's production plan.[12] More generally, it might be assumed that a group requires more than a fraction δ of a firm's shares to control the firm, where δ is some exogenous parameter lying between 0 and 1. Obviously the smaller δ is, the easier it is for a production plan to be changed, and the smaller the equilibrium set becomes.

Unfortunately, it turns out that if $\delta < 1$ and we continue to allow sidepayments, the equilibrium set becomes too small. In fact, except in very special cases, only *trivial* allocations will qualify as equilibria.[13]

To see this, consider a particular firm k. Assume that this firm has chosen its input vector and must now choose what distribution of output over states of the world to produce in period 1. Let us suppose that the possible output vectors can be parameterized as $y_k^1(\lambda)$ where λ is a real number lying between 0 and 1. Assume (A.3) and that $x_{i1}^0 > 0$ for all i.

Suppose that in equilibrium firm k chooses λ equal to λ_0, and assume that $0 < \lambda_0 < 1$. Define

$$b_i = \frac{(\partial U_i(x_i^0, \sum_{j \neq k} s_{ij} y_j^1 + s_{ik} y_k^1(\lambda))/\partial \lambda)}{(\partial U_i(x_i^0, \sum_{j \neq k} s_{ij} y_j^1 + s_{ik} y_k^1(\lambda))/\partial x_{i1}^0)},$$ (3.1)

where the derivatives are evaluated at $\lambda = \lambda_0$. The quantity $(b_i \, d\lambda)$ represents the maximum amount of the first good in period 0 that consumer i is prepared to give up to change the parameter λ from λ_0 to $\lambda_0 + d\lambda$, given that shareholdings are fixed (b_i may be positive or negative).

Now, if sidepayments• in the form of period 0 consumption goods are allowed, we know that, for $\lambda = \lambda_0$ to be an equilibrium, it cannot be the case that all shareholders of firm k can be made better off by changing firm k's production plan and redistributing period 0 consumption. Hence, defining $I_k = \{i \in I \mid s_{ik} > 0\}$, we must have $(\sum_{i \in I_k} b_i) \, d\lambda \leqslant 0$ for all feasible $d\lambda$, from which it follows, since $0 < \lambda_0 < 1$, that

$$\sum_{i \in I_k} b_i = 0.$$ (3.2)

[12] A majority rule equilibrium has been analyzed by Gevers [6]. However, Gevers does not permit sidepayments between shareholders.

[13] The set of equilibria will not be empty since there always exist trivial equilibria in which one consumer owns all the firms and all the endowment implicit assumption that the initial distribution of wealth is not specified a priori.

Suppose, however, that any coalition with more than a fraction δ of firm k's shares can change λ. Then, since coalitions give positive weight only to those terms on the left-hand side of (3.2) applying to their own members, we must have, for any such coalition B,

$$\sum_{i \in B} b_i = 0. \tag{3.3}$$

Let i be an individual shareholder who owns less than a fraction $(1 - \delta)$ of firm k's shares and let B be the coalition of all other shareholders. Then, subtracting (3.3) from (3.2), we obtain

$$b_i = 0. \tag{3.4}$$

Now since we expect different shareholders to have different preferences (as a result, in particular, of different attitudes toward risk and probability beliefs), it would be a complete coincidence if (3.4) could be satisfied for more than one individual at any particular value of λ.[14] Thus, we may conclude that, barring accidents, there can be at most one shareholder who owns less than a fraction $(1 - \delta)$ of firm k's shares. From this it immediately follows that firm k must have fewer than $(1/(1 - \delta)) + 1$ shareholders.

We see then that only very special allocations can qualify as equilibria when $\delta < 1$. In particular, if $\delta = \frac{1}{2}$, our argument tells us that, barring accidents, no firm can have more than two shareholders!

It is disturbing to have arrived at a conclusion which is so obviously at variance with what is observed in reality. Of course, in reaching this conclusion, we have made a number of unrealistic assumptions. For example, we have ignored the costs of forming coalitions. Also, we have assumed that shareholders are perfectly informed about firms' production possibilities whereas in reality shareholders often have little idea of what firms are presently doing, let alone of what they are capable of doing.

In addition, it might be argued that the notion of equilibrium which we have proposed is inappropriate when $\delta < 1$. For example, even though a coalition of shareholders can change a firm's production plan, individuals may be unwilling to join the coalition because they fear that other coalitions, from which they will be excluded, will then form to make further changes. This suggests that it might be desirable to incorporate some features of the bargaining set (see [1]) into our concept of equilibrium when $\delta < 1$.[15]

---

[14] An exception would be if the spanning condition holds (see [5]).

[15] One might also expect a system of contingent sidepayments to evolve if $\delta < 1$. For example, consumer i might make a sidepayment to consumer j in return for consumer j voting for a particular production plan, where there is an added condition that j must return the sidepayment if he later votes for another production plan.

We will not pursue these issues here. However, we do believe that the study of cooperative equilibria when $\delta < 1$ is an interesting topic for future research.

4. TAKE-OVER BID EQUILIBRIA

A criticism of the cooperative equilibria considered in the last section is that they depend too heavily on the idea that possibly large groups of individuals can get together at shareholders' meetings to carry out changes in production. In practice, it may be difficult to alter production plans in this way. An alternative method of changing a firm's production plan is through a take-over bid; that is, an individual or group of individuals can purchase enough shares of the firm to gain control, change the firm's production plan, and then resell shares at the new market price.

In this section we will analyze a notion of equilibrium based on the idea of a take-over bid. Throughout we will assume that only individual agents can mount take-over bids (the analysis can be easily modified to allow for group take-over bids, however). Also we will assume that an individual requires 100 % of the firm's shares to gain control.[16]

As a first step, we introduce market prices into our concept of an exchange equilibrium.

DEFINITION. A price-allocation array (x, y, S, p) is a competitive exchange equilibrium if

$$(x, y, S) \text{ is a stock market allocation;} \tag{4.1}$$

$$p = (w, v), \text{ where } w \in R_+^M \text{ and } v \in R_J^+; \tag{4.2}$$

if

$$s'_{ij} \geqslant 0 \text{ for } j = 1,\dots, J$$

and

$$\left(x_i'^0, \sum_j s'_{ij} y_j^1\right) >_i \left(x_i^0, \sum_j s_{ij} y_j^1\right),$$

then

$$wx_i'^0 + \sum_j s'_{ij} v_j > wx_i^0 + \sum_j s_{ij} v_j (i = ,\dots, I). \tag{4.3}$$

Here w is a vector of consumption good prices in period 0 and v_j is the market value of firm j. Condition (4.3) says that, given firms' production

---

[16] This assumption can be relaxed without substantially altering our results. Moreover, since the equilibrium notion which we now consider differs from that of Section 3, it is no longer the case that only trivial equilibria exist once the 100 % requirement is dropped.

plans, consumers maximize utility subject to their budget constraints. Note that consumers' wealths are defined with respect to the final allocation (x, y, S) rather than with respect to an initial allocation. Condition (4.1) ensures that (w, v) is a market-clearing vector of prices and market values, given the production plans y_j.

DEFINITION. Let (x, y, S, p) be a competitive exchange equilibrium. Then, a take-over bid is possible if there exists $k \in I$, an allocation $(x_i')_{i \in I}$, $(y_j')_{j \in J}$, $(s_{ij}')_{i \in I, j \in J}$ and prices $(\bar{v}_j)_{j \in J}$, $(v_j')_{j \in J}$ such that:

$$x_i' \in R_+^{M+T} \qquad \text{for all } i \in I, \tag{4.4}$$

$$y_j' \in Y_j \qquad \text{for all } j \in J; \tag{4.5}$$

$$s_{ij}' \geqslant 0 \qquad \text{for all } i \in I, j \in J; \tag{4.6}$$

$$x_i'^1 = \sum_{j \in J} s_{ij}' y_j'^1 \qquad \text{for all } i \in I; \tag{4.7}$$

$$\bar{v}_j \in R, \qquad v_j' \in R_+ \qquad \text{for all } j \in J; \tag{4.8}$$

$$\bar{v}_j = v_j' = v_j \qquad \text{if } y_j' = y_j; \tag{4.9}$$

$$\sum_{i \in I} s_{ij}' = 1 \qquad \text{for all } j \in J^* = \{j \in J \mid y_j' \neq y_j\}; \tag{4.10}$$

$$wx_i'^0 + \sum_{j \in J} s_{ij}' v_j' \leqslant wx_i^0 + \sum_{j \in J} s_{ij} \bar{v}_j \qquad \text{for all } i \neq k; \tag{4.11}$$

$$s_{ij}'' \geqslant 0 \qquad \text{for } j = 1,...,J \qquad \text{and} \qquad \left(x_i''^0, \sum_{j \in J} s_{ij}'' y_j'^1 \right)$$

$$\succ_i \left(x_i'^0, \sum_{j \in J} s_{ij}' y_j'^1 \right) \Rightarrow wx_i''^0 + \sum_{j \in J} s_{ij}'' v_j' > wx_i^0$$

$$+ \sum_{j \in J} s_{ij} \bar{v}_j \qquad \text{for all } i \neq k; \tag{4.12}$$

$$wx_k'^0 + \sum_{j \in J} s_{kj}' v_j' \leqslant wx_k^0 + \sum_{j \in J} s_{kj} \bar{v}_j - \sum_{j \in J} \bar{v}_j + \sum_{j \in J} v_j' - w \left(\sum_{j \in J} (y_j'^0 - y_j^0) \right); \tag{4.13}$$

$$x_i' \succcurlyeq_i x_i \qquad \text{for all} \quad i \in I, x_k' \succ_k x_k. \tag{4.14}$$

DEFINITION. We will say that (x, y, S, p) is a take-over bid equilibrium if (1) it is a competitive exchange equilibrium; (2) no take-over bid is possible.

The easiest way to understand a take-over bid is as follows. Individual k announces that he is going to take over some subset of firms $j \in J^*$ and to change the production plans of these firms from y_j to y_j'. Individual k offers to buy the shares in these firms at price $\bar{v}_j$ per 100 % (to be general we allow $\bar{v}_j$

to be negative) and to sell the shares after the change in production plan at price v_j' per 100 % (if $j \notin J^*$, we set $y_j' = y_j$ and $v_j' = \bar{v}_j = v_j$). Each shareholder of the firms $j \in J^*$ then calculates on the basis of these prices and the proposed changes in production plan, *and on the assumption that prices in all other markets remain the same*, whether he will be made better off or at least no worse off by these changes. If a shareholder is made no worse off, it is assumed that he will agree to sell his shares to individual k.[17] Individual k will carry out the take-over bid if, given the cost of purchasing shares at $\bar{v}_j$ and the cost of financing the additional inputs in production ($y_j'^0 - y_j^0$), he is made better off.

Note that k is permitted to take over several firms simultaneously. Note also that k must select the v_j' so that the share markets of firms $j \in J^*$ clear after the take-over bid. (This assumption is embodied in (4.10)–(4.13). Equations (4.11) and (4.12) say that consumers $i \neq k$ maximize utility subject to their post-take-over budget constraints. Equation (4.13) says that k satisfies his budget constraint. Finally (4.10) is the market-clearing condition.) *However, other markets need not clear*; this assumption is not particularly satisfactory but it can be justified on the grounds that share transactions in firms $j \in J^*$ are consummated before offsetting transactions are made in other markets. Of course, when these offsetting transactions are carried out, some agents will be disappointed and will realize that their assumption that market prices would remain the same was false.

While all individuals apart from k are assumed to act as price-takers, k acts as a price-setter on the share markets for firms in J^*, that is, k's actions must satisfy his budget constraint (4.13) but need not satisfy the usual first-order conditions.

Note that we do not permit shareholders to hold on to their shares during a take-over bid. However, this possibility can easily be incorporated into the analysis. For example, assume that individual k finances the cost of inputs $w(y_j'^0 - y_j^0)$ by floating new shares in firm j. Then, the initial shares in firm j will be worth $v_j' - w(y_j'^0 - y_j^0)$ after the take-over bid. Clearly, all shareholders will prefer to hold on to their shares and sell them after the take-over bid rather than before unless $\bar{v}_j \geqslant v_j' - w(y_j'^0 - y_j^0)$. Hence, a new constraint on $\bar{v}_j$ is now imposed. An interesting consequence of this constraint is that it might pay k to conceal what v_j' will be so that he can buy up initial shares at a lower price.

Let B be the set of take-over bid equilibrium allocations; that is, $B = \{(x, y, S) \mid$ there exists p such that (x, y, S, p) is a take-over bid equilibrium$\}$. Note that the initial distribution of wealth does not enter into the definition

---

[17] There is a problem here. Since a take-over bid will fail unless it has the agreement of all shareholders, it is possible that, even if they are made better off, some shareholders will refuse to sell their shares because they hope thereby to force k to raise $\bar{v}_j$. We ignore this possibility.

of a take-over bid equilibrium; budget constraints are determined with respect to the final distribution of wealth, which is taken to be a variable. For this reason one expects the set B to be large. However, while it is easy to show that B is nonempty (one considers the allocation in which one agent owns everything), I have been unable to find general conditions which ensure that B contains nontrivial allocations.

We turn now to the optimality of a take-over bid equilibrium. It is often argued that take-over bids will bring about efficiency in the stock market. In general, this proposition is false as the next example shows, a take-over bid equilibrium allocation may not be constrained Pareto optimal.

EXAMPLE 2. There are three consumers, one firm, two states, and $M = 2$. Good 2 is used only as an input in production (we ignore this good from now on). With all of this input allocated to the firm, either two units of output in state 1 or two units of output in state 2 can be produced (for simplicity we assume that convex combinations of these production plans are *not* feasible). Consumers' utility functions are given by $U_1 = x_1^0 + 2(x_1^1)^{1/2}$, $U_2 = x_1^0 + 4(x_1^1)^{1/4}$, $U_3 = x_1^0 + 11(x_2^1/2)^{1/2}$ (here x_1^0 is consumption of good 1 in period 0 and x_t^1 is consumption of the single period 1 good in state t; we leave out the i subscript). $\overline{X}^0 = 9$.

Consider the allocation A in which the firm produces two units of output in state 1; consumers 1 and 2 each hold 50% of the firm's shares and each consumes one unit of good 1 in period 0; consumer 3 consumes the remaining seven units of good 1 in period 0. It is easy to check that A is a competitive exchange equilibrium with $v_1 = £2$ and $w_1 = £1$. We show that A is a take-over bid equilibrium allocation.

Consider first whether consumer 3 can organize a take-over bid. If consumer 3 wishes to change the firm's production plan, he must compensate consumer 2 for the loss of all the benefits from holding the firm's shares — to the tune of £4. Since there is a uniform price for shares, this means that consumer 1 must be paid the same amount, hence $\bar{v}_1 = 8$. Thus consumer 3 must pay out £8 altogether, which is more than he possesses. Hence no take-over bid by consumer 3 is possible.

Can consumer 1 organize a take-over bid? In order to do so, consumer 1 must pay consumer 2 £4 for his shares. Also consumer 1 requires £2 to compensate for his own loss of benefits from holding shares. Therefore consumer 1 needs at least £6 to make the take-over bid worthwhile. But if consumer 1 sells the firm's shares to consumer 3 in the open market after implementing production of output in state 2, he will receive only $(\partial U_3/\partial s_{31})/(\partial U_3/\partial x_{31}^0)$, evaluated at $s_{31} = 1$, i.e., £5½. The same argument shows that it does not pay consumer 2 to mount a take-over bid.

This establishes that A is a take-over bid equilibrium. However, it is easy to check that A is Pareto dominated by the allocation $\overline{A}$ in which the firm produces output in state 2; consumer 3 holds 100% of the shares; consumer 1 consumes $3\frac{1}{2}$ units of good 1 in period 0 and consumer 2 consumes $5\frac{1}{2}$ units of good 1 in period 0.

It is clear from Example 2 that the reason for the inefficiency of take-over bid equilibria lies in the fact that price discrimination has been ruled out. For if consumer 3 could pay consumer 1 £2 for his shares and consumer 2 £4 for his shares, a take-over bid would be profitable: consumers 1 and 2 would agree to the offer since they are made no worse off, while consumer 3, by implementing production of output in state 2 and retaining 100% of the firms' shares, could increase his utility from 7 to 12.[18] Similarly, if either consumers 1 or 2 could charge consumer 3 more for inframarginal shares than for marginal shares, they could obtain more than the £6 which is necessary to compensate them for carrying out a take-over bid. In fact it can easily be shown in general that, if price discrimination is permitted, the inefficiency of take-over bid equilibria disappears.

We can use Example 2 to make another point. In the allocation A, the market value of the firm is 2 (in terms of the numeraire, good 1), while in the allocation $\bar{A}$ the market value of the firm is $5\frac{1}{2}$. Hence we see that the possibility of take-over bids does not ensure that the market value of the firm is maximized. The reason for this is clear. The market value of the firm in the allocation A represents the benefits of holding shares in the firm *at the margin*. In order to purchase the shares of the firm, however, one must pay the shareholders according to the *total* benefits from holding shares (see also [11] on this point).

We have seen that a take-over bid equilibrium allocation is not generally constrained Pareto optimal. It is also not generally true that every constrained Pareto optimum can be sustained as a take-over bid equilibrium allocation.

EXAMPLE 3.   There are three consumers, one firm, two states, and $M = 3$. Good 3 is used only as an input in production (we ignore this good from now on). With all of this input allocated to the firm, λ units of output are produced in state 1 and $(1 - \lambda)$ units in state 2, where $0 \leqslant \lambda \leqslant 1$ is the firm's decision variable. Consumers' utility functions are given by $U_1 = x_1{}^0 + x_1{}^1$, $U_2 = x_2{}^0 + x_2{}^1$, $U_3 = x_1{}^0 x_2{}^0$ (here $x_k{}^0$ is consumption of good k in period 0). $\bar{X}_1{}^0 = \bar{X}_2{}^0 = 2$.

Consider the allocation A in which $\lambda = 1$; consumer 1 owns 100% of firm 1's shares and consumes $\frac{1}{2}$ unit of good 1 in period 0; consumer 2 consumes $1\frac{1}{3}$ units of good 2 in period 0; consumer 3 consumes $1\frac{1}{2}$ units

---

[18] One way in which consumer 3 could proceed is by buying consumer 1's shares first at a low price and then consumer 2's shares at a higher price. However, if consumer 1 realizes what is going to happen, he will hold out for the higher price. In the present analysis, we ignore the possibility of discriminating between shareholders through the timing of transactions.

of good 1 and $\frac{2}{3}$ units of good 2 in period 0. It is easy to check that this allocation is constrained Pareto optimal. Consider the competitive exchange equilibrium prices $p = (w, v)$ which sustain this allocation. It is clear from consumer 3's utility function that $w_2 > w_1$. Let consumer 2 offer to pay £$(w_2 - \epsilon)$ to consumer 1 in exchange for consumer 1's shares. For small positive ϵ, consumer 1 will accept this offer since he can use the money to obtain more than one unit of good 1 at current prices. Moreover, consumer 2 will also be made better off since, once he has control, he can set $\lambda = 0$ and hold 100% of the firm's shares. Hence the allocation A is not a take-over bid equilibrium.

The fact that constrained Pareto optima may not be sustainable as take-over bid equilibria is a consequence of our assumption that consumers do not take into account the effect of a take-cover bid on prices in other markets. A constrained Pareto optimum is blocked because there are changes in production which make all consumers better off, subject to compensating transactions being made on other markets at current prices. However, when these compensating transactions are actually carried out, prices will change and some consumers will be made worse off (in Example 3, consumer 1 will find that when he enters the market for good 1, w_1 will rise and he will obtain less than one unit of good 1 for his £$(w_2 - \epsilon)$). What is interesting is that this phenomenon can be traced directly to the nonconvexities in the stock market economy. For in a convex economy, if there was any feasible take-over bid, there would also be a take-over bid which involved small changes in production and shareholdings and hence small compensating changes on other markets. With respect to such small changes, the price-taking assumption would be (approximately) correct and therefore an allocation could only be blocked by a take-over bid if it was not constrained Pareto optimal.

In view of the above, it is not surprising to find that a constrained Pareto optimum *can* be sustained as a take-over bid equilibrium in the convex Diamond model. In fact, in the Diamond model, it is also the case that every take-over bid equilibrium is constrained Pareto optimal; in other words, $B = P$.

To show this, let (x, y, S, p) be a competitive exchange equilibrium in the Diamond model. As noted in Section 2, we can think of firm j as supplying the composite commodity a_j. If $f_j(y_j^0) > 0$, the "price" of the composite commodity a_j, π_j, is given by $\pi_j = v_j/f_j(y_j^0)$. If $f_j(y_j^0) = 0$, however, we cannot deduce the price of a_j from market data—instead we shall in this case define the price of a_j to be

$$\pi_j = w_1\{\max_{i \in I} [(\partial U_i(x_i^0, x_i^1 + \lambda a_j)/\partial\lambda)/(\partial U_i(x_i)]/\partial x_{i1}^0)\}, \qquad (4.15)$$

evaluated at $\lambda = 0$ (we assume (A.2) and (A.3) and adopt the convention that $(\partial U_i/\partial\lambda)/(\partial U_i/\partial x_{i1}^0) = 0$ if $x_{i1}^0 = 0$). The expression on the right-hand

side of (4.15) represents the maximum marginal willingness to pay by consumers for a_j in the exchange equilibrium. Of course, if $f_j(y_j^0) > 0$, this
expression is just equal to $v_j/f_j(y_j^0)$ by the first-order conditions for utility
maximization.

There is a natural definition of competitive behavior by firms in the
Diamond model: taking π_j and w as fixed, each firm j maximizes net market
value or "profit" given by $\pi_j f_j(y_j^0) - wy_j^0 = v_j - wy_j^0$. We show below in
Propositions 4.1 and 4.2 that competitive behavior in this sense is a necessary
and sufficient condition for a competitive exchange equilibrium to be a
take-over bid equilibrium.

PROPOSITION 4.1. *Assume* (A.1)–(A.3). *Let* (x, y, S, p) *be a take-over
bid equilibrium in the Diamond model. For each* $j \in J$, *define* π_j *as in* (4.15).
Then, for each $j \in J$:

$$\pi_j f_j(y_j^0) - wy_j^0 \geqslant \pi_j f_j(y_j'^0) - wy_j'^0 \qquad \text{for all } y_j'^0 \in R_+^M. \qquad (4.16)$$

Proof. Suppose that (4.16) is violated for some $k \in J$ and some $y_k'^0$.
Assume first that $f_k(y_k^0) > 0$. Let $y_k^0(\lambda) = (1 - \lambda) y_k^0 + \lambda y_k'^0$, $0 \leqslant \lambda \leqslant 1$.
Consider the following take-over bid by some consumer i with $s_{ik} > 0$: buy
up firm k's shares at v_k per 100 %, change firm k's inputs from y_k^0 to $y_k^0(\lambda)$,
sell new shares in firm k at $v_k (f_k(y_k^0(\lambda))/f_k(y_k^0))$ per 100 %, and set $s_{ik}' =$
$\{s_{ik}f_k(y_k^0) + f_k(y_k^0(\lambda)) - f_k(y_k^0)\}/f_k(y_k^0(\lambda))$, $x_{i1}'^0 = x_{i1}^0 - (w(y_k^0(\lambda) - y_k^0)/w_1)$.
((A.2) implies that $w_1 > 0$).) For λ close to 0, this is feasible for i and will
receive the support of other shareholders (their position is unaffected since
they can buy the same composite commodities a_j at the same prices π_j
after the take-over bid as before). Moreover,

$$\frac{dU_i}{d\lambda} = \frac{\partial U_i}{\partial x_i^1}\left(\frac{df_k}{d\lambda}\right) a_k - \frac{\partial U_i}{\partial x_{i1}^0}\frac{w}{w_1}(y_k'^0 - y_k^0), \qquad (4.17)$$

where we evaluate these derivatives at $\lambda = 0$ and

$$\frac{df_k}{d\lambda} = \lim_{\substack{\lambda \to 0 \\ \lambda > 0}} \left(\frac{f_k(y_k^0(\lambda)) - f_k(y_k^0)}{\lambda}\right)$$

is well-defined since f_k is concave in λ. Substituting the first-order conditions
for consumer i,

$$\left(\frac{\partial U_i/\partial x_i^1}{\partial U_i/\partial x_{i1}^0}\right) f_k(y_k^0) a_k = \frac{v_k}{w_1}, \qquad (4.18)$$

into (4.17), we obtain

$$\frac{dU_i}{d\lambda} = \frac{1}{w_1}\frac{\partial U_i}{\partial x_{i1}^0}\left(\frac{v_k}{f_k(y_k^0)}\frac{df_k}{d\lambda} - w(y_k'^0 - y_k^0)\right). \qquad (4.19)$$

However, since (4.16) is violated by $y_k'^0$, the right-hand of (4.19) is positive and so $dU_i/d\lambda > 0$. Hence, the take-over bid is in consumer i's interest, which contradicts $(x, y, S) \in B$.

This disposes of the case $f_k(y_k{}^0) > 0$. If $f_k(y_k{}^0) = 0$, we consider a consumer i for whom

$$\frac{\pi_k}{w_1} = \left[\frac{\partial U_i}{\partial \lambda}(x_i{}^0, x_i{}^1 + \lambda a_k) \Big/ \frac{\partial U_i}{\partial x_i{}^0}(x_i) \right].$$

Then it is easy to see that this consumer will gain by taking over firm k, changing the inputs to $y_k{}^0(\lambda)$ for small λ, and holding 100% of the firm's shares. Again $(x, y, S) \in B$ is contradicted.   Q.E.D.

Proposition 4.1 tells us that, in the Diamond model, take-over bids *do* lead to net market value maximizing behavior by firms, where net market value maximizing behavior is defined taking the prices $\pi_1, ..., \pi_J$ as given.

PROPOSITION 4.2. *Assume* (A.1)–(A.3). *Let* (x, y, S, p) *be a competitive exchange equilibrium in the Diamond model. For each* $j \in J$, *define* π_j *as in* (4.15). *Then if* (4.16) *holds for all* $j \in J$, (x, y, S, p) *is a take-over bid equilibrium.*

Proof. Since (x, y, S, p) is a competitive exchange equilibrium, we must have for each i:

$$z_{ij} \geqslant 0 \qquad \text{for } j = 1, ..., J \text{ and } \left(x_i'^0, \sum_j z_{ij} a_j \right) >_i$$

$$\left(x_i{}^0, \sum_j s_{ij} f_j(y_j{}^0) \, a_j \right) \Rightarrow wx_i'^0 + \sum_j z_{ij}\pi_j > wx_i{}^0 + \sum_j s_{ij}f_j(y_j{}^0)\,\pi_j \,. \tag{4.20}$$

Here z_{ij} represents consumer i's purchases of the composite commodity a_j. Condition (4.20) simply says that consumer i is maximizing utility at the prices $\pi_1, ..., \pi_J$.

Let i^* mount a take-over bid. Then, summing the budget constraints (4.11) and (4.13) and using the fact that $v_j = \pi_j f_j(y_j{}^0)$, we find that the post-take-over bid allocation must satisfy

$$w \left\{ \sum_{i \in I} (x_i'^0 - x_i{}^0) + \sum_{j \in J} (y_j'^0 - y_j{}^0) \right\} + \sum_{i \in I} \sum_{j \notin J^*} (s_{ij}' - s_{ij}) f_j(y_j{}^0)\,\pi_j \leqslant 0.$$

Substituting (4.20) with z_{ij} set equal to $s_{ij}' f_j(y_j'^0)$ for all $j \in J$, we get

$$-\sum_{i \in I} \sum_{j \in J^*} s_{ij}' f_j(y_j'^0)\,\pi_j + \sum_{i \in I} \sum_{j \in J^*} s_{ij}' f_j(y_j{}^0)\,\pi_j + w \sum_{j \in J^*} (y_j'^0 - y_j{}^0) < 0,$$

which, together with the condition that $\sum_{i \in I} s_{ij} = \sum_{i \in I} s_{ij}' = 1$ if $j \in J^*$, contradicts (4.16).   Q.E.D.

We can now prove

THEOREM 4.3. *Assume* (A.1).(A.3). *Suppose the Diamond model; that is, for each j,* Y_j *is given by* $\{(y_j^0, f_j(y_j^0)a_j) \mid y_j^0 \in R_+^M\}$ *where* $a_j \in R_+^T$, $a_j \neq 0$ *and* f_j *is a real-valued, increasing, continuous, concave function, with* $f_j(0) = 0$. *Then* $B = P$.

Proof. We know from Proposition 4.1 that any take-over bid equilibrium satisfies the "profit" maximization condition (4.16). A standard argument implies that the allocation is constrained Pareto optimal. Hence $B \subset P$. On the other hand, again by a standard argument, every constrained Pareto optimum must satisfy (4.16). Hence, by Proposition 4.2, every constrained Pareto optimum is a take-over bid equilibrium allocation and $B \supset P$. Q.E.D.

5. LARGE ECONOMIES

In the last section we saw that except in the Diamond model the potential for take-over bids ensures neither that the stock market allocation is constrained Pareto optimal nor that firms maximize net market value, given by $(v_j - wy_j^0)$. In this section we will show that these results are due to the fact that the economy is "small." In particular, if the number of consumers is increased in such a way that each firm becomes small relative to the aggregate economy, then a take-over bid equilibrium is (approximately) constrained Pareto optimal and firms do (approximately) maximize net market value.

To simplify matters, we will assume from now on that $M = 1$. We will retain all the assumptions of Section 2 except those applying to firms. We now make the number of operating firms an endogenous variable of the model. We assume that there is a finite number, K, of *types* of firms.[19] A firm of type k is assumed to have the production set $Y_k \subset R_+^{T+1}$. We assume:

(A.6) $0 \in Y_k(k = 1,..., K)$;
(A.7) if $y_k \in Y_k$ and $y_k \neq 0$, then $y_k^0 \geq \bar{y}^0 > 0$ $(k = 1,..., K)$;
(A.8) Y_k is bounded $(k = 1,..., K)$.

Assumption (A.7) states that any firm which operates must pay a set-up cost greater than or equal to $\bar{y}^0$. As a result of this set-up cost, Y_k will, of course, not be convex. Assumption (A.8) is made in order to ensure that each firm remains small as the number of consumers is made large. It can be replaced by a weaker assumption that firms have U-shaped average cost curves (see [9]). (Note that if two firms of the same type choose the same production plan, then their returns in period 1 will be perfectly correlated since they will produce the same amount of output in each state. Thus the law of large numbers does not apply here.)

---

[19] This assumption is made only for simplicity (see Hart [9]).

We will assume that, in principle, there is no limit to the number of firms of any type that can set up, i.e., there is free entry.[20] Let N be the set of positive integers and let $J = K \times N$. Then, J will represent the set of firms, with the understanding that the firm $j = (k, n)$ stands for the nth firm of type k and $Y_j = Y_k$. Of course, in practice, most of the firms in J will decide not to set up. Thus J should be understood as the set of *potential* firms.

We will continue to assume that there are I types of consumers. We will make the number of consumers large by replicating the consumers of each type. At the same time we will increase the aggregate endowment of the economy.

DEFINITION. Let ^rE represent the economy in which there are r consumers of each type $i = 1,..., I$; the aggregate endowment of the single good in period 0 is $r\overline{X}^0 \in R_{++}$; and the set of firms is $J = K \times N$.

We define a stock market allocation for the economy ^rE in the same way as in Section 2. Now the consumption plan of the lth consumer of type i is represented by $x_{il} \in R_+^{T+1}$ ($l = 1,..., r$); production plans are represented by an array $y = (y_j)_{j \in J}$ which specifies the production plan of each firm whether it operates or not; and shareholdings are represented by the array $(s_{ilj})_{i \in I, j \in J, l=1,...,r}$, where s_{ilj} is the shareholding of the lth consumer of type i in firm j. We also add the condition

$$y_j = 0 \qquad \text{except for a finite number of } j \in J \qquad (5.1)$$

in the definition of a stock market allocation. Given the existence of set-up costs, this condition must hold if (2.5) is to be satisfied in an economy with finite aggregate resources.

The definition of constrained Pareto optimality given in Section 2 carries over to the present context, as does the definition of a competitive exchange equilibrium. In the latter, prices are represented by $p = (w, v)$ where $v = (v_j)_{j \in J}$ is a list of the market values of every firm and it is to be understood that $v_j = 0$ if $y_j = 0$.

We define a take-over bid equilibrium for the economy ^rE as in Section 4 except that we will now add the condition

$$y_j' = y_j \qquad \text{for all} \quad j \in J, j \neq j^*. \qquad (5.2)$$

In other words we now restrict agents carrying out take-over bids to take over only one firm at a time; we will call this a simple take-over bid. Of course this makes a successful take-over bid more difficult, and hence makes the results proved below stronger. Note that the definition of a take-over bid now incorporates the possibility of an agent starting up a new firm ($y_j = 0$, $y_j' \neq 0$) or closing down an old firm ($y_j \neq 0$, $y_j' = 0$).

---

[20] This assumption is again made only for simplicity. (see [9]).

PROPOSITION 5.1. *Assume the conditions of this section. Let* (x, y, S, p) *be a simple take-over bid equilibrium for the economy* ^rE. *Then, for each* $j \in J$, $(v_j - wy_j^0) \leqslant 0$.

Proof. Suppose $(v_j - wy_j^0) > 0$. Let some consumer A set up a new firm of the same type as j with the same production plan y_j. This costs A y_j^0. Let A announce that the market value of the new firm will be v_j. Then consumers who were holding shares in firm j will be willing to transfer their shares to the new firm. Moreover, A will be better off since his wealth will have increased by $(v_j - wy_j^0)$.   Q.E.D.

Proposition 5.1 is a consequence of our Bertrand-like assumption that consumers ignore the effect of a take-over bid on prices in other markets. Note that Proposition 5.1 allows for the possibility that the net market value of a firm is negative in equilibrium; this possibility can arise because v_j represents the marginal benefits obtained by shareholders from holding the firm's shares and not the total benefits.

We consider now the limiting properties of take-over bid equilibria in the economies ^rE as $r \to \infty$. As r gets larger the aggregate endowment of the economy increases and more firms can set up. As a result a greater number of different types of shares can be made available to consumers. This means that the set of feasible consumption allocations is a function of r.

We will confine our attention to equilibrium allocations where consumers of the same type are treated equally. Under (A.3), this means that all consumers of type i consume the same bundle; that is, x_{il} is independent of l. In this case, we will write x_i as the common value of x_{il}.

PROPOSITION 5.2. *Assume* (A.1)–(A.3), (A.6)–(A.8) *and the conditions of this section. Let* $((^rx, {}^ry, {}^rS, {}^rp))$ *be a sequence of simple take-over bid equilibria for the economies* ^rE, $r = 1, 2, \ldots$. *Assume that, for each* $i \in I$, $^rx_{il} = {}^rx_i$ *is independent of* l *for all* r. *Assume also that, for each* $i \in I$, *the sequence* $(^rx_i^0)$ *is bounded away from zero. Then,* $\min_{j \in J}(^rv_j - {}^rw^ry_j^0) \to 0$ *as* $r \to \infty$.

We already know from Proposition 5.1 that a firm's net market value is nonpositive in a take-over bid equilibrium. Proposition 5.2 tells us that the net market value of every firm tends to zero as $r \to \infty$ (and the convergence is uniform). The requirement that every firm's net market value be zero has been proposed as a condition of long-run competitive equilibrium by Leland [11]. Note, however, that this condition will only hold exactly when $r = \infty$.

Proof of Proposition 5.2. Without loss of generality (w.l.o.g.) we may normalize so that $^rw = 1$. We prove first that $(^rv_j - {}^ry_j) \to 0$ for each j. Assume that this is not true for some firm $j \in J$. Use (A.8) and Proposition 5.1 to choose convergent subsequences so that $^ry_j \to y_j$ and $^rv_j \to v_j$ where $(v_j - y_j) < 0$. We will assume that each type i consumer has the same shareholding in firm j: denote this by $^rs_{ij}$; the more general case where different type i consumers have different shares in firm j is dealt with similarly and we will omit the details (the more general case can arise if firm j's production plan is a linear combination of other firms' production plans).

First it is useful to establish

LEMMA 5.3.   *The sequence $(^rx_1, ..., ^rx_I)$ is bounded.*

Proof.   Follows directly from conditions (2.3)–(2.5) and (A.8).

By Lemma 5.3 we may assume that $^rx_i \to$ some x_i for each i. We ask now how much a type-i consumer must be compensated for closing firm j down. Clearly this amount cannot exceed £^rb_i where

$$U_i(^rx_i^0 + {}^rb_i, {}^rx_i^1 - {}^rs_{ij}{}^ry_j^1) = U_i(^rx_i). \qquad (5.3)$$

For if the consumer receives £^rb_i, he can purchase ^rb_i units of period 0 consumption and this makes up for the loss of share benefits in firm j.

Let some consumer A carry out the following take-over bid. Offer each type-i consumer (including himself) £^rb_i to part with his shares; then close firm j down. The cost to A of buying up shares is $r \sum_i {}^rb_i$, while the return from closing firm j down and selling off firm j's assets is $^ry_j^0$. All shareholders will agree to this proposal, and A will be better off if

$$r \sum_i {}^rb_i < {}^ry_j^0. \qquad (5.4)$$

Now since $r \sum_i {}^rs_{ij} = 1$ and $^rs_{ij} \geqslant 0$, we know that $^rs_{ij} \to 0$ for each i. Hence, using the fact that Y_j is bounded, we may form the Taylor expansion

$$U_i(^rx_i^0 + {}^rb_i, {}^rx_i^1 - {}^rs_{ij}{}^ry_j^1) = U_i(^rx_i) + ((\partial U_i(^rx_i)/\partial x_i^0) + \epsilon_1)^rb_i$$
$$-((\partial U_i(^rx_i)/\partial x_i^1) + \epsilon_2)\, {}^rs_{ij}{}^ry_j^1, \qquad (5.5)$$

where ϵ_1, $\epsilon_2 \to 0$ as $r \to \infty$. Substituting (5.5) into (5.3), we get

$$r\, {}^rb_i = \frac{r\, {}^rs_{ij}((\partial U_i(^rx_i)/\partial x_i^1) + \epsilon_2)\, {}^ry_j^1}{(\partial U_i(^rx_i)/\partial x_i^0) + \epsilon_1}. \qquad (5.6)$$

Since $0 \leqslant r\, {}^rs_{ij} \leqslant 1$, we may assume that $^rrs_{ij} \to$ some number a_{ij}. Therefore taking limits in (5.6) we get

$$\lim_{r \to \infty} r\, {}^rb_i = a_{ij}[(\partial U_i(x_i)/\partial x_i^1)/(\partial U_i(x_i)/\partial x_i^0)]\, y_j^1. \qquad (5.7)$$

Now we know from the first-order conditions for utility maximization in the competitive exchange equilibrium $(^rx, ^ry, ^rS, ^rp)$ that

$$[(\partial U_i(^rx_i)/\partial x_i^1)/(\partial U_i(^rx_i)/\partial x_i^0)]\ ^ry_j^1 = {}^rv_j^1 \qquad \text{if}\quad {}^rs_{ij} > 0. \qquad (5.8)$$

Taking limits in (5.8) and substituting in (5.7), we get, using the fact that $\sum_i a_{ij} = 1$,

$$\lim_{r\to\infty} r \sum_{i\in I} {}^rb_i = v_j. \qquad (5.9)$$

Equation (5.9) and the fact that, by assumption, $(v_j - y_j^0) < 0$ imply that (5.4) holds for large r. Hence, for large r, it will be profitable for consumer A to carry out the take-over bid, which violates the assumption that $(^rx, ^ry, ^rS, ^rp)$ is a take-over bid equilibrium.

This shows that $(^rv_j - {}^ry_j^0) \to 0$ for each j. To prove uniform convergence, assume the contrary. Then we can find a sequence (j_r) such that $(^rv_{j_r} - y_{j_r})$ converges to a negative number. Since y_{j_r} must lie in the union of $Y_1,\dots, Y_K$ we may assume that (y_{j_r}) has a limit. The rest of the proof proceeds as before. $\qquad\qquad$ Q.E.D.

We turn now to the Pareto optimality of a take-over bid equilibrium. For each r, let ^rC denote the set of feasible consumption allocations in the economy ^rE in which consumers of the same type are treated equally; i.e., $^rC = \{(x_1,\dots, x_I)\mid \text{there exist } S \text{ and } y \text{ such that } (x, y, S) \text{ is a stock market allocation in } ^rE \text{ and } x_{il} = x_i \text{ for all } l = 1,\dots, r \text{ and for all } i \in I\}$. We define the limiting set of stock market consumption allocations, as $r \to \infty$, as follows:

$$^\infty C = \{x \mid x \text{ is a limit point of some sequence } (^rx) \text{ with } ^rx \in {}^rC \text{ for all } r\}.$$

THEOREM 5.4. *Assume (A.1)–(A.3), (A.6)–(A.8) and the conditions of this section. Let $((^rx, ^ry, ^rS, ^rp))$ be a sequence of simple take-over bid equilibria for the economies ^rE, $r = 1, 2,\dots$. Assume that, for each $i \in I$, $^rx_{il} = {}^rx_i$ is independent of l for all r. Assume also that, for each $i \in I$, the sequence $(^rx_i^0)$ is bounded away from zero. Then, if $x = (x_1,\dots, x_I)$ is a limit point of the sequence $((^rx_1,\dots, ^rx_I))$, x is Pareto optimal relative to the set $^\infty C$.*

Remark. Theorem 5.4 tells us that any take-over bid equilibrium is approximately constrained Pareto optimal when r is large. For given the take-over bid equilibrium allocation $^rx \in {}^rC$, define $^r\alpha(^rx) = \max\{U_1(\tilde{x}_1) - U_1(^rx_1) \mid \tilde{x} \in {}^rC \text{ and } U_i(\tilde{x}_i) \geqslant U_i(^rx_i) \text{ for all } i\}$ to be the maximum possible increase in the utility of each type 1 consumer in the economy ^rE, given that no consumer can be made worse off than in the allocation ^rx; $^r\alpha$ is a per capita measure of how far the allocation ^rx is from being constrained Pareto optimal. Then it follows from Theorem 5.4 that $^r\alpha \to 0$ as $r \to \infty$. For if not, we can find a sequence $({}^r\tilde{x})$ of points in ${}^rC$ with a limit point $\tilde{x}$ which Pareto dominates x. This contradicts the fact that x is Pareto optimal relative to ${}^\infty C$.[21]

Proof of Theorem 5.4. We will first establish a preliminary result. W.l.o.g., we may assume that ${}^rx_i \to x_i$ for each i. Define

$$q^i = (\partial U_i(x_i)/\partial x_i{}^1)/(\partial U_i(x_i)/\partial x_i{}^0). \tag{5.10}$$

LEMMA 5.5.   *For each* $k = 1,\dots, K$,

$$W_k \stackrel{\text{def}}{=} \max_{y \in Y_k} [\max_{i \in I} (q^i y^1 - y^0)] = 0. \tag{5.11}$$

Proof.   Since $0 \in Y_k$, we know that $W_k \geqslant 0$. Suppose

$$q^i y^1 - y^0 > 0 \tag{5.12}$$

for some $i \in I$ and $y \in Y_k$. We will show that it pays somebody to start up another firm of type k and implement the production plan y when r is large.

Let some consumer A do this and sell off shares in the new firm, call it firm j, after the production plan has been implemented at price ${}^rv_j$ per 100 %. Assume that A chooses not to retain any shares in the firm himself. Then it is easy to show that, under (A.1)–(A.3), the excess demand correspondence for the firm's shares is a convex-valued, upper semicontinuous correspondence for positive ${}^rv_j$, prices in other markets remaining fixed. Moreover, as ${}^rv_j \to 0$ excess demand becomes positive, and as ${}^rv_j \to \infty$ excess demand becomes negative. It follows from standard arguments that the market clears for at least one positive value of ${}^rv_j$.

Let ${}^r\tilde{x}_i$ be the common consumption bundle of each type i consumer (excluding consumer A) after equilibrium in the market for firm j's shares has been established, where consumers adjust their purchases on other markets optimally at the given market prices. Clearly

$${}^r\tilde{x}_i \gtrsim_i {}^rx_i \tag{5.13}$$

since no consumer is forced to buy the new firm's shares (we continue to exclude consumer A). Moreover, letting ${}^rs_{ij}$ stand for each type-i consumer's common shareholding in firm j, we have

$${}^rx_i \gtrsim_i ({}^r\tilde{x}_i{}^0 + {}^rs_{ij}{}^rv_j, {}^r\tilde{x}_i{}^1 - {}^rs_{ij} y^1) \gtrsim_i ({}^r\tilde{x}_i{}^0, {}^r\tilde{x}_i{}^1 - {}^rs_{ij} y^1) \tag{5.14}$$

---

[21] A partial converse of Theorem 5.4 can also be shown to hold. If $({}^rx)$ is a sequence of equal treatment constrained Pareto optima for the economies ${}^rE$, then, for large r, $({}^rx)$ will be approximately a simple take-over bid equilibrium allocation, in the sense that the gain from organizing a take-over bid will be small.

since the bundle $({}^r\tilde{x}_i{}^0 + {}^r s_{ij}{}^r v_j , {}^r\tilde{x}_i{}^1 - {}^r s_{ij} y^1)$ could have been achieved by a type i consumer before the new firm was set up (the second part of (5.14) follows from monotonicity).

We wish to show that the sequence $({}^r\tilde{x}^i)$ has the same limit as the sequence $({}^r x^i)$. First we may assume w.l.o.g., that $({}^r\tilde{x}^i)$ is bounded (if not replace ${}^r\tilde{x}^i$ by a suitably chosen convex combination of ${}^r\tilde{x}^i$ and ${}^r x^i$). Let $\tilde{x}^i$ be any limit point of $({}^r\tilde{x}^i)$. Then it follows from (5.13), (5.14), (A.8), and the fact that ${}^r s_{ij} \to 0$ that

$$\tilde{x}_i \sim_i x_i .$$

But by the strict convexity of preferences this means that $\tilde{x}_i = x_i$ since otherwise a type-i consumer could do better by choosing $\frac{1}{2}({}^r\tilde{x}_i + {}^r x_i)$ instead of ${}^r\tilde{x}_i$ after firm j has been set up.

The final step of the proof is to apply the first order conditions for utility maximization. These tell us that

$$ {}^r v_j = [(\partial U_i({}^r\tilde{x}_i)/\partial x_i{}^1)/(\partial U_i({}^r\tilde{x}_i)/\partial x_i{}^0)] \, y^1 \qquad \text{if} \quad {}^r\tilde{s}_{ij} > 0, $$

i.e.,

$$ {}^r v_j = \max_{i \in I} \, [(\partial U_i({}^r\tilde{x}_i)/\partial x_i{}^1)/(\partial U_i({}^r\tilde{x}_i)/\partial x_i{}^0)] \, y^1. \tag{5.15}$$

Taking limits we get

$$\lim_{r \to \infty} {}^r v_j = \max_{i \in I} (q^i y^1).$$

Hence, from (5.12), ${}^r v_j - y^0 > 0$ for large r, which means that consumer A will gain from setting up the new firm. This contradicts the fact that $({}^r x, {}^r y, {}^r S, {}^r p)$ is a take-over bid equilibrium. $\qquad$ Q.E.D.

We return now to the proof of Theorem 5.4. Suppose x is Pareto dominated by $\tilde{x} \in {}^\infty C$. By (A.3) we may assume w.l.o.g. that $\tilde{x}_i >_i x_i$ for all $i \in I$. Then the quasi-concavity of U_i implies that

$$\tilde{x}_i{}^0 + q_i \tilde{x}_i{}^1 > x_i{}^0 + q_i x_i{}^1 \tag{5.16}$$

for all i.

From the definition of ${}^\infty C$ we can, choosing subsequences if necessary, find $({}^r\tilde{x})$ such that ${}^r\tilde{x} \in {}^r C$ for each r and ${}^r\tilde{x} \to \tilde{x}$. Define

$$ {}^r q_i = (\partial U_i({}^r x_i)/\partial x_i{}^1)/(\partial U_i/\partial x_i{}^0)({}^r x_i).$$

Let the shareholdings and production plans corresponding to the allocation ${}^r x_i$ (resp. ${}^r\tilde{x}_i$) be $({}^r y_j)$, $({}^r s_{ij})$ (resp. $({}^r\tilde{y}_j)$, $({}^r\tilde{s}_{ij})$) where w.l.o.g. each type-i consumer has the same shareholding ${}^r s_{ij}$ (resp. ${}^r\tilde{s}_{ij}$) in firm j. Then

$$ {}^r x_i{}^0 + {}^r q_i \, {}^r x_i{}^1 = {}^r x_i{}^0 + {}^r q_i \sum_{j \in J} {}^r s_{ij} \, {}^r y_j{}^1 $$

$$ = {}^r x_i{}^0 + \sum_{j \in J} {}^r s_{ij} \, {}^r v_j $$

by (5.8). Summing over i, we get from (2.5) that

$$\sum_{i \in I} ({}^r x_i{}^0 + {}^r q_i \, {}^r x_i{}^1) = \overline{X}{}^0 + (1/r) \sum_{j \in J} ({}^r v_j - {}^r y_j{}^0). \qquad (5.17)$$

Equation (5.17) and Proposition 5.1 imply that

$$\overline{X}{}^0 + ({}^r N/r) \min_{j \in J} ({}^r v_j - {}^r y_j{}^0) \leqslant \sum_{i \in I} ({}^r x_i{}^0 + {}^r q_i \, {}^r x_i{}^1) \leqslant \overline{X}{}^0, \qquad (5.18)$$

where ${}^r N$ is the number of firms j with ${}^r y_j{}^0 > 0$. However, from (2.5) and (A.7),

$$ {}^r N \bar{y}{}^0 \leqslant r \overline{X}{}^0, $$

so that the sequence $({}^r N/r)$ is bounded. Therefore, taking limits in (5.18) and using Proposition 5.2, we get

$$\lim_{r \to \infty} \sum_{i \in I} ({}^r x_i{}^0 + {}^r q_i \, {}^r x_i{}^1) = \sum_{i \in I} (x_i{}^0 + q_i x_i{}^1) = \overline{X}{}^0. \qquad (5.19)$$

We consider now the expression

$$\sum_{i \in I} ({}^r \tilde{x}_i{}^0 + q_i \, {}^r \tilde{x}_i{}^1).$$

We may rewrite this as

$$\sum_{i \in I} {}^r \tilde{x}_i{}^0 + \sum_{i \in I} q_i \sum_{j \in J} {}^r \tilde{s}_{ij} \, {}^r \tilde{y}_j{}^1$$

and, substituting (2.5), we get

$$\overline{X}{}^0 + \sum_{i \in I} q_i \sum_{j \in J} {}^r \tilde{s}_{ij} \, {}^r \tilde{y}_j{}^1 - (1/r) \sum_{j \in J} {}^r \tilde{y}_j{}^0. \qquad (5.20)$$

From Lemma 5.5, we know that $q_i {}^r \tilde{y}_j{}^1 \leqslant {}^r \tilde{y}_j{}^0$. Hence $(5.20) \leqslant \overline{X}_0$ and so

$$\sum_{i \in I} ({}^r \tilde{x}_i{}^0 + q_i \, {}^r \tilde{x}_i{}^1) \leqslant \overline{X}_0. \qquad (5.21)$$

Taking limits in (5.21) we get

$$\sum_{i \in I} (\tilde{x}_i{}^0 + q_i \tilde{x}_i{}^1) \leqslant \overline{X}_0 = \sum_{i \in I} (x_i{}^0 + q_i x_i{}^1),$$

which contradicts (5.16). Q.E.D.

We end this section with a number of remarks.

Remark 1. The intuition behind Proposition 5.2 and Theorem 5.4 is the following. As consumers are replicated, each firm becomes small relative to the aggregate economy and in particular relative to the market for its shares. Since consumers of the same type have the same utility, we may assume without loss of generality that they have the same shareholding in a particular firm; this means that each consumer's shareholding in any firm j tends to zero as $r \to \infty$. As a result, the difference between the marginal utility and average utility from holding shares in firm j also tends to zero.

Figure 1 shows how the utility of a shareholder varies with the number of shares held. If $0C$ is the total number of shares in the firm, then, when

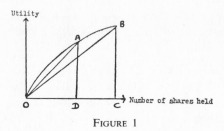

FIGURE 1

there is only one shareholder, the marginal utility from holding shares is given by the slope of the curve at B while the average utility is given by the slope of the line $0B$. If there are two identical shareholders, the marginal utility is given by the slope of the curve at A and the average utility is given by the slope of $0A$, where $0D = DC$. Clearly as the number of shareholders tends to infinity, the marginal and average utility both tend to the slope of the curve at 0, and their difference tends to zero (the assumption that firms' production plans are bounded is important here, as is the assumption that the marginal utility is finite at the origin). To put it another way, the demand curve for the firm's shares becomes horizontal.

Since the average and marginal utilities are equal in the limit, the consumer surplus from holding any firm's shares tends to zero. *Note that this does not mean that consumers do not obtain surplus from all their share investments taken together*—rather it means that the contribution of an individual firm to the surplus is zero, so that if any single firm is deleted from the economy each shareholder will require only the market value of his shares in compensation.[22]

It is important to emphasize that our argument does not apply only to the case where different consumers of the same type have the same shareholding in firm j. If firms' production plans are linearly dependent, consumers of the same type might hold different portfolios and a consumer's shareholding in any particular firm might not tend to zero as $r \to \infty$. It is easy to show that our conclusions still hold under these conditions.

[22] Thus each firm satisfies the no-surplus condition proposed by Ostroy [13] as a characterization of competitive behavior.

As a result of the elimination of consumer surplus, when r is large the net market value of a firm represents the total benefits provided by the firm to the economy. Thus if the net market of a firm is negative, this is a signal that the firm should be closed down—this is the content of Proposition 5.2. On the other hand, if an allocation is not constrained Pareto optimal, then this means that some firm could be choosing a production plan which provides higher total benefits. But this means that the net market value of this firm is not being maximized, and it will pay somebody to take over the firm and implement the new production plan. (Note that, since there is no consumer surplus, the agent who is carrying out the take-over bid will find that he does not have to raise the price of shares above v_j to get other shareholders to part with them.)

Remark 2.   It is interesting to develop further the relationship between take-over bids and net market value maximizing behavior by firms. Proposition 5.2 tells us that, in a sequence of take-over bid equilibria, each firm's net market value tends to zero as $r \to \infty$. Lemma 5.5 tells us that zero is the maximum possible net market value for any firm as $r \to \infty$, *if we take the limiting marginal rate of substitution vectors q^i as given* (see (5.10), (5.15) and note that w has been normalized to be 1 in Lemma 5.5). But Lemma 5.5 leaves open the possibility that a single firm could increase its net market value by changing the q^i.

To see that this is not possible, consider the consequences of a single firm j changing its production plan from $^r y_j$ to $^r y_j'$. Assume that any new inputs that the firm requires are financed by the shareholders according to their shareholdings $^r s_{ij}$, where $^r s_{ij}$ is the common shareholding of a type-i consumer in firm j (there is a difficulty here if firm j is setting up; we assume that the shareholders of all firms, even those which are not yet operating, have been specified). Assume that, after the change in production plan, markets for all firms' shares and for the period 0 good reopen. Let the equal treatment consumption allocation in the new competitive exchange equilibrium be $(^r x_1', ..., ^r x_I')$. Then, we must have

$$^r x_i' \gtrsim_i (^r x_i^0 - ^r s_{ij}(^r y_j'^0 - ^r y_j^0), ^r x_i^1 + ^r s_{ij}(^r y_j'^1 - ^r y_j^1)) \qquad (5.22)$$

since the bundle on the right-hand side of (5.22) is a type-i consumer's new endowment after firm j changes its production plan. By Lemma 5.3, we may assume w.l.o.g. that $^r x_i' \to x_i'$, $^r x_i \to x_i$ for each i. Using (A.8) and the fact that $^r s_{ij} \to 0$, we get, taking limits in (5.22), that

$$x_i' \gtrsim_i x_i . \qquad (5.23)$$

We show that $x_i' = x_i$ for all i. Suppose first that $x_i' >_i x_i$ for all i. Then since the allocation $(^r x_1', ..., ^r x_I')$ can be achieved with the new production plan $^r y_j{}'$, it follows that the allocation $(^r \tilde{x}_1, ..., {}^r \tilde{x}_I)$, where $^r \tilde{x}_i{}^0 = {}^r x_i{}'^0 + {}^r s_{ij} \ (^r y_i{}'^0 - {}^r y_j{}^0)$, $^r \tilde{x}_i{}^1 = {}^r x_i{}'^1 - {}^r s_{ij} \ (^r y_i{}'^1 - {}^r y_j{}^1)$, is feasible when firm j produces $^r y_j$. But if $x_i{}' >_i x_i$, then, since $^r \tilde{x}_i \to x_i{}'$, it follows that $^r \tilde{x}_i >_i {}^r x_i$ for all i when r is large, which contradicts the fact that the competitive exchange equilibrium allocation $(^r x_1, ..., {}^r x_I)$ must be Pareto optimal relative to the production plans $(^r y_j)_{j \in J}$.

This shows that $x_i{}' >_i x_i$ for all i is impossible. A similar argument shows that $(x_1{}', ..., x_I{}')$ cannot Pareto dominate $(x_1, ..., x_I)$. Hence, by (5.23), $x_i{}' \sim_i x_i$ for all i. Finally, the strict quasiconcavity of U_i implies that $x_i{}' = x_i$ for all i.

We see then that a single firm cannot affect the limiting consumption allocation $(x_1, ..., x_I)$. Hence it cannot affect the limiting $q_i = (\partial U_i / \partial x_i{}^1)(x_i)/(\partial U_i / \partial x_i{}^0)$ (x_i). (For further discussion of this, see [9].)

Remark 3. The results of this section have been obtained under the assumption that there is no short selling of firms' shares. The introduction of short sales does not alter the results as long as the short sales are bounded below and we continue to insist that consumers are solvent in every state of the world at date 1. If we put no a priori bounds on short sales, however, the situation changes. For now, even if r is large, an individual firm may have a significant influence on the economy. Suppose, for example, that all firms except for j choose the same production plan y. Let firm j choose the plan y' where y'^1 and y^1 are linearly independent. Then, if there is no lower bound on short sales, the dimensionality of the set of feasible consumption allocations is changed by the presence of firm j. Under these conditions the net market value of firm j does not represent firm j's total contribution to the economy.

Remark 4. There is no reason in general to expect convergence of a take-over bid equilibrium to an unconstrained Arrow–Debreu Pareto optimum as $r \to \infty$. For example, suppose that there is only one type of firm ($K = 1$) and its production set exhibits multiplicative uncertainty as in the Diamond model. Then increasing r does not increase the variety of shares that consumers can be offered, and so the gains from opening contingent commodity markets will remain high.

Remark 5. We noted in Section 3, that, in general, there does not exist a nontrivial stock market equilibrium when coalitions with less than 100 % of a firm's shares can determine a firm's production plan and sidepayments are permitted. In large economies this problem becomes considerably less acute. For since the consumer surplus that a shareholder obtains from holding a particular firm's shares tends to zero as the size of the economy tends to infinity, the utility yielded by the firm is represented simply by the market value of the consumer's shares. As a result, the shareholders will unanimously support any change in production plan which increases the net market value of the firm, and the disagreement which was responsible for the nonexistence of equilibrium in Section 3 is eliminated.

The above remark is unrigorous. We hope to make the argument precise in a forthcoming paper.

Remark 6. Large stock market economies have also been studied by Jensen and Long (J–L) [10] and Merton and Subrahmanyam (M–S) [12] for the case where consumers have mean-variance utility functions. J–L and M–S assume that firms have zero set-up costs and face constant returns to scale. They make the economy large by increasing the number of firms but they do not increase the number of consumers. However, as soon as we allow the existence of set-up costs, the number of operating firms cannot be increased without also increasing the size of the consumption sector. Thus, our way of making the economy large is more general than that of J–L and M–S.

6. CONCLUSION

In this paper, we have analyzed various notions of equilibrium in a stock market economy. In Section 3, we considered a notion of cooperative equilibrium based on the idea that a firm's production plan is determined by a vote at a meeting of shareholders. Under the assumption that sidepayments are permitted, we showed that in general only trivial allocations can qualify as equilibria unless support from all the shareholders is required to effect a new production plan.

In Section 4, we studied a notion of noncooperative equilibrium based on the idea of a take-over bid. In order to take over a firm, it was assumed that an individual must buy up 100 % of the firm's shares, change the firm's production plan, and then resell some (or all) of the shares at the new market price. We found that, except in the case of multiplicative uncertainty, take-over bids lead neither to constrained Pareto optimal outcomes nor to net market value maximizing behavior by firms.

In Section 5, we showed that the reason for the suboptimality of a take-over bid equilibrium is that individual firms are too large relative to the aggregate economy. We proved that in an economy where there is a large number of consumers and where each firm is small relative to the aggregate economy, a take-over bid equilibrium is approximately constrained Pareto optimal. In addition the possibility of take-over bids leads firms to choose production plans which are approximately net market value maximizing. The reason for this is that, in a large economy, the consumer surplus which a shareholder obtains from investing in any firm is close to zero. As a result the net market of a firm's shares represents the total contribution of the firm to the economy, and a take-over bid is profitable as long as this contribution is not being maximized.

REFERENCES

1. R. J. AUMANN AND R. MASCHLER, The bargaining set for cooperative games, *in* "Advances in Game Theory," (M. Dresher, L. S. Shapley, A. W. Tucker, Eds.), Annals of Mathematical Studies (52), Princeton Univ. Press, Princeton, N.J., 1964.
2. G. DEBREU, "Theory of Value," Wiley, New York, 1959.
3. P. A. DIAMOND, The role of a stock market in a general equilibrium model with technological uncertainty, *Amer. Econ. Rev.* 57 (1967), 759–776.
4. J. DRÈZE, Investment under private ownership: optimality, equilibrium and stability, *in* "Allocation under Uncertainty: Equilibrium and Optimality" (J. Drèze, Ed.), Chap. 9, Macmillan, London, 1974.
5. S. EKERN AND R. WILSON, On the theory of the firm in an economy with incomplete markets, *Bell J. Econ. Manage. Sci.* 5 (1974), 171–180.
6. L. GEVERS, Competitive equilibrium of the stock exchange and Pareto efficiency, Chapter 10 *in* "Allocation under Uncertainty: Equilibrium and Optimality" (J. Drèze, Ed.), Chap. 10, Macmillan, London, 1974.
7. S. J. GROSSMAN AND O. D. HART, "A Theory of Competitive Equilibrium in Stock Market Economies," Technical Report No. 230, I.M.S.S.S., Stanford University, 1976.
8. O. D. HART, "Production Decisions in Stock Market Economies," Working Paper No. 76, I.M.S.S.S. Stanford University, 1976.
9. O. D. HART, "Monopolistic Competition in a Large Economy with Differentiated Commodities," mimeo, 1977.
10. M. C. JENSEN AND J. B. LONG, Corporate investment under uncertainty and Pareto optimality in the capital markets, *Bell J. Econ. Manage. Sci.* 3 (1972), 151–174.
11. H. LELAND, Production theory and the stock market, *Bell J. Econ. Manage. Sci.* 5 (1974), 125–144.
12. R. MERTON AND M. SUBRAHMANYAM, The optimality of a competitive stock market, *Bell J. Econ. Manage. Sci.* 5 (1974), 145–170.
13. J. OSTROY, "The No-surplus condition as a Characterization of Perfectly Competitive Equilibrium," mimeo, 1976.
14. R. RADNER, A note on unanimity of stockholders' preferences among alternative production plans: A reformulation of the Ekern–Wilson model, *Bell J. Econ. Manage. Sci.* 5 (1974), 181–186.
15. Symposium on the optimality of competitive stock markets, *Bell J. Econ. Manage. Sci.* 5 (1974).

Printed by the St Catherine Press Ltd., Tempelhof 37, Bruges, Belgium.

discussion | Strategic Analyses of Takeover Bids

Chester S. Spatt

Graduate School of Industrial Administration
Carnegie-Mellon University

I. INTRODUCTION

The study of the market processes for takeover of firms has yielded important insights on basic aspects of the theory of the firm, clarifying the operation of the market for firms and the extent to which firms are disciplined by the capital market to behave in a profit-maximizing fashion.These analyses have been spurred by developments in game theory, the theory of auctions, and the theory of agency as well as observed practices and empirical studies. This commentary evaluates the theoretical modeling of markets for firm takeover and identifies some important issues raised by this line of research.[1]

Models of the takeover process typically specify the incentives of shareholders, management, and bidders. The numbers of each type of agent are indicated along with the structure of information. Each agent receives a signal of his valuation of the firm. In some cases the signal also provides information on the valuation to the others, and inferences are drawn in equilibrium about any privately observed signals of others from the equilibrium pattern of behavior. The rules of the game specify the permissible mechanisms and the mapping from strategies to outcomes. Equilibrium strategies and allocations are then studied.[2] The models of takeover analyzed specialize this general framework (e.g., ignoring the conflict between shareholders and management in most problems with multiple bidders, and assuming the presence of a single potential bidder and the impotence of management in the takeover process in much of the analysis of the free-rider problem confronting a bidder) to understand particular aspects of the takeover problem.

In Section II we discuss the free-rider problem in tender offers and alternative solutions to it. We examine takeover auctions involving multiple bidders in Section III in particular discussing the effect of the information and bidding structure, advantages of bidder elimination, the nature of preemptive bidding, the use of securities and cash offers, and managerial entrenchment in

---

I wish to thank, without implicating, Ken Dunn, Ron Giammarino, Dan Kovenock, and Bart Lipman for useful discussions and, especially, Sudipto Bhattacharya for helpful suggestions and detailed comments. The support of the National Science Foundation is also gratefully acknowledged.

takeover bidding. Our discussion contrasts alternative approaches to takeover auctions modeling and synthesizes these directions. We offer concluding comments in Section IV.

II. THE FREE-RIDER PROBLEM AND ITS RESOLUTION

The recent literature on the takeover process began with the widely discussed paper of Grossman and Hart (1980a). They consider a model with a single bidder who can improve the deployment of the target firm's resources while privately incurring a cost. The shares of the target firm are assumed to be owned by a continuum of holders who each own a negligible portion of the firm. The firm's allocation of resources can be changed only by a successful takeover. We denote the value of a share under the initial resource deployment as q and the value of a share under the improved allocation of resources as v $(v > q)$. Following Grossman and Hart (1980a), we examine an unconditional tender offer in which the bidder offers a price of p $(v > p > q)$ per share for all shares tendered. If each shareholder believes the tender will be unsuccessful, then tendering is advantageous $(p > q)$, whereas if each shareholder believes the tender will succeed, then all shareholders have an incentive not to tender their shares $(v > p)$. Hence, a pure-strategy Nash equilibrium does not exist, and therefore it is unclear that the unconditional tender offer can provide an equilibrium basis for a free-rider interpretation. However, the free-rider interpretation does arise using an alternative form of the tender offer—that is, where the offer is conditional upon the minimum number of shares required for control actually tendering their shares. If the tender bid is conditional upon the raider winning control, then under $p < v$ (which is necessary for the bidder to recover any prebid costs) it is a dominant strategy for each shareholder not to tender his shares. Each small holder views himself as not influencing the aggregate tender decisions of the shareholders, so each would prefer to free-ride and the tender fails in the unique Nash solution (also the dominant strategy equilibrium). Although the free-rider problem arises using this form of a conditional bid, Dunn and Spatt (1984) argue that a two-tiered conditional offer can overcome the free-rider problem. An important aspect of the modeling of tender offers is the design of optimal forms for the bids. Bagnoli and Lipman (1985a, 1986) discuss in detail the distinctive implications of tender bids for any and all shares compared to conditional tender bids.

Grossman and Hart (1980a) allow the free-rider problem to be resolved by permitting a successful bidder to dilute the value of minority (holdout) shares. The main substantive distinction between dilution and two-part bids is a potential signaling role in two-part bids.[3] By the choice of the backend (as well as front-end) price the bidder potentially can use two-tiered offers to communicate separate signals concerning undervaluation and private synergies.[4] Therefore, in light of the information structure assumed, there is little formal distinction (though some interpretative differences) between dilution and two-part bids in both Grossman and Hart (1980a) and Bradley and Kim (1985).

The use of the two-part tender offer as an alternative form of dilution is identified in Dunn and Spatt (1984, p. 418) and analyzed by Bradley and Kim (1985). The two-part bid can eliminate the incentive to free-ride on the improvement resulting from the raid without the "voluntary dilution of shareholder property rights" emphasized in Grossman and Hart (1980a, pp. 46–47). Bradley and Kim (1985) also explore whether a bidder can force the acceptance of an unsatisfactory tender by a prisoner's dilemma game. If each shareholder takes the strategies of the rivals as given, then the threat of dilution or a front-loaded two-part tender forces each shareholder to tender his shares as a dominant strategy.[5] The tender succeeds in the resulting dominant strategy equilibrium as a consequence of dilution and occurs even if the offer makes the target worse off than the initial status quo value of a share. Bradley and Kim (1985) argue that permitting the current management to compete against the bidder (or allowing multiple bidders) protects the shareholders against such inferior offers. However, their analysis does not incorporate the private information of the various bidders, and it exploits an exogenously assumed probability that the competing bids will succeed (see note 5).

The inability of the shareholders to redeploy the firm's assets is the direct result of the types of mechanisms permitted by Grossman and Hart (1980a). The free-rider problem associated with the tender process can be eliminated in several ways by making individual shareholders recognize the effect of individual tender responses upon the aggregate tender outcome (see footnote 33 in Easterbrook and Fischel 1981), though this is outside a "competitive" framework in that individual agents affect the aggregate outcome. For example, a requirement that all shareholders must tender for the raid to succeed guarantees that each shareholder is pivotal and tenders his shares only if he prefers the tender to be accepted rather than rejected.[6] Of course, requiring a successful tender to be unanimously accepted would impose considerable difficulties in practice and emphasizes the problem in ignoring the differential information and taxation of investors.

In a model with a finite set of shareholders, the firm can eliminate the nonexistence and free-rider problems even with unconditional bids good for any number of shares tendered. The shareholder's payoff is p if he accepts the tender regardless of the decisions of the other owners. The shareholder's payoff is v if he does not tender but the bidder acquires control, and q if the shareholder does not tender and the tender is unsuccessful, $v > p > q$ (see Bagnoli and Lipman 1985a, 1986 and Kovenock 1984). This is consistent with equilibrium for some probability of the tender succeeding strictly between 0 and 1. When the shareholders own the same number of shares, there exists an equilibrium in which each tenders his shares with a common probability.

The role of the distribution of ownership is examined by Shleifer and Vishny (1986b), who analyze the incentives of a large holder to monitor management when the remaining shares are owned by a continuum of small owners. The large holder monitors the firm's management and thereby increases the value to the small holders. The acquisition of the large position in the market to achieve this discipline itself could be difficult as a result of a free-rider problem. The intention of an investor to acquire a large stake in the firm raises the value to the small shareholders and the cost of acquisition (a reason in practice that investors are unwilling to identify their large holdings or intentions until legally required). This raises the question of how to design adequate incentives for investors to acquire these large holdings and bear the costs of monitoring the firm (see discussion of the effect of taxation in the concluding section). In fact, Spiegel (1985) recently attempts to endogenize this equilibrium in an analysis of mergers. Kyle and Vila (1986) examine the ability of a single large trader to acquire a large position while masking his intentions (because of "noise" trading).

The value of various financial securities also depends on the distribution of holdings, and, in some instances, free-rider problems similar to those in the takeover setting emerge. For example, under several alternatives for reinvesting warrant exercise proceeds, a sequential exercise strategy by a monopoly warrantholder is advantageous.[7,8] The ability of a monopolist to coordinate in setting his optimal sequential exercise strategy is a benefit to monopolization of the warrant position. The increasing returns to larger holdings lead to a free-rider problem similar to that in the takeover problem, potentially preventing the cornering of the market and the acquisition of monopoly power. When there is a single large warrantholder and a competitive fringe (analogous to Shleifer and Vishny 1986b), the competitors possess an incentive to free-ride on the exercise policy of the dominant player, but the dominant player does not internalize the full effect of his exercise decision. This eliminates much of the potential advantage of sequential exercise (see Constantinides 1984, pp. 393–94).[9]

III. MULTIPLE-BIDDER AUCTIONS

An important aspect of many recent studies of the takeover process is the interplay among multiple bidders for the firm. In addition to predicting bidding behavior, focusing on the strategic interaction of bidders can shed light on issues as diverse as the pure theory of auctions with transaction costs (in particular, modeling the takeover bid process illustrates the impact of bidding and investigative costs upon both bidder behavior and the design of auctions that maximize the seller's revenue) and the robustness of the free-rider analysis of Grossman and Hart (1980a) (e.g., under what conditions will competition eliminate both bidder profit and the divergence between social and private incentives in determining allowed dilution levels).

A. The Impact of Bidder Elimination

An interesting theme in recent analyses of takeover bidding is the target's potential advantage in eliminating some potential bidders so as to increase ex ante the frequency of bidding competition (in these models there is no incentive to restrict competition once the bidders are determined). For example, Shleifer and Vishny (1986a) explore these issues in a model in which two potential bidders have high synergies with the target while another potential bidder has a lower synergy. Under some conditions it is profit maximizing for the target to eliminate a bidder with low synergies in order to increase the intensity with which a higher-synergy firm attempts to identify the target, raising the probability that the firm bids (see also Berkovitch and Khanna 1986). Otherwise, this potential bidder would not search very intensively because the target would collect much of the synergy as a result of the bidding competition with the lower-synergy bidder. The target also has available a white knight—that is, a potential bidder for whom the target can identify the high synergy with the bidder. A high-synergy bidder is required for the target to collect all the rents from the white knight. It can be optimal for the target to pay a premium to eliminate a low-synergy bidder ("greenmail") only when it does not possess a white knight. In the model the price of the target declines after the payment of greenmail because the firm has signaled that it does not possess a white knight and hence is unlikely to collect much of the potential synergy, though the payment of greenmail is in the shareholder interest.[10] A closely related analysis from a legal viewpoint is Macey and McChesney (1985), who emphasize the potential advantage for the target's shareholders in the raider's production of information. They argue that the payment of greenmail deals with the free-rider problem in producing costly information and can allow the target to obtain a more efficient match than with the initial bidder. Tiemann (1986) argues that there is a potential advantage to the target in increasing the competitiveness of the bidding game by the target announcing that it has provided private information to a white knight. From the perspective of the free-rider problem, Bagnoli and Lipman (1985b) provide an example in which the elimination of one of the raiders increases the monopoly power of individual shareholders and the price received by the target.

Interestingly, the potential advantage to bidder elimination can arise with identical synergies by all potential bidders, simultaneous bidding, and the absence of signaling.[11] In an example due to Bhattacharya (1985) it is common knowledge that the synergistic gain is identical for each of the *potential n* bidders. Each must pay an investigative (or bidding) cost c in order to learn this expected gain v and participate in the bidding. The game has two stages. In the first stage each potential bidder specifies his probability of paying the investigative cost and bidding; in the second stage an auction occurs among those who bid using the first-stage bidding probabilities. If there are at least two bidders in the ex post bidding game, then competition between them causes the target to receive v. If there is only a single actual bidder, then the bidder receives the entire value v and the target receives zero. Finally, if there are no bidders ex post, then the value is lost and the target receives zero. Each bidder's expected profit can then be expressed as

$$\pi_i = v p_i \prod_{\substack{j=1 \\ j \neq i}}^{n} (1 - p_j) - p_i c,$$

where p_j is the probability that potential bidder j bids in the takeover auction. In the symmetric solution to this game,[12] each potential bidder uses a mixed bidding strategy in which each is indifferent to bidding. Then each receives a zero incremental expected payoff from bidding so that the common bidding probability, p, satisfies

$$(1 - p)^{n-1} = \frac{c}{v}.$$

It is straightforward to show that the target's profit strictly declines with n for $n \geq 2$ (i.e., bidder elimination is advantageous).[13]

Although eliminating potential bidders helps the target under the assumption of a fixed number of potential bidders, the target's expected payoff decreases in the symmetric solution with an increase in the common cost of bidding. An increase in the individual cost of bidding reduces the probability that an individual potential bidder chooses to bid in equilibrium and, hence, reduces the target's expected revenue by reducing the aggregate probability that at least two potential bidders choose to bid. Therefore, in this example the comparative statics of the effect of the ease of bidding differs between reducing the exogenous number of potential bidders and increasing the cost of bidding.

Bhattacharya's example raises the question of the robustness of the advantage to bidder elimination for situations in which the bidders have independent values (e.g., Vickrey 1961) or signals of a common value (e.g., Milgrom and Weber 1982). We have extended the result on bidder elimination to a simultaneous move, n-bidder version of the information structure explored by P'ng (1985). Each bidder's valuation has two components, a common component ($u = 0$ or $u = 1$) and an independent component ($v = 0$ or $v = 1$). P'ng (1985) defines m as the reservation value of the firm (which we restrict to $1 < m < 2$). All potential bidders observe their own signals for a cost c (in P'ng 1985 only the second of the two bidders needed to incur the cost). Following Bhattacharya (1985), we use a two-stage game model: in the first stage the bidders simultaneously determine investigation probabilities, and in the second stage those who bid participate in a progressive auction. After defining the target's profit function, the reasoning in note 13 for the symmetric equilibrium can be extended to this case. The advantage of bidder elimination is clearly also present if we drop the common component in the P'ng (1985) information structure (so that the overall signals across bidders are independent). The results extend to these alternative information structures in that the possibility of low signals indirectly scales back the probability of a bidding rivalry and leads to endogenous adjustment of the investigation probability of each bidder. In these examples an increase in the number of potential bidders reduces the target's profit, even though an increase in the number actually investigating improves the efficiency of the takeover market. The robustness of these findings is an open question.

A different conclusion emerges if the actual number of bidders is determined to eliminate the incentive for profitable entry in an auction setting in which each potential bidder observes a private signal of the common value after incurring a bidding cost (e.g., French and McCormick 1984). In such a setting the number of bidders is determined endogenously as a function of the bidding cost and the other parameters. In contrast, in Bhattacharya (1985) the number of potential bidders is fixed exogenously, but the equilibrium probability that each bid is determined within the model. Increasing the bidding cost cannot increase the target's expected revenue under either model. However, within a setting in which the actual number of bidders is fixed by the cost of bidding, there is no analogy to the exogenous elimination of bidders. These alternative approaches to prebid costs also raise the question of which method is more suitable in various circumstances.[14]

B. Preemptive Bidding

Another interesting feature of several of the recent studies of auctions is the explanation for initial tender bids substantially in excess of the previous prevailing price for the security. Both Fishman (1986a) and P'ng (1985) assume that the bidders receive a signal of their valuation of the target. An exogenous order for the bidders is specified in which the second bidder decides whether to pay an investigative cost in order to observe a signal and bid (suppose it is not optimal to bid without observing the signal after observing the initial bidder's bid). In Fishman (1986a) the valuations are independent across bidders, and in P'ng (1985) there is both an independent component and an identical common component (each bidder directly observes only the sum of these).[15] In light of the investigative cost of the second bidder, in Fishman (1986a) it can be optimal for the first bidder to bid above the target's reservation price in order to signal a high private value to the potential rival so that the potential rival does not investigate and bid.[16] Khanna (1985) examines an alternative approach to preemptive bidding in which each bid stays outstanding for a minimum time (according to the actual requirement on tender bids) and bidders arrive at the market at exogenous discrete increments of time. A preemptive bid by the initial bidder reduces the probability that the second potential bidder will bid and force the initial bidder to potentially compete with later potential bidders (the auction is terminated if the second bidder declines to respond to the initial bid). The effect of the requirement that the offer remain outstanding for a fixed period of time (e.g., 30 days) raises some interesting issues and should be studied in more detail. An offer required to be outstanding for a long time gives the target a valuable option, even though the bid might be rejected ultimately. If the value of the option is substantial (e.g., if the anticipated volatility following the offer is high), the requirement seems to raise substantially the transaction cost of bidding and to reduce the frequency of takeover.

Some of the models of preemptive bidding (e.g., Fishman 1986a and P'ng 1985) predict that the bidder never unsuccessfully attempts to preempt.[17] Yet, in practice most initial takeover bids are at a substantial premium above the prior market value for the target. However, the attempt to preempt is often unsuccessful. We suspect this can be illustrated by introducing into the model (e.g., Fishman 1986a) a signal that the second bidder observes without cost after observing the bid of the first bidder and prior to deciding whether to investigate in order to observe an additional signal. We conjecture that the following intuition can be formalized. The second bidder's investigation decision is a function of his first signal. A higher initial bid by the first bidder then would result in a reduced probability of investigation by the second bidder. The trade-off confronting the first bidder in determining his equilibrium preemptive bid depends on his own valuation for the target. For example, an initial bidder with a higher valuation bids more aggressively in order to deter with higher probability investigation by the second bidder. Such an approach would seem to yield a variety of empirical insights about the role of rivalry among the bidders.

The potential advantage of preemptive bidding in retarding competition gives earlier bidders an advantage that can make it useful to precommit by bidding early rather than waiting to infer common information contained in rival bids.[18] This could lead to an interesting theory of the endogenous timing of bids in an environment in which bidder signals contain both private and common information (both components play an important role in this intuition). An alternative perspective on the endogenous timing of information acquisition and bidding is in Bagnoli and Lipman (1985b).

C. Securities and Cash Bidding

In addition to the unconditional bids typically analyzed in the theory of auctions, observed bids often are contingent (e.g., bidders often use securities of the combined firm as part of their offer). With no private information on the part of the target, the target increases the auction price by restricting the bidding to an equity share in the merged firm.[19] Hansen (1985) shows that in a progressive auction in which the bidders offer a share of the resulting merged firm, the seller obtains greater revenue because the seller captures part of the surplus of the winning bidder. For example, suppose all potential bidders have identical market value prior to bidding for the target and independently drawn private values for the target. The second highest valuation bidder stops bidding when the share of his own firm to be paid to the target eliminates the bidder's surplus. However, at that share a bidder with the highest valuation pays more than the second highest reservation price because his share is applied to a larger valuation than the second highest bidder's is. The nature of the private information of the target about its value in a merger also influences the bidding mechanism used by the acquirer. To the extent that the target has considerable private information about the synergy of a bidder, the bidder could benefit by conditioning the target's acceptance upon his signal of the synergy (potentially overcoming the adverse selection that results from the bidder's private information about the synergies as described in note 19). Because the target retains a position in the project by accepting a security offer, the target evaluates such an offer with respect to his private signal of the potential synergy as well as the information contained in the form of the bidder's offer (see Fishman 1986b and Hansen 1987).

The form of the takeover offer will also be influenced by tax considerations because a cash purchase forces the recognition of capital gains and losses. The resulting cost (i.e., if recognition was not otherwise optimal) suggests an additional advantage of a nontaxable securities exchange. The preferences of the target shareholders concerning the form of the offer can vary with their tax bases (see related discussion in Dreyfus 1984). However, tax considerations alone cannot make the taxable purchase advantageous because investors always possess the option of recognizing the capital gain or loss (additional discussion of the effect of taxation is in the concluding section).

D. Managerial Entrenchment, Takeover, and Bidding

Baron's (1983) model of managerial resistance and bidding examines a two-stage bidding game in which rejection by the manager of the high bid in the first stage triggers a second auction among new bidders (whose valuations are independent of the bidders in the first round). The manager's reservation price for the firm is determined by his privately observed signal of the value of the firm (which is a component of the value to bidders), his privately observed preference for perquisites, and the stage of the auction game. Therefore, the bidders are unsure about management's reservation value and confront a distribution of possible values. Second-stage bidders learn about the distribution of reservation prices they face from the level of the rejected first-stage bid. The model emphasizes the inability of outsiders to deduce whether management rejected a takeover bid in an attempt to generate a higher offer (e.g., if they have a high signal of the value of the firm) or to protect themselves (i.e., managerial entrenchment).[20] The formal analysis in Baron (1983) indirectly raises some interesting methodological issues.[21]

IV. CONCLUDING COMMENTS

A. Legal Regulation

A number of important policy questions concerning the legal regulation of takeover have not been exhaustively explored in the literature. They include the protection of minority shareholders, disclosure requirements, management resistance, payment of greenmail, and restrictions on the form of takeover bidding (including the use of front-loaded bids and requirements that the bid be outstanding for a minimum period). Policy prescriptions in takeover contexts are quite sensitive to model specification as alternative theoretical approaches lead to opposite conclusions. Empirical evidence on the importance of various factors is critical for obtaining policy conclusions.

An illustration of the difficulty in drawing policy conclusions from highly stylized models is the debate on the management entrenchment hypothesis and the desirability of management playing an active role in determining the firm's response to a takeover offer. There has been a strong tendency for authors to draw general conclusions concerning legal rules on this issue as a result of stylized models that look at special aspects of the problem (e.g., Easterbrook and Fischel 1981 and Bebchuk 1982).

Grossman and Hart (1980a, b, 1981) take a strong position in support of eliminating statutory impediments to dilution. For example, they emphasize optimal dilution in order to ensure adequate disciplining of incumbent management by takeover threats. A variety of the issues discussed in this commentary and in the papers cited herein suggest this interpretation may be too rigid. Grossman and Hart (1980b) even argue against mandatory federal *disclosure* requirements of the intentions of bidders to dilute minority shareholders *because* it would facilitate prosecution of these bidders under state laws. They argue that such disclosure requirements would be redundant in light of antifraud statutes in an environment in which the target shareholders (but apparently not state prosecutors) could deduce these intentions. A similar argument relating disclosure and antifraud legislation is also offered by Grossman (1981) in analyzing warranties.

B. Taxes and the Free-Rider Problem

Shleifer and Vishny (1986b) attempt to explain firm dividend payments as compensation for the monitoring costs of large shareholders. They argue that large shareholders (e.g., corporations) prefer dividends to capital gains because of the statutory exclusion from taxation of 85 percent of intercompany dividends, whereas individual investors prefer capital gains to dividends. Without this compensation for monitoring costs, the large investor could have an incentive to sell his holding, thereby reducing the value of the holdings of the small investors by more than the tax costs of their dividends. Yet most large positions are not held by such investors with a strict tax preference for dividends (e.g., pension funds). Further, the tax costs (to individual investors) of this transfer to large corporate investors are quite large.

C. Reputation and Sequential Gaming

A potentially important approach that has not yet been explored in the takeover literature is the role of the reputation of the economic players. To what extent does concern about future reputation affect the tactics and strategies of both management and raiders as well as the valuation of firms? For example, information that a "knowledgeable" raider is purchasing shares in a firm can potentially affect its market value. The observed price decline after a firm pays greenmail, though consistent with Shleifer and Vishny (1986a), is also potentially (and perhaps more plausibly) consistent with an agency and reputation model in which the payment of greenmail both wastes firm resources and causes the market to update its assessment of the management's type and future behavior (somewhat related to Baron 1983). The reputational effect of aggressive management efforts to block raiders (e.g., Unocal's repurchase offer that discriminated against the raider) also could be important. In a more technical vein such studies of reputation as well as models of sequential bidding often have a host of sequential equilibria. Often the interpretation of the results of such models rests in an unsatisfactory fashion upon selecting a particular sort of equilibrium for detailed study. These selections are sometimes biased (e.g., selecting an equilibrium with the desired property) and often arbitrary. It is useful to motivate equilibrium selection by, for example, game-theoretic refinements of the sequential equilibria concept (see, e.g., Banks and Sobel 1987, Kreps 1984, and Grossman and Perry 1986 and some of the references in those papers).[22] For example, Shleifer and Vishny (1986b), Bagnoli, Gordon, and Lipman (1986), and Fishman (1986b) use versions of the Grossman and Perry (1986) refinement to restrict the equilibria.

NOTES

[1] In light of both space limitations and the orientation of this book, we shall focus the discussion upon theoretical developments. This neglects the extensive and important set of empirical studies on firm takeover. These identify numerous stylized facts about takeovers. Several of these studies are provided in the *Journal of Financial Economics* Symposium (1983). Similarly, our discussion of the extensive legal debate on various restrictions on firm takeover is also limited (see concluding section). In addition, we will assume that takeover is potentially advantageous, and we will not explore detailed informational and game-theoretical modeling of the potential gains from mergers (e.g., Baldwin 1983a, b, Grossman and Hart 1986, Kihlstrom 1986, and Stoughton 1984) in order to focus upon other issues.

[2] In some cases in which a particular equilibrium solution is described, uniqueness is not demonstrated.

[3] In practice, bidders often make a tender offer for a prespecified fraction of the firm. If more shares are tendered than sought by the bidder, the acquirer can accept the shares tendered on a pro rata basis and decline the excess. A two-part tariff specifies the price to be paid for shares until a critical level (e.g., needed for control) and another (lower) price for the remainder. The three parameters of this schedule are the two price levels and the fraction that is paid the higher price.

[4] Grossman and Hart (1981) permit mergers because of market undervaluation of the target and because of the presence of synergistic opportunities. Undervaluation cannot be the sole basis for mergers (i.e., there must be an allocational role for mergers) because otherwise adverse selection would cause the target to reject any offer (discussions of adverse selection in other contexts include Akerlof 1970 and Milgrom and Stokey 1982).

[5] For a fixed set of probability beliefs about which tender will succeed, the rivals will maximize the differential payoff between the two parts in order to maximize the cost to shareholders of declining to tender compared to the cost of declining to accept a rival's offer. Without limits on the permissible dilution, or signaling of private information held by bidders, the price on the back part of the offer would be zero.

[6] Another procedure that attempts to resolve the free-rider problem is the approving and disapproving tender suggested by Bebchuk (1984). He argues that shareholders should be permitted to choose among three alternatives: (1) tender one's own shares and approve the tender; (2) tender one's own shares but disapprove the tender; and (3) do not tender one's shares and disapprove the tender. For such a tender

to be successful, a majority of the shareholders must approve the tender [i.e., strategy (1)], and the tender outcome is allocated among all shares tendered, whether approving or disapproving [i.e., strategies (1) and (2)]. Bebchuk (1984) argues that all shares should be tendered, whether approvingly or disapprovingly, because the dilution of minority shareholders ensures that strategy (2) dominates strategy (3). But this relies upon dilution and implicitly rules out the possibility that shareholders (4) do not tender their shares and approve the tender.

[7] Emanuel (1983) first pointed out the advantage to sequential exercise strategies under some circumstances. This discussion has been expanded by Constantinides (1984), Cox and Rubinstein (1985), and Spatt and Sterbenz (1986).

[8] Another financial security for which there is a gain to market cornering is a sinking fund bond issue. A hoarder can squeeze the firm and obtain an artificially high price for bonds needed by the issuer to fulfill his sinking fund requirement (see Dunn and Spatt 1984). If all investors receive an inflated price only on those bonds on which they are the unique supplier (following the equilibrium payoff pattern in Dunn and Spatt 1984), then *given* the distribution of holdings there is no potential for small investors to free-ride.

[9] Other specific reasons why cornering of warrants and convertibles would not occur are that (1) the firm can use a reinvestment policy on exercise proceeds to eliminate the advantage due to sequential strategies and market cornering, and (2) with incomplete hoarding due to rivalry the hoarders' payoff can decline (see Spatt and Sterbenz 1986).

[10] In many financial signaling models the managerial objective function depends on future as well as current compensation to create a potential cost of falsely signaling. Therefore, the immediate price decline after the adverse signal can be consistent with the manager acting in the shareholder's interest.

[11] A study with sequential bidding that illustrates that the target may not wish to assist bidders is P'ng (1985). Assistance to a rival can eliminate the incentive of an earlier bidder to bid aggressively so as to deter the rival's investigation.

[12] Using the payoff functions to this Nash game, one can show that the only other equilibrium occurs when someone bids with probability 1 and all others bid with probability 0, which is an inferior outcome for the seller.

[13] Because the target's revenue is v unless ex post there is either zero or one actual bidder, the target's expected revenue is

$$\pi = v[1 - (1 - p)^n - np(1 - p)^{n-1}].$$

Substituting the equilibrium bidding probability, we express the target's revenue as a function of the number of potential bidders.

$$\pi = v - c\left\{\left[1 - \left(\frac{c}{v}\right)^{1/(n-1)}\right]n + \left(\frac{c}{v}\right)^{1/(n-1)}\right\}.$$

Twice differentiating this expression with respect to n, we obtain

$$\frac{\partial \pi}{\partial n} = -c\left\{1 - \left(\frac{c}{v}\right)^{1/(n-1)} + \frac{1}{n-1}\ln\frac{c}{v}\left(\frac{c}{v}\right)^{1/(n-1)}\right\}$$

$$\frac{\partial^2 \pi}{\partial n^2} = c\left(\frac{c}{v}\right)^{1/(n-1)}\left(\ln\frac{c}{v}\right)^2\left(\frac{1}{n-1}\right)^3 > 0$$

so the derivative with respect to n is strictly increasing. But

$$\lim_{n \to \infty}\left[1 - \left(\frac{c}{v}\right)^{1/(n-1)} + \frac{1}{n-1}\ln\frac{c}{v}\left(\frac{c}{v}\right)^{1/(n-1)}\right] = 0.$$

Since the derivative with respect to *n* is increasing and at the limit is zero, the derivative is negative for finite *n*, so the target's profit declines in *n* (for finite *n* and $n > 1$).

[14] The issue of prebid costs raises an interesting concern about the literature on dilution and the free-rider problem. Grossman and Hart (1980a, 1981) observe that if investigative costs are borne (unrealistically) only by the winning bidder, then competition among bidders (who earn zero profit) implies that the social and private optimal levels of dilution are identical. However, they also point out that the presence of investigative costs borne by all bidders need not undercut their single-bidder conclusion that there is an inadequate private incentive for dilution. The study of the comparison between the social and private optimal dilution levels should be linked to bidding environments that consider sunk prebid costs of each bidder (e.g., French and McCormick 1984 and Bhattacharya 1985), taking into account the effect of dilution levels upon bidding behavior.

[15] In P'ng (1985) a rival bidder uses the observed bid to draw an inference about the independent component of the earlier bidder's valuation in order to decide whether to investigate and bid. Any rival who chooses to investigate learns his overall valuation and draws no further inference from the bidding behavior of the other bidder in a sequential auction. In contrast, Giammarino and Heinkel (1986) study a market in which the valuation of the target is identical for an informed and uninformed bidder so that the uninformed draws inferences about the common valuation from the bidding behavior of the informed. Their specific conclusions exploit the assumed timing of bidder moves (i.e., the uninformed bidder has the tactical advantage of the last move) and restriction to a discrete bidding grid. It would be useful to understand in other settings the effect of the inferences drawn from individual bids upon equilibrium bidder behavior.

[16] Fishman (1986a) allows the bidders to engage in a progressive auction if the second bidder decides to participate. The motivation for preemption in P'ng is slightly different, since he restricts the initial bidder to a single bid (so that a second bidder wins the auction provided that his valuation exceeds the first bidder's bid rather than the first bidder's valuation). The common value component in P'ng (1985) is also not crucial for his analysis.

[17] In Khanna (1985) preemption need not succeed in that later bidders always observe their valuation and bid provided their valuation exceeds the current bid.

[18] Existing bidding models of takeover with "common" signals are somewhat specialized and do not have multiple bidders drawing inferences from rival bids. In P'ng (1985) the common component is identical across bidders, and in Giammarino and Heinkel (1986) only the single informed bidder observes the common signal (see also the discussion in note 15).

[19] Without this restriction on the form of the bids, bidders could make a cash offer to avoid the adverse inference drawn from such a conditional offer (and the resulting adverse selection). The evaluation of any bid would reflect the market's assessment of the type of the bidders who would make such an offer (e.g., Fishman 1986b and Hansen 1987).

[20] A related analysis of managerial entrenchment is offered in Bagnoli, Gordon, and Lipman (1986), who examine defensive stock repurchases in a model in which the incumbent management and a raider have private (but correlated) signals of the value of the firm. Another interesting analysis of managerial entrenchment is in Harris and Raviv (1985), who examine a model in which managers set the firm's capital structure to minimize the manager's total cost of loss of control of the firm due to either bankruptcy or a successful takeover bid. The analysis trades off the advantage of incremental equity in reducing the probability of loss of control due to bankruptcy risk against the cost of incremental equity of reducing the proportion of the voting stock retained by management and thereby increasing the probability of a successful takeover. Of course,

if nonvoting equity were permitted in the model, debt would be dominated by it and never utilized.

[21] In auction models with a reserve price, the final bid price can depend on the highest valuation as well as the second highest valuation. For example, if the high-valuation bidder knew the target's reserve price, then he would offer to pay the reserve level when it exceeded the second highest valuation (bid). Even in the presence of an uncertain reservation value, the final bid of the highest-valuation bidder can be influenced by both his own valuation and the second highest one. Intuitively, because of the influence of the final bid on its probability of acceptance, the final bid should depend on one's own valuation. Yet, Baron (1983) restricts the final offer in any round of the bidding game to a function solely of the second highest valuation of all investors in that round while permitting management to reject that offer using a reserve price rule.

[22] Because game-theoretic results are often sensitive to the modeling of the game, it is also important to consider alternative specifications and endogenize the form of the game. For example, Berkovitch and Khanna (1986) compare a bargaining game (which they call a "merger" attempt) and an auction game (a "tender offer"). The tender offer, unlike the merger negotiations, is assumed to reveal the presence of a positive synergy, whose size varies across prospective partners, to these rival bidders.

REFERENCES

Akerlof, G. 1970. "The Market for 'Lemons': Quality Uncertainty and the Market Mechanism." *Quarterly Journal of Economics* 84: 488–500.

Bagnoli, M.; Gordon, R.; and Lipman, B. 1986. "Takeovers and Defensive Stock Repurchase under Incomplete Information." University of Michigan, manuscript.

Bagnoli, M., and Lipman, B. 1985a. "An Economic Analysis of Restrictions on Takeover Bids." University of Michigan, manuscript, July.

———. 1985b. "Takeover Bids, Multiple Raiders, and Information Acquisition: A Game-Theoretic Analysis." University of Michigan, manuscript.

———. 1986. "Successful Takeovers without Exclusion." University of Michigan, manuscript, revised June.

Baldwin, C. 1983a. "Innovation and the Vertical Structure of Industry." Working paper HBS 84-16, Harvard Business School, October.

———. 1983b. "Productivity and Labor Unions: An Application of the Theory of Self-enforcing Contracts." *Journal of Business* 56: 155–85.

Banks, J., and Sobel, J. 1987. "Equilibrium Selection in Signaling Games." *Econometrica*, forthcoming.

Baron, D. 1983. "Tender Offers and Management Resistance." *Journal of Finance* 38: 331–43.

Bebchuk, L. 1982. "The Case for Facilitating Competing Tender Offers." *Harvard Law Review* 95: 1028–56.

———. 1984. "A Model of the Outcome of Takeover Bids." Unpublished manuscript, December.

Berkovitch, E., and Khanna, N. 1986. "A Theory of Acquisition Markets: Mergers Vs. Tender Offers, Golden Parachutes and Greenmail." Unpublished manuscript, revised May.

Bhattacharya, S. 1985. Private communication, September.

Bradley, M., and Kim, E. H. 1985. "The Tender Offer as a Takeover Device: Its Evolution, the Free Rider Problem, and the Prisoner's Dilemma." Unpublished manuscript, revised April.

Constantinides, G. 1984. "Warrant Exercise and Bond Conversion in Competitive Markets." *Journal of Financial Economics* 13: 371–97.

Cox, J., and Rubinstein, M. 1985. *Options Markets*. Englewood Cliffs, N.J.: Prentice-Hall.

Dreyfus, J. 1984. "Takeover Bids and Personal Income Taxes." Unpublished manuscript, November.

Dunn, K., and Spatt, C. 1984. "A Strategic Analysis of Sinking Fund Bonds." *Journal of Financial Economics* 13: 399–423.

Easterbrook, F., and Fischel, D. 1981. "The Proper Role of a Target's Management in Responding to a Tender Offer." *Harvard Law Review* 94: 1161–1204.

Emanuel, D. 1983. "Warrant Valuation and Exercise Strategy." *Journal of Financial Economics* 12: 211–35.

Fishman, M. 1986a. "A Theory of Preemptive Takeover Bidding." Northwestern University, manuscript, revised February.

———. 1986b. "Preemptive Bidding and the Role of the Medium of Exchange in Acquisitions." Northwestern University, manuscript, July.

French, K., and McCormick, R. 1984. "Sealed Bids, Sunk Costs and the Process of Competition." *Journal of Business* 57: 417–41.

Giammarino, R., and Heinkel, R. 1986. "A Model of Dynamic Takeover Behavior." *Journal of Finance* 41: 465–80.

Grossman, S. 1981. "The Informational Role of Warranties and Private Disclosure about Product Quality." *Journal of Law and Economics* 24: 461–83.

Grossman, S., and Hart, O. 1980a. "Takeover Bids, the Free-Rider Problem, and the Theory of the Corporation." *Bell Journal of Economics* 11: 42–64.

———. 1980b. "Disclosure Laws and Takeover Bids." *Journal of Finance* 35: 323–34.

———. 1981. "The Allocational Role of Takeover Bids in Situations of Asymmetric Information." *Journal of Finance* 36: 253–70.

———. 1986. "The Costs and Benefits of Ownership: A Theory of Vertical and Lateral Integration." *Journal of Political Economy* 94: 691–719.

Grossman, S., and Perry, M. 1986. "Perfect Sequential Equilibrium." *Journal of Economic Theory* 39: 97–119.

Hansen, R. 1985. "Auctions with Noncontingent Payments." *American Economic Review* 75: 862–65.

———. 1987. "A Theory for the Choice of Exchange Medium in Mergers and Acquisitions." *Journal of Business* 60: 75–95.

Harris, M., and Raviv, A. 1985. "Corporate Control Contests and Capital Structure." Northwestern University, manuscript, August.

Journal of Financial Economics. 1983. "Symposium on the Market for Corporate Control: The Scientific Evidence." 11.

Khanna, N. 1985. "Optimal Bidding for Tender Offers." University of Michigan, manuscript.

Kihlstrom, R. 1986. "The Informational Role of Mergers in the Context of a Complete Securities Market." In Lacy G. Thomas, ed., *The Economics of Strategic Planning: Essays in Honor of Joel Dean*. Lexington, Mass.: Lexington Books.

Kovenock, D. 1984. "A Note on Takeover Bids." Purdue University, manuscript, September.

Kreps, D. 1984. "Signalling Games and Stable Equilibria." Stanford University, manuscript.

Kyle, A., and Vila, J. 1986. "Noise Trading and Takeovers." Princeton University, manuscript, September.

Macey, J., and McChesney, F. 1985. "A Theoretical Analysis of Corporate Greenmail." *Yale Law Journal* 95: 13–61.

Milgrom, P., and Stokey, N. 1982. "Information, Trade and Common Knowledge." *Journal of Economic Theory* 26: 17–27.

Milgrom, P., and Weber, R. 1982. "A Theory of Auctions and Competitive Bidding."

Econometrica 50: 1089–1122.

P'ng, I. 1985. "The Information Conveyed by a Tender Offer and the Takeover Price of a Target Firm." University of California at Los Angeles, manuscript, revised February.

Shleifer, A., and Vishny, R. 1986a. "Greenmail, White Knights, and Shareholders' Interest." *Rand Journal of Economics* 17: 293–309.

———. 1986b. "Large Shareholders and Corporate Control." *Journal of Political Economy* 94: 461–88.

Spatt, C., and Sterbenz, F. 1986. "Warrant Exercise, Dividends and Reinvestment Policy." Carnegie-Mellon University, manuscript, revised August.

Spiegel, M. 1985. "A Theory of the Corporation: Mergers and Acquisitions." Princeton University, manuscript, December.

Stoughton, N. 1984. "The Information Content of Corporate Merger and Acquisition Offers." University of British Columbia, manuscript, revised December.

Tiemann, J. 1986. "Applications of Auction Games in Mergers and Acquisitions: The White Knight Takeover Defense." Harvard Business School, manuscript.

Vickrey, W. 1961. "Counterspeculation, Auctions and Competitive Sealed Tenders." *Journal of Finance* 16: 8–37.

On the Impossibility of Informationally Efficient Markets

By Sanford J. Grossman and Joseph E. Stiglitz*

If competitive equilibrium is defined as a situation in which prices are such that all arbitrage profits are eliminated, is it possible that a competitive economy always be in equilibrium? Clearly not, for then those who arbitrage make no (private) return from their (privately) costly activity. Hence the assumptions that all markets, including that for information, are always in equilibrium and always perfectly arbitraged are inconsistent when arbitrage is costly.

We propose here a model in which there is an equilibrium degree of disequilibrium: prices reflect the information of informed individuals (arbitrageurs) but only partially, so that those who expend resources to obtain information do receive compensation. How informative the price system is depends on the number of individuals who are informed; but the number of individuals who are informed is itself an endogenous variable in the model.

The model is the simplest one in which prices perform a well-articulated role in conveying information from the informed to the uninformed. When informed individuals observe information that the return to a security is going to be high, they bid its price up, and conversely when they observe information that the return is going to be low. Thus the price system makes publicly available the information obtained by informed individuals to the uniformed. In general, however, it does this imperfectly; this is perhaps lucky, for were it to do it perfectly, an equilibrium would not exist.

In the introduction, we shall discuss the general methodology and present some con-

jectures concerning certain properties of the equilibrium. The remaining analytic sections of the paper are devoted to analyzing in detail an important example of our general model, in which our conjectures concerning the nature of the equilibrium can be shown to be correct. We conclude with a discussion of the implications of our approach and results, with particular emphasis on the relationship of our results to the literature on "efficient capital markets."

I. The Model

Our model can be viewed as an extension of the noisy rational expectations model introduced by Robert Lucas and applied to the study of information flows between traders by Jerry Green (1973); Grossman (1975, 1976, 1978); and Richard Kihlstrom and Leonard Mirman. There are two assets: a safe asset yielding a return R, and a risky asset, the return to which, u, varies randomly from period to period. The variable u consists of two parts,

$$(1) \qquad u = \theta + \varepsilon$$

where θ is observable at a cost c, and ε is unobservable.[1] Both θ and ε are random variables. There are two types of individuals, those who observe θ (informed traders), and those who observe only price (uninformed traders). In our simple model, all individuals are, *ex ante*, identical; whether they are informed or uninformed just depends on whether they have spent c to obtain information. Informed traders' demands will depend on θ and the price of the risky asset P. Uninformed traders' demands

*University of Pennsylvania and Princeton University, respectively. Research support under National Science Foundation grants SOC76-18771 and SOC77-15980 is gratefully acknowledged. This is a revised version of a paper presented at the Econometric Society meetings, Winter 1975, at Dallas, Texas.

[1]An alternative interpretation is that θ is a "measurement" of u with error. The mathematics of this alternative interpretation differ slightly, but the results are identical.

will depend only on P, but we shall assume that they have rational expectations; they learn the relationship between the distribution of return and the price, and use this in deriving their demand for the risky assets. If x denotes the supply of the risky asset, an equilibrium when a given percentage, λ, of traders are informed, is thus a price function $P_\lambda(\theta, x)$ such that, when demands are formulated in the way described, demand equals supply. We assume that uninformed traders do not observe x. Uninformed traders are prevented from learning θ via observations of $P_\lambda(\theta, x)$ because they cannot distinguish variations in price due to changes in the informed trader's information from variations in price due to changes in aggregate supply. Clearly, $P_\lambda(\theta, x)$ reveals some of the informed trader's information to the uninformed traders.

We can calculate the expected utility of the informed and the expected utility of the uninformed. If the former is greater than the latter (taking account of the cost of information), some individuals switch from being uninformed to being informed (and conversely). An overall equilibrium requires the two to have the same expected utility. As more individuals become informed, the expected utility of the informed falls relative to the uninformed for two reasons:

(a) The price system becomes more informative because variations in θ have a greater effect on aggregate demand and thus on price when more traders observe θ. Thus, more of the information of the informed is available to the uninformed. Moreover, the informed gain more from trade with the uninformed than do the uninformed. The informed, on average, buy securities when they are "underpriced" and sell them when they are "overpriced" (relative to what they would have been if information were equalized).[2] As the price system becomes more informative, the difference in their information—and hence the magnitude by

which the informed can gain relative to the uninformed—is reduced.

(b) Even if the above effect did not occur, the increase in the ratio of informed to uninformed means that the relative gains of the informed, on a per capita basis, in trading with the uninformed will be smaller.

We summarize the above characterization of the equilibrium of the economy in the following two conjectures:

Conjecture 1: The more individuals who are informed, the more informative is the price system.

Conjecture 2: The more individuals who are informed, the lower the ratio of expected utility of the informed to the uninformed.

(Conjecture 1 obviously requires a definition of "more informative"; this is given in the next section and in fn. 7.)

The equilibrium number of informed and uninformed individuals in the economy will depend on a number of critical parameters: the cost of information, how informative the price system is (how much noise there is to interfere with the information conveyed by the price system), and how informative the information obtained by an informed individual is.

Conjecture 3: The higher the cost of information, the smaller will be the equilibrium percentage of individuals who are informed.

Conjecture 4: If the quality of the informed trader's information increases, the more their demands will vary with their information and thus the more prices will vary with θ. Hence, the price system becomes more informative. The equilibrium proportion of informed to uninformed may be either increased or decreased, because even though the value of being informed has increased due to the increased quality of θ, the value of being uninformed has also increased because the price system becomes more informative.

Conjecture 5: The greater the magnitude of noise, the less informative will the price system be, and hence the lower the expected utility of uninformed individuals. Hence, in equilibrium the greater the magnitude of noise, the larger the proportion of informed individuals.

---

[2]The framework described herein does not explicitly model the effect of variations in supply, i.e., x on commodity storage. The effect of futures markets and storage capabilities on the informativeness of the price system was studied by Grossman (1975, 1977).

Conjecture 6: In the limit, when there is no noise, prices convey all information, and there is no incentive to purchase information. Hence, the only possible equilibrium is one with no information. But if everyone is uninformed, it clearly pays some individual to become informed.[3] Thus, there does not exist a competitive equilibrium.[4]

Trade among individuals occurs either because tastes (risk aversions) differ, endowments differ, or beliefs differ. This paper focuses on the last of these three. An interesting feature of the equilibrium is that beliefs may be precisely identical in either one of two situations: when all individuals are informed or when all individuals are uninformed. This gives rise to:

Conjecture 7: That, other things being equal, markets will be thinner under those conditions in which the percentage of individuals who are informed (λ) is either near zero or near unity. For example, markets will be thin when there is very little noise in the system (so λ is near zero), or when costs of information are very low (so λ is near unity).

In the last few paragraphs, we have provided a number of conjectures describing the nature of the equilibrium when prices convey information. Unfortunately, we have not been able to obtain a general proof of any of these propositions. What we have been able to do is to analyze in detail an interesting example, entailing constant absolute risk-aversion utility functions and normally distributed random variables. In this example, the equilibrium price distribution can actually be calculated, and all of

the conjectures provided above can be verified. The next sections are devoted to solving for the equilibrium in this particular example.[5]

II. Constant Absolute Risk-Aversion Model

A. *The Securities*

The ith trader is assumed to be endowed with stocks of two types of securities: $\overline{M}_i$, the riskless asset, and $\overline{X}_i$, a risky asset. Let P be the current price of risky assets and set the price of risk free assets equal to unity. The ith trader's budget constraint is

$$(2) \qquad PX_i + M_i = W_{0i} \equiv \overline{M}_i + P\overline{X}_i$$

Each unit of the risk free asset pays R "dollars" at the end of the period, while each unit of the risky asset pays u dollars. If at the end of the period, the ith trader holds a portfolio (M_i, X_i), his wealth will be

$$(3) \qquad W_{1i} = RM_i + uX_i$$

B. *Individual's Utility Maximization*

Each individual has a utility function $V_i(W_{1i})$. For simplicity, we assume all individuals have the same utility function and so drop the subscripts i. Moreover, we assume the utility function is exponential, i.e.,

$$V(W_{1i}) = -e^{-aW_{1i}}, \qquad a > 0$$

where a is the coefficient of absolute risk aversion. Each trader desires to maximize expected utility, using whatever information is available to him, and to decide on what information to acquire on the basis of the consequences to his expected utility.

Assume that in equation (1) θ and ε have a multivariate normal distribution, with

$$(4) \qquad E\varepsilon = 0$$

$$(5) \qquad E\theta\varepsilon = 0$$

$$(6) \qquad Var(u^*|\theta) = Var\,\varepsilon^* \equiv \sigma_\varepsilon^2 > 0$$

---

[3]That is, with no one informed, an individual can only get information by paying c dollars, since no information is revealed by the price system. By paying c dollars an individual will be able to predict better than the market when it is optimal to hold the risky asset as opposed to the risk-free asset. Thus his expected utility will be higher than an uninformed person gross of information costs. Thus for c sufficiently low all uninformed people will desire to be informed.

[4]See Grossman (1975, 1977) for a formal example of this phenomenon in futures markets. See Stiglitz (1971, 1974) for a general discussion of information and the possibility of nonexistence of equilibrium in capital markets.

[5]The informational equilibria discussed here may not, in general, exist. See Green (1977). Of course, for the utility function we choose equilibrium does exist.

since θ and ε are uncorrelated. Throughout this paper we will put a * above a symbol to emphasize that it is a random variable. Since W_{1i} is a linear function of ε, for a given portfolio allocation, and a linear function of a normally distributed random variable is normally distributed, it follows that W_{1i} is normal conditional on θ. Then, using (2) and (3) the expected utility of the *informed* trader with information θ can be written

(7) $\quad E(V(W_{1i}^*)|\theta) =$

$$- \exp\left(-a\left\{ E[\,W_{1i}^*|\theta\,] - \frac{a}{2}\,Var[\,W_{1i}^*|\theta\,]\right\}\right)$$

$$= -\exp\left(-a\left[RW_{0i} + X_I\{E(u^*|\theta) - RP\}\right.\right.$$

$$\left.\left. - \frac{a}{2}\,X_I^2\,Var(u^*|\theta)\right]\right)$$

$$= -\exp\left(-a\left[RW_{0i} + X_I(\theta - RP)\right.\right.$$

$$\left.\left. - \frac{a}{2}\,X_I^2\sigma_\varepsilon^2\right]\right)$$

where X_I is an informed individual's demand for the risky security. Maximizing (7) with respect to X_I yields a demand function for risky assets:

(8) $\qquad X_I(P,\theta) = \dfrac{\theta - RP}{a\sigma_\varepsilon^2}$

The right-hand side of (8) shows the familiar result that with constant absolute risk aversion, a trader's demand does not depend on wealth; hence the subscript i is not on the left-hand side of (8).

We now derive the demand function for the uninformed. Let us assume the only source of "noise" is the per capita supply of the risky security x.

Let $P^*(\cdot)$ be some particular price function of (θ, x) such that u^* and P^* are jointly normally distributed. (We will prove that this exists below.)

Then, we can write for the uninformed individual

(7') $E(V(W_{1i}^*)|P^*) = -\exp\left[-a\left\{ E[\,W_{1i}^*|P^*\,]\right.\right.$

$$\left.\left. - \frac{a}{2}\,Var[\,W_{1i}^*|P^*\,]\right\}\right]$$

$$= -\exp\left[-a\left\{ RW_{0i} + X_U(E[\,u^*|P^*\,] - RP)\right.\right.$$

$$\left.\left. - \frac{a}{2}\,X_U^2\,Var[\,u^*|P^*\,]\right\}\right]$$

The demands of the uninformed will thus be a function of the price function P^* and the actual price P.

(8') $\quad X_U(P;P^*)$

$$= \frac{E[\,u^*|P^*(\theta, x) = P\,] - RP}{a\,Var[\,u^*|P^*(\theta, x) = P\,]}$$

C. Equilibrium Price Distribution

If λ is some particular fraction of traders who decide to become informed, then define an equilibrium price system as a function of $(\theta, x), P_\lambda(\theta, x)$, such that for all (θ, x) per capita demands for the risky assets equal supplies:

(9) $\quad \lambda X_I(P_\lambda(\theta, x), \theta)$

$$+ (1 - \lambda)X_U(P_\lambda(\theta, x); P_\lambda^*) = x$$

The function $P_\lambda(\theta, x)$ is a statistical equilibrium in the following sense. If over time uninformed traders observe many realizations of (u^*, P_λ^*), then they learn the joint distribution of (u^*, P_λ^*). After all learning about the joint distribution of (u^*, P_λ^*) ceases, all traders will make allocations and form expectations such that this joint distribution persists over time. This follows from (8), (8'), and (9), where the market-clearing price that comes about is the one which takes into account the fact that uninformed traders have learned that it contains information.

We shall now prove that there exists an equilibrium price distribution such that P^* and u^* are jointly normal. Moreover, we shall be able to characterize the price distribution. We define

(10a) $\quad w_\lambda(\theta, x) = \theta - \dfrac{a\sigma_\varepsilon^2}{\lambda}(x - Ex^*)$

for $\lambda > 0$, and define $w_0(\theta, x)$ as the number:

(10b) $\quad w_0(\theta, x) = x \quad$ for all (θ, x)

where w_λ is just the random variable θ, plus noise.[6] The magnitude of the noise is inversely proportional to the proportion of informed traders, but is proportional to the variance of ε. We shall prove that the equilibrium price is just a linear function of w_λ. Thus, if $\lambda > 0$, the price system conveys information about θ, but it does so imperfectly.

D. Existence of Equilibrium and a Characterization Theorem

THEOREM 1: *If $(\theta^*, \varepsilon^*, x^*)$ has a nondegenerate joint normal distribution such that θ^*, ε^*, and x^* are mutually independent, then there exists a solution to (9) which has the form $P_\lambda(\theta, x) = \alpha_1 + \alpha_2 w_\lambda(\theta, x)$, where α_1 and α_2 are real numbers which may depend on λ, such that $\alpha_2 > 0$. (If $\lambda = 0$, the price contains no information about θ.) The exact form of $P_\lambda(\theta, x)$ is given in equation (A10) in Appendix B. The proof of this theorem is also in Appendix B.*

The importance of Theorem 1 rests in the simple characterization of the information in the equilibrium price system: P_λ^* is informationally equivalent to w_λ^*. From (10) w_λ^* is a "mean-preserving spread" of θ; i.e., $E[w_\lambda^*|\theta] = \theta$ and

(11) $\quad Var[w_\lambda^*|\theta] = \dfrac{a^2\sigma_\varepsilon^4}{\lambda^2} Var\, x^*$

[6]If $y' = y + Z$, and $E[Z|y] = 0$, then y' is just y plus noise.

For each replication of the economy, θ is the information that uninformed traders would like to know. But the noise x^* prevents w_λ^* from revealing θ. How well-informed uninformed traders can become from observing P_λ^* (equivalently w_λ^*) is measured by $Var[w_\lambda^*|\theta]$. When $Var[w_\lambda^*|\theta]$ is zero, w_λ^* and θ are perfectly correlated. Hence when uninformed firms observe w_λ^*, this is equivalent to observing θ. On the other hand, when $Var[w_\lambda^*|\theta]$ is very large, there are "many" realizations of w_λ^* that are associated with a given θ. In this case the observation of a particular w_λ^* tells very little about the actual θ which generated it.[7]

From equation (11) it is clear that large noise (high $Var\, x^*$) leads to an imprecise price system. The other factor which determines the precision of the price system $(a^2\sigma_\varepsilon^4/\lambda^2)$ is more subtle. When a is small (the individual is not very risk averse) or σ_ε^2 is small (the information is very precise), an informed trader will have a demand for risky assets which is very responsive to changes in θ. Further, the larger λ is, the more responsive is the total demand of informed traders. Thus small $(a^2\sigma_\varepsilon^4/\lambda^2)$ means that the aggregate demand of informed traders is very responsive to θ. For a fixed amount of noise (i.e., fixed $Var\, x^*$) the larger are the movements in aggregate demand which are due to movements in θ, the more will price movements be due to movements in θ. That is, x^* becomes less important relative to θ in determining price movements. Therefore, for small $(a^2\sigma_\varepsilon^4/\lambda^2)$ uninformed traders are able to confidently know that price is, for example, unusually high due to θ being high. In this way information from informed traders is transferred to uninformed traders.

[7]Formally, w_λ^* is an experiment in the sense of Blackwell which gives information about θ. It is easy to show that, *ceteris paribus*, the smaller $Var(w_\lambda^*|\theta)$ the more "informative" (or sufficient) in the sense of Blackwell, is the experiment; see Grossman, Kihlstrom, and Mirman (p. 539).

E. *Equilibrium in the Information Market*

What we have characterized so far is the equilibrium price distribution for given λ. We now define an *overall* equilibrium to be a pair (λ, P^*_λ) such that the expected utility of the informed is equal to that of the uninformed if $0 < \lambda < 1$; $\lambda = 0$ if the expected utility of the informed is less than that of the uninformed at P^*_0; $\lambda = 1$ if the expected utility of the informed is greater than the uninformed at P^*_1. Let

(12a) $\quad W^\lambda_{Ii} \equiv R(W_{0i} - c)$

$\qquad + [u - RP_\lambda(\theta, x)]X_I(P_\lambda(\theta, x), \theta)$

(12b) $\quad W^\lambda_{U1} \equiv RW_{0i}$

$\qquad + [u - RP_\lambda(\theta, x)]X_U(P_\lambda(\theta, x); P^*_\lambda)$

where c is the cost of observing a realization of θ^*. Equation (12a) gives the end of period wealth of a trader if he decides to become informed, while (12b) gives his wealth if he decides to be uninformed. Note that end of period wealth is random due to the randomness of W_{0i}, u, θ, and x.

In evaluating the expected utility of W^λ_{Ii}, we do not assume that a trader knows which realization of θ^* he gets to observe if he pays c dollars. A trader pays c dollars and then gets to observe some realization of θ^*. The overall expected utility of W^λ_{Ii} averages over all possible θ^*, ε^*, x^*, and W_{0i}. The variable W_{0i} is random for two reasons. First from (2) it depends on $P_\lambda(\theta, x)$, which is random as (θ, x) is random. Secondly, in what follows we will assume that $\overline{X}_i$ is random.

We will show below that $EV(W^\lambda_{Ii})/EV(W^\lambda_{Ui})$ is independent of i, but is a function of λ, a, c, and σ^2_ε. More precisely, in Appendix B we prove

THEOREM 2: *Under the assumptions of Theorem 1, and if $\overline{X}_i$ is independent of (u^*, θ^*, x^*) then*

(13) $\quad \dfrac{EV(W^\lambda_{Ii})}{EV(W^\lambda_{Ui})} = e^{ac}\sqrt{\dfrac{Var(u^*|\theta)}{Var(u^*|w_\lambda)}}$

F. *Existence of Overall Equilibrium*

Theorem 2 is useful, both in proving the uniqueness of overall equilibrium and in analyzing comparative statics. Overall equilibrium, it will be recalled, requires that for $0 < \lambda < 1$, $EV(W^\lambda_{Ii})/EV(W^\lambda_{Ui}) = 1$. But from (13)

(14) $\quad \dfrac{EV(W^\lambda_{Ii})}{EV(W^\lambda_{Ui})}$

$\qquad = e^{ac}\sqrt{\dfrac{Var(u^*|\theta)}{Var(u^*|w_\lambda)}} \equiv \gamma(\lambda)$

Hence overall equilibrium simply requires, for $0 < \lambda < 1$,

(15) $\qquad \gamma(\lambda) = 1$

More precisely, we now prove

THEOREM 3: *If $0 \leqslant \lambda \leqslant 1$, $\gamma(\lambda) = 1$, and P^*_λ is given by (A10) in Appendix B, then (λ, P^*_λ) is an overall equilibrium. If $\gamma(1) < 1$, then $(1, P^*_1)$ is an overall equilibrium. If $\gamma(0) > 1$, then $(0, P^*_0)$ is an overall equilibrium. For all price equilibria P_λ which are monotone functions of w_λ, there exists a unique overall equilibrium (λ, P^*_λ).*

PROOF:

The first three sentences follow immediately from the definition of overall equilibrium given above equation (12), and Theorems 1 and 2. Uniqueness follows from the monotonicity of $\gamma(\cdot)$ which follows from (A11) and (14). The last two sentences in the statement of the theorem follow immediately.

In the process of proving Theorem 3, we have noted

COROLLARY 1: $\gamma(\lambda)$ *is a strictly monotone increasing function of λ.*

This looks paradoxical; we expect the ratio of informed to uninformed expected utility to be a decreasing function of λ. But, *we have defined utility as negative.* Therefore as λ rises, the expected utility of informed traders does go down relative to uninformed traders.

Note that the function $\gamma(0) = e^{ac}(Var(u^*|\theta))/Var u^*)^{1/2}$. Figure 1 illustrates the determination of the equilibrium λ. The figure assumes that $\gamma(0) < 1 < \gamma(1)$.

G. Characterization of Equilibrium

We wish to provide some further characterization of the equilibrium. Let us define

$$(16a) \qquad m = \left(\frac{a\sigma_\epsilon^2}{\lambda}\right)^2 \frac{\sigma_x^2}{\sigma_\theta^2}$$

$$(16b) \qquad n = \frac{\sigma_\theta^2}{\sigma_\epsilon^2}$$

Note that m is inversely related to the informativeness of the price system since the squared correlation coefficient between P_λ^* and θ^*, ρ_θ^2 is given by

$$(17) \qquad \rho_\theta^2 = \frac{1}{1+m}$$

Similarly, n is directly related to the quality of the informed trader's information because $n/(1+n)$ is the squared correlation coefficient between θ^* and u^*.

Equations (14) and (15) show that the cost of information c, determines the equilibrium ratio of information quality between informed and uninformed traders $(Var(u^*|\theta))/Var(u^*|w_\lambda)$. From (1), (A11) of Appendix A, and (16), this can be written as

$$(18)$$

$$\frac{Var(u^*|\theta)}{Var(u^*|w_\lambda)} = \frac{1+m}{1+m+nm} = \left(1 + \frac{nm}{1+m}\right)^{-1}$$

Substituting (18) into (14) and using (15) we obtain, for $0 < \lambda < 1$, in equilibrium

$$(19a) \qquad m = \frac{e^{2ac}-1}{1+n-e^{2ac}}$$

or

$$(19b) \qquad 1 - \rho_\theta^2 = \frac{e^{2ac}-1}{n}$$

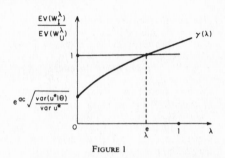

FIGURE 1

Note that (19) holds for $\gamma(0) < 1 < \gamma(1)$, since these conditions insure that the equilibrium λ is between zero and one. Equation (19b) shows that the equilibrium informativeness of the price system is determined completely by the cost of information c, the quality of the informed trader's information n, and the degree of risk aversion a.

H. Comparative Statics

From equation (19b), we immediately obtain some basic comparative statics results:

1) An increase in the quality of information (n) increases the informativeness of the price system.

2) A decrease in the cost of information increases the informativeness of the price system.

3) A decrease in risk aversion leads informed individuals to take larger positions, and this increases the informativeness of the price system.

Further, all other changes in parameters, such that n, a, and c remain constant, do not change the equilibrium degree of informativeness of the price system; other changes lead only to particular changes in λ of a magnitude to exactly offset them. For example:

4) An increase in noise (σ_x^2) increases the proportion of informed traders. At any given λ, an increase in noise reduces the informativeness of the price system; but it increases the returns to information and leads more individuals to become informed; the remarkable result obtained above establishes that *the two effects exactly offset each*

other so that the equilibrium informativeness of the price system is unchanged. This can be illustrated diagrammatically if we note from (16a) that for a given λ, an increase in σ_x^2 raises m which from (18) lowers $(Var(u^*|\theta))/Var(u^*|w_\lambda)$. Thus from (14) a rise in σ_x^2 leads to a vertical downward shift of the $\gamma(\lambda)$ curve in Figure 1, and thus a higher value of λ^e.

5) Similarly an increase in σ_e^2 for a constant n (equivalent to an increase in the variance of u since n is constant) leads to an increased proportion of individuals becoming informed—and indeed again just enough to offset the increased variance, so that the degree of *informativeness* of the price system remains unchanged. This can also be seen from Figure 1 if (16) is used to note that an increase in σ_e^2 with n held constant by raising σ_θ^2 leads to an increase in m for a given λ. From (18) and (14) this leads to a vertical downward shift of the $\gamma(\lambda)$ curve and thus a higher value of λ^e.

6) It is more difficult to determine what happens if, say σ_θ^2 increases, keeping σ_u^2 constant (implying a fall in σ_e^2), that is, *the information obtained is more informative.* This leads to an increase in n, which from (19b) implies that the equilibrium informativeness of the price system rises. From (16) it is clear that m and nm both fall when σ_θ^2 rises (keeping $\sigma_u^2 = \sigma_\theta^2 + \sigma_e^2$ constant). This implies that the $\gamma(\lambda)$ curve may shift up or down depending on the precise values of c, a, and n.[8] This ambiguity arises because an

improvement in the precision of informed traders' information, with the cost of the information fixed, increases the benefit of being informed. However, some of the improved information is transmitted, via a more informative price system, to the uninformed; this increases the benefits of being uninformed. If n is small, both the price system m is not very informative *and* the marginal value of information to informed traders is high. Thus the *relative* benefits of being informed rises when n rises; implying that the equilibrium λ rises. Conversely when n is large the price system is very informative and the marginal value of information is low to informed traders so the relative benefits of being uninformed rises.

7) From (14) it is clear that an increase in the cost of information c shifts the $\gamma(\lambda)$ curve up and thus decreases the percentage of informed traders.

The above results are summarized in the following theorem.

THEOREM 4: *For equilibrium λ such that $0 < \lambda < 1$:*

A. *The equilibrium informativeness of the price system, ρ_θ^2, rises if n rises, c falls, or a falls.*

B. *The equilibrium informativeness of the price system is unchanged if σ_x^2 changes, or if σ_u^2 changes with n fixed.*

C. *The equilibrium percentage of informed traders will rise if σ_x^2 rises, σ_u^2 rises for a fixed n, or c falls.*

D. *If $\bar{n}$ satisfies $(e^{2ac} - 1)/(\bar{n} - (e^{2ac} - 1)) = \bar{n}/(\bar{n}+1)$, then $n \overset{<}{>} \bar{n}$ implies that λ falls (rises) due to an increase in n.*

PROOF:

Parts A—C are proved in the above remarks. Part D is proved in footnote 8.

I. *Price Cannot Fully Reflect Costly Information*

We now consider certain limiting cases, for $\gamma(0) \leqslant 1 \leqslant \gamma(1)$, and show that equilibrium does not exist if $c > 0$ and price is fully informative.

1) As the cost of information goes to zero, the price system becomes more infor-

---

[8]From (14) and (18) it is clear that λ rises if and only if $Var(u^*|\theta) + Var(u^*|w_\lambda)$ falls due to the rise in σ_θ^2 for a given λ. This occurs if and only if $nm/(1+m)$ rises. Using (16) to differentiate $nm/(1+m)$ with respect to σ_e^2 subject to the constraint that $d\sigma_u^2 = 0$ (i.e., $d\sigma_\theta^2 = -d\sigma_e^2$), we find that the sign of

$$\frac{d}{d\sigma_\theta^2}\left(\frac{nm}{1+m}\right) = sgn\left[m\left(\frac{n+1}{n}\right) - 1\right]$$

$$= sgn\left[\left(\frac{\gamma}{n-\gamma}\right)\left(\frac{n+1}{n}\right) - 1\right]$$

where $\gamma \equiv e^{2ac} - 1$ and the last equality follows from equation (19a). Thus for n very large the derivative is negative so that λ falls due to an increase in the precision of the informed trader's information. Similarly if n is sufficiently small, the derivative is positive and thus λ rises.

mative, but at a positive value of c, say $\hat{c}$, all traders are informed. From (14) and (15) $\hat{c}$ satisfies

$$e^{a\hat{c}}\sqrt{\frac{Var(u^*|\theta)}{Var(u^*|w_1)}} = 1$$

2) From (19a) as the precision of the informed trader's information n goes to infinity, i.e., $\sigma_\epsilon^2 \to 0$ and $\sigma_\theta^2 \to \sigma_u^2$, σ_u^2 held fixed, the price system becomes perfectly informative. Moreover the percentage of informed traders goes to zero! This can be seen from (18) and (15). That is, as $\sigma_\epsilon^2 \to 0$, $nm/(1+m)$ must stay constant for equilibrium to be maintained. But from (19b) and (17), m falls as σ_ϵ^2 goes to zero. Therefore nm must fall, but nm must not go to zero or else $nm/(1+m)$ would not be constant. From (16) $nm = (a/\lambda)^2\sigma_\epsilon^2\sigma_x^2$, and thus λ must go to zero to prevent nm from going to zero as $\sigma_\epsilon^2 \to 0$.

3) From (16a) and (19a) it is clear that as noise σ_x^2 goes to zero, the percentage of informed traders goes to zero. Further, since (19a) implies that m does not change as σ_x^2 changes, the informativeness of the price system is unchanged as $\sigma_x^2 \to 0$.

Assume that c is small enough so that it is worthwhile for a trader to become informed when no other trader is informed. Then if $\sigma_x^2 = 0$ or $\sigma_\epsilon^2 = 0$, there exists no competitive equilibrium. To see this, note that equilibrium requires either that the ratio of expected utility of the informed to the uninformed be equal to unity, or that if the ratio is larger than unity, no one be informed. We shall show that when no one is informed, it is less than unity so that $\lambda = 0$ cannot be an equilibrium; but when $\lambda > 0$, it is greater than unity. That is, if $\sigma_x^2 = 0$ or $\sigma_\epsilon^2 = 0$, the ratio of expected utilities is not a continuous function of λ at $\lambda = 0$.

This follows immediately from observing that at $\lambda = 0$, $Var(u^*|w_0) = Var\,u^*$, and thus by (14)

$$(20) \quad \frac{EV(W_{Ii}^0)}{EV(W_{Ui}^0)} = e^{ac}\sqrt{\frac{\sigma_\epsilon^2}{\sigma_\epsilon^2 + \sigma_\theta^2}}$$

$$= e^{ac}\sqrt{\frac{1}{1+n}}$$

while if $\lambda > 0$, by (18)

$$\frac{EV(W_{Ii}^\lambda)}{EV(W_{Ui}^\lambda)} = e^{ac}\sqrt{\frac{1}{1+n\dfrac{m}{m+1}}}$$

But if $\sigma_x^2 = 0$ or $\sigma_\epsilon^2 = 0$, then $m = 0$, $nm = 0$ for $\lambda > 0$, and hence

$$(21) \quad \lim_{\lambda \to 0} \frac{EV(W_{Ii}^\lambda)}{EV(W_{Ui}^\lambda)} = e^{ac}$$

It immediately follows that

THEOREM 5: (a) *If there is no noise* $(\sigma_x^2 = 0)$, *an overall equilibrium does not exist if (and only if)* $e^{ac} < \sqrt{1+n}$. (b) *If information is perfect* $(\sigma_\epsilon^2 = 0, n = \infty)$, *there never exists an equilibrium.*

PROOF:

(a) If $e^{ac} < \sqrt{1+n}$, then by (20) and (21), $\gamma(\lambda)$ is discontinuous at $\lambda = 0$; $\lambda = 0$ is not an equilibrium since by (20) $\gamma(0) < 1$; $\lambda > 0$ is not an equilibrium since by (21) $\gamma(\lambda) > 1$.

(b) If $\sigma_\epsilon^2 = 0$ and $\sigma_\theta^2 = \sigma_u^2$ so that information is perfect, then for $\lambda > 0$, $nm = 0$ by (16) and hence $\gamma(\lambda) > 1$ by (21). From (20) $\gamma(0) = 0 < 1$.

If there is no noise and some traders become informed, then *all* their information is transmitted to the uninformed by the price system. Hence each informed trader acting as a price taker thinks the informativeness of the price system will be unchanged if he becomes uninformed, so $\lambda > 0$ is not an equilibrium. On the other hand, if no traders are informed, then each uninformed trader learns nothing from the price system, and thus he has a desire to become informed (if $e^{ac} < (1+n)^{1/2}$). Similarly if the informed traders get perfect information, then their demands are very sensitive to their information, so that the market-clearing price becomes very sensitive to their information and thus reveals θ to the uninformed. Hence all traders desire to be uninformed. But if all traders are uninformed, each trader can eliminate the risk of his portfolio by the purchase of information, so each trader desires to be informed.

In the next section we show that the non-existence of competitive equilibrium can be thought of as the breakdown of competitive markets due to lack of trade. That is, we will show that as σ_x^2 gets very small, trade goes to zero and markets serve no function. Thus competitive markets close for lack of trade "before" equilibrium ceases to exist at $\sigma_x^2 = 0$.

III. On the Thinness of Speculative Markets

In general, trade takes place because traders differ in endowments, preferences, or beliefs. Grossman (1975, 1977, 1978) has argued that differences in preferences are not a major factor in explaining the magnitude of trade in speculative markets. For this reason the model in Section II gave all traders the same risk preferences (note that none of the results in Section II are affected by letting traders have different coefficients of absolute risk aversion). In this section we assume that trade requires differences in endowments or beliefs and dispense with differences in risk preference as an explanatory variable.[9]

There is clearly some fixed cost in operating a competitive market. If traders have to bear this cost, then trade in the market must be beneficial. Suppose traders have the same endowments and beliefs. Competitive equilibrium will leave them with allocations which are identical with their initial endowments. Hence, if it is costly to enter such a competitive market, no trader would ever enter. We will show below that in an important class of situations, there is continuity in the amount of net trade. That is, when initial endowments are the same and peo-

ples' beliefs differ *slightly*, then the competitive equilibrium allocation that an individual gets will be only *slightly* different from his initial endowment. Hence, there will only be a slight benefit to entering the competitive market. This could, for sufficiently high operating costs, be outweighed by the cost of entering the market.

The amount of trade occurring at any date is a random variable; a function of θ and x. It is easy to show that it is a normally distributed random variable. Since one of the primary determinants of the size of markets is differences in beliefs, one might have conjectured that markets will be thin, in some sense, if almost all traders are either informed or uninformed. This is not, however, obvious, since the amount of trade by any single trader may be a function of λ as well, and a few active traders can do the job of many small traders. In our model, there is a sense, however, in which our conjecture is correct.

We first calculate the magnitude of trades as a function of the exogenous parameters, θ and x. Let $h \equiv \sigma_\epsilon^2$, $\bar{x} = Ex^*$, and $\bar{\theta} \equiv E\theta^*$. (The actual trades will depend on the distribution of random endowments across all of the traders, but these we shall net out.) Per capita net trade is [10]

$$(22) \quad X_I - x = (1-\lambda)\left[\left(nm + \frac{ah}{\lambda}\right)(x - \bar{x})\right.$$
$$\left. + [(m+1)n - 1](\theta - \bar{\theta}) + \bar{x}nm\right]$$
$$+ [1 + m + \lambda nm]$$

[9]In the model described in Section II it was assumed that an individual's endowment $\bar{X}_i$ is independent of the market's per capita endowment x^*. This was done primarily so there would not be useful information in an individual's endowment about the total market endowment. Such information would be useful in equilibrium because an individual observes $P_\lambda(\theta, x)$. If due to observing $\bar{X}_i$, he knows something about x, then by observing $P_\lambda(\theta, x)$, $\bar{X}_i$ is valuable in making inferences about θ. To take this into account is possible, but would add undue complication to a model already overburdened with computations.

[10]Calculation of distribution of net trades

$$\frac{\lambda}{ah}(\theta - RP_\lambda)$$

$$+ \frac{(1-\lambda)\left[(\bar{\theta} - RP_\lambda)(1+m)n + \theta - \bar{\theta} - \frac{ah}{\lambda}(x - \bar{x})\right]}{ah(1 + m + nm)n} = x$$

$$\text{or} \quad \frac{(\theta - RP_\lambda)}{ah}\left(\lambda + \frac{(1-\lambda)(1+m)}{1 + m + nm}\right)$$

$$= \left(\frac{\theta - RP_\lambda}{ah}\right)\left(\frac{1 + m + \lambda nm}{1 + m + nm}\right)$$

$$= x + \frac{(1-\lambda)\left([(m+1)n - 1](\theta - \bar{\theta}) + \frac{ah}{\lambda}(x - \bar{x})\right)}{ah(1 + m + \lambda nm)n}$$

Thus, the mean of total informed trade is

$$(23) \qquad E\lambda(X_I - x) = \frac{(1-\lambda)\lambda m\bar{x}}{1 + m + \lambda nm}$$

and its variance is

$$(24) \qquad \sigma_\theta^2(1-\lambda)^2\lambda^2\left[\left[(m+1)n - 1\right]^2\right.$$

$$\left. + \left(nm + \frac{a\sigma_\epsilon^2}{\lambda}\right)^2 \frac{\sigma_x^2}{\sigma_\theta^2}\right] + (1+m+\lambda nm)^2 n^2$$

In the last section we considered limiting values of the exogenous variables with the property that $\lambda \to 0$. The following theorem will show that the mean and variance of trade go to zero as $\lambda \to 0$. That is, the distribution of $\lambda(X_I - x)$ becomes degenerate at zero as $\lambda \to 0$. This is not trivial because as $\lambda \to 0$ due to $n \to \infty$ (very precise information), the informed trader's demand $X_I(P,\theta)$ goes to infinity at most prices because the risky asset becomes riskless with perfect information.

THEOREM 6: (a) *For sufficiently large or small c, the mean and variance of trade is zero.* (b) *As the precision of informed traders' information n goes to infinity, the mean and variance of trade go to zero.*

PROOF:

(a) From remark 1) in Section II, Part I, $\lambda = 1$ if $c \leqslant \hat{c}$, which from (23) and (24) implies trade is degenerate at zero. From (14), for c sufficiently large, say c^0, $\gamma(0) = 1$, so

---

or $X_I = \dfrac{1 + m + nm}{1 + m + \lambda nm}$

$$\times \left[x + \frac{(1-\lambda)\left([(m+1)-1](\theta-\bar{\theta}) + \frac{ah}{\lambda}(x-\bar{x})\right)}{ah(1+m+nm)n} \right]$$

$X_I - x =$

$$\frac{(1-\lambda)\left[\left(nm+\frac{ah}{\lambda}\right)(x-\bar{x}) + [(m+1)-1](\theta-\bar{\theta}) + \bar{x}nm\right]}{(1+m+\lambda nm)n}$$

---

the equilibrium $\lambda = 0$. As c goes to c^0 from below $\lambda \to 0$, and from (14), (15), and (18) $\lim_{c \uparrow c^0}(1 + nm/(1+m))^{-1/2} = e^{-ac^0}$. Hence $\lim_{c \uparrow c^0}(nm/1+m)$ is a finite positive number. Thus from (22) mean trade goes to zero as $c \uparrow c^0$. If the numerator and the denominator of (24) are divided by $(1+m)^2$, then again using the fact that $m/1+m$ has a finite limit gives the result that as $c \uparrow c^0$, $\lambda \to 0$, and variance of trade goes to zero.

(b) By (14), (15), and (18), $nm/(1+m)$ is constant as $n \to \infty$. Further, from remark 2) of Section II, Part I, $\lambda \to 0$ as $n \to \infty$. Hence from (23) and (24), the mean and variance of trade go to zero.

(c) From remark 3) in Section II, Part I, m is constant and λ goes to zero as $\sigma_x^2 \to 0$. Therefore mean trade goes to zero. In (24), note that $(nm + a\sigma_\epsilon^2/\lambda)^2\sigma_x^2/\sigma_\theta^2 = (nm\sigma_x/\sigma_\theta + (m)^{1/2})^2$ by (16a). Hence the variance of trade goes to zero as $\sigma_x^2 \to 0$.

Note further that $\lambda(X_I - x) + (1-\lambda)(X_U - x) = 0$ implies that no trade will take place as $\lambda \to 1$. Thus, the result that competitive equilibrium is incompatible with informationally efficient markets should be interpreted as meaning that speculative markets where prices reveal a lot of information will be very thin because it will be composed of individuals with very similar beliefs.

IV. On the Possibility of Perfect Markets

In Section II we showed that the price system reveals the signal w_λ^* to traders, where

$$w_\lambda \equiv \theta - \frac{a\sigma_\epsilon^2}{\lambda}(x - Ex^*)$$

Thus, for given information of informed traders θ, the price system reveals a noisy version of θ. The noise is $(a\sigma_\epsilon^2/\lambda)(x - Ex^*)$. Uninformed traders learn θ to within a random variable with mean zero and variance $(a\sigma_\epsilon^2/\lambda)^2 Var x^*$, where σ_ϵ^2 is the precision of informed traders' information, $Var x^*$ is the amount of endowment uncertainty, λ the fraction of informed traders, and a is the degree of absolute risk aversion. Thus, in general the price system does not reveal all the information about "the true value" of the risky asset. (θ is the true value of the risky asset in that it reflects the best available information about the asset's worth.)

The only way informed traders can earn a return on their activity of information gathering, is if they can use their information to take positions in the market which are "better" than the positions of uninformed traders. "Efficient Markets" theorists have claimed that "at any time prices fully reflect all available information" (see Eugene Fama, p. 383). If this were so then informed traders could not earn a return on their information.

We showed that when the efficient markets hypothesis is true and information is costly, competitive markets break down. This is because when $\sigma_\epsilon^2 = 0$ or $Var\, x^* = 0$, w_λ, and thus price, does reflect all the information. When this happens, each informed trader, because he is in a competitive market, feels that he could stop paying for information and do as well as a trader who pays nothing for information. But all informed traders feel this way. Hence having any positive fraction informed is not an equilibrium. Having no one informed is also not an equilibrium, because then each trader, taking the price as given, feels that there are profits to be made from becoming informed.

Efficient Markets theorists seem to be aware that costless information is a *sufficient* condition for prices to fully reflect all available information (see Fama, p. 387); they are not aware that it is a *necessary* condition. But this is a *reducto ad absurdum*, since price systems and competitive markets are important only when information is costly (see Fredrick Hayek, p. 452).

We are attempting to redefine the Efficient Markets notion, not destroy it. We have shown that when information is very inexpensive, or when informed traders get very precise information, then equilibrium exists and the market price will reveal most of the informed traders' information. However, it was argued in Section III that such markets are likely to be thin because traders have almost homogeneous beliefs.

There is a further conflict. As Grossman (1975, 1977) showed, whenever there are differences in beliefs that are not completely arbitraged, there is an incentive to create a market. (Grossman, 1977, analyzed a model of a storable commodity whose spot price did not reveal all information because of the presence of noise. Thus traders were left with differences in beliefs about the future price of the commodity. This led to the opening of a futures market. But then uninformed traders had two prices revealing information to them, implying the elimination of noise.) But, because differences in beliefs are themselves endogenous, arising out of expenditure on information and the informativeness of the price system, the creation of markets eliminates the differences of beliefs which gave rise to them, and thus causes those markets to disappear. If the creation of markets were costless, as is conventionally assumed in equilibrium analyses, equilibrium would never exist. For instance, in our model, were we to introduce an additional security, say a security which paid

$$z = \begin{cases} 1 & \text{if} \quad u > E\theta^* \\ 0 & \text{if} \quad u \leqslant E\theta^* \end{cases}$$

then the demand y for this security by the informed would depend on its price, say q on p and on θ, while the uninformed demand depends only on p and q:

$$\lambda y_I(q,p,\theta) + (1-\lambda)y_u(q,p) = 0$$

is the condition that demand equals (supply is zero for a pure security). Under weak assumptions, q and p would convey all the information concerning θ. Thus, the market would be "noiseless" and no equilibrium could exist.

Thus, we could argue as soon as the assumptions of the conventional perfect capital markets model are modified to allow even a slight amount of information imperfection and a slight cost of information, the traditional theory becomes untenable. There *cannot* be as many securities as states of nature. For if there were, competitive equilibrium would not exist.

It is only because of costly transactions and the fact that this leads to there being a limited number of markets, that competitive equilibrium can be established.

We have argued that because information is costly, prices cannot perfectly reflect the information which is available, since if it did, those who spent resources to obtain it would receive no compensation. There is a fundamental conflict between the efficiency with which markets spread information and the incentives to acquire information. However, we have said nothing regarding the social benefits of information, nor whether it is socially optimal to have "informationally efficient markets." We hope to examine the welfare properties of the equilibrium allocations herein in future work.

APPENDIX A

Here we collect some facts on conditional expectations used in the text. If X^* and Y^* are jointly normally distributed then

$$(A1) \quad E[X^*|Y^*=Y]$$
$$= EX^* + \frac{Cov(X^*,Y^*)}{Var(Y^*)}\{Y - EY^*\}$$

$$(A2) \quad Var[X^*|Y^*=Y]$$
$$= Var(X^*) - \frac{[Cov(X^*,Y^*)]^2}{Var(Y^*)}$$

(See Paul Hoel, p. 200.) From (A1) note that $E[X^*|Y^*]$ is a function of Y. If the expectation of both sides of (A1) is taken, we see that

$$(A3) \quad E\{E[X^*|Y^*=Y]\} = EX^*$$

Note that $Var[X^*|Y^*=Y]$ is not a function of Y, as $Var(X^*)$, $Cov(X^*,Y^*)$, and $Var(Y^*)$ are just parameters of the joint distribution of X^* and Y^*.

Two other relevant properties of conditional expectation are

$$(A4) \quad E\{E[Y^*|F(X^*)]|X^*\} = E[Y^*|F(X^*)]$$

$$(A5) \quad E\{E[Y^*|X]|F(X^*)\} = E[Y^*|F(X^*)]$$

where $F(\cdot)$ is a given function on the range of X^* (see Robert Ash, p. 260).

APPENDIX B

PROOF of Theorem 1:
  (a) Suppose $\lambda = 0$; then (9) becomes

$$(A6) \quad X_U(P_0(\theta,x),P_0^*) = x$$

Define

$$(A7) \quad P_0(\theta,x) \equiv \frac{E\theta^* - ax\sigma_u^2}{R}$$

where σ_u^2 is the variance of u. Note that $P_0(\theta^*,x^*)$ is uncorrelated with u^*, as x^* is uncorrelated with u^*. Hence

$$(A8) \quad E[u^*|P_0^* = P_0(\theta,x)] = Eu^* = E\theta^*$$

and $\quad Var[u^*|P_0^* = P_0(\theta,x)] = Var[u^*]$

Substitution of (A8) in (8) yields

$$(A9) \quad X_U(P_0^*,P_0(\theta,x)) = \frac{E\theta^* - RP_0(\theta,x)}{a\,Var\,u}$$

Substitution of (A7) in the right-hand side of (A9) yields $X_U(P_0^*(\theta,x),P_0^*) = x$ which was to be shown.
  (b) Suppose $0 < \lambda \leqslant 1$. Let

$$(A10)$$
$$P_\lambda(\theta,x) = \frac{\dfrac{\lambda w_\lambda}{a\sigma_\epsilon^2} + \dfrac{(1-\lambda)E[u^*|w_\lambda]}{a\,Var[u^*|w_\lambda]} - Ex^*}{R\left[\dfrac{\lambda}{a\sigma_\epsilon^2} + \dfrac{(1-\lambda)}{a\,Var[u^*|w_\lambda]}\right]}$$

Note that from equations (1), (10), (A1) and (A2):

$$(A11a)$$
$$E(u^*|w_\lambda) = E\theta^* + \frac{\sigma_\theta^2}{Var\,w_\lambda} \cdot (w_\lambda - E\theta^*)$$

$$(A11b) \quad Var(u^*|w_\lambda) = \sigma_\theta^2 + \sigma_\epsilon^2 - \frac{\sigma_\theta^2}{Var\,w_\lambda}$$

$$(A11c) \quad Var\,w_\lambda = \sigma_\theta^2 + \left(\frac{a\sigma_\epsilon^2}{\lambda}\right)^2 Var\,x^*$$

Since $P_\lambda(\theta, x)$ is a linear function of w_λ, it is immediate that $E(u^*|w_\lambda) \equiv E(u^*|P_\lambda)$, $Var(u^*|w_\lambda) = Var(u^*|P_\lambda)$, etc. To see that P_λ^* is an equilibrium, we must show that the following equation holds as an identity in (θ, x), for $P_\lambda(\cdot)$ defined by (A10):

(A12)

$$\lambda \cdot \frac{\theta - RP_\lambda}{a\sigma_e^2} + (1 - \lambda) \frac{E[u^*|w_\lambda] - RP_\lambda}{a\,Var[u^*|w_\lambda]} = x$$

It is immediate from (10) that (A12) holds as an identity in θ and x.

PROOF of Theorem 2:

(a) *Calculation of the expected utility of the informed.* Using the fact that W_{Ii}^λ is normally distributed conditional on $(\bar{X}_i, \theta, x)$

(A13) $\quad E[V(W_{Ii}^\lambda)|\bar{X}_i, \theta, x]$

$$= \exp\left[-a\left\{E[W_{Ii}^\lambda|\bar{X}_i, \theta, x]\right.\right.$$

$$\left.\left. - \frac{a}{2} Var[W_{Ii}^\lambda|\bar{X}_i, \theta, x]\right\}\right]$$

Using (8), (12), and the fact that (θ, x) determines a particular P,

(A14a) $\quad E[W_{Ii}^\lambda|\bar{X}_i, \theta, x] = R(W_{0i} - c)$

$$+ \frac{(E[u^*|\theta] - RP_\lambda)^2}{a\sigma_e^2}$$

(A14b)

$$Var[W_{Ii}^\lambda|\bar{X}_i, \theta, x] = \frac{(E[u^*|\theta] - RP_\lambda)^2}{a^2\sigma_e^2}$$

Substitution of (A14) into (A13) yields

(A15) $\quad E[V(W_{Ii}^\lambda)|\bar{X}_i, \theta, x]$

$$= -\exp\left[-aR(W_{0i} - c)\right.$$

$$\left. - \frac{1}{2\sigma_e^2}(E[u^*|\theta] - RP_\lambda)^2\right]$$

Note that, as $P_\lambda^*(\cdot) = P_\lambda(\theta, x)$,

(A16) $\quad E\left(E[V(W_{Ii}^\lambda)|\bar{X}_i, \theta, x]|P_\lambda, \bar{X}_i\right)$

$$= E[V(W_{Ii}^\lambda)|P_\lambda, \bar{X}_i]$$

(see (A5)). Note that since W_{0i} is nonstochastic conditional on $(P_\lambda, \bar{X}_i)$, equation (A15) implies

(A17)

$$E[V(W_{Ii}^\lambda)|P_\lambda, \bar{X}_i] = -\exp[-aR(W_{0i} - c)] \cdot$$

$$E\left[\left\{\exp\left[-\frac{1}{2\sigma_e^2}(E[u|\theta] - RP_\lambda)^2\right]\right\}|P_\lambda, \bar{X}_i\right]$$

Note that by Theorem 1, conditioning on w_λ^* is equivalent to conditioning on P_λ^*. Define

(A18) $\quad h_\lambda \equiv Var(E[u^*|\theta]|w_\lambda)$

$$= Var(\theta|w_\lambda), h_0 \equiv \sigma_e^2 \equiv h$$

(A19) $\quad Z \equiv \dfrac{E[u^*|\theta] - RP_\lambda}{\sqrt{h_\lambda}}$

Using (3) and (A18), equation (A17) can be written as

(A20) $\quad E[V(W_{Ii}^\lambda)|P_\lambda, \bar{X}_i]$

$$= e^{ac}V(RW_{0i})E\left[\exp\left[-\frac{h_\lambda}{2\sigma_e^2}Z^2\right]|w_\lambda\right]$$

since $\bar{X}_i$ and w_λ are independent. Conditional on w_λ, P_λ is nonstochastic and $E[u^*|\theta]$ is normal. Hence conditional on w_λ, $(Z^*)^2$ has a noncentral *chi*-square distribution (see C. Rao, p. 181). Then for $t > 0$ the moment generating function for $(Z^*)^2$ can be written

(A21) $\quad E[e^{-tZ^2}|w_\lambda]$

$$= \frac{1}{\sqrt{1+2t}}\exp\left[\frac{-(E[Z|w_\lambda])^2 t}{1+2t}\right]$$

Note that $E[u^*|\theta] = E[u^*|\theta, x]$. Hence

(A22) $\quad E\big[\,E[\,u^*|\theta]|w_\lambda\,\big] = E\big[\,u^*|w_\lambda\,\big]$

$$= E\theta^* + \frac{\sigma_\theta^2}{Var\,w_\lambda}(w_\lambda - E\theta^*)$$

since w_λ is just a function of (θ, x). Therefore

(A23) $\quad E\big[\,Z^*|w_\lambda\,\big] = \dfrac{E[\,u^*|w_\lambda\,] - RP_\lambda}{\sqrt{h_\lambda}}$

Since $u = \theta + \varepsilon$

(A24)
$$Var(u^*|w_\lambda) = \sigma_\varepsilon^2 + Var(\theta^*|w_\lambda) = \sigma_\varepsilon^2 + h_\lambda$$

The nondegeneracy assumptions on $(x^*, \varepsilon^*, u^*)$ imply $h_\lambda > 0$. Set $t = (h_\lambda/2\sigma_\varepsilon^2)$; and evaluate (A21) using (A23) and (A24):

(A25)

$$E\left[\exp\left[-\frac{h_\lambda}{2\sigma_\varepsilon^2}Z^2\right]\bigg|w_\lambda\right] = \sqrt{\frac{Var(u^*|\theta)}{Var(u^*|w_\lambda)}}$$

$$\cdot \exp\left(\frac{-\big(E(u^*|w_\lambda) - RP_\lambda\big)^2}{2\,Var(u^*|w_\lambda)}\right)$$

This permits the evaluation of (A20).

(b) *Calculation of expected utility of the uninformed.* Equations (8), (5), and the normality of W_{Ui}^λ conditional on w_λ can be used to show, by calculations parallel to (A13)–(A25), that

(A26) $\quad E\big[\,V(W_{Ui}^\lambda)|w_\lambda, \overline{X}_i\,\big]$

$$= V(RW_{0i})\exp\left(\frac{-\big(E(u^*|w_\lambda) - RP_\lambda\big)^2}{2\,Var(u^*|w_\lambda)}\right)$$

Hence

(A27)

$$E\big[\,V(W_{Ii}^\lambda)|w_\lambda, \overline{X}_i\,\big] - E\big[\,V(W_{Ui}^\lambda)|w_\lambda, \overline{X}_i\,\big]$$

$$= \left[e^{ac}\sqrt{\frac{Var(u^*|\theta)}{Var(u^*|w_\lambda)}} - 1\right]$$

$$\times E\big[\,V(W_{Ui}^\lambda)|w_\lambda, \overline{X}_i\,\big]$$

Taking expectations of both sides of (A27) yields:

(A28) $\quad E\big[\,V(W_{Ii}^\lambda)\,\big] - E\big[\,V(W_{Ui}^\lambda)\,\big]$

$$= \left[e^{ac}\sqrt{\frac{Var(u^*|\theta)}{Var(u^*|w_\lambda)}} - 1\right]EV(W_{Ui}^\lambda)$$

Equation (13) follows immediately from (A28).

REFERENCES

Robert B. Ash, *Real Analysis and Probability*, New York 1972.

E. Fama, "Efficient Capital Markets: A Review of Theory and Empirical Work," *J. Finance*, May 1970, 25, 383–417.

J. R. Green, "Information, Efficiency and Equilibrium," disc. paper no. 284, Harvard Inst. Econ Res., Mar. 1973.

_____, "The Non-Existence of Informational Equilibria," *Rev. Econ. Stud.*, Oct. 1977, 44, 451–64.

S. Grossman, "Essays on Rational Expectations," unpublished doctoral dissertation, Univ. Chicago 1975.

_____, "On the Efficiency of Competitive Stock Markets Where Traders Have Diverse Information," *J. Finance*, May 1976, 31, 573–85.

_____, "The Existence of Futures Markets, Noisy Rational Expectations and Informational Externalities," *Rev. Econ. Stud.*, Oct. 1977, 64, 431–49.

_____, "Further Results on the Informational Efficiency of Competitive Stock Markets," *J. Econ. Theory*, June 1978, 18, 81–101.

_____, R. Kihlstrom, and L. Mirman, "A Bayesian Approach to the Production of Information and Learning by Doing," *Rev. Econ. Stud.*, Oct. 1977, 64, 533–47.

F. H. Hayek, "The Use of Knowledge in Society," *Amer. Econ. Rev.*, Sept. 1945, 35, 519–30.

Paul G. Hoel, *Introduction to Mathematical Statistics*, New York 1962.

R. Kihlstrom and L. Mirman, "Information and Market Equilibrium," *Bell. J. Econ.*, Spring 1975, 6, 357–76.

R. E. Lucas, Jr., "Expectations and the Neutrality of Money," *J. Econ. Theory*, Apr. 1972, *4*, 103–24.

C. Rao, *Linear Statistical Inference and Its Applications*, New York 1965.

J. E. Stiglitz, "Perfect and Imperfect Capital Markets," paper presented to the Econometric Society, New Orleans 1971.

———, "Information and Capital Markets," mimeo., Oxford Univ. 1974.

discussion | # Information in Financial Markets: The Rational Expectations Approach

Anat R. Admati

**Graduate School of Business
Stanford University**

I. INTRODUCTION

It is evident that asymmetry and diversity of information among traders are important elements of financial markets. For example, at least some of the trading volume in financial markets seems to be due to diversity of beliefs— optimists trading with pessimists. Many fund managers claim to trade on the basis of superior information. Traders expend resources to acquire information, and there are active markets in advisory services and other forms of information (e.g., investment newsletters). Finally, the regulation of insider trading, pubiic disclosure of information, and the organization of financial markets are undertaken in response to the welfare implications of the allocation of public and private information.

Because of their size and the relative lack of trading frictions, financial markets are usually thought of as being, at least to a good approximation, perfectly competitive. The notion of a rational expectations equilibrium is a natural extension of the competitive Walrasian equilibrium that is particularly appropriate to situations of asymmetric and diverse information.[1] In light of the above, this concept seems well suited to the analysis of financial markets.

This chapter surveys some recent developments in the theory of rational expectations equilibrium and its applications to financial economics. Due to space limitations,.the survey is not exhaustive. Our focus will be on models that are appropriate for applications.

The paper is organized as follows. In Section II we review the basic concept of a rational expectations equilibrium. Fully revealing equilibria and their accompanying paradoxes are discussed in Section III. Noisy rational expectations equilibrium models are the topic of Section IV. In Section V we discuss various applications of rational expectations equilibrium models to topics in finance, including volume of trade, performance measurement, insider trading, and the production, sale, and acquisition of public and private information.

I am grateful to Sudipto Bhattacharya, David Kreps, and Paul Pfleiderer for helpful discussions and comments. This paper was mostly written at the Institute for Advanced Studies, Hebrew University, Jerusalem, Israel.

II. THE CONCEPT OF A RATIONAL EXPECTATIONS EQUILIBRIUM

Quite often, particularly in financial markets, agents have private information concerning events of common interest. When agents interact through prices, prices reflect the information utilized in their decisions. If a piece of information is initially held by some agents and not by others, then equilibrium prices may reveal some or all of this information to the initially uninformed. Intuitively, competition among investors who possess good news about a particular security will cause its price to rise.[2] A trader not possessing this information can then look at the price and suspect that others have received this good news. He may, in consequence, be less willing to sell this security than he would if he made no inference from the rise in the price.

In the usual Walrasian equilibrium, prices enter the individual's choice problem only through their effect on the budget set. Agents form expectations "outside" the market place, based on their private information only. Although market clearing prices aggregate the private information of others, agents in the Walrasian model do not change their beliefs with observed prices. Parties that are identical except that one possesses superior information may trade even though the uninformed party is, on average, worse off for participating in the exchange, and even if the equilibrium terms of trade (prices) change with the private information of the informed party. Clearly, the uninformed agent is not behaving optimally in this case.

Consider, in contrast, a model in which agents infer some information from prices. One could specify the effect of prices on expectations in an ad hoc fashion.[3] In a rational expectations equilibrium, however, *this effect is not ad hoc but is part of the equilibrium*. In the usual definition of a rational expectations equilibrium, equilibrium prices are a function of the ensemble of agents' information, and each trader knows the joint distribution of his information, payoff-relevant variables, and the equilibrium prices. For every realization of agents' information, which determines the realization of equilibrium prices, (i) each agent formulates expectations and chooses net trades based on the (correct) conditional distribution of payoff-relevant variables given all the information available to him, including equilibrium prices, and (ii) markets clear when the expectations and demands of traders are so formed. Agents take the distribution of prices and the price realization as given to capture the notion that markets are competitive.

This equilibrium has the desirable property that expectations are self-fulfilling: if agents base their expectations and actions on the joint distribution (of exogenous and endogenous variables) implied by the rational expectations equilibrium, then this distribution will actually emerge as a result of agents' actions. Moreover, having observed (equilibrium) prices, agents do not wish to change their demands, since their actions optimally account for all the relevant information.

The following important example illustrates these ideas. In a two-period financial market economy, trade takes place in the first period and consumption of a single good in the second. A riskless asset (in units of the consumption good) and one risky asset are traded. The riskless asset is in perfectly elastic supply at an exogenously given price; the risky asset is in fixed supply. The payoff of the risky asset is denoted by $\tilde{F}$. There are N agents indexed by $i = 1, \ldots, N$. Prior to trading, agents receive diverse private signals concerning the risky payoff, which have the following structure: agent i observes the realization of $\tilde{Y}_i = \tilde{F} + \tilde{\varepsilon}_i$, where $\tilde{F}$ and $(\tilde{\varepsilon}_i)_{i=1}^{N}$ are mutually independent and normally distributed. Agents have exponential utility functions. Following Lintner (1969), one can calculate the Walrasian equilibrium of this economy for every realization of the private signals $(\tilde{Y}_i, \ldots, \tilde{Y}_N)$: having observed that $\tilde{Y}_i = y_i$, agent i computes the conditional distribution of $\tilde{F}$ given that $\tilde{Y}_i = y_i$. Under the parametric assumption of this model, the demand for the risky asset by agent i is linear in the observed signal and the price of the risky asset, say $D_i(y_i, p) = g_0^i + g_1^i y_i + g_2^i p$, with coefficients depending on the model's parameters. Adding up individual demands gives a market clearing price that is a linear function of all the private signals:

$$P(\tilde{Y}_1, \ldots, \tilde{Y}_N) = \alpha_0 + \sum_{i=1}^{N} \alpha_i \tilde{Y}_i.$$

This price aggregates the private information held in the economy.

The above equilibrium is unstable in the following sense. In order to trade, agents must know the equilibrium price, because their demands depend on the price. If agents understand the equilibrium relation between the price and the joint signal $(\tilde{Y}_1, \ldots, \tilde{Y}_N)$ (which, for example, would happen if the economy was repeated and agents paid attention to history), then they would realize that, through its dependence on other agents' signals, the equilibrium price provides additional payoff-relevant information. Agents could (and should), therefore, take this extra information into account when forming beliefs. If they do, then the naive demands based on the conditional distribution of $\tilde{F}$, given that $\tilde{Y}_i = y_i$ alone, are no longer optimal, and the above equilibrium breaks down.

Imagine instead that the equilibrium price is a linear function of the private signals $P^*(\tilde{Y}_1, \ldots, \tilde{Y}_N) = \alpha_0^* + \sum \alpha_i^* \tilde{Y}_i$ such that, for every realization $(y_1, \ldots, y_N)$ of $(\tilde{Y}_1, \ldots, \tilde{Y}_N)$, if agent i calculates his demand on the basis of the conditional distribution of $\tilde{F}$, given that $Y_i = y_i$ and that $P^*(\tilde{Y}_1, \ldots, \tilde{Y}_N) = P^*(y_1, \ldots, y_N)$, then markets clear. This would be a rational expectations equilibrium for this economy. Grossman (1976) shows that such an equilibrium exists; its properties are discussed more fully in the next section.

III. FULLY REVEALING EQUILIBRIA

Grossman's (1976) equilibrium for the foregoing example has a remarkable property. If private signals are identically distributed, then for every realization of the private signals $(y_1 \ldots y_N)$ the equilibrium price reveals $\bar{y}$, their simple average, which is a *sufficient statistic* for $\tilde{F}$ given $(y_1 \ldots y_N)$.[4] Two important conclusions follow: (i) since the equilibrium price provides statistically superior information to any private signal, private information becomes redundant given the price; and (ii) the rational expectations equilibrium is identical to the Walrasian equilibrium of an artificial economy where agents share all their information before trading. These properties characterize *fully revealing rational expectations equilibria* on which much of the early literature on rational expectations equilibrium was focused.[5]

Fully revealing equilibria may seem very appealing: "...the competitive allocations are as if an invisible hand with all the economy's information allocated resources" (Grossman 1981, p. 555). With complete markets this implies that equilibrium allocations are ex post Pareto efficient.[6] Also, the way that information is aggregated in a fully revealing equilibrium seems to formalize the idea of efficient markets (Fama 1970). However, a closer look reveals serious problems.

To see these problems most clearly, note first that in Grossman's (1976) model (the example above) the equilibrium demand functions of traders are constant, independent of initial wealth, private information, and prices. Consider these phenomena in turn. The independence of initial wealth is least troublesome. It is due to the assumption of constant absolute risk aversion, which implies that there are no income effects in this model.

The sufficient statistic property of the price is the reason that private information does not affect demands. This leads to the most well-known paradox associated with fully revealing prices, which is discussed in detail in Grossman and Stiglitz (1980). If private information is costly and agents do not use their private information then they have no incentives to collect it. In other words, with fully revealing prices there is no return to private information. Moreover, if information acquisition is endogenous and private information is relatively inexpensive (but not free), then an overall equilibrium may not exist.

Most surprising is that demands are independent of prices. To understand this, note that in a rational expectations equilibrium, in addition to the usual income and substitution effects, there is an *information effect* that a change in (equilibrium) price has on demands. Besides changing the terms of trade, a price change in a rational expectations equilibrium model directly affects the *desirability* of the commodity. With one risky asset, the substitution and information effects work in opposite directions. If agent's expectations are held fixed, a rise in the price of the risky asset would cause agents to substitute the riskless asset for it. But here a price rise is also taken as a signal that the risky asset is worth more (because others have, presumably, received good news about its payoff). In this specific model, agents change their *expectations* if the price changes, but the simultaneous change in the terms of trade *precisely* offsets this, so at every price agents have the same demand for the risky asset, namely a fixed (identical) fraction of its total supply.[7]

With constant demands, it is difficult to see how private information ever comes to be reflected in prices. Certainly this equilibrium could not emerge if demand functions were collected in order to find a market clearing price— *every* price is market clearing. This fundamental problem, noted first by Beja (1977), has two potential solutions: One can require, as in Anderson and

Sonnenschein (1982) and Diamond and Verrecchia (1981), that price is measurable in excess demand functions. Then fully revealing equilibria fail this requirement, at least under conditions identified by Beja (1977). (The noisy rational expectations equilibrium models of the next section do satisfy this requirement.) Alternatively, one can investigate explicitly the price-setting mechanism; see comments on implementation in the concluding remarks.

Another problem with fully revealing prices, especially in the context of financial markets, is that they preclude speculative trading on the basis of diverse beliefs. This is related to the well-known "no trade" results discussed by Tirole in this volume. As noted by Grossman (1978), if it is costly to operate the market, then markets will close down if there is little trading, and thus fewer prices will be available for the transmission of information. Prices will then not be fully revealing, since their dimension will be less than that of a sufficient statistic of all privately held information.

IV. NOISY RATIONAL EXPECTATIONS EQUILIBRIUM MODELS

The difficulties discussed above are resolved within the rational expectations framework if prices are not fully revealing. Prices that are not fully revealing ("noisy") can be obtained by postulating the existence of random variables (e.g., aggregate supply or endowments) that affect equilibrium prices but that are unknown to all the agents. In this case, agents are not able to identify whether a high price is due to optimistic predictions by others or, say, a low supply realization. As a result, private information is generally useful, and it may be collected even if it is costly, and trading on the basis of different beliefs may take place. [The random element is usually related to the existence of gains from trade (e.g., if it is the result of liquidity motivated trading by some agents).]

A typical example of a noisy rational expectations model is developed in Grossman and Stiglitz (1980). In their model some agents acquire a single piece of private information and become "informed" while the rest remain privately uninformed.[8] The signal observed by the informed, perturbed by supply noise, is partially revealed to the uninformed by the price. This model is used to discuss information acquisition and derive some comparative static results, as discussed in the next section.

Because there is only one piece of information in the market, the model of Grossman and Stiglitz does not capture the *aggregation* of information in financial markets. Differences of beliefs are only possible between an informed agent and an uninformed agent; all informed agents hold identical beliefs, and prices do not affect *their* beliefs.

In contrast to this, models that involve both noisy transmission of information by prices and the aggregation of diverse information are analyzed by Hellwig (1980) and Diamond and Verrecchia (1981). As in Grossman and Stiglitz, noise is introduced through the lack of perfect information about the aggregate supply of the risky asset. But, unlike Grossman and Stiglitz, private signals are not the same; they are conditionally independent of each other given the true payoff, as in Grossman (1976) (the example discussed in Section II). The diversity of the information combined with the noise in the price imply that *every* agent uses *both* private information and the equilibrium price to create expectations.

In Hellwig's (1980) model, agents may vary in their risk attitudes and in the precision of their information. For a finite-agent economy Hellwig proves the existence of a linear rational expectations equilibrium and analyzes how an agent's characteristics affect his weight in the equilibrium price. He goes on to consider the limit of this equilibrium as the number of agents grows to infinity, and obtains particularly interesting and useful results. First, the effect on the equilibrium price of the error terms in individual signals becomes negligible. Thus the price reflects only what is common to many signals, and the competitive price-taking assumption makes more sense than in the finite-agent economy (in which each trader's private signal realization affects the price). Second, the price function obtained in the limit is solved in closed form. This model provides the basis for a number of subsequent extensions and applications, such as Admati (1985), Pfleiderer (1984), Grinblatt and Ross (1985), discussed below.

In Grossman and Stiglitz (1980), Hellwig (1980), and others, the source of the supply noise is unmodeled.[9] It is assumed, for simplicity and tractability, to be independent of agents' private information. Most naturally, the randomness in supply can be interpreted as a result of trade that is motivated by non-speculative reasons: life-cycle, liquidity, or private income hedging all come to mind. Since the preferences of "noise traders" are unspecified, this interpretation is unsatisfactory for certain purposes, especially welfare analysis.

The model of Diamond and Verrecchia (1981) is similar to Hellwig's finite-agent model (with identical agents) except that the source of aggregate supply noise is explicit: agents' endowments in the risky asset are random, and aggregate supply is the sum of these endowments. Private endowments are assumed i.i.d. Agents can (and do) use the realization of their private endowment to draw inferences about aggregate supply and hence about others' payoff-relevant information (from the price).

Note that, because individual endowments are i.i.d., if the number of agents grows but the variance of each endowment is bounded, then by the law of large numbers per capita supply becomes constant; the model of Diamond and Verrecchia would therefore approach Grossman's (1976) fully revealing model. If the variance of individual endowments grows with the number of agents, the limit is Hellwig's (1980) model, but this may be hard to interpret. One way to keep the flavor of Diamond and Verrecchia's model and prevent full revelation without restoring to unbounded variances is to have private endowments subject to a common shock (that must affect the price); but this is not so tractable analytically.

The noisy rational expectations equilibrium models discussed above involve a safe asset and one risky asset and lead to the following intuitive results: (i) the price of the risky asset increases in its true payoff and decreases in its actual supply; (ii) both equilibrium price and private information have positive regression coefficients in agents' expectation functions; and (iii) the demand for the risky asset is strictly decreasing in its (equilibrium) price.[10]

Admati (1985) shows that these intuitive results are not generally true in a model with many risky assets. Admati's model is like Hellwig's (1980), but with many assets and a large (infinite) number of agents. The equilibrium functions are derived in closed form, and their properties are examined, showing the complex interactions among the assets that are possible. For example, a change in one asset's price generally provides information about *other* assets' payoffs as well as the asset's own payoff. It is possible that when the price of one asset increases and a second stays fixed, investors infer that the payoff of the first is likely to be *lower*—the lack of change in the second may contain important (and counterintuitive) information that is used in drawing inferences about the first change. One may also find equilibrium prices that are decreasing in an asset's own payoff and increasing in an asset's own supply, and demand functions that are increasing in an asset's own price (i.e., assets that are "Giffen goods"). This analysis illustrates that, in addition to the correlations between financial assets' returns (which play a central role in modern asset pricing theories), the correlations between the prediction errors in traders' information and between the amount of "noise trading" across assets are important in determining equilibrium relations.

V. APPLICATIONS TO FINANCIAL MARKETS

If one believes that asymmetric information and diverse beliefs exist and are important in financial markets, then models that either assume homogeneous beliefs or in which prices are fully revealing cannot capture important features of these markets. Noisy rational expectations equilibrium models, on the other hand, provide a natural framework for analyzing a variety of issues. This section discusses some recent applications of these models.

A. Volume of Trading

Pfleiderer (1984) uses Hellwig's (1980) model of noisy rational expectations equilibrium with an infinite number of (identical) agents and some extensions to multiperiod models to analyze price variability and trading volume. One interesting comparative static result is that the volume of trade is generally *increasing* in the precision of private signals; that is, other things equal, the less precise the private signals (therefore, the "more dispersed" are pretrade expectations), the lower is the volume of trade. Note two things here. First, equilibrium *beliefs* are not always more homogeneous if private signals are more precise; with more precise (diverse) signals, there is less reliance on the public information in equilibrium price. Second, traders take much bolder positions on the basis of more precise private information, and this works to increase the volume.[11] Pfleiderer also discusses a few multiperiod models of futures markets and examines conditions on preferences and information and price processes under which, for example, the variability of prices or the trading volume increases as the futures contract matures.

B. Performance Measurement

Do some agents, such as mutual fund managers, trade on the basis of superior information? The measurement of investment performance has received much attention in the literature. This question is naturally cast within an equilibrium model that captures asymmetries (as well as diversity) in information among traders, as is done in Admati and Ross (1985), using the model in Admati (1985). It is shown first that traditional risk return measures, such as the reward-to-variability ratio, are inappropriate to measure superior information.[12] The performance measurement problem is then set up as a class of statistical inference problems (depending, among other things, on the nature of the observations), and valid statistical tools are developed. The regression models that arise in this model have a special structure that allows, for example, the identification of both risk aversion and the precision of private information when either the portfolio weights or only the portfolio's returns are observable (together with prices).

C. Insider Trading

Insider trading is another topic that has received considerable attention in the literature and that inherently involves asymmetric information. To capture the idea that insiders may have market power and to investigate the consequences for equilibrium, Grinblatt and Ross (1985) modify Hellwig's (1980) model, adding an informed risk-neutral insider, who acts as a Stackelberg leader. The insider, by choosing how to use his private information, effectively chooses the rational expectations equilibrium, doing so to maximize his expected profits. The rest of the traders behave competitively, realizing the implications of the insider's strategy for the informational content of equilibrium prices. Restricting to linear strategies, Grinblatt and Ross obtain an equilibrium and show, for example, that among such strategies the insider does not need to add noise to his information. Grinblatt (1985) discusses the implications of this model for the regulation of insider trading and shows that speculators (but not necessarily liquidity motivated traders) prefer a ban on insider trading.

D. The Provision of Information

Investors in real financial markets undertake numerous activities to improve the information they bring to the market. In all the papers discussed above, except for Grossman and Stiglitz (1980), this feature is missing; the allocation of pretrading information is specified exogenously. Recent papers have set out to model the activity of information acquisition, where the decision to acquire information is made in view of the value it has for the subsequent trading in financial markets.

Grossman and Stiglitz (1980) is the pioneering effort in this direction. In their model each agent decides whether to acquire, at a given cost, a particular piece of information. As more traders are informed, the (incremental) value of information declines, since the price reveals more of it to the uninformed. In equilibrium the proportion of the traders that are informed is such that the value of information exactly equals its cost.

Verrecchia (1982) analyzes a model of information acquisition that is similar in spirit to Grossman and Stiglitz (1980). However, private signals (and hence the equilibrium) in this model follow Hellwig's (1980) specification; each agent can acquire a signal that is conditionally independent (given the payoff) of other private signals. Agents can also choose the precision of their private signals according to a given cost function. Verrecchia proves the existence of equilibrium with endogenous information acquisition and shows (among other things) that more risk-averse agents will choose less precise private signals.

Information acquisition decisions generally depend on the amount of public information available. If assets are shares in firms, firms can alter the incentives to collect private information by releasing information. Using the model of Hellwig (1980) and Verrecchia (1982), Diamond (1985) characterizes the public information release policy that maximizes the ex ante expected utility of speculators. Because the firm can generally produce and release the information more cheaply than can the aggregate of all traders, and since (in this model) ex ante expected utility is *decreasing* in the precision of public information if no private information is collected, the optimal amount of public information just eliminates the incentives to acquire private information. Public release of information may also benefit traders if there is no cost saving, particularly when the amount of supply noise is large.

In the papers cited above, the nature and cost of available information are exogenously specified. In most cases this is consistent either with the private production of the information or with a market in which the information is bought.[13] If information is bought in a market, however, then the nature and cost of the information would depend in part on its seller(s). Admati and Pfleiderer (1986a, b) analyze the case of a monopolistic seller of information. Since prices partially reveal what informed traders know, those who do not purchase information (and sometimes those who do) can free-ride on others who do, limiting the price the monopolist can charge. This externality is more severe when the amount of noise in the price is low, and particularly when the information sold is very precise, since such information is used very aggressively and, therefore, is more clearly reflected in prices. Admati and Pfleiderer (1986a) show that if information is sold *directly,* so that the buyer observes the signal sold and can use it to trade in the financial market, then the seller may prefer to sell noisier information than the information he has. Within a large class of allocations of information the optimal way for the seller to add noise is such that added noise realizations do not affect the equilibrium price. For example, the seller can sell "personalized" (conditionally independent) signals to all the traders (with the appropriate level of added noise). Another way to sell information is for the seller to create a fund whose investment portions depend on the information, and to sell shares in this fund to traders. This *indirect* selling method is explored and compared to the direct selling method in Admati and Pfleiderer (1986b). This paper shows, for example, that (with one risky asset) selling information indirectly and charging only a per share price leads to higher profits than selling it directly if and only if the externality implied by informative prices is relatively intense.[14]

A critical ingredient in all the studies of the provision of information is the value of information to traders. Under the assumptions of normal distributions and exponential utility functions (made in all the noisy rational expectations models discussed above), Admati and Pfleiderer (1987) show that the value of information is always a simple function of the (generalized) variance of the prediction errors obtained using the private information and that obtained without the private information (in both cases). This is used to investigate which allocations of information are viable in the sense that they can be sustained in a nondiscriminatory market in information. The fact that prices transmit information has important implications for the viability of various allocations. For example, the information in prices affects whether different pieces of information are substitutes or complements, which in turn determines whether viable allocations involving these signals are "concentrated" or "dispersed." It is shown that viable allocations of information may require that all information is concentrated (resp. dispersed) in the economy even though traders are ex ante identical and the pieces of information, viewed in isolation (i.e., absent price information), are substitutes (resp. complements). Some situations where viability implies concentration (or dispersion) are developed.

VI. CONCLUDING REMARKS

Although some of the empirical literature on efficient markets is relevant to the models discussed above, little of it relates directly to rational expectations equilibrium models with diverse information or to their application. One exception is the study of Huberman and Schwert (1985) on indexed bonds, which gives support to a noisy rational expectations equilibrium model. Also, rational expectations models perform well in experimental markets (see, for example, Plott and Sunder 1982 and Sunder 1984).

Much foundational research remains to be done. Like the Walrasian equilibrium, the rational expectations equilibrium concept is static; it does not explain how prices are formed. Further, this equilibrium concept involves a stronger than usual assumption of price taking, namely that agents take both the distribution of prices and the price realization as given. We need to understand better the appropriateness of these assumptions.

As discussed in Section III, these issues are most apparent in the context of fully revealing equilibria. But the question of *implementation* of rational expectations equilibria is generally important: do there exist mechanisms (games) of a general or a specific kind whose Nash equilibria correspond to the rational expectations equilibria of the economy? It is particularly important to investigate realistic mechanisms (e.g., auctions, trading via market makers or specialists and sequential trading procedures) and to relate their equilibria to the rational expectations equilibria.[15] A related area of research concerns the issue of "learning": how do agents come to know the correct distributions of endogenous variables?[16]

Rational expectations equilibrium models where prices are not fully revealing can be very complex. For tractability, all the models of noisy rational expectations equilibrium discussed above assume exponential utility functions and normal distributions. Although these models capture many important phenomena, this limitation should be noted. Needless to say, tractable models with different parametric assumptions are sorely needed.

The applications described in Section V illustrate that rational expectations equilibrium models provide a useful framework for various analyses. However, many of the applications are only first steps toward understanding the issues involved. Much research remains, for example, in the area of the provision of information, including analyses of the trade-offs between selling information and trading on it, competition, and the credibility of information sellers.

Finally, multiperiod models with asymmetric information are needed. With few exceptions, the intertemporal and continuous-time models in the literature assume a representative agent. The importance of information has been emphasized (see, for example, Hansen and Richard 1984), but little has been done to develop models where agents are heterogeneous, particularly with respect to their private information.[17] The development of such models is particularly important in making connections with empirical research.

NOTES

[1] The concept of a rational expectations equilibrium, also referred to as a perfect foresight or self-fulfilling equilibrium, was developed and applies also to situations where beliefs are homogeneous but are endogenously determined. See, for example, Lucas (1972). We do not cover such models, which are mostly in the macroeconomic literature. For a further discussion of the rational expectations equilibrium concept and its development, see Grossman (1981).

[2] See the discussion of Admati (1985) where it is shown that the direction of the change in prices can be counterintuitive.

[3] This is the idea of temporary equilibrium; see Grandmont (1977), for example.

[4] Grossman (1976) only treats the symmetric case, where $\tilde{\varepsilon}_i$ are i.i.d. and agents have identical risk tolerance. However, the existence of a linear rational expectations equilibrium price and its sufficient statistic property hold more generally; see Hellwig (1980). Moreover, the equilibrium is unique within those that are linear in the private signals. See also Danthine (1978) for a similar result in a futures market context.

[5] Some early references include Green (1973), Grossman (1977), Kihlstrom and

Mirman (1975), and Kreps (1977). The existence of fully revealing (and other) rational expectations equilibria in general economies was investigated particularly extensively. This literature is beyond the scope of this survey and will not be discussed further; see the discussion and references in Jordan and Radner (1982).

[6] Ex post Pareto efficiency is a very weak optimality concept under incomplete information, however. There has been relatively little research on welfare properties of rational expectations equilibria in general. See Laffont (1985) for a general discussion and Allen (1984) and Kealhofer (1984) for applications of the model of Grossman and Stiglitz (1980) (or generalizations) to welfare issues.

[7] This may remind the reader of the conclusion of the traditional CAPM, where everyone holds the market portfolio. Indeed, Grossman (1978) shows that under joint normality (and other minor assumptions), an extended version of the CAPM holds. Homogeneous beliefs, which are assumed in the standard CAPM, are now induced endogenously at the equilibrium.

[8] Much of the early literature on rational expectations equilibrium models was based on models with two groups of agents: informed and uninformed; see the references in note 5.

[9] Bray (1981) develops a model of futures markets where the second-period endowments of producers are random, resulting in prices that are generally not sufficient statistics.

[10] Compare (iii) with Grossman's (1976) flat demand functions: the existence of noise weakens the information effect so that it only partially offsets the substitution effect.

[11] This conclusion seems to be contrary to Theorem 6 in Grossman and Stiglitz (1980). However, in their model (i) there is no diversity of beliefs among the informed traders, since they all observe the same signal, and (ii) the fraction of informed traders is endogenous and becomes smaller as the precision of private information increases. In Pfleiderer's model all agents are privately informed, and the comparison is made when the precision of their diverse information changes.

[12] These results are similar to Dybvig and Ross (1985), who do not use a rational expectations equilibrium model.

[13] In either interpretation, agents always use their information for trading in the financial market; if the information could be resold (or shared) costlessly and instantaneously, then obviously a market in information would break down. Resale may be problematic for a number of reasons (e.g., moral hazard), but this has not been explored.

[14] For further discussion of markets in information, see the essay by Allen in this volume.

[15] Kyle (1985) analyzes a model like Hellwig (1980) with imperfect competition among traders. For models that involve explicit price formation mechanisms, see Milgrom (1981) and Dubey, Geanakoplos, and Shubik (1985). The essay by Kyle in this volume discusses models with marketmakers and specialists; see the references there. The more abstract implementation problem (with incomplete information) is the subject of much ongoing research.

[16] See Blume, Bray, and Easley (1982) and the references there.

[17] Two exceptions (in the rational expectations context) are Pfleiderer (1984) and Singleton (1986). Duffie and Huang (1985) focus mostly on fully revealing equilibria in a continuous-time model.

REFERENCES

Admati, Anat R. 1985. "A Noisy Rational Expectations Equilibrium for Multi-Asset Securities Markets." *Econometrica* 53: 629–57.

Admati, Anat R., and Pfleiderer, Paul. 1986a. "A Monopolistic Market for Information." *Journal of Economic Theory* 39: 400–38.

———. 1986b. "Direct and Indirect Sale of Information." Working paper 899, Graduate School of Business, Stanford University.

———. 1987. "Viable Allocations of Information in Financial Markets." *Journal of Economic Theory*, forthcoming.

Admati, Anat R., and Ross, Stephen A. 1985. "Measuring Investment Performance in a Rational Expectations Equilibrium Model." *Journal of Business* 58: 1–26. "Corrigendum," 59: 367.

Allen, Franklin. 1984. "The Social Value of Asymmetric Information." Working paper, University of Pennsylvania.

Anderson, Robert, and Sonnenschein, Hugo. 1982. "On the Existence of Rational Expectations Equilibrium." *Journal of Economic Theory* 26: 261–78.

Beja, Avraham. 1977. "The Limits of Price Information in Market Processes." Working paper 61, Research Program in Finance, University of California, Berkeley.

Blume, Laurance E.; Bray, Margaret M.; and Easley, David. 1982. "Introduction to the Stability of Rational Expectations Equilibrium." *Journal of Economic Theory* 26: 313–17.

Bray, Margaret M. 1981. "Futures Trading, Rational Expectations and the Efficient Market Hypothesis." *Econometrica* 49: 575–96.

Danthine, J. 1978. "Information, Futures Prices, and Stabilizing Speculation." *Journal of Economic Theory* 17: 79–98.

Diamond, Douglas W. 1983. "Optimal Release of Information by Firms." *Journal of Finance* 40: 1071–94.

Diamond, Douglas W., and Verrecchia, Robert E. 1981. "Information Aggregation in a Noisy Rational Expectations Economy." *Journal of Financial Economics* 9: 221–35.

Dubey, Pradeep; Geanakoplos, John, and Shubik, Martin. 1985. "The Revelation of Information in Strategic Market Games: A Critique of Rational Expectations Equilibrium." Working paper, Cowles Foundation, Yale University.

Duffie, Darrell, and Huang, Chi-fu. 1985. "Multiperiod Security Markets with Differential Information: Martingales and Resolution Times." Working paper 812, Stanford Graduate School of Business.

Dybvig, Philip, and Ross, Stephen A. 1985. "Differential Information and Performance Measurement Using a Security Market Line." *Journal of Finance* 40: 383–99.

Fama, Eugene F. 1970. "Efficient Capital Markets: A Review of Theory and Empirical Work." *Journal of Finance* 25: 383–417.

Grandmont. Jean Michel. 1977. "Temporary General Equilibrium Theory." *Econometrica* 45: 535–72.

Green, Jerry R. 1973. "Information, Efficiency, and Equilibrium." Harvard Institute of Economic Research, Harvard University, manuscript.

Grinblatt, Mark S. 1983. "On the Regulation of Insider Trading." Working paper, University of California, Los Angeles, October.

Grinblatt, Mark S., and Ross, Stephen A. 1985. "Market Power in a Securities Market with Endogenous Information." *Quarterly Journal of Economics* 100: 1143–67.

Grossman, Sanford. 1976. "On the Efficiency of Competitive Stock Markets Where Agents Have Diverse Information." *Journal of Finance* 18: 81–101.

———. 1977. "The Existence of Futures Markets, Noisy Rational Expectations and Informational Externalities." *Review of Economic Studies* 64: 431–49.

———. 1978. "Further Results on the Informational Efficiency of Competitive Stock Markets." *Journal of Economic Theory* 18: 81–101.

———. 1981. "An Introduction to the Theory of Rational Expectations under Asymmetric Information." *Review of Economic Studies* 48: 541–59.

Grossman, Sanford, and Stiglitz, Joseph E. 1980. "On the Impossibility of Informationally Efficient Markets." *American Economic Review* 70: 393–408. Reprinted Chapter 4, this volume.

Hansen, Lars Peter, and Richard, Scott F. 1984. "A General Approach for Deducing Testable Restrictions Implied by Asset Pricing Models." Working paper, Department of Economics, University of Chicago.

Hellwig, Martin F. 1980. "On the Aggregation of Information in Competitive Markets." *Journal of Economic Theory* 22: 477–98.

Huberman, Gur, and Schwert, G. William 1985. "Information Aggregation, Inflation and the Pricing of Indexed Bonds." *Journal of Political Economy* 93: 92–114.

Jordan, James S., and Radner, Roy. 1982. "Rational Expectations in Microeconomic Models: An Overview." *Journal of Economic Theory* 26: 201–23.

Kealhofer, Stephen. 1984. "Costly Private Information and Social Welfare." Working paper, Columbia University.

Kihlstrom, Richard, and Mirman, Leonard J. 1975. "Information and Market Equilibrium." *Bell Journal of Economics* 6: 357–76.

Kreps, David M. 1977. "A Note on Fulfilled Expectations Equilibria." *Journal of Economic Theory* 14: 32–43.

Kyle, Albert S. 1985. "Informed Speculation with Imperfect Competition." Working paper, Woodrow Wilson School, Princeton University.

Laffont, Jean-Jacques. 1985. "On the Welfare Analysis of Rational Expectations Equilibria with Asymmetric Information." *Econometrica* 53: 1–30.

Lintner, John. 1969. "The Aggregation of Investors' Diverse Judgements and Preferences in Purely Competitive Security Markets." *Journal of Financial and Quantitative Analysis* 4: 103–24.

Lucas, Robert E. 1972. "Expectations and the Neutrality of Money." *Journal of Economic Theory* 4: 103–24.

Milgrom, Paul R. 1981. "Rational Expectations, Information Acquisition, and Competitive Bidding." *Econometrica* 49: 921–44.

Pfleiderer, Paul. 1984. "Private Information, Price Variability and Trading Volume." Working paper, Stanford University.

Plott, Charles R., and Sunder, Shayam. 1982. "Efficiency of Experimental Security Markets with Insider Information: An Application of Rational Expectations Models." *Journal of Political Economy* 90: 663–98.

Singleton, Kenneth J. 1986. "Asset Prices in a Time Series Model with Disparately Informed, Competitive Traders." Conference volume from the 1985 Austin Symposium in Economics on "New Approaches to Monetary Economics."

Sunder, Shyam. 1985. "Rational Expectations Equilibrium in Asset Markets with Costly Information: Experimental Evidence." Working paper 1984-3, Graduate School of Management, University of Minnesota.

Verrecchia, Robert. 1982. "Information Acquisition in a Noisy Rational Expectations Economy." *Econometrica* 50: 1415–30.

discussion | **Imperfect Competition, Market Dynamics, and Regulatory Issues**

Albert S. Kyle

University of California, Berkeley

The Grossman and Stiglitz paper emphasizes the role speculative market prices can play in communicating information about asset values from informed to uninformed traders. Their simple model is based upon the assumptions of perfect competition, one-shot trading, and a Walrasian auction mechanism. Although standard in the rational expectations literature and useful for discussing the informational role of prices in an abstract setting, these assumptions do not describe exactly how markets for stocks, bonds, and commodities work. In actual financial markets, the largest players probably do have the ability to influence price (if only temporarily), because no market is infinitely liquid or infinitely deep; the dynamic nature of trading creates a role for market makers; and the decentralized trading of over-the-counter markets, the specialist system of the New York Stock Exchange, and the crowd system of the commodities exchanges each represent market microstructures distinctly different from the textbook Walrasian auction.

The following comments discuss informally the informational role of prices when the special assumptions of Grossman and Stiglitz are replaced by ones designed to capture more fully the flavor of actual trading in financial assets. The discussion is divided into separate sections dealing with imperfect competition and market liquidity, market making and the bid/asked spread, dynamic trading, continuous trading, and regulatory issues.

IMPERFECT COMPETITION AND MARKET LIQUIDITY

To examine how the results obtained by Grossman and Stiglitz depend on the assumption of perfect competition, consider a modified model in which all of the informed traders are merged together into one large trading unit, and let the equilibrium be a Nash equilibrium in demand curves. A generalized version of this modified model is examined in detail by Kyle (1986). Imperfect competition is present because the informational monopolist takes account of his effect on prices in determining the demand curve he submits (even though the uninformed traders continue to trade as perfect competitors). When the assumptions of Grossman and Stiglitz are maintained, the Nash equilibrium in demand curves yields exactly their competitive rational expectations equilibrium. Furthermore, even when imperfect competition is allowed, the market microstructure looks "Walrasian" in the sense that the market clearing price is determined as if a nontrading auctioneer simply aggregated the demand curves submitted by various traders. This makes the modified model a good vehicle for examining how Grossman and Stiglitz's results depend on their assumption of perfect competition.

The resulting equilibrium has the property that the equilibrium price reveals less information than the corresponding competitive price, and it is easy to see why. The large informed trader faces a residual supply curve whose slope is positive, not zero. Like a textbook monopolist who reduces output in order to raise price, the informational monopolist trades a smaller quantity in order to make the price more favorable. This reduces the signal-to-noise ratio in prices and therefore makes prices less informative.

The resulting equilibrium also has the property that prices never become fully revealing, even in the limit as noise trading vanishes and even in the limit as the informed trader becomes risk neutral. In the limit as noise trading vanishes, the profits of the large informed trader are driven to zero, not because the price becomes fully revealing but because the quantity traded by the large informed trader goes to zero. This occurs because the slope of the residual supply curve faced by the large informed trader becomes infinitely steep. It is tempting to define the "depth" of the market as the reciprocal of the slope of a trader's residual supply curve—that is, as the quantity a trader must buy or sell to make the price rise or fall by one dollar. This definition of market depth is different from what Grossman and Stiglitz call market "liquidity." For Grossman and Stiglitz, market liquidity is proportional to trading volume, which serves as a proxy for the transactions fee necessary to cover the fixed costs of operating a market. With either definition, however, vanishing noise trading leads to a market that is infinitely illiquid.

When the informed trader is risk neutral, a well-defined equilibrium exists in which the informed trader's residual supply curve has a positive slope, he continues to restrict his trading so that prices do not become fully revealing, and his profits are proportional to the amount of noise trading. In the limit as informed traders become risk neutral in the competitive model, by contrast, prices become fully revealing, the profits of informed traders vanish, and incentives to acquire private information thus disappear. With endogenous informed trading, informed traders would exit until there was only one left, in which case a model with imperfect competition would become appropriate.

MARKET MAKING AND THE BID/ASKED SPREAD

Now let us consider modifying the "market microstructure"—that is, the rules governing the structure of the trading process—to allow for the existence of market makers. Market makers serve as intermediaries who quote a bid price and an asked price, buy when other traders want to sell, sell when other traders want to buy, and profit by turning over positions quickly on relatively small margins. Their profits come from the bid/asked spread, not from speculation; they make money by knowing where other traders would like to buy and sell, not by acquiring unique fundamental information of their own. Their information comes from observing the "order flow" (i.e., by observing the trading activities of other traders in the marketplace). It seems hard for a Walrasian mechanism to accommodate market makers because the Walrasian mechanism treats all traders symmetrically. Market making, however, appears to involve an inherent asymmetry between traders in which market makers know more, at any given moment, about what is going on in the marketplace than other traders are able to know.

One can attempt to understand the economic role of market makers by asking what service market makers provide. Do they provide execution immediacy by being willing to buy and sell when other traders are not present in the market? Do they reduce search costs by matching buyers with sellers? Do they provide a temporary risk-bearing service by holding positions for short periods of time? Are they monopolists who solve an inventory problem? Do they provide a price discovery service by quoting prices that represent a consensus of others' intentions to buy and sell? Are they information processors who calculate the best estimate of the value of an asset based upon the trading activities of other buyers and sellers in the marketplace? Or do they provide no service at all, functioning instead like an externality or tax on other buyers and sellers in the marketplace? Perhaps a complete understanding of market making requires examining market making from all of these perspectives. Stoll (1985) discusses intuitively several of them. A large "market microstructure" literature has come into existence discussing various perspectives. Cohen et al. (1981) emphasize immediacy, whereas Amihud and Mendelson (1980) emphasize inventory costs. Other useful references are Ho (1984) and Kahn (1982). Amihud, Ho, and Schwartz (1985) contains several interesting papers.

The perspective most closely related to the Grossman-Stiglitz paper, however, treats market makers as information processors, and this is the perspective we shall emphasize here. This perspective was first discussed systematically by Bagehot (1971) and Black (1971).

When market makers are modeled as information processors, the bid/asked spread is derived from information asymmetries in the following manner.

Consider a market in which market makers trade with both informed traders who, on average, earn speculative profits and with uninformed "noise traders" motivated either by liquidity or life-cycle needs, by risk aversion (and endowment shocks), or even by irrationality. The market maker is assumed to be unable to distinguish informed traders from uninformed traders. If the market maker quotes a single price at which he is willing to both buy and sell the asset, he breaks even on average with noise traders (because their trading is random in an appropriate sense), but he loses money systematically on transactions with informed traders, because informed traders only buy when the price is about to rise (on average) and they only sell when the price is about to fall (on average). On average, therefore, the market maker loses money when he is willing to buy and sell at the same price, and these losses can be traced to "adverse selection" from informed traders.

For a market maker to stay in business when informed traders are present, he must set his bid price lower than his asked price. Although the market maker still loses on trades made with informed traders, he now earns profits proportional to the bid/asked spread on transactions with noise traders. The market maker thus becomes a conduit through which transactions costs for noise traders are converted into profits for informed traders. In equilibrium, the spread is set wide enough so that profits on transactions with noise traders cover all losses with informed traders plus leave enough left over to pay per unit transactions fees, compensate the market maker for risk bearing, cover the opportunity cost of the market maker's time and trouble, and allow the market maker to earn any monopoly rents (presumably capitalized into exchange memberships and specialists' privileges) to which the market microstructure entitles him.

As Bagehot (1971) points out, the informational component of the spread (that is, the part of the spread that compensates the market maker for losses with informed traders) will be proportional to the probability of a transaction occurring with an informed trader and also proportional to the profit the informed trader would expect to make if he held the position for a long time. In general, there will be different bid and asked prices (and therefore a different spread) for different quantities. The spread for small quantities will typically be smaller than the spread for large quantities either because small quantities tend to be more likely to be traded by noise traders or because informed traders who trade small quantities tend to have small amounts of private information. Thus, as Black (1971) points out, in a market where trading frictions are otherwise negligible and market makers are competitive, a trader who wishes to trade a tiny quantity should be able to buy or sell at approximately the same price, whereas a trader who wishes to trade a large quantity should expect his transaction to have an appreciable impact on the market. The bid and offer prices, together with attached quantities, form a supply schedule for other traders, and because traders with private information are present in the market, this supply schedule is not as elastic as it would otherwise be.

Although motivated differently, this approach to informed trading has much in common with the approach taken by Grossman and Stiglitz. The primary difference is that Grossman and Stiglitz emphasize prices as signals operating through a Walrasian market clearing mechanism, whereas the market-maker approach emphasizes quantities as signals processed by the market maker. Both approaches, however, capture the basic idea that the buying and selling of traders in the marketplace lead to prices that contain information about the value of the traded asset.

DYNAMIC TRADING

This approach to market making makes just as much sense in a dynamic setting with sequential trading as in an atemporal setting with one-shot trading.

In a dynamic setting, the price changes resulting from the adverse-selection component of the bid/asked spread are permanent, and this leads to a martingale result that we now discuss.

Suppose that market makers are risk neutral and expect to break even on every transaction. Then the market makers' bid price for a particular quantity is the expectation of the fundamental value (to be interpreted as a liquidation value or value in the distant future) conditional on information about all past transactions and on the next transaction's being a sell order for the particular quantity. The offer prices are determined analogously. Since the sequence of actual transaction quantities defines a sequence of constantly improving information sets about the value of the asset, the sequence of conditional expectations—the sequence of actual transactions prices—automatically follows a martingale. Glosten and Milgrom (1985) discuss precisely the mathematics of this result in the context of a particular model where transactions are always for one unit of the asset. Kyle (1985a) discusses the same idea in a context where normal random variables allow the sequence of transactions prices to be determined in a simple intuitive manner by iterated linear projections.

Now in actual markets, of course, we do not expect market makers to be risk-neutral agents who provide their services for free, and, therefore, we do not expect the sequence of transactions prices to be precisely a martingale. The martingale result does, however, make operational the distinction between the adverse-selection component of the bid/asked spread and the other components (for example, per unit transactions fees, monopoly power, risk aversion, and finite tick size, all of which should make the bid/asked spread larger but have little effect on prices that persist for very many transactions. It is well known that transaction-by-transaction stock price fluctuations tend to have a powerful negative correlation at one lag, and this indicates that much of the bid/asked spread, especially for small quantities, is due to factors other than adverse selection. It does not, however, imply that the permanent component due to adverse selection is unimportant, especially for large transactions.

CONTINUOUS TRADING

Consider now a market in which a large trader with private information chooses strategically the quantities he trades through time. In a dynamic setting like this, it is possible to ask a richer set of questions about the informational and liquidity characteristics of the market than is possible in an atemporal context with one-shot trading. Instead of asking how much private information is revealed in prices, one can ask how quickly new private information is incorporated into prices. It becomes possible to discuss other aspects of market liquidity besides the "depth" of the market—that is, the quantity it takes to move prices by one dollar. These other aspects of market liquidity include the "tightness" of the market (that is, the cost of turning over a position in a very short period of time) and the "resiliency" of the market (that is, the speed with which prices tend to converge towards the underlying value of the commodity when perturbed by noise trading).

Kyle (1985a) describes a model with noise trading in which market makers earn zero profits on every transaction and the informational characteristics of prices and the liquidity characteristics of the market are determined endogenously along with the trading strategy of the informed trader. The "continuous auction equilibrium"—that is, the limiting equilibrium in which trading takes place continuously and noise trading follows Brownian motion—has the following properties. The informed trader, by buying or selling in the marketplace, continuously pushes prices towards his private valuation of the asset. The speed with which he pushes prices towards their underlying value measures the resiliency of the market. This speed is equal to the difference between his private valuation and the current price, divided by the amount of trading time left until markets close. The depth of the market, which is constant over time, is proportional to the amount of noise trading present in the market and inversely proportional to the amount of private information in the hands of the large informed trader. The expected profits of the informed trader, which equal the expected losses of the noise trader, are proportional to the amount of noise trading and proportional to the amount of information in the hands of the informed trader. The market is "infinitely tight," because with continuous trading the informed trader can break any transaction down into many tiny pieces, on each of which the bid/asked spread is small. In effect, this enables him to move up and down along his residual supply curve like a perfectly discriminating monopolist without generating any additional transactions costs. The informed trader's private information is incorporated into prices gradually, such that by the end of trading prices converge exactly to the informed trader's private valuation of the asset. Thus, the informed trader would have no interest in having markets reopened after they close. Prices follow a Brownian motion process, and in this sense the market looks like a textbook "efficient market." Until the market closes, however, prices are only efficient in the "semistrong" sense, because the informed trader has private information not yet incorporated into prices. One cannot infer from looking at prices alone that there is an informed trader present in the market. The presence of information trading can be indirectly inferred, however, from the contemporaneous correlation between quantities traded in the market and permanent changes in prices.

Now Grossman and Stiglitz emphasize in their paper that when private information is costly, profitable informed trading is incompatible with prices that reveal it perfectly. The price "cannot perfectly reflect the information which is available, since if it did, those who spent resources to obtain it would receive no compensation. There is a fundamental conflict between the efficiency with which markets spread information and the incentives to acquire information." With continuous trading this informational efficiency paradox must be interpreted carefully. In the model discussed in the previous paragraph, prices do reveal all the informed trader's private information, but only by the end of trading. But alternative models of continuous trading exist in which the difference between private valuations of the asset and the market price are at all times arbitrarily small, yet the profits of the informed trader or traders do not vanish! Hellwig (1982) describes a competitive model with this property. Kyle (1985b) describes a model with a monopolistic informed trader with this property. Thus, with continuous trading, it is, in principle, possible for markets to spread information arbitrarily quickly without undermining incentives to acquire private information.

REGULATORY ISSUES

Markets for financial assets are regulated both by government institutions like the Securities and Exchange Commission (SEC), the Commodity Futures Trading Commission (CFTC), and the Federal Reserve Board, and by private institutions like stock and commodities exchanges. The following discussion of regulatory issues is applicable to both government regulatory institutions and self-regulation by the exchanges themselves. This discussion covers material in Kyle (1984), but the underlying economic problem is much the same as that described by Hirshleifer (1971).

A marketplace for financial assets provides two distinct services to the economy. On the one hand, it provides an exchange mechanism that allows buyers and sellers to internalize gains from trade by redistributing risk and transferring liquidity. Because we refer to these buyers and sellers as noise traders here should not be taken to mean that they have no economic motive in trading, but that, given their trading pattern, the dynamics of price formation do not depend on exactly what this economic motive is. On the other hand, the prices generated by the marketplace reveal useful information that may influence beneficially the allocation of resources (e.g., investment decisions) even by those who do not trade in the marketplace. The kind of informational externality described by Grossman and Stiglitz clearly affects the efficiency with which these two services are provided. The information revealed publicly through announced prices is, in effect, a public good to those who use this information to make resource allocation decisions unrelated to their trading decision. The noise traders who use the marketplace for exchanging assets in effect pay for this information, even though they may not use it. The payment takes the form of transactions costs or expected trading losses (extracted perhaps through the bid/asked spread), which are necessary because informed traders make profits trading in the market. In other words, the adverse-selection component of trading costs is like a tax on noise traders that subsidizes the acquisition of private information and its subsequent dissemination through the price system. As with other taxes, there is an associated deadweight cost: As trading costs increase because increased informed trading erodes market liquidity, noise traders will decrease their trading activity, thus reducing the usefulness of the exchange service provided by the marketplace.

Because of these externalities associated with information trading, there is no presumption that an unregulated marketplace leads to a socially efficient amount of private information being incorporated into prices. If an informative price system has little social value (because the decisions made upon the basis of the information contained in prices are not important) but a liquid marketplace has great value, then increased information trading will tend to reduce welfare. If, however, there is little noise trading but the information produced by the price system has great value, then increased information trading will tend to increase welfare.

Regulators can attempt to influence the liquidity of the market and the informativeness of prices by appropriate policies. For example, suppose regulators adopt a policy of collecting information and announcing it publicly themselves or requiring public disclosure of information collected privately. If public disclosure takes place before transactions based upon this information are made in the marketplace, then prices can adjust from the public announcement without adverse consequences for market liquidity. Such a policy may also discourage some private acquisition of information by making it less valuable. Of course, the resources necessary to pay for collecting and disseminating this information publicly must come from somewhere. The presumption behind these policies must be that other sources of tax revenues (e.g., general revenues for the government or lump-sum levies on exchange members for private exchanges) involve less distortion than the gains from a more informative, more liquid price mechanism.

Regulators can also attempt to reduce informed trading by banning insider trading upon the basis of certain kinds of private information. Effective enforcement of such prohibitions is likely to be difficult, however. Considerations of economic efficiency suggest that the kind of information upon the basis of which trade should be prohibited is information that would otherwise soon be incorporated into prices through public announcements. This suggests banning trading based on leaks of government statistics, earnings announcements, SEC filings, and other close substitutes for publicly announced data, but not banning trade upon the basis of private research that complements public sources of information.

A regulator may attempt to reduce noise trading on the grounds that noise trading destabilizes prices. Remember, however, that noise trading is the fodder that attracts informed traders into the marketplace, and exit of noise traders will induce exit of informed traders as well. In the context of the Grossman-Stiglitz model, the informativeness of prices does not depend on the amount of noise trading when entry and exit of informed traders are taken into account. In the context of a more general model (see Kyle 1986) where different informed traders produce different information and imperfect competition is possibly present, exit of noise traders actually leads to so much exit of informed traders that prices become less informative! In this sense, more noise trading promotes a more informative price system by attracting informed traders into the marketplace. A regulator seeking to increase the informativeness of prices should attempt to increase the liquidity of the market by attracting more noise traders, not by driving noise traders away.

REFERENCES

Amihud, Y.; Ho, T.; and Schwartz, R. 1985. *Market Making and the Changing Structure of the Securities Industry*. Lexington, Mass: Lexington Books.

Amihud, Y., and Mendelson, H. 1980. "Dealership Market: Market Making with Inventory." *Journal of Financial Economics* 8: 31–53.

Bagehot, W. (pseud.) 1971. "The Only Game in Town." *Financial Analysts Journal* 27 (March–April).

Black, F. 1971. "Towards a Fully Automated Exchange. I, II. *Financial Analysts Journal* (July–August, November–December).

Cohen, K.; Maier, S.; Schwartz, R.; and Whitcomb, D. 1981. "Transaction Costs, Order Placement Strategy, and the Existence of the Bid-Asked Spread." *Journal of Political Economy* 89: 287–305.

Demsetz, H. 1968. "The Cost of Transacting." *Quarterly Journal of Economics* 82: 33–53.

Glosten, L. R., and Milgrom, P. R. 1985. "Bid, Ask, and Transaction Prices in a Specialist Market with Heterogeneously Informed Traders." *Journal of Financial Economics* 14: 71–100.

Grossman, S. J., and Stiglitz, J. E. 1980. "On the Impossibility of Informationally Efficient Markets." *American Economic Review* 70: 393–408. Reprinted Chapter 4, this volume.

Hellwig, M. 1982. "Rational Expectations Equilibrium with Conditioning on Past Prices." *Journal of Economic Theory* 22: 477–98.

Hirshleifer, J. 1971. "The Private and Social Value of Information and the Reward to Inventive Activity." *American Economic Review* 61: 561–74.

Ho, T. 1984. "Dealer Market Structure: A Dynamic Competitive Model." Working paper, New York University, March.

Kahn, C. 1982. "Market Microstructure: A Dynamic Competitive Model." University of Chicago (mimeo), June.

Kyle, A. S. 1984. "Market Structure, Information, Futures Markets, and Price Formation." In Gary G. Storey, Andrew Schmitz, and Alexander H. Sarris, eds., *International Agricultural Trade: Advanced Readings in Price Formation, Market Structure, and Price Instability*. Boulder: Westview, pp. 45–65.

———. 1985a. "Continuous Auctions and Insider Trading." *Econometrica* 53: 1335–55.

———. 1985b. "On Incentives to Acquire Private Information with Continuous Trading." Unpublished manuscript, December.

———. 1986. "Informed Speculation with Imperfect Competition." Memorandum No. 66, Princeton University, Financial Research Center, January.

Stoll, H. 1985. "Alternative Views of Market Making." In Amihud, Ho, and Schwartz, *Market Making*, pp. 67–92.

Reprinted from JOURNAL OF ECONOMIC THEORY
All Rights Reserved by Academic Press, New York and London

Vol. 36, No. 1, June 1985
Printed in Belgium

Delegated Portfolio Management*

SUDIPTO BHATTACHARYA

University of California at Berkeley, Berkeley, California 94720

PAUL PFLEIDERER

Stanford University, Stanford, California 94305

Received November 12, 1983; revised October 8, 1984

A problem of screening agents with privately known forecasting abilities and reservation utilities and then eliciting truthful information from these agents once they are employed is considered. For the case of risk averse agents and large principals, an approximately optimal solution is constructively characterized under the assumption that payoffs are normally distributed. A significant extension of the deFinnetti–Savage probability elicitation result is developed. Under this extension knowledge of agent preferences is not required (when the underlying conditional distributions are symmetric) and this fact is exploited to solve the screening problem in a mean-variance formulation. *Journal of Economic Literature* Classification Numbers: 022, 026, 522. © 1985 Academic Press, Inc.

1. INTRODUCTION

In this paper we address an important problem in agency theory. This problem occurs whenever agents are heterogeneous and the attraction of better agents and the motivation of actions in the principal's interest are joint objectives. In our specification of the problem agents have two elements of private information; the first is received at the precontracting stage, while the second is received after contracting takes place but before actions that affect the principal's welfare are taken. Although actions are *observable* at the second stage (in addition to the outcomes of such actions), deviations from optimal risk-sharing arrangements are required to

* We would like to thank the seminar participants at Chicago, Northwestern, Pennsylvania, Columbia, MIT, Santa Barbara, London School of Economics, Nuffield College (Oxford), Churchill College (Cambridge), and London Business School for their comments. Special thanks are due to Franklin Allen, Ed Green, Milt Harris, Oliver Hart, Bengt Holmström, David Kreps, Jim Mirrlees, and Robert Wilson; all responsibility for errors rests with us. The first author received support from a Batterymarch fellowship while the second was supported by the Stanford Program in Finance.

0022-0531/85 $3.00
Copyright © 1985 by Academic Press, Inc.
All rights of reproduction in any form reserved.

induce revelation of information at the initial stage. Thus, the problem combines those of delegation and screening.

One obvious context in which these considerations arise is the employment of portfolio managers. Here a principal must hire from a pool of managers having unobservable forcasting abilities. Once a manager is hired he receives private pieces of information about security returns which he then uses to make portfolio decisions. By considering the general problem in this setting we are able to establish some useful connections between, as well as extensions of, the literatures on agency theory (Ross [17]), contingent contracting (Bhattacharya [4]), and the elicitation of probability beliefs (Savage [19]). Constructive solutions are derived under the assumption that payoffs are normally distributed and these provide a rich basis for developing models of dencentralized investment management under asymmetric information.[1] At this point, however, our results should be seen as suggestive ones for normative applications, rather than predictions about actual practice in complex environments.

Several very recent papers in the information economics literature are related to our work in this paper, and two of these, in particular, should be mentioned as alternative approaches. Along with us, Holmström [9] has examined an agency theory problem in which (nonpecuniary) effort-dis-utility costs to the agent are nonexistent, and risk-sharing with the agent is unimportant for a large principal (e.g., a syndicate). All difficulties in motivating principal-optimal actions arise because of the heterogeneity of agents. Holmström's focus is quite different from ours, however, since in his formulation of the problem all parties have symmetric information about abilities at the precontracting stage. Over time learning about this ability variable occurs. The wage revisions which result create a conflict between the risk-neutral principal's desired action-choice criterion and that of the risk-averse agent. Holmström does not consider (even approximately) optimal principal-agent contracts in this multiperiod model. Instead, he shows that in a multiperiod world in which beliefs about abilities are revised, contracts which would be optimal in a single-period setting produce suboptimal action choices.

Since we restrict our investigation to a one period setting, learning about ability has no role to play in our analysis. More general formulations will, of course, permit reward structures to depend upon an agent's historical performance. However, in some contexts, especially in the portfolio delegation problem we consider here, the opportunity to observe historical performance may have little value. In a companion paper (Pfleiderer and Bhatacharya [14]) we have discussed some of the difficulties encountered

[1] Previous work in this area, by Heckerman [8] and Sharpe [20], assumed that the precision of the manager's forecasts was common knowledge.

in identifying superior forecasting ability through the statistical evaluation of portfolio returns. We conclude that in many realistic cases it will be difficult to distinguish between agents who react to past returns ("chartists") and agents who have truly valuable information and act in anticipation of future returns. Moreover, to obtain accurate appraisals of ability, inordinately long time series of data may be required.[2] Given these problems, a compensation scheme which encourages managers to reveal truthfully their own beliefs about their predictive abilities as well as their actual predictions should be incrementally useful. In this paper we therefore explicitly account for the fact that a manager's behavior will be endogenously determined by the evaluation and reward schemes employed.

The second piece of related work is Allen [2]. Considered in that paper is the problem of finding the optimal contract design for a risk-averse seller of information who must convince buyers that he is indeed informed. This differs from what follows in two importnt ways. First, Allen's informed sellers are the mechanism designers who know all their private information at the time of contract choice. Second, buyers in his model are sufficiently numerous so that their quantitative willingness to pay is not an additional constraint for the seller's maximization problem. In contrast, our approach focuses much more on the information buyer's (principal's) problem of surplus extraction from the agent. The two approaches differ in the resulting characterizations and information requirements in ways that are of interest to any potential general equilibrium extensions of these types of models. These connections are discussed following the presentation of our results.

Finally, we comment on the relation between the results obtained here and the voluminous statistics literature on truthful elicitation of probability beliefs.[3] Oftentimes these elicitation procedures employ scoring rules which make use of all the moments of the elicited distribution in a rather inflexible fashion. Use of these rules in contract design leaves little room for the attainment of other goals. We show here that far less information (and inflexibility) is required for the elicitation of means in the case of symmetric distributions. As a result, our model admits a rather simple parameterization that allows one to meet both the screening and surplus extraction objectives. In addition to its immediate application to the portfolio delegation problem, this simplification may prove useful in other contexts as well. Our results augment those that have been obtained for other payoff distributions which have special supports, e.g., the two-outcome supports in Matthews [11] and the framework found in Page [13].

The organization of this paper is as follows. In Section 2, we set out the

---

[2] Related problems have been considered in Roll [15], Dybvig and Ross [6], and Admati and Ross [1].

[3] See, e.g., Savage [19] and deFinetti [7].

general problem and show that sharing rules that are optimal without *ex ante* (precontracting) heterogeneity of agents can lead to perverse results with heterogeneity. This section is closely related to the work of Wilson [21], which stimulated our initial thinking on the problem. In Section 3, we introduce an alternative scheme, and prove its ability to elicit truthfully an agent's forecasts when the underlying distribution is symmetric. This is done *without* knowledge of the (risk-averse) agent's preferences. In Section 4, we fully characterize the screening model that is based on this structure. Given knowledge of agents' preferences, one can write contracts which induce agents to self-select by predictive ability, i.e., precision of forecasts. In Section 5, which concludes the paper, we briefly discuss the possibility of incorporating into the model (a) unknown agent preferences, (b) the employment of multiple agents, and (c) unobservable precision-augmenting actions which the agent might take and which have nonpecuniary costs, i.e., moral hazard.

2. Model Structure and Linear Sharing Rules

We consider the problem faced by a principal, with wealth W_0, who has the opportunity to invest in two assets. For simplicity, each asset has constant returns to scale payoffs. One asset is riskless and pays a gross rate of return R. The second is risky with normally distributed gross rate of return $\tilde{P}$,

$$\tilde{P} \sim N(\bar{P}, \sigma_P^2). \tag{1}$$

Thus, $\bar{P}$ is the *ex ante* expected return and σ_P^2 is the unconditional variance of this return.

Our principal is aware of the existence of agents who are capable, if employed in portfolio management activity, of receiving noisy signals about $\tilde{P}$, given by

$$\tilde{S} = \tilde{P} + \tilde{\varepsilon}, \tag{2a}$$

where $\tilde{\varepsilon}$ is uncorrelated with $\tilde{P}$, and normally distributed with mean zero and variance σ_ε^2.

$$\tilde{\varepsilon} \sim N(0, \sigma_\varepsilon^2). \tag{2b}$$

It is assumed that both σ_ε^2 and $\tilde{S}$ are private information to the agent. It is useful to state the same specification in terms of the normal posterior distribution of $\tilde{P}$ conditional on $\tilde{S} = S$, given by

$$(\tilde{P} \mid \tilde{S} = S) \sim N\left(M(S), \frac{1}{H}\right), \tag{3}$$

where $M(S)$ is the conditional mean, obtained from (1), (2a), (2b) and Bayes rule. That is,

$$\mathbf{M}(S) = KS + (1 - K)\,\bar{P},\qquad(4)$$

where K is the regression coefficient of $\tilde{P}$ on $\tilde{S}$, given by

$$K = \frac{\sigma_P^2}{\sigma_P^2 + \sigma_\varepsilon^2} \equiv \rho^2.\qquad(5)$$

In the same fashion the agent's precision H, the inverse of his conditional variance of returns, is given by

$$H^{-1} = \mathrm{Var}(\tilde{P} \mid \tilde{S} = S) = \mathrm{Var}(\tilde{P}) - K^2\,\mathrm{Var}(\tilde{S})$$

$$= \sigma_P^2 - \frac{\sigma_P^4}{(\sigma_P^2 + \sigma_\varepsilon^2)^2}(\sigma_P^2 + \sigma_\varepsilon^2)$$

$$= \frac{\sigma_P^2 \sigma_\varepsilon^2}{(\sigma_P^2 + \sigma_\varepsilon^2)}.\qquad(6)$$

Since all random variables are normally distributed, the conditional variance of $\tilde{P}$ does not depend on the particular realized value of $\tilde{S}$.

It is also common knowledge that agents of differing precision are ranked by the criterion of (Blackwell [5]) sufficiency, so that hiring more than one agent is unproductive for a principal. In the present context, this means that if for two agents A and B, $H_A = H_B$, then $\tilde{\varepsilon}_A = \tilde{\varepsilon}_B$ and if $H_A > H_B$, then there exists a normal random variable $\tilde{\pi}$, uncorrelated with $\tilde{P}$ and $\tilde{\varepsilon}_A$, such that $\tilde{\varepsilon}_B = \tilde{\varepsilon}_A + \tilde{\pi}$.[4] The principal also believes that in the population, agents of differing precision H are distributed according to a distribution function $\mathbf{F}(H)$, having continuous density $\mathbf{f}(H)$, and compact support $[\underline{H}, \bar{H}]$. Further the principal is either himself capable, or is aware of an agent who is capable, of receiving information with precision level H_0, where $H_0 \in (\underline{H}, \bar{H})$. The principal's goal is to attract agents with precision levels at least as high as H_0, while screening out agents with lower precision levels. At the same time the principal wants to ensure that (i) the hired agent is not paid too much, and that (ii) the agent accurately reveals information about $\tilde{P}$ once hired, given his reward structure.

The principal knows that agents of higher ability or precision are also more capable in alternative employment, and therefore have nonstochastic reservation wages $r(H)$ that are increasing in H. The function $r(\cdot)$ is common knowledge. For a given reward scheme offered by the principal, the

---

[4] We shall consider relaxing this assumption in Section 5.

supply of agents attracted is drawn only from the subset of $[\underline{H}, \bar{H}]$ for which the maximized expected utility of the agent exceeds the utility of receiving $r(H)$. If the principal falls back on the reservation precision level (by managing the portfolio himself), he incurs a direct or an opportunity cost of $r(H_0)$. We discuss some essential properties of the sampling process from this acceptance set before setting out the formal structure in more detail.

In most of our detailed results to follow, we shall be concerned with a large principal (e.g., a syndicate of investors), for whom the efficiency of risk-sharing (payment) arrangements with the agent is unimportant, relative to the task of screening out agents with precisions below H_0. If the sample size of agents that a reward scheme elicited were independent of the size (measure w.r.t. $F(H)$) of the associated acceptance set, a rather simple contract might arise. Our large principal would offer to pay an agent $r(\bar{H})$, no matter what he said about his precision, but put him to work managing his portfolio only if his disclosed precision exceeds H_0. (An obvious extension exists if disutility of monitorable work requires differential wage D; the nonworking agent is paid $r(\bar{H}) - D$.) We rule out this solution by assuming that the number of sampled agents who would need to be paid is an increasing function of the measure of the acceptance set with the limit being infinite as that measure approaches unity.[5] Of course, the size of the sampled set will also be important in any screening scheme. We abstract from these problems by assuming that N, the number of agents sampled, is equal to one when agents with abilities less than H_0 are screened out.[6]

Having explained the nature of the sampling process for agents, we now describe the principal's problem of designing a suitable reward scheme as below. We shall assume in this section, as well as Section 4, that the Von Neuman–Morgenstern utility function shared by all potential agents, $U_A(\cdot)$, is common knowledge and is given by

$$\mathbf{U}_A(\tilde{W}_A) = -\exp(-a\tilde{W}_A). \tag{7a}$$

---

[5] We are grateful to Oliver Hart for discussions on this issue. It illustrates the degree to which one must be careful when dealing with a principal who does not care about risk-sharing (efficiency of payments to agent) because of his size, rather than inherent risk-neutrality.

[6] Allowing for more than one agent in the sampled set (i.e., $N > 1$) would merely complicate each agent's objective function and the conditions for screening since each agent would need to calculate and account for the probability of being the highest precision agent sampled. Incentives for strategic misrepresentation of precision would arise in some situations. Note that this will not be a problem if the reward structure extracts all of the agent's surplus. The scheme developed in Section 4 does just that and would therefore be viable in settings where $N > 1$. Further discussion of this point follows Proposition 3.

W_A is the agent's (stochastic) wealth, paid at the end of the period and given by

$$\tilde{W}_A = f(h, m(\tilde{M}, h), \tilde{P}). \tag{8}$$

The function $f: [\underline{H}, \bar{H}] \times \Re^2 \to \Re$ is the payoff scheme for the agent, determining his reward as a function of (a) his announced precision h, (b) his announced conditional mean $m(M, h)$, and (c) the *ex post* return on the asset $\tilde{P}$.

We can now turn to the principal's problem. We shall assume that the principal, like the agent, has constant absolute risk aversion:

$$U_B(\tilde{W}_B) = -\exp(-b\tilde{W}_B), \tag{7b}$$

where $\tilde{W}_B$ is the principal's end of period wealth. This wealth is in part determined by the principal's rule for portfolio construction. Such a rule gives for each report (m, h) which the agent might submit, the amount of money to be invested in the risky asset. Let this amount be denoted by $\omega(m, h)$ and recall that the remaining wealth, $W_0 - \omega(m, h)$, will be invested in the riskless asset. This portfolio policy can be implemented directly by the principal. In that case, the agent's only role is one of passing information to the principal. Alternatively, one can assume that the agent himself adjusts the portfolio position for the principal after having stated his claimed precision h. *Ex post*, the principal observes both the total dollar amount in his account, and the portfolio composition the agent had picked. The agent's announced $m(M, h)$ is then recovered using the principal's preannounced portfolio choice function $\omega(m, h)$. Since no problems of commitment by the principal to the payoff scheme exist, we can without loss of generality restrict ourselves to truthful direct revelation mechanisms (Myerson [12]) which satisfy, for all M,

$$M \in \text{Arg} \max_m \, \mathscr{E}^H_{(\tilde{P})} \{ U_A(f(H, m, \tilde{P})) \mid \tilde{M} = M \}, \tag{9a}$$

and the additional condition that

$$H \in \text{Arg} \max_h \, \mathscr{E}^H_{(\tilde{M}, \tilde{P})} \{ U_A(f(h, \bar{m}(M, h), \tilde{P})) \}, \tag{10}$$

where the function $\bar{m}(M, h)$ embodies the possibility that the agent might prefer to lie about M in the second stage if he does not tell the truth about H in the first, i.e.,

$$\bar{m}(M, h) \in \text{Arg} \max_m \, \mathscr{E}^H_{(\tilde{P})} \{ U_A(f(h, m, \tilde{P})) \mid \tilde{M} = M \}. \tag{9b}$$

In Eqs. (9a), (9b), and (10) the superscript H on the expectations operator $\mathscr{E}\{\cdot\}$ serves to remind us that the joint distribution, $(\tilde{P}, \tilde{M})$, and the conditional distribution, $(\tilde{P} \mid \tilde{M} = M)$, depend upon the agent's precision; the functional dependence of (m, h) on H is implicit.

The acceptance set of agents that results from a particular reward scheme $f(\cdot)$ is then given by

$$\mathscr{H}(f(\cdot)) = \{H \mid \mathscr{E}^H_{(\tilde{M},\tilde{P})}\{\mathbf{U}_A(f(H, \tilde{M}, \tilde{P}))\} \geqslant \mathbf{V}(H)\}, \qquad (11a)$$

where

$$\mathbf{V}(H) = \mathbf{U}_A(r(H)) = -\exp(-ar(H)) \qquad (11b)$$

The principal's problem then is to find functions $f(h, m, \tilde{P})$ and $\omega(m, h)$ that maximize his expected utility subject to the constraints of Eqs. (9a), (9b), (10), and (11). We shall write this objective function under the assumptions that a single agent is randomly sampled, learns about $f(\cdot)$, and accepts employment if his $H \in \mathscr{H}$. The agent then reveals his H and is put to work managing the portfolio. For this problem we shall find an approximately optimal solution (for a large principal) which screens out all $H \leqslant H_0$, i.e., $\mathscr{H} = [H_0, \bar{H}]$.

Formally, the principal chooses $f(H, \tilde{M}, \tilde{P})$ and $\omega(M, H)$, subject to the constraints already mentioned, to maximize

$$C_1 + C_2 \Pr\{H \notin \mathscr{H}(f(\cdot))\}, \qquad (12a)$$

where

$$C_1 = \int_{H \in \mathscr{H}(f(\cdot))} \mathscr{E}^H_{(\tilde{M},\tilde{P})}\{\mathbf{U}_B(W_0 R + \omega(\tilde{M}, H)(\tilde{P} - R) - f(H, \tilde{M}, \tilde{P}))\} \, d\mathbf{F}(H) \qquad (12b)$$

represents the principal's expected utility from hiring outside agents with superior forecasting ability, and

$$C_2 = \mathscr{E}^{H_0}_{(\tilde{M},\tilde{P})}\{\mathbf{U}_B(W_0 R + \omega(\tilde{M}, H_0)(\tilde{P} - R) - r(H_0))\} \qquad (12c)$$

represents his expected utility from managing with the inside agent having precision H_0. As mentioned above, the latter option incurs an opportunity cost of $r(H_0)$. Screening out agents with H below H_0 will often be achieved by deviating from first-best risk-sharing, and since the H_0-agent can be employed at a sure cost of $r(H_0)$, the principal might well optimize by screening out agents with precisions H somewhat above H_0. These subtleties will be eliminated in our approximately optimal solution for a large principal, having (in effect) a very low risk-aversion coefficient. Essentially, as we increase the size of the principal by increasing the number of investors in the syndicate, the cost of paying the agent per principal will tend to decline to zero, and it is only the screening properties of the scheme that will matter. When the principal is not large, a more elaborate scheme which allows the probability of employment to vary with the H disclosed might be desirable.[7]

We now examine the performance (under our type of agent heterogeneity) of first-best optimal reward schemes that would be incentive compatible if H were common knowledge and only $\tilde{M}$ were private information. Wilson [21] has shown that whenever first-best optimal sharing rules are linear, truthful revelation of information, followed by a first-best optimal action is incentive compatible when the distribution of information signals *and* reservation utility are common knowledge.[8] If we assume that the principal, like the agent, has preferences represented by a negative exponential utility function, then first-best sharing rules are linear. An optimal reward scheme in this setting (with constant returns to scale investments) simply consists of giving the agent a current fee A and allowing him to invest in the risky asset as he wishes. Truthful revelation of $\{H, M\}$ by the agent is (weakly) incentive compatible. Since the agent is allowed to invest, his total second-period wealth will be given by

$$f(M, H, \tilde{P}) = AR + \omega_A(M, H)(\tilde{P} - R), \tag{13a}$$

where $\omega_A(M, H)$ is the amount invested. The optimal investment rule solves,

$$\max_{\omega} \mathscr{E}^H_{(\tilde{P})} \{ -\exp - a[AR + \omega(\tilde{P} - R)] \mid \tilde{M} = M \}$$

$$= \max_{\omega} -\exp - a\left[AR + \omega(M - R) - \frac{a\,\omega^2}{2\,H} \right]. \tag{13b}$$

This is maximized at $\omega(M, H)$ given by

$$\omega_A(M, H) = \frac{H(M - R)}{a}. \tag{13c}$$

---

[7] The optimal auction design model of Matthews [11] has this characteristic. This, however, is derived in a simple setting where (a) the principal is risk-neutral, and where (b) no adverse selection problem exists, i.e., the seller is concerned only with the payments received from the buyer, and not with the buyer's attributes *per se*. In addition, the auction outcome is dichotomous for each agent.

[8] This is related to Ross's [17] result that there is unanimity regarding the optimal action whenever the Pareto-efficient sharing rules are linear. One can think of revelation of information followed by choice of (conditionally) Pareto-efficient action as delegated choice of action.

The agent's resulting conditional expected utility is

$$\mathscr{E}\{\mathbf{U}_A(\cdot) \mid M, H\} = -\exp - a\left(AR + \frac{(M-R)^2 H}{2a}\right). \tag{14}$$

Clearly, this scheme is incentive-compatible when H is privately known to the agent if and only if $A(H)$ does not depend on H. This simple observation is formalized as Proposition 1, following which we look at the structure of the acceptance set $\mathscr{H}$ that results from such a (naive) scheme.

PROPOSITION 1. *Let the reward scheme for the agent be described by*

$$f(h, m, \tilde{P}) = \alpha(h, m) + \beta(h, m)(\tilde{P} - R), \tag{15a}$$

where $\alpha(\cdot)$, $\beta(\cdot)$ are differentiable functions of their arguments. Then, $f(\cdot)$ is incentive-compatible (truth-revealing) and consistent with first-best risk-sharing if and only if $\alpha(h, m) = A$, some constant.

Proof. As in Eq. (14), the agent's expected utility conditional on H and M is easily computed to be

$$\mathscr{E}\{\mathbf{U}_A(f(h, m, \tilde{P})) \mid M, H\}$$

$$= -\exp - a\left[\alpha(h, m) + \beta(h, m)(M - R) - \frac{\alpha(\beta(h, m))^2}{2H}\right]. \tag{15b}$$

Maximizing in (15b) with respect to m gives the first-order condition (dropping arguments of functions),

$$\frac{\partial \alpha(\cdot)}{\partial m} + \frac{\partial \beta(\cdot)}{\partial m}\left[(M - R) - \frac{\alpha\beta(\cdot)}{H}\right] = 0$$

or

$$\beta(h, m(M)) = \frac{H}{a}\left[(M - R) + \frac{\partial \alpha(\cdot)/\partial m}{\partial \beta(\cdot)/\partial m}\right]. \tag{15c}$$

If (15c) is to be consistent with (13c) for every M, then $\partial \alpha/\partial m = 0$. Thus $\alpha(h, m) = \hat{\alpha}(h)$. The agent's expected utility unconditional on M is therefore given by

$$\mathscr{E}^H_{(\tilde{P},\tilde{M})}\{\mathbf{U}_A(f(\cdot))\} = [-\exp - a(\hat{\alpha}(h))]$$

$$\times \left[\mathscr{E}^H_{(\tilde{P},\tilde{M})}\left\{\exp - a\left(\frac{H}{a}(\tilde{P} - R)(\tilde{M} - R)\right)\right\}\right]. \tag{15d}$$

From this it is clear that only $\hat{\alpha}(h) = A$, some constant, is incentive compatible for direct revelation of H. ∎

Proposition 1 illustrates the importance of the incentive-compatibility constraints (9b) and (10). Namely, the agent can (with this type of linear scheme) always compensate for the lie about H by also misrepresenting M, so that $\beta(M, h)$ continues to satisfy (15c). In the next section, we consider a structure in which such compensating lies are not possible, i.e., $m(M, h) = M$ is optimal no matter what claimed h is, thus allowing for a separation of the problems of probability elicitation and screening of H by self-selection. Before doing so, we conclude this section with a diagrammatic look at the nature of the acceptance set $\mathcal{H}(f(\cdot))$ brought about by $f(\cdot)$ satisfying Eq. (13a). This makes clear the problems which arise when only $A(h) = A$ is incentive compatible. To determine the acceptance set one must first evaluate the H-type agent's unconditional expected utility.

$$\mathcal{E}^H U_A(f(\cdot)) \equiv \mathcal{E}^H_{(\tilde{P},\tilde{M})}\left\{ -\exp - a\left[AR + \frac{H}{a}(\tilde{M} - R)(\tilde{P} - R) \right]\right\}$$

In Appendix A we show that this is equal to

$$\mathcal{E}^H U_A(f(\cdot)) = \frac{-1}{\sigma_P H^{1/2}} \exp - a\left[AR + \frac{(\bar{P} - R)^2}{2a\sigma_P^2} \right]. \tag{16}$$

The acceptance set of the agents can be graphed by asking the *minimum* $A(H)$ for which the H-type agent will work. This minimum level, call it $A_0(H)$, satisfies

$$aA_0(H)R + \frac{(\bar{P} - R)^2}{2\sigma_P^2} + \log \sigma_P + \tfrac{1}{2}\log H = -\log(-V(H)). \tag{17}$$

Similarly, we can calculate the *ex ante* payment $B_0(H)$ made to an agent having precision H that leaves the principal indifferent between hiring that agent and hiring an agent of ability H_0 and paying him $r(H_0)$ ex post. Using the fact that the principal's optimal investment in the risky asset is $H(M - R)/b$, it can be shown that $B_0(H)$ must solve

$$\frac{-1}{\sigma_P H^{1/2}} \exp - b\left[(W_0 - B_0(H))R + \frac{(\bar{P} - R)^2}{2b\sigma_P^2} \right]$$

$$= \frac{-1}{\sigma_P H_0^{1/2}} \exp - b\left[\left(W_0 - \frac{r(H_0)}{R}\right)R + \frac{(\bar{P} - R)^2}{2b\sigma_P^2} \right]. \tag{18a}$$

Solving this we obtain

$$B_0(H) = \frac{1}{2bR} \log\left(\frac{H}{H_0}\right) - \frac{r(H_0)}{R}. \tag{18b}$$

It is clear from (18b) that $B_0(H)$ is increasing in H. However, from Eq. (17), we see that $A_0(H)$ can either be decreasing in H or increasing in H. If $V(H)$—equivalently $r(H)$—is either constant or rises sufficiently slowly in H, $A_0(H)$ decreases in H. This is shown in Fig. 1a. If, however, $r(H)$ increases sufficiently rapidly with H, then $A_0(H)$ is an increasing function. This gives us Case II which is plotted in Fig. 1b. These two cases have quite different screening properties.

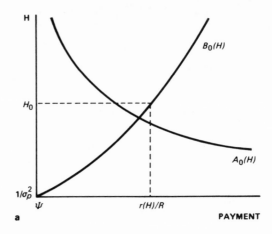

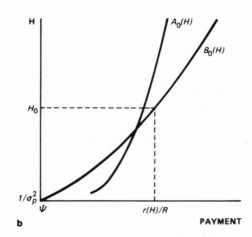

FIG. 1. Screening with linear sharing rules.

In Case I a high precision agent is willing to accept a lower fee than a lower precision agent. This willingness to accept lower nominal compensation is a consequence of our assumption that managers only acquire their private information about investment opportunities when they are employed in portfolio management. Since the reward scheme being discussed allows agents to use the information they uncover in constructing their own portfolios, they realize directly the value of their information. In Case I the difference between the value of the information received by a high precision manager and the same for a low precision manager is greater than the difference between their alternative employment wages. For this reason the less competent will demand higher payment. In this situation, it is clear that the principal can easily screen out all the agents for whom $A_0(H) \leqslant B_0(H)$ by offering a suitably chosen A. The same is not true for Case II. Any A that attracts $H \geqslant H_0$, for example, also attracts agents with $H < H_0$. In its spirit, Case I is similar to the problem analyzed in Matthews [11], where a small principal has then the further problem of maximizing expected residual gain by deviating from this optimal risk-sharing arrangement. Here, we are much more concerned with Case II. Note that the horizontal coordinate of the origin in Fig. 1b, Ψ, can be significantly negative. This possibility shows why screening out agents with $H < H_0$ is important to the principal. In the next two sections we develop a scheme that can achieve this screening.

3. Revelation of Means for Symmetric Distributions

In the last section it was shown that linear reward structures are not always successful in discriminating against low ability agents. Their limited range of application is due to the fact that contracts which meet first best risk sharing objectives and which vary their terms in response to announced precision are not incentive compatible. An agent can correct for the consequences of misrepresenting his ability in the first stage by lying about his forecast in the second stage. In this section we find a reward scheme, $f(h, m, \tilde{P})$, that guarantees truthful revelation of means no matter what was said about ability in the first stage. This separates the agency and screening problems. The form of $f(h, m, \tilde{P})$, does not depend on the details of agents preferences and therefore has a certain degree of robustness, i.e., adaptability to other preferences structures. Moreover, it induces truthful revelation in any case where the underlying conditional distribution is symmetric. Normality is not necessary. One such scheme is presented in Proposition 2 and a general class of schemes is identified in Proposition 4 following a discussion of the screening problem.

PROPOSITION 2. *Let the reward scheme $f(m, \tilde{P})$ be given by*

$$f(m, \tilde{P}) = \gamma_1 - \gamma_2(\tilde{P} - m)^2 \tag{19a}$$

with $\gamma_2 > 0$, and assume that the distribution function of $\tilde{P}$ conditional on $\tilde{M} = M$ is symmetric. Then, for any weakly risk-averse agent, $m = M$ is an optimal revelation.

Proof. To show that

$$M \in \text{Arg} \max_m \mathscr{E}^H_{(\tilde{P})}\{ U_A(f(h, m, \tilde{P})) \mid \tilde{M} = M \},$$

we can complete the square in Eq. (19a) and note that

$$f(m, \tilde{P}) = \gamma_1 - \gamma_2[(\tilde{P} - M)^2 + 2(\tilde{P} - M)(M - m) + (M - m)^2]. \tag{19b}$$

For symmetric distributions

$$\mathscr{E}[(\tilde{P} - M) \mid (\tilde{P} - M)^2 = \delta] = 0, \qquad \forall \delta \geqslant 0. \tag{19c}$$

Thus, from Rothschild–Stiglitz [18], the $f(m, \tilde{P})$ distribution obtained by telling the truth, i.e., setting $m = M$, dominates that obtained from lying, in the sense of second-degree stochastic dominance. Hence, any (weakly) risk-averse agent optimizes by setting $m = M$. ∎

Notice that for the case of a conditionally normally distributed $\tilde{P}$, the log likelihood ratio rule of Savage [19] would set the *utility* of the agent given P equal to the logarithm of normal density at P given (h, m). This payoff, for the case of a *risk-neutral* agent, is indeed proportional to $(P - m)^2$ for the normal. What we have in Proposition 2 is a far more robust result that can be utilized for (i) any risk-averse preference structure, and (ii) an associated screening problem in which predictive ability (precision H) is not only elicited, but also where it is important to screen out agents with low H, by making sure that they do not receive their opportunity expected utility in this activity.

Before taking up this screening problem, we wish to point out a simple but useful extension of Proposition 2. If $\tilde{P}$ is not symmetrically distributed, but some exogenously given function of it is, then $\tilde{P}$ can be replaced by that function. For example, $\log(\tilde{P})$ could be substituted for $\tilde{P}$ if the conditional distribution were log-normal. This will induce truthful revelation of $\mathscr{E}(\log(\tilde{P}))$ and since the forecast variance of $\log(\tilde{P})$ will also be truthfully revealed, $\mathscr{E}(\tilde{P})$ will also be recoverable.

4. SCREENING AGENTS WITH PRIVATELY KNOWN PRECISIONS

For the purposes of screening of truthful precision H, the structure discussed previously in Proposition 2 must be modified to a parametric form that inherits the truthful revelation of M property. Consider the reward structure

$$f(m, h, \tilde{P}) = \frac{1}{a} \log \gamma_1(h) - \frac{1}{a} \gamma_2(h)(\tilde{P} - m)^2, \tag{20}$$

where $\gamma_1(\cdot)$, $\gamma_1(\cdot)$ are functions that are endogenized below. Given the implication that $m(M, h) = M$ for all M in (9b), we can investigate satisfaction of (10), i.e., truthful revelation of H, by computing the expected utility of an agent of type H who claims to be of type h, i.e.,

$$\mathbf{E}(h, H; \gamma_1(\cdot), \gamma_2(\cdot)) \equiv \mathscr{E}^H_{(\tilde{P}, \tilde{M})} \left\{ -\exp -a \left[\frac{1}{a} \log \gamma_1(h) - \frac{1}{a} \gamma_2(h)(\tilde{P} - \tilde{M})^2 \right] \right\}$$

$$= \frac{-1}{\gamma_1(h)(1 - 2\gamma_2(h)/H)^{1/2}}. \tag{21}$$

The calculations implicit in Eq. (21) are to be found in Appendix B. It is assumed in this calculation that $\gamma_2(h) < H/2$. This is required for convergence of the expected utility integrals. It is easy to show that the distribution of wealth obtained by the agent when this inequality is violated is dominated by every distribution which can be obtained when the inequality is observed.

Let us first find conditions under which Eq. (10) is satisfied, i.e.,

$$H \in \operatorname*{Arg\,max}_{h} \mathbf{E}(h, H; \gamma_1(h), \gamma_2(h)), \tag{22}$$

and the agent's reservation utility schedule is achieved as an equality for all H, i.e., complete surplus extraction (given the contract form) occurs. For the latter condition to hold, $\gamma_1(\cdot)$ and $\gamma_2(\cdot)$ must satisfy

$$\forall H, \qquad \mathbf{E}(H, H; \gamma_1(\cdot), \gamma_2(\cdot)) = \mathbf{V}(H). \tag{23}$$

Observe that if (22) and (23) can be satisfied, the principal can easily exclude agents with $H \leqslant H_0$ by modifying $\gamma_1(h)$ to $\gamma_1(h) - e$ for some $e > 0$ and for all $h \leqslant H_0$; the condition (23) is not necessary for this exclusion however.

Assuming that $\gamma_1(\cdot)$ and $\gamma_1(\cdot)$ are twice-differentiable, the necessary conditions for (22) and (23) to hold can be expressed as follows. From the first-order condition in (22), letting $\mathbf{E}_1 \equiv \partial \mathbf{E}/\partial h$ and $\mathbf{E}_2 \equiv \partial \mathbf{E}/\partial H$, it must be that along $h(H) = H$,

$$\mathbf{E}_1 = 0. \tag{24a}$$

From the total differential of (22), we know that along $h(H) = H$,

$$\mathbf{E}_1 + \mathbf{E}_2 = \mathbf{V}'(H). \tag{24b}$$

If we combine (24b) with (24a), we see that

$$\forall H, \qquad \mathbf{E}_2(h = H, H; \gamma_1(\cdot), \gamma_2(\cdot)) = \mathbf{V}'(H). \tag{25}$$

Equations (21), (23), and (25) turn out to be sufficient to solve explicitly for $\gamma_1(h)$ and $\gamma_2(h)$. Using (21), Eq. (25) can be re-expressed as

$$\mathbf{E}_2 = -\mathbf{E} \times \left[\frac{\gamma_2(H)}{H^4(1 - 2\gamma_2(H)/H)} \right].$$

This can be combined with (23) to yield

$$\frac{\gamma_2(H)}{H^2(1 - 2\gamma_2(H)/H)} = -\frac{\mathbf{V}'(H)}{\mathbf{V}(H)},$$

or

$$\gamma_2(H) = \left[\frac{2}{H} - \frac{\mathbf{V}(H)}{H^2 \mathbf{V}'(H)} \right]^{-1}. \tag{26}$$

Note that our earlier restriction that $\gamma_2(h)$ be less than $H/2$ is satisfied along the equilibrium schedule $h(H) = H$, since $\mathbf{V}' > 0$ and $\mathbf{V} < 0$. The solution for $\gamma_1(H)$ is now obtained, using (23) and (26) as

$$\gamma_1(H) = \frac{-1}{\mathbf{V}(H)[1 - 2\gamma_2(H)/H]^{1/2}}. \tag{27}$$

We now examine the conditions which guarantee that the agent achieves the global optimum when the announced precision h is set equal to the true precision H. We do this on two teps. First, we show that under a contract using the functions $\gamma_1(\cdot)$ and $\gamma_2(\cdot)$ given in (27) and (26), the first-order condition (24a) for a critical point can be met only at $h = H$. Second, we evaluate the second-order condition for a maximum at this critical point. This condition depends upon the shape of the reservation utility schedule and we find it easy to show that it is satisfied for a broad class of schedules.

For the first step, we use (21) to note that

$$\mathbf{E}_1(h, H) = -\mathbf{E}\left[\frac{\gamma_1'(h)}{\gamma_1(h)} - \frac{\gamma_2'(h)}{H(1 - 2\gamma_2(h)/H)}\right]. \tag{28}$$

We know from the derivation of $\{\gamma_1(H), \gamma_2(H)\}$ that $\mathbf{E}_1(h = H, H) = 0$. Suppose there also exists $\bar{h} \neq H$, such that $\mathbf{E}_1(\bar{h}, H) = 0$. Using (28), this contrapositive implies that

$$\left[\frac{\gamma_2'(\bar{h})}{H - 2\gamma_2(\bar{h})}\right] = \left[\frac{\gamma_1'(\bar{h})}{\gamma_1(\bar{h})}\right] = \left[\frac{\gamma_2'(\bar{h})}{\bar{h} - 2\gamma_2(\bar{h})}\right], \tag{28'}$$

since $\mathbf{E}_1((\bar{h}, \bar{h}) = 0$, by construction of $\gamma(\cdot)$ and $\gamma_2(\cdot)$. Clearly, for $\gamma_2'(\bar{h}) \neq 0$, (28') cannot be met.

Now look at the second-order condition for a (local) maximum at $h = H$ in (22). This condition is simply

$$\mathbf{E}_{11} < 0, \tag{29a}$$

and it can be used to obtain conditions on E_{12} and E_{22}. To do that we look at the total differential of (24a) along $h(H) = H$, i.e.,

$$\mathbf{E}_{11} + \mathbf{E}_{12} = 0, \tag{29b}$$

and the same for (24b), i.e.,

$$\mathbf{E}_{12} + \mathbf{E}_{22} = \mathbf{V}''(H). \tag{29c}$$

Combining (29a), (29b), (29c), we find that

$$\forall H, \qquad \mathbf{V}''(H) - \mathbf{E}_{22}(h = H, H; \gamma_1(\cdot), \gamma_2(\cdot)) > 0. \tag{30}$$

These conditions are closely related to those derived in Bhattacharya [4].

Since $\mathbf{E}_{22}$ is completely determined by the contract structure, (30) should be viewed as a condition which must be met by the reservation utility schedule if the reward structure given in (26) and (27) is to be viable. From (21) we obtain that

$$\mathbf{E}_2 = -\mathbf{E} \times \left[\frac{\gamma_2(h)}{H^2(1 - 2\gamma_2(h)/H)}\right], \tag{31a}$$

$$\mathbf{E}_{22} = \mathbf{E} \times \left[\frac{3(\gamma_2(h))^2}{H^4(1 - 2\gamma_2(h)/H)^2} + \frac{2\gamma_2(h)}{H^3(1 - 2\gamma_2(h)/H)}\right]. \tag{31b}$$

Since $\mathbf{E} < 0$, it follows that $\mathbf{E}_{22} < 0$. Hence (30) can be met even if $\mathbf{V}'' < 0$. Write $\mathbf{V}(H)$ in terms of the agent's alternative (end-of-period) wage as

$$\mathbf{V}(H) = -\exp - [ar(H)]. \tag{11b}$$

Using this, one can show that

$$\mathbf{V}''(H) = -ar''(H)\,\mathbf{V}(H) + a^2(r'(H))^2\,\mathbf{V}(H). \tag{32}$$

In interpreting (32) it should be remembered that $\mathbf{V}(H)$ is a negative quantity. Using our solution for $\gamma_2(\cdot)$ given in (26), (31b) can be simplified to to

$$\mathbf{E}_{22} = \mathbf{V}(H)\left[3\left(\frac{-\mathbf{V}'(H)}{\mathbf{V}(H)}\right)^2 + \frac{2}{H}\left(\frac{-\mathbf{V}'(H)}{\mathbf{V}(H)}\right)\right]. \tag{33}$$

Using the fact that

$$\left[\frac{\mathbf{V}'(H)}{\mathbf{V}(H)}\right] = ar'(H),$$

we now see that for (30) to be satisfied, the alternative wage schedule must satisfy

$$2a^2 r'(H)^2 + \frac{2}{H} ar'(H) + ar''(H) > 0$$

or

$$(ar'(H))^2 + \left(\frac{ar'(H)}{H}\right) > -\frac{ar''(H)}{2}. \tag{34}$$

Equation (34) is clearly satisfied if $r''(H) > 0$. Even if $r''(H) < 0$, many common concave functions like the power and the logarithmic functions, satisfy Eq. (34). More picturesquely, a sufficient condition for satisfaction of (34) is that $-Hr''(H)/r'(H) < 2$, i.e., that the relative risk aversion coefficient of the $r(H)$ function be less than 2. We have,

PROPOSITION 3. *A solution to Eqs. (22) and (23) exists if and only if the reservation wage schedule $r(H)$ satisfies Eq. (34).*

Remarks. As noted before, satisfaction of (34) everywhere is not essential to screen out agents with $H \leqslant H_0$, since agents with $H > H_0$ can be paid a surplus, if necessary. If $r''(H)$ is too concave then it is sufficient for such screening to have (22), (23) hold for the chord passing through $r(\underline{H})$ and $r(H_0)$, where $\underline{H}$ is the lowest possible precision, e.g., $1/\sigma_P^2$. However, if more than one agent is sampled, agents may have an incentive to lie in order to increase the probability of being hired from the sample set. Complete surplus extraction is sufficient to eliminate this incentive, since then every agent in the accepted set is indifferent between being hired by the principal and remaining in the alternative occurpation.

As a final step, we may come back to the principal's problem that we started with in Section 2 and ask what are the implications of a screening structure like (22), (23) for a principal's problem. As noted before, satisfaction of the screening objective imposes risks on the agent in a second-best fashion, thus implying that the expected wage payment from the principal to the agent is higher than with first-best risk-sharing. Thus, even a nearly risk-neutral principal does not necessarily wish to use this screening structure to eliminate all agents with $H < H_0$. This is counterbalanced, however, by the fact that more precise information is worth more to a less risk-averse principal, since he will be inclined to make larger investments based on it. This argument can be easily formalized by letting the principal be a syndicate of N investors, each with utility $-\exp[-bW]$ and wealth W_0, and taking the limit as $N \to \infty$ of the per capita expected utility net of wage payments to the agent which are equally shared among principals. These expected utility integrals approach the same limit for the quadratic scheme of Sections 3 and 4 and the (first-best) linear scheme of Section 2, for $H \geqslant H_0$. But, of course, the linear scheme (flat fee) is not, in Case II of Section 2 (Fig. 1), able to screen out agents with $H < H_0$. The quadratic scheme is successful in meeting this goal. Thus, for a large enough principal, the quadratic scheme dominates strictly. Details of this argument are tedious, but available on request.

5. Caveats, Qualifications, and Extensions

We believe that the simple probability elicitation *cum* screening model outlined above captures some realistic special features of portfolio management problems. Given the difficulties of evaluating accurately the precision of managerial forecasts (regarding stocks especially) with any reasonable amount of time series data, contract structures like that examined here have a serious role to play. However, several basic features of our model are restrictive, and here we wish to discuss three of them: (i) knowledge of agents' preferences by the principal, (ii) the importance of multimanager contracts, and (iii) the role of unobservable precision-augmenting actions taken by agents.

We have assumed, for the purposes of screening of H, that the principal knows that agents have exponential preferences with known risk-aversion coefficient a. In a related model, Allen [2] has considered contracts designed by information sellers, who optimize under the (credibility) constraint that even risk-neutral sellers would not offer such schedules were they uninformed. However, to infer (only) from the seller's choice of schedule something about his conditional mean and precision, the buyers have to know the seller's preferences. This is especially important (i.e., the seller cannot just tell buyers what mean and precision are) if in the aggregate buyers' willingness to pay is a function of the seller's unknown precision, a case which Allen does not emphasize.

The optimal reward scheme schedules obtained by Allen in the exponential utility and normal distributions case have the same quadratic structure as ours, but the details are different. Suppose it is assumed that the buyer knows a class restriction on the seller's preferences, i.e., it is exponential. Then the problem of solving for $\{a, M, H\}$ of the seller from the observed reward schedule, in particular its three coefficients of $(P^0, \tilde{P}, \tilde{P}^2)$, as well as prior information like $(\bar{P}, \sigma_P^2)$, is a simple linear algebra exercise in his model. (Note again that buyers' willingness to pay is not a function of inferred precision, so strategic manipulation of preferences is ignored.)

In our scheme, the principal's willingness to pay is a function of precision, not so much for the payment involved (per capita for a large syndicate) but for the associated screening and resulting management efficiency reasons. As a result, the reward structure of our model depends upon knowledge of the risk aversion parameter a, and is not robust to strategic misrepresentation of privately known preferences. However, extensions of the screening structure in Propositions 2 and 3 should be capable of eliciting unknown preferences from a finite-dimensional parametric class, as suggested by the following result.

PROPOSITION 4. *Assume that the agent's reward scheme is given by*

$$f(m, \tilde{P}) = \gamma_1 - \gamma_2 g(\tilde{P} - m) \qquad (35)$$

with $\gamma_2 > 0$ and $g(\cdot)$ a symmetric, convex (measurable) function. Assume that the distribution of $\tilde{P}$ conditional upon $\tilde{M} = M$ is symmetric. Then, for any weakly risk averse agent, $m = M$ is an optimal revelation.

Proof. Consider any pair $\{P_+, P_-\}$, such that $(P_+ - M) = (M - P_-) = \delta \geqslant 0$. By the convexity and symmetry of $g(\cdot)$ and the symmetry of $\tilde{P}$ around M, we have that

$$\mathscr{E}_{\tilde{P}}[g(\tilde{P} - M) \mid \tilde{P} \in \{P_+, P_-\}] = g(\delta)$$

and

$$\mathscr{E}_{\tilde{P}}[g(\tilde{P}-m) \mid \tilde{P} \in \{P_{+}, P_{-}\}] = \tfrac{1}{2}g(\delta + |m - M|) + \tfrac{1}{2}g(\delta - |m - M|)$$
$$\geqslant g(\delta).$$

Thus, given that the distribution of the random variable $g(\tilde{P} - M)$ conditional on $P \in \{P_{+}, P_{-}\}$ is degenerate, we have shown that

$$\mathscr{E}_{\tilde{P}}[U(f(M, \tilde{P})) \mid \tilde{P} \in \{P_{+}, P_{-}\}] \geqslant \mathscr{E}_{\tilde{P}}[U(f(m, \tilde{P})) \mid \tilde{P} \in \{P_{+}, P_{-}\}]$$

for all concave $U(\cdot)$. Since this is true for all $\delta \geqslant 0$, we have by the law of iterated expectations that

$$\mathscr{E}_{\tilde{P}}[U(f(M, \tilde{P}))] \geqslant \mathscr{E}_{\tilde{P}}[U(f(m, \tilde{P}))]. \quad \blacksquare$$

The result in Proposition 4 suggests the following type of generalization of Proposition 3. Suppose, for example, that agents' utility functions belong to an exponential family with privately known risk aversion parameter a. Then by designing a reward structure of the form

$$f(m, p, h, \hat{a}) = \gamma_1(h, \hat{a}) - \gamma_2(h, \hat{a})\, g_1(m - \tilde{P}) - \gamma_3(h, \hat{a})\, g_2(m - \tilde{P}),$$

where $g_1(\cdot)$ and $g_2(\cdot)$ are symmetric, convex functions, and $\hat{a}$ is the announced risk aversion parameter, one might be able to elicit truthfully both H and a, possibly along the lines suggested in Kohlleppel [10].

In our work, we have assumed that hiring only one agent made sense, since agents were ranked by Blackwell [5] sufficiency. If, on the other hand, multiple agents are hired, and they receive normal signals that are conditionally independent given $\tilde{P} = P$, then again it is easy to show—using the methods of Wilson [21]— that the first-best linear risk-sharing scheme has no screening by precision properties. Here again the *ex ante* payment of a flat fee, followed by both the agent and the principal taking a portfolio position based upon all (reported) information is not implementable if the fee is a nontrivial function of reported h. Indeed, unless one agent's precision communicates information about that of another's, there is no reason to expect a major change in our results when several agents are hired.

We have also assumed that agents' forecasting abilities are exogenously given, rather than being a result of unobservable, privately costly actions taken by them. Recently, Baron [3] has provided some solutions for a problem where both moral hazard and precontract heterogeneity are present. These solutions are obtained under the strong restrictions of (a) risk-neutral agents, and (b) contracts linear in other observable actions and payoffs. The linearity restriction, in particular, seems inappropriate for our problem with its two stages of private information. (Under such a restriction, the agent is able to tell compensating lies to extract surplus form the principal, and frustrate the screening objective.) It would be interesting to compare the type of restricted contracts we consider with those examined by Baron, in a setting with multiple stages of private information and moral hazard. In a setting like ours, quadratic contracts would *not* necessarily function badly in providing incentives to improve the accuracy of forecasts, since it is the *precision* of the conditional distribution that would be determined through effort.

APPENDIX A

In this appendix we calculate the agent's *ex ante* expected utility under a linear reward scheme. (The principal's calculation is nearly identical.)

$$\mathscr{E}U_A(H, W) \equiv \mathscr{E}^H_{(\tilde{P},\tilde{M})} \left\{ -\exp - a\left[WR + \frac{H}{a}(\tilde{M} - R)(\tilde{P} - R) \right] \right\} \quad (A1)$$

We know that $\tilde{M} = (1 - K)\bar{P} + K(\tilde{P} + \tilde{\varepsilon})$, where $K = \sigma_P^2/(\sigma_P^2 + \sigma_\varepsilon^2)$. The agent's wealth will be determined by the realization of two random variables $\tilde{P}$ and $\tilde{\varepsilon}$,

$$\text{wealth} = WR + \frac{H}{a}(\bar{P} - R + K(\tilde{P} - \bar{P}) + K\tilde{\varepsilon})(\tilde{P} - \bar{P} + \bar{P} - R). \quad (A2)$$

Let $v = \{\tilde{P} - \bar{P}, \tilde{\varepsilon}\}$ and $Q = \{H(K + 1)(\bar{P} - R), HK(\bar{P} - R)\}$. Define Ω to be a matrix, where

$$\Omega = \begin{pmatrix} \dfrac{2}{\sigma_\varepsilon^2} + \dfrac{1}{\sigma_P^2} & \dfrac{1}{\sigma_\varepsilon^2} \\ \dfrac{1}{\sigma_\varepsilon^2} & \dfrac{1}{\sigma_\varepsilon^2} \end{pmatrix} \quad (A3)$$

Since Ω is positive definite, it can be factored: $\Omega = \Upsilon\Upsilon'$. Let $w = \Upsilon'v + \Upsilon^{-1\prime}Q$. Then

$$\mathscr{E}U_A(H, W) = \frac{-\exp - aWR - H(\bar{P} - R)^2}{2\pi\sigma_P\sigma_\varepsilon} \int_{\mathbb{R}^2} \exp - \tfrac{1}{2}w'w + \tfrac{1}{2}Q'\Omega^{-1}Q \, dw. \quad (A4)$$

The determinant of Ω is H/σ_ε^2 and

$$Q'\Omega^{-1}Q = (\bar{P} - R)^2 \left(2H - \frac{1}{\sigma_P^2} \right). \tag{A5}$$

These, when substituted into (A4), give us (16).

APPENDIX B

In this appendix we determine the *ex ante* expected utility of a manager with precision H who reports precision h under the quadratic reward scheme. We assume that $\gamma_2(h) < H/2$. It is shown in the body of the paper that wealth distributions obtained when this condition is not satisfied are inferior to those obtained when it is.

We know by Proposition 1 that the agent will truthfully report the conditional mean no matter what precision level has been reported. *Ex ante* expected utility will equal

$$\frac{-1}{\gamma_1(h)} \mathscr{E}^H_{(\tilde{P},\tilde{M})} \exp[\gamma_2(h)(\tilde{P} - \tilde{M})^2]. \tag{A6}$$

Since $\tilde{M} = (1 - K)\,\bar{P} + K(\tilde{P} + \tilde{\varepsilon})$,

$$
\begin{aligned}
(\tilde{P} - \tilde{M})^2 &= (1 - K)^2(\tilde{P} - \bar{P})^2 + 2K(1 - K)(\tilde{P} - \bar{P})\,\tilde{\varepsilon} + K^2\tilde{\varepsilon}^2 \\
&= \frac{1}{\sigma_P^2 + \sigma_\varepsilon^2} [\sigma_\varepsilon^4(\tilde{P} - \bar{P})^2 - 2\sigma_\varepsilon^2\sigma_P^2(\tilde{P} - \bar{P})\,\tilde{\varepsilon} + \sigma_P^4\tilde{\varepsilon}^2].
\end{aligned} \tag{A7}
$$

Let

$$\Omega = \begin{pmatrix} \dfrac{1}{\sigma_P^2} - \dfrac{2\gamma_2(h)\,\sigma_\varepsilon^4}{(\sigma_P^2 + \sigma_\varepsilon^2)^2} & \dfrac{2\gamma_2(h)\,\sigma_P^2\sigma_\varepsilon^2}{(\sigma_P^2 + \sigma_\varepsilon^2)^2} \\[2ex] \dfrac{2\gamma_2(h)\,\sigma_P^2\sigma_\varepsilon^2}{(\sigma_P^2 + \sigma_\varepsilon^2)^2} & \dfrac{1}{\sigma_\varepsilon^2} - \dfrac{2\gamma_2(h)\,\sigma_P^4}{(\sigma_P^2 + \sigma_\varepsilon^2)^2} \end{pmatrix}. \tag{A8}$$

Using the definition for H, it is easy to show that

$$|\Omega| = \frac{1}{\sigma_P^2 + \sigma_\varepsilon^2} [H - 2\gamma_2(h)].$$

We now show that if $\gamma_2(h) < H/2$, Ω will be positive definite. Clearly the determinant will be positive. If the condition is satisfied, then

$$\Omega_{11} = \frac{\sigma_\varepsilon^2}{\sigma_P^2 + \sigma_\varepsilon^2} \left[H - \frac{2\gamma_2(h)}{H\sigma_P^2} \right] > \frac{\sigma_\varepsilon^2}{\sigma_P^2 + \sigma_\varepsilon^2} \left[H - \frac{1}{\sigma_P^2} \right] > 0,$$

and

$$\Omega_{22} = \frac{\sigma_P^2}{\sigma_P^2 + \sigma_\varepsilon^2} \left[H - \frac{2\gamma_2(h)}{H\sigma_\varepsilon^2} \right] > \frac{\sigma_P^2}{\sigma_P^2 + \sigma_\varepsilon^2} \left[H - \frac{1}{\sigma_\varepsilon^2} \right] > 0.$$

Thus the diagonal elements of Ω are positive and Ω is positive definite. Let $\tilde{v} = \{ \tilde{P} - \bar{P}, \tilde{\varepsilon} \}$. Then

$$
\begin{aligned}
\mathscr{E}\mathbf{U}_A &= \frac{-1}{\gamma_1(h)\, 2\pi\sigma_P\sigma_\varepsilon} \int_{\Re^2} \exp -\tfrac{1}{2}v'\Omega v \, dv = \frac{-1}{\gamma_1(h)\, |\Omega|^{1/2}\, \sigma_P\sigma_\varepsilon} \\
&= \frac{-1}{\gamma_1(h)\, \sigma_P\sigma_\varepsilon \left(\dfrac{1}{\sigma_P^2\sigma_\varepsilon^2} - \dfrac{2\gamma_2(h)}{\sigma_P^2 + \sigma_\varepsilon^2} \right)^{1/2}} \\
&= \frac{-1}{\gamma_1(h) \left(1 - \dfrac{2\gamma_2(h)}{H} \right)^{1/2}}. \qquad (A9)
\end{aligned}
$$

REFERENCES

1. A. R. ADMATI AND S. A. ROSS, Measuring investment performance in a rational expectations equilibrium model, *J. Bus.* **58** (1985), 1–26.
2. F. ALLEN, Contracts to sell information, unpublished, Nuffield College, Oxford, 1982.
3. D. P. BARON, A model of the demand for investment banking advising and distribution services for new issues, *J. Finance* **37** (1982), 955–976.
4. S. BHATTACHARYA, Nondissipative signaling structures and dividend policy, *Quart. J. Econ.* **95** (1980), 1–24.
5. D. BLACKWELL, Comparison of experiments, *in* J. Neyman, "Proceedings of the Second Berkeley Symposium on Mathematical Statistics and Probability" (J. Neyman, Ed.), Univ. of California Press, Berkeley, 1951.
6. P. H. DYBVIG AND S. A. ROSS, The simple analytics of performance measurement, unpublished, Yale University, 1981.
7. B. DE FINNETTI, Does it make sense to speak of good probability appraisers? *in* "The Scientist Speculates: An Anthology of Partly-Baked Ideas" (J. J. Good, Ed.), Basic Books, New York, 1962.
8. D. HECKERMAN, Motivating managers to make investment decisions, *J. Finan. Econ.* **2** (1975), 273–292.
9. B. HOLMSTRÖM, Managerial incentive problems—a dynamic perspective, unpublished, Northwestern University, 1982.

10. L. KOHLLEPPEL, "Properties of Sorting Equilibria," Working Paper No. 113, Universität Bonn, 1983.
11. S. MATTHEWS, Selling to risk adverse buyers with unobservable tastes, *J. Econ. Theory* **30** (1983), 370–400.
12. R. MYERSON, Incentive compatibility and the bargaining problem, *Econometrica* **47** (1979), 61–74.
13. T. PAGE, Incentive compatibility in risk assessment, unpublished, California Institute of Technology, 1982.
14. P. PFLEIDERER AND S. BHATTACHARYA, Parametric aprroaches to portfolio performance measurement: The continuous case, unpublished, Stanford University, 1984.
15. R. ROLL, Ambiguity when performance is measured by the security market line, *J. Finance* **33** (1978), 1051–1069.
16. B. ROSENBERG, Institutional investment management with multiple portfolio managers, unpublished, University of California, Berkeley, 1977.
17. S. A. ROSS, The economic theory of agency: The principal's problem, *Amer. Econ. Rev.* **63** (1973), 135–139.
18. M. ROTHSCHILD AND J. E. STIGLITZ, Increasing risk: a definition, *J. Econ. Theory* **2** (1970), 225–243.
19. L. J. SAVAGE, Elicitation of personal probabilities and expectations, *J. Amer. Statist. Assoc.* **66** (1971), 783–801.
20. W. F. SHARPE, Decentralized investment management, *J. Finance* **36** (1981), 217–234.
21. R. WILSON, Incentive compatible risk sharing, unpublished, Stanford, 1979.

discussion | Information Contracting in Financial Markets

Franklin Allen

The Wharton School
University of Pennsylvania

Bhattacharya and Pfleiderer (1985) (henceforth BP) analyze contracts between a group of uninformed investors and an informed agent hired to manage their wealth for them. The paper contributes to at least two areas. The contracts considered effectively allow the informed person to sell his information. It is thus concerned with the operation of markets for information. Section I concentrates on this aspect. In addition, BP extends the literature on the principal-agent problem and managerial contracts. Section II deals with this.

I. MARKETS FOR INFORMATION

Casual observation suggests that information about the returns to securities is often sold. This can take a direct form, such as market newsletters. Alternatively, it can be indirect: many forms of financial intermediation are intimately connected with the provision of information. For example, actively managed mutual funds perform research, and the resulting information is used to invest clients' funds. One of the features of full-service stockbrokers is that they give investment advice as well as executing orders. Similarly with many other types of intermediary, information comes as part of a package of services. In addition to being important in its own right, a full understanding of the market for information is therefore necessary for explaining the existence and operation of many of the intermediaries that are observed. Despite this, markets for information about securities are only rarely even mentioned. BP is one of the first papers to contain a formal analysis of how such markets work. This section starts by considering some of the special features of information markets and relates BP and other recent work to these markets. It then goes on to consider the role of this type of analysis in explaining intermediation.

    Information is unlike any other commodity. As a result, information markets differ substantially from markets for other commodities. The first problem in selling information was pointed out by Hirshleifer (1971). Anybody

I am grateful to Anat Admati and Sudipto Bhattacharya for helpful comments and suggestions.

can claim to have superior forecasting ability or to have done research on the returns to securities. How can a buyer be sure that the seller's claimed information has not simply been fabricated? This adverse-selection/moral-hazard problem is the central focus of BP and Allen (1985).

BP is concerned with the problem faced by investors who have formed a mutual fund. They wish to hire a manager to do research and then use the information acquired to manage their funds for them. There are two assets: a safe one and a risky one. The payoff to the risky asset is normally distributed. When managers do research, they observe a signal that is the sum of the risky asset's payoff and an independent normally distributed error: the higher a manager's ability, the greater the precision of his payoff estimate and also the greater his exogenous alternative earnings opportunities. The utility functions of managers and portfolio owners are exponential in final wealth and are observable. The portfolio owners' problem is to design a contract that ensures that a manager has a greater precision than their own and obtains at least as high a utility as in his alternative opportunity. BP's main result is to show that by using a payment schedule that is a quadratic function of the risky asset's payoff, it is possible to ensure that a manager correctly reveals his true conditional mean and precision. Moreover, the contract they derive is shown to be approximately optimal if the portfolio owners, taken together as a syndicate, are almost risk neutral.

Allen (1985) also focuses on the adverse-selection/moral-hazard problem. The structure of the model used is similar to BP in terms of the nature of the informed person's information and, there being two assets, normally distributed returns and exponential utility functions. However, rather than looking at the problem in the context of portfolio owners hiring managers, the informed person has a monopoly over the information he acquires and sells it directly to uninformed people. Thus the informed person obtains the surplus from his information, whereas in BP the portfolio owners receive it. Instead of the manager's alternative opportunity being exogenous, it is assumed that the informed person can either sell his information or use it to just invest in the two assets. Also the informed person's utility function is unobservable.

The sequence of events when information is sold is the following. Before the signal is observed, the seller announces a set of payment schedules to potential buyers, where the payment depends on the risky asset's payoff. There is one schedule for each possible signal. The buyers then decide whether or not to purchase the information. After contracts are signed, the seller observes the signal and announces the corresponding payment schedule to the buyer. Markets meet and the risky asset's payoff is realized. Finally, the buyers make a payment to the seller, determined by this and the announced schedule.

The main problem for the seller is to convince buyers that he will actually observe the signal after the contract is signed. This is achieved by constraining each of the payment schedules so that if the seller did not observe the signal, he would not be any better off from selling information than from just investing in the two assets. If he sells information, his total receipts come from two sources: payments from the information buyers and returns on his portfolio. Both his portfolio and the contracts he has signed with other buyers are assumed to be observable. Therefore, given a utility function for the seller, every buyer can work out for each schedule the seller's expected utility if he were uninformed, from going ahead and selling information. They can also work out his expected utility if he were uninformed and were to just invest in the two assets. Provided the latter is greater than the former for every payment schedule, buyers know that if the seller had the given utility function he must be going to observe the signal. Otherwise he would be worse off than if he had not tried to sell information. Since the seller's utility function is unobservable, this constraint must be satisfied for all the possible utility functions the seller could have.

Although this set of constraints has a complex form in general, the assumption of exponential utility allows a tractable version to be found. The schedule that maximizes the seller's utility and satisfies the constraints can then be derived for each possible signal. As in BP's analysis, it involves a quadratic function of the risky asset's payoff, but the differences in assumptions mean the details are not at all similar. It turns out that the resulting set of schedules is such that it is possible for buyers to uniquely deduce the precision of the seller's signal and his degree of absolute risk aversion. Given these, a unique signal can be associated with each schedule. Thus the schedules themselves convey the seller's information. The payment to the seller is shared equally by the buyers. There must be enough buyers so that the cost to each makes the information worth purchasing. Since every buyer's benefit from the information is finite, only a finite number of buyers is necessary. Finally, it can also be shown that selling information is the informed person's optimal course of action: he is always better off doing this than simply using his information to invest in the two assets.

At the end of their paper BP make a conjecture concerning the situation where managerial utilities are unobservable (see Proposition 4). This case is similar to the problem solved by Allen (1985). A full analysis of their conjecture should shed further light on the relationship between the approaches.

The adverse-selection/moral-hazard problem is not the only important difference between markets for information and those for other commodities. Another results from the fact that the prices of assets can signal investors' private information (see Admati this volume). Usually, the more people that have a particular piece of information, the better prices reveal it and the less valuable it is. In contrast to standard commodities, there is thus a relationship between the amount that is sold and the value of that information to individual traders. This relationship does not arise in BP or Allen (1985). The model in BP is partial equilibrium in nature, and asset prices are taken to be exogenous. In Allen (1985) the number of information buyers is finite, but there is a continuum of asset traders, so the price of the risky asset is unaffected by the information market. As a result, the analysis of the adverse-selection/moral-hazard problem is greatly simplified.

Admati and Pfleiderer (henceforth AP) (1984, 1986) take the opposite approach. They focus on some of the implications of the link between the information market and the price of the risky asset in a similar framework with exponential utility and normally distributed returns. The adverse-selection/moral-hazard problem is avoided by assuming it is possible to observe directly whether people are informed.

AP (1984) considers the buyer's side of the information market. It looks at the value of the information contained in a noisy private signal given that prices are also noisy signals of the same information. There are thus externalities: even if a private signal is unaltered, any change in the noisiness of the price signal can affect the value of the information it contains. AP show that one implication of these externalities is that there may be a nonconcavity in the value of information: taken together two signals may be worth more than the sum of the values of each taken separately.

In AP (1986) the authors go on to consider the optimal strategy of a monopolist seller of information. The problem is that the more people the monopolist sells to, the more the price reflects his information and the less buyers are prepared to pay for it. One possibility for improving this trade-off is for the monopolist to add noise to his signal when he sells it. This has the advantage that the price reflects less information for a given number of sales, and so the seller can sell to more people. It has the disadvantage that it lowers the price that can be charged. AP show that if a seller has precise information he should randomize, but otherwise, he should not. They also demonstrate the seller is better off using individualized randomization, where different noise is added to each buyer's information, than "xerox" randomization where the same noise is added.

As argued initially, understanding information markets is important in explaining the operation and role of many financial intermediaries. An illustration of this is the paper by Ramakrishnan and Thakor (1984a). In their model, firms issuing securities hire information producers to certify their value. Similarly to BP and Allen (1985), the focus is on the moral-hazard problem, but they assume there is a direct noisy indicator of information producers' effort. Their resolution of this problem leads to a theory of intermediation that is not based on transaction costs (for a further discussion of this, see Diamond this volume).

Other examples of the relationship between the operation of markets for information and the role of intermediaries come from AP (1984) and Allen (1985). The nonconcavity in the value of information identified in AP (1984) suggests that information producers may find it profitable to join together and form an intermediary to sell the information. In Allen (1985) the continuum of traders implies that the value of the informed person's information is unbounded. However, the constraints necessary to solve the adverse-selection/moral-hazard problem cause his expected utility to be finite. An implication of this is that intermediation will be profitable: by reselling the information an intermediary can capture part of the value that the original seller cannot.

One of the differences between BP and AP (1986) and Allen (1985), which arises from the public good nature of information, suggests one possible explanation for why actively managed mutual funds exist as intermediaries. BP assume exogenously that portfolio managers do not transmit their information to portfolio owners: instead the owners initially specify the investments to be made in each possible situation, and the managers simply carry out the appropriate set of instructions once they have observed their information. In contrast, in AP (1986) and Allen (1985) the information is transmitted directly to buyers, and they make their own investments.

Since information is a public good, buyers may be able to resell it. In this case the original seller would have to compete with the resale, and this may severely limit the price he can obtain. This possibility is ruled out in AP (1986) and Allen (1985). One assumption that guarantees this is that resale is observable because the original seller can then outlaw it. Another possibility is that information transmission takes time. This implies information is more valuable to early buyers, and competition from resale is less severe. Where markets meet only once before asset payoffs are received, the seller can eliminate the problem by timing the transmissions to buyers so late that they cannot resell. However, in many other situations, resale can pose a serious problem for sellers. One way this can be avoided is for the seller to set up an actively managed mutual fund that would operate as in BP. Hence, taking account of the public good aspect of information provides an explanation for the existence of mutual funds. This differs substantially from the usual transaction cost theories.

In conclusion, it can be seen from the above discussion that work on information markets is still at an early stage. Much remains to be done before a full understanding of them is obtained.

II. PRINCIPAL-AGENT RELATIONSHIPS

The second contribution of BP is to the literature on the principal-agent problem in general and managerial contracts in particular. As Ross (1973) points out (p. 135): "for some questions the *raison d'être* for an agency relationship is that the agent (or the principal) may possess different (better or finer) information about the states of the world than the principal (agent)." BP is one of the first papers to consider a situation where the motivation for the agency relationship is differences in information. This section relates their approach to other recent work on the principal-agent problem and managerial incentives.

Ross (1973) considers a model where the agent takes an unobservable action that determines the probability distribution of output that accrues to the principal. The agent incurs no disutility from taking this action: in the context of the shareholder-manager relationship, actions can be interpreted as investments. The principal's payment to the agent is a function of the level of output, which is observable. This schedule is chosen to maximize the principal's utility but must be such that the agent can obtain his reservation expected utility. If actions were observable, the optimal contract would specify the agent's first-best action, and the payment schedule would share the risk associated with that action optimally.

However, when actions are unobservable, this schedule may not provide the correct incentives for the agent to choose the first-best action. He may be better off choosing another action that gives him a higher expected return at the expense of the principal. In such cases the principal must design a second-best contract that takes into account that the agent chooses his action to maximize his expected utility. The resulting payment schedule optimally trades off the allocation of risk and the provision of incentives.

In Ross's model the principal knows the probability distribution associated with each possible action or investment but cannot observe which one the agent chooses. In contrast, in BP's model the principal knows the investment the agent makes but does not know the associated probability distribution. The principal must therefore choose the payment schedule to ensure that the agent has a precise estimate of the returns to the possible investments.

Much of the principal-agent literature subsequent to Ross's paper focuses on the case where the agent's action requires unpleasant effort (see, for example, Mirrlees 1974, Harris and Raviv 1979, Holmstrom 1979, Shavell 1979, and Grossman and Hart 1983). In the simplest version of this type of model, a risk-averse agent takes an action, and this action together with a random variable determines the output that accrues to a risk-neutral principal. The structure of the principal's problem is similar to that in Ross's model. If the agent's actions were observable, the optimal contract would specify the agent's first-best action and the principal would pay him a fixed fee: since the principal is risk neutral, it is optimal for him to absorb all the risk.

If the agent's actions cannot be observed directly and cannot be deduced from output because the random variable is also unobservable, this type of scheme is no longer desirable: If the agent is paid a fixed fee no matter what he does, he has an incentive to shirk. In order to make him work, it is necessary for his compensation to depend on his actions. This can be achieved by making his payment a function of output, but it has the disadvantage that he must bear some of the risk associated with the random variable. Usually the second-best contract will involve his receiving a higher expected wage and working less than with the first-best contract. This compensates him for the increased risk, so he still obtains his reservation utility. As for the principal, he is worse off than in the first-best case by an amount that depends on how reliably the output indicates the agent's action. The less reliable an indicator it is, the worse off the principal is. If there exist any proxies for the agent's effort in addition to output, then Holmstrom (1979) and Shavell (1979) have shown that the agent's compensation should also be based on these.

Many authors use variants of the principal-agent model to analyze managerial compensation schemes in more detail. For example, Diamond and Verrecchia (1982) adapt an example of Holmstrom (1982a) to include a capital market. In addition to the output being a proxy for managerial effort, it is shown how stock price and a measure of systematic risk may also be useful. The stock price reflects the private information of investors; taking it and the indicator of systematic risk together with output gives a better signal of managers' effort than does output alone. A closed-form solution is obtained for the optimal contract, and it is shown that the risk-neutral principal bears all the systematic risk. However, the agent must bear the nonsystematic risk, since it is this that prevents his actions being perfectly deduced from output. In contrast to standard valuation theories, such as the arbitrage pricing theory (APT) or the capital asset pricing model (CAPM), this implies that nonsystematic risk becomes important for capital budgeting decisions. The greater the nonsystematic risk, the less effective the proxies are as indicators of managerial effort, and the more risk the manager must bear to have incentives to work. The cost of this greater risk is borne by the shareholders, who therefore prefer projects with less nonsystematic risk. Ramakrishnan and Thakor (1984b) demonstrate similar results on the role of nonsystematic risk, in the context of a more general model. Whereas Diamond and Verrecchia make very specific assumptions concerning the risk neutrality of the principal, the utility function of the agent, and the distribution of asset returns, Ramakrishnan and Thakor consider the case where the principal is risk averse, the agent has a separable utility function, and asset returns are determined in an APT framework. (For other aspects of managerial incentives see Marcus 1982 and Beck and Zorn 1982.)

In contrast to analyses of the principal-agent problem that assume the agent's actions involve unpleasant effort, BP assume the agent expends no costly effort in acquiring his superior information. Instead their focus is on the screening problem caused by the fact that people have different abilities and hence different precisions. An interesting variant of BP's model would be the case where everybody has the same ability, but obtaining more precise information involves greater disutility. This analysis would involve the agent's choice of precision in the same way that the agent chooses effort in the standard models discussed above.

Holmstrom (1982b) suggests another type of situation in which the interests of a principal and agent may diverge. Similar to BP, the agent's role is to provide information to the principal. However, in contrast to BP, the reason interests differ is that the manager is concerned with the effect of investment outcomes on his future reputation, whereas the firm is interested in the profitability of investments. In Holmstrom's example, the job of the agent or manager is to find investment projects and suggest them to superiors, who make the actual decisions. He cannot misrepresent information about any project he suggests, but he can refrain from suggesting them. Initially his ability, which is associated with his expected marginal product, is unknown by himself and by the firm. This symmetry is preserved throughout. Further information on his ability is provided by the outcomes of projects. If the manager is paid his expected marginal product, undertaking projects that reveal a lot of information about his ability makes his future income stream riskier. If he is risk averse, he may be better off hiding such projects. They may be profitable, however, and hence desirable from the firm's point of view.

In a subsequent paper Holmstrom and Ricart i Costa (1984) (henceforth HR) consider the same issue in a more general model and derive the optimal contracts firms should use. The ideal way of solving the problem would be to fully insure the manager's human capital risk. This would involve paying everybody the initial expected marginal product no matter what their ability turned out to be. However, this type of solution is not usually feasible because the legal system prohibits contracts that tie employees to a firm. Consequently, it is optimal to pay a reduced wage during the first period and then partially insure in subsequent periods. Those who turn out to have an ability below a certain level receive a downwardly rigid wage; those above receive their marginal product to ensure they do not leave the firm. However, it may be optimal to pay bonuses for investing, since this can provide incentives to bring forward proposals. The rules for investment decisions are also part of the insurance provided to managers. These rules require that the hurdle rate is above the opportunity cost of capital, and there may also be capital rationing.

HR's analysis differs substantially from those of other repeated principal-agent problems. Fama (1980) suggests managers' concern for their reputation can, in contrast, play a significant role in providing incentives to work. In his model, a manager's ability, which is again associated with his expected marginal product, cannot be directly observed and is subject to random change. If a manager reduces his effort below the optimal level, output will also be reduced on average. A low output will be taken as a signal that a manager's ability has declined. As a result, his compensation in subsequent periods will fall. Fama gives an example with a zero discount rate where, in the long run, managers bear the full cost of any deviation from the optimal effort level. They therefore have the correct incentives even though contracts are not used at all.

If there were no repetition of the relationship in HR's model, there would be no divergence of interests. Thus, time is a cause of the problem. However, in many other recent papers repetition improves efficiency (see, e.g., Radner 1981, Rubinstein and Yaari 1983, and Rogerson 1985). For example, Radner (1981) considers a standard principal-agent relationship where effort causes disutility. He shows that if there is no discounting and the principal is risk neutral, then as the number of repetitions goes to infinity the first-best can be arbitrarily closely achieved. Repetition improves efficiency for two reasons. First, it allows risk to be diversified across time. Second, it provides valuable information about the distribution of output and, hence, about the agent's actions.

Holmstrom and Milgrom (1985) suggest another type of repeated principal-agent model. In this the agent produces a sequence of observable outputs that accrue to the principal. The level of each output in the sequence depends on the cost spent by the agent and a random variable, neither of which can be observed by the principal. At the end of the sequence the principal makes a payment to the agent, which is a function of the history of outputs. The agent's utility depends on this payment less the total costs expended in producing the sequence. In this model, repetition is not a cause of the divergence of interests, as in HR. Neither does it increase efficiency, as in Radner (1981). Instead, repetition results in a rich set of actions for the agent to choose from.

Holmstrom and Milgrom are able to show that this richness can lead to optimal incentive schemes where payments are simple linear functions of aggregate output.

As the quotation from Ross (1973) at the beginning of the section stresses, the existence of many principal-agent relationships is due to the fact that the agent has, or can acquire, superior information. Despite this, only a few papers have considered situations of this type. As with markets for information, research in this area is still at an early stage.

REFERENCES

Admati, A. R., and Pfleiderer, P. 1984. "The Value of Information in Speculative Trading." Working paper 782, Graduate School of Business, Stanford University.
———. 1986. "A Monopolistic Market for Information." *Journal of Economic Theory* 39: 400–38.
Allen, F. 1985. "Contracts to Sell Information." Working paper 12–85, Rodney L. White Center, University of Pennsylvania.
Beck, P. J., and Zorn, T. S. 1982. "Managerial Incentives in a Stock Market Economy." *Journal of Finance* 37: 1151–67.
Bhattacharya, S., and Pfleiderer, P. 1985. "Delegated Portfolio Management." *Journal of Economic Theory* 36: 1–25. Reprinted Chapter 5, this volume.
Diamond, D. W., and Verrecchia, R. E. 1982. "Optimal Managerial Contracts and Equilibrium Security Prices." *Journal of Finance* 37: 275–87.
Fama, E. F. 1980. "Agency Problems and the Theory of the Firm." *Journal of Political Economy* 88: 288–307.
Grossman, S. J., and Hart, O. D. 1983. "An Analysis of the Principal-Agent Problem." *Econometrica* 51: 7–46.
Harris, M., and Raviv, A. 1979. "Optimal Incentive Contracts with Imperfect Information." *Journal of Economic Theory* 20: 231–59.
Hirshleifer, J. 1971. "The Private and Social Value of Information and the Reward to Inventive Activity." *American Economic Review* 61: 561–74.
Holmstrom, B. 1979. "Moral Hazard and Observability." *Bell Journal of Economics* 10: 74–91.
———. 1982a. "Moral Hazard in Teams." *Bell Journal of Economics* 13: 324–40.
———. 1982b. "Managerial Incentive Problems—A Dynamic Perspective." In *Essays in Economics and Management in Honor of Lars Whalbeck*. Helsinki: Swedish School of Economics.
Holmstrom, B., and Milgrom, P. 1985. "Aggregation and Linearity in the Provision of Intertemporal Incentives." Working paper D-5, School of Organization and Management, Yale University.
Holmstrom, B., and Ricart i Costa, J. E. 1984. "Managerial Incentives and Capital Management." Working paper D-4, School of Organization and Management, Yale University.
Marcus, A. J. 1982. "Risk Sharing and the Theory of the Firm." *Bell Journal of Economics* 13: 369–78.
Mirrlees, J. A. 1974. "Notes on Welfare Economics, Information and Uncertainty." In M. Balch, D. McFadden, and S. Wu, eds., *Essays on Economic Behavior under Uncertainty*. Amsterdam: North-Holland.
Radner, R. 1981. "Monitoring Cooperative Agreements in a Repeated Principal-Agent Relationship." *Econometrica* 49: 1127–48.

Ramakrishnan, R. T. S., and Thakor, A. V. 1984a. "Information Reliability and a Theory of Financial Intermediation." *Review of Economic Studies* 51: 415–32.

———. 1984b. "The Valuation of Assets under Moral Hazard." *Journal of Finance* 34: 229–38.

Rogerson, W. P. 1985. "Repeated Moral Hazard." *Econometrica* 53: 69–76.

Ross, S. A. 1973. "The Economic Theory of Agency: The Principal's Problem." *American Economic Review* 63: 134–39.

Rubinstein, A., and Yaari, M. E. 1983. "Repeated Insurance Contracts and Moral Hazard." *Journal of Economic Theory* 30: 74–97.

Shavell, S. 1979. "Risk Sharing and Incentives in the Principal and Agent Relationship." *Bell Journal of Economics* 10: 55–73.

Journal of Financial Economics 15 (1986) 187–212. North-Holland

WHY NEW ISSUES ARE UNDERPRICED*

Kevin ROCK

Harvard Business School, Boston, MA 02163, USA

Received November 1984, final version received August 1985

This paper presents a model for the underpricing of initial public offerings. The argument depends upon the existence of a group of investors whose information is superior to that of the firm as well as that of all other investors. If the new shares are priced at their expected value, these privileged investors crowd out the others when good issues are offered and they withdraw from the market when bad issues are offered. The offering firm must price the shares at a discount in order to guarantee that the uninformed investors purchase the issue.

1. Introduction

Several years ago, Grossman (1976) showed that if one class of investors has superior information about the terminal value of an asset, the information can be read by anyone from the equilibrium price. This result produces a paradox. If anyone can infer private information from the equilibrium price, no one pays to collect information. Yet if no one collects information, the price reveals none, and an incentive emerges to acquire it.

The key to the paradox is the assumption of a noiseless environment. If noise is present in the equilibrium price, privileged information is secure. For the uninformed cannot be sure whether a high price reflects favorable information or extraneous factors, such as a change in risk aversion or a need for liquidity.

This paper takes an alternative approach. If price, which is observable, does not correspond to a unique level of demand, which is unobservable, then the main channel by which inside information is communicated to the market is destroyed. Until the channel is re-established, the informed investor has an opportunity to profit from his knowledge by bidding for 'mispriced' securities. In this way, the investor is compensated for his costly investigations into the asset's value, and obtains some remuneration for showing where capital should best be allocated.

*This paper is based on Chapter 1 of my Ph.D. dissertation at the University of Chicago in 1982. I would like to thank the members of my Committee: Jonathan Ingersoll, Merton Miller (inside members), Douglas Diamond, Tom Garcia, and Willard Zangwill (outside members). I owe a special thanks to George Constantinides (chairman), as well as to Jay Ritter of the University of Michigan. In addition, Michael Jensen provided many helpful comments and suggestions.

0304-405X/86/$3.50©1986, Elsevier Science Publishers B.V. (North-Holland)

The setting for this model is the new issues market, in particular, the market for 'firm commitment offerings'. In a firm commitment offering, the firm and its investment bank agree on a price and quantity for the firm's first issuance of equity. Once the price is set, typically on the morning of the offer, no further adjustments are allowed. If there is excess demand, the underwriter rations the shares, sometimes exercising an 'overallotment option' which permits as many as 10% more to be sold. If there is excess supply, the offer concludes with unsold shares. The investment bank pays the firm for the surplus shares and disposes of them later at market prices. Each condition – excess supply or demand – is not observed until after the 'offering date'. Only then does the presence or absence of informed trading become apparent.

The new issue market resembles an auction, but the resemblance is not exact. Price is not determined by the bidding of investors. In particular, the investor with the highest valuation need not obtain the shares, even if the valuation exceeds the issuer's reservation (offer) price. That investor may simply not receive an allocation of rationed shares from the underwriter. Moreover, the issuing firm is both a bidder, who submits a price in consultation with the underwriting investment bank, and a seller, who exchanges an asset for cash. Nevertheless, the spirit of the model and its methodology belong to the auction literature.

This model is directed toward an explanation of an anomaly in the new issue market. New shares appear to be issued at a discount. Ibbotson (1975) tested this hypothesis and found, on average, an 11.4% discount in the offer price which disappeared within weeks in the aftermarket. Using a simpler model, Ibbotson and Jaffe (1975) found a 16.8% average excess return relative to the market. Both were unable to account for their findings. After suggesting several explanations, Ibbotson termed the phenomenon a 'mystery'.

The discount is a natural consequence of the present model, which incorporates asymmetric information and rationing. Ibbotson and Jaffe themselves notice that underpriced shares can be severely rationed. They mention that it is not uncommon for underwriters to receive, prior to the effective data, 'indications of interest' for five times the number of shares available. This phenomenon has an effect upon the uninformed investor. If an investor finds that he receives none of the underpriced issues due to rationing brought on by informed demand, and all of the overpriced issues, then the investor revises downwards his valuation of new shares. He does not participate in the new issue market until the price falls enough to compensate for the 'bias' in allocation.

The analysis shows that the equilibrium offer price includes a finite discount to attract uninformed investors. This result is not a foregone conclusion. It is not immediately clear what advantage accrues to the issuer from uninformed participation. Nor is it clear if any discount is sufficient to attract them to the offering. It is conceivable that reducing the offer price could elicit greater informed demand, exacerbate the bias, and further disadvantage the uninformed.

The analysis also shows that the optimal offer price is but one of a continuum of feasible prices. Different prices have different levels of uninformed investment and different probabilities of receiving rationed shares. Contrary to intuition, a small change in price does not produce a large uninformed response, even as the number of investors goes to infinity. The limiting demand schedule is easy to compute and does not depend upon the degree of risk aversion of the investors.

2. Relation to other work

Ritter (1984) has developed an implication of the current model and applied it to the 'hot issue' market of 1980. In general, the greater the uncertainty about the true price of the new shares, the greater the advantage of the informed investors and the deeper the discount the firm must offer to entice uninformed investors into the market. Ritter tested to see whether the predictable occurrence of market cycles in which initial offerings are deeply discounted could be explained as a change in the composition of the firms going public. The hypothesis is that during one phase, the initial uncertainty about firm values is low while during the other the uncertainty is high. While Ritter finds a significant statistical relation between the price variability of an issue in the aftermarket (which serves as a proxy for initial uncertainty) and the size of the discount, he concludes that the hot issue market of 1980 is attributable to another factor, the sudden appearance of natural resource firms going public.

In addition to Ibbotson and Ritter, several other authors find new issues to be underpriced, notably, Reilly (1977), Logue (1973), McDonald and Fisher (1972) and Reilly and Hatfield (1969). Among those offering explanations for the underpricing phenomenon, Baron (1980) argues that the discount is due to the superior information of the investment banker who sets the price and distributes the issue. Later, Parson and Raviv (1985) argue that the discount is a result of asymmetric information among investors, and they explain how both seasoned and unseasoned offerings are, on average, underpriced.

3. The model

Consider a market in which there are two assets available for investment. One is a safe asset whose return is normalized to 1. The other is an asset whose value per share, $\tilde{v}$, is uncertain. It is the latter asset which is being issued. The issuer pre-selects an offer price, p, and an offer quantity, Z shares. Once selected, the issuer receives offers to buy in quantities that vary according to the investor. Because no re-adjustment of price or quantity is allowed, the issuer can experience demand in excess of supply. In this case, the issuer can fill only a fraction of the incoming orders. Thus, in the new issue market, the probability that an order is filled can be less than one.

When oversubscription occurs, it is assumed to result exclusively from large orders placed by investors who have favorable information about the prospects of the offering. This privileged segment of the market is called 'the informed'. All other investors, including the issuer, are called 'the uninformed'.

There are several reasons for regarding the issuer as uninformed, notwithstanding the fact that the firm and its agent, the investment banker, know a considerable amount about the company's future. First, the firm gives up its informational advantage by revealing its proprietary knowledge to the market. The firm discloses 'material information' about its plans and activities directly through the prospectus. Indirectly, the firm and the underwriter disclose their assessment of the firm's financial future through how aggressively they price the issue relative to 'comparable' offerings. Indeed, one role of the investment banker is to certify, by means of his reputation, that the proposed price accurately reflects the firm's prospects [see Beatty and Ritter (1986)]. Second, even though the firm and its agent know more than any single individual in the market, they know less than all the individuals in the market combined. While the investment banker is the one agent best suited to price the offering, his information and expertise are inferior to the pooled talents and knowledge of all the agents. Some individuals may have inside information about a competitor that could have a significant impact upon the firm's product. Others may know better than the firm or the investment banker the appropriate rate to discount the firm's cash flows in the capital market. Indeed, it is almost tautological that the firm and its banker are at a considerable informational disadvantage relative to the market as a whole. It is not unusual for the price set by the underwriter to be off by more than 20% when compared to the price established at the end of the first trading month. In fact, if the initial returns from the offer price to the closing price on the first trading day are averaged across all the firms going public in a given month, there are 18 months between 1/75 and 1/81 in which the average exceeds 20%. There are 5 months in which the average exceeds 40%. The firm and its underwriter, then, seem to be in substantial disagreement with the market over what the stock is 'truly' worth.

To emphasize the informational advantage which the market enjoys over the firm and the underwriter, it is assumed that:

A.1. The informed investors have perfect information about the realized value of the new issue.

In addition:

A.2. Informed investors cannot borrow securities or short-sell. They cannot sell their private information.

The first part of the second assumption is true almost by definition. To sell the shares short, an investor must physically borrow them, which is impossible on or before the issue date unless the shares are received from the firm itself. If the issuer, however, loans the stock, it is guilty of pre-issuing the offer and circumventing the securities laws.

The other assumptions are:

A.3. Informed demand, I, is no greater than the mean value of the shares offered, $\bar{v}Z$.

A.4. Uninformed investors have homogeneous expectations about the distribution of $\tilde{v}$.

A.5. All investors have the same wealth (equal to 1) and the same utility.

In addition to these five assumptions, the investment bank is implicitly regarded as an invisible intermediary. The firm is assumed to dictate the price of the offering, not the underwriter. In addition, the firm rather than the investment bank bears the risk of having the issue undersubscribed.

By A.1, the informed submit orders for the new shares whenever the realized value per share, $\tilde{v}$, exceeds the offer price, P. By A.2, the informed order to the full extent of their wealth (equal to 1). And by A.3, when the informed order, they order a constant dollar amount:

$$I \quad \text{if} \quad p < \tilde{v},$$
$$0 \quad \text{if} \quad p > \tilde{v}.$$

Unlike the informed, the uninformed, who are N in number, cannot predicate the size of their order upon the realization of $\tilde{v}$. By A.4 and A.5, each uninformed investor wants to submit the same fraction, T, of his wealth (equal to 1) for the new issue. Since short-selling is impossible, each investor submits the positive share $T^* = \max(0, T)$. The combined dollar demand of the informed and uninformed is

$$NT^* + I \quad \text{if} \quad p < \tilde{v},$$
$$NT^* \quad \quad \text{if} \quad p > \tilde{v}.$$

Since the demand fluctuates according to whether $\tilde{v}$ is above or below p, the issuer must experience either excess supply or excess demand in one of the two states. In the state $\tilde{v} > p$, let the probability that an order is filled be denoted b. If $\tilde{v} < p$, designate the probability b'. To relate b and b' to fundamental magnitudes, a particular mechanism for allocating rationed shares must be devised.

The incoming orders are assigned a lottery number upon arrival. These numbers are drawn at random, and the corresponding orders are filled in their entirety. The drawings conclude when there are either no more orders or no more shares. Clearly, under this rationing scheme, the probability that an order is filled is independent of its size, as implicitly assumed in the definition of b and b'.

In some countries, for example, England, the underwriter *must* allocate the shares in an even-handed fashion. In the U.S., however, the underwriter has more discretion. This latitude leads to a common complaint that domestic underwriters tend to favor their established customers. To the extent that these customers are better informed than the rest, this arrangement exacerbates the bias against the uninformed and leads to larger discounts.

The discretionary power of the underwriter, however, holds some benefit for the uninformed investor. If underwriters deny allocations to customers who quickly traded out of their positions at a large gain in the past, they diminish the bias against the uninformed and decrease the size of the discount. Indeed, one might speculate that the successful underwriter is the one who can best discriminate among potential investors, giving first priority to the uninformed and second place to informed customers of longstanding who can rebate some of their profits via commissions on future trades.

If rationing occurs, the value of the issue equals the value of the orders filled, plus some small excess if the last order chosen cannot be totally accommodated. Upon ignoring the small 'round-off' error, we have

$$\tilde{N}_u T^* + \tilde{N}_i = pZ \quad \text{if} \quad b < 1,$$

where $\tilde{N}_u$ is the number of uninformed orders filled and $\tilde{N}_i$ is the number of informed orders filled.

Taking expectations,

$$bNT^* + bI = pZ \quad \text{if} \quad b < 1,$$

or

$$b = \min\left(\frac{pZ}{NT^* + I}, 1 \right). \tag{1}$$

Similarly,

$$b' = \min\left(\frac{pZ}{NT^*}, 1 \right) \tag{2}$$

Observe that $b < b'$, which says directly that the probability of receiving an allocation of an underpriced issue ($\tilde{v} > p$) is less than or equal to the probability of receiving an allocation of an overpriced issue ($\tilde{v} < p$). This bias in

Table 1

Terminal wealth of investor as a function of the aftermarket value of the new issue and the probability of obtaining an allocation.

	Aftermarket value[a]			
	$\tilde{v} > p$ (underpriced)		$\tilde{v} < p$ (overpriced)	
Allocation	yes	no	yes	no
Wealth	$p^{-1}\tilde{v}T + (1 - T)$	1	$p^{-1}\tilde{v}T + (1 - T)$	1
Probability	$b_e p(\tilde{v} > p)$	$(1 - b_e)p(\tilde{v} > p)$	$b'_e p(\tilde{v} < p)$	$(1 - b'_e)p(\tilde{v} < p)$

[a]Aftermarket value is the price, v, realized on the first trade; the aftermarket price differs from the offering price, p, according to whether the issue is underpriced ($v > p$) or overpriced ($v < p$). The probabilities of these two events from the viewpoint of the uninformed investor are denoted $p(v > p)$ and $p(v < p)$, respectively. Given the issue is underpriced, the probability of an allocation is b_e; given the issue is overpriced, the probability of an allocation is b'_e. The uninformed investor has unit wealth initially, and chooses a fraction, T, to invest in the new issue.

allocation causes the uninformed investors to revise downward their valuation of the new shares. Therefore, to attract uninformed investors to the offering, the issuer must price the shares at a discount, which can be interpreted as compensation for receiving a disproportionate number of overpriced stocks.[1]

When uninformed investors decide on the fraction of their wealth to be placed in the new issue, they base the decision upon their prior beliefs regarding b and b'. To emphasize that prior expectations are involved, b and b' are temporarily subscripted by 'e'. Uninformed investors calculate T by maximizing their expected utility of terminal wealth. Table 1 presents the investor's terminal wealth as a function of the aftermarket value of the new issue and the probability of receiving an allocation. In table 1, if an investor submits an order which is not transacted because of rationing, the order is transformed into an equal dollar amount of the safe asset.

From the table, the uninformed investor has the expected terminal utility:

$$b_e p(\tilde{v} > p) E\left[U\left(1 + T\left(p^{-1}\tilde{v} - 1\right)\right) | \tilde{v} > p\right]$$

$$+ b'_e p(\tilde{v} \leq p) E\left[U\left(1 + T\left(p^{-1}\tilde{v} - 1\right)\right) | \tilde{v} \leq p\right]$$

$$+ \left[1 - b_e p(\tilde{v} > p) - b'_e p(\tilde{v} \leq p)\right] U(1). \qquad (3)$$

[1]For an investor to experience a biased allocation, it is not necessary that others be perfectly informed. It is sufficient that aggregate demand be more informative than his personal observation. For example, let investor i derive a noisy estimate, $\tilde{v}_i$, of the true value per share, v. The estimate is $\tilde{v}_i - v + \tilde{\varepsilon}_i$. Suppose i's demand is an increasing function of the ratio (v_i/p). If the errors, $\tilde{\varepsilon}_i$, are independent and the market is large, aggregate demand is a non-stochastic, increasing function of (v/p). Thus, underpriced shares are more strictly allocated than overpriced shares.

Therefore, the optimal T satisfies the first-order condition

$$(b_e/b_e')p(\tilde{v} > p)\mathrm{E}\big[U'(1 + T(p^{-1}\tilde{v} - 1))(p^{-1}\tilde{v} - 1)|\tilde{v} > p\big]$$

$$+ p(\tilde{v} \le p)\mathrm{E}\big[U'(1 + T(p^{-1}\tilde{v} - 1))(p^{-1}\tilde{v} - 1)|\tilde{v} \le p\big) = 0.$$

A small insight into the economics of the offering process can be extracted from the form of the first-order condition. As far as the investor is concerned, it is not rationing *per se* which lowers his estimate of the value of the offering when he obtains an allocation. If rationing occurs to the same degree for both underpriced and overpriced issues, uninformed demand is the same as if there is no rationing. Rather, it is the *bias* in rationing good issues relative to bad issues which is important, the bias being measured by the ratio (b_e/b_e') in the optimality condition.

To finish the description of the equilibrium, it only remains to require that the expectations of the investors be rational. Investors' beliefs about the chances of being dealt a good or bad offer must equal the actual probabilities which arise from the allocation mechanism. Upon equating investors' beliefs to the actual outcomes given by eqs. (1) and (2), the complete equilibrium is

$$b = \min\left(\frac{pZ}{NT^*(b/b', p) + I}, 1\right), \tag{4}$$

$$b' = \min\left(\frac{pZ}{NT^*(b/b', p)}, 1\right), \tag{5}$$

$$0 = (b/b')p(\tilde{v} > p)\mathrm{E}\big[U'(1 + T(p^{-1}\tilde{v} - 1))(p^{-1}\tilde{v} - 1)|\tilde{v} > p\big]$$

$$+ p(\tilde{v} \le p)\mathrm{E}\big[U'(1 + T(p^{-1}\tilde{v} - 1))(p^{-1}\tilde{v} - 1)|\tilde{v} \le p\big], \tag{6}$$

$$T^*(b/b', p) = \max(0, T(b/b', p)).$$

In examining the equilibrium close attention is paid to how the uninformed change their demand in dollar terms as the offer price changes. The major question is whether uninformed investment increases as the offer price is reduced. This question involves more than whether the price is in the elastic portion of the demand curve. The additional consideration is that uninformed investment, $T(b, p)$, depends not only upon the price but also upon the probability of receiving an allocation of underpriced shares. The probability of receiving an allocation *declines* as the price is lowered and, hence, counteracts the usual effect of price on demand.

The reason why the probability declines is that, as the issue is made less expensive, the informed investors can purchase a larger fraction of it. Other things equal, the informed become relatively more influential and, as a consequence, worsen the bias against the uninformed. To see this point analytically, hold uninformed investment, $T(b, p)$, fixed while decreasing the price. Then the denominator of eq. (4), which determines b, does not change while the numerator declines. Thus, the probability, b, must also decline. As a result, while uninformed demand may be stimulated by a decrease in the offer price, it is diminished by the smaller probability of obtaining desirable shares.

Establishing that uninformed investment increases with a price reduction is essential. There are two principal reasons why a company enters the new issue market. One reason is to refinance the firm. After several years of successful operation, the founders, venture capitalists and employees holding stock options have a considerable amount of wealth invested in the enterprise. Not only are they interested in adding some liquidity to their investments, they are also anxious to diversify their portfolios. The same motive applies to older companies with employee stock ownership plans. As employees retire, they want to diversify their pension assets and convert their holdings into cash in order to consume. Since selling shares back to the company requires the firm to use up valuable funds and negotiate with employees about the terms of repurchase, a simpler procedure for all the parties involved is to take the company public.

A second reason to go public is to obtain new funds. Having gone several rounds with the banks and the venture capitalists, a firm may have no alternative but to seek funds in the public market to finance new investment. Even if bank financing or venture funding is available, the equity market allows larger sums to be raised more efficiently, without the need for complex convenants and restrictions.

The first motive for going public is risk aversion on behalf of the owners, pensioners and financial backers of the firm. The second motive is the desire to take advantage of a positive net present value investment opportunity. In both cases, the firm faces a tradeoff. If uninformed demand increases as the price is reduced, the lower the price, the larger the payment guaranteed to the firm from the offering. This guarantee offers protection to risk-avoiding claimants who otherwise are exposed to declines in the value of their assets. Moreover, it assures the firm which is contemplating an investment opportunity that the funds which are necessary to undertake the project will be available. The task facing the issuer, therefore, is to trade the guaranteed payment against the expected proceeds from the offering. That is, the issuer must trade higher minimum proceeds for a lower average take.

4. The opportunity set facing the issuer

Before investigating whether uninformed demand slopes downward like a proper demand curve, the first proposition to establish is that an equilibrium exists. The chief concern is whether there are any sets of beliefs that are consistent with the actual probabilities of receiving an allocation.

A useful heuristic is to consider what happens when the number of investors is very large. In this case, the risky asset represents a small fraction of each investor's total wealth. Since individuals are approximately risk-neutral with respect to small gambles, any uninformed investor who buys the initial public offering expects a return which is close to the risk-free rate.

The fact that an uninformed investor earns approximately the risk-free rate in a large market essentially determines his chances of receiving an allocation of good shares. If an uninformed investor submits a bid, his expected profit is[2]

$$bp(\tilde{v} > p)\mathrm{E}(\tilde{v} - p|\tilde{v} > p) + p(\tilde{v} < p)\mathrm{E}(\tilde{v} - p|\tilde{v} < p).$$

Upon requiring zero abnormal profits, we have

$$b \equiv b_0(p) = \frac{p(\tilde{v} > p)\mathrm{E}(\tilde{v} - p|\tilde{v} > p)}{p(\tilde{v} < p)\mathrm{E}(p - \tilde{v}|\tilde{v} < p)}.$$

This is the smallest probability an uninformed investor will tolerate of obtaining rationed shares before withdrawing from the new issue market, given the offering price is p. The function, $b_0(p)$, therefore, is called the 'zero demand probability'. Since, for large markets, each uninformed investor is on the verge of demanding zero, the resulting probability of receiving an allocation should be close to the zero demand probability. For large markets, at least, the existence of a consistent set of beliefs is guaranteed because $b_0(p)$ depends only upon the offer price and not upon the particulars of the investor's utility function.

For markets of arbitrary size, the existence of a consistent set of beliefs – called $b(p, N)$ to emphasize the dependence upon both the price and the number of investors – is proven in the following theorem:

Theorem 1. Let $0 < p < \bar{v}$. Then

$$b = \min\left(\frac{pZ}{NT^*(b, p) + I}, 1\right)$$

has the unique solution $b(p, N)$. It satisfies $b(p, N) > b_0(p) > 0$.

---

[2] See table 1. We assume that bad shares are not rationed (i.e., $b' = 1$).

Proof. See appendix.

The following lemma confirms the conjecture that as the number of investors tends to infinity, their beliefs about the chances of being rationed converge to the 'zero demand probability'. The lemma also shows that when the number of investors is large, the zero demand probability gives an accurate picture of how beliefs *change* with the offer price.

Lemma. Let $(\partial^2/\partial b \partial p)T(b, p)$ and $(\partial^2/\partial b^2)T(b, p)$ be continuous in the region $0 < b < 1, 0 < p < \bar{v}$. Then, the following limits hold uniformly:

$$\lim_{N \to \infty} b(p, N) = b_0(p),$$

$$\lim_{N \to \infty} \frac{\mathrm{d}}{\mathrm{d}p} b(p, N) = \frac{\mathrm{d}}{\mathrm{d}p} b_0(p).$$

Proof. See appendix.

Our interest in the function $b(p, N)$ stems from a desire to understand how uninformed demand changes in response to a change in the offer price. If the probability of obtaining good issues does not fall too much as the offer price declines, then uninformed demand increases. The fact that the probability $b(p, N)$ converges uniformly, with its derivatives, to $b_0(p)$ simplifies the study of uninformed demand for large markets because the zero demand probability can be so easily computed. This enables us to prove:

Theorem 2. For large markets and any price below $\bar{v}$,

$$\frac{\mathrm{d}}{\mathrm{d}p} T(b(p, N), p) < 0.$$

Proof. See appendix.

We can now completely describe the opportunity set. Suppose the market price is initially set equal to the mean value of the shares, $\bar{v}$, and the informed are not numerous enough to buy the entire issue, even if they wanted to. At this price, there is no rationing. The informed orders do not cause rationing by themselves, and the uninformed are unexcited by the chance to earn the risk-free rate on a small but risky investment. As the price is lowered, the uninformed become more interested, and they start to submit orders. At some critical price, the issue is fully subscribed in the state of the world where the informed know the issue is worth purchasing ('the good state'). At this price, uninformed demand plus informed demand exactly equals the dollar value of the offering.

Further reductions in price elicit even larger uninformed orders, according to Theorem 2. The uninformed and informed are now competing for shares whose offer price is growing smaller as the value of their orders is growing larger. The result is that all orders must be rationed more strictly in the good state of the world.

As a result of the uninformed, demand is also growing in the state of the world where the informed do not find the shares worth purchasing ('the bad state'). At some point the price is so low that the uninformed by themselves can fully account for the issue. This is called the 'full subscription price' – the price at which the issuer can rely on selling all the shares in the bad state, as well as in the good state.

For prices lower than the full subscription price, continued growth in uninformed demand causes rationing in both states but the amount of rationing in the good state *relative* to the bad state declines. Indeed, as the uninformed begin to dominate the market, the chances of being rationed in each state become the same. As a result, the informativeness of receiving an allocation tends to zero, since the market realizes that a successful bid does not necessarily mean a lack of interest on the part of the informed.

This effect produces a curious result. The more nearly equal the chances are of receiving an allocation in the good and bad state, the larger is the demand of the uninformed, who care only about the *bias* in the rationing. The larger the uninformed demand, however, the smaller the bias, which calls forth even greater uninformed demand, ad infinitum. Uninformed demand literally *explodes* when the price goes below the full subscription amount, as the example below demonstrates.

Before considering an example, it is important to verify that the 'full subscription' price always exists and to have some simple formula for computing it when the number of investors is large. By definition of the full subscription price, p_f,

$$p_f Z = NT(b(p_f, N), p_f).$$

Upon substituting this into the defining relation for $b(p, N)$, eq. (4), we have

$$b(p_f, N) = p_f Z / (p_f Z + I).$$

For large markets, the probability of receiving an allocation, $b(p, N)$, is uniformly close to the 'zero demand probability', $b_0(p)$. The full subscription price, then, must be close to the solution of

$$b_0(p) = pZ / (pZ + I), \tag{7}$$

which can always be shown to exist.

5. An example

This section verifies some of the important assertions made in the preceding section. The first assertion is that uninformed demand increases as the offer price is lowered. Second, the probability of receiving an allocation of under-priced shares converges to the 'zero demand probability' as the market grows larger. Third, the full subscription price is easy to calculate and nears the specified limit. Finally, demand 'explodes' when the offer price goes below the full subscription point.

For this example,

–the value of the issue per share, $\bar{v}$, is uniformly distributed on the interval $(0, 2\bar{v})$;

–investors have identical quadratic utilities,

$$U(w) = w - gw^2/2.$$

The first step is to calculate the uninformed demand from eq. (6). Since the utility is quadratic, the equation is linear in T and easily yields the solution

$$T(b/b', p) = 3\frac{(1-g)}{g} \left\{ \frac{(b/b')(2\bar{v}/p - 1)^2 - 1}{(b/b')(2\bar{v}/p - 1)^3 + 1} \right\}. \tag{8}$$

Eqs. (4) and (5) are not in a form that can be readily solved. They can be replaced by the equivalent relations

$$b = \min\left[\frac{pZ}{NT^*(b, p) + I}, 1 \right] \quad \text{if} \quad b' = 1, \tag{9}$$

$$(b/b') = \frac{NT^*(b/b', p)}{NT^*(b/b', p) + I} \quad \text{if} \quad b' < 1. \tag{10}$$

Observe from the form of T in eq. (8) that eqs. (9) and (10) lead to quadratics in b and (b/b'), for a given p. The eqs. (9) and (10) are, accordingly, straightforward to solve.

Table 2 calculates the uninformed demand and the probability of receiving an allocation under two sets of assumptions about the parameters. In each case, the uninformed have the expectation that overpriced shares are not rationed, an expectation which is analytically equivalent to $b' = 1$. Later, these expectations will be examined to see whether they can be maintained over the whole range of prices and, if so, whether other expectations also make sense.

The table confirms that as the offer price falls, uninformed demand increases both in absolute dollar amount and as a percentage of the market value of the issue. The increase occurs notwithstanding the fact that good issues are harder to get, i.e., b is decreasing.

Table 2

Uninformed demand and probability of an allocation of underpriced shares to an uninformed investor, as a function of offer price and number of investors; large (A) and small (B) markets.

Offer price as percentage of mean price/share $100 \times p/\bar{v}$	Uninformed demand as percentage of mean value of issue $100 \times NT^*/\bar{v}Z$		Uninformed demand as percentage of market value of issue $100 \times NT^*/\bar{p}Z$		Probability of an allocation of underpriced shares b		Zero demand probability $b_0(p)$
	(A)	(B)	(A)	(B)	(A)	(B)	
95%	14%	17%	15%	18%	84%	86%	82%
90	27	25	30	28	71	72	67
85	41	30	50	35	59	66	55
80	56	34	70	43	51	60	44
75	71	40	96	53	43	53	36
70	86	47	123	67	38	47	29
65	100	55	154	85	33	42	23
60	114	62	190	103	29	37	18
55	129	71	235	129	25	32	14
50	143	80	286	160	21	28	11

If the discount is kept fixed while the size of the market increases, the probability of receiving an allocation of underpriced shares falls. For instance, when the offer price is 80% of the mean price per share, the chances of being rationed go down from 60% to 51% as the market goes from small to large. This result is found along the row corresponding to the 80% offer price in the leftmost column of table 2. By moving from small to large under the heading b, the probabilities decrease from 60% to 51%. Eventually, as the market becomes infinitely large, the chances approach the 'zero demand probability', shown in the rightmost column.

As the name implies, the 'zero demand probability' makes the demand in eq. (8) zero:

$$b_0(p) = \frac{1}{(2\bar{v}/p - 1)^2}.$$

The usefulness of this schedule extends beyond the calculation of the asymptotic probabilities of obtaining a share of a good issue. According to eq. (7), solving

$$b_0(p) = \frac{1}{(2\bar{v}/p - 1)^2} = \frac{p}{p + \bar{v}}$$

yields the price at which uninformed demand is sufficient to subscribe the entire offering. That solution involves a 20% discount from the mean. Although the solution is exact only for markets with infinitely many uninformed investors, it provides an approximation to the full subscription price for markets of any size. For instance, in the large market case, the full subscription price is 74% of the mean price per share. At this price, uninformed demand is 100% of the market value of the issue. The price, accordingly, is obtained from table 2 by interpolating between the uninformed demands in the center column until one is found which equals the market value of the issue. For large markets, equality occurs somewhere between 75% and 70% of the unconditional mean price per share; say, at 74%. Thus, a 26% discount, rather than a 20% one, is needed to insure that all the shares are sold in every state of the world.

If, for each offer price, we graph the probability of receiving an allocation of underpriced shares when the market is 'large', we obtain curve A, B shown in fig. 1. Observe that the solid segment stops at point B. Below point B, the offer price is so low that uninformed demand exceeds the market value of the offering (see the large market column in the center of table 2). In this region, the shares are always oversubscribed. This contradicts our explicit assumption in forming table 2, that investors do not expect overpriced shares to be rationed. As a result, points along the dotted segment can never be observed. The question remains, then, what happens if the issuer insists on lowering the price below that corresponding to point B? If the issuer insists on having such large discounts, investors must revise their expectations and submit different orders.

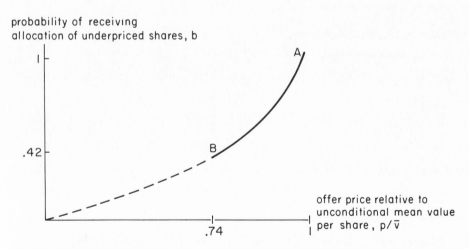

Fig. 1. Probability of receiving an allocation of underpriced shares as function of the offer price per share. For prices less than 74% of the mean value per share, shown as the dotted portion of the graph below point B, the probability of receiving an allocation of overpriced shares is less than one.

Earlier, we observed that uninformed demand depends only upon the bias in allocating shares. We measured this bias by the probability of being rationed in the good state relative to the probability of being rationed in the bad state ($= b/b'$). Upon graphing the 'relative' probability of being rationed versus the offer price, we obtain a complete picture of the new issue market. (See fig. 2.)

Fig. 2 looks much like fig. 1. The segment A, B is the same since only underpriced shares are rationed along its length. As the price drops below B, however, oversubscription occurs for bad shares as well as good shares. Demand by the uninformed actually increases because good shares become *relatively* easier to obtain than bad shares. As uninformed demand rises, the bias in allocating good shares relative to bad shares is further attenuated, raising uninformed demand still more. Uninformed demand jumps discontinuously, which is reflected in the discontinuous change from B to C when the price falls incrementally below the point of full subscription.

Analytically, the multiplicity of expectations at a given price arises from the fact the expectations are defined by two quadratic equations. Eq. (9), which defines segment A, B, always has one positive root, while eq. (10) generally has two.

It is interesting to speculate whether there is any connection between the multiplicity of solutions and observed behavior in the new issue market. A very tentative connection can be made with the hot/cold cycles of initial public

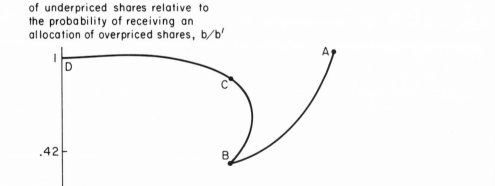

Fig. 2. Relative probability of receiving an allocation of underpriced shares as function of offer price per share. Points B and C correspond to two distinct equilibria at the same offer price. At point C, uninformed demand is significantly larger than at point B, causing both underpriced and overpriced shares to be rationed.

offerings. During the cold issue cycles, discounts are large, but the number of offerings are few. Several offerings are even undersubscribed. This is exactly what happens along the lower branch from A to B (see fig. 2). During the hot issue cycles, however, demand is heavy and discounts are smaller than in the cold cycle. This behavior corresponds to the upper branch from B, C, D where all offerings are fully subscribed.

6. The optimal offer price

As mentioned in section 3, there are two motives for going public. Here, we will investigate only one: risk aversion on the part of the founders, employees and financial backers of the firm.[3] Given this motive, the offer price cannot exceed the unconditional mean value of the shares, $\bar{v}$. If the price is greater than $\bar{v}$, the uninformed never submit an order. The issuer sells exclusively to the informed. Thus, when the shares are bad, the issuer ends up holding them, and when the shares are good, the issuer sells them off. No matter what the degree of risk aversion, the 'owners' are clearly better off to retain the shares rather than sell in this range.

Suppose the collective preferences of the owners can be represented by a utility function, say,

$$U(w) = -w^{-1}.$$

Table 3 shows the owners' terminal wealth as a function of the 'true price' which is revealed in the aftermarket.

The expected utility of the owners is, accordingly,

$$EU(w) = p(\tilde{v} > p)U(pZ) + p(\tilde{v} < p)$$

$$\times E(U(NT(b, p) + \tilde{v}(Z - NT(b, p)/p)))|\tilde{v} < p).$$

Under the assumption that $\tilde{v}$ is uniform on $(0, 2\bar{v})$, we have

$$EU(w) = \frac{-1}{pZ} + \frac{1}{2\bar{v}Z}\left\{1 + \frac{\log(NT(b, p)/pZ)}{1 - (NT(b, p)/pZ)}\right\}.$$

---

[3] For greater realism, we drop the fiction that the underwriting investment bank is an invisible intermediary. Henceforth, 'owners' refer either to the founders of the company or to the investment banking firm which acquires the shares prior to a public offering as part of a firm commitment arrangement.

Table 3

Issuer's terminal wealth, as a function of the realized value of the shares in the aftermarket.

	Aftermarket value[a]	
	$\tilde{v} > p$ (underpriced)	$\tilde{v} < p$ (overpriced)
Issuer's wealth	pZ	$NT(b, p) + \tilde{v}(Z - NT(b, p)/p)$

[a]Aftermarket value is the price, v, realized on the first trade; this price differs from the offering price, p, according to whether the issue is underpriced ($v > p$) or overpriced ($v < p$). The number of shares offered is Z, the number of uninformed investors is N, and T is the fraction of wealth the uninformed investor allocates to the new issue.

This expression is easily interpreted. The first term, $(-1/pZ)^{-1}$, is the utility of the owners, given the issue is completely subscribed at the price p. The second term is a correction that depends upon the fraction of the issue subscribed by the uninformed:

$$NT(b, p)/pZ.$$

Observe that the issuer will not choose a price at which uninformed demand is zero. If the true value of the shares is lower than p, none of the shares are sold. The owners – either the investment bank which takes the shares public or the original organizers of the company – retain by default an issue which might be completely worthless. Given the form of the owners' utility function, the prospect of a total loss makes their expected utility equal to $-\infty$. Consequently, the owners are willing to offer the shares at a discount to enjoy the benefits of risk-sharing.[4]

Using the definition of $b(p, N)$, the probability of receiving an allocation, the maximization problem can be written

$$\max_{p > p_f} \frac{-1}{pZ} + \frac{1}{2\bar{v}Z}\left\{ 1 + \frac{\log\left(\dfrac{1}{b(p, N)} - \dfrac{\bar{v}}{p}\right)}{1 + \dfrac{\bar{v}}{p} - \dfrac{1}{b(p, N)}} \right\}.$$

[4] The fact that the owners are phobic about losing all their money does not mean they are unwilling to initiate such a project; they must simply expect to trade out before the ultimate outcome is known.

If the number of investors is large, then $b(p, N)$ is approximately equal to the zero demand probability, $b_0(p)$. For the example considered in section 4, the zero demand probability is calculated explicitly. In this instance, the maximization problem becomes

$$
\max_{p > 0.8\bar{v}} \frac{-1}{pZ} + \frac{1}{2\bar{v}Z} \left\{ 1 + \frac{p^2 \log((4\bar{v} - p)(\bar{v} - p)p^{-2})}{5\bar{v}(p - 0.8\bar{v})} \right\}.
$$

The solution to the constrained maximization occurs at the boundary, $0.8\bar{v}$. The owners choose the smallest discount which guarantees full subscription in every state of the world.

7. Conclusion and empirical tests

The model presented here is designed to explain the well-established phenomenon of the underpricing of initial public offerings. Insofar as the underpricing feature is the focus of the model, it can hardly be considered the definitive test.

The crucial test of the model involves observing the degree to which shares are rationed on the offer date. If the model is correct, weighting the returns by the probabilities of obtaining an allocation should leave the uninformed investor earning the riskless rate.

Evidence on the degree of rationing, however, is hard to obtain for several reasons. First, underwriters are sensitive to the question of allocational fairness. They are generally hostile to the suggestion that shares are rationed in a preferential way, or, indeed, rationed at all. Second, the degree to which shares are rationed reflects directly on the underwriter's ability. If the shares are undersubscribed, the underwriter is either negligent in pricing them or lax in promoting and distributing the offer. If, however, the shares are heavily oversubscribed, the underwriter appears to be underpricing the issue to make it easier to sell. Finally, not all the orders the underwriter receives are firm. Orders are slightly inflated because the investor can renege on the deal for several day after the offer date. Hence, the degree of rationing is overstated.

Since direct evidence on the occurrence of rationing is hard to obtain, indirect evidence must be used instead. One indicator of the extent of rationing can be found in the sample of stocks which are offered with overallotment options. If, in this sample, the overallotment option is rarely exercised, then it is safe to say that rationing seldom occurs for initial public offerings as a whole. If, however, the overallotment provision is used frequently to obtain additional shares, then it seems that oversubscription is a common event. Of course, the mere existence of rationing is not sufficient to explain the discount. The important additional consideration is that rationing occurs more often for good shares than for bad shares. To confirm the presence of a bias, those shares for which the issuer exercises the option must be shown to appreciate more in price than those shares for which the option expires unused. Such a test is easy to perform by simply measuring the price change of each class of shares on the offering date.

An alternative to measuring the extent of rationing in new issue markets is to find evidence of a similar effect in other markets. The same argument which predicts a discount for initial public offerings predicts a premium for tender offers. Briefly, uninformed investors expect the tender to be oversubscribed if the tender price is too high and undersubscribed if the tender price is too low. Thus, by participating in the offer, the uninformed give up their good shares and keep their bad shares. That is, the informed crowd the uninformed out of those tender offers for which the premium is too high and they withdraw from those tenders for which the premium is too low. To induce a sufficient number of uninformed investors to tender, therefore, the firm making the offer must add a premium to overcome the bias.

The advantage of using tender offers as a 'proof of principle' for initial public offerings is that the degree of rationing is a matter of public record. Firms announce, at the close of the offer, the number of tenders they receive. An additional advantage is that the allocation mechanism is explicit. In the case of oversubscription, the offers to tender are placed in a pool from which they are drawn in a prescribed way.[5] Finally, the premium is easy to measure; it is the simply ratio of the tender price to the *post-tender* trading price.

The model presented here for firm commitment offerings can be generalized considerably. Suppose that, instead of the orders *all* being received on one day and filled by lot, the orders arrive over a period of many days and are filled in order of arrival. Such an arrangement is typical of a 'best efforts underwriting'. If the issuer closes the offer as soon as the last share is subscribed, the rationing is 'invisible' because the unfilled orders can't be seen. Nevertheless, the unfilled orders exist; they belong to the disappointed buyers who arrive after all the shares are sold.

Invisible rationing exerts the same downward pressure on the offering price as the more overt kind. Uninformed investors who arrive in time suspect their success is due as much to lack of interest on the part of informed investors as it is to good luck. Conditional upon receiving an allocation, the uninformed find the shares to be worth less than their unconditional value. Therefore, just as in a firm commitment offering, the shares must be priced at a discount to attract uninformed buyers.

---

[5] In one type of tender offer [Federal Register (1984)]: 'The bidder states a maximum number of shares to be purchased in addition to a minimum condition. If the offer is oversubscribed, the tendered shares will be subject to prorationing. When the offer is executed under prorationing, each tendering account has the same fraction accepted. Prorationing requirements insure that each target shareholder receives proportionate share of the terms of the tender offer.'

Such an extension is satisfying because it suggests that the institutional mechanism for delivering the shares to the public is irrelevant as far as the offer price discount is concerned. Whether the shares are sold sequentially, as in the best efforts arrangement, or all at once, as in the firm commitment underwriting, the essentials are the same. The uninformed compete with the informed, and the issuer must ultimately compensate them for their disadvantage.

Appendix

First, we must prove some miscellaneous results.

Lemma 1. $T(b, p)$ *is strictly increasing in* b, *for* $p, b > 0$.

Proof.   Differentiate eq. (6) with respect to b:

$$p(\tilde{v} > p)\mathrm{E}\left[U'\left(1 + T\left(p^{-1}\tilde{v} - 1\right)\right)\left(p^{-1}\tilde{v} - 1\right)|\tilde{v} > p\right]$$

$$+ (b)p(\tilde{v} > p)\mathrm{E}\left[U''\left(1 + T\left(p^{-1}\tilde{v} - 1\right)\right)\left(p^{-1}\tilde{v} - 1\right)^2|\tilde{v} > p\right]\frac{\mathrm{d}T(b, p)}{\mathrm{d}b}$$

$$+ p(\tilde{v} < p)\mathrm{E}\left[U''\left(1 + T\left(p^{-1}\tilde{v} - 1\right)\right)\left(p^{-1}\tilde{v} - 1\right)^2|\tilde{v} < p\right]\frac{\mathrm{d}T(b, p)}{\mathrm{d}b} = 0.$$

Note that

$$U''\left(1 + T\left(p^{-1}\tilde{v} - 1\right)\right)\left(p^{-1}\tilde{v} - 1\right)^2 < 0 \quad \text{if} \quad U'' < 0.$$

Also

$$U'\left(1 + T\left(p^{-1}\tilde{v} - 1\right)\right)\left(p^{-1}\tilde{v} - 1\right) > 0 \quad \text{when} \quad \tilde{v} > p,$$

provided $U' > 0$. Thus, the first term above is positive while the coefficients of $\mathrm{d}T(b, p)/\mathrm{d}b$ are negative when $b, p > 0$. This implies

$$\mathrm{d}T(b, p)/\mathrm{d}b > 0 \quad \text{for} \quad p, b > 0.$$

proving the lemma.

Lemma 2. $p\dfrac{\mathrm{d}}{\mathrm{d}p}\ln b_0(p) > 1$.

Proof. Upon taking the logarithm of eq. (11), which defines $b_0(p)$, and differentiating,

$$\frac{\mathrm{d}}{\mathrm{d}p}\ln b_0(p) = \frac{1}{p(\tilde{v}<p)\mathrm{E}(p-\tilde{v}|\tilde{v}<p)}\frac{\mathrm{d}}{\mathrm{d}p}\mathrm{E}(p-\tilde{v}|\tilde{v}<p)p(\tilde{v}<p)$$

$$= \frac{1}{p(\tilde{v}>p)\mathrm{E}(p-\tilde{v}|\tilde{v}>p)}\frac{\mathrm{d}}{\mathrm{d}p}\mathrm{E}(p-\tilde{v}|\tilde{v}>p)p(\tilde{v}>p).$$

Notice

$$\frac{\mathrm{d}}{\mathrm{d}p}\mathrm{E}(p-\tilde{v}|\tilde{v}<p)p(\tilde{v}<p) = p(\tilde{v}<p),$$

and

$$\frac{\mathrm{d}}{\mathrm{d}p}\mathrm{E}(\tilde{v}-p|\tilde{v}>p)p(\tilde{v}>p) = p(\tilde{v}>p).$$

Therefore,

$$p\frac{\mathrm{d}}{\mathrm{d}p}\ln b_0(p) = \frac{p}{\mathrm{E}(p-\tilde{v}|\tilde{v}<p)} + \frac{p}{\mathrm{E}(p-\tilde{v}|\tilde{v}>p)}.$$

Since $\tilde{n}>0$, $\mathrm{E}(p-\tilde{v}|\tilde{v}<p)<p$. Hence

$$p\frac{\mathrm{d}}{\mathrm{d}p}\ln b_0(p) > \frac{p}{p} = 1,$$

proving the lemma. We can now prove the following theorem.

Theorem 1

$$b = \frac{pZ}{NT^*(b,p)+I} \tag{11}$$

has the unique solution $b(p,N) > b_0(p) > 0$.

Proof. Write the tautology

$$b_0(p) = b_0(\bar{v})\exp\left[\int_{\bar{v}}^{p}\frac{\mathrm{d}}{\mathrm{d}t}\ln b_0(t)\,\mathrm{d}t\right].$$

By Lemma 2 and assumption A.3,

$$b_0(p) < b_0(\bar{v})\exp\left[\int_{\bar{v}}^{p}t^{-1}\,\mathrm{d}t\right] = b_0(\bar{v})p\bar{v}^{-1} = \frac{pZ}{\bar{v}Z} < \frac{pZ}{I}.$$

Because $T(b_0(p), p) = 0$ by definition, the inequality above implies

$$b_0(p) < \frac{pZ}{NT*(b_0(p), p) + I} = \frac{pZ}{I}. \tag{12}$$

By Lemma 1, $T(b, p)$ is strictly increasing in b. Therefore, for any $b > (pZ/I)$,

$$b > \frac{pZ}{NT*(b, p) + I}. \tag{13}$$

Both sides of expression (13) are continuous in b. By (12) and (13), the functions cross on $(b_0(p), \infty)$. Therefore, at some point, $b(p, N)$, which lies in the interval $(b_0(p), \infty)$, the functions are equal. Since the function on the left-hand side is strictly increasing, while the function on the right-hand side is decreasing, necessarily the solution $b(p, N)$ is unique.

Lemma 3. Let $(\partial^2/\partial b \partial p)T(b, p)$ and $(\partial^2/\partial b^2)T(b, p)$ be continuous in the region $0 < b < 1$, $0 < p < \bar{v}$. Then, for all p in any closed subinterval of $(0, \bar{v})$ which does not contain 0, the following limits hold uniformly:

$$\lim_{N \to \infty} b(p, N) = b_0(p), \qquad \lim_{N \to \infty} \frac{d}{dp} b(p, N) = \frac{d}{dp} b_0(p).$$

Proof. Differentiate eq. (11), which defines $b(p, N)$, with respect to N. Upon re-arranging,

$$\frac{d}{dN} b(p, N) = \frac{-pZ}{D^2} T(b(p, N), p)\left(1 + \frac{pNZ}{D^2} T_b\right)^{-1},$$

where

$$D = NT(b(p, N), p) + I,$$

$$T_b = \frac{\partial}{\partial b} T(b(p, N), p).$$

By Lemma 1, T_b is positive, which implies

$$\frac{d}{dN} b(p, N) < 0 \quad \text{for} \quad p > 0.$$

Since $b(p, N)$ is decreasing in N, a limit exists which satisfies

$$\lim_{N \to \infty} b(p, N) = \lim_{N \to \infty} \left[\frac{pZ}{NT(b(p, N), p) + I} \right].$$

From the above equation, either $b(p, N)$ or $T(b(p, N), p)$ goes to zero. The former possibility can be excluded by Theorem 1, for $b(p, N) > b_0(p) > 0$. Thus,

$$\lim_{N \to \infty} T(b(p, N), p) = T\left(\lim_{N \to \infty} b(p, N), p \right) = 0,$$

which means that $b(p, N)$ converges to the zero demand probability. That is,

$$\lim_{N \to \infty} b(p, N) = b_0(p).$$

Since the convergence is monotone in N, and the limit is continuous, 'Dini's Theorem' yields that the approach is uniform on any closed subinterval of $(0, \bar{v})$ which does not contain zero [see Dieudonné (1969)].

To show that the derivatives are uniformly convergent, differentiate eq. (11) with respect to p, and re-arrange,

$$\frac{d}{dp} b(p, N) = \frac{-T_p + (Z/b(p, N)N)}{T_b + (pZ/b^2(p, N)N)}, \qquad p > 0,$$

where

$$T_p = \frac{\partial}{\partial p} T(b(p, N), p).$$

Observe that upon totally differentiating the identity $T(b_0(p), p) = 0$, we obtain

$$\frac{d}{dp} b_0(p) = - \frac{\partial}{\partial p} T(b_0(p), p) \bigg/ \frac{\partial}{\partial b} T(b_0(p), p).$$

Compare the expressions for $(d/dp)b(p, N)$ and $(d/dp)b_0(p)$. Since $(\partial/\partial b)T(b_0(p), p) > 0$ for $p > 0$ by Lemma 1, it suffices to show the following limits are uniform on any closed subinterval of $(0, \bar{v})$ which does not contain zero:

$$\lim_{N \to \infty} \frac{\partial}{\partial p} T(b(p, N), p) = \frac{\partial}{\partial p} T(b_0(p), p),$$

$$\lim_{N \to \infty} \frac{\partial}{\partial b} T(b(p, N), p) = \frac{\partial}{\partial b} T(b_0(p), p).$$

By assumption, $(\partial^2/\partial p\,\partial b)T(b, p)$ is continuous and bounded for $0 < x \le p \le \bar{v}$, $0 < b \le 1$. Let

$$M_x = \max_{\substack{0 < b < 1 \\ x < p < b}} \frac{\partial^2}{\partial p\,\partial b} T(b, p) < \infty.$$

By the Mean Value Theorem,

$$\frac{\partial}{\partial p} T(b(p, N)\,p) - \frac{\partial}{\partial p} T(b_0(p), p) < M_x b(p, N) - b_0(p).$$

Since $b(p, N)$ converges uniformly to $b_0(p)$ on $0 < x \le p \le \bar{v}$, then $(\partial/\partial p)T(b(p, N), p)$ must converge uniformly to $(\partial/\partial p)T(b_0(p), p)$. An identical argument establishes that $(\partial/\partial b)T(b_0(p), p)$ converges uniformly to $(\partial/\partial b)T(b_0(p), p)$, completing the proof of the lemma.

The uniform convergence of the function $b(p, N)$ and its derivatives to $b_0(p)$ is an important ingredient in the next theorem, which is the key to characterizing the issuer's opportunity set.

Theorem 2. $(\mathrm{d}/\mathrm{d}p)T(b(p, N), p) < 0$, *for N sufficiently large.*

Proof. Re-arrange eq. (11),

$$T(b(p, N), p) = \frac{pZ}{Nb(p, N)} - \frac{I}{N}.$$

This equation is an identity which can be differentiated with respect to p:

$$\frac{\mathrm{d}}{\mathrm{d}p} T(b(p, N), p) = \frac{Z}{b(p, N)N} 1 - p\frac{\mathrm{d}}{\mathrm{d}p} \ln b(p, N). \qquad (14)$$

Since $b(p, N)$ converges uniformly with its derivatives to $b_0(p)$, then

$$\lim_{N \to \infty} p\frac{\mathrm{d}}{\mathrm{d}p} \ln b(p, N) = p\frac{\mathrm{d}}{\mathrm{d}p} \ln b_0(p), \qquad (15)$$

uniformly for all p in any closed subinterval of $(0, \bar{v})$ which does not contain zero. By Lemma 2, the right-hand side of eq. (15) is greater than 1. Therefore, on any closed subinterval of $(0, \bar{v})$ which excludes 0, N can be chosen large enough that the right-hand side of (14) is negative.

References

Baron, D., 1982, A model of the demand for investment banking advising and distribution services for new issues, Journal of Finance, 955–976.

Beatty R. and J. Ritter, 1986, Investment banking, reputation, and the underpricing of initial public offerings, Journal of Financial Economics, this issue.

Dieudonne, J., 1969, Foundations of modern analysis (Academic Press, New York).

Federal Register, 1984, Proposed Rules, v. 49, no. 127.

Going public: The IPO Reporter, 1975–1980 (Howard & Co., Philadelphia, PA).

Grossman, S.J., 1976, On the efficiency of competitive stock markets where traders have diverse information, Journal of Finance 31, 573–585.

Halloran, M.J., 1979, Going public, 3rd ed. (Sorg Printing Co., New York).

Ibbotson, R.G., 1982, Common stock new issues revisited, Working paper 84 (Center for Research in Security Prices, University of Chicago, Chicago, IL).

Ibbotson, R.G., 1975, Price performance of common stock new issues, Journal of Financial Economics, 2, 235–272.

Ibbotson, R.G. and J. Jaffe, 1975, 'Hot issue' markets, Journal of Finance 30, 1027–1042.

Logue, D., 1973, On the pricing of unseasoned equity issues, 1965–69, Journal of Financial and Quantitative Analysis 8, 91–103.

McDonald, J. and A.K. Fisher, 1972, New issue stock price behavior, Journal of Finance, 97–102.

Myerson, R.B., 1981, Mechanism design by an informed principal, Discussion paper 481 (J.L. Kellogg Graduate School of Management, Northwestern University, Evanston, IL).

Parsons, J. and A. Raviv, 1985, Alternative methods for floating new issues, forthcoming.

Reilly, F., 1977, New issues revisited, Financial Management, 28–42.

Reilly, F. and K. Hatfield, 1969, Investor experience with new stock issues, Financial Analysts Journal, 73–80.

Ritter, J., 1984, The 'hot issue' market of 1980, Journal of Business 57, 215–240.

discussion | Alternative Models of Investment Banking

Artur Raviv

Northwestern University and Tel Aviv University

We survey several models dealing with the marketing of new securities. No attempt is made to provide an exhaustive review of the fast-growing literature related to investment banking and the capital acquisition process (see Smith 1986). We concentrate instead on the decisions to be made after the firm has decided on the type and number of securities to be issued. In particular, we focus on the choice of method for floating new issues (rights versus underwritten offerings), the contract between the issuer and the investment banker in cases where the firm uses an underwriter, and the pricing of new issues.[1]

Two methods exist for raising equity capital on financial markets: the rights and underwritten offerings. In the rights offering, current shareholders receive a "right" from the firm giving them an option to purchase additional shares at a prespecified exercise price. Under this method the firm receives capital from the sale of new shares to holders of the rights. Current shareholders either use their rights to purchase new shares or sell the rights in the financial markets. In a firm commitment underwritten offering, the investment banker purchases the new shares from the firm and then offers the shares for sale to the public. The firm's proceeds are guaranteed, and the risk is borne by the underwriter.

Several interesting features regarding issues of new shares have been noted in recent research and provide the motivation for the studies discussed.

1. In the United States underwriters are employed in over 80 percent of the offerings (see Smith 1977). Recent studies that have analyzed the costs of employing each method of issue do not provide a convincing explanation for the prevalence of the underwritten offerings. Moreover, Marsh (1979) found that in the United Kingdom, during 1975, 99 percent of the new equity was raised through rights offers.

2. In rights offers the subscription price is typically set slightly below the prevailing market price, despite the fact that by setting the subscription arbitrarily low the issuer can ensure the success of the offer.

3. If the issuer uses the services of an investment banker, the most common contractual agreement is a "firm commitment" contract. Other arrangements observed in practice are the "best efforts" and "standby" contracts.

4. Both seasoned and unseasoned issues appear to be underpriced. Ibbotson (1975) and Ibbotson and Jaffe (1975) found that on average unseasoned issues are sold at an 11.4 percent and 16.8 percent, respectively, discount relative to their price in the aftermarket. Furthermore, Smith (1977) found that in the underwritten issue of seasoned securities the initial offering price is below both the market price prevailing prior to arrival of the new issue and the price following the distribution of the new issue.

We survey several models that have been proposed to explain the above features. We start (Section I) with models dealing with the pricing of new issues. An understanding of the underpricing phenomena is necessary to the analysis of alternative methods for floating new issues, since the pricing decision may affect the choice of the selling method. Section II provides a comparison between rights and underwritten offerings. The design of the contract between the issuer and the investment banker is the subject of Section III. Concluding remarks are contained in the last section.

I. PRICING OF NEW SHARES

In this section we discuss models of underwritten offerings of new shares of both seasoned and unseasoned securities. The purpose of these models is to explain why the offering price chosen by the underwriter may be below the market value of the securities. The explanations of Rock (1986) and Parsons and Raviv (1986) are based on the characteristics of the selling mechanism employed in marketing the securities. The explanation of Baron (1982) stresses the incentives problems in the principal-agent relationship between the issuer and the underwriter.

Rock (1986) provides a nice model explaining why unseasoned issues are, on average, sold at a discount. In his model the discount is a consequence of the asymmetrically informed investors and the rationing that occurs if the issue is oversubscribed. The population consists of informed and uninformed investors. Informed investors know the "true" value of the firm and purchase shares only if the price does not exceed this value. Uninformed investors attempt to purchase shares based on the comparison between the share's expected value and its price. The uninformed investor recognizes that the fraction of the order he receives is inversely related to the value of the share. Whenever the issue is undersubscribed, he receives the whole order, but the undersubscription arises precisely because the informed investors choose not to purchase (i.e., in cases where the issue is overpriced). On the other hand, when the share is highly valued by the informed investors, then the issue is oversubscribed and the uninformed investor receives a small fraction of his order. This consideration lowers the price that the uninformed investor is willing to pay for the new issue below its expected value. This is the essence of Rock's (1986) explanation of the underpricing phenomenon. The equilibrium offer price of new equity has to compensate for the bias resulting from the uneven rationing of high- and low-quality shares.

Rock's explanation of underpricing is very appealing. It is also robust to changes in the assumptions of the formal model he develops. The driving force behind the result is the uneven rationing of shares. Investors have to be compensated (through lower offer price) for the "winner's curse" effect; they receive the "worst" shares with the highest probability. As a result, the offer price has to be below the expected value of the shares.

As mentioned above, this explanation depends only on the bias in rationing "good" issues relative to "bad" issues. It is, therefore, crucially dependent on the selling mechanism. For all selling schemes resulting in biased rationing, the issuer has to offer a discount to the uninformed investors. But how about alternative selling methods? Can one design a selling method that will not result in a biased allocation? Why do we not observe these schemes being used to enhance the revenue from selling new issues? An example of such a mechanism is similar to the weekly auction used to sell Treasury bills. Suppose that the issuer announces that all buyers can place their orders as either a competitive or a noncompetitive bid. A noncompetitive bidder will receive his full order at the average price of all accepted competitive bids. The competitive bidders will be allocated all shares that were not sold to noncompetitive buyers based on their bid price; higher-price bidders will be allocated before those that submitted lower bids. If this scheme was employed in the environment described by Rock's (1986) model, all uninformed and informed investors would be sold their shares without any allocational bias. Thus, on average, issues would not be underpriced if this scheme were used.

The more general point illustrated by this simple example is that Rock (1986) takes the selling mechanism as exogenously given. The question that arises is whether one can design a better mechanism, one that alleviates the biased allocation to the uninformed investor and thus obviates the underpricing. In the simple environment described by Rock (1986), I have proposed such a mechanism. It is interesting to investigate the "best"—that is, expected revenue-maximizing—mechanism for selling securities in an environment characterized by asymmetric information. (See Milgrom and Weber 1982, Harris and Raviv 1981, and Parsons and Raviv 1986 for a beginning of such a treatment.)

Rock's (1986) model dealt with the underpricing of unseasoned securities. Parsons and Raviv (1986) provide a model of the underwritten offerings of new shares of seasoned securities. In this model an existing firm has a new project to be financed by asymmetrically informed investors. Each investor is assumed to know his own valuation but not that of any other investor, except, of course, the incomplete information revealed through the markets. Neither the firm nor the investment banker knows the valuation of any investor. The model distinguishes between two market stages. First, there exists a competitive market in the "old" shares that is affected by the announcement of the new issue. Second, the new issue is sold by the underwriter and enters the market. The equilibrium solution recognizes the interdependence between the markets in the two stages. Therefore the first-stage competitive solution results from investors' demands/supplies derived in anticipation of the events in the second stage. Parsons and Raviv (1986) prove that the equilibrium price in the competitive market operating prior to the arrival of the new issue will always be *higher* than the price at which the new issue will be sold. This result helps explain the empirical observation that new issues of seasoned securities are underpriced.

The major insight gained about the pricing of a new issue is that market prices and the underwriter's offer price are jointly determined in the equilibrium. The investment banker, then, cannot simply set the initial offer price to correspond to the current market price. In the model the banker sets on *optimal* offer price, and the market reacts to this choice. Thus, according to Parsons and Raviv's (1986) theory, the underpricing phenomenon should not be interpreted as an irrational setting of the offering price below the market value; it is a reaction of the market to an anticipated offering price, the potential for oversubscription and the rationing that will follow. In this model the underwriter chooses the initial offering price, attempting to attract investors with a high valuation of the firm's new project. This price is set low enough to encourage high-valuation investors to purchase at this initial price rather than to attempt to buy at a subsequently lowered price. The high-valuation investors recognize that they will be successful in purchasing at a lower price only in the event that the issue is undersubscribed at the initial price. The underwriter uses this threat to charge an initial price that extracts some of the surplus from high-valuation investors, but due to asymmetric information he cannot set it high enough to extract all of the surplus. Therefore, since investors can purchase a share with certainty in the market for old securities taking place before the new issue arrives, the competitive price will be driven to a level higher than the initial offering price.

The Parsons and Raviv (1986) analysis views the selling of new shares as an auction in which asymmetrically informed investors bid for shares. They employ results from auction theory to analyze the optimal offering price and compare among alternative selling schemes. The above explanation of underpricing is derived for the independent valuations model, in which the heterogeneity among investors is exogenously imposed, and the dependent valuations model, in which the source for the divergence in valuations and its resolution are explicitly incorporated.

A different explanation for the underpricing phenomena is offered by Baron (1982), who focuses on the principal-agent relationship between the issuer and the investment banker. In Baron's model the banker has better information about the likely market demand than does the issuer. The offer price decision is delegated to the banker so that he can utilize his superior information. This delegation is complicated because the proceeds from the sale of the issue are assumed to depend also on the distribution effort of the banker. Since this distribution effort is costly to the banker, the issuer has to design an optimal compensation scheme to deal with the banker's "moral hazard." Baron (1982) investigates the optimal contract in this agency relationship. The analysis is complicated by the informational asymmetry between the banker and the issuer. In an example, Baron succeeds in showing that it might be in the interest of the issuer to delegate the offer-price decision to the banker. This offer price is shown to be below the first-best offer price, the offer price that would be set under symmetric information. This underpricing increases as the issuer becomes more uncertain about the market demand for his securities. Note that Baron's (1982) model is the only explanation of underpricing within a framework in which there is a positive role for the investment banker. In contrast, the investment banker played no essential role in Rock (1986) and Parsons and Raviv (1986).

II. RIGHTS VERSUS UNDERWRITTEN OFFERINGS

In this section we discuss the choice of the method for issuing new securities. In particular, we seek to understand the relative costs and benefits of issuing new shares via the rights offerings and firm commitment underwritten offerings described in the Introduction.

The most commonly cited reasons for employing an investment banker are to underwrite the issue, to market the new shares, and to advise the issuer in the difficult pricing decision. It appears that all three of these functions are rendered unnecessary in the rights issue. If the subscription price is set sufficiently low, the success of the new issue can be virtually guaranteed, the subscription price appears to be an insignificant parameter of the offer because a low subscription price is equivalent to a stock split without any economic consequences, and the marketing of new shares is accomplished by existing shareholders exercising their rights or selling them to new investors. Thus, it seems that rights offerings dominate the underwritten offerings. The problem is made even more difficult since a careful examination by Smith (1977) of the costs involved in rights and underwritten offerings showed that the out-of-pocket expenses of an underwritten equity issue are from 3 to 30 times higher than the costs of a rights offering.

In an attempt to explain the prevalence of the underwritten offerings, Parsons and Raviv (1986) investigated the revenue generated from the alternative selling methods. Their model was discussed in Section I in connection with the pricing decision of the underwriter. Interpreting the underwritten issue as a priority pricing scheme (see Harris and Raviv 1981), they were able to compare its expected revenue to the expected revenue from a rights issue that was viewed as a competitive (single-price) auction. To clarify the auction analogy, we now discuss each method of selling securities.

In an underwritten offering the underwriter sets an initial offer price, but may drop the price in case shares are unsold. Each investor chooses his demand at each of the two prices, knowing the "priority" allocation rule used by the underwriter: investors requesting to purchase at the initial offering price are allocated their shares first, and only after all demands at this price have been fulfilled are investors waiting to purchase at the lower price allocated a share or fraction thereof. The optimal pricing strategy for the underwriter is to set the prices to induce investors with high valuation of the firm's shares to purchase at the initial offering price, whereas those with a lower valuation will wait and purchase only if the price is lowered. In the rights issue it is known at the time of announcement that the competitive equilibrium price for an ex rights share will be equal to the value of this share to either a high- or a low-valuation investor, depending on their relative demand. This price is identical to the price that would obtain in a competitive auction for the shares. Therefore, the expected total revenue received for the sale of the new shares in the rights issue is equal to the expected revenue from a competitive auction. This expected revenue and the revenue in a "priority pricing" scheme are equal in the independent valuations model, and therefore the underwritten and rights offerings are equivalent with respect to the expected revenue raised.

The above discussion should not be viewed as a definite claim that the two methods are equivalent. First, dependent valuations introduce new considerations into the comparison between the two methods of sale, making the expected revenue comparison ambiguous. Second, current shareholders are concerned with more than just the revenue raised by the new issue. A complete treatment of their welfare has not been achieved.

Heinkel and Schwartz (1986) also address the problem of choosing a flotation method. They view the choice among underwritten and rights offerings as an attempt by the issuing firms to signal their quality. In their model, when the equity offer is announced, the issuer knows more about the stock price than investors or underwriters do. The highest-quality firms choose a standby rights issue in which the underwriter becomes informed, at a fixed exogenous cost, about the quality of the firm. The intermediate-quality firms choose an uninsured rights issue with optimally selected subscription price. Since failure of a rights offering is costly, a higher-quality firm using this method can credibly distinguish itself by choosing a high subscription price and, by doing so, subject itself to the risk of a costly failure. In equilibrium the quality of the intermediate group firms is ranked by the subscription price. The lowest-quality group of firms chooses an uninformed underwriter to sell their shares at a common offer price. These lower-quality firms are better off using the apparently more costly underwriting method because the costs of signaling and the costs of investigation in a rights offer would be even higher.

The Heinkel and Schwartz (1986) model explains two empirical regularities. First, they explain why firms use the costly underwritten offer method of selling equity. Second, they provide a reason why firms using uninsured rights offers do not set arbitrarily low subscription prices to ensure the success of the issue, even though shareholder wealth is unaffected by the level of the subscription price in a perfect market. The only weakness of the model is in the crucial assumption about the source of the asymmetric information signaled through the choice of the flotation method. It is assumed that the distribution of the stock price at the expiration of the right is known to the firm and unknown to the investment banker and the investors. The whole model is based upon this information asymmetry. The question is whether the asymmetry regarding the stock price in the next three to four weeks is significant enough to give rise to the signaling equilibrium and determine the choice of the selling method.

III. THE UNDERWRITING CONTRACT

Several forms of underwriting contracts are observed in practice. The major ones are "firm commitment" contract, "best-efforts" contract, and "standby" contract. In a firm commitment contract the underwriter purchases the entire issue outright and thus ensures the issuer of receiving a fixed amount of funds. If the issue does not sell well, the underwriter, and not the issuer, takes a loss. In a best-efforts contract only the distribution facilities of the investment banker are employed, without any insurance function. In a standby contract the banker binds himself to purchase all the securities that the issuing corporation may be unable to sell at a prespecified price. In this form of agreement the risk is shared by the issuer and the investment banker.

The economic analysis of the underwriting contract applies the results of the general agency theory. In all the following studies the issuer is viewed as the principal engaging the services of the investment banker as an agent. The contract is designed to resolve optimally the conflicts between the two parties involved. The literature focuses on various aspects of the agency relationship. Mandelker and Raviv (1977) view the underwriting contract as an optimal risk-sharing arrangement. In their analysis the issuer and the investment banker have symmetric information about the *exogenously* determined stochastic proceeds from the new issue. Baron (1979, 1982) and Baron and Holmstrom (1980) investigate the incentive problem resulting from the inability of the issuer to observe the effort expended by the banker in distributing the securities. To mitigate the incentive problem, the issuer must design an incentive contract to induce the banker to expend more effort. This optimal incentive contract is investigated under various assumptions about the information structure. Baron (1979) assumed that the issuer and the investment banker have symmetric information at the time of contracting as well as during the selling of the issue. Baron and Holmstrom (1980) also assumed symmetric information at the time of contracting but recognized that thereafter the banker is able to acquire private information. In Baron (1982) the contract design problem is analyzed under the assumption that prior to contracting the banker has superior information about the likely market demand.

A general statement about the optimal contract in all of the above environments is difficult to make. In all symmetric information models the firm commitment contract is optimal if the underwriter is risk neutral. Otherwise some kind of risk sharing and decision delegation is optimal, which is also true in the asymmetric information cases. In these cases the models developed provide an insight into the nature of the conflict between the banker and the issuer and the ways in which the compensation scheme resolves part of this conflict.

IV. CONCLUSION

We have attempted to review some papers related to investment banking. The focus was on formal models dealing with the choice of the method for floating and pricing new issues, and the contract between the issuer and the investment banker. Each paper discussed analyzes some aspect of these problems. None of the papers, however, provides a framework in which all of these issues can be investigated simultaneously. The next step in the inquiry is the construction of a model in which the choice of the method for selling a new issue is investigated simultaneously with the contract design question and in anticipation of the pricing strategies available to the banker and the issuer.

NOTES

[1] The important problem of choosing the security to be floated and the announcement effects are not discussed here. See Smith (1986) for a survey of the literature on this issue.

REFERENCES

Baron, David P. 1979. "The Incentive Problem and the Design of Investment Banking Contracts." *Journal of Banking and Finance* 3: 157–75.
———. 1982. "A Model of the Demand for Investment Banking Advising and Distribution Services for New Issues." *Journal of Finance* 37: 955–76.
Baron, David P., and Holmstrom, Bengt. 1980. "The Investment Banking Contract for New Issues under Asymmetric Information: Delegation and the Incentive Problem." *Journal of Finance* 35: 1115–38.
Harris, Milton, and Raviv, Artur. 1981. "A Theory of Monopoly Pricing Schemes with Demand Uncertainty." *American Economic Review* 71: 347–65.
Heinkel, Robert, and Schwartz, Eduardo S. 1986. "Rights Versus Underwritten Offerings: An Asymmetric Information Approach." *Journal of Finance* 41: 1–18.
Ibbotson, Roger. 1975. "Price Performance of Common Stock New Issues." *Journal of Financial Economics* 2: 235–72.
Ibbotson, Roger G., and Jaffe, Jeffrey F. 1975. " 'Hot Issue' Markets." *Journal of Finance* 30: 1027–42.
Mandelker, Gershon, and Raviv, Artur. 1977. "Investment Banking: An Economic Analysis of Optimal Underwriting Contracts." *Journal of Finance* 32: 683–94.
Marsh, Paul. 1979. "Equity Rights Issues and the Efficiency of the UK Stock Market." *Journal of Finance* 34: 839–62.
Milgrom, Paul, and Weber, Robert. 1982. "A Theory of Auctions and Competitive Bidding." *Econometrica* 50: 1089–1122.
Parsons, John, and Raviv, Artur. 1986. "Underpricing of Seasoned Issues." *Journal of Financial Economics* 14: 377–97.
Rock, Kevin. 1986. "Why New Issues Are Underpriced." *Journal of Financial Economics* 15: 187–212.
Smith, Clifford. 1977. "Alternative Methods for Raising Capital: Rights Versus Underwritten Offerings." *Journal of Financial Economics* 5: 273–307.
———. 1986. "Investment Banking and the Capital Acquisition Process." *Journal of Financial Economics* 15: 3–29.

Reprinted from THE BELL JOURNAL OF ECONOMICS

Vol. 10, No. 1, Spring 1979

Copyright © 1979, American Telephone and Telegraph Company

Imperfect information, dividend policy, and "the bird in the hand" fallacy

Sudipto Bhattacharya
Graduate School of Business
University of Chicago

This paper assumes that outside investors have imperfect information about firms' profitability and that cash dividends are taxed at a higher rate than capital gains. It is shown that under these conditions, such dividends function as a signal of expected cash flows. By structuring the model so that finite-lived investors turn over continuing projects to succeeding generations of investors, we derive a comparative static result that relates the equilibrium level of dividend payout to the length of investors' planning horizons.

1. Introduction

■ This article develops a model in which cash dividends function as a signal of expected cash flows of firms in an imperfect-information setting. We assume that the productive assets in which agents invest stay in place longer than the agents live and that ownership of the assets is transferred, over time, to other agents. The latter are *a priori* imperfectly informed about the profitability of assets held by different firms. The major signaling costs that lead dividends to function as signals arise because dividends are taxed at the ordinary income tax rate, whereas capital gains are taxed at a lower rate. Within this framework, this paper explains why firms may pay dividends despite the tax disadvantage of doing so.

Recently, Leland and Pyle (1977) and Ross (1977) have used the paradigm of Spence's signaling model (1974) to examine financial market phenomena related to unsystematic risk borne by entrepreneurs and firm debt-equity choice decisions, respectively. In its spirit and cost structure, our model is closely related to the Ross model (1977). The essential contributions of our model are the following. First, we develop a tax-based signaling cost structure founded on the observation that signaling equilibria are feasible, even if signaling cost elements that are negatively related to true expected cash flows are small, provided there are other signaling costs that are not related to true cash flow levels. Second, we develop the model in an intertemporal setting that allows

This paper is a revised version of a chapter of my Ph.D. dissertation at the Sloan School of Management, Massachusetts Institute of Technology (1977). I wish to thank Professors Carliss Baldwin, Jonathan Ingersoll, Stanley Kon, Joseph Williams, and, especially, Professors Robert C. Merton, Stewart C. Myers, Merton H. Miller, and an anonymous referee and the Editorial Board of this Journal for discussions and for helpful comments. I alone bear the responsibility for any remaining errors.

us to identify the relative weights placed on the benefits (increase in value) and costs of signaling with dividends. Our model suggests an interesting comparative static result concerning the shareholders' planning horizon; namely, the shorter the horizons over which shareholders have to realize their wealth, the higher is the equilibrium proportion of dividends to expected earnings.[1] Other comparative static properties of the dividend-signaling equilibrium, with respect to major variables like the personal income tax rate and the rate of interest, are also developed and are shown to be in accord with the empirical results of Brittain (1966).

To keep the analysis manageable, and to highlight the essential characteristics, we employ two major analytical simplifications. First, we assume that the valuation of cash flow streams is done in a risk-neutral world. Second, we allow the "urgency" of the agents' need to realize their wealth to be parameterized by the length of the planning horizons over which they maximize expected discounted realized wealth, with no detailed consideration of the intertemporal pattern of asset disposal. These assumptions are further discussed below, after the basic model is developed. The general structure of the dividend-signaling model and the conditions for the existence of dividend-signaling equilibria are developed in Section 2. In Section 3 we analyze an example with uniformly distributed cash flows to facilitate discussion of comparative static properties and issues related to multiperiod planning horizons and dynamic learning possibilities. Section 4 contains the concluding remarks and suggestions for further research.

2. Dividends as signals

■ In this section we outline the nature of the dividend-signaling model and the signaling cost structure. The model applies to a setting in which outside investors cannot distinguish (*a priori*) the profitability of productive assets held by a cross section of firms. Existing shareholders of firms care about the market value "assigned" by outsiders, because the planning horizon over which they have to realize their wealth is shorter than the time span over which the firms' assets generate cash flows. The simplifying assumption of risk-neutrality eliminates the diversification motive. The usual noncooperative evolution arguments of the Spence-type (1974) suggest a signaling equilibrium, if a signal with the appropriate cost-structure properties exists. Dividends are shown to satisfy the requirements.

We ignore the incorporation of other sources of information (e.g., accountants' reports) on the ground that, taken by themselves, they are fundamentally unreliable "screening" mechanisms because of the moral hazard involved in communicating profitability. Hence, the model of this paper is somewhat exploratory in nature, a property that it shares with most other signaling models in which the costliness of signals derives from exogenous considerations.[2]

---

[1] The old "bird in the hand" argument that agents have to realize their wealth for consumption and that, somehow, dividends are "superior" to capital gains for this purpose is, of course, fallacious in a perfectly informed, competitive financial market, even under uncertainty. For a proof, refer to Miller and Modigliani (1961).

[2] A complementary approach to the dividend-signaling problem, which deals with signaling of insiders' information in the presence of indicators of *ex post* profitability that are *not* exogenously costly, is developed in Bhattacharya (1977). A synthesis of the two types of models would provide a richer framework that could incorporate an interesting "partial" role for sources of information like accounting reports.

To preserve the simplicity of the model's structure, we assume that assets owned by firms generate cash flows that are perpetual streams, which are, in most of what follows, taken to be intertemporally independently identically distributed. In this section, and for most of the paper, we assume that existing shareholders have a single-period planning horizon. The firms are assumed to have sufficient investment opportunities, so that *all* of the cash flows from existing assets can be rationally reinvested. This simplifying assumption can be relaxed somewhat. The communication of even *ex post* cash flows from existing assets is assumed to be costly, because cash payouts in the form of dividends on regular share repurchases are assumed to be taxed at a higher personal tax rate than capital gains.[3] In the absence of explicit cash payout, before taking on outside financing for new investments, *ex post* cash flows *cannot* be communicated without moral hazard, because one of the "inside" variables that a firm cannot readily communicate without moral hazard is the level of new investment.

It is assumed that the signaling benefit of dividends derives from the rise in *liquidation* value $V(D)$ caused by a *committed*, and actually paid, dividend level D. We develop the model in terms of a marginal analysis for a new project taken on by a firm. This simplification serves two purposes. First, not analyzing dividend decisions *vis-à-vis* existing and new asset cash flows enables us to postpone discussion of dynamic learning issues to the example in Section 3. Second, this mode of analysis permits us to retain simplicity and flexibility with respect to the modeling of costs incurred in making up shortfalls of cash flows relative to promised dividends. For example, one way of making up such shortfalls is likely to be the postponement of investment/replacement plans, although fundamentally we adhere to the sound partial equilibrium practice of analyzing the dividend decision when the investment policy is given.[4] It is assumed that dividend decisions are taken by shareholders' agents, whom we term insiders or managers. These agents optimize the after-tax objective function of shareholders, possibly because their own incentive compensation is tied to the same criterion. The insiders are the only people who know the cash flow distributions of their projects.

Let X represent the uncertain cash flow from the new project being considered at the end of the period that corresponds to the current shareholders' planning horizon. It is assumed that dividends paid to shareholders are taxed at a personal income tax rate of $(1 - \alpha)$ and, for simplicity, that capital gains are not taxed at all. Let D denote the incremental dividend commitment made on account of the new project, and $V(D)$ the signaling response of incremental liquidation value. If X is above D, D in dividends is paid, current shareholders receive αD after taxes, and the extent of outside financing required for reinvestment is reduced by $(X - D)$, relative to a state of nature in which X equals D. If X is below

---

[3] In a recent paper Miller and Scholes (1978) have pointed out that the tax disadvantage of dividends is reduced by investors' ability to offset dividend income by interest deductions on borrowings, combined with investment of the proceeds from the borrowing in tax-sheltered means of accumulation like life insurance contracts and retirement accounts. Whether or not this effect has more than inframarginal implications empirically, and, if the effect is valid at the margin, then the reconciliation of this model with other tax-based models of financial structure like that of Miller (1977), are very much unresolved issues at present.

[4] In fact, the model only requires that there be sufficient investment opportunities for the cash flows.

D, D in dividends is still paid, and it is assumed that making up the "shortfall" $(D - X)$ results in costs to current shareholders amounting to $(1 + \beta)(D - X)$, relative to a state of nature in which X equals D.

The essential justification for our assumption that the cost of making up a cash-flow deficit is more than the benefit of a cash-flow surplus of the same size is that frictionless access to extra external financing is assumed to be unavailable. Basically, we are assuming, realistically, that one of the "market conventions" that prevails in a dividend-signaling equilibrium is that a firm "should" be able to meet its dividend commitment without recourse to extra, "unanticipated" new financing. Thus, the possibility of X's being low means that to pay the committed level of dividends the firm is forced to incur the costs of either the organization and transaction costs of selling real, physical assets in the secondary market or postponing, but not necessarily canceling, investment/ replacement programs of positive net present value. Similar dissipative costs are assumed to arise if the firm can cope by keeping buffer stocks of liquid assets earning less than the discount rate or if it has the ability to negotiate, at extra cost, some unanticipated "bail-out" financing.[5] If the substitution of cash-flow surpluses for previously planned external financing is costly—because the surplus has to be temporarily kept as liquid assets or because the cancellation of planned external financing is costly—, then there is an effect in the same direction on the cost structure. As we shall see, these "frictional" costs play an essential role in making for a feasible signaling equilibrium.[6]

Given the foregoing discussion, we can write the incremental part of the objective function of current shareholders and their agents as:

$$E(D) = \frac{1}{1 + r}\left[V(D) + \alpha D + \int_{D}^{\bar{X}} (X - D)f(X)dX \right.$$

$$\left. + \int_{\underline{X}}^{D} (1 + \beta)(X - D)f(X)dX \right] \quad (1a)$$

$$= \frac{1}{1 + r}\left[V(D) + M - (1 - \alpha)D - \beta \int_{\underline{X}}^{D} F(X)dX \right], \quad (1b)$$

where $f(X)$ and $F(X)$ represent the density and distribution functions of X assumed to be distributed over $(\underline{X}, \bar{X})$, M represents the mean cash flow, and r is the per period rate of interest after personal income taxes. In our economy with only one class of investors, r can be either the interest rate on a tax-exempt bond, or α times the before-tax interest rate on taxable bonds.[7]

Current shareholders' agents choose D to maximize $E(D)$. In equilibrium, the endogenous $V(D)$ schedule provides consistent valuation of cash flows beyond the planning horizon. That is, given the equilibrium $V(D)$ schedule and the optimizing dividend decision, all shareholders make a competitive after-tax

---

[5] For simplicity we exclude using cash flow surpluses relative to dividend commitments for other assets assuming, essentially, perfect correlation of cash flows. Adding that factor would not alter the basic nature of the structure.

[6] A similar cost of making up the deficit of liquid assets relative to deposit withdrawals plays a critical role in bank asset management models (see e.g., Pyle (1972)).

[7] The assumption of a flat and nonstochastic term structure is solely for simplicity, although a partial equilibrium model like ours does not go into the details of how r is affected by agents' time preferences and endowments in this economy. Note also that the risk-neutrality assumption has been useful for valuing the "truncated" deficit makeup cost.

market return of r on their investments in firms.[8] The critical existence condition for a Spence-type (1974) signaling equilibrium is that the marginal signaling cost—which in our model is seen to be $[(1 - \alpha) + \beta F(D)]$, from (1b)—must be strictly negatively related to the source of true value, the mean cash flow M. If the cross section of projects is such that the "family" of distribution functions $\{F(Z)\}$ has the same ordering across the cross section for all Z, and the ordering is possibly weak only where at least some $F(Z) = 1$, then this existence condition is satisfied for $D < \bar{X}$, since M is lower for a project whose cash-flow distribution function F strictly dominates that of the other in comparison. Of course, the assertion that this condition is sufficient in our model assumes that the equilibrium implications of today's dividends for future dividends are such that the true *value* of future cash flows, taking account of the personal income tax implications of future dividends, is positively related to M. This seems very reasonable, and it holds in all the examples of Section 3.

In the next section—specifically in equations (6c) and footnote 13—I derive the asymptotic distribution-free equilibrium solutions for D as a function of mean cash flow M (denoted $t/2$ there), and the signaling cost and interest rate parameters for single- and multiperiod shareholder planning horizons. It is technically possible for a solution for D to lie between M and $\bar{X}$ and satisfy the maximization and consistency criteria defined above. But it is difficult to justify the survival of an exogenously costly signaling equilibrium that "requires" D to be greater than M, since *ex post* cash flows can be disclosed by paying out *before* taking on outside financing for new investment, at a lower average tax cost.

3. An example of comparative statics

■ Having discussed the general structure of the model and the costs that permit dividends to function as a signal, we now use a simple example to examine in more detail the nature of equilibrium and its comparative statics. Suppose the incremental cash flow of the project whose value is being signaled is, in any given period, distributed uniformly over $[0, t]$ with mean $t/2$. All projects are perpetuities and, for the time being, the cash flows of each project are taken to be intertemporally independently identically distributed. In the cross section of firms the value of t is assumed to vary between t_{min} and t_{max}, but investors cannot discriminate among projects with different t's held by different firms. It is further assumed that $t_{min} = 0$. This is partly for analytical convenience but, *vis-à-vis* a marginal project in any given firm, this is a natural assumption since one of the "inside" variables that a firm cannot costlessly communicate to the market without moral hazard is the amount of investment it undertakes. Initially, we continue to assume shareholders have a one-period planning horizon.

Using equation (1b), we find that, given a market signaling value function $V(D)$, the current shareholders' agents choose D to maximize

$$\underset{D}{\text{Max }} E(D) = \frac{1}{(1 + r)} \left[\frac{t}{2} + V(D) - (1 - \alpha)D - \beta \frac{D^2}{2t} \right]. \tag{2}$$

---

[8] In our model we consider only all-equity firms. Introducing debt would not alter the basic nature of the results. However, the simultaneous optimization of debt and dividend policy would be complex. If substantial dividend payments exist, then the simple Miller-type (1977) equilibrium in which only aggregate corporate debt is determinate is not likely to hold. We should note that introducing different shareholder tax rates into the signaling model is very tricky, if both shareholder unanimity and the consistency condition are to be preserved.

As in Section 2, $V(D)$ is the exdividend value associated with committing and later paying dividends D, at the *end* of the one-period horizon. Maximization of $E(D)$ with respect to D yields the first-order condition,

$$V'(D^*) - (1 - \alpha) - \beta \frac{D^*}{t} = 0, \tag{3}$$

where the optimum D^* is, of course, conditional on t.

The market signaling value function $V(D)$ survives in equilibrium only if expectations are fulfilled, i.e., only if $V(D^*)$ is the true value of *future* (post-horizon) cash flows for the project whose cash flows are signaled with dividend D^*. To impose this requirement, future levels of dividends to be paid by the firm on account of the project must be specified because $V(D^*)$ should only reflect the value that is not dissipated by taxes and other losses of future dividends. In a model with genuine time structure, this is a difficult issue to decide. The perpetuity structure of our model, in conjunction with an assumption that succeeding generations of shareholders will also have one-period horizons, would suggest a stationary dividend for any given t, given the intertemporally independently identically distributed nature of cash flows. On the other hand, there is the argument that in a model with genuine time structure, there should be some learning about t from the observed *ex post* frequency of asset sales or unanticipated new financing needed for making up shortfalls of cash flows compared with promised dividends. Therefore, as time goes on, outside investors' ability to discriminate among project cash flows of different firms should improve.

There appears to be no simple way to incorporate dynamic learning phenomena into an imperfect information signaling model, and we do not attempt to make any contributions to that area. In the context of intertemporally independently identically distributed project cash flows, dynamic learning may be ignored if outside investors cannot observe unanticipated, deficit makeup financing as such, although the extra cost of such financing is an integral part of our model. In addition, a strong argument in favor of a stationary structure—which is perceived most clearly in the case of a corner solution of full payout—is that a firm cannot, without moral hazard, distinguish (for outsiders) an early-in-life payout from a new project from payouts supported by later-in-life cash flows from an old project.

An equilibrium $V(D)$ schedule predicated on a stationary dividend assumption is defined by the consistency condition, along the equilibrium schedule $D^*(t)$, that

$$V(D^*(t)) = K\left[\frac{t}{2} - (1 - \alpha)D^*(t) - \beta \frac{D^{*2}(t)}{2t}\right], \tag{4}$$

where $K = 1/r$. It can be shown[9] that the same consistency condition (4) is

---

[9] Consider the case in which, for any given project, t follows a random walk without drift over time, so that a continuing dividend signal is "required" in the future. Given the random walk, the expected value of any future t is just today's t, for any today. Now consider the following convergence argument. Let $V(D)$ now represent the response of *current* value to the committed level of dividends D. Assume for a moment that, in a fulfilled (rational) expectations equilibrium, the current shareholders' agents assume that $V(D)$ is linear in D and that equilibrium $D^*(t)$ is proportional to t. Then, the following implications for conditional expected values of future levels

implied when the mean cash flows of projects follow random walks without drift over time, so no significant learning can take place. Although this is a strong assumption, it is at least fully internally consistent to ignore dynamic learning in this situation. It should be noted that, because of the perpetuity structure and the stationary dividend assumption, the same equilibrium consistency condition (4) applies to the *current* market value of the project. The analysis that follows applies to the intertemporally independently identically distributed cash flows case with dynamic learning ignored as well as to the driftless random walk case.

Equations (3) and (4) provide us with sufficient information to solve for the equilibrium $V(D)$ and $D^*(t)$ schedules and to check that the second-order condition for the maximization problem of equation (2) is satisfied. In Section 4 we discuss possible mechanisms by which the consistency condition (equation (4)) may be arrived at in this setting. Here we work out the detailed implications of our model.

Totally differentiating equation (4), and substituting for $V'(D)$ from equation (3), we obtain

$$(K + 1)\left[(1 - \alpha) + \beta \frac{D}{t}\right]\frac{dD}{dt} = K\left[\frac{1}{2} + \beta \frac{D^2}{2t^2}\right] \qquad (5)$$

as the equation that must hold along the equilibrium schedule $D^*(t)$. Given our assumption that $t_{min} = 0$, the boundary condition to equation (5) for the surviving Pareto-superior schedule, which corresponds to the "lowest" member incurring no dissipative costs of signaling, as in Riley (1975), is given by

$$D^*(0) = 0. \qquad (5a)$$

To solve equation (5) subject to the boundary condition (5a), we try a solution of the form

$$D^*(t) = At, \qquad (6a)$$

which obviously satisfies (5a). Substituting from (6a) into (5), we get the quadratic

---

of the variables are immediate:

$$\epsilon[V(D)] = V(\epsilon[D]) = V(D)$$

$$\epsilon[(1 - \alpha)D] = (1 - \alpha)D$$

$$\epsilon\left[\beta \frac{D^2}{2t}\right] = \beta \frac{D^2}{2t},$$

where ϵ is the conditional expectations operator with respect to any future period, and the right-hand-side terms refer to current values of the variables. Given these implications, it is evident that the agents' objective function, which should reflect expected next-period liquidation values, formally remains the same as that in equation (2), and the same equilibrium consistency condition, equation (4), must hold for the *current* value schedule $V(D)$. We show in the text below that, given the structure provided by equations (2) and (4), the equilibrium dividend $D^*(t)$ is indeed proportional to t and that $V(D)$ is linear in D, for the uniform distribution case here. Thus, the same formal solution is also an internally consistent fulfilled-expectations signaling equilibrium when t's follow a random walk. It should also be clear from the linearity of the distribution-free asymptotic ($\beta \to 0$) solutions below, and the conditional expectations arguments above, that a similar argument holds for the "asymptotic case."

equation for A

$$\frac{(K + 2)}{(K + 1)} A^2 + \frac{2(1 - \alpha)}{\beta} A - \frac{K}{\beta(K + 1)} = 0.$$

The positive root for A is given by

$$A = -\frac{(1 - \alpha)}{\beta} \cdot \frac{(K + 1)}{(K + 2)} + \frac{(1 - \alpha)}{\beta}$$

$$\times \frac{(K + 1)}{(K + 2)} \sqrt{1 + \frac{\beta K(K + 2)}{(1 - \alpha)^2 (K + 1)^2}}. \quad (6b)$$

Given equation (3), together with the boundary condition $V(0) = 0$, equilibrium $V(D)$ is given by

$$V(D) = ((1 - \alpha) + \beta A)D. \quad (7)$$

It is easy to verify that, given this $V(D)$, the first-order condition for the maximization problem of equation (2) is satisfied at $D/t = A$, and that the second-order condition for a maximum is also satisfied for $\beta > 0$. The solution for $\beta = 0$ or the binomial approximation for $\beta \ll (1 - \alpha)^2$ is given by

$$A = \frac{1}{2} \cdot \frac{K}{(K + 1)(1 - \alpha)}. \quad (6c)$$

Of course, if $\beta = 0$, then the "equilibrium" $V(D) = (1 - \alpha)D$ does not result in a strict maximum for the shareholders' maximization problem. In practice, β is likely to be small and the resulting convexity "weak." The implications of this are further discussed in Section 4.[10]

Two important comparative statics of the equilibrium solution $D^*(t)$ are as follows. First, equilibrium A is decreasing in the tax rate $(1 - \alpha)$ in both (6b) and (6c). Second, since $(K + 1)/(K + 2)$, $K(K + 2)/(K + 1)^2$, and $K/(K + 1)$ are all increasing functions of K, the equilibrium A is an increasing function of K, and thus a decreasing function of the rate of interest r. On a note of casual empiricism, both of these comparative-static results are in accord with the empirical results of Brittain's comprehensive study (1966) of corporate dividends.

To provide an intuitive understanding of these comparative statics, it is helpful to develop the notion of what is needed in the way of signaling cost for insiders to "tell the truth," i.e., for there to be an optimum $D^*(t)$ solution which satisfies a consistency condition of the type in equation (4). (The task is a little tricky because $V(D)$ is endogenized and thus responds to parameter variation.) The essence of the notion is captured by the following description of the role that the tax cost of dividends plays in making for a feasible signaling equilibrium. In the absence of the tax costs, an interior optimum $D^*(t)$ would be produced only by a $V(D)$ that had a very low response to D—but then $V(D^*(t))$ would be a gross underestimate of undissipated value. The tax costs help make for:

---

[10] The asymptotic solution (6c) is useful only to the extent that if its comparative statics are the same as those of (6b), then we may assert that the comparative statics derived for this example have general validity for other distribution function examples for β in some neighborhood of zero. This is possible because the asymptotic solution (6c) is independent of the distributional characteristics of cash flows (substituting mean cash flow M for $t/2$), and because of the continuity of solutions in parameters.

(i) a higher response of $V(D)$ to D that still provides an interior optimum $D^*(t)$, and (ii) $V(D^*(t))$'s being equal to undissipated value because of the higher costs of signaling.

In the case of the tax rate comparative static, it is clear that if for a higher tax rate $V(D)$ responded only to the new $(1 - \alpha)$ in (7), then the optimizing $D(t)$ would continue to equal A^*t, with the same A as in the equilibrium for a lower tax rate. At this "old" $D(t)$, $V(D(t))$ would be an overestimate of undissipated future value, since the tax cost of the same proportionate dividend is now higher, whereas $V(D(t))$ would have changed in just the reverse direction relative to the "old" equilibrium. In equilibrium this is resolved by a lower interior optimum A, induced by an appropriate response of $V(D)$ to D, in accordance with equations (6b) and (7). For the asymptotic solution (6c), the net effect is to leave $V(D^*(t))$, the equilibrium value of cash flows less tax costs, unaffected. In the same manner, when K is higher, the higher relative magnitude of the value of future cash flows requires in equilibrium a higher response of $V(D)$ to D, which induces a higher A — "to tell the truth."

It may be pointed out that the response of equilibrium dividend payout to the rate of interest has not, to our knowledge, received strong theoretical support in previous research (see, e.g., Pye (1972)). Attempts to explain it by arguing that debt financing is more "expensive" when interest rates are high, and thus internal financing is increased, are in conflict with leverage indifference propositions of either the Modigliani and Miller (1958) or Miller (1977) type.[11] For the sake of completeness, it should also be pointed out that for the equilibrium solution (6b), $\partial A/\partial \beta < 0$, as would be expected from the intuition behind the comparative static result with respect to $(1 - \alpha)$.

So far, both in Section 2 and here, we have developed our model in terms of a one-period planning horizon for shareholders. This is somewhat unsatisfactory, however, for the following reasons. First, in reality, shareholder horizons are far longer than the time periods over which corporations can change their dividends. Second, as a consequence, the low response of $V(D)$ to D in equation (7) appears to be unrealistic, and it also raises doubts about the assumption that shortfalls of cash flows compared to dividends can be made up by selling assets — although this is partially remedied by letting cash flow distributions lie over shorter ranges, e.g., $t/4$ to $3t/4$.[12]

In what follows, we briefly consider a simple extension to a multiperiod horizon case, and mention the problems that exist with respect to keeping the structure of the model simple and tractable. This extension also hints at a comparative static result with respect to shareholders' planning horizons that is reminiscent, in its effects as opposed to its reasoning, of the "bird in the hand" fallacy notion associated with dividends. *Ceteris paribus*, the shorter is the planning horizon, or the higher the "urgency" to realize wealth for consumption, the higher is the equilibrium dividend-payout ratio.

Suppose the current shareholders have an $(n + 1)$-period planning horizon

---

[11] If the Miller-type (1977) equilibrium does not obtain, and optimum debt levels are chosen by the familiar tradeoff between tax deductibility of interest payments and bankruptcy costs, then, *ceteris paribus*, higher interest rates would tend to make expected bankruptcy costs higher by making bankruptcy more likely, and this may result in lower debt levels and more retention. (The value of the tax "shield" of debt should not be significantly affected in a perpetuity-type model.) Note also that these comparative statics are of the partial equilibrium type.

[12] It can be shown that the simple linear form of the equilibrium solution holds in this case too.

and that their objective function (and hence their agents' objective) is given by

$$E(D) = \frac{1}{1+r}\left[\left(1 + \frac{1}{(1+r)} + \ldots + \frac{1}{(1+r)^n}\right)\right.$$

$$\left. \times \left(\frac{t}{2} - (1-\alpha)D - \beta\frac{D^2}{2t}\right) + \frac{1}{(1+r)^n}\cdot V(D)\right]. \quad (8)$$

Let

$$\mu = 1 + (1+r) + (1+r)^2 + \ldots + (1+r)^n.$$

Then the equation corresponding to equation (5) for the equilibrium $D^*(t)$ schedule is given by

$$(K + \mu)\left[(1-\alpha) + \beta\frac{D}{t}\right]\cdot\frac{dD}{dt} = K\left[\frac{1}{2} + \beta\frac{D^2}{2t^2}\right]. \quad (9)$$

Now, for $\mu > 1$, $K/(K + \mu) = K^*/(K^* + 1)$ for some $K^* < K$, and K^* clearly declines with a rise in μ caused by an increase in n. Thus the results of the one-period horizon case can be used to assert that the A of the equilibrium solution decreases with an increase in n.

The intuition behind the result is similar to that for the earlier comparative static result with respect to K. A longer planning horizon implies that the relative weight of intrahorizon cash flows increases and that of the end-of-period "return of capital" declines in the current shareholders' objective function. A given response of $V(D)$ to D results in a lower $D(t)$'s being chosen, at which $V(D(t))$ is lower than true undissipated value. In equilibrium, a somewhat higher response of $V(D)$ to D, which nevertheless results in a lower $D^*(t)$, constitutes the appropriate adjustment.

It is also easily shown that, in equilibrium

$$V(D) = \mu[(1-\alpha) + \beta A]D. \quad (10)$$

Equation (10), for large values of μ, is consistent with the assumption that deficits of cash flows compared with dividends can be made up. The comparative statics for the tax rate and the interest rate for the one-period horizon case also carry over to the multiperiod horizon case.[13]

However, multiperiod horizons raise many new issues, especially with any general equilibrium treatment in an overlapping generations setting. We briefly catalog them below, leaving them as open questions for further research. First, there are problems with shareholders of different horizons existing concurrently (because people have shorter horizons as calendar time passes); shareholder unanimity regarding corporate decision rules is not obtained. Second, to preserve

---

[13] As $\beta \to 0$, the equilibrium dividend payout approaches

$$\frac{t}{2}\cdot\frac{K}{(K+\mu)(1-\alpha)},$$

and the undissipated value approaches

$$\frac{Kt}{2}\left[1 - \frac{K}{(K+\mu)}\right] = \frac{Kt}{2}\left[\frac{\mu}{K+\mu}\right].$$

With $r = 0.10$ per "year," $K = 10$, $\mu \approx 18.3$ for $n = 10$ or an 11-"year" horizon. $(\mu/K + \mu)$, the fraction of asset value that is *not* dissipated by the tax cost of dividends, is nearly two-thirds. The equilibrium level of dividends is smaller than $t/2$ for $(1-\alpha) > 10/28.3$.

the simplicity of the model in terms of the stationarity of optimal response D conditional on t as calendar time passes and horizons become shorter, we have to impose some *ad hoc* restriction of choice among the class of stationary decision rules only; this is also a remedy for the unanimity problem. Third, describing the shareholders' objective function as simply as in (8), in the presence of interim consumption needs, depends critically on developed consumption-loan markets and risk neutrality. Fourth, for equation (8) to correctly represent current shareholders' objective functions, i.e., to ensure that *ex post* intra-horizon actions do not affect the effective horizon of shareholders in out-of-equilibrium situations, it is necessary to assume: (i) that possible asset sales in the secondary market are made at true undissipated values and not at signaled values, and (ii) that, with the exception of possible short-term borrowing to finance dividend deficits, all corporate financing is done through rights issues to *existing* shareholders. Essentially, we have to rule out *intrahorizon* market transactions with outsiders whose values to current shareholders, in their relevant metric given their horizons, depend on the signaling decision chosen by the firm. The basic intuition behind the horizon result may, however, carry over to more elaborate models.[14]

4. Concluding remarks

■ Two unfinished tasks are taken up in this section. First, we discuss the signaling cost structure of our model in relation to other financial-signaling models in the literature and possible alternatives. Second, we provide a brief discussion of convergence to equilibrium in financial-signaling models.

The signaling cost structure that we have developed is not only realistic (dividends linked only to *expected* cash flows), but also the only simple structure consistent with the assumption of an exogenously costly dividend-signaling equilibrium. Superficially, another simple possibility that satisfies the marginal-cost characteristics required for signaling is a "lower-truncated" structure with cash flow X in dividends paid if and only if X is *less* than some "promised" D! Since the moral hazard in costlessly communicating X to outsiders is the basis for the dissipative signaling equilibrium, this is not going to be a very enforce-able structure. In a different context Ross (1977) has developed a financial-signaling model of leverage based on a "lower-truncated" cost structure of significant bankruptcy penalties *for managers*. A difficulty with such a structure is that unless enforceable penalties of similar magnitude relative to the benefits of nonbankruptcy exist for shareholders, there is an incentive for shareholders to make side payments to managers to induce false signaling by employing higher levels of debt. In another paper (Bhattacharya, 1977), I have developed a model of nondissipative—not exogenously costly—signaling of insiders' information about future cash flows, based on expectations revision in the market, in a setting in which there is no tax cost to directly communicating *ex post* cash flows. As noted in Section 2, it is my belief that a synthesis of the two types of models, which should allow us to provide a partial role for sources of *ex post* earnings information like accounting reports, is an interesting, if difficult, problem for further research.

---

[14] These problems do, of course, make the planning horizon comparative static analysis somewhat *ad hoc*. In particular, it is difficult to attach any meaning in terms of different-horizon "clienteles," since we have not explained how an economy with different-horizon "clienteles" attached to different firms would evolve in its ownership structure.

Convergence to equilibrium in financial-signaling models is an interesting issue primarily because the time structure of events is likely to be different from that in the job-market signaling model of Spence (1974). In both our model and that of Ross (1977), the signaling cost arises in the future, whereas the benefit, the rise in value, is likely to get established in current as well as liquidation values. If unconstrained liquidation with no effect on value is posited, then current shareholders, and their agents, clearly have an incentive to signal falsely and sell out at an inconsistently high value. One must assume that premature or excessive—relative to normal trading by "retiring" stockholders—liquidation bids by shareholders would significantly affect market value so as to virtually eliminate such problems.[15] It is also likely that observations of insider trading, conditional on their signaling decisions in the current shareholders' interest, or eliciting (conditional) insider bids in a *tâtonnement* model, will play a significant role in convergence to the equilibrium valuation schedule as a function of the signal.[16] These are clearly issues that need further study, as do the issues related to multiperiod planning horizons discussed in Section 3.

References

BHATTACHARYA, S. "An Exploration of Nondissipative Dividend-Signaling Structures." Working paper, Graduate School of Business, University of Chicago, November 1977.

BRITTAIN, J.A. *Corporate Dividend Policy*. Washington, D.C.: The Brookings Institution, 1966.

GROSSMAN, S.J. AND STIGLITZ, J.E. "Information and Competitive Price Systems." *The American Economic Review*, Vol. 66, No. 2 (May 1976).

LELAND, H. AND PYLE, D.H. "Informational Asymmetries, Financial Structure, and Financial Intermediation." *Journal of Finance* (May 1977).

MILLER, M.H. "Debt and Taxes." *Journal of Finance* (May 1977).

―――― AND SCHOLES, M. "Dividends and Taxes." Working paper, Graduate School of Business, University of Chicago, January 1978.

―――― AND MODIGLIANI, F. "Dividend Policy, Growth, and the Valuation of Shares." *Journal of Business* (October 1961).

MODIGLIANI, F. AND MILLER, M.H. "Cost of Capital, Corporation Finance, and the Theory of Investment." *The American Economic Review*, Vol. 48, No. 3 (June 1958).

PYE, G. "Preferential Tax Treatment of Capital Gains, Optimal Dividend Policy, and Capital Budgeting." *Quarterly Journal of Economics* (May 1972).

PYLE, D.H. "Descriptive Theories of Financial Institutions Under Uncertainty." *Journal of Financial and Quantitative Analysis* (December 1972).

RILEY, J. "Competitive Signaling." *Journal of Economic Theory* (April 1975).

ROSS, S.A. "The Determination of Financial Structure: The Incentive Signaling Approach." *The Bell Journal of Economics*, Vol. 8, No. 1 (Spring 1977).

SPENCE, A.M. "Competitive and Optimal Responses to Signals: Analysis of Efficiency and Distribution." *Journal of Economic Theory* (March 1974).

---

[15] This is essentially a "no-Ponzie-game" type assumption. Informational aspects of prices and bids have been noted by Grossman and Stiglitz (1976) among others.

[16] Liquidation bids in response to overvaluation will be continuous functions in a risk-averse setting. For the same time-structure reasons, our model, with its weak convexity provided by the deficit makeup cost (β), may be "stable" because although setting a $D(t)$ different from equilibrium $D^*(t)$ may reduce the objective function conditional on the assumed horizon by only a small amount, it will also tend to provide an incentive to liquidate currently.

The model of Leland and Pyle (1977) does not share the time-structure characteristics discussed here. In the model of Ross (1977) the relative weights of *current* value and end of period payoff (including bankruptcy penalties) in *managers'* objective functions is exogenously given.

discussion | **Signaling with Dividends, Investment, and Debt**

Joseph Williams

Graduate School of Business
New York University

Since the publication of Bhattacharya (1979), problems of signaling with dividends, investment, and debt have attracted considerable attention among financial economists. Most work on financial signaling has been based on the seminal papers by Spence (1973) and Riley (1979).

I. DIVIDENDS

Dividends continue to puzzle financial economists. Most perplexing are the large, apparently avoidable personal taxes paid on dividends. For example, in 1977 individual stockholders incurred $8 billion in taxes on $26 billion in dividends.[1] To reduce these taxes, corporations could have repurchased shares nonproportionally, thereby imposing at most capital gains on their stockholders.[2] Alternatively, stockholders could have sold shares on personal account and thereby raise cash equal to the forgone dividends. In the latter case, firms would have retained all their cash and subsequently sold fewer securities to raise external funds. Finally, individuals could have held their stocks that pay dividends through tax-managed funds. As corporations, these funds avoid taxes on 85 percent of all corporate dividends, distribute no dividends to their stockholders, and, instead, generate at most capital gains.[3]

In turn, these problems raise related questions. Why do firms pay dividends and sometimes almost simultaneously sell new securities? Why do mature firms apparently distribute larger dividends than growth firms? Who do so many companies seem to smooth dividends relative to corporate cash inflows? Also, why do investors who demand cash, like retirees, evidently hold stocks that pay dividends, despite the adverse personal taxes? In addition, when can dividends compete with other signals, like repurchases of either stock or senior corporate securities? Can dividends coexist as signals with other, presumably less costly mechanisms for revealing private information, like audited financial statements and reports of security analysts? Finally, can conflicts of interest between managers, bondholders, stockholders, and other corporate claimants explain dividends?

Recently, signaling equilibria with dividends have attracted considerable attention. An important, early paper in this literature is Bhattacharya (1979). In his signaling equilibrium, corporate insiders distribute a taxable dividend, rather than repurchasing stock, in an environment without taxes on capital gains. This dividend maximizes stockholders' after-tax cash flows during their holding period plus their stock's liquidation value, conditional on insiders' private information about their firm's present value. Thus, the dividend maximizes the wealth of current stockholders, given their policy of selling shares. In turn, outside investors correctly value each firm and then pay in the perfectly competitive capital market the correct prices for all stock.

Bhattacharya's signaling model is driven by an asymmetric transaction cost. By assumption, larger values of each firm's private attribute produce first-order stochastically dominant distributions for the firm's future cash inflow. Also, if the firm has a subsequent cash inflow insufficient to cover its promised dividend, then it must borrow and incur a proportional transaction cost. This transaction cost is asymmetric; a cash inflow exceeding the promised dividend has no corresponding benefit. Hence, larger values of the firm's private attribute decrease the present value of its future transaction costs and thereby decrease the marginal signaling costs. This condition on marginal signaling costs, due originally to Spence (1973), guarantees the existence of a signaling equilibrium.[4]

Although Bhattacharya's signaling model requires an asymmetric transaction cost, its properties also reflect the proportional personal taxes on dividends. For example, additional dividends have a marginal impact on the firm's market value approximately equal to the constant tax rate. Also, for his example with a uniformly distributed future cash flow, higher tax rates induce lower optimal dividends. Consequently, realistic dividends and associated announcement effects can occur even with surprisingly small asymmetric transaction costs.

Subsequently, John and Williams (1985) constructed a signaling equilibrium with dividends and single dissipative cost: a proportional tax on dividends. In this model, taxes are assessed only on dividends, and no transaction costs are incurred when issuing, retiring, or trading shares. Nevertheless, there exists a signaling equilibrium with dissipative dividends. In this equilibrium, corporate insiders distribute a taxable dividend and thereby reveal to outside investors the present value of their firm's future cash inflows if and only if the demand for cash by both their firm and its current stockholders exceeds the supply of internal funds. Thus, some firms distribute dividends, whereas others do not. Of those firms that pay dividends, some simultaneously sell new shares to outside investors. These dividends benefit current shareholders by supporting a firm's stock price when either the firm or its stockholders sell shares to new investors.

The intuition behind this signaling equilibrium is as follows. When raising funds for investment, a firm must either issue new shares or retire fewer outstanding shares. Similarly, to raise cash on personal account, current stockholders must sell existing shares. In either case stockholders suffer some dilution in their fractional ownership of the firm. Reducing this dilution on either corporate or personal account is more valuable to current shareholders when inside information is more favorable. Thus, insiders, who maximize their stockholders' wealth, may distribute a taxable dividend if outsiders recognize this relationship, bid up the stock price, and thereby reduce current stockholders' dilution. In the resulting signaling equilibrium, insiders control dividends optimally, and outsiders pay the correct price for the firm's stock.

The signaling equilibrium of John and Williams exists because the marginal benefit from distributing dividends differs across firms. For firms with more valuable inside information, the premium paid in the market for stocks with marginally larger dividends, and thereby the reduction in dilution for current shareholders, just compensates stockholders for the incremental personal taxes on dividends. For firms with less favorable inside information the dissipative costs of the same dividend exceed at the margin the gains from reducing dilution. Consequently, there exists in the market a pricing function for stock that separates firms with more favorable inside information from those with less. In the resulting signaling equilibrium, firms with better inside information optimally pay higher dividends, other things equal, and receive appropriately higher prices for their stock. Current stockholders then capture all economic rents net of taxes on dividends. Costs are critical in this application of Riley (1979); without taxes or other costs of paying dividends, there is no signaling equilibrium. However, these costs need not satisfy the marginal conditions familiar from Spence (1973).

In the two previous papers, costly dividends are distinguished from costless repurchases of stock by the additional personal taxes assessed on dividends relative to capital gains. Alternatively, these costs can be interpreted as the present value of stockholders' forgone returns from avoiding personal taxes on dividends through a trading scheme as in Miller and Scholes (1978).[5] In addition, these dissipative costs need not be produced by taxes nor be linear in dividends. Any other cost that increases in dividends can support a signaling equilibrium.

The previous papers also help to explain observed positive announcement effects of dividends. Empirically, when a firm increases its dividend, its stock price on average increases. In signaling equilibria, positive announcement effects follow from a pricing function for stock that increases in dividends, other things equal. Although most empirical studies support positive announcement effects for dividends, some suggest that dividends convey no information not revealed by reported earnings.[6] Surprisingly, even the latter evidence can be consistent with announcement effects. Because corporate insiders can manipulate reported earnings, credible reports must serve insiders' interests. No such incentive compatibility condition holds for reported earnings—at least within the limits imposed by accounting standards.[7] Thus, insiders must support any credible report of earnings with a signal, like dividends, for which an incentive compatibility condition exists. This signal supports a separating equilibrium with positive announcement effects even though it contains no information not revealed by reported earnings.

Recently other authors have attempted to explain dividends as a partial resolution of agency problems. For example, Easterbrook (1984) argues that stockholders can exert effective control over corporate managers only when they buy the firm's stock. Hence, if managers distribute dividends, then they force their firm to raise external capital more frequently and thereby reduce the agency costs from conflicts of interest between managers and stockholders. However, dividends are tangential to his argument. Repurchases of stock are not only equally effective in reducing conflicts but also less costly when extra taxes are assessed on dividends relative to capital gains.[8]

II. INVESTMENT

Firms can also signal by altering corporate investment. Miller and Rock (1985) construct a model that works as follows. By assumption, outside investors cannot observe firms' current cash flows. Also, all firms have identical investment opportunities with diminishing marginal returns, and raise external funds solely through sales of riskless corporate debt. Finally, individuals pay no additional taxes on dividends relative to capital gains. In this case, dividends and repurchases of bonds are perfect substitutes. Consequently, corporate insiders signal by distributing cash and then satisfy their firm's sources and uses of funds by altering investment. In particular, insiders in firms with larger cash inflows can distribute more cash and still match the investment of firms with smaller cash inflows. If insiders in the latter, less valuable firms attempt to mimic more valuable firms, then they must invest less and thereby forgo projects with higher marginal returns than the projects forgone at the margin by more valuable firms. Thus, there exists a signaling equilibrium in which corporate distributions reveal cash inflows and firms forgo projects with positive net present values.

John and Kalay (1985) study signaling with investment from a different perspective. In practice, bond indentures often contain covenants constraining both dividends and repurchases of stock. In effect, these covenants commit firms to minimum levels of future investment. Also, with both corporate and personal taxes, firms' investments in financial securities have negative net present value to stockholders. This then restricts profitable corporate investments to real assets. As a result, insiders in firms with more profitable prospective projects may choose to constrain more tightly their future dividends and repurchases relative to firms with fewer opportunities. Because these commitments to invest are more costly to firms with fewer future opportunities, the latter firms are induced not to mimic more valuable firms. Thus, there exists a signaling equilibrium in which corporate insiders reveal their firms' future opportunities to invest, and thereby their true market values, through constraints on dividends and repurchases.[9]

The multiplicity of signaling instruments raises another interesting question. Why should corporate insiders signal with one instrument as opposed to another—for example, dividends versus investment?[10] If insiders seek to maximize their stockholders' wealth, then dividends can exist in equilibrium only if dividends and investment credibly convey private information at lower cost than investment alone. Thus, dividends must be efficient to survive in the signaling equilibrium. Efficient signaling with dividends and investment is addressed in a recent paper by Ambarisha, John, and Williams (1987).[11] In their model, mature firms optimally forgo projects with positive net present value, whereas growth firms adopt projects with negative net present value. For all firms, announced increments in dividends increase stock prices, with investment held constant. By contrast, announced new issues of stock, with dividends held constant, decrease stock prices for mature firms but increase stock prices for growth firms. For firms listed on the New York and American Stock Exchanges—mainly mature firms—supporting empirical evidence appears in Asquith and Mullins (1983) and the references cited therein. Additional evidence appears in Schipper and Smith (1986) for equity carve-outs, which have characteristics of growth firms.

The above signaling equilibria have dissipative, deadweight costs relative to the corresponding solutions with symmetric information. Thus, if all investors hold completely diversified portfolios, then a pooling equilibrium, in which no firms signal and all stock prices equal the average value, may produce greater wealth for all investors. Nevertheless, a signaling equilibrium may still Pareto-dominate this pooling equilibrium by producing a more efficient allocation of capital in which firms with more profitable projects raise and invest more funds. In addition, a pooling equilibrium is unstable. From Riley (1979), any uninformed investor can offer to buy stock conditional on dividends, investment, or any feasible signal, and induce only insiders in truly more valuable firms to accept. Thereby, this investor makes profits, imposes losses on other investors, and unravels the pooling equilibrium.[12]

III. DEBT

Corporate insiders can also signal with debt. In Ross (1977), corporate insiders' compensation is tied to their firm's market price, with a personal penalty for bankruptcy. Because outside investors conjecture correctly that additional debt conveys favorable inside information, managers with more favorable information issue more debt. This increases their firm's market price and thereby their personal compensation. Given the personal penalty for bankruptcy, insiders in firms with less favorable information are induced not to mimic. Thus, there exists a signaling equilibrium satisfying the marginal cost conditions familiar from Spence (1973).[13]

Many variations of Ross (1977) are possible. For example, the loss of tax-deductible interest expenses, as in DeAngelo and Masulis (1980), can substitute for bankruptcy costs and thereby support a signaling equilibrium with debt. Alternatively the loss of managers' perquisites when their firm fails, much as in Grossman and Hart (1982), can support a separating equilibrium. In both cases, a cost induces insiders in less valuable firms not to mimic more valuable firms by issuing more debt. Also, Narayanan (1985) argues that the voluntary withdrawal from the market of firms with unprofitable investments prevents the unraveling of a signaling equilibrium with debt, as in Riley (1979). In particular, it precludes the profitability of alternative pooling offers for firms with virtually only riskless debt outstanding.

Recently, signaling with debt has been studied in sequential equilibria, as developed by Kreps and Wilson (1982). For example, in Diamond (1986), defaults reveal borrowers' types, induce lenders to cut off credit, and thereby reduce borrowers' incentive to pick risky projects. Over time, as borrowers with risky projects default and drop out of the cohort, the interest rate charged by competitive lenders to borrowers in the cohort falls. This raises the value of the remaining borrowers' reputation and reduces their incentive to pick risky projects. Consequently, the value of the cohort's reputation can first rise and then fall as the time horizon nears.

Harris and Raviv (1985) construct a sequential equilibrium of calling convertible corporate bonds. In their equilibrium, insiders with unfavorable information call their corporate bonds and thereby force early conversion. This transfers wealth from bondholders to stockholders. By contrast, stockholders in truly more valuable firms gain less from forcing early conversion because their bondholders subsequently convert voluntarily with greater probability. Thus, insiders who act for their stockholders optimally delay calling their firm's bonds when they possess favorable private information. In the resulting equilibrium, calling convertible bonds reveals unfavorable inside information and thereby reduces stock prices.

IV. DISCUSSION

Most signaling models share in common a few critical components. One is the source of asymmetric information. With few exceptions the previous papers identify as inside information managers' forecasts of future cash flows. This focus on future, rather than current, cash flows is critical. In practice, forecasts of future cash inflows from either assets in place or opportunities to invest cannot be verified through mechanical examination of corporate records. Thus, a signaling equilibrium with dividends can coexist with examinations by public auditors, security analysts, and rating agencies. For current cash flows, however, all these alternatives are likely to be less costly than dissipative dividends. Moreover, the most valuable information—forecasts conditional on proprietary corporate data—most likely exists only in the minds of successful senior management. Consequently, this information can be communicated credibly only through mechanisms compatible with managerial incentives. Finally, because future cash inflows depend statistically on current forecasts, corporate claimants can design contingent contracts that support signaling equilibria. These contingent contracts can only reduce the dissipative costs of dividends.

In the above models managers maximize either their stockholders' wealth or their personal wealth. In either case, the clientele is assumed to be homogeneous with respect to two critical components: personal tax rates and sales of personal shares. Sales of shares determine the weight attached in the maximand to current distributions of cash, the firm's stock price, and its true value as assessed by insiders. Moreover, managers must be prevented in either case from trading privately on personal account. Otherwise, they can signal falsely, adjust their personal portfolios, realize sizable gains, and thereby break any signaling equilibrium.

In this literature many important problems remain unresolved. In practice, not all stockholders are identical with respect to either personal tax rates or demands for liquidity. With heterogeneous stockholders, clienteles must somehow match themselves with firms. Do investors with lower personal tax rates and greater demands for liquidity purchase in equilibrium stocks paying larger dividends? In equilibrium, do mature firms supply these larger dividends? Similarly, do investors with higher tax rates and lower demands for liquidity buy stocks of growth firms that pay lower dividends? How are stocks then priced in equilibrium? Also, how is this equilibrium affected by other securities, such as corporate bonds and preferred stock?

Why should insiders signal with dividends, investment, or debt if other, less costly mechanisms can convey credible private information to the market? True, dividends and investment do maximize the wealth of current shareholders in signaling equilibria, but only when outside investors ignore other pertinent information. For example, security analysts most likely can infer any private information implicit in a firm's dividends and aggregate investment from its net new issues of securities and announced portfolio of investments. In other words, neither dividends, investment, nor debt has been shown to be an efficient signal, competitive with other technologies for conveying credible private information to the market.

Efficient signaling with multiple signals and a single private attribute is a special case of a more general problem: multidimensional signaling. In practice, firms can have more than a single private attribute. For example, corporate insiders can possess private information about their firm's future returns on both assets in place and opportunities to invest. In turn, many combinations of, say, dividends, investment, and debt can convey insiders' information to the market. Again, this produces a problem of picking the least costly combination of signals. To date, problems of multidimensional signaling have been solved only for some special technologies.

NOTES

[1] See Feenberg (1981, p. 265).

[2] To not be taxed as a dividend, stock repurchases must be sufficiently nonproportional, as defined in the Internal Revenue Code, Sec. 302.

[3] By realizing short-term capital losses, tax-managed funds often can offset the remaining 15 percent of dividends and thereby avoid any taxable corporate income. An alternative scheme for avoiding personal taxes on dividends is described in Miller and Scholes (1978). Following their scheme, stockholders can borrow, offset all dividends

with interest expenses, and use the proceeds to purchase tax-deferred annuities.

[4] In addition, Bhattacharya (1980) has a nondissipative model of signaling with dividends. In his model, if outside investors can observe after some time a firm's private attribute, then there exists a pricing function for settling up ex post that induces corporate insiders initially to signal truthfully.

[5] Without some costs, either explicit or implicit, the trading scheme of Miller and Scholes (1978) is inconsistent with plausible tax equilibria—most notably, Miller (1977)—and the associated empirical evidence of Schaefer (1982), Trczinka (1982), and others. The argument is simple. Apply the above trading scheme to interest on corporate bonds rather than dividends on stock. If the scheme is completely costless, then corporate bonds must be priced in equilibrium with all implicit tax rates equal to zero, in contrast to the above empirical evidence. Moreover, in Miller's tax equilibrium all firms then issue only bonds and no stock. Thus, without explicit costs, the trading scheme must entail an implicit cost: the difference in the yield to maturity between taxable and tax-exempt bonds.

[6] Recent examples of empirical studies reporting positive announcement effects from dividends include Aharony and Swary (1980), Asquith and Mullins (1983), and Patell and Wolfson (1984). By contrast, Penman (1983) argues that dividends reveal little information not reported with earnings.

[7] If the report is verifiable, but the decision to disclose is not, then disclosure must be compatible with insiders' incentives, as in Milgrom (1981).

[8] Precisely the same problem appears in Green and Feldstein (1983).

[9] John and Kalay (1985) complicate their signaling model with a tangential issue: corporate debt and the subsequent incentive of stockholders to invest less than the value-maximizing level. This issue is familiar from Myers (1977).

[10] The multiplicity of potential signals is illustrated by Leland and Pyle (1977), in which the signal is the fraction of insiders' wealth invested in their firm. Efficient signaling with advertising and price is studied in Milgrom and Roberts (1986).

[11] Also see Ofer and Thakor (1987).

[12] See Riley (1979, Theorem 5). Under some conditions the signaling equilibrium can also be unraveled, as indicated in Riley's Theorems 3 and 4. This problem of unraveling a pooling equilibrium appears in Myers and Majluf (1984).

[13] In Ross (1977) corporate insiders maximize their personal wealth, conditional on the hypothesized managerial compensation function. Several authors have criticized this assumption because it induces stockholders in large firms to make side agreements with managers that break the signaling equilibrium. However, this criticism applies to any signaling model. If managers can trade privately on personal account, then they can signal falsely and receive sizable benefits. Also, Ross's model applies equally well to altruistic managers who maximize stockholders' wealth net of their bankruptcy costs.

REFERENCES

Aharony, J., and Swary, I. 1980. "Quarterly Dividend and Earnings Announcements and Stockholders' Returns: An Empirical Analysis." *Journal of Finance* 35: 1–12.

Ambarisha, R.; John, K.; and Williams, J. 1987. "Efficient Signaling with Dividends and Investment." *Journal of Finance* 42: forthcoming.

Asquith, P., and Mullins, D. 1983. "The Impact of Initiating Dividend Payments on Stockholders' Wealth." *Journal of Business* 56: 77–96.

Bhattacharya, S. 1979. "Imperfect Information, Dividend Policy and the Bird in the Hand Fallacy." *Bell Journal of Economics* 10: 259–70. Reprinted Chapter 7, this volume.

————. 1980. "Nondissipative Signalling Structures and Dividend Policy." *Quarterly Journal of Economics* 95: 1–24.

DeAngelo, H., and Masulis, R. 1980. "Optimal Capital Structure under Corporate and Personal Taxation." *Journal of Financial Economics* 8: 3–29.

Diamond, D. 1986. "Reputation Acquisition in Debt Markets." Working paper, Graduate School of Business, University of Chicago.

Easterbrook, F. 1984. "Two Agency-Cost Explanations of Dividends." *American Economic Review* 74: 650–59.

Feenberg, D. 1981. "Does the Investment Interest Limitation Explain the Existence of Dividends?" *Journal of Financial Economics* 9: 265–69.

Green, J., and Feldstein, M. 1983. "Why Do Companies Pay Dividends?" *American Economic Review* 73: 17–30.

Grossman, S., and Hart, O. 1982. "Corporate Financial Structure and Managerial Incentives." In J. McCall, ed., *The Economics of Information and Uncertainty*. Chicago: University of Chicago Press.

Harris, M., and Raviv, A. 1985. "A Sequential Signaling Model of Convertible Debt Call Policy." *Journal of Finance* 40: 1263–81.

John, K., and Kalay, A. 1985. "Informational Content of Optimal Debt Contracts." In E. Altman and M. Subrahmanyam, eds., *Recent Advances in Corporate Finance*. Homewood, Ill.: Irwin.

John, K., and Williams, J. 1985. "Dividends, Dilution, and Taxes: A Signaling Equilibrium." *Journal of Finance* 40: 1053–70.

Kreps, D., and Wilson, R. 1982, "Sequential Equilibria." *Econometrica* 50: 1767–97.

Leland, H., and Pyle, D. 1977. "Informational Asymmetries, Financial Structure, and Financial Intermediation." *Journal of Finance* 32: 371–87. Reprinted Chapter 8, this volume.

Milgrom, P. 1981. "Good News and Bad News: Representation Theorems and Applications." *Bell Journal of Economics* 12: 380–91.

Milgrom, P., and Roberts, J. 1986. "Price and Advertising as Signals of Product Quality." *Journal of Political Economy* 94: 796–821.

Miller, M. 1977. "Debt and Taxes." *Journal of Finance* 32: 261–75. Reprinted Chapter 2, this volume.

Miller, M., and Rock, K. 1985. "Dividend Policy under Asymmetric Information." *Journal of Finance* 40: 1031–51.

Miller, M., and Scholes, M. 1978. "Dividends and Taxes." *Journal of Financial Economics* 6: 333–64.

Myers, S. 1977. "The Determinants of Corporate Borrowing." *Journal of Financial Economics* 5: 147–75.

Myers, S., and Majluf, N. 1984. "Corporate Financing and Investment Decisions When Firms Have Information That Investors Do Not Have." *Journal of Financial Economics* 13: 187–221.

Narayanan, M. 1985. "Signaling with Capital Structure: A General Model." Working paper, Graduate School of Business Administration, University of Florida.

Ofer, A., and Thakor, A. 1987. "A Theory of Stock Price Responses to Alternative Corporate Cash Disbursement Methods: Stock Repurchases and Dividends." *Journal of Finance* 42: forthcoming.

Patell, J., and Wolfson, M. 1984. "The Intraday Speed of Adjustment of Stock Prices to Earnings and Dividend Announcements." *Journal of Financial Economics* 13: 223–52.

Penman, S. 1983. "The Predictive Content of Earnings Forecasts and Dividends." *Journal of Finance* 38: 1181–99.

Riley, J. 1979. "Informational Equilibrium." *Econometrica* 47: 331–59.

Ross, S. 1977. "The Determination of Financial Structure: The Incentive-Signalling

Approach." *Bell Journal of Economics* 8: 23–39.

Schaefer, S. 1982. "Tax-Induced Leverage Clientele Effects in the Market for British Government Securities: Placing Bounds on Security Values in an Incomplete Market." *Journal of Financial Economics* 10: 121–59.

Schipper, K., and Smith, A. 1986. "A Comparison of Equity Carve-outs and Seasoned Equity Offerings: Share Price Effects and Corporate Restructuring." *Journal of Financial Economics* 15: 153–86.

Spence, M. 1973. "Job Market Signaling." *Quarterly Journal of Economics* 87: 355–79.

Trczinka, C. 1982. "The Pricing of Tax-Exempt Bonds and the Miller Hypothesis." *Journal of Finance* 37: 907–32.

Vishwanathan, S. 1986. "A Multiple Signaling Model of Corporate Finance." Working paper, Graduate School of Business, Duke University.

Reprinted from
THE JOURNAL OF FINANCE · VOL. XXXII, NO. 2 · MAY 1977

SESSION TOPIC: INVESTMENTS—THEORETICAL ISSUES

SESSION CHAIRPERSON: RICHARD BREALEY*

INFORMATIONAL ASYMMETRIES, FINANCIAL STRUCTURE, AND FINANCIAL INTERMEDIATION

HAYNE E. LELAND AND DAVID H. PYLE**

INTRODUCTION AND SUMMARY

NUMEROUS MARKETS ARE characterized by informational differences between buyers and sellers. In financial markets, informational asymmetries are particularly pronounced. Borrowers typically know their collateral, industriousness, and moral rectitude better than do lenders; entrepreneurs possess "inside" information about their own projects for which they seek financing.

Lenders would benefit from knowing the true characteristics of borrowers. But moral hazard hampers the direct transfer of information between market participants. Borrowers cannot be expected to be entirely straightforward about their characteristics, nor entrepreneurs about their projects, since there may be substantial rewards for exaggerating positive qualities. And verification of true characteristics by outside parties may be costly or impossible.

Without information transfer, markets may perform poorly. Consider the financing of projects whose quality is highly variable. While entrepreneurs know the quality of their own projects, lenders cannot distinguish among them. Market value, therefore, must reflect *average* project quality. If the market were to place an average value greater than average cost on projects, the potential supply of low quality projects may be very large, since entrepreneurs could foist these upon an uninformed market (retaining little or no equity) and make a sure profit. But this argues that the average quality is likely to be low, with the consequence that even projects which are known (by the entrepreneur) to merit financing cannot be undertaken because of the high cost of capital resulting from low average project quality. Thus, where substantial information asymmetries exist and where the supply of poor projects is large relative to the supply of good projects, venture capital markets may fail to exist.

For projects of good quality to be financed, information transfer must occur. We have argued that moral hazard prevents direct information transfer. Nonetheless, information on project quality may be transferred if the *actions* of entrepreneurs ("which speak louder than words") can be observed. One such action, observable because of disclosure rules, is the willingness of the person(s) with inside information to invest in the project or firm. This willingness to invest may serve as a signal to the lending market of the true quality of the project; lenders will place a value on the project that reflects the information transferred by the signal.

As shown by the seminal work of Akerlof [1970] and Spence [1973], and by the

* London Graduate School of Business Studies.

** University of California, Berkeley. We have greatly benefited from discussion with Avraham Beja and James Ohlson.

subsequent contributions of Rothschild and Stiglitz [1975] and Riley [1975, 1976], equilibrium in markets with asymmetric information and signalling may have quite different properties from equilibrium either with no information transfer, or with direct and costless information transfer. Signalling equilibria may not exist, may not be sustainable, and may not be economically efficient.

In subsequent sections, we develop a simple model of capital structure and financial equilibrium in which entrepreneurs seek financing of projects whose true qualities are known only to them. We show that the entrepreneur's willingness to invest in his own project can serve as a signal of project quality. The resulting equilibrium differs importantly from models which ignore informational asymmetries. The value of the firm increases with the share of the firm held by the entrepreneur. In contrast with Modigliani and Miller [1958], the financial structure of the firm typically will be related to project or firm value even when there are no taxes.[1] And firms with riskier returns will have lower debt levels even when there are no bankruptcy costs. Signaling incurs welfare costs by inducing entrepreneurs to take larger equity positions in their own firms than they would if information could be directly transferred; we show, however, that the set of investment projects which are undertaken will coincide with the set which would be undertaken if direct information transfer were possible. Finally, we suggest that financial inter-mediation, which is difficult to explain in traditional models of financial equilibrium, can be viewed as a natural response to asymmetric information.

FINANCIAL STRUCTURE AND INSIDE INFORMATION: A SIGNALING MODEL

Consider an investment project which involves a capital outlay K and a future return $\mu + \tilde{x}$, where μ is the expected end-of-period value of the project and $\tilde{x}$ is a random variable with zero mean and variance σ^2. We shall consider an entrepreneur who wants to undertake this investment project and plans to hold a fraction α of the firm's equity, raising the remainder of the equity from other lenders. Throughout our analysis, the firm and the entrepreneur (on personal account) are both assumed to be able to issue debt at the riskless rate.[2]

The entrepreneur has information that leads him to assign a specific value to μ, but he has no credible way to convey this information directly to other potential shareholders, who have a subjective probability distribution for μ. However, other potential shareholders will respond to a signal by the entrepreneur regarding his evaluation of μ if they know that it is in the self-interest of the entrepreneur to send true signals. The signal which we shall examine is α, the fraction of the equity in the project which is retained by the entrepreneur. This will be taken by other lenders as a (noiseless) signal of the true μ. That is, the market perceives μ to be a function of α.

Assuming that capital markets are competitive and that there is no uncertainty

1. A recent study by Jensen and Meckling [1975] emphasizing management costs without consideration of informational asymmetries, and a study by Ross [1976] emphasizing managerial incentives in the presence of informational asymmetries, provide examples of alternative approaches to some of the financial structure questions addressed in this paper.

2. This assumption is not unreasonable if entrepreneurs have substantial initial wealth and project returns are bounded below.

about the project's mean, given signal α, we can express the *total market value of the project*, V, as

$$V(\alpha) = \frac{1}{(1+r)} [\,\mu(\alpha) - \lambda\,], \qquad (1)$$

where r = the riskless interest rate;

$\mu(\alpha)$ = the market valuation schedule, expressing the market's perception of the true expected return as a function of α, the fraction of equity retained by the entrepreneur.

λ = the market's adjustment for the risk of the project with returns $\tilde{x}$ about the mean.[3]

We shall assume that $\mu(\alpha)$ is a differentiable function.[4]

In addition to the possibility of investing in his own project, the entrepreneur can invest in the *market portfolio*. Define

$\tilde{M}$ = the random (gross) return of the market portfolio;

V_M = the value of the market portfolio;

β = the fraction of the market portfolio held by the entrepreneur.

We shall make the "perfect competition" assumption that the project is small relative to the market as a whole; the entrepreneur perceives his decisions with respect to the project to have a negligible effect on the returns and value of his share of the market portfolio.

The entrepreneur is presumed to maximize his expected utility of wealth with respect to (a) the financial structure of the project or firm; (b) his holding of equity in the project or firm; and (c) his holding of the market portfolio and the riskless asset. His choices must satisfy his budget constraint

$$W_0 + D + (1-\alpha)[\,V(\alpha) - D\,] - K - \beta V_M - Y = 0, \qquad (2)$$

if he undertakes the project.[5] In this case, end of period wealth $\tilde{W}_1$ is determined

3. Equation (1) can be shown by arbitrage, since in competitive markets an asset with return $\mu + \tilde{x}$ will have the value of an asset with sure return μ plus the value of an asset with return $\tilde{x}$. In the case of the capital asset pricing model, $\lambda = \lambda^* \operatorname{Cov}(\tilde{x}, \tilde{M})$, where λ^* is the "market price of risk" and M is the return of the market portfolio.

4. At considerable complication, our theorems can be shown to hold when $\mu(\alpha)$ is differentiable almost everywhere. Thus continuity of the optimal schedule is not an essential assumption.

5. Some attention to the entrepreneur's budget constraint is required. He is assumed to have initial wealth W_0. The undertaking of his investment project requires an investment of K, and generates returns $\tilde{x} + \mu$. The entrepreneur can sell claims to this return. Let D represent the amount of priority claims sold (debt), paying a sure return $(1+r)D$. The returns to equity after debt service will be $\tilde{x} + \mu - (1+r)D$, with value $V(\alpha) - D$. If the entrepreneur sells a proportion $(1-\alpha)$ of his equity (retaining a proportion α), he will receive $(1-\alpha)[V(\alpha) - D]$. His initial wealth after transactions related to the project is

$$W_0 + D + (1-\alpha)[\,V(\alpha) - D\,] - K.$$

This will be divided between investments in the market (which cost βV_M) and his private holdings of the riskless asset (which cost Y). Thus, the entrepreneur's budget constraint satisfies the equation (2).

by his returns from investments in the project, market, and riskless security:

$$\tilde{W}_1 = \alpha[\tilde{x} + \mu - (1+r)D] + \beta\tilde{M} + (1+r)Y.$$

Substituting for Y from (2) and for $V(\alpha)$ from (1) yields

$$\tilde{W}_1 = \alpha[\tilde{x} + \mu - \mu(\alpha) + \lambda] + \beta[\tilde{M} - (1+r)V_M] + (W_0 - K)(1+r) + \mu(\alpha) - \lambda. \quad (3)$$

The decision problem

$$\text{Maximize } E[U(\tilde{W}_1)] \quad (4)$$

will, for any given $\mu(a)$ schedule, determine an optimal portfolio which depends upon μ:

$$\alpha^* = \alpha^*(\mu),$$

$$\beta^* = \beta^*(\mu);$$

where α^* and β^* are the optimal holdings of the project and the market portfolio, respectively.[6]

We are not interested in arbitrary functions $\mu(\alpha)$; rather, we shall restrict our attention to schedules which have an equilibrium property. More precisely, we define an

Equilibrium Valuation Schedule: A market valuation schedule $\mu(\alpha)$ is said to be an equilibrium valuation schedule if the entrepreneur's true μ is correctly identified by the market for all values of μ for which the entrepreneur undertakes the project. That is,

$$\mu[\alpha^*(\mu)] = \mu, \quad (5)$$

for all levels of μ which induce the entrepreneur to undertake the project, given the schedule $\mu(\alpha)$.

Condition (5) is a natural notion of equilibrium given competitive capital markets. If the imputed $\mu(\alpha)$ were greater than the actual μ of an entrepreneur retaining α, outside investors would on average receive less than the return required for the project's risk, and equity financing would not continue on such terms. If, on the other hand, $\mu(\alpha)$ consistently underestimated the entrepreneur's true μ, given α, excess returns would exist for outside investors. Competitive forces would eliminate

---

6. Note D has disappeared from equation (3), and therefore from the maximization problem. Substituting the optimal holdings α^* and β^* into the budget constraint (2) determines

$$H^* \equiv \alpha^* D - Y$$

only. Any combination of borrowing D through the firm or $-Y$ on personal account which satisfies the above equation will generate the same expected utility to the entrepreneur, if there are no transactions costs. Discussion of an optimal D is deferred until pp. 14 ff.

these excess returns. Thus, for levels of μ for which entrepreneurs undertake their projects, (5) must hold in equilibrium.[7]

Properties of Equilibrium Valuation Schedules

We shall not address the difficult problem of whether an equilibrium schedule $\mu(\alpha)$ exists.[8] Rather, we shall presume that at least one equilibrium schedule exists, and examine its properties. In the subsequent section, we consider an example in which we can actually compute an equilibrium valuation schedule.

Consider now any equilibrium schedule $\mu(\alpha)$. Given this schedule and value of μ in the relevant range, the entrepreneur chooses α and β to maximize expected utility (4). First-order necessary conditions require that

$$\partial E\left[U\left(\tilde{W}_1 \right) \right]/\partial\alpha = E\left[U'\left(\tilde{W}_1 \right) \left[\tilde{x} + \mu - \mu(\alpha) + \lambda + (1-\alpha)\mu_\alpha \right] \right] = 0; \qquad (6)$$

$$\partial E\left[U\left(\tilde{W}_1 \right) \right]/\partial\beta = E\left[U'\left(\tilde{W}_1 \right) \left[\tilde{M} - (1+r)V_M \right] \right] = 0; \qquad (7)$$

where $\tilde{W}_1$ is given by (3) and $\mu_\alpha \equiv d\mu(\alpha)/d\alpha$.

Note that condition (6) diverges from the usual portfolio optimization condition because the "price" of the project, $V(\alpha)$, depends upon α through the equilibrium valuation schedule $\mu(\alpha)$. Using the equilibrium condition (5) and rearranging terms, we may rewrite (6) as

$$(1-\alpha)\mu_\alpha = -E\left[U'\left(\tilde{W}_1 \right)(\tilde{x}+\lambda) \right]/E\left[U'\left(\tilde{W}_1 \right) \right]. \qquad (8)$$

Equation (7) can now be used to solve for β as a function of α and μ.

---

7. Because condition (5) is key to the analysis which follows, it behooves us to make more precise the values of μ for which projects will be undertaken, given an equilibrium schedule $\mu(\alpha)$. Let us define the *reservation utility level* U^* as the maximum expected utility the entrepreneur could achieve without undertaking the project. Let $\mu(\alpha)$ be an assumed equilibrium valuation function. Then condition (5) need hold only for values of μ such that

$$\underset{\alpha,\beta}{\text{Max}} \, E\left[U\left(\tilde{W}_1 \right) \right] \geqslant U^*,$$

Let μ^* represent the minimum level of μ for which the inequality holds. Clearly μ^* depends on the schedule $\mu(\alpha)$.

It can be shown that, for a given equilibrium valuation function $\mu(\alpha)$, the project will be undertaken if and only if $\mu \geqslant \mu^*$. Thus, the *relevant range* $R[\mu(\alpha)]$ of the equilibrium schedule $\mu(\alpha)$ is given by

$$R[\mu(\alpha)] = \{ \mu \mid \mu \geqslant \mu^* \}$$

and the *relevant domain* $D[\mu(\alpha)]$ by

$$D[\mu(\alpha)] = \{ \alpha \epsilon [0,1] \mid \mu(\alpha) \geqslant \mu^* \}.$$

Note that, in equilibrium, we will never find more productive projects being rejected while less productive projects are undertaken.

8. Clearly this assumption is nontrivial. In the example considered in the subsequent section, however, a schedule exists which satisfies the equilibrium conditions. See also Riley [1976].

Substituting this relationship for β into (8) yields a differential equation relating μ and α. *Any equilibrium schedule must satisfy this differential equation over the relevant domain.*

In addition to the necessary first-order conditions, the entrepreneur's optimal choice of α and β must satisfy second-order optimizing conditions. Defining

$$A \equiv \partial^2 E\left[U(\tilde{W}_1) \right] / \partial\alpha^2 = E\left[U''(\tilde{W}_1)\left[\tilde{x} + \lambda + (1-\alpha)\mu_\alpha \right]^2 \right]$$

$$+ E\left[U'(\tilde{W}_1)\left[-2\mu_\alpha + (1-\alpha)\mu_{\alpha\alpha} \right] \right];$$

$$B \equiv \partial^2 E\left[U(\tilde{W}_1) \right] / \partial\beta^2 = E\left[U''(\tilde{W}_1)\left[\tilde{M} - (1+r)V_M \right]^2 \right];$$

$$C \equiv \partial^2 E\left[U(\tilde{W}_1) \right] / \partial\alpha\partial\beta = E\left[U''(\tilde{W}_1)\left[\tilde{x} + \lambda + (1-\alpha)\mu_\alpha \right]\left[\tilde{M} - (1+r)V_M \right] \right],$$

second-order conditions require

$$A < 0; \qquad B < 0; \qquad AB - C^2 > 0. \tag{9}$$

The necessary conditions (8) and (9) will be used to examine properties of equilibrium valuation schedules. But first, we need a definition:

Normal Asset Demand: An individual's demand for an asset is said to be *normal* if, in a portfolio choice situation without signaling, the individual will always demand a larger amount of that asset when its price falls.

THEOREM I. *The equilibrium valuation function $\mu(\alpha)$ is strictly increasing with α over the relevant domain, if and only if the entrepreneur's demand for equity in his project is normal.*

Proof. See Appendix.

Theorem I provides a fairly strong characterization of equilibrium schedules: under normal conditions they are monotonically increasing with the fraction of ownership α retained by the entrepreneur. The market reads higher entrepreneurial ownership as a signal of a more favorable project. And the entrepreneur is motivated to choose a higher fraction of ownership in more favorable projects, given the equilibrium valuation function.

THEOREM II. *In equilibrium with signaling by α, entrepreneurs with normal demands will make larger investments in their own projects than would be the case if they could costlessly communicate their true mean.*

Proof. See Appendix.

Theorem II can be viewed as a welfare result: the "cost" of signaling the true μ to the market through α is the welfare loss resulting from investment in one's own project beyond that which would be optimal if the true μ could be communicated costlessly. Of course, less costly communication may not be possible. And, as argued in the introduction, equilibrium with no communication could result in *no* projects being undertaken.

To examine further aspects of equilibrium valuation schedules and their implications for financial structure, we turn our attention to a specific example.

THE SIGNALING MODEL: AN EXAMPLE

Let us assume

(a) Entrepreneur's expected utility can be expressed in the form

$$E\left[U\left(\tilde{W}_1 \right) \right] = G\left[E\left(\tilde{W}_1 \right) - (b/2)\sigma^2\left(\tilde{W}_1 \right) \right], \tag{10}$$

where G is a monotonically increasing function and $\sigma^2(\tilde{W}_1)$ is the variance of end-of-period wealth;[9]

(b) The risk adjustment coefficient can be expressed as $\lambda = \lambda^* \operatorname{Cov}(\tilde{x}, \tilde{M})$, where

$$\lambda^* = \frac{E(\tilde{M}) - (1+r)V_M}{\sigma_M^2} \tag{11}$$

is the "market price of risk." Assumption (b) is consistent with the valuation implied by the capital asset pricing model.[10]

Using (10), first-order maximizing conditions (6) and (7) can be expressed as

$$\left[\mu - \mu(\alpha) + \lambda^* \operatorname{Cov}(\tilde{x}, \tilde{M}) \right] + (1 - \alpha)\mu_\alpha - \alpha b \sigma_x^2 - \beta b \operatorname{Cov}(\tilde{x}, \tilde{M}) = 0; \tag{12}$$

$$\left[E(\tilde{M}) - (1+r)V_M \right] - \alpha b \operatorname{Cov}(\tilde{x}, \tilde{M}) - \beta b \sigma_M^2 = 0, \tag{13}$$

where σ_x^2 and σ_M^2 are the variance of the project and market returns, respectively. Substituting for βb from (13) and using (11) and (5) permits us to rewrite (12) as a special case of (8):

$$(1 - \alpha)\mu_\alpha = b\alpha\left[Z \right], \tag{14}$$

where

$$Z = \frac{\sigma_x^2 \sigma_M^2 - \left[\operatorname{Cov}(\tilde{x}, \tilde{M}) \right]^2}{\sigma_M^2}.$$

Note that Z will always be nonnegative, and can be interpreted as the *specific risk* of the project. If the project is independent of the market returns, $\operatorname{Cov}(\tilde{x}, \tilde{M}) = 0$ and Z is simply the variance of $\tilde{x}$. If the market and project returns are perfectly correlated, $Z = 0$. In most cases, of course, Z will lie between these extremes.

The solution to the differential equation (14) is a family of functions

$$\mu(\alpha) = -bZ\left[\log(1 - \alpha) + \alpha \right] + C \tag{15}$$

---

9. Such a representation of expected utility is possible whenever indifference curves are linear in mean and variance. An example of this representation is when utility is exponential and returns are normally distributed.

10. See the models of Sharpe [1964] and Mossin [1966], for example.

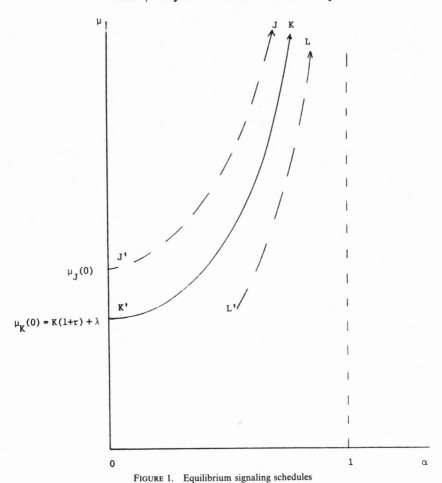

FIGURE 1. Equilibrium signaling schedules

where C is an arbitrary constant. It can be verified that the second-order conditions (9) are also satisfied for schedules in the family.

Figure 1 shows some examples of valuation functions satisfying the equilibrium form (15). We will now show that further equilibrium arguments can be used to reduce this family of curves to a single schedule which will be viable in the market.

First, consider a curve above and to the left of KK', such as JJ'. Because such a curve intersects the $\alpha = 0$ axis at $\mu_J(0) > (1+r)K + \lambda$, an entrepreneur could undertake a project with arbitrarily low true μ, retain zero equity, and have

$$\text{Max}_\beta E\left[U\left[\beta\left[\tilde{M} - (1+r)V_M \right] + (1+r)\left[V_J(0) - K + W_0 \right] \right] \right]$$

$$> \text{Max}_\beta E\left[U\left[\beta\left(\tilde{M} - (1+r)V_M \right) + W_0(1+r) \right] \right],$$

since

$$V_J(0) - K = \frac{1}{1+r} [\mu_J(0) - \lambda] - K > 0.$$

Thus, at $\alpha = 0$, schedules such as JJ' have the property that entrepreneurs with true $\mu < \mu_J(0)$ could undertake the project, retain zero equity, and be better off than they would if they abandoned the project. Lenders offering the schedule JJ' would lose money on projects in which the entrepreneur held zero equity. And indeed, even if lenders attach a minimum permissible $\alpha > 0$ to the schedule JJ', there will always be some "freeloaders" at α whose μ's are less than those expected by the market. Schedules such as JJ' therefore will *not* satisfy the equilibrium condition (5) at their left endpoint.

If the schedule KK' is offered, the same freeloading problem as above may arise at $\alpha = 0$. (Since $\alpha = 0$ implies $V_K(0) = K$, entrepreneurs with $\mu < \mu_K(0)$ are indifferent between undertaking (holding zero equity) or not undertaking their projects.) But for $\alpha > 0$, no freeloading will take place, since even the smallest amount of required equity holding would reduce potential freeloaders to a level of utility less than that which would result if they did not undertake the project.

Now consider schedules below and to the right of KK', such as LL'. (These schedules do not reach $\alpha = 0$ because the relevant domain does not include α's associated with levels of μ less than μ^*.) Such schedules would indeed satisfy the equilibrium requirement (5). But they will not be competitive with schedule KK', in the sense that, if KK' were offered by some lenders when others were offering LL', all entrepreneurs would do business with lenders offering schedule KK'. This is because the entrepreneur will have a higher level of expected utility along KK', since the required α to signal any given level of μ is less with KK' than with LL'. *The cost of signaling is less along KK' than along any other schedule which satisfies the equilibrium requirement everywhere.*[11]

Thus, of all the family of functions (15), we have identified the unique equilibrium schedule

$$\mu(\alpha) = -bZ[\log(1-\alpha) + \alpha] + (1+r)K + \lambda; \qquad \alpha > 0. \tag{16}$$

Using (1),

$$V(\alpha) = \frac{1}{1+r} [-bZ[\log(1-\alpha) + \alpha]] + K; \qquad V_\alpha = \frac{bZ}{1+r} \left[\frac{\alpha}{1+\alpha} \right] > 0,$$

implying

$$V(0) = K; \qquad V(\alpha) > K \quad \text{for} \quad \alpha > 0. \tag{17}$$

An immediate implication of (17) is

---

11. Riley [1975] argues along similar lines to reduce multiple schedules to a single schedule. If the number of projects offering a true value μ or more falls rapidly as μ increases, we need not be concerned by the unravelling problem considered by Rothschild and Stiglitz [1975] and by Riley [1975; amended 1976]. Even the left endpoint is immune to unravelling since there is by assumption a number of projects whose true μ lies below cost K.

PROPOSITION I. *A project will be undertaken if, and only if, its true market value, given μ, exceed its cost.*[12]

This result implies that information transfer through signaling possesses a key *efficiency property*: the set of projects which are undertaken will coincide with that set which would be undertaken if information could be communicated costlessly.[13]

We now consider the effects of parametric changes on the signaling equilibrium.

PROPOSITION II. *An increase either in the specific risk Z of the project or in the risk aversion b of the entrepreneur will reduce the entrepreneur's equilibrium equity position α*(μ), for any value of μ at which the project is undertaken.*

Proof. For any fixed value of μ, we have from the equilibrium requirement $\mu(\alpha) = \mu$

$$\frac{d}{d(bZ)}\left[\mu(\alpha)\right] = 0; \quad \text{or}$$

$$\frac{d\alpha}{d(bZ)}\left[-bZ\left[\log(1-\alpha)+\alpha\right]+(1+r)K+\lambda\right] = 0;$$

implying

$$\frac{d\alpha}{d(bZ)} = \frac{(1-\alpha)\left[\log(1-\alpha)+\alpha\right]}{\alpha bZ} < 0,$$

since

$$\left[\log(1-\alpha)+\alpha\right] < 0 \quad \text{for} \quad \alpha > 0.$$

A more fundamental question concerns entrepreneurial welfare: does the expected utility "cost" of signaling vary with Z? We can show

PROPOSITION III. *An increase in specific risk Z results in greater expected utility for the entrepreneur, for any level μ at which the project is undertaken.*

Proof. Tedious calculations show that

$$\frac{dE[U]}{dZ} = G'(\cdot)\left[-b(1-\alpha)\left[\log(1-\alpha)+\alpha\right]\right] > 0$$

Thus projects which are "more distinct" (higher specific risk) from the market are relatively easier to signal, in the sense that they result in lower signaling costs in equilibrium.

12. This result can be generalized to arbitrary utility functions, *only* if (as in this example) the optimal holding of the project is zero when μ is directly communicated. Such will be the case if the entrepreneur (like other investors) wishes to hold "the market portfolio" in the absence of signaling.

13. This is not quite correct: since we require $\alpha > 0$, only projects with $\mu > K$ will be undertaken. With costless information transfer, projects with $\mu = K$ might be undertaken, since entrepreneurs would be indifferent between acceptance or rejection of these projects. But since projects with $\mu = K$ are truly marginal to society, there is no social loss associated with their exclusions. Note that, as $\alpha \to 0$ and $\mu \to K$, the expected utility loss associated with signaling approaches zero. This explains why the acceptance sets are identical.

Optimal Debt Levels and the Modigliani-Miller Theorem

We have shown that in equilibrium the entrepreneur's equity position α in his project is related to the value of his project. We now address the relationship between the value of the project (or firm) V and the financing decision D. In a world of symmetric information, the Modigliani-Miller theorem suggests that there will be no systematic relationship between the financing decision and the value of the firm. In a world with asymmetric information, we show that this will not always be the case. But our results must be interpreted with considerable caution.

From the budget constraint (2), we observe

$$H \equiv \alpha D - Y = K - W_0 - (1 - \alpha)V(\alpha) + \beta V_M. \tag{18}$$

For the subsequent discussion, we consider the example introduced in the previous section, with the additional assumption that the project's returns are independent of the market returns. This implies $\text{cov}(\tilde{x}, \tilde{M}) = 0$, which in turn can be shown to imply that β is independent of α. Thus we can talk of Z as the variance of the project's returns, and can treat βV_M as a constant with respect to the choice α.

We shall make the assumption that (as both debt and lending are at the riskless rate) the entrepreneur will not simultaneously borrow and lend: borrowing will be done through the firm, and lending will be done privately. Institutional arrangements and (even small) transactions costs can be invoked to support the realism of this argument.

We focus upon the domain of α where the debt of the firm is positive. In this domain, $Y = 0$, and assuming for simplicity $r = 0$, we can rewrite (18) as

$$D = \left[K - W_0 + \beta V_M - (1 - \alpha)V(\alpha) \right] / \alpha$$

$$= \left[K - W_0 + \beta V_M - (1 - \alpha) \left[-bZ[\log(1 - \alpha) + \alpha] + K \right] \right] / \alpha, \tag{19}$$

using (16). Differentiating with respect to α gives

$$\text{sign}(\partial D / \partial \alpha) = \text{sign} \left\{ -bZ \left[\log(1 - \alpha) + \alpha + \alpha^2 \right] + W_0 - \beta V_M \right\}. \tag{20}$$

$\partial D / \partial \alpha$ will not be positive for all values of α, W_0, and bZ. Calculations show, however, that if

$$\frac{W_0 - \beta V_M}{K} \geqslant .186$$

then $\partial D / \partial \alpha > 0$ for all levels of α such that $D \geqslant 0$. This is true regardless of the absolute levels of K and W_0, as well as the level of bZ. Therefore debt will be an increasing function of the entrepreneur's equity position α, whenever the entrepreneur's financial contribution to the firm is at least 18.6 percent of the cost of the project.[14] We shall assume this to be the case, and henceforth limit our attention to debt which is monotonically increasing in α.

14. In most cases, $\partial D / \partial \alpha > 0$ even when entrepreneurs own considerably less than 18.6 percent of the firm. But this fraction ownership guarantees under all circumstances that debt increases with equity share, when debt is positive.

PROPOSITION IV. *For any level of* μ, *greater project variance* σ_X^2 *implies lower optimal debt.*

Proof. Differentiating (19) with respect to $Z(=\sigma_X^2)$, keeping μ constant, yields

$$dD/dZ = (\partial D/\partial\alpha)(d\alpha/dZ) + \partial D/\partial Z$$

$$= (\partial D/\partial\alpha)(d\alpha/dZ) + [(1-\alpha)b[\log(1-\alpha)+\alpha]]/\alpha.$$

By our previous analysis, $\partial D/\partial\alpha > 0$; by Proposition II, $d\alpha/dZ < 0$. Since $[\log(1-\alpha)+\alpha] < 0$ for all $\alpha > 0$, it follows that $dD/dZ < 0$.

Proposition IV shows that, *independent of possible bankruptcy costs*, firms with riskier returns will have lower optimal debt levels.[15]

Consider now the relationship between value V and debt D of *seemingly similar* projects. By "seemingly similar," we mean that observers without inside information on μ view the projects as identical. Since both V and D are positive functions of α, and therefore of μ, *a regression of value on debt would show a positive relationship*.

Does this invalidate the Modigliani-Miller theorem that value is independent of capital structure? Not really. In the MM world with symmetric information, a change in D will not change the project's perceived returns, and financial structure will be irrelevant. In a world with asymmetric information in which α can be observed, a change in D *with α constant* will not change perceived returns, and financial structure will also be irrelevant. But we have argued that observed D, given small transactions costs, will be related to α. And a change in α *does* give rise to a change in perceived returns and therefore in market value. Thus there is a *statistical* but not a *causal* relation between V and D of seemingly similar firms.

If transactions costs were sufficiently high, or institutions such that borrowing through the firm entirely precluded lending privately, then D itself could serve as a signal of μ and therefore of firm value, since a choice of D would (through the budget constraint) determine a unique choice of α; D as well as α would then be a function of μ and could serve as a signal. But when transactions costs are minimal, D cannot serve as a signal, since entrepreneurs with any μ would be willing to incur small transactions costs to have (say) high D's in order to receive a high project value, while at the same time choosing Y so that α remained at a level appropriate to their true μ. Thus D could not serve as a signal with equilibrium properties.

INFORMATION AND FINANCIAL INTERMEDIATION: SOME PRELIMINARY THOUGHTS

Traditional models of financial markets have difficulty explaining the existence of financial intermediaries, firms which hold one class of securities and sell securities of other types. If transactions costs are not present, ultimate lenders might just as well purchase the primary securities directly and avoid the costs which intermediation must involve. Transactions costs could explain intermediation, but their

---

15. Note that this result would follow in a normal portfolio model (without signaling), if we assumed as here that transactions costs linked debt to the entrepreneur's choice of α, and further assumed that optimal holding α increased with μ.

magnitude does not in many cases appear sufficient to be the sole cause. We suggest that informational asymmetries may be a primary reason that intermediaries exist.

For certain classes of asset—typically, those related to individuals, such as mortgages or insurance—information which is not publicly available can be obtained with an expenditure of resources.[16] This information can benefit potential lenders; if there are some economies of scale, one might expect organizations to exist which gather and sell information about particular classes of assets.

Two problems, however, hamper firms which might try to sell information directly to investors. The first is the appropriability of returns by the firm—the well known "public good" aspect of information. Purchasers of information may be able to share or resell their information to others, without diminishing its usefulness to themselves.[17] The firm may be able to appropriate only a fraction of what buyers in totality would be willing to pay.

The second problem in selling information is related to the credibility of that information. It may be difficult or impossible for potential users to distinguish good information from bad. If so, the price of information will reflect its average quality. And this can lead to market failure, if entry is easy for firms offering poor quality information. Firms which expend considerable resources to collect good information will lose money because they will receive a value reflecting the low average quality. When they leave the market, the average quality will further fall, and equilibrium will be consistent only with poor quality information, much as Akerlof's market for used cars will result in only "lemons" for sale.

Both these problems in capturing a return to information can be overcome if the firm gathering the information becomes an intermediary, buying and holding assets on the basis of its specialized information. The problem of appropriability will be solved because the firm's information is embodied in a private good, the returns from its portfolio. While information alone *can* be resold without diminishing its returns to the reseller, claims to the intermediary's assets *cannot* be. Thus, a return to the firm's information gathering can be captured through the increased value (over cost) of its portfolio.[18]

Of course, a return to information can be gathered only if the buyers of the intermediary's claims believe that the intermediary uses good information. Without

16. We do not consider information of this type to be a normal "transactions cost." Securities can be exchanged in many cases independently of how much the buyer may know about the precise nature of that security. Costs of exchange are considered transactions costs. We do not consider better information or "sorting costs" to be a cost *necessary* for exchange. Our approach can be contrasted with that of Benston [1976]. By emphasizing informational asymmetries, we can show not only why financial intermediaries exist, but also why they tend to be characterized by high leverage.

17. This, of course, depends on the nature of the information. If information provides a competitive advantage, its usefulness may be diminished by resale. If it simply provides better decisions internally, its usefulness may not be.

18. We presume that outsiders cannot profit from the firm's information merely be examining the portfolio chosen by the firm. Note that some loss in the potential value of information may occur because the portfolio weights chosen by the firm may not coincide with the weights which individual investors would have chosen by themselves, given the information. If there is competition for assets which have been sorted, firms may have difficulty in achieving a return to their information unless the borrowers directly pay for their sorting: see Stiglitz [1974].

some signal of quality, the average return may be low. But, just as in previous sections, this problem can be overcome through signaling. The organizers' willingness to invest in their firm's equity serves as a signal of the quality of the firm's information and the assets selected on the basis of this information. We previously have shown that the financial structure of the firm—the types and amounts of securities it issues—will be related to the owner's equity share. If, as seems often the case, most intermediaries' assets have low specific risk, Proposition IV implies the high degrees of leverage (through debt or deposits) which characterize most intermediaries.

It is of interest to note that, once an organization or group of organizations becomes more capable than other lenders of sorting a class of risks, there is a natural tendency for such assets to be sorted—even when the information costs of doing the sorting may be relatively high. Sellers of risks with favorable characteristics wish to be identified, and would deal with an informationally-efficient intermediary rather than with an uninformed set of lenders offering the value of the average risk. With the best risks "peeled off," the average risk will be less valuable, inducing owners of the next best risks to deal with the intermediary. The end of this chain of logic is that sellers of all types of risks will sell to the intermediary, except perhaps the group at the bottom of the barrel. An open question is whether, in equilibrium, an optimal amount of sorting occurs.

REFERENCES

G. Akerlof. "The Market for 'Lemons': Qualitative Uncertainty and the Market Mechanism," *Quarterly Journal of Economics*, 89 (August 1970), 488–500.

G. Benston. "A Transactions Cost Approach to the Theory of Financial Intermediation," *Journal of Finance* 31 (May 1976), 215–231.

M. Jensen and W. Meckling. "The Theory of the Firm: Managerial Behavior, Agency Costs and Ownership Structure," University of Rochester, Graduate School of Management Working Paper No. GPB-75-3. December 1975.

F. Modigliani and M. Miller. "The Cost of Capital, Corporation Finance, and the Theory of Investment," *American Economic Review*, 48 (June 1958), 261–97.

J. Riley. "Competitive Signalling," *Journal of Economic Theory*, 10 (1975).

———. "Informational Equilibrium." Rand Working Paper R-2059. September 1976.

S. Ross. "Some Notes on Financial Incentive-Signalling Models, Activity Choice and Risk Preferences," Working Paper. University of Pennsylvania, September 1976.

M. Rothschild and J. Stiglitz. "Equilibrium in Competitive Insurance Markets: An Essay on the Economics of Imperfect Information," *Quarterly Journal of Economics*.

A. M. Spence. "Job Market Signaling," *Quarterly Journal of Economics*, 87 (August 1973), 355–79.

———. *Market Signaling* (Cambridge: Harvard University Press, 1974a).

———. "Competitive and Optimal Responses to Signals: Analysis of Efficiency and Distribution," *Journal of Economic Theory*, (March 1974b).

J. E. Stiglitz. "Information and Economic Analysis," Technical Report No. 155, Institute for Mathematical Studies in the Social Sciences, Stanford University, 1974.

APPENDIX

Proof of Theorem I

We first shall show that normality implies μ_α is positive over the relevant domain. Differentiating the first-order conditions (6) and (7) totally with respect to μ and using the equilibrium condition (5) gives

$$\begin{bmatrix} A & C \\ C & B \end{bmatrix} \begin{bmatrix} d\alpha^*/d\mu \\ d\beta^*/d\mu \end{bmatrix} = -\begin{bmatrix} D \\ G \end{bmatrix},$$

where A, B, and C are given on page 8, and

$$\begin{aligned} D &\equiv E\left[U'(\tilde{W}_1) \right] + E\left[U''(\tilde{W}_1)[\tilde{x} + \lambda + (1-\alpha)\mu_\alpha]\alpha \right] \\ G &\equiv E\left[U''(\tilde{W}_1)[M - (1+r)V_M]\alpha \right], \end{aligned} \tag{A.1}$$

evaluated at $\alpha = \alpha^*$. Solving for the unknowns gives

$$\begin{bmatrix} d\alpha^*/d\mu \\ d\beta^*/d\mu \end{bmatrix} = \left(\frac{1}{AB - C^2} \right) \begin{bmatrix} B & -C \\ -C & A \end{bmatrix} \begin{bmatrix} -D \\ -G \end{bmatrix} \tag{A.2}$$

or

$$d\alpha^*/d\mu = -R[DB - CG], \tag{A.3}$$

where $R = 1/(AB - C^2) > 0$ by (9).

$R > 0$ is required for a regular local maximum of expected utility. For a set of measure zero in which the second-order condition vanished (but higher-order conditions were satisfied), we would have $\mu_\alpha = 0$.

Differentiating (5), we see that $(\mu_\alpha)(d\alpha^*/d\mu) = 1$; therefore,

$$\text{sign}\,\mu_\alpha = \text{sign}(d\alpha^*/d\mu). \tag{A.4}$$

We shall now show that sign $(d\alpha^*/d\mu)$ is positive by showing $DB - CG$ is negative. Consider the regular portfolio problem

$$\underset{\alpha,\beta}{\text{Max}}\, E\left[U(\tilde{W}_1) \right]$$

subject to the budget constraint

$$\alpha p_x + \beta p_M + Y = W_0, \tag{A.5}$$

where α and β are holdings of the project and market portfolio (with returns $\tilde{x} + \mu$ and $\tilde{M}$, as before), and p_x and p_M are arbitrary prices of these assets.

Final wealth $\tilde{W}_1$ will, after substitution for Y through (A.5), be given by

$$\tilde{W}_1 = \alpha\left[\tilde{x} + \mu - (1+r)p_x \right] + \beta\left[\tilde{M} - (1+r)p_M \right] + W_0(1+r),$$

and first-order maximizing conditions by

$$\begin{aligned} E\left[U'(\tilde{W}_1)[\tilde{x} + \mu - (1+r)p_x] \right] &= 0; \\ E\left[U'(\tilde{W}_1)[\tilde{M} - (1+r)V_M] \right] &= 0. \end{aligned} \tag{A.6}$$

Consider now the optimal choice of α and β in this setting if

$$p_x = \frac{1}{1+r}\left[\mu(\alpha^*) - \lambda - (1-\alpha^*)\mu_\alpha(\alpha^*)\right]$$

$$p_m = V_M \tag{A.7}$$

$$W_0 = (W_0 - K) + \frac{1}{1+r}\left[\mu(\alpha^*) - \lambda + (1-\alpha^*)\mu_\alpha(\alpha^*)\right]\alpha^*,$$

where α^* is the optimal α chosen by the entrepreneur (given μ) in the signaling environment. Substitution of these values into the first order conditions (A.6) yield precisely the conditions (6) and (7) when (5) holds; therefore, the same α^*, β^* *will be chosen in this regular portfolio problem*, given the prices and wealth specified by (A.7).

Finally, consider a change in the price p_x from that specified in (A.7). Differentiating (A.6) totally with respect to p_x, we find

$$\begin{bmatrix} \hat{A} & C \\ C & B \end{bmatrix}\begin{bmatrix} d\alpha/dp_x \\ d\beta/dp_x \end{bmatrix} = \begin{bmatrix} (1+r)D \\ (1+r)G \end{bmatrix},$$

where B and C are as given on page 8, D and G are given by (A.1), and

$$\hat{A} = E\left[U''(\tilde{W}_1)\left[\tilde{x} + \lambda + (1-\alpha^*)\mu_\alpha^*\right]^2\right].$$

Solving for $d\alpha/dp_x$ gives (after matrix inversion)

$$d\alpha/dp_x = R(1+r)\left[DB - CG\right],$$

where $R = \hat{A}B - C^2 > 0$ by the regular second-order portfolio conditions. But by the assumption of normality, $d\alpha/dp_x < 0$. Therefore,

$$DB - CG < 0,$$

which with (A.3) and (A.4) implies $\mu_\alpha > 0$.

Proof of Theorem II

Consider $\alpha(k)$ and $\beta(k)$, the holdings of the project and the riskless asset for given μ which satisfy

$$E\left[U'(\tilde{W}_1)(\tilde{x} + \lambda)\right] = k;$$

$$E\left[U'(\tilde{W}_1)\left[\tilde{M} - (1+r)V_M\right]\right] = 0, \tag{A.8}$$

when the value of μ is known to the public (costlessly) and does not depend upon α. We note two special cases:

a) $k = 0$. In this case, the resulting solution to (A.8), $\alpha(0)$, is the optimal holding of the project by the entrepreneur if he could communicate μ costlessly to the public.

b) $k = -[(1-\alpha^*)\mu_\alpha^*]E[U'(W_1^*)]$ where $\alpha^* = \alpha^*(\mu)$, the optimal holding of the project when the market perceives μ through the equilibrium schedule $\mu(\alpha)$, and $EU'(W_1^*)$ is expected utility when $\alpha = \alpha^*$, $\beta = \beta^*$. The solution $\alpha(k)$ is simply α^*, since (A.8) in this case coincides with the conditions (6) and (7) when (5) holds.

What we shall now show is that $d\alpha(k)/dk < 0$, for any μ. Totally differentiating the conditions (A.8), we have

$$
\begin{bmatrix} M & N \\ N & P \end{bmatrix} \begin{bmatrix} d\alpha/dk \\ d\beta/dk \end{bmatrix} = \begin{bmatrix} 1 \\ 0 \end{bmatrix}, \tag{A.9}
$$

where $M \equiv E[U''(W_1)(x+\lambda)^2] < 0$; $N \equiv E[U''(W_1)(x+\lambda)[M-(1+r)V_M]]$; and $P \equiv E[U''(W_1)[M-(1+r)V_M]^2] < 0$. By the concavity of U, $MP - N^2 > 0$, for all possible (α, β). Solving (A.9) for $d\alpha/dk$ yields

$$
d\alpha/dk = \frac{1}{MP - N^2}(P) < 0, \quad \text{which was to be shown.}
$$

We finally observe that, in going from costless communication of μ to signaling, the relevant first-order conditions go from $k = 0$ to $k = -(1-\alpha^*)\mu_\alpha^* E[U'(W_1^*)] < 0$, by Theorem I. Since $d\alpha/dk < 0$, α will be larger with signalling.

discussion | # Asset Services and Financial Intermediation

Douglas W. Diamond

Yale University

I. INTRODUCTION

Financial intermediaries are agents, or groups of agents, who are delegated the authority to invest in financial assets. In particular, they issue securities in order to buy other securities. A first step in understanding intermediaries is to describe the features of the financial markets in which they are important and the technology that allows them to provide beneficial services. In particular settings where intermediation is important, it is possible to obtain an endogenous specification of the form of the contracts written by the intermediaries, allowing predictions about how changes in the economy or in regulations affect the behavior of intermediaries and the markets in which they operate.

A major focus of recent literature on intermediation has been on the types of services supplied by intermediaries and how their organizational form facilitates providing these services.[1] Intermediaries provide services: this is clear because intermediaries issue "secondary" financial assets to buy "primary" financial assets. If the intermediary provided no services, those investors who buy the secondary securities issued by the intermediary might as well directly purchase the primary securities and save the intermediary's costs.

Microeconomic studies of intermediaries have integrated the study of financial institutions into the economics of corporation finance and the theory of optimal contracts. Most of the advances involve understanding the role of intermediaries when there are financial contracting problems caused by private information.[2] Much of the motivation for recent work comes from the suggestion in Leland and Pyle (1977) (LP, hereafter) that information collection by intermediaries might help to improve on the costly signaling equilibrium in markets for new issues that they analyze. Although LP do not model intermediaries, their suggestions have proved to be insightful in identifying a specific role for intermediaries. A review and extension of their approach is presented in Section III.

I am grateful to Sudipto Bhattacharya, Charlie Jacklin, and Andrei Shleifer for useful comments on an earlier draft.

A. Three Types of Intermediary Services

To explain the sorts of services that intermediaries offer, we categorize them in terms of a simplified balance sheet. Asset services are those provided to the issuers of the assets held by an intermediary (e.g, to bank borrowers). An intermediary that provides asset services is distinguished by its atypical asset portfolio. Relative to intermediaries not providing asset services, its portfolio will be specialized in assets that the intermediary has a comparative advantage in "holding." The literature that we discuss develops a foundation for understanding this aspect of intermediation.[3] There are two other important aspects of intermediation that we do not survey here: liability services and transformation services. *Liability services* are those provided to the holder of intermediary liabilities in addition to the services provided by most other securities. Examples include the ability to use bank demand deposits as a means of payment and the personalization of contingent contracts available from life insurance companies. Some liability services, for example check clearing, are well understood, and others relate to unresolved issues about the role of money in microeconomic theory; see Townsend (1979, 1983). Some services do not fit into this balance sheet dichotomy because they relate to both assets and liabilities. *Transformation services* involve the conversion of illiquid assets into liquid liabilities, offering improved risk sharing compared with nontraded direct investment in the assets that intermediaries hold (see Diamond and Dybvig 1983); these are discussed by Jacklin after Chapter 9.

If intermediaries provide asset services, then they provide services to borrowers who issue assets to them. That is, it matters to the issuer of an asset that the asset is to be held by an intermediary rather than directly by investors. This means there are some costs that are lower if the asset is held by an intermediary rather than by numerous individuals. We examine how a financial intermediary acting as a middleman can reduce these costs, and we develop the implications of this role for the structure of intermediaries.

Whether intermediaries are viable depends on their *net* cost saving. The imperfections that give rise to costs of issuing securities by primary borrowers could also give rise to similar costs to an intermediary that issues deposits. The goal of a theory of financial intermediation is to show how intermediaries help, even when they face the same technology as others in the economy (or to explain why they have access to a better technology).

II. FINANCIAL INTERMEDIATION AND MONITORING

A. The Value of Information in Loan Contracts

Theories based on the collection of private information by an intermediary require that there be some benefit to using this additional information in lending. A key result in the agency theory literature is that monitoring by a principal can allow improved contracts.[4] In Section III we review results that show that additional information can be useful when the problem is adverse selection (private information of a borrower about his default prospects). Whether there is a net demand for this monitoring depends on the cost of monitoring as well. This cost depends on the number of lenders who contract with a given borrower.

In contracting situations involving a single lender and a single borrower, one compares the physical cost of monitoring with the resulting savings of contracting costs. Let K be the cost of monitoring and S the savings from monitoring. When there are multiple lenders involved, either each must be able to monitor the additional information directly at a total cost of $M \times K$, where M is the number of lenders per borrower, or the monitoring must be delegated to someone. Delegating the monitoring gives rise to a new private information problem: the person doing the monitoring as agent now has private information, and perhaps even the fact that he actually monitored is not directly verifiable. Delegated monitoring can lead to delegation costs. Let D denote the delegation cost per borrower. A complete financial intermediary theory based on contracting costs of borrowers must model the delegation costs and explain why intermediation leads to an overall improvement in the set of available contracts. That is, delegated monitoring pays when

$$K + D \leqslant \min [S, M \times K],$$

because $K + D$ is the cost using an intermediary, S is the cost without monitoring, and $M \times K$ is the cost of direct monitoring.

Diamond (1984) presents a model of monitoring by a financial intermediary. The model analyzes delegation costs and the organizational structure and contractual form that minimizes these costs. Although the points developed there are more general, the analysis is carried out in the simplest setting where there is an obvious need for monitoring additional information.

To study the benefits of intermediation, we must first find the best available contracts between borrowers and lenders if there is no intermediary and no monitoring. This is an input in determining the value of S. The complication assumed is that the ex post profitability of each investment project is observed only by risk-neutral potential borrowers who have limited wealth. All other information, such as the expected return of the project, is symmetric. The project is large, so capital is needed from many lenders. Because the return of the investment project is not observed by potential lenders, then, if there is no monitoring, the contracts written by borrowers cannot be contingent on the realized return and must be uncontingent (debt) contracts. The optimal financial contract between borrowers and lenders is shown to be a debt contract that involves positive expected deadweight bankruptcy costs, which are necessary to provide incentives for repayment.[5] The gross demand for monitoring arises because one can use lower cost contracts (with reduced bankruptcy costs) if the project's return can be made observable, with a saving of S. In practice, the type of contract that could be used with monitoring is one with a more restrictive set of convenants that are renegotiated on the basis of costly information if there is a potential default on a covenant.

Monitoring is costly, especially if duplicated. The act of monitoring, if delegated, and the information then obtained by the intermediary are not publicly observed. As a result, there are delegation costs associated with providing incentives for the intermediary to monitor the information and to take the appropriate actions based on that information. Because the depositors in the intermediary do not observe the intermediary's information, the claims they hold on the intermediary are also simple debt contracts (for the same reason that debt contracts are best when lenders and borrowers contract directly).

B. Diversification and Delegation Costs

If the intermediary did not diversify and monitored a single lender, it would have delegation costs just as high as the contracting costs the borrower would incur if it borrowed directly without monitoring. In any situation where the borrower would have defaulted and incurred bankruptcy costs, the intermediary would also default and incur the same cost, implying that $D \geqslant S$.

Diversification within the intermediary is shown to reduce delegation costs. If the returns of borrowers' projects are mutually independent and bounded, the per-borrower delegation cost, D, approaches zero as the number of borrowers grows. If there are systematic risks influencing many borrowers' projects, then the intermediary will condition the required payments on these observable risks. If the contracts are not conditioned on these variables, then the intermediary (or the borrowers themselves) will hedge as many of those risks as possible in futures markets. This provides a positive theory of within-the-intermediary diversification (that cannot be replaced by diversification by depositors) and of hedging by publicly held intermediaries or firms.

C. The Role of Diversification

One explanation for the value of the diversification is that it helps to remove the information asymmetry between the intermediary and its depositors. The realization of any given project's return is private information, but the distribution of project outcomes is public information. With diversification over a large number of independent projects, the realization of the average converges in probability to its expected value. Even limited diversification can suffice for viable intermediation based on collection of private information.

The diversification discussed above involves an intermediary making and monitoring loans to many borrowers and issuing debt deposits to many depositors. All investors and bankers are assumed to be risk neutral: the diversification is useful because it reduces delegation costs. The intermediary was assumed to have a single manager (or top manager who provides incentives to lower-level employees). If intermediary managers are risk averse, diversification might be thought to also make their income stream less risky. However, the value of diversification to a risk-averse agent is traditionally due to the ability to subdivide risks and share them with others: it is less risky for each of two agents to bear 50 percent of two independent identical gambles than to bear either one alone. With a single manager there is no subdivision of risks—increasing the number of loans made increases the number of independent risks added rather than subdividing any risk; see Samuelson (1963). A class of risk-averse preferences for which diversification by adding risks does improve expected utility of wealth is characterized in Diamond (1984) (decreasing absolute risk aversion and positive fourth derivative of utility of consumption). This allows a motivation in addition to saving on delegation/bankruptcy costs for diversification in single-top-manager inter-mediaries when there is risk aversion.

Another way to model diversification with an intermediary is to assume that there are no incentive problems within the intermediary itself, and that as a result there can be substantial risk sharing (subdivision) among agents working together in the intermediary. If there is a trade-off between risk sharing and incentives or self-selection, then risk sharing within an inter-mediary can reduce the magnitude of the trade-off. Risk sharing then provides another reason why there could be an overall improvement in the set of available contracts when an intermediary spends resources to monitor private information.

Ramakrishnan and Thakor (1984) generalize the analysis of adding risks in Diamond (1984), providing a model of delegated information production based on risk subdivision, assuming there is no incentive problem within the intermediary. They examine the feasibility of delegating the production of reliable information when the act of investing in information and the information itself are not publicly observed. The main result is that if the information is produced about N firms with independently distributed returns and there are N risk-averse agents who all directly observe each other's actions and information, then the risk-bearing cost of providing incentives for producing information and revealing it truthfully is a decreasing function of N. If N grows very large, then there is perfect risk sharing among the agents working within the intermediary, and the risk-sharing cost of providing incentives to them approaches zero. If the agents working within the intermediary cannot directly observe each other's actions and information, then there is no benefit to diversification, because large amounts of risk must be imposed on each agent to provide incentives to produce the information.

The contracts to provide incentives to information producers make the compensation of each employee of the information producer depend directly on the average of the information announced by all employees of the producer and on the information that subsequently becomes available about each firm investigated. These contracts need not have any special structure common to financial intermediaries. As a result, it appears that the value of diversification by subdivision is quite general in reducing costs of moral hazard or adverse selection caused by suboptimal risk sharing, and that it could also provide a useful basis for a theory of conglomerate firms. The most troubling aspect of the analysis is the assumption that there are no moral-hazard or adverse-selection problems within an organization. It would be interesting to integrate the analysis of diversification by adding risks (that implies concentration of risk bearing by a "top manager" of an organization) with some limited risk sharing within an organization made incentive compatible by effort monitoring by the top manager. The analysis in Mookherjee (1984) of the possibilities for internal monitoring when various agents within a firm optimally break up tasks provides a promising foundation for such an integration.

III. SELF-SELECTION AND INTERMEDIARY INFORMATION PRODUCTION

Another factor that complicates contracting between borrowers and lenders is a borrower's possession of private information about his ex ante ability to repay. This implies that there is an adverse-selection problem where borrowers with unpromising projects are the most likely to sell securities to outsiders. Such problems can result in market failure, as in Akerlof (1970), or in possibly costly signaling equilibria, as in LP. Boyd and Prescott (1986) presents an intermediation model based on adverse selection, which we describe next. The implications for intermediation of LP are developed in Section III.B, where the related work of Chan (1983) is discussed.

Boyd and Prescott (1986) analyzes a model where risk-neutral individuals have private information about the prospects for their production projects, and the information is useful for deciding whether to fund the projects. Projects require outside financing, and even individuals with bad projects have an incentive to borrow to operate them. There is a project evaluation technology that can reveal to the public, at a cost, some information about a project's prospects. The paper characterizes an optimal contractual mechanism that generally involves contracting for the use of the evaluation technology and uses the ability to commit. This implies that agents are promised different ex post treatment than they would receive in a security market for the purpose of facilitating self-selection of agents with profitable projects. All can observe whether an evaluation takes place and the outcome of the evaluation.

Under certain conditions there is a role in this environment for diversified financial intermediaries, rather than for contingent contracts between groups of agents. This occurs when the evaluation technology reveals some information that is not known even to the project owner. The evaluation serves two purposes: one as a signal (to reveal the individual's confidence that he will get a good evaluation), and one as a further input to production decisions, even given the signal of the individual's information. Intermediaries are modeled as large coalitions where diversification is useful because it allows the coalition to use the information about the proportion of each type of agent (i.e., the number who will receive good evaluations and the number who will receive bad evaluations) before contracts are written. Diversification is useful in this environment because it facilitates commitment by the agents. Agents contract for investment decisions and contingent payments between agents that differ from what an ex post market would produce. Without diversification, the realized fraction of each type of agent is random, and if too many agents have promising projects, the coalition may have insufficient capital to fund them all. This can force some agents into the ex post market, which increases the costs of producing self-selection. If the evaluation served only to enforce truthful signaling and did not reveal useful new information, diversification would not be necessary because any size coalition would have a nonstochastic proportion of each type of agent, conditional on the self-selection actions of the agents.

This approach, with intermediaries performing a screening function, appears promising and realistic. The role of diversification in the Boyd-Prescott (1986) model is similar to that in Diamond (1984): it allows the population (rather than sample) parameters to be those used in contracting. It suggests an interesting extension: diversification allows an intermediary to get around incentive problems when the outcome of its evaluation is not observed to the public. It simply commits to give a certain fraction of each type of evaluation, knowing that someone will deserve each type: this is similar to the advantages of rank order tournament or a seniority system (see Bhattacharya 1983 and Carmichael 1983). If the outcome of the evaluation is not observed by the public, then the intermediary must have incentives to reveal or at least take acts based on the information. This would provide a theory of screening by intermediaries in an environment similar to the monitoring theory in Diamond (1984). Next we review the LP paper, which presents an environment where screening could be useful. Then we show how it can serve as a foundation for a screening-based intermediary theory in a way consistent with the original conjectures in LP.

A. Project Specific Risk and Signalling Costs in the Leland-Pyle Model

The LP paper shows how private information observed by a firm going public, but facing unlimited liability, can lead to costs of excessive bearing of specific (diversifiable) risk compared to a situation of no private information. The only private information the firm's owner possesses is about the project's mean; the model assumes that the variance of the project and its covariance with the exogenously specified "market" are common knowledge.

The LP paper shows that the fraction of equity an entrepreneur will retain in his project is increasing in his assessment of its mean and that there is strict overinvestment in the project by the manager relative to full information. The other results in the paper use the assumption of a normal distribution of project returns and exponential utility for the entrepreneur. The assumption of normal distributions and the restriction to the linear risk sharing offered by equity and unlimited liability debt imply that the covariance with the market will not affect signaling costs or contractual forms because the entrepreneur can eliminate the "market risk" by trading in the "market portfolio."[6] The entrepreneur cannot sell off the firm-specific risk separately from the return of the project itself (because the firm specific component is not observed elsewhere), so the entrepreneur must bear some of it to enforce truthful signaling.

Signaling costs are never prohibitive because any project that has a positive net present value under full information will be financed (the entrepreneur will invest at least a small amount in any favorable lottery, and because the outsiders know the specific risk, a smaller investment in a project with high specific risk will indicate that the entrepreneur has a given amount of good news). The amount of equity retained by the entrepreneur is decreasing in the specific risk and in the entrepreneur's coefficient of risk aversion because high specific risk or risk aversion implies outsiders are impressed with even small investments. One other result, Proposition III, contains an error.

Proposition III as stated claims that increased specific risk increases the entrepreneur's expected utility. In fact, it is shown in Diamond (1984) that the reverse is true; it decreases expected utility (Barclay 1984 also notes this error). The intuitive reason behind the correct result is that a small increase in specific risk increases the variance of the entrepreneur's wealth in equilibrium but leaves its mean unchanged. Referring to the proof of Proposition III in LP, Diamond (1984) shows that the correct expression for the derivative of expected utility with respect to specific risk, Z, is

$$\frac{dE[U]}{dZ} = -b\left\{(1-\alpha)\left[\log(1-\alpha)+\alpha\right]+\frac{\alpha^2}{2}\right\} < 0.$$

LP obtained a positive sign for the derivative by omitting the final $\alpha^2/2$ term.

B. Financial Intermediation in the Leland-Pyle Model

In addition to providing a model of the determinants of the cost of signaling, LP propose the basis of a financial intermediation theory. No analysis is presented, but they make two suggestions about such a theory. They suggest that opportunities for reselling information is one reason why delegating ex ante information production to an intermediary may be important. Chan (1983) constructs a search model extending this notion of a public-good problem with information collection: information collectors capture only a fraction of the social benefit of higher effort by entrepreneurs. This is an alternative model of the gross demand for intermediation. Delegation costs are assumed to be absent.

The second suggestion is that information collection might be reliably delegated to an intermediary if the intermediary itself were required to signal. Rather than entrepreneurs' signaling directly, the information could be collected at a cost by an intermediary and then signaled by the intermediary. For this suggestion to be useful, one must analyze the associated delegation costs. Are the signaling costs of the intermediary, per project, less than the costs of directly signaling the information by the individual project entrepreneurs? If not, intermediation would not be viable even if the intermediary could observe each firm's information at no cost. Campbell and Krackaw

(1980) recognizes a related problem and presents a model quite different from that of LP, providing an example where intermediation cannot be explained by information collection. The Campbell-Krackaw analysis neither considers diversification nor permits intermediaries to write observable optimal contracts. As a result, it is an incomplete analysis of the feasibility of "delegated signaling."

An analysis of the feasibility of intermediation in the LP model, based on diversification, is presented in Diamond (1984). Diversification by adding risks (many independent projects investigated by a single top intermediary manager who signals with retained equity) is shown to be neutral: under the assumed preferences in LP, the per project signaling costs are exactly the same for the intermediary as they would be if the individual project managers signaled directly by retaining their own equity. This implies that this does not lead to viable intermediation, because there are no cost savings to offset the intermediary's information production costs.[7] For other valid risk-averse preferences that would complicate solving the model but not violate its logic, this type of diversification is beneficial. Diversification by subdividing risks (many independent projects investigated by many employees in an intermediary who observe each other's information and effort) does allow delegated signaling, because the variance of specific risk per employee is a decreasing function of the number of independent projects investigated. The corrected version of Proposition III shows that this will reduce signaling costs. Delegated signaling is potentially viable in the LP structure, but this conclusion depends on the information structure within the intermediary.

IV. CONCLUSION

The recent literature on asset services and the role of intermediation has produced a large crop of positive implications about the structure of intermediaries. The importance of diversification and the collection of private information help explain the reasons for the comparative advantage possessed by intermediaries in some financial markets.

Many fundamental aspects of intermediation remain unexplored. The collection of private information by an intermediary often implies that its assets will be illiquid, perhaps because the information asymmetry results in the absence of any secondary market for them. In multiperiod models with private liquidity shocks received by depositors, exogenous illiquidity of assets leads to the desirability of demand deposits and potential problems with bank runs (see the chapter by Jacklin). It would be interesting to integrate these two approaches and examine bank runs and optimal multiperiod contracts when intermediaries collect private information. In addition, private information about the ex ante risk and value of assets can create moral-hazard problems with deposit insurance. Most studies of these problems (e.g., Kareken and Wallace 1978, Merton 1978, and Dothan and Williams 1980) assume complete markets where intermediaries provide no services. This implies that any distortion caused by deposit insurance is a net social loss. It would be interesting to investigate the second-best optimum with useful intermediaries and the moral-hazard constraint on deposit insurance pricing.

Finally, some results on the determinants of the demand for intermediation by different sorts of borrowers would be useful. The analysis in Diamond (1985) suggests that moral-hazard and adverse-selection problems are most severe for borrowers with a short track record (and an implied low value of reputation capital), implying that these borrowers receive the greatest benefit from the asset services of intermediaries. This hints at a possible "life-cycle" model where borrowers have a choice each period between borrowing through an intermediary and issuing securities directly. Analysis of the competing roles of financial markets and financial institutions should help us understand the microeconomic structure of corporate and individual financial decisions.

NOTES

[1] The older literature on banking focused on liability services by linking the demand for bank assets to the demand for money, without modeling the rationale for the demand for intermediation. The motivation was an understanding of the demand for high-powered money by profit-maximizing banks. Important examples of work in this area include Edgeworth (1881), Tobin (1963), Tobin and Brainard (1963), and Gurley and Shaw (1960).

[2] The literature builds on the work on contract theory with both moral hazard (e.g., Jensen and Meckling 1976, Harris and Raviv 1979, Holmström 1979, and Shavell 1979) and adverse selection (Townsend 1979, Myerson 1979, and Harris and Townsend 1981).

[3] Fama (1985) notes that banks issue large certificates of deposit that pay market rates of interest for their risk but are also subject to reserve requirements, implying that the costs of reserve requirements are passed along to borrowers. This is evidence in favor of the idea that banks provide asset services.

[4] See Holmström (1979) and Shavell (1979).

[5] This analysis of optimal debt contracts is extended in Gale and Hellwig (1985). On the value of monitoring in this situation, see Townsend (1979).

[6] The "market portfolio" is an exogenously specified security that might not be the optimal choice for the manager with private information. It has an exogenous market price of risk.

[7] The necessary conditions for beneficial diversification by adding risks are decreasing absolute risk aversion and a positive forth derivative of utility of consumption. The preferences in LP have constant absolute risk aversion.

REFERENCES

Akerlof, G. 1970. "The Market for 'Lemons': Quality Uncertainty and the Market Mechanism." *Quarterly Journal of Economics* 84: 488–500.

Barclay, M. 1984. "Diversification and Financial Market Signalling." Working paper, Stanford University.

Bhattacharya, S. 1983. "Tournaments and Incentives: Heterogeneity and Essentiality." Research paper No. 695, Graduate School of Business, Stanford University.

Boyd, J. H., and Prescott, E. C. 1986. "Financial Intermediary-Coalitions." *Journal of Economic Theory* 38: 211–32.

Campbell, T., and Krackaw, M. 1980. "Information Production, Market Signalling, and the Theory of Financial Intermediation." *Journal of Finance* 54: 863–82.

Carmichael, L. 1983. "Firm-Specific Human Capital and Promotion Ladders." *Bell Journal of Economics* 14: 251–58.

Chan, Y. 1983. "On the Positive Role of Financial Intermediation in Allocation of Venture Capital in a Market with Imperfect Information." *Journal of Finance* 38: 1543–68.

Diamond, D. W. 1984. "Financial Intermediation and Delegated Monitoring." *Review of Economic Studies* 51: 393–414.

———. 1985. "Reputation Acquisition in Debt Markets." Working paper, University of Chicago, May.

Diamond, D. W., and Dybvig, P. H. 1983. "Bank Runs, Deposit Insurance, and Liquidity." *Journal of Political Economy* 91: 410–19.

Dothan, U., and Williams, J. 1980. "Banks, Bankruptcy and Public Regulation." *Journal of Banking and Finance* 4: 65–87.

Edgeworth, F. Y. 1881. *Mathematical Psychics.* London: Kegan Paul.

Fama, E. F. 1985. "What's Different about Banks?" *Journal of Monetary Economics* 15: 29–39.

Gale, D., and Hellwig, M. 1985. "Incentive-Compatible Debt Contracts: The One-Period Problem." *Review of Economic Studies* 52: 647–64.

Gurley, J. G., and Shaw, E. S. 1960. *Money in a Theory of Finance.* Washington: Brookings Institution.

Harris, M., and Raviv, A. 1979. "Optimal Incentive Contracts with Imperfect Information." *Journal of Economic Theory* 20: 231–59.

Harris, M., and Townsend, R. 1981. "Resource Allocation under Asymmetric Information." *Econometrica* 49: 33–64.

Holmström, B. 1979. "Moral Hazard and Observability." *Bell Journal of Economics* 10: 324–40.

Jensen, M., and Meckling, W. 1976. "Theory of the Firm: Managerial Behavior, Agency Costs and Ownership Structure." *Journal of Financial Economics* 3: 305–60.

Kareken, J., and Wallace, N. 1978. "Deposit Insurance and Bank Regulation: A Partial Equilibrium Exposition." *Journal of Business* 51: 412–38.

Leland, H., and Pyle, D. 1977. "Informational Asymmetries, Financial Structure and Financial Intermediation." *Journal of Finance* 32: 371–87. Reprinted Chapter 8, this volume.

Merton, R. 1978. "On the Cost of Deposit Insurance When There Are Surveillance Costs." *Journal of Business* 51: 429–52.

Mookherjee, D. 1984. "Optimal Incentive Schemes with Many Agents." *Review of Economic Studies* 51: 433–46.

Myerson, R. 1979. "Incentive Compatibility and the Bargaining Problem." *Econometrica* 47: 61–74.

Ramakrishnan, R., and Thakor, A. 1984. "Information Reliability and a Theory of Financial Intermediation." *Review of Economic Studies* 51: 415–32.

Samuelson, P. 1963. "Risk and Uncertainty: A Fallacy of Large Numbers." *Sciencia* (April–May).

Shavell, S. 1979. "Risk Sharing and Incentives in the Principal and Agent Relationship." *Bell Journal of Economics* 10: 55–73.

Tobin, J. 1963. "Commercial Banks as Creators of 'Money'." In D. Carson, ed., *Banking and Monetary Studies.* Homewood, Ill.: Irwin.

Tobin, J., and Brainard. W. 1963. "Financial Intermediaries and the Effectiveness of Monetary Control." *American Economic Review* 53: 383–400.

Townsend, R. M. 1979. "Optimal Contracts and Competitive Markets with Costly State Verification." *Journal of Economic Theory* 21: 265–93.

———. 1983. "Theories of Intermediated Structures." In *Carnegie-Rochester Conference Series on Public Policy* 18, pp. 221–72.

Bank Runs, Deposit Insurance, and Liquidity

Douglas W. Diamond

University of Chicago

Philip H. Dybvig

Yale University

This paper shows that bank deposit contracts can provide allocations superior to those of exchange markets, offering an explanation of how banks subject to runs can attract deposits. Investors face privately observed risks which lead to a demand for liquidity. Traditional demand deposit contracts which provide liquidity have multiple equilibria, one of which is a bank run. Bank runs in the model cause real economic damage, rather than simply reflecting other problems. Contracts which can prevent runs are studied, and the analysis shows that there are circumstances when government provision of deposit insurance can produce superior contracts.

I. Introduction

Bank runs are a common feature of the extreme crises that have played a prominent role in monetary history. During a bank run, depositors rush to withdraw their deposits because they expect the bank to fail. In fact, the sudden withdrawals can force the bank to liquidate many of its assets at a loss and to fail. In a panic with many bank failures, there is a disruption of the monetary system and a reduction in production.

Institutions in place since the Great Depression have successfully prevented bank runs in the United States since the 1930s. Nonethe-

We are grateful for helpful comments from Milt Harris, Burt Malkiel, Mike Mussa, Art Raviv, and seminar participants at Chicago, Northwestern, Stanford, and Yale.

[*Journal of Political Economy*, 1983, vol. 91, no. 3]
© 1983 by The University of Chicago. All rights reserved. 0022-3808/83/9103-0004$01.50

less, current deregulation and the dire financial condition of savings and loans make bank runs and institutions to prevent them a current policy issue, as shown by recent aborted runs.[1] (Internationally, Eurodollar deposits tend to be uninsured and are therefore subject to runs, and this is true in the United States as well for deposits above the insured amount.) It is good that deregulation will leave banking more competitive, but we must ensure that banks will not be left vulnerable to runs.

Through careful description and analysis, Friedman and Schwartz (1963) have provided substantial insight into the properties of past bank runs in the United States. Existing theoretical analysis has neglected to explain why bank contracts are less stable than other types of financial contracts or to investigate the strategic decisions that depositors face. The model we present has an explicit economic role for banks to perform: the transformation of illiquid assets into liquid liabilities. The analyses of Patinkin (1965, chap. 5), Tobin (1965), and Niehans (1978) provide insights into characterizing the liquidity of assets. This paper gives the first explicit analysis of the demand for liquidity and the "transformation" service provided by banks. Uninsured demand deposit contracts are able to provide liquidity but leave banks vulnerable to runs. This vulnerability occurs because there are multiple equilibria with differing levels of confidence.

Our model demonstrates three important points. First, banks issuing demand deposits can improve on a competitive market by providing better risk sharing among people who need to consume at different random times. Second, the demand deposit contract providing this improvement has an undesirable equilibrium (a bank run) in which all depositors panic and withdraw immediately, including even those who would prefer to leave their deposits in if they were not concerned about the bank failing. Third, bank runs cause real economic problems because even "healthy" banks can fail, causing the recall of loans and the termination of productive investment. In addition, our model provides a suitable framework for analysis of the devices traditionally used to stop or prevent bank runs, namely, suspension of convertibility and demand deposit insurance (which works similarly to a central bank serving as "lender of last resort").

The illiquidity of assets enters our model through the economy's riskless production activity. The technology provides low levels of output per unit of input if operated for a single period but high levels

---

[1] The aborted runs on Hartford Federal Savings and Loan (Hartford, Conn., February 1982) and on Abilene National Bank (Abilene, Texas, July 1982) are two recent examples. The large amounts of uninsured deposits in the recently failed Penn Square Bank (Oklahoma City, July 1982) and its repercussions are another symptom of banks' current problems.

of output if operated for two periods. The analysis would be the same if the asset were illiquid because of selling costs: one receives a low return if unexpectedly forced to "liquidate" early. In fact, this illiquidity is a property of the financial assets in the economy in our model, even though they are traded in competitive markets with no transaction costs. Agents will be concerned about the cost of being forced into early liquidation of these assets and will write contracts which reflect this cost. Investors face private risks which are not directly insurable because they are not publicly verifiable. Under optimal risk sharing, this private risk implies that agents have different time patterns of return in different private information states and that agents want to allocate wealth unequally across private information states. Because only the agent ever observes the private information state, it is impossible to write insurance contracts in which the payoff depends directly on private information, without an explicit mechanism for information flow. Therefore, simple competitive markets cannot provide this liquidity insurance.

Banks are able to transform illiquid assets by offering liabilities with a different, smoother pattern of returns over time than the illiquid assets offer. These contracts have multiple equilibria. If confidence is maintained, there can be efficient risk sharing, because in that equilibrium a withdrawal will indicate that a depositor should withdraw under optimal risk sharing. If agents panic, there is a bank run and incentives are distorted. In that equilibrium, everyone rushes in to withdraw their deposits before the bank gives out all of its assets. The bank must liquidate all its assets, even if not all depositors withdraw, because liquidated assets are sold at a loss.

Illiquidity of assets provides the rationale both for the existence of banks and for their vulnerability to runs. An important property of our model of banks and bank runs is that runs are costly and reduce social welfare by interrupting production (when loans are called) and by destroying optimal risk sharing among depositors. Runs in many banks would cause economy-wide economic problems. This is consistent with the Friedman and Schwartz (1963) observation of large costs imposed on the U.S. economy by the bank runs in the 1930s, although they attribute the real damage from bank runs as occurring through the money supply.

Another contrast with our view of how bank runs do economic damage is discussed by Fisher (1911, p. 64).[2] In this view, a run occurs because the bank's assets, which are liquid but risky, no longer cover the nominally fixed liability (demand deposits), so depositors withdraw quickly to cut their losses. The real losses are indirect, through

---

[2] Bryant (1980) also takes this view.

the loss of collateral caused by falling prices. In contrast, a bank run in our model is caused by a shift in expectations, which could depend on almost anything, consistent with the apparently irrational observed behavior of people running on banks.

We analyze bank contracts that can prevent runs and examine their optimality. We show that there is a feasible contract that allows banks both to prevent runs and to provide optimal risk sharing by converting illiquid assets. The contract corresponds to suspension of convertibility of deposits (to currency), a weapon banks have historically used against runs. Under other conditions, the best contract that banks can offer (roughly, the suspension-of-convertibility contract) does not achieve optimal risk sharing. However, in this more general case there is a contract which achieves the unconstrained optimum when government deposit insurance is available. Deposit insurance is shown to be able to rule out runs without reducing the ability of banks to transform assets. What is crucial is that deposit insurance frees the asset liquidation policy from strict dependence on the volume of withdrawals. Other institutions such as the discount window ("lender of last resort") may serve a similar function; however, we do not model this here. The taxation authority of the government makes it a natural provider of the insurance, although there may be a competitive fringe of private insurance.

Government deposit insurance can improve on the best allocations that private markets provide. Most of the existing literature on deposit insurance assumes away any real service from deposit insurance, concentrating instead on the question of pricing the insurance, taking as given the likelihood of failure (see, e.g., Merton 1977, 1978; Kareken and Wallace 1978; Dothan and Williams 1980).

Our results have far-reaching policy implications, because they imply that the real damage from bank runs is primarily from the direct damage occurring when recalling loans interrupts production. This implies that much of the economic damage in the Great Depression was *caused* directly by bank runs. A study by Bernanke (in press) supports our thesis, as it shows that bank runs give a better predictor of economic distress than money supply.

The paper proceeds as follows. In the next section, we analyze a simple economy which shows that banks can improve the risk sharing of simple competitive markets by transforming illiquid assets. We show that such banks are always vulnerable to runs. In Section III, we analyze the optimal bank contracts that prevent runs. In Section IV, we analyze bank contracts, dropping the previous assumption that the volume of withdrawals is deterministic. Deposit insurance is analyzed in Section V. Section VI concludes the paper.

II. The Bank's Role in Providing Liquidity

Banks have issued demand deposits throughout their history, and economists have long had the intuition that demand deposits are a vehicle through which banks fulfill their role of turning illiquid assets into liquid assets. In this role, banks can be viewed as providing insurance that allows agents to consume when they need to most. Our simple model shows that asymmetric information lies at the root of liquidity demand, a point not explicitly noted in the previous literature.

The model has three periods ($T = 0$, 1, 2) and a single homogeneous good. The productive technology yields $R > 1$ units of output in period 2 for each unit of input in period 0. If production is interrupted in period 1, the salvage value is just the initial investment. Therefore, the productive technology is represented by

$$
\begin{array}{ccc}
T = 0 & T = 1 & T = 2 \\
-1 & \begin{cases} 0 \\ 1 \end{cases} & \begin{array}{c} R \\ 0, \end{array}
\end{array}
$$

where the choice between $(0, R)$ and $(1, 0)$ is made in period 1. (Of course, constant returns to scale implies that a fraction can be done in each option.)

One interpretation of the technology is that long-term capital investments are somewhat irreversible, which appears to be a reasonable characterization. The results would be reinforced (or can be alternatively motivated) by any type of transaction cost associated with selling a bank's assets before maturity. See Diamond (1980) for a model of the costly monitoring of loan contracts by banks, which implies such a cost.

All consumers are identical as of period 0. Each faces a privately observed, uninsurable risk of being of type 1 or of type 2. In period 1, each agent (consumer) learns his type. Type 1 agents care only about consumption in period 1 and type 2 agents care only about consumption in period 2. In addition, all agents can privately store (or "hoard") consumption goods at no cost. This storage is not publicly observable. No one would store between $T = 0$ and $T = 1$, because the productive technology does at least as well (and better if held until $T = 2$). If an agent of type 2 obtains consumption goods at $T = 1$, he will store them until $T = 2$ to consume them. Let c_T represent goods "received" (to store or consume) by an agent at period T. The privately observed consumption at $T = 2$ of a type 2 agent is then what he stores from $T = 1$ plus what he obtains at $T = 2$, or $c_1 + c_2$. In terms of this publicly observed variable c_T the discussion above implies that each agent has a state-dependent utility function (with the state private information), which we assume has the form

$$U(c_1, c_2; \Theta) = \begin{cases} u(c_1) & \text{if } j \text{ is of type 1 in state } \Theta \\ \rho u(c_1 + c_2) & \text{if } j \text{ is of type 2 in state } \Theta, \end{cases}$$

where $1 \geq \rho > R^{-1}$ and $u:R_{++} \to R$ is twice continuously differentiable, increasing, strictly concave, and satisfies Inada conditions $u'(0) = \infty$ and $u'(\infty) = 0$. Also, we assume that the relative risk-aversion coefficient $-cu''(c)/u'(c) > 1$ everywhere. Agents maximize expected utility, $E[u(c_1, c_2; \Theta)]$, conditional on their information (if any).

A fraction $t \in (0, 1)$ of the continuum of agents are of type 1 and, conditional on t, each agent has an equal and independent chance of being of type 1. Later sections will allow t to be random (in which case, at period 1, consumers know their own type but not t), but for now we take t to be constant.

To complete the model, we give each consumer an endowment of 1 unit in period 0 (and none at other times). We consider first the competitive solution where agents hold the assets directly, and in each period there is a competitive market in claims on future goods. It is easy to show that because of the constant returns technology, prices are determined: the period 0 price of period 1 consumption is 1, and the period 0 and 1 prices of period 2 consumption are R^{-1}. This is because agents can write only uncontingent contracts as there is no public information on which to condition. Contracting in period $T = 0$, all agents (who are then identical) will establish the same trades and each will invest his endowment in the production technology. Given this identical position of each agent at $T = 0$, there will be trade in claims on goods for consumption at $T = 1$ and at $T = 2$. Each has access to the same technology and each can choose any positive linear combination of $c_1 = 1$ and $c_2 = R$. Each individual's production set is proportional to the aggregate set, and for there to be positive production of both c_1 and c_2, the period $T = 1$ price of c_2 must be R^{-1}. Given these prices, there is never any trade, and agents can do no better or worse than if they produced only for their own consumption. Letting c_k^i be consumption in period k of an agent who is of type i, the agents choose $c_1^1 = 1, c_2^1 = c_1^2 = 0$, and $c_2^2 = R$, since type 1's always interrupt production but type 2's never do.

By comparison, if types were *publicly* observable as of period 1, it would be possible to write optimal insurance contracts that give the ex ante (as of period 0) optimal sharing of output between type 1 and type 2 agents. The optimal consumption $\{c_k^{i*}\}$ satisfies

$$c_1^{2*} = c_2^{1*} = 0 \tag{1a}$$

(those who can, delay consumption),

$$u'(c_1^{1*}) = \rho R u'(c_2^{2*}) \tag{1b}$$

(marginal utility in line with marginal productivity), and

$$t c_1^{1*} + [(1 - t) c_2^{2*}/R] = 1 \tag{1c}$$

(the resource constraint).

By assumption, $\rho R > 1$, and since relative risk aversion always exceeds unity, equation (1) implies that the optimal consumption levels satisfy $c_1^{1*} > 1$ and $c_2^{2*} < R$.[3] Therefore, there is room for improvement on the competitive outcome ($c_1^1 = 1$ and $c_2^2 = R$). Also, note that $c_2^{2*} > c_1^{1*}$ by equation (1b), since $\rho R > 1$.

The optimal insurance contract just described would allow agents to insure against the unlucky outcome of being a type 1 agent. This contract is not available in the simple contingent-claims market. Also, the lack of observability of agents' types rules out a complete market of Arrow-Debreu state-contingent claims, because this market would require claims that depend on the nonverifiable private information. Fortunately it is potentially possible to achieve the optimal insurance contract, since the optimal contract satisfies the self-selection constraints.[4] We argue that banks can provide this insurance: by provid-

---

[3] The proof of this is as follows:

$$\rho R u'(R) < R u'(R)$$

$$= 1 \cdot u'(1) + \int_{\gamma=1}^{R} \frac{\partial}{\partial \gamma} [\gamma u'(\gamma)] d\gamma$$

$$= u'(1) + \int_{\gamma=1}^{R} [u'(\gamma) + u''(\gamma)] d\gamma$$

$$< u'(1),$$

as $u' > 0$ and $(\forall \ \gamma) \ -u''(\gamma)\gamma/u'(\gamma) > 1$. Because $u'(\cdot)$ is decreasing and the resource constraint (1c) trades off c_1^{1*} against c_2^{2*}, the solution to (1) must have $c_1^{1*} > 1$ and $c_2^{2*} < R$.

[4] The self-selection constraints state that no agent envies the treatment by the market of other indistinguishable agents. In our model, agents' utilities depend on only their consumption vectors across time and all have identical endowments. Therefore, the self-selection constraints are satisfied if no agent envies the consumption bundle of any other agent. This can be shown for optimal risk sharing using the properties described after (1). Because $c_1^{1*} > 1$ and $c_1^{2*} = 0$, type 1 agents do not envy type 2 agents. Furthermore, because $c_1^{2*} + c_2^{2*} = c_2^{2*} > c_1^{1*} = c_1^{1*} + c_2^{1*}$, type 2 agents do not envy type 1 agents. Because the optimal contract satisfies the self-selection constraints, there is necessarily a contract structure which implements it as a Nash equilibrium—the ordinary demand deposit is a contract which will work. However, the optimal allocation is not the unique Nash equilibrium under the ordinary demand deposit contract. Another inferior equilibrium is what we identify as a bank run. Our model gives a real-world example of a situation in which the distinction between implementation as a Nash equilibrium and implementation as a *unique* Nash equilibrium is crucial (see also Dybvig and Spatt, in press, and Dybvig and Jaynes 1980).

ing liquidity, banks guarantee a reasonable return when the investor cashes in before maturity, as is required for optimal risk sharing. To illustrate how banks provide this insurance, we first examine the traditional demand deposit contract, which is of particular interest because of its ubiquitous use by banks. Studying the demand deposit contract in our framework also indicates why banks are susceptible to runs.

In our model, the demand deposit contract gives each agent withdrawing in period 1 a fixed claim of r_1 per unit deposited at time 0. Withdrawal tenders are served sequentially in random order until the bank runs out of assets. This approach allows us to capture the flavor of continuous time (in which depositors deposit and withdraw at different random times) in a discrete model. Note that the demand deposit contract satisfies a *sequential service constraint*, which specifies that a bank's payoff to any agent can depend only on the agent's place in line and not on future information about agents behind him in line.

We are assuming throughout this paper that the bank is mutually owned (a "mutual") and liquidated in period 2, so that agents not withdrawing in period 1 get a pro rata share of the bank's assets in period 2. Let V_1 be the period 1 payoff per unit deposit withdrawn which depends on one's place in line at $T = 1$, and let V_2 be the period 2 payoff per unit deposit not withdrawn at $T = 2$, which depends on total withdrawals at $T = 1$. These are given by

$$V_1(f_j, r_1) = \begin{cases} r_1 & \text{if } f_j < r_1^{-1} \\ 0 & \text{if } f_j \geq r_1^{-1} \end{cases} \tag{2}$$

and

$$V_2(f, r_1) = \max \{R(1 - r_1 f)/(1 - f), 0\}, \tag{3}$$

where f_j is the number of withdrawers' deposits serviced before agent j as a fraction of total demand deposits; f is the total number of demand deposits withdrawn. Let w_j be the fraction of agent j's deposits that he attempts to withdraw at $T = 1$. The consumption from deposit proceeds, per unit of deposit of a type 1 agent, is thus given by $w_j V_1(f_j, r_1)$, while the total consumption, from deposit proceeds, per unit of deposit of a type 2 agent is given by $w_j V_1(f_j, r_1) + (1 - w_j)V_2(f, r_1)$.

Equilibrium Decisions

The demand deposit contract can achieve the full-information optimal risk sharing as an equilibrium. (By equilibrium, we will always refer to pure strategy Nash equilibrium[5]—and for now we will assume all agents are required to deposit initially.) This occurs when $r_1 = c_1^{1*}$, that is, when the fixed payment per dollar of deposits withdrawn at $T = 1$ is equal to the optimal consumption of a type 1 agent given full information. If this contract is in place, it is an equilibrium for type 1 agents to withdraw at $T = 1$ and for type 2 agents to wait, provided this is what is anticipated. This "good" equilibrium achieves optimal risk sharing.[6]

Another equilibrium (a bank run) has all agents panicking and trying to withdraw their deposits at $T = 1$: if this is anticipated, all agents will prefer to withdraw at $T = 1$. This is because the face value of deposits is larger than the liquidation value of the bank's assets.

It is precisely the "transformation" of illiquid assets into liquid assets that is responsible both for the liquidity service provided by banks and for their susceptibility to runs. For all $r_1 > 1$, runs are an equilibrium.[7] If $r_1 = 1$, a bank would not be susceptible to runs because $V_1(f_j, 1) < V_2(f, 1)$ for all values of $0 \leqslant f_j \leqslant f$; but if $r_1 = 1$, the bank simply mimics direct holding of the assets and is therefore no improvement on simple competitive claims markets. A demand deposit contract which is not subject to runs provides no liquidity services.

The bank run equilibrium provides allocations that are worse for all agents than they would have obtained without the bank (trading in the competitive claims market). In the bank run equilibrium, everyone receives a risky return that has a mean one. Holding assets directly provides a riskless return that is at least one (and equal to $R > 1$ if an agent becomes a type 2). Bank runs ruin the risk sharing between agents and take a toll on the efficiency of production because all production is interrupted at $T = 1$ when it is optimal for some to continue until $T = 2$.

If we take the position that outcomes must match anticipations, the inferiority of bank runs seems to rule out observed runs, since no one would deposit anticipating a run. However, agents will choose to deposit at least some of their wealth in the bank even if they anticipate a positive probability of a run, provided that the probability is small enough, because the good equilibrium dominates holding assets di-

---

[5] This assumption rules out a mixed strategy equilibrium which is not economically meaningful.

[6] To verify this, substitute $f = t$ and $r_1 = c_1^{1*}$ into (2) and (3), noting that this leads to $V_1(\cdot) = c_1^{1*}$ and $V_2(\cdot) = c_2^{2*}$. Because $c_2^{2*} > c_1^{1*}$, all type 2's prefer to wait until time 2 while type 1's withdraw at 1, implying that $f = t$ is an equilibrium.

[7] The value $r_1 = 1$ is the value which rules out runs and mimics the competitive market because that is the per unit $T = 1$ liquidating value of the technology. If that liquidating value were $\Theta < 1$, then $r_1 = \Theta$ would have this property. It has nothing directly to do with the zero rate of interest on deposits.

rectly. This could happen if the selection between the bank run equilibrium and the good equilibrium depended on some commonly observed random variable in the economy. This could be a bad earnings report, a commonly observed run at some other bank, a negative government forecast, or even sunspots.[8] It need not be anything fundamental about the bank's condition. The problem is that once they have deposited, anything that causes them to anticipate a run will lead to a run. This implies that banks with pure demand deposit contracts will be very concerned about maintaining confidence because they realize that the good equilibrium is very fragile.

The pure demand deposit contract is feasible, and we have seen that it can attract deposits even if the perceived probability of a run is positive. This explains why the contract has actually been used by banks in spite of the danger of runs. Next, we examine a closely related contract that can help to eliminate the problem of runs.

III. Improving on Demand Deposits: Suspension of Convertibility

The pure demand deposit contract has a good equilibrium that achieves the full-information optimum when t is not stochastic. However, in its bank run equilibrium, it is worse than direct ownership of assets. It is illuminating to begin the analysis of optimal bank contracts by demonstrating that there is a simple variation on the demand deposit contract which gives banks a defense against runs: suspension of allowing withdrawal of deposits, referred to as suspension of convertibility (of deposits to cash). Our results are consistent with the claim by Friedman and Schwartz (1963) that the newly organized Federal Reserve Board may have made runs in the 1930s worse by preventing banks from suspending convertibility: the total week-long banking "holiday" that followed was more severe than any of the previous suspensions.

If banks can suspend convertibility when withdrawals are too numerous at $T = 1$, anticipation of this policy prevents runs by removing the incentive of type 2 agents to withdraw early. The following contract is identical to the pure demand deposit contract described in (2) and (3), except that it states that any agent will receive nothing at $T = 1$ if he attempts to withdraw at $T = 1$ after a fraction $\hat{f} < r_1^{-1}$ of all deposits have already been withdrawn—note that we

---

[8] Analysis of this point in a general setting is given in Azariadis (1980) and Cass and Shell (1983).

redefine $V_1(\cdot)$ and $V_2(\cdot)$,

$$V_1(f_j, r_1) = \begin{cases} r_1 & \text{if } f_j \leq \hat{f} \\ 0 & \text{if } f_j > \hat{f} \end{cases}$$

$$V_2(f, r_1) = \max\left\{\frac{(1 - fr_1)R}{1 - f}, \frac{(1 - \hat{f}r_1)R}{1 - \hat{f}}\right\},$$

where the expression for V_2 assumes that $1 - \hat{f}r_1 > 0$.

Convertibility is suspended when $f_j = \hat{f}$, and then no one else "in line" is allowed to withdraw at $T = 1$. To demonstrate that this contract can achieve the optimal allocation, let $r_1 = c_1^{1*}$ and choose any $\hat{f} \in \{t, [(R - r_1)/r_1(R - 1)]\}$. Given this contract, no type 2 agent will withdraw at $T = 1$ because no matter what he anticipates about others' withdrawals, he receives higher proceeds by waiting until $T = 2$ to withdraw; that is, for all f and $f_j \leq f$, $V_2(\cdot) > V_1(\cdot)$. All of the type 1's will withdraw everything at period 1 because period 2 consumption is worthless to them. Therefore, there is a unique Nash equilibrium which has $f = t$. In fact, this is a dominant strategy equilibrium, because each agent will choose his equilibrium action even if he anticipates that other agents will choose nonequilibrium or even irrational actions. This makes this contract very "stable." This equilibrium is essentially the good demand deposit equilibrium that achieves optimal risk sharing.

A policy of suspension of convertibility at $\hat{f}$ guarantees that it will never be profitable to participate in a bank run because the liquidation of the bank's assets is terminated while type 2's still have an incentive not to withdraw. This contract works perfectly only in the case where the normal volume of withdrawals, t, is known and not stochastic. The more general case, where t can vary, is analyzed next.

IV. Optimal Contracts with Stochastic Withdrawals

The suspension of convertibility contract achieves optimal risk sharing when t is known ex ante because suspension never occurs in equilibrium and the bank can follow the optimal asset liquidation policy. This is possible because the bank knows exactly how many withdrawals will occur when confidence is maintained. We now allow the fraction of type 1's to be an unobserved random variable, $\bar{t}$. We consider a general class of bank contracts where payments to those who withdraw at $T = 1$ are any function of f_j and payments to those who withdraw at $T = 2$ are any function of f. Analyzing this general class will show the shortcomings of suspension of convertibility.

The full-information optimal risk sharing is the same as before, except that in equation (1) the actual realization of $\tilde{t} = t$ is used in place of the fixed t. As no single agent has information crucial to learning the value of t, the arguments of footnote 3 still show that optimal risk sharing is consistent with self-selection, so there must be some mechanism which has optimal risk sharing as a Nash equilibrium. We now explore whether banks (which are subject to the constraint of sequential service) can do this too.

From equation (1) we obtain full-information optimal consumption levels, given the realization of $\tilde{t} = t$, of $c_1^{1*}(t)$ and $c_2^{2*}(t)$. Recall that $c_2^{1*}(t) = c_1^{2*}(t) = 0$. At the optimum, consumption is equal for all agents of a given type and depends on the realization of t. This implies a unique optimal asset liquidation policy given $\tilde{t} = t$. This turns out to imply that uninsured bank deposit contracts cannot achieve optimal risk sharing.

PROPOSITION 1: Bank contracts (which must obey the sequential service constraint) cannot achieve optimal risk sharing when t is stochastic and has a nondegenerate distribution.

Proposition 1 holds for all equilibria of uninsured bank contracts of the general form $V_1(f_j)$ and $V_2(f)$, where these can be any function. It obviously remains true that uninsured pure demand deposit contracts are subject to runs. Any run equilibrium does not achieve optimal risk sharing, because both types of agents receive the same consumption. Consider the good equilibrium for any feasible contract. We prove that no bank contract can attain the full-information optimal risk sharing. The proof is straightforward, a two-part proof by contradiction. Recall that the "place in line" f_j is uniformly distributed over $[0, t]$ if only type 1 agents withdraw at $T = 1$. First, suppose that the payments to those who withdraw at $T = 1$ is a nonconstant function of f_j over feasible values of t: for two possible values of $\tilde{t}$, t_1 and t_2, the value of a period 1 withdrawal varies, that is, $V_1(t_1) \neq V_1(t_2)$. This immediately implies that there is a positive probability of different consumption levels by two type 1 agents who will withdraw at $T = 1$, and this contradicts an unconstrained optimum. Second, assume the contrary: that for all possible realizations of $\tilde{t} = t$, $V_1(f_j)$ is constant for all $f_j \in [0, t]$. This implies that $c_1^1(t)$ is a constant independent of the realization of $\tilde{t}$, while the budget constraint, equation (1c), shows that $c_2^2(t)$ will vary with t (unless $r_1 = 1$, which is itself inconsistent with optimal risk sharing). Constant $c_1^1(t)$ and varying $c_2^2(t)$ contradict optimal risk sharing, equation (1b). Thus, optimal risk sharing is inconsistent with sequential service.

Proposition 1 implies that no bank contract, including suspension convertibility, can achieve the full-information optimum. Nonetheless, suspension can generally improve on the uninsured demand deposit contract by preventing runs. The main problem occurs when convertibility is suspended in equilibrium, that is, when the point $\hat{f}$ where suspension occurs is less than the largest possible realization of $\bar{t}$. In that case, some type 1 agents cannot withdraw, which is inefficient ex post. This can be desirable ex ante, however, because the threat of suspension prevents runs and allows a relatively high value of r_1. This result is consistent with contemporary views about suspension in the United States in the period before deposit insurance. Although suspensions served to short-circuit runs, they were "regarded as anything but a satisfactory solution by those who experienced them, which is why they produced so much strong pressure for monetary and banking reform" (Friedman and Schwartz 1963, p. 329). The most important reform that followed was federal deposit insurance. Its impact is analyzed in Section V.

V. Government Deposit Insurance

Deposit insurance provided by the government allows bank contracts that can dominate the best that can be offered without insurance and never do worse. We need to introduce deposit insurance into the analysis in a way that keeps the model closed and assures that no aggregate resource constraints are violated. Deposit insurance guarantees that the promised return will be paid to all who withdraw. If this is a guarantee of a real value, the amount that can be guaranteed is constrained: the government must impose real taxes to honor a deposit guarantee. If the deposit guarantee is nominal, the tax is the (inflation) tax on nominal assets caused by money creation. (Such taxation occurs even if no inflation results; in any case the price level is higher than it would have been otherwise, so some nominally denominated wealth is appropriated.) Because a private insurance company is constrained by its reserves in the scale of unconditional guarantees which it can offer, we argue that deposit insurance probably ought to be governmental for this reason. Of course, the deposit guarantee could be made by a private organization with some authority to tax or create money to pay deposit insurance claims, although we would usually think of such an organization as being a branch of government. However, there can be a small competitive fringe of commercially insured deposits, limited by the amount of private collateral.

The government is assumed to be able to levy any tax that charges every agent in the economy the same amount. In particular, it can tax those agents who withdrew "early" in period $T = 1$, namely, those with low values of f_j. How much tax must be raised depends on how many deposits are withdrawn at $T = 1$ and what amount r_1 was promised to them. For example, if every deposit of one dollar were withdrawn at $T = 1$ (implying $f = 1$) and $r_1 = 2$ were promised, a tax of at least one per capita would need to be raised because totally liquidating the bank's assets will raise at most one per capita at $T = 1$. As the government can impose a tax on an agent *after* he or she has withdrawn, the government can base its tax on f, the realized total value of $T = 1$ withdrawals. This is in marked contrast to a bank, which must provide sequential service and cannot reduce the amount of a withdrawal after it has been made. This asymmetry allows a potential benefit from government intervention. The realistic sequential-service constraint represents some services that a bank provides but which we do not explicitly model. With deposit insurance we will see that imposing this constraint does not reduce social welfare.

Agents are concerned with the after-tax value of the proceeds from their withdrawals because that is the amount that they can consume. A very strong result (which may be too strong) about the optimality of deposit insurance will illuminate the more general reasons why it is desirable. We argue in the conclusion that deposit insurance and the Federal Reserve discount window provide nearly identical services in the context of our model but confine current discussion to deposit insurance.

PROPOSITION 2: Demand deposit contracts with government deposit insurance achieve the unconstrained optimum as a unique Nash equilibrium (in fact, a dominant strategies equilibrium) if the government imposes an optimal tax to finance the deposit insurance.

Proposition 2 follows from the ability of tax-financed deposit insurance to duplicate the optimal consumptions $c_1^1(t) = c_1^{1*}(t)$, $c_2^2(t) = c_2^{2*}(t)$, $c_2^1(t) = 0$, $c_1^2(t) = 0$ from the optimal risk sharing characterized in equation (1). Let the government impose a tax on all wealth held at the beginning of period $T = 1$, which is payable either in goods or in deposits. Let deposits be accepted for taxes at the pretax amount of goods which could be obtained if withdrawn at $T = 1$. The amount of tax that must be raised at $T = 1$ depends on the number of withdrawals then and the asset liquidation policy. Consider the proportionate tax as a function of f, $\tau: [0, 1] \rightarrow [0, 1]$ given by

$$\tau(f) = \begin{cases} 1 - \dfrac{c_1^{1*}(f)}{r_1} & \text{if } f \leqslant \bar{t} \\ 1 - r_1^{-1} & \text{if } f > \bar{t}, \end{cases}$$

where $\bar{t}$ is the greatest possible realization of $\bar{t}$.

The after-tax proceeds, per dollar of initial deposit, of a withdrawal at $T = 1$ depend on f through the tax payment and are identical for all $f_j \leq f$. Denote these after-tax proceeds by $\hat{V}_1(f)$, given by

$$
\hat{V}_1(f) = \begin{cases} c_1^{1*}(f) & \text{if } f \leq \bar{t} \\[2mm] 1 & \text{if } f > \bar{t}. \end{cases}
$$

The net payments to those who withdraw at $T = 1$ determine the asset liquidation policy and the after-tax value a withdrawal at $T = 2$. Any tax collected in excess of that needed to meet withdrawals at $T = 1$ is plowed back into the bank (to minimize the fraction of assets liquidated). This implies that the after-tax proceeds, per dollar of initial deposit, of a withdrawal at $T = 2$, denoted by $\hat{V}_2(f)$, are given by

$$
\hat{V}_2(f) = \begin{cases} \dfrac{R\{1 - [c_1^{1*}(f)f]\}}{1 - f} = c_2^{2*}(f) & \text{if } f \leq \bar{t} \\[4mm] \dfrac{R(1 - f)}{1 - f} = R & \text{if } f > \bar{t}. \end{cases}
$$

Notice that $\hat{V}_1(f) < \hat{V}_2(f)$ for all $f \in [0, 1]$, implying that no type 2 agents will withdraw at $T = 1$ no matter what they expect others to do. For all $f \in [0, 1]$, $\hat{V}_1(f) > 0$, implying that all type 1 agents will withdraw at $T = 1$. Therefore, the unique dominant strategy equilibrium is $f = t$, the realization of $\bar{t}$. Evaluated at a realization t,

$$
\hat{V}_1(f = t) = c_1^{1*}(t)
$$

and

$$
\hat{V}_2(f = t) = \frac{[1 - tc_1^{1*}(t)]R}{1 - t} = c_2^{2*}(t),
$$

and the optimum is achieved.

Proposition 2 highlights the key social benefit of government deposit insurance. It allows the bank to follow a desirable asset liquidation policy, which can be separated from the cash-flow constraint imposed directly by withdrawals. Furthermore, it prevents runs because, for all possible anticipated withdrawal policies of other agents, it never pays to participate in a bank run. As a result, no strategic issues of confidence arise. This is a general result of many deposit insurance schemes. The proposition may be too strong, as it allows the government to follow an unconstrained tax policy. If a nonoptimal tax must be imposed, then when t is stochastic there will be some tax distortions and resource costs associated with government deposit insurance. If a sufficiently perverse tax provided the revenues for insurance, social welfare could be higher without the insurance.

Deposit insurance can be provided costlessly in the simpler case where t is nonstochastic, for the same reason that there need not be a suspension of convertibility in equilibrium. The deposit insurance guarantees that type 2 agents will never participate in a run; without runs, withdrawals are deterministic and this feature is never used. In particular, so long as the government can impose *some* tax to finance the insurance, no matter how distortionary, there will be no runs and the distorting tax need never be imposed. This feature is shared by a model of adoption externalities (see Dybvig and Spatt, in press) in which a Pareto-inferior equilibrium can be averted by an insurance policy which is costless in equilibrium. In both models, the credible promise to provide the insurance means that the promise will not need to be fulfilled. This is in contrast to privately provided deposit insurance. Because insurance companies do not have the power of taxation, they must hold reserves to make their promise credible. This illustrates a reason why the government may have a natural advantage in providing deposit insurance. The role of government policy in our model focuses on providing an institution to prevent a bad equilibrium rather than a policy to move an existing equilibrium. Generally, such a policy need not cause distortion.

VI. Conclusions and Implications

The model serves as a useful framework for analyzing the economics of banking and associated policy issues. It is interesting that the problems of runs and the differing effects of suspension of convertibility and deposit insurance manifest themselves in a model which does not introduce currency or risky technology. This demonstrates that many of the important problems in banking are not necessarily related to those factors, although a general model will require their introduction.

We analyze an economy with a single bank. The interpretation is that it represents the financial intermediary industry, and withdrawals represent net withdrawals from the system. If many banks were introduced into the model, then there would be a role for liquidity risk sharing between banks, and phenomena such as the Federal Funds market or the impact of "bank-specific risk" on deposit insurance could be analyzed.

The result that deposit insurance dominates contracts which the bank alone can enforce shows that there is a potential benefit from government intervention into banking markets. In contrast to common tax and subsidy schemes, the intervention we are recommending provides an institutional framework under which banks can operate smoothly, much as enforcement of contracts does more generally.

The riskless technology used in the model isolates the rationale for deposit insurance, but in addition it abstracts from the choice of bank loan portfolio risk. If the risk of bank portfolios could be selected by a bank manager, unobserved by outsiders (to some extent), then a moral hazard problem would exist. In this case there is a trade-off between optimal risk sharing and proper incentives for portfolio choice, and introducing deposit insurance can influence the portfolio choice. The moral hazard problem has been analyzed in complete market settings where deposit insurance is redundant and can provide no social improvement (see Kareken and Wallace 1978; Dothan and Williams 1980), but of course in this case there is no trade-off. Introducing risky assets and moral hazard would be an interesting extension of our model. It appears likely that some form of government deposit insurance could again be desirable but that it would be accompanied by some sort of bank regulation. Such bank regulation would serve a function similar to restrictive covenants in bond indentures. Interesting but hard to model are questions of regulator "discretion" which then arise.

The Federal Reserve discount window can, as a lender of last resort, provide a service similar to deposit insurance. It would buy bank assets with (money creation) tax revenues at $T = 1$ for prices greater than their liquidating value. If the taxes and transfers were set to be identical to that of the optimal deposit insurance, it would have the same effect. The identity of deposit insurance and discount window services occurs because the technology is riskless.

If the technology is risky, the lender of last resort can no longer be as credible as deposit insurance. If the lender of last resort were *always* required to bail out banks with liquidity problems, there would be perverse incentives for banks to take on risk, even if bailouts occurred only when many banks fail together. For instance, if a bailout is anticipated, all banks have an incentive to take on interest rate risk by mismatching maturities of assets and liabilities, because they will all be bailed out together.

If the lender of last resort is not required to bail out banks unconditionally, a bank run can occur in response to changes in depositor expectations about the bank's credit worthiness. A run can even occur in response to expectations about the general willingness of the lender of last resort to rescue failing banks, as illustrated by the unfortunate experience of the 1930s when the Federal Reserve misused its discretion and did not allow much discounting. In contrast, deposit insurance is a binding commitment which can be structured to retain punishment of the bank's owners, board of directors, and officers in the case of a failure.

The potential for multiple equilibria when a firm's liabilities are more liquid than its assets applies more generally, not simply to banks. Consider a firm with illiquid technology which issues very short-term bonds as a large part of its capital structure. Suppose one lender expects all other lenders to refuse to roll over their loans to the firm. Then, it may be his best response to refuse to roll over his loans even if the firm would be solvent if all loans were rolled over. Such liquidity crises are similar to bank runs. The protection from creditors provided by the bankruptcy laws serves a function similar to the suspension of convertibility. The firm which is viable but illiquid is guaranteed survival. This suggests that the "transformation" could be carried out directly by firms rather than by financial intermediaries. Our focus on intermediaries is supported by the fact that banks directly hold a substantial fraction of the short-term debt of corporations. Also, there is frequently a requirement (or custom) that a firm issuing short-term commercial paper obtain a bank line of credit sufficient to pay off the issue if it cannot "roll it over." A bank with deposit insurance can provide "liquidity insurance" to a firm, which can prevent a liquidity crisis for a firm with short-term debt and limit the firm's need to use bankruptcy to stop such crises. This suggests that most of the aggregate liquidity risk in the U.S. economy is channeled through its insured financial intermediaries, to the extent that lines of credit represent binding commitments.

We hope that this model will prove to be useful in understanding issues in banking and corporate finance.

References

Azariadis, Costas. "Self-fulfilling Prophecies." *J. Econ. Theory* 25 (December 1980): 380–96.

Bernanke, Ben. "Nonmonetary Effects of the Financial Crisis in the Propagation of the Great Depression." *A.E.R.* (in press).

Bryant, John. "A Model of Reserves, Bank Runs, and Deposit Insurance." *J. Banking and Finance* 4 (1980): 335–44.

Cass, David, and Shell, Karl. "Do Sunspots Matter?" *J.P.E.* 91 (April 1983): 193–227.

Diamond, Douglas W. "Financial Intermediation and Delegated Monitoring." Working Paper, Graduate School Bus., Univ. Chicago, 1980.

Dothan, U., and Williams, J. "Banks, Bankruptcy and Public Regulations." *J. Banking and Finance* 4 (March 1980): 65–87.

Dybvig, Philip H., and Jaynes, G. "Microfoundations of Wage Rigidity." Working Paper, Yale Univ., 1980.

Dybvig, Philip H., and Spatt, Chester S. "Adoption Externalities as Public Goods." *J. Public Econ.* (in press).

Fisher, Irving. *The Purchasing Power of Money: Its Determination and Relation to Credit, Interest and Crises.* New York: Macmillan, 1911.

Friedman, Milton, and Schwartz, Anna J. *A Monetary History of the United States, 1867–1960.* Princeton, N.J.: Princeton Univ. Press (for Nat. Bur. Econ. Res.), 1963.

Kareken, John H., and Wallace, Neil. "Deposit Insurance and Bank Regulation: A Partial-Equilibrium Exposition." *J. Bus.* 51 (July 1978): 413–38.

Merton, Robert C. "An Analytic Derivation of the Cost of Deposit Insurance and Loan Guarantees: An Application of Modern Option Pricing Theory." *J. Banking and Finance* 1 (June 1977): 3–11.

———. "On the Cost of Deposit Insurance When There Are Surveillance Costs." *J. Bus.* 51 (July 1978): 439–52.

Niehans, Jürg. *The Theory of Money.* Baltimore: Johns Hopkins Univ. Press, 1978.

Patinkin, Don. *Money, Interest, and Prices: An Integration of Monetary and Value Theory.* 2d ed. New York: Harper & Row, 1965.

Tobin, James. "The Theory of Portfolio Selection." In *The Theory of Interest Rates,* edited by Frank H. Hahn and F. P. R. Brechling. London: Macmillan, 1965.

discussion | **Imperfect Information, Credit Markets, and Macroeconomic Fluctuations**

Andrew Weiss

Boston University

I. INTRODUCTION

In a series of recent papers Joseph Stiglitz and I have explored the implication of informational asymmetries on the operation of credit markets (see Weiss 1977, Stiglitz and Weiss 1980, 1981, 1983, 1986a, b, c).[1] Our main concern was the existence of rationing equilibria in credit markets. We showed that competitive credit markets could be characterized by credit rationing in either of two senses: (a) among observationally identical borrowers some are given credit while others are denied loans even though the latter are willing to pay a higher interest rate than are the borrowers being denied credit; (b) potential borrowers are denied credit even though borrowers that are nearly identical to them are getting loans, and the borrowers denied credit would (if they got loans) have their welfare discretely improved. (Type (b) rationing is often referred to as redlining.) We also showed that there exist reasonable conditions under which the borrowers that were denied credit would, if given loans, choose projects or techniques with higher expected gross returns than the projects chosen in equilibrium. These resource misallocations are due to the different incentives of borrowers and lenders—borrowers are unconcerned with the bottom tail of the distribution of returns; lenders are unconcerned with the upper tail of the distribution.[2]

This paper reviews both the micro- and macroeconomic implications of informational asymmetries in credit markets. We show that the possession of different information by borrowers and lenders and the lack of control by lenders over important decisions of borrowers can cause the aggregate level of investment to be too low.

Informational asymmetries also cause macroeconomic fluctuations to have dramatically different effects on interest rates and on the allocation of credit among borrowers from the effects predicted by the standard macroeconomic models. (These effects may be in closer accord with observed phenomena than are the predictions of the perfect information models.) In particular, an increase in the success probabilities of all investments may cause either a rise or a fall in the interest rate paid to depositors and in the average interest rate charged to borrowers. Similarly an expansion in the supply of loanable funds may cause a *rise* in the average interest rate charged to borrowers. These results differ from those of the standard *IS-LM* analysis. As a policy prescription it also follows that government intervention in the setting of interest rates and the allocation of credit may affect Pareto improvements (see Stiglitz and Weiss 1980 and Ordover and Weiss 1981).

In what follows we first discuss the source of informational asymmetries in credit markets and the effect these asymmetries have on the terms of standard loan contracts. We show why competition among banks will result in contracts that cause inefficiencies in the allocation of credit: when redlining and credit rationing are practiced by banks, these welfare losses are likely to be relatively large. Finally, we explore the macroeconomic implications of these informational asymmetries.

II. INCENTIVE EFFECTS

When lenders offer contracts to potential borrowers, they are concerned not just with choosing the highest interest rate that will attract borrowers, but also with the effect the interest rate and other nonprice terms of the contract have on the default rate of the loans the lender is making. Although banks usually know in broad terms how the money they are lending is being spent—for example, to dig an irrigation well—there are many decisions made by the borrower that affect the lender but which the lender does not directly control. A farmer borrowing money to dig an irrigation well is also choosing whether to use disease-resistant seeds, how much fertilizer to use, how much pesticide to spray, and when to harvest the crops. These "choices of techniques" are made to maximize the expected utility of the borrower; they may adversely affect the utility of the lender. The interests of borrowers and lenders frequently conflict. The lender is concerned with the loan being repaid and with the value of the assets in the case of default. The borrower is concerned with the value of his assets when the loan is repaid. Ignoring reputation effects, he is unconcerned with the value of those assets in the case of default. (For example, a heavy use of fertilizer may increase the expected return to the farmer but may also increase the probability of default in the case of a drought or insect infestation.) Borrowers often choose techniques different from those preferred by the lender.[3]

Lenders do not have the degree of knowledge needed for them to control all the relevant decisions of their borrowers. Even if they had that knowledge, monitoring all those decisions would be prohibitively expensive. Consequently, lenders will exercise some degree of indirect control. That is, in addition to direct screening of projects and borrowers and direct monitoring of loans, lenders will choose the terms of the contracts they offer borrowers in order to influence the default rate on the loans they make.

This influence takes two forms. Lenders wish to affect both the distribution of borrowers that apply to them for loans and the choice of technique by each borrower. High collateral requirements discourage applications from poor borrowers. If borrowers' utility functions are characterized by decreasing absolute risk aversion, poor borrowers would tend to favor relatively safe projects (see Stiglitz and Weiss 1981). High interest rates encourage borrowers to choose techniques with higher probabilities of default—interest rates are only paid in states when the project is successful, so the expected cost of the high interest rate is lower when a technique with a high default probability is used by the borrower.

These effects follow directly from the return functions of borrowers and lenders. The utility to a risk-averse borrower from a loan of one unit is

$$(1) \qquad U^* = \int_0^{R*} f(R)dR \, U(A - C) + \int_{R*}^{\infty} f(R)U(R + A - r)dR,$$

where A is the assets of the borrower, C is the collateral on the loan, r is 1 plus the interest rate charged the borrower, R is the gross return on a loan, $f(R)$ is the density of R, and R^* is the gross return at which the borrower is indifferent about repaying the loan. R^* is chosen to maximize the borrower's expected utility so that $R^* + A - r = A - C$ or $R^* = r - C$. The expected return to a risk-neutral lender is

$$(2) \qquad \pi = \int_0^{R*} (f(R)R + C)dR + \int_{R*}^{\infty} f(R)r \, dR - i$$

where i is the interest rate paid to depositors. We assume a competitive market for deposits, so in equilibrium i is driven to the level at which $\pi = 0$. In equilibrium all banks earn zero profits. We also assume that all projects require one unit of credit; alternatively we could instead have assumed a region of increasing returns to scale for projects. Some form of increasing returns to scale is necessary for a credit rationing equilibrium.

Much of the literature on credit markets with asymmetric information is concerned with the effect of contracts on the distribution of borrowers (the sorting effect) and the effect on the choice of technique (the incentive effect). In the analysis of these effects it is useful to illustrate the divergent interests of borrowers and lenders by examining the preferences of the risk-neutral

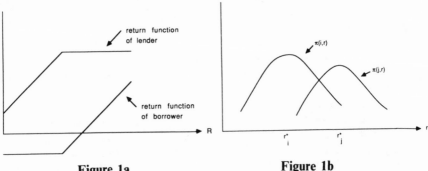

Figure 1a   Figure 1b

borrowers and lenders over a mean-preserving spread of techniques. We can easily show that risk-neutral borrowers prefer the risky technique, risk-neutral lenders the safe one. These effects are illustrated in Fig. 1, where we graph the return functions of borrowers and lenders. Because the return function of borrowers is convex, a mean-preserving spread of the distribution of gross returns of a project will increase their expected return. Conversely, a mean-preserving spread of the distribution of gross returns of lenders will decrease their expected gross returns.

In general, the distributions of returns over different techniques are not mean-preserving spreads. However, the general effects illustrated in Fig. 1 remain for more general distributions. Lenders favor contract terms that decrease the default rate of their loans either by discouraging applications from those borrowers that would tend to use risky techniques or by inducing borrowers to use safe techniques.

Let us begin by analyzing simple contracts, contracts that only mandate an interest rate. From equation (1) we can see that if borrowers are initially indifferent between two techniques, an increase in the interest rate will cause them to choose the technique with the higher probability of bankruptcy. This adverse incentive effect of interest rates can outweigh the direct effect on the bank's profits. An increase in the interest rate charged borrowers could then cause a fall in the lender's profits. The conditions for this to occur are presented in the following theorem, a proof of which appears in Stiglitz and Weiss (1981).

THEOREM 1. *The expected return to the bank is lowered by an increase in the interest rate at r; if at r the firm is indifferent between two projects j and k with distributions $F_j(R)$ and $F_k(R)$, j having a higher probability of bankruptcy than k, and there exists a distribution $F_l(R)$ such that*
(a) $F_j(R)$ represents a mean-preserving spread of the distribution $F_l(R)$, and
(b) $F_k(R)$ satisfies a first-order dominance relationship with $F_l(R)$.

When the relationship between the interest rate charged borrowers and the return to the bank is not monotonic, competitive equilibrium in the credit market could be characterized by credit rationing. For instance, suppose the conditions described in Theorem 1 are satisfied, and suppose for simplicity that all borrowers are identical and have the same set of available projects (these assumptions are relaxed immediately below). Let $L^D(r)$ and $L^S(i)$, respectively, denote the aggregate demand and supply for loanable funds when banks are charging borrowers interest rate r and depositors are paid i. Let r^* denote the interest rate that maximizes π, a bank's return per dollar loaned, and assume the supply of loanable funds is not infinitely elastic. Then, if $L^D(r^*) > L^S(\pi(r^*))$, the market equilibrium is characterized by credit rationing. Although all the banks face an excess demand for credit, no bank would increase the interest rate it charged borrowers above r^*; to do so would lower its return per dollar loaned.

In equilibrium, competition for depositors implies $i = \pi(r^*)$. If a bank increased the interest rate it paid depositors, it would lose money. A bank lowering the interest rate it paid depositors would fail to attract deposits. A bank increasing the interest rate it charged borrowers would fail to attract borrowers. Hence, the market equilibrium is characterized by rationing at interest rates $r = r^*$ and $i = \pi(r^*)$. There may be interest rates charged borrowers at which the market would clear, but if the loan supply-and-demand curves have the usual shapes (upward and downward sloping, respectively), these Walrasian interest rates would not be offered in a competitive banking system.

If there were several types of borrowers and banks were perfectly informed about the attributes of each borrower, the market equilibrium could be characterized both by (a) rationing of the form described above and by (b) rationing or redlining. The relationship between π and r would differ across borrowers according to the techniques available to each borrower and the risk aversion of the borrower. Even if banks could costlessly distinguish among borrowers so that every borrower were a distinct type, the qualitative features of the rationing equilibrium would remain. Borrowers would be excluded from the credit market who were nearly identical to those who were getting loans. The excluded borrowers would suffer a discrete loss in utility. The market equilibrium could have the additional unfortunate feature that the expected gross return on the projects of the excluded borrowers could be higher than the expected return on the projects that were getting loans.

The relationship between interest rates and the bank's return is affected both by the risk preferences of the different borrowers and by the techniques available to each borrower. Suppose all borrowers had the same set of available techniques. Then, if all borrowers were offered the same contract and assuming decreasing absolute risk aversion, the richer borrowers would choose riskier techniques. In general, the same interest rate would induce a different technique and hence generate a different return to the bank if offered to borrowers with different degrees of risk aversion. The interest rate that maximizes the bank's return to a rich borrower would differ from the interest rate that maximizes the bank's return to a poor borrower.

Similarly if different techniques are available to different borrowers, then, even if all borrowers were risk neutral, the function mapping the interest rate charged a type of borrower to the profits of the bank would differ across borrowers. In equilibrium each borrower that gets a loan would, in general, be charged a different interest rate. Competition among banks would cause the return π to be the same from loans to different observationally distinguishable types of borrowers. Type j borrowers that are excluded from the credit market are those for whom there is no interest rate r_j that generates a return to the bank greater than or equal to the interest rate i paid to depositors. Type j borrowers could be excluded either because they are less risk averse than other borrowers or because they have techniques with higher expected returns but also higher default probabilities available to them. One can easily present examples in which, if excluded type j borrowers were given credit at the interest rate r_j^* that maximized the bank's return on loans to those borrowers, the

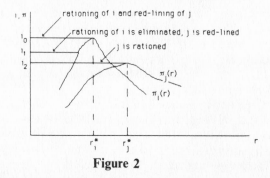

Figure 2

expected gross return on the projects undertaken by the type j borrowers would exceed the expected gross return on the average investment.

Suppose the supply of loanable funds function shifted outward. The interest rate paid to depositors would fall, and type j borrowers would get credit. If r_j^* were greater than the average interest rate charged to borrowers, then an outward shift in the supply of loanable funds function could cause an increase in the average interest rate charged to borrowers. This situation is illustrated in Fig. 2.

Although at $\pi = i_1$ there is not credit rationing in the sense that among observationally *identical* borrowers some are getting credit and some are being denied credit, if type i and j borrowers are similar there may be credit rationing in the sense that among *nearly identical* borrowers some are getting loans while others are being denied credit. There is a discontinuity in the utility of borrowers that are getting loans and borrowers that are denied loans whether the excluded borrowers are of the same or different types.

Note that regardless of the relationship between the gross return on the projects undertaken by the marginal and the inframarginal borrowers, the standard debt contract leads to underinvestment in competitive loan markets. Loans are only made if the return to the bank is greater than or equal to the bank's cost of funds. The surplus generated to borrowers is ignored by the market determination of the volume of loans.

III. ADVERSE SELECTION

In a more realistic representation of the economy, it is unlikely that banks would know all the attributes of particular groups of borrowers. They would partition applicants according to easily observed attributes. In that case each type of borrower represented by i or j in Fig. 2 would represent a class of observationally indistinguishable borrowers.

To focus on adverse-selection effects, let us assume that within each class of borrowers there is a continuous distribution of borrowers each of whom has only one available technique, enabling us to ignore the incentive effects of contracts. Projects either succeed in generating a gross return R with probability $p(R)$ or fail, thus generating a return of D. R lies on the closed interval $[0, K]$, and D is a constant. We will define a class of projects as being of the same type i if $p(R)R + (1 - p(R))D = T_i$. When a project fails, there is a bankruptcy cost of X which is the same for all projects. Let $g_i(R)$ denote the normalized density of type i borrowers: each borrower is defined by the technique available to him.

From our discussion in Section II, it is clear that if there is an interior interest rate r_i^* that maximizes the banks' returns on loans to a group of buyers, then the market equilibrium could be characterized by both redlining and credit rationing in the sense of arbitrary exclusion of borrowers that are identical to borrowers that are getting credit. The analysis is the same as in Section II, except that the shape of the $\pi_i(r)$ function is determined by adverse selection rather than incentive effects. The crucial question for the existence of an equilibrium with arbitrary rationing of borrowers is thus whether the $\pi(r)$ functions have interior maxima. In Stiglitz and Weiss (1981) the following result is proved.

THEOREM 2. *If $g_i(K) = g_i'(K) = 0$, and $g_i''(K) \neq 0$, then a sufficient condition for $\pi_i(r)$ to have an interior maximum is that $X > (K - D)/3$. If $g_i(K) = 0$ and $g_i'(K) \neq 0$, then a sufficient condition for $\pi_i(r)$ to have an interior maximum is that $X > (K - D)/2$.*

As in the case of incentive effects of interest rates redlining may cause an inefficient allocation of funds. For example, suppose all type j borrowers are identical; their projects generate a return, if successful, of R_j with probability p_j such that $p_j R_j + (1 - p_j)D = T_j$. Banks maximize their returns on loans to type j borrowers by charging those borrowers an interest rate $r = R_j$ and get an expected return of $T_j - (1 - P_j)X$. Consider type i borrowers with a distribution of projects (one for each borrower) $g_i(R)$. The projects available to type i borrowers each have the property that $p_i(R)R + (1 - p_i(R))D = T_i$, where $T_i > T_j$, and R is on the closed interval $[0, K]$. If $g_i(K) = 0$ and $X > (K - D)/2$, then the return to the bank per dollar ioaned is maximized at an interest rate $r_i^* < T_i$. The interest rate r_i^* that maximizes the expected return to the bank will generate a return strictly less than $T_i - (1 - P_i)X$. Hence, type j borrowers may be getting loans while type i borrowers are being denied credit even if $T_i - (1 - P_i)X > T_j - (1 - P_j)X$. To see this suppose the demand for loans by j borrowers at interest rate $r = R_j$ is greater than the supply of funds forthcoming at an interest rate paid to depositors $i = T_j - (1 - P_j)X$. Then if $P_i r_i^* + (1 - P_i)(D - X) < T_j - (1 - P_j)X$, market equilibrium will be characterized by credit rationing: some type j borrowers would be arbitrarily excluded, and no type i borrowers would get credit.

Type i borrowers are excluded because there is no interest rate at which banks could profitably make loans to them when the interest rate paid to depositors is $T_j - (1 - P_j)X$. Type j borrowers are arbitrarily rationed because at any interest rate $r > R_j$ all type j borrowers would default and the banks would have to bear the fixed costs of bankruptcy, lowering their profits.

If we start from that rationing equilibrium with redlining, and if the supply of funds function were to move outward, the interest rate paid to depositors and the interest rate charged to type j borrowers would both fall. A sufficiently large outward movement in the supply of loanable funds could cause the type i borrowers to get credit at r_i^*. As in the incentive case, if $r_i^* > T_j$, an outward shift in the supply of loanable funds function could cause an increase in the average interest rate charged to borrowers.

IV. RATIONING WITH COLLATERAL

In Stiglitz and Weiss (1987b) banks not only choose the interest rate they offer borrowers but also collateral requirements and the equity they demand from borrowers. Under those conditions an increase in the probability of success of every technique could cause a *decrease* in the interest rate charged at every collateral requirement, while causing an increase in the average interest rate charged borrowers. The intuition generating this somewhat perverse result is that when success probabilities increase, bank profits on low-collateral–high-interest-rate contracts increase by more than do their profits on high-collateral–low-interest-rate contracts. Consequently, if the new equilibrium is characterized by rationing, there will be an increase in the proportion of low-collateral–high-interest-rate loans made by banks.

Enriching the strategy space of banks has other interesting consequences for our model. There may be as many contracts offered as types of borrowers. There may be equilibria in which all types of borrowers choose the same contract (pooling equilibria). In either case there may be an excess demand for credit at each contract.

To simplify the analysis, consider a model of the following form. There are two types of borrowers i and j. A type of borrower is defined so that all borrowers of the same type k have the same collateralizable wealth C_k and noncollateralizable wealth A_k, where $C_i > C_j$ and $A_i > A_j$. Lenders know the distribution of borrowers of each type and the wealth of each type. Lenders do not know the identity (type) of borrowers.

All borrowers have the same utility function, characterized by decreasing absolute risk aversion, and the same two techniques available to them, which are known to lenders. The "safe" technique has a payoff R^s if successful; the "risky" technique has a payoff of R^r if successful. They each have a payoff of zero if unsuccessful. The safe technique succeeds with probability bp^s; the risky technique succeeds with probability abp^r. Both b and a vary procyclically, have means of unity, and $(a - 1)(b - 1) > 0$. Thus the success probability of the risky technique has greater cyclical variability than the success probability of the safe technique. Finally, we assume that for all values of a, $p^s R^s \gg ap^r R^r$, and that lenders always prefer to finance a safe project at the interest-rate–collateral-requirement pair that induces borrowers to choose the safe technique. The function $r(C, i)$ describes the maximum interest rate that induces type i borrowers to choose the safe technique when collateral C is required.

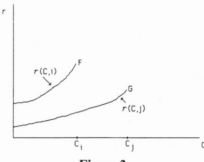

Figure 3

Under these conditions there may exist partial sorting equilibria with rationing in which two contracts are offered, F and G requiring collateral of C_i and C_j and interest rates $r(C_i, i)$ and $r(C_j, j)$, respectively. The wealthy borrowers apply for loans at F and G. If they are denied credit at G and are offered a loan at the low-collateral contract F, they take the low-collateral loan and choose the risky technique (this choice is a consequence of decreasing absolute risk aversion). All the poor borrowers given low-collateral loans choose the safe technique, as do the rich borrowers given high-collateral loans. The returns to the bank from risky and safe loans at F and G are such that there exists a proportion of wealthy borrowers taking low-collateral loans that equates the returns to the bank from contracts F and G. In particular, decreasing absolute risk aversion and $A_i > A_j$ must be sufficient for the return to a bank from a safe loan at F to exceed its return from a safe loan at G.

The switch lines $r(C, i)$ and $r(C, j)$ move downward during booms and upward during slumps. This is a consequence of our assumption that the probability of the safe technique succeeding varies less over the business cycle than does the probability of the risky technique succeeding. The same interest rate that would induce a borrower to choose the safe technique during a slump would induce the borrower to choose the risky technique during a boom. Because lower interest rates encourage borrowers to choose safer projects, during booms the interest rates charged at both collateral requirements C_i and C_j must fall to prevent borrowers from switching to the riskier technique.

On the other hand, the change in the distribution of low- and high-collateral loans over the business cycle could cause the average interest rate charged to borrowers to move procyclically. During booms the return on the low-collateral loans rises more than the return on the high-collateral loans. This is because the risky techniques have become relatively more profitable compared to the safe techniques (in the partially separating equilibrium only the low-collateral loans are financing risky techniques) and because collateral is less valuable to a lender when the success probability is high. Consequently, in a rationing equilibrium, the proportion of wealthy borrowers among those taking the low-collateral loans increases to equate the lenders' returns on high- and low-collateral contracts. This can only occur if fewer high-collateral loans were being made. Since the interest rate on the high-collateral loans is lower than the interest rate on the low-collateral loans, in a boom the proportion of high-interest-rate–low-collateral loans increases. This effect could offset the fall in the interest rate charged on both the high- and low-collateral loans. Consequently, the average interest rate charged to borrowers could move either procyclically or countercyclically.

If a is a constraint so that business cycles have equiproportionate effects on the success probabilities of the safe and risky projects, then the $r(C, i)$ and $r(C, j)$ functions do not vary with changes in b. As in the previous case, increases in the success probabilities will have a smaller effect on the profitability of the high-collateral contracts than on the profitability of the low-collateral contracts. Thus, following the argument developed above, equiproportionate increase in the success probabilities of the safe and risky projects causes the average interest rate charged to borrowers to move procyclically.[4]

The analysis thus far has assumed that the economy is characterized by credit rationing both during booms and slumps. If macroeconomic fluctuations were to eliminate rationing, by decreasing the demand for funds during slumps or increasing the supply of funds during booms, then the analysis would change fundamentally.

For example, suppose a boom not only increased the success probability of all techniques, but also increased demand for investment relative to the supply, thus eliminating credit rationing. In that case, lenders would compete for borrowers by decreasing both the interest rate and collateral requirements on their loans. Not only would the $r(C, i)$ and $r(C, j)$ functions shift cyclically and the proportion of low- and high-collateral loans change, but also contracts would move along $r(C, i)$ and $r(C, j)$ in response to aggregate demand shocks. Consequently, shifts in aggregate demand have indeterminate effects on the interest rates charged to borrowers.

Similarly, shifts in the aggregate supply of loans function could increase or decrease the average interest rate charged to borrowers. Starting from a separating equilibrium with rationing, an increase in the supply of funds would increase the proportion of contract F loans being made. This is because the number of G loans determines the banks' returns on the F loans, and in equilibrium the return on the two contracts must be equal. Consequently, small outward shifts in the supply of loanable funds function will cause an increase only in the volume of high-interest-rate F loans. Outward shifts in the supply of loanable funds function that eliminate rationing would cause southwest movements along the $r(C, i)$ and $r(C, j)$ curves as banks compete for borrowers. Therefore, small increases in the supply of loanable funds would increase the average interest rate charged to borrowers, while large increases in the supply of loanable funds would decrease the average interest rate charged to borrowers.

V. EXTENSIONS

This paper has focused on a static model of competitive credit markets. In Stiglitz and Weiss (1983) we included some simple dynamics: borrowers lived for more than one period, and lenders were allowed to make contingency contracts. This enrichment of the strategy space of lenders accentuates the inefficiencies generated in the static model.

Suppose (identical) experienced borrowers were better than (identical) inexperienced borrowers in the sense that a one-period loan to the former would be more profitable than a one-period loan to the latter and that the expected gross return to experienced borrowers was greater than the expected gross return to inexperienced borrowers. Equilibrium might be characterized by rationing of experienced borrowers and no rationing of inexperienced borrowers. This occurs if lenders use the denial of credit to borrowers whose projects failed as an incentive mechanism to induce borrowers to choose safe techniques.

Stiglitz and Weiss (1980) presented a sequence of government interventions for this dynamic model that makes everyone strictly better off.

Given these inefficiencies in credit markets, one might wonder why we see debt contracts used. Gale and Hellwig (1985) show that monitoring costs can make the standard debt contract optimal. Stiglitz and Weiss (1981) argue that other methods of financing such as equity contracts generate inefficiencies that are perhaps more important than those generated by the standard debt contracts. The analysis of markets with imperfect information suggests that enriching the strategy space of lenders will not necessarily result in socially optimal contracts being offered or even in Pareto improvements.

VI. CONCLUSIONS

Here are the main results of our analysis:

1. Competitive credit markets may be characterized by arbitrary rationing of borrowers and by redlining. These phenomena are robust to changes in the strategy space of lenders.

2. The allocation of funds is likely to be inefficient both in the sense that too few loans are being made and in the sense that the wrong borrowers are getting credit.

3. There is unlikely to be a monotonic or even consistent relationship between movements of interest rates and either cyclical demand fluctuations or monetary policy.

NOTES

[1] William Keeton (1979) independently analyzed the incentive effects of interest rates. Interesting extensions and other lines of inquiry have been pursued by Hildegarde Wette (1983). Alan Blinder (1984), K. Vandell (1984), David Besanko and Anjor Thakor (1984), Gerhard Clemenz (1985), Carol Such (1985), Douglas Gale and Martin Hellwig (1985), and Hellmuth Milde and John Riley (1986), to mention but a few of the many recent contributions to this literature. The literature on the sorting and incentive effects of labor contracts generates similar results to those obtained for credit markets (see Salop 1973 and Weiss 1980, respectively, for treatments of the incentive and sorting effects of wages).

[2] The market imperfections generated by informational imperfections are robust to finer partitions of the set of borrowers such as those suggested by Riley (1987) (see Stiglitz and Weiss 1981, 1987a) and to increases in the number of instruments available to lenders (see Stiglitz and Weiss 1986).

[3] One can argue that the terms of the loan contract could dictate all the choices of the borrowers. That would require lenders (a) to write complete contingency contracts that dictated each borrower's behavior under all contingencies (writing such contracts would be prohibitively expensive); (b) to have perfect and instantaneous control over all decisions made by the borrower (delayed monetary penalties would be insufficient since these penalties would have no force when the borrower defaults); and (c) to know which future decisions should be dictated by the contingency contracts. These conditions would never all be satisfied. For them to even be nearly satisfied the required knowledge and control by lenders of the optimal decisions of borrowers would be so great that the lender would be exerting total managerial control. Effectively the lender would have to become the entrepreneur.

[4] These procyclical effects would be accentuated if the success probability of the safe technique varied more drastically over the business cycle than did the success probability of the risky technique.

REFERENCES

Besanko, D., and Thakor, A. 1984. "Competition, Collateral and Rationing: Sorting Equilibria in the Credit Market." Working paper, Northwestern University.

Blinder, A. 1984. "Notes on the Comparative Statics of a Stiglitz-Weiss Bank" (mimeo).

Clemenz, G. 1986. "Credit Markets with Asymmetric Information." Working paper, University of Vienna.

Gale, D., and Hellwig, M. 1985. "Incentive-Compatible Debt Contracts: The One-Period Problem." *Review of Economic Studies* 52: 647–63.

Keeton, W. 1979. *Equilibrium Credit Rationing.* New York: Garland Press.

Milde, H., and Riley, J. 1986. "Signalling in Credit Markets." Working paper, UCLA.

Ordover, J., and Weiss, A. 1981. "Information and the Law: Evaluating Legal Restrictions on Competitive Contracts." *American Economic Review* 71: 399–404.

Riley, J. 1987. "Credit Rationing, A Further Remark." *American Economic Review* 77: 224–27.

Salop, S. 1973. "Wage Differentials in a Dynamic Theory of the Firm." *Journal of Economic Theory* 6: 321–44.

Such, C. 1985. "Interactions between Signaling and Repeated Play with Borrower Default." IMSSS Technical report 480, Stanford University.

Stiglitz, J., and Weiss, A. 1980. "Credit Rationing in Markets with Imperfect Information. Part II: A Theory of Contingency Contracts." Working paper, Bell Laboratories.

———. 1981. "Credit Rationing in Markets with Imperfect Information." *American Economic Review* 71: 393–409.

———. 1983. "Incentive Effects of Terminations: Applications to the Credit and Labor Markets." *American Economic Review* 73: 919–27.

———. 1986. "Credit Rationing with Collateral." In *Recent Advances in Corporate Finance*, ed. Jeremy Edwards, Julian Franks, Colin Mayer, and Stephen Schaefer. Cambridge: Cambridge University Press.

———. 1987a. "Credit Rationing with Many Borrowers." *American Economic Review* 77: 228–31

———. 1987b. "Macro-Economic Equilibrium and Credit Rationing." NBER working paper no. 2164.

Vandell, K. 1984. "Imperfect Information, Uncertainty, and Credit Rationing: Comment and Extension." *Quarterly Journal of Economics* 98: 841–63.

Weiss, A. 1977. "Credit Rationing in Markets with Imperfect Information." Bell Laboratories technical memorandum.

———. 1980. "Job Queues and Layoffs in Labor Markets with Flexible Wages." *Journal of Political Economy* 72: 526–38.

Wette, H. 1983. "Collateral in Credit Rationing in Markets with Imperfect Information: Note." *American Economic Review* 73: 442–45.

discussion | **Banks and Risk Sharing:**
Instabilities and Coordination

Charles J. Jacklin

Graduate School of Business
Stanford University

I. INTRODUCTION

The coincidence of the collapse of the banking system and the beginning of the Great Depression led to extensive restructuring and regulation of banking, including the initiation of federally sponsored deposit insurance. If the objective of the regulations and deposit insurance were to stabilize the banking system, then it is undeniable that they were successful. However, the cost and efficiency of the stabilization has been an issue of concern for many years. Examples related to this issue are many. That non-risk-adjusted deposit insurance induces banks to hold portfolios that are "too risky" has been an ongoing concern. The effect of the separation of investment and commercial banking on the competitiveness of investment banking is another issue. That geographic and portfolio restrictions lead to banks that are not sufficiently diversified is another. Finally, it has been argued the banking system became too stable. Restrictions on competition—in particular, deposit rate ceilings—allow inefficient banks to exist. One would naturally expect to see failures of poorly run institutions in any industry; however, until recently bank failures have been practically nonexistent.

For a variety of reasons, only one of which is a concern for efficiency, the existing regulatory and insurance structure has come into question, and recent legislation has dramatically altered or eliminated many of the old regulations.[1] Understandably, this has stimulated new theoretical and empirical research focusing on the impact of these or additional potential changes either by analyzing models that attempt to capture the salient features of the banking system or by examining data from preregulatory periods. Diamond and Dybvig's paper, which has stimulated much other work, focuses on the role of deposit insurance in preventing costly (in a social sense) bank runs as well as the role of demand deposits in the improvement of risk sharing. Note that both ingredients are essential to a thorough analysis of this sort. Before one argues

I wish to thank Sudipto Bhattacharya, Doug Diamond, and Andrei Shleifer for helpful comments on an earlier draft.

that bank runs are costly and therefore should be prevented, it must be established that the features of banking that lead to runs, such as fixed-rate demand deposits, uniquely serve an important economic function and thus warrant preservation. If it were the case that the economic service of banks that leads to the possibility of costly runs could be provided in another way, without introducing costly bank runs, then the alternative mechanism would be preferred. For example, Fama (1980) argues that unregulated banks would offer deposits that represented proportional claims on a well-specified portfolio of assets. Cone (1983) has demonstrated that deposits of this type would not be subject to panics.

The discussion in the previous paragraph sets the tone of what I hope to accomplish in this piece. I examine recent theoretical literature on bank regulation and deposit insurance with the following questions in mind:

1. What characteristics of banking lead to the potential instability we fear?

2. What economic functions hinge on these characteristics?

3. Can alternative, more stable mechanisms provide these same functions?

4. What is the precise role of deposit insurance in the prevention of panics?

5. What other aspects of regulatory policy can be better understood on the basis of extant models of banking?

Keeping this context in mind, in Section II I briefly discuss Diamond and Dybvig's paper as well as important extensions by Jacklin (1987). In this section, I also discuss the papers of Bryant (1980) and Waldo (1985). Bryant (1980) differs from Diamond and Dybvig (1983) and Waldo (1985) in that he emphasizes the role of interim private information about risky bank portfolios as the key ingredient in the propagation of bank runs, whereas the other authors model pure panic bank runs. In Section III I discuss papers that build on the ideas of Bryant (1980) and/or Diamond and Dybvig (1983) and provide additional insights into the implications of a banking framework with similar or identical characteristics. Included in these are Jacklin and Bhattacharya (1985), Bhattacharya and Gale (1985), Chari and Jagannathan (1984), Postlewaite and Vives (1986), Bernanke and Gertler (1985), Smith (1984), and Gorton (1985). The primary focus of the work mentioned to this point is on the liability side of the balance sheet. In Section IV I turn to the asset side and briefly discuss some of the recent work related to credit markets, giving particular emphasis to the credit rationing work of Stiglitz and Weiss (1981, 1983). I also attempt to relate some of this work to work that emphasizes the role of intermediation and financing constraints to business cycles and more general macroeconomic phenomena. Section V contains a brief summary.

II. THE ECONOMIC FUNCTION OF DEMAND DEPOSITS

Theories of banking panics have been around for many years. What distinguishes recent work from the earlier theories is the recognition that a credible theory must not only explain why panics occur but must also demonstrate that the characteristics of deposit contracts that lead to panics have an economic function in their own right.

Bryant (1980) first recognized the role of demand deposits in providing insurance against unobservable risks (for example, preference shocks). There are many ingredients necessary if deposit contracts are to have a unique role in providing insurance for risks that are not directly insurable. At this point I focus those ingredients required to establish a role for deposit contracts relative to no contracting whatsoever. Later I discuss the additional assumptions required if deposits are to have a unique role relative to other forms of contracting (such as equitylike contracts). Two key ingredients for the existence of this insurance role are (a) the unobservability of the risk to be insured and (b) some inherent illiquidity in the assets supporting the deposit contracts.[2]

The following example illustrates the nature of this risk in a setting similar to that used by Bryant (1980), Diamond and Dybvig (1983), and several others. Ex ante (at time $T = 0$) depositors are identical. At $T = 1$ some depositors find out that they are going to die before $T = 2$, and others discover they will live for both periods. The ex post type of a depositor is assumed to be externally unobservable; therefore, this risk cannot be insured by conventional means. The need for an insurance mechanism hinges on an underlying technological illiquidity. That is, long-term investments have a higher yield than short-term investments, but if long-term investments are liquidated early, the yield over the short time horizon is inferior to (or no better than) that on short-term investments. One can think of the role of deposit contracts as giving the early diers in the economy a share in the benefit of the long-term technology.

The deposit contract is constructed so that both ex post types self-select — that is, the early diers withdraw all their money at $T = 1$, and the late diers leave their money in the bank until the second period. In this context Bryant focuses on informationally based bank runs. He assumes that the long-term technology is risky and that interim information about the distribution of the technology's payoff may lead to both early and late diers withdrawing early.

On the other hand, Diamond and Dybvig (1983) and Waldo (1985) focus on pure panic runs. That is, in their models there are multiple (Pareto-ordered) Nash equilibria. To illustrate the two equilibria, consider the Diamond-Dybvig model further. They assume that there is a single *riskless* technology that has a total payoff of $R > 1$ if held for two periods, yet returns only the initial investment if liquidated after one period. If depositors are sufficiently risk averse, Diamond and Dybvig show that ex ante they are willing to trade off some consumption in the second period if they turn out to be late diers for additional consumption in the first period if they turn out to be early diers. The deposit contract in essence "insures" depositors against being early diers by offering a strictly positive return over the first period. However, the bank can provide this return if only the early diers withdraw at time $T = 1$ (since liquidation at $T = 1$ only yields one unit per unit invested).

The deposit contract is constructed so that depositors self-select appropriately as long as they assume everyone else is doing so. Diamond and Dybvig show that if this is the case and if the proportion of early diers is a known constant, then the deposit contract leads to the same degree of risk sharing that would be accomplished if there were no informational asymmetries in the economy. However, if for some reason the late diers believe that all the other late diers are going to withdraw at $T = 1$, then they too will want to withdraw because there will not be any money left in the bank at $T = 2$. This "bad" equilibrium is characterized as a bank run by Diamond and Dybvig. Although they do not characterize what exactly leads the late diers to conjecture that other late diers are going to run the bank, their discussion suggests that it could be the observation of an event (for example, a sunspot or a run at another bank) or even a rumor that leads to the run. Since the investments of the bank are riskless, they have explicitly ruled out any fundamental weakness in the bank as a source of concern.

Given the possibility of multiple equilibria, Diamond and Dybvig then show how different mechanisms can eliminate the bad equilibrium. If the proportion of depositors who ultimately are early diers is known in advance, then suspension of convertibility eliminates the bank run equilibrium. After the appropriate proportion of depositors has withdrawn their money at $T = 1$, the bank allows no further withdrawals. This guarantees that there will be funds available for the late diers at $T = 2$ and thus eliminates any desire to run the bank, even if a given late dier believes all the other late diers are withdrawing at $T = 1$. On the other hand, if the proportion of early diers is stochastic, then the suspension mechanism is less effective. In this case Diamond and Dybvig argue that "deposit insurance" eliminates the bad equilibrium and leads to first-best risk sharing. Essentially their deposit insurance mechanism amounts to an ex post tax (or subsidy) levied by the government after the proportion of early diers is observed. The tax is structured as a wealth transfer from the early diers to the late diers (or vice versa) so that the ex ante first-best risk sharing is achieved; that is, only the early diers withdraw at $T = 1$. Given the tax, the late diers again have no incentive to run the bank regardless of their conjectures about other late diers. Banks are assumed to be unable to design and implement such a contingent payment mechanism.

Diamond and Dybvig (1983) emphasize the risk-sharing aspects of demand deposits, focusing on ex ante expected utility maximization. In a slightly different framework. Waldo (1985) focuses on an alternative welfare criterion—productive efficiency. In Waldo's model there are long- and short-term riskless investment technologies as well as currency as a store of value. Like Diamond and Dybvig (1983), Waldo (1985) models bank runs as a Pareto-dominated equilibrium that is driven by the conjectures of the late diers regarding the withdrawal behavior of other late diers. Yet Waldo differs from Diamond and Dybvig in that he emphasizes the impact of the possibility of bank runs on aggregate investment. Given the possibility of a bank run, depositors hold currency to mitigate the impact of "being at the end of the line" and not being able to withdraw. By holding currency, depositors reduce the amount of investment in the productive short-term technology. Thus, the fear of bank runs leads to inefficiency. Waldo also suggests that, given his model, the deposit-currency ratio should be a leading indicator of banking panics.

In the introduction of this discussion, I emphasized the necessity of combining the analysis of bank runs with an economic role for demand deposits, since the demand nature of deposits is what ultimately makes runs possible. Diamond and Dybvig (1983) and Waldo (1985) establish a role for demand deposits relative to no contracting whatsoever. On the other hand, Fama (1980) argues that if banks were totally unregulated, then they would offer deposits that were, in essence, proportional claims on portfolios. With this in mind, Jacklin (1987) takes the issue of the economic role of demand deposits a step further by comparing demand deposits to equitylike contracts.[3] That paper shows (when the proportion of each type is known) that both the nature of preferences and the trading environment are crucial variables in determining whether demand deposits have a unique economic function. Specifically, it shows that, given the preference assumptions made by Diamond and Dybvig (1983) and Waldo (1985), a dividend-paying traded equity contract can achieve the same allocations as demand deposits without the possibility of a bad equilibrium like bank runs. The basic idea here is that, instead of making deposits in a bank, individuals all invest in a firm that invests just like the bank would. At $T = 0$ the firm pays a dividend that is equivalent in the aggregate amount that would have been withdrawn from the bank in the good equilibrium. The (now realized) type 1s and type 2s then trade their dividends and ex dividend shares to reach a final allocation that is identical to that achieved using demand deposits.

Jacklin (1987) goes on to show that this equivalence (between demand deposits and equity) depends on the assumed nature of preference and the trading environment. In particular, I show that deposit contracts can achieve greater risk sharing than the described equity contract for essentially all but the preferences assumed in the previously mentioned papers *if* trading opportunities are sufficiently restricted. Rather than assuming that the type 1s actually die at the end of the first period, assume that both types live for two periods, but the type 1s prefer consumption in the first period relatively more than consumption in the second period (and vice versa for type 2s). [Call this preference assumption *smooth preferences*.] If this occurs, then deposits can provide greater risk sharing than the equity contract in a restricted trading environment. One way to think of the advantage deposit contracts have over equity is in reference to the insurance role of deposits discussed earlier. Given the illiquid (yet more productive) long-term technology, the deposit contract was described as providing insurance against being of type 1 and hence unable to enjoy (fully) the fruits of the long-term technology. One can think of this insurance as providing a wealth transfer from type 2s to type 1s. Such a wealth transfer cannot be freely accomplished if trading opportunities are unrestricted and individual preferences are smooth. Since type is unobservable, each type will claim to be the type that receives the most valuable allotment and trade if need be. More technically, without trading restrictions only the competitive equilibrium from equal endowments can be achieved (also see Varian 1974 and Hammond 1983), whereas ex ante optimality entails maximizing the representative depositor's expected utility.

In this section I have reviewed several papers that consider the economic function of deposit contracts as well as model bank runs. Two alternative views regarding the source of bank runs have been discussed — the pure-panic view of Diamond and Dybvig (1983) and Waldo (1985) and the information-based view of Bryant (1980). As for the economic function of deposit contracts, the three papers mentioned in the previous sentence all measure the deposit contracts relative to no contracting. On the other hand, Jacklin (1987) demonstrates that the economic role of deposit contracts exceeds that of equity contracts (that are not subject to runs), provided restricted trading of deposit contracts could be enforced.

III. RELATED RESEARCH

In this section I discuss several papers that are related to the research discussed in Section II. These papers do not constitute an all-inclusive list of current research in this area. Hopefully, they are a representative sample of such.

In Section II two alternative views of bank runs are discussed — the information-based view and the pure-panic view. Jacklin and Bhattacharya (1985) contrast these two alternatives while considering the relative merits of deposit and equity contracts in a framework substantially more complex than those discussed in Section II. We model information-based bank runs in an economy where depositors have smooth preferences and where the underlying assets of the bank are risky. The model is characterized by two sources of asymmetric information — the bank cannot observe the true liquidity needs (type) of depositors and the depositors are asymmetrically informed about the quality of the bank's assets. Bank "runs" occur as a *unique* equilibrium when some of the depositors get bad news about the return on the risky asset. Suspension of convertibility eventually is used to stop a run, but not without cost. Since some of the type 2 depositors (those who prefer consumption in period 2) have run the bank, some type 1 depositors are unable to withdraw before convertibility is suspended. In this scenario deposit contracts no longer have a clear-cut advantage over equity contracts (as shown for riskless bank investments in Jacklin 1987) even if trading opportunities are restricted. The choice of risk-sharing instrument (deposit or equity) is shown to depend on the underlying attributes of and information about the bank asset's returns. For example, deposit contracts are better for financing relatively low-risk assets, whereas equity contracts are better for financing relatively high-risk assets. This happens essentially because deposit contracts suffer from interim information to a greater extent in the lower tail of asset returns (signals).

The role played by deposit insurance in the prevention of bank "runs" depends on whether you view runs as being pure panics or information based. In the pure-panic setting one can think of deposit insurance as a mechanism that keeps an aggregate shock (the sunspot) from destabilizing banking and, thus, the economy in general. On the other hand, in the information-based setting deposit insurance reduces the incentive to collect unproductive interim information about the assets of the bank.

Chari and Jagannathan (1984) and Postlewaite and Vives (1986) also focus on modeling bank runs as a single equilibrium as opposed to one of a multiplicity of equilibria (as in Diamond and Dybvig 1983 and Waldo 1985). In Chari and Jagannathan (1984) the proportion of type 1 depositors as well as the investment returns of the bank are stochastic. In their model people can observe the initial withdrawal demands at the bank and act conditional on this observation. The line at the bank may be long because some people have bad news about the bank's investments; however, there can be confusion about whether high withdrawal demands reflect bad news or high liquidity demands. Thus, counterproductive runs can occur. Postlewaite and Vives (1986) also model runs as an equilibrium phenomenon. Given the "standard" deposit contract (i.e., you can withdraw all your money on demand), they show in a model with two depositors, who may each end up as one of three types, that a "counterproductive" bank run may result because for some combinations of realized types the two depositors may end up in a "prisoner's dilemma" situation. Although they modeled a bank run as an equilibrium phenomenon, the economic function of deposits in their economy is not clear.[4]

Several additional examples of theoretical work in this area are Bhattacharya and Gale (1985), Bernanke and Gertler (1985), and Smith (1984). Bhattacharya and Gale (1985) examine the implications of preference shock-based models of banking on issues of interbank coordination and central bank policy. Their model is the same as Diamond and Dybvig's except that there are many banks. Each bank faces uncertain liquidity demands, but there are many banks and no aggregate uncertainty about liquidity demand. They show that an unregulated interbank funds market for coordinating liquidity demands can be improved upon by a central bank that offers restricted borrowing and lending opportunities at nonmarket rates.[5] Furthermore, they show that individual banks would typically underinvest in liquid assets relative to the first-best level. This underinvestment suggests a role for central bank reserve requirements based on imperfect monitoring of bank asset portfolios.

Bernanke and Gertler (1985) model banks in an overlapping generations framework. In their model, banking panics can be thought of as a response to the deterioration of bank capital to the point that depositors no longer have confidence in the ability of the bank to withstand additional losses. They assume that banks cannot augment their initial equity capital through refinancing.

Smith (1984) examines the role of deposit interest rate ceilings in equilibrium in banking when banks face potential adverse-selection problems in the market for depositors. Banks want to attract depositors that are not likely to withdraw soon. Without deposit rate ceilings, Smith argues that equilibrium in the market for deposits may not exist for reasons akin to market failure in insurance markets as modeled by Rothschild and Stiglitz (1976); alternatively, interest rate ceilings may lead to the attainment of a Pareto-superior "pooling" equilibrium across depositor types.

Gorton (1985) presents a model in which suspension of convertibility is used as a communication mechanism. The basic idea behind this model is that depositors have imperfect information, relative to that of banks, regarding the quality of bank assets. Given such information, depositors may withdraw when they mistakenly believe that the return on the bank's assets will be low. In this model, banks suspend convertibility only when they know that the bank's assets are sound, because suspension is linked to costly verification of the state of the bank's portfolio. The equity-holders are assumed not to have limited liability with respect to the cost of verification. Thus, if the assets were unsound, then the owners of the bank would not only have to pay depositors to the extent they could from the assets of the bank, they would also have had to pay for the costly verification.

IV. CREDIT MARKETS AND MACROECONOMIC PHENOMENA

In the previous two sections the discussion focuses on the demand nature of bank deposit liabilities and the implications of this demand nature for risk sharing as well as the stability and regulation of banking. The asset side of banks' balance sheets, which consists primarily of loans, also plays a key role in understanding the economic function of banks. The need for financial intermediation in credit markets is derived from informational asymmetries that exist between borrowers and lenders (see Diamond's discussion in this volume for a survey of research on this issue). In this section I first briefly discuss other microeconomic models of borrower-lender informational asymmetries in the market for credit. Then, I discuss several recent papers that examine the effect of imperfect credit markets on macroeconomic behavior.

Stiglitz and Weiss (1981, 1983, 1986)[6] model the adverse-selection and incentive problems that exist in credit markets when lenders are imperfectly informed about the characteristics or actions of borrowers. They demonstrate that *equilibrium* in credit markets may be characterized by rationing. That is, interest rates (or collateral requirements) may not rise to the point where there is no excess demand for loans. This is the case when banks maximize their profits by offering loans at lower rates (or collateral requirements). The intuition behind rationing in equilibrium is either that raising interest rates or collateral requirements may discourage loan applications from good credit risks more than poor credit risks (adverse selection) or that higher interest rates may encourage borrowers to pursue riskier strategies in the operation of their businesses (moral hazard).

The macroeconomic implications of imperfect credit markets has been the topic of several recent papers of interest. Bernanke (1983) argues that the collapse of the banking system helped propel the economy from a severe, yet not unprecedented, recession into the Great Depression. His thesis is that, with the collapse of the financial system, the intermediary role played by banks (which mitigates the informational asymmetries in credit markets) was assumed by other, less efficient, intermediaries. This loss of the efficiency in the resource allocation mechanism of the economy, Bernanke argues, resulted in the severe depression.

Woodford (1986) and Greenwald and Stiglitz (1986) both present models in which imperfections (finance constraints) help explain macroeconomic fluctuations (business cycles). Woodford (1986) models an economy populated with infinitely lived agents in which the impact of finance constraints (consumers can lend but not borrow, or consumers buy debt but not equity of firms) on the possibility of sunspot equilibria around stationary deterministic equilibria is investigated. He characterizes the stochastic process of capital stock, the length of business cycles, and the elasticity of labor supply required for such sunspot equilibria to exist. He also characterizes the comovement of aggregate variables across fluctuating equilibria.

Greenwald and Stiglitz (1986) model an economy with constraints on the amount of equity capital that firms can raise. Their justification for the assumption of equity finance constraints is based on the works of Greenwald, Stiglitz, and Weiss (1984), Majluf and Myers (1984), and Leland and Pyle (1977), all of whom provide suggestive models in which informational asymmetries lead to de facto equity finance constraints. In the context of this model they show that equity finance constraints help explain many "stylized facts" regarding macroeconomic fluctuations. For example, their theory is consistent with the fact that banks claim to have an excess of loanable funds in the trough of a recession. They argue that firms ration themselves in fear of being severely credit constrained in the future if they extend themselves too far at present and end up defaulting on their debt.

V. SUMMARY

I have attempted to provide a brief review of some of the current research concerned with the impact of imperfect information on financial intermediation. Much of the chapter is devoted to addressing bank runs as well as the characteristics of demand deposits that lead to bank runs. Many contributions that help improve our understanding of the substantive issues were cited. Further modeling of liquidity is necessary as well as the incorporation of alternative stores of value in models of bank runs (i.e., the juxtaposition of sectors with and without trading restrictions). The pairing of the lending function with the function of liquidity transformation should also be examined in more detail, taking into account the informational characteristics of loans and the potential impact these informational characteristics may have on the stability of banking.[7]

In Section IV I briefly describe some recent work that examines the impact of informationally based market imperfections on the macroeconomy. Although this area is in the very early stages of development, the potential for significant contributions to our understanding of the macroeconomic fluctuations appears promising, as the discussion by Weiss in this volume suggests.

NOTES

[1] For example, the Depository Institutions Deregulation and Monetary Control Act of 1980 and the Garn–St. Germain Depository Institutions Act of 1982. Also see Kareken (1986) for a history of federal bank regulation.

[2] Given deposit contracts are supported to a large degree by loan portfolios, the assumption that the assets supporting deposits are illiquid seems to be justified. The asymmetry of information about the quality of loans between the lending bank and any potential purchaser leads to a "lemon" (see Akerlof 1970) problem in a secondary market for loans. Thus, it is quite natural to think of loans as illiquid assets.

[3] Haubrich and King (1983) consider the use of market-based and depositlike mechanisms for insuring against endowment shocks.

[4] The authors recognize this point in their paper.

[5] The interbank market can be thought of as the equity share market in Jacklin (1983). Just as the deposit contract in Jacklin (1983) could provide additional risk sharing if trading opportunities were restricted, so too can the central bank by offering restricted borrowing and lending opportunities at nonmarket rates.

[6] See Jaffee (1971), Jaffee and Russell (1976), and Keeton (1979) as well.

[7] Black (1975) (as well as Fama 1985 and Nakamura 1984) argues that the link between demand deposits and lending is important in that the observation of the cash flows of a firm helps banks deal with adverse-selection problems.

REFERENCES

Akerlof, George A. 1970. "The Market for Lemons: Quality Uncertainty and the Market Mechanism." *Quarterly Journal of Economics* 84: 488–500.

Bernanke, Ben S. 1983. "Nonmonetary Effects of the Financial Crisis in the Propagation of the Great Depression." *American Economic Review* 73: 257–76.

Bernanke, Ben S., and Gertler, Mark. 1985. "Banking in General Equilibrium." In *Austin Symposium on New Approaches to Monetary Economics*.

Bhattacharya, Sudipto, and Gale, Douglas. 1985. "Preference Shocks, Liquidity, and Central Bank Policy." University of California at Berkeley (mimeo), May.

Black, Fischer. 1975. "Bank Funds Management in an Efficient Market." *Journal of Financial Economics* 2: 323–39.

Bryant, John. 1980. "A Model of Reserves, Bank Runs, and Deposit Insurance." *Journal of Banking and Finance* 4: 335–44.

Chari, V. V., and Jagannathan, Ravi. 1984. "Banking Panics, Information and Rational Expectations Equilibrium." Kellogg School of Management, Northwestern University (mimeo), July.

Cone, Kenneth R. 1983. "Regulation of Depository Financial Institutions." Ph.D. Dissertation, Stanford University.

Diamond, Douglas W. 1987. "Asset Services and Financial Intermediation." Discussion, Chapter 8, this volume.

Diamond, Douglas, and Dybvig, Philip. 1983. "Bank Runs, Deposit Insurance, and Liquidity." *Journal of Political Economy* 91: 401–19.

Fama, Eugene F. 1980. "Banking in the Theory of Finance." *Journal of Monetary Economics* 6: 39–57.

———. 1985. "What's Different about Banks?" *Journal of Monetary Economics* 15: 29–39.

Gorton, Gary. 1985. "Bank Suspension of Convertibility." *Journal of Monetary Economics* 15: 177–93.

Greenwald, Bruce, and Stiglitz, Joseph. 1986. "Information, Finance Constraints and Business Fluctuations." Bellcore (mimeo).

Greenwald, Bruce; Stiglitz, Joseph; and Weiss, Andrew. 1984. "Information Imperfections and the Capital Markets." *American Economic Review* 74: 194–99.

Hammond, Peter. 1983. "Multilateral Incentive Compatibility in Continuum Economies." Stanford University (mimeo), December.

Haubrich, Joseph, and King, Robert. "Banking and Insurance." University of Rochester (mimeo).

Jacklin, Charles J. 1987. "Demand Deposits, Trading Restrictions, and Risk Sharing." Stanford (mimeo). In Ed Prescott and Neil Wallace, eds., *Financial Intermediation and Intertemporal Trade*. Minneapolis: University of Minnesota Press.

———. 1985. "Essays in Banking." Ph.D. Dissertation, Stanford University.

Jacklin, Charles J., and Bhattacharya, Sudipto. 1985. "Distinguishing Panics and Information-Based Bank Runs: Welfare and Policy Implications." CRSP Working paper No. 163, University of Chicago, Graduate School of Business; forthcoming in the *Journal of Political Economy*.

Jaffee, Dwight. 1971. *Credit Rationing and the Commercial Loan Market*. New York: John Wiley.

Jaffee, Dwight, and Russell, T. 1976. "Imperfect Information and Credit Rationing." *Quarterly Journal of Economics* 90: 651–66.

Kareken, John H. 1986. "Federal Bank Regulatory Policy: A Description and Some Observations." *Journal of Business* 59: 3–48.

Keeton, W. 1979. *Equilibrium Credit Rationing*. New York: Garland Press.

Leland, Hayne, and Pyle, David. 1977. "Informational Asymmetries, Financial Structure, and Financial Intermediation." *Journal of Finance* 32: 371–87. Reprinted Chapter 8, this volume.

Majluf, Nicholas S., and Myers, Stewart C. 1984. "Corporate Financing and Investment Decisions When Firms Have Information That Investors Do Not Have." *Journal of Financial Economics* 13: 187–221.

Nakamura, Leonard I. 1984. "Bankruptcy and the Informational Problems of Commercial Bank Lending." Princeton financial research memorandum No. 51, November.

Postlewaite, Andrew, and Vives, Xavier. 1986. "Bank Runs as an Equilibrium Phenomenon." University of Pennsylvania (mimeo).

Rothschild, Michael, and Stiglitz, Joseph E. 1976. "Equilibrium in Competitive Insurance Markets: The Economics of Incomplete Information." *Quarterly Journal of Economics* 90: 629–50.

Smith, Bruce. 1984. "Private Information, Deposit Interest Rates, and the Stability of the Banking System." *Journal of Monetary Economics* 14: 293–318.

Stiglitz, Joseph, and Weiss, Andrew. 1981. "Credit Rationing in Markets with Imperfect Information." *American Economic Review* 71: 393–410.

———. 1983. "Incentive Effects of Terminations: Applications to the Credit and Labor Markets." *American Economic Review* 73: 912–27.

———. 1986. "Credit Rationing and Collateral." Bellcore working paper.

Varian, Hal R. 1974. "Envy, Equity, and Efficiency." *Journal of Economic Theory* 9: 63–91.

Waldo, Douglas. 1985. "Bank Runs, the Deposit-Currency Ratio and the Interest Rate." *Journal of Monetary Economics* 15: 269–77.

Woodford, Michael. 1986. "Expectations, Finance and Aggregate Instability." Columbia University (mimeo).

Market Anticipations of Government Policies and the Price of Gold

Stephen W. Salant and Dale W. Henderson

Board of Governors, Federal Reserve System

This paper is an analysis of the effects of anticipations of government sales policies on the real price of gold. Although the risk of a future government gold auction depresses the price, it also causes the price to rise in percentage terms faster than the real rate of interest and at an increasing rate. Even risk-neutral investors require this rate of return as inducement to hold gold in the face of the asymmetric risk of a price collapse. Announcements making a government auction more probable cause a sudden drop in the price. Government attempts to peg the price or to defend a price ceiling with sales from its stockpile must result eventually in a sudden attack by speculators.

Between March 1968, when central banks stopped their pegging operations, and December 1974, when the U.S. government announced its first gold auction, the path of the real gold price (shown in fig. 1) exhibited two striking features. First, the price rose at a rate much greater than the real rate of interest for intervals as long as 8 months. Second, each upward surge was interrupted by a sharp setback. During that 6-year period, little or no gold was actually decumulated from the massive stockpiles controlled by world governments. But since the role of gold in the international monetary system had been reduced, the possibility persisted that significant sales to the private market might some day occur. Because of its profound

Our colleague, Jeffrey Shafer, showed us that, if there were some reason why price might fall to a constant floor, observed prices would accelerate away from that floor. For his initial idea and subsequent insights, we wish to acknowledge our debt. Helpful comments on Salant and Henderson (1974) and several memoranda by us which formed the basis for this paper were received from Ralph Bryant, George Henry, Walter Salant, Steven Salop, Charles Siegman, Edwin Truman, and Henry Wallich. No one but the authors is responsible for the paper's remaining shortcomings. This paper represents the views of the authors and should not be interpreted as reflecting the views of the Federal Reserve System or other members of its staff.

[*Journal of Political Economy*, 1978, vol. 86, no. 4]
© 1978 by The University of Chicago. 0022-3808/78/8604-0006$01.93

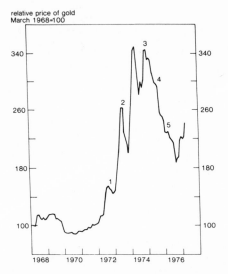

Fig. 1.—Monthly index of the dollar price of gold relative to the U.S. Consumer Price Index. *1*, First explicit reports that the United States and the IMF were considering gold sales. *2*, Reports of impending agreement to permit central bank sales. *3*, Announcement of first U.S. auction. *4*, Announcement of second U.S. auction. *5*, Agreement reached in Jamaica on IMF gold sales.

consequences, this possibility could not be disregarded by market participants owning gold. Government stocks are about 25 times as large as global annual production at its peak and are roughly equal to estimates of the entire stock remaining underground on the planet.[1] In our view, market anticipations that governments would sell a portion of these stocks at an unpredictable time exerted a significant influence on the gold price during this period. Since then, the United States and the International Monetary Fund have publicly sold, or announced schedules to sell, about 4 percent of the total stock overhang. It seems reasonable to expect further sales in the future.

The purpose of this paper is to explain the effects of anticipations of government gold policies on the path of the gold price. Since gold, like any other ore, can be depleted (through use in dentistry and industry) but not created, the conventional theory of depletable resources should be useful in understanding the behavior of the gold price.[2] However, it is argued

---

[1] Data on annual world gold extraction appear in Samuel Montagu & Co. (1977), and data on gold reserves held by world governments and international organizations are included in International Monetary Fund (1977).

[2] The basic theory of exhaustible resources was developed by Hotelling (1931). Solow (1974) provides a lucid exposition of this theory. Analyses of gold as an exhaustible resource can be traced to Paish (1938). Thomas Wolfe, the former director of the Office of Domestic Gold and Silver Operations of the Treasury, has emphasized that "[g]old is among the few minerals that could reach a critical supply situation within this century, taking account of available reserves above and below ground" (1977, p. 35).

in Section I that without some modification the standard theory cannot be used to explain how the price of a resource traded by competitive speculators could persistently rise by more than the rate of interest, nor can it be employed to account persuasively for the timing of the observed breaks in the price. In Section II, the standard Hotelling model is extended to the case where risk-neutral agents anticipate an auction of an additional stock at an unknown time. Properties of the anticipations model are established in Section III. The consequences of anticipations of other government policies involving gold sales are considered in Section IV. Section V contains concluding remarks.

I. The Inability of the Standard Model of Exhaustible Resources to Explain the Observed Movements in the Gold Price

To review the simplest model of an extraction industry, suppose a collection of competitive firms with zero extraction costs and fixed stocks of known size sell to consumers whose demand at any time depends only on the price then prevailing in the market.[3] Under such circumstances, only one sequence of prices will make the optimal decisions of extractors and consumers consistent at all times. The equilibrium price path must begin at a specified level and rise at the rate of interest during all periods of positive sales. If the price did not rise at that rate, some prices would have lower discounted values than others. Mine owners maximizing the present value of their profits would sell nothing in those periods, and excess demand would then result. Similarly, if the initial price were set too low (high), the cumulative amount demanded by consumers would exceed (fall short of) the cumulative supply, an indication that some of the intertemporal sequence of markets would fail to clear.

When speculators with neither costs of storage nor initial inventories are added to this model, the equilibrium price path does not change. Extraction in a period where speculators buy (sell) exceeds (falls short of) gold consumption, the difference going into (coming from) speculative inventories. While competitive extractors make profits because of the rents on the scarce resource they own, competitive speculators make no profits.

In this simple form, the exhaustible-resource model fails to capture the most salient characteristics of the price path of gold since 1968. It does not predict persistent increases in the price at greater than the rate of interest, nor can it explain either the existence or timing of most drops in the price.[4]

---

[3] Consumers, who purchase goods and services produced using gold, ultimately determine how much gold is bought by jewelry fabricators, dentists, and electronics firms. It is these derived demands which add up to the flow demand curve. Gold used for these purposes is assumed not to be used again, either because of the taboos of society or because of prohibitive costs of recovery.

[4] It does suggest that gold extraction might fall as price rises, a phenomenon which has occurred, to the puzzlement of some analysts.

However, since the assumptions of this naive model do not reflect several prominent features of the gold market, the omission of some important characteristic may account for the poor predictive performance of the model.

Three characteristics of gold distinguish it from the exhaustible resource of the simple model. First, extraction costs in the gold industry are not negligible and have risen. Second, the gold market is not competitive but is dominated by one seller, the South African Reserve Bank.[5] Third, gold holders cannot know with certainty the size of the stock which will be available for private use since the possibility always exists that governments may sell to the private market some of their enormous holdings.

Of these three distinguishing features of the gold market,[6] only the third could account for the basic characteristics of the observed gold price path. For, while the presence of soaring extraction costs or of monopolistic behavior could conceivably give rise to the observed pattern of prices in

---

[5] The Reserve Bank acquires and markets all South African production, an amount equal to three-quarters of the world total. This arrangement creates a presumption that the Reserve Bank takes account of its influence on market price as Machlup (1969) speculated. Since, in 1970 and 1971, the bank sold part of its supply to the IMF and some central banks in order to avoid reducing the higher price on the free market, the inference that it considers its market power in its sales decisions seems inescapable. The prices the Reserve Bank received from the two different sets of buyers may be used to infer the bank's estimate of the elasticity of the demand for gold at the time. In both 1970 and 1971, South Africa sold gold to the IMF and some central banks at $35 an ounce and to the free market at the higher market price of $40. Such behavior implies that South Africa estimated the marginal revenue of selling another unit on the private market to be $35 or, equivalently, estimated the elasticity of the (excess) demand facing it to be about 8. To infer the elasticity of *aggregate* demand from this information requires an additional assumption about how South Africa perceived its dominant position in the gold market. If it did not take into consideration how other sellers would react to changes in its sales (the "Cournot" assumption), the elasticity of aggregate demand would simply equal the elasticity of excess demand, estimated above, multiplied by South Africa's market share at the time. If it considered that other extractors would sell more when it sold less (the "Stackelberg" assumption), the implied elasticity of aggregate demand would be lower. For models of a dominant resource extractor which utilize the "Cournot" and the "Stackelberg" solution concepts, see Salant 1976 and 1978, respectively.

[6] There may be a fourth characteristic of gold which distinguishes it from the exhaustible resource of the simple model. In the simple model speculators and zero-cost extractors are willing to hold the existing stock of gold only if its price is increasing at the rate of interest. However, it has been suggested that some people may derive services from the mere presence of bullion. Such individuals would be willing to rent gold from its owners in order to obtain these services. As long as gold owners receive a positive rental income, the rate of increase in the gold price sufficient to induce them to hold title to the gold stock would be even *smaller* than the rate of interest. (In fact, industrial depletion may eventually be choked off altogether, and owners of the remaining stock would then earn only a rental income.) Hence, although the introduction of a demand for services derived from the presence of gold would increase the realism and complexity of the model, it would contribute nothing to an explanation of the observed, rapid surges in the price. An analysis of the effects of introducing a demand for services derived from the stock of an exhaustible resource into the simple model is available on request.

the absence of speculators,[7] *neither factor could explain the observed pattern in a world where competitive speculators can enter and do operate.* Since competitive gold speculators have no extraction costs and negligible storage costs, they prevent the price from persistently rising in percentage terms faster than the rate of interest. For, if speculators came to foresee a more rapid increase, they would attempt to make unlimited profits by borrowing, buying gold in one period, and selling it in the next—thereby carrying cheaper ore into a period in which it would have been more expensive. Such actions would cause the price path to change until all foreseeable opportunities for profitable arbitrage were eliminated.

II. An Alternative Model to Explain Gold Price Movements

Since competitive speculators place an upper bound on the rate of increase of the gold price under the circumstances considered so far, a model which purports to explain movements in these prices must explain why speculators did not flood the gold market when persistently faced with apparently unexploited profit opportunities. We believe the key ingredient in such an explanation is the persistent anticipation of gold holders that a portion of the large stocks held by the world's governments would be sold on the private market at an unpredictable time. This possibility had been mentioned repeatedly in trade journals, official statements, and newspapers long before the U.S. government finally announced its first gold auction.[8] In the words of the *New York Times* (May 24, 1974), "The 'sword of Damocles' over gold's high price is the huge dormant supply in the central banks." It is argued here that the threat that this sword would drop would have been sufficient to cause rapid increases in the gold price even in the absence of rising extraction costs and South African market power.

To clarify how the risk of government selling affects the path of the gold

[7] Hotelling (1931) and Solow (1974) study competitive extractors with positive marginal extraction costs. The behavior of a single monopolistic extractor is analyzed in Hotelling (1931), Weinstein and Zeckhauser (1975), Lewis (1976), and Stiglitz (1976). Although both Weinstein and Zeckhauser (1975) and Lewis (1976) indicate that an unconstrained monopolistic extractor might set a price path rising faster than the rate of interest, Salant (1976) and Stiglitz (1976) show that such paths cannot characterize an equilibrium in the presence of speculators. The constraints imposed on a monopolist by competitive speculators are completely analogous to those considered by Smithies (1941). He considered the single producer of a commodity who wishes to sell it in spatially separated markets at different prices but who knows he cannot (because of arbitrageurs) let prices diverge between markets by more than transportation costs. In an intertemporal model the markets are separated in time, and the cost of transporting through time is the rate of interest.

[8] For example, Samuel Montagu & Co., Ltd. cautioned, "Serious consideration has therefore also been given to sales of gold by monetary authorities, and these cannot be excluded in the future" (1973, p. 12). A year later, the warning was renewed that "the very large gold holdings of investors and central banks cannot be ignored" (1974, p. 13).

price, we retain most of the assumptions of the simple model discussed in the previous section. It is assumed that mine owners have an initial gold stock of known size ($\bar{I}$) which they extract costlessly and sell competitively. Speculators without storage costs or initial inventories are free to purchase gold and subsequently resell it. The consumers' demand curve for gold [$D(\cdot)$] is assumed to be stationary and downward sloping with a "choke" price (P_c) above which demand is zero.

What makes the modified model different is the possibility of government gold sales. To treat the simplest case, we assume a known amount ($\bar{G}$) may be sold in a single auction at an unknown date.[9] Mine owners and speculators are assumed to assess the odds of a sale in the next period,[10] given that none has so far been announced, as some constant α.[11] Let P_t be the price which will emerge at time t in the absence of an auction and f_t be the real price which will result if the auction occurs. Since agents are assumed to be risk-neutral, they act to maximize discounted expected profits. The stock of gold in private hands at the beginning of period t in the absence of an auction is denoted S_t.

Under these assumptions, five conditions determine the equilibrium paths of the variables in the model. In the initial period the private sector has what gold is in the mines:

$$S_0 = \bar{I} \qquad \text{(initial condition)}. \tag{1}$$

[9] The extension to the case of anticipations of multiple auctions announced at random times is available on request.

[10] The simplifying assumption that market participants regard the timing of government gold sales as an entirely exogenous random process implies that agents cannot use market variables (like price) to improve their forecasts of government behavior. Although this assumption eliminates interesting considerations of game theory—which may well be relevant in the future—we think that market participants have had no reasonable basis for believing that government sales decisions to date were related to market behavior. For a not dissimilar view, see Wolfe (1977, p. 35).

[11] Alternatively, agents might have reasons to believe that the probability of an auction at t, given none has occurred before then, will vary over time. This complication can be incorporated merely by adding a time subscript to α in eq. (4). If this alternate specification implies that an auction will occur "soon enough" with probability one, the market would fully discount the event and the stock overhang would not have the effects described in the text. This point has occasionally been adduced as an objection to our analysis. We believe it to be valid as a logical possibility but demonstrably false as an empirical proposition. That is, as long as the market anticipates with probability one that the government will sell its stock some time before the date when $\bar{I}$ units would be depleted along a path rising at the rate of interest and generating cumulative demand of $\bar{G} + \bar{I}$, then the auction would occur soon enough, and the uncertainty about the exact timing of the auction would not matter. In such a situation, however, the announcement of an auction would not affect the price since the market would already have discounted the event that it would receive the stock in sufficient time. In reality, however, the announcement of each auction has triggered precipitous price declines. *This indicates that the market did not fully discount such announcements before they occurred.* Therefore, the overhang *should* have the effects described in the text.

Private gold holders sell all their gold before the endogenously determined terminal period (T) when price chokes off demand:

$$P_T = P_c,$$
$$S_T = 0, \qquad \text{(terminal conditions)}. \qquad (2)$$

If an auction occurs at time t, the private sector then owns $S_t + \bar{G}$ units of gold and, by assumption, no longer operates under the threat of a future auction. Hence, price grows over time at the real rate of interest (r) from the auction price (f_t) to the choke price. The potential auction price is determined by the condition that cumulative consumption along the price path exactly equals the stock in private hands:

$$\sum_{x=0}^{\infty} D[f_t(1 + r)^x] = \bar{G} + S_t \qquad \begin{array}{l}\text{(equation determining} \\ \text{potential auction price)}.\end{array} \qquad (3)$$

Equation (3) determines the potential auction price as an implicit function of the stock remaining in private hands at the time of the auction.

Since consumers demand gold in every period before T, mine owners and speculators must be willing both to sell gold and to carry some inventory of the metal. Risk-neutral private gold holders will be indifferent between these two activities only when they yield the same discounted expected profit. Opportunities for profitable arbitrage exist unless the price in period t is equal to the discounted value of the price then expected to prevail in period $t + 1$:[12]

$$P_t = \frac{\alpha f_{t+1} + (1 - \alpha)P_{t+1}}{(1 + r)} \qquad \text{(arbitrage equation)}. \qquad (4)$$

The private stock is depleted between period t and period $t + 1$ by the amount of nonrecoverable consumption in period t:

$$S_{t+1} = S_t - D(P_t) \qquad \text{(depletion equation)}. \qquad (5)$$

---

[12] Eq. (4) indicates that the discounted price expected in period t to prevail one period in the future is equal to the price in period t. It can be verified that a similar relation holds for the price expected in period t to prevail k periods in the future. That is,

$$\frac{E(X_{t+k} \mid P_t)}{(1 + r)^k} = P_t,$$

where X_{t+k} is the random price in period $t + k$. The verification is accomplished by showing that each side of the equation above is equal to the same intermediate expression: X_{t+k} may take on the following $k + 1$ values: $f_{t+i}(1 + r)^{k-i}$ with probability $\alpha(1 - \alpha)^{i-1}$, $i = 1, k$; P_{t+k} with (complementary) probability $(1 - \alpha)^k$. Thus,

$$\frac{E(X_{t+k} \mid P_t)}{(1 + r)^k} = \sum_{i=1}^{k} f_{t+i}(1 + r)^{-i} \alpha(1 - \alpha)^{i-1} + P_{t+k} \left[\frac{(1 - \alpha)}{(1 + r)}\right]^k.$$

That P_t is equal to the expression on the right-hand side of this equation can be verified by starting with the arbitrage eq. (4) and iterating $k - 1$ times to obtain P_t as a function of f_{t+i} $(i = 1, k)$ and P_{t+k}.

The model of equations (1) through (5) generates time paths for the price of gold in anticipation of an auction (P_t), the potential auction price (f_t), demand $[D(P_t)]$, and the private stock of gold (S_t). The number of periods (T) required to consume the initial private stock $(\bar{I})$ if the anticipated auction does not occur prior to its exhaustion is also determined.

To show that equations (1) through (5) determine these variables a backward solution is utilized. At the end, the private stock (S_T) and the price (P_T) in the absence of an anticipated auction are indicated by the terminal conditions. Using the private stock and equation (3), f_T—the price that would occur in the final period if there were an auction—can be calculated. Substituting P_T and f_T into equation (4) yields P_{T-1}, the price that must prevail at the beginning of the previous period in the absence of an auction. The stock in private hands in the previous period can then be determined from equation (5).

It has been shown that starting with the final values of the private stock (S_T) and price (P_T) in the absence of an auction, values for those same two variables one period earlier can be obtained. The process can be repeated to construct the time paths of the endogenous variables. Eventually, the private stock reaches the level specified by the initial condition,[13] and the backward iteration is terminated; T is calculated by counting the number of backward steps required for termination.[14]

---

[13] If the procedure described in the text is followed, the private stock may never build up exactly to the initial inventory since the analysis of the text is in discrete rather than continuous time. Formally, the arbitrage eq. (4) linking the price at $T - 1$ to the expected price at T holds with an inequality rather than equality because zero stock is carried into period T. Thus, $P_{T-1} \epsilon \{[\alpha f_T + (1 - \alpha)P_c]/[1 + r], P_c\}$. To insure that cumulative demand builds up exactly to the initial inventory, set P_{T-1} at the lower end of this interval and work backward in the manner described in the text, stopping in the first period in which cumulative demand exceeds $\bar{I}$. Then increase P_{T-1} until cumulative demand over the same number of periods is reduced exactly to $\bar{I}$. That this can be accomplished for P_{T-1} less than the upper limit of the interval is a consequence of the following observation: cumulative demand along a path of a given length beginning with P_{T-1} at the upper end of the interval is identical with cumulative demand along a path one period shorter beginning with P_{T-1} at the lower end of the interval. Since, by assumption, demand along the latter path was found to be smaller than I, raising P_{T-1} to the upper end of the interval and working back one period more will reduce cumulative demand too much. Since cumulative demand over a given number of periods is a continuous function of P_{T-1}, there exists some P_{T-1} in the closed interval above for which cumulative demand exactly matches the initial stock.

[14] It might be assumed that gold holders are uncertain about the amount of gold the government might sell but that the distribution of possible auction sizes is independent of the time of the auction and the size of the private stock. Under these assumptions the solution technique is only slightly different. For every auction size $(\tilde{g})$, the initial price of the auction $[f_t(g)]$ can be obtained from the following equation:

$$\sum_{x=0}^{\infty} D[f_t(\tilde{g}) \cdot (1 + r)^x] = \tilde{g} + S_t.$$

Using the probability distribution on $\tilde{g}$, the expected auction price (m_t) can be computed. This number replaces f_t in the backward solution described in the text.

III. Properties of the Model with Anticipations of an Auction

The most striking property of the anticipations model is that, prior to the auction, the price must rise in percentage terms by more than the rate of interest and at an increasing rate. Risk-neutral extractors and speculators require this rate of return to induce them to hold gold in the face of the asymmetric risk of a price collapse which would result if the government announced a sale. According to the arbitrage equation, the *expected* price in $t + 1$ must have the same discounted value as the price in period t. Given the intuitive proposition that a government auction in any period would reduce the price ($f_t < P_t$, for all t),[15] the price which would occur in period $t + 1$ in the absence of the government sale must have a larger discounted value than the price prevailing in the previous period:

$$P_t(1 + r) = \alpha f_{t+1} + (1 - \alpha)P_{t+1} < \alpha P_{t+1} + (1 - \alpha)P_{t+1} = P_{t+1}.$$

(6)

If the price were ever to rise at a slower rate prior to the auction, the expected discounted capital gain from owning gold would be negative, and no one would be willing to hold it as an asset.

The percentage increase in the price in anticipation of an auction must itself increase as time passes. To establish this property, we use the result proved below that the potential auction price rises by less than the rate of interest $[f_{t+1} < f_t(1 + r)]$. The arbitrage equation can be rearranged to yield an expression for R_t—the percentage increase in the price between period t and period $t + 1$:

$$R_t \equiv \frac{P_{t+1} - P_t}{P_t} = r + \frac{\alpha}{1 - \alpha}\left[(1 + r) - \frac{f_{t+1}}{P_t}\right].$$

(7)

Since it has been shown that the actual price prior to the auction rises by more than the rate of interest and since it is being supposed for the moment that the potential auction price rises by less than the rate of interest, the ratio (f_{t+1}/P_t) in the expression above must decline over time. Hence, R_t increases over time. From equation (7), it also is evident that there is an

---

[15] To prove that $P_t > f_t$ for all t, we assume the contrary $(P_t \leq f_t)$ for some t. It can then be shown that if $P_t \leq f_t$ for some t, $P_{t+i} \leq f_{t+i}$ for $i = 1, T - t$. But since $P_T > f_T$ (assuming $\bar{G} > 0$, this follows from [2] and [3]), the hypothesis generating this implication must be false, and $P_t > f_t$ for all t. Specifically, if $P_t \leq f_t$ for some t, (A) $f_{t+1} \geq f_t(1 + r)$. *Proof:* This result is established by changing the premise in the argument in the text used to establish that $f_{t+1} < f_t(1 + r)$ from $P_t > f_t$ to $P_t \leq f_t$. However, A implies that (B) $P_{t+1} \leq P_t(1 + r)$. *Proof:* $(1 + r)P_t = \alpha f_{t+1} + (1 - \alpha)P_{t+1} \geq \alpha P_t(1 + r) + (1 - \alpha)P_{t+1}$. Hence, the potential auction price would have to be greater than or equal to the price in anticipation of an auction in the next period: (C) $P_{t+1} \leq f_{t+1}$. *Proof:* $f_{t+1} \geq f_t(1 + r) \geq P_t(1 + r) \geq P_{t+1}$. By induction, the potential auction price would have to be greater than or equal to the price in anticipation of an auction for all subsequent t; but this generates a contradiction since $f_T < P_c = P_T$.

upper bound to the percentage increase in the price in anticipation of the auction:

$$R_t \leq \frac{\alpha + r}{1 - \alpha}.\tag{8}$$

It has been shown that market participants who are risk-neutral require the gold price to rise by more than the interest rate in order for them to hold gold in the face of the possible capital loss. If holders of gold were *averse* to risk and therefore preferred a safe return to a risky one with the same expected value, the return to gold holders would have to include a risk premium. In that case, the rise of the gold price would have to be even steeper, and R_t could exceed the upper bound given by (8).

To show that the potential auction price rises by less than the rate of interest $[f_{t+1} < f_t(1 + r)]$, we utilize equations (3) and (5). If the government auction occurs at t, the price drops to f_t; depletion equals $D(f_t)$; and the price consequently rises in the following period to $f_t(1 + r)$. A price path rising at the rate of interest from this initial level generates a cumulative demand equal to the stock then in private hands $[S_t + \bar{G} - D(f_t)]$. In the absence of an auction at t, however, the price is higher $(P_t > f_t)$, the depletion is consequently lower $[D(P_t) < D(f_t)]$, and the stock remaining at $t + 1$, $[S_t - D(P_t)]$, is therefore larger. If the government then auctions $\bar{G}$ units, the price (f_{t+1}) must fall below $f_t(1 + r)$ for the market to absorb the larger total stock. Since this argument applies to any period, the potential auction price must always grow by less than the rate of interest $[f_{t+1} < f_t(1 + r)$ for *all* $t]$.

An important consequence of this result is that the longer the government waits to auction its gold, the smaller the real discounted value of its proceeds. The exact magnitude of the loss cannot be determined without knowledge of the demand curve and various exogenous magnitudes. However, a lower bound to the loss can be deduced without such information under fairly general assumptions as shown in the Appendix.

The three paths in figure 2 illustrate what has been learned so far about the effects of the anticipation of government sales when gold holders are risk-neutral. Path AA is the path of prices which would emerge with no possibility of government selling. Along this path, price rises at the rate of interest. Since the natural logarithm of price is plotted against time, this path is represented by a straight line. Path BB is the path that emerges in the continued anticipation of sales *which have not yet occurred*. The slope of BB is always greater than the slope of AA, and rises as time passes. Path CC shows the path of the natural logarithm of f_t, the price which would potentially emerge each period if the government auctioned its stock in that period. It rises at a rate which is always below the rate of interest. Prior to the auction, the gold price moves along BB. If the auction occurs, the price jumps to CC and rises from it along a line parallel to AA.

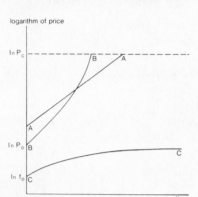

FIG. 2.—Price paths when a single auction is anticipated

In figure 2, the price path with risk (BB) begins lower, cuts the no-risk path (AA), and chokes demand sooner. To understand why this is so, recall that since the same stock $(\bar{I})$ must be depleted along both paths, cumulative demand along each path must be the same. Suppose the two paths began together. Since prices on the path with risk rise at a faster rate, this path would remain above the other and less would be consumed along it in each period. For the cumulative demand along each path to match, the price path with risk must begin lower. This implies that private gold stocks will be exhausted more quickly than they would be without the risk of government selling which fails to materialize.

That the price path with a risk of government sales should start lower and rise more steeply is intuitively appealing. Suppose society had a fixed stock of some exhaustible resource and had some chance, each period, of discovering a single additional deposit of known size. In that case, depleting more of the fixed stock in the early period than if there were no prospect of finding the additional amount would be sensible. However, if the additional stock were not "found," what remained after the early phase of rapid depletion should be rationed tightly. A group of competitive mine owners and speculators, acting in self-interest, would solve this planning problem by selling at low prices in early periods and very high prices later. Of course, in the case of government sales of gold, the "problem" solved by the market is artificial and man made; however, that makes the risk that additional supplies will topple the price no less real to private holders of gold.

It is helpful to consider what the model predicts will happen to the path of prices when unanticipated information becomes available. Suppose an official statement is made about the sale of monetary gold. If this statement causes speculators and mine owners to revise upward their estimate of the probability of government sales, the price of gold must fall and begin a new ascent;[16] if the intervention does not occur, the new path eventually rises above the old one and chokes off demand sooner. Figure 2 provides an illustration of this. When the odds of government selling increase (from zero to a positive fraction), the price immediately drops and follows the lower, steeper path. The reason for the drop, of course, is that holders of gold sell more quickly when faced with a higher probability of capital loss.

In fact, the sudden price declines of August 1972 and July 1973 (see fig. 1) appear to have resulted from exactly such revisions in the market's estimate of the odds of government sales. In the former episode, the revision was prompted by reports (*New York Times* August 2 and August 7, 1972) during the first week of August that the U.S. Treasury might consider selling gold to domestic users and by reports (*London Financial Times* August 4, 1972; *New York Times* August 7, 1972) in the second week of August that the Fund would ᵣecommend selling gold from its stocks (or from those of central banks) to the private market. In the latter episode, it was reported (*Washington Star News* July 14, 1973; *London Financial Times* July 21, 1973) during the second week of July 1973 that the Committee of 20 Deputies was in favor of official sales of gold in the free market as part of the reformed international monetary system.[17] In both episodes, the unanticipated reports triggered price declines although no official sales in fact took place; eventually, as the theory predicts, the price resumed its upward surge and surpassed its previous high.

The current discounted revenue which a mine owner or speculator can expect from the sale of a given amount of gold at any time in the future is equal to its current market value. When the odds of government sales increase, the market value of the existing stock falls. This serves to remind us that while the better prospect of additional supplies is socially beneficial the increased likelihood does injure owners of the existing stock. A country like South Africa, for example, would be injured by actions or announcements of world governments which substantially depress the gold price— just as it has benefitted substantially from previous international payments arrangements among nations which, in effect, constituted a commodity support program for gold.

---

[16] Suppose instead that the price path were initially *higher* after α increased. Then, as will be argued, eqq. (3) through (5) imply this path would have to *remain* higher until the choke price is reached. But then cumulative demand along the path with increased risk would be smaller than the initial stock, and excess supply would result. Hence, the path with increased risk must begin *strictly below* the other path, as is asserted in the text. Specifically, eqq. (3) through (5) imply that the path with increased risk must *remain* above the other path *if* it begins higher. From (7), the percentage increase in the price (R_t) is larger the larger is α and P_t and the smaller is f_{t+1}. If the path with increased risk ever approached the other path from above, it would have a larger α and P_t and a smaller f_{t+1}. Hence its percentage rate of increase in the next period would be higher, and the paths would never cross.

[17] As a noted market analyst observed, these reports "were instrumental in changing investors' attitudes to the gold market" (Samuel Montagu & Co., Ltd. 1974, p. 6).

IV. The Consequences of Market Anticipations of Alternative Government Policies

Up to now, the analysis has focused on the implications of market anticipations of a particular type of government gold policy, a single auction. In this section, the effects of market anticipations of three alternative gold policies are considered: a sequence of auctions, a price ceiling, and a pegged price.

It is worth considering the consequences of market anticipations of these alternative government policies for two reasons. First, since analysis of these cases involves the same methodology as that used in analyzing the case of anticipations of the announcement of a single auction, the general applicability of the approach is illustrated.[18] Second, it is conceivable that at some point in the future market participants might be given some reason to anticipate a government gold policy other than an auction. In addition, any analysis of the effects of anticipations of a policy requires a description of the effects of that policy when it is actually announced. Such a description provides a basis for understanding what happened in the gold market when the same policy or a similar policy was pursued in the past even if it had not been anticipated.

The approach used to analyze the effects of anticipations of each of the three alternative policies is essentially the same as that utilized in Sections II and III. In each case the first step in the analysis is to determine the initial price on the path which emerges if an announcement is actually made in any period that the government will undertake a particular action. It is shown for each policy how this price depends on the size of the private stock at the time of the announcement. In each case the time path of all variables could then be computed by replacing equation (3) with this new relationship, retaining the other equations of the model, and utilizing a backward solution as in Section II. For the three policies considered, the properties of the price path in anticipation of the policy announcement are described as they were in Section III for the case of a single auction.

To begin, consider the consequences of market anticipations of an announcement by the government that it will conduct two auctions at which $\bar{G}_0$ and $\bar{G}_1$ will be sold, respectively, where $\bar{G}_0 + \bar{G}_1 = \bar{G}$. Suppose it is known that the first auction will take place at the time of the announcement and that the second will take place $k + 1$ periods later. For any given private stock, the post-announcement price path will not depend on how the fixed total stock ($\bar{G}$) is allocated between the two separate auctions provided one condition is met. Assume first that the private stock is zero and let DD in figure 3, top, represent the post-announcement price path

---

[18] Two interesting examples of this approach have recently become available (see Long 1975 and Dasgupta and Stiglitz 1976).

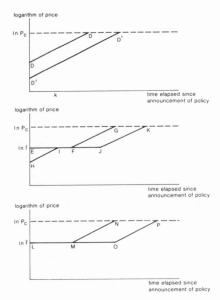

F$_{IG}$. 3.—Post-announcement price paths associated with alternative government policies. Top, sequence of auctions. Middle, price ceiling. Bottom, price peg.

which would result if the entire government stock were sold in the first
auction ($\bar{G}_0 = \bar{G}$). Now, suppose that $\bar{G}_0 < \bar{G}$. Provided the amount sold
at the first auction, $\bar{G}_0$, equals or exceeds the cumulative consumption
along DD for the $k + 1$ periods before the second auction occurs,[19] the
post-announcement price path is still DD. Furthermore, as long as $\bar{G}_0$
meets this condition, that is, as long as a sufficient amount of gold is sold
at the first auction, for any strictly positive private stock the post-announcement price path is the same no matter whether the government announces
one auction or two.[20] In such cases, the first price on the post-announcement price path, f_t, is determined by equation (3), and the set of equations
determining all the variables in each period is the same as in the case when
a single auction is anticipated.

[19] If $\bar{G}_0$ is smaller than the cumulative consumption along DD for the $k + 1$ periods
before the second auction occurs, the description of how to determine the post-announcement price path is considerably more involved. A complete analysis of the implications of
market anticipations of the announcement of a pair of auctions when $\bar{G}_0$ takes on small
values (including zero) is available from the authors on request. Assuming that $\bar{G}_0 = 0$
is equivalent to assuming that market participants anticipate that a single auction might
be announced but that there will be a delay between the announcement of the auction
and its execution.

[20] That is, as long as $\bar{G}_0$ meets the condition of the text, the post-announcement price
path will have only a single segment with price growing at the rate of interest, for all positive private stocks. The alternative possibility, that such a path has a downward jump,
can easily be ruled out.

Under such circumstances, therefore, the price path in anticipation of an announcement of a pair of auctions is *identical* with the case in which a single auction is anticipated. An analogous proposition can be established when a sequence of more than two auctions is anticipated.

Suppose instead that the market anticipates an announcement by the government that it will defend a real price ceiling, f, by standing ready to sell an amount of previously acquired gold, $\bar{G}$. Two possible post-announcement price paths are shown in figure 3, middle. If the private stock at the time of the announcement is zero, the post-announcement price path is a path like *EFG*.[21] The initial price on the post-announcement price path, f_t, is equal to f, and the government satisfies consumption demand at f for several periods as shown by *EF*. Eventually, private market participants realize that the remaining government stock can be exhausted along *FG*, a path which begins at f and rises at the rate of interest to the choke price.[22] Then the remaining government gold is purchased by market participants in a swift speculative "attack."[23] Consumption demand is satisfied from the newly acquired private stock.

If the private stock at the time of the announcement is strictly positive, the post-announcement price path is a path like *HIJK*. The first segment of the price path, *HI*, is a path which rises at the rate of interest and along which the entire private stock is just depleted by the time the price reaches f. If a ceiling is announced, private market participants realize that when f is reached the government will satisfy demand for some time at that price and that they will receive no capital gains during this time. Since private market participants have no incentive to hold gold in the absence of capital gains, they attempt to sell gold, and the price drops to the first price on *HI*. The rest of the price path is *IJK* which is a lateral translation of *EFG*. For a while the government satisfies demand from its stock; then there is a speculative attack in which private market participants buy up the rest

---

[21] It is assumed in the text that the stock the government is willing to sell to defend the ceiling exceeds the cumulative demand along a price path beginning at the specified ceiling price and rising to the choke price at the rate of interest. Suppose, instead, that the government reserves were smaller:

$$\bar{G} < \sum_{x=0}^{\infty} D[\bar{f}(1 + r)^x].$$

In that case, the post-announcement price path would have no flat segment, and the initial price on that path would be determined by eq. (3). The price path in anticipation of an announcement that the government will defend a ceiling would then be indistinguishable from the price path in anticipation of an auction.

[22] Actually, the market price which prevails in the period in which the attack occurs may be anywhere in the closed interval between $\bar{f}$ and $\bar{f}(1 + r)$. Of course, if the market price lies above f, those lucky enough to be able to purchase gold from the government make an immediate capital gain.

[23] The analysis implies that selling gold at a fixed real price results in a speculative attack. Of course, selling at a declining real price (or, equivalently, at a fixed nominal price in an inflationary world) makes the inevitable occur more quickly.

of the government stock. The larger the initial private stock, the lower the first price on the post-announcement price path, f_t, and the longer the time between the announcement and the time $\bar{f}$ is reached.[24] After $\bar{f}$ is reached the price path is the same no matter what the size of the private stock at the time of the announcement since only the government stock remains. Hence, by announcing that it is willing to defend a ceiling the government determines how much it will receive for its gold, but the timing of the required government sales and, therefore, the present value of the proceeds, is determined endogenously.

The properties of the price path which emerges in anticipation of an announced ceiling can now be summarized. At termination, when the private stock is zero, $P_T > f_T$ since $P_c > \bar{f}$. Using this condition, it can be demonstrated by repeating the proofs of Section III that in each period the price which emerges in the absence of an announcement is greater than the price which emerges if an announcement is made; that the first price on the post-announcement price path rises at less than the rate of interest; that the path of prices which emerges in the absence of an announcement rises at a rate greater than the rate of interest; and that this rate of increase itself increases over time. In short, the price path which emerges in anticipation of an announcement that a ceiling will be defended has properties similar to the corresponding price path when the event anticipated is an announcement of an auction.

Finally, consider the consequences of an announcement by the government that it will attempt to peg the gold price at a fixed real value, $\bar{f}$, by buying whatever gold is offered to it or by selling at that price whatever it has acquired plus its initial inventory of $\bar{G}$. Two possible post-announcement price paths are shown in figure 3, bottom. If the private stock at the time of the announcement is zero, the post-announcement price path is a path like LMN.[25] The government satisfies consumption demand for

---

[24] The first price on the post-announcement price path can be determined as follows:

A. If $S_t = 0$, $\qquad f_t = \bar{f}$;

B. If $S_t > 0$, $\qquad f_t$ solves $\sum_{x=0}^{\infty} E[f_t(1 + r)^x] = S_t$,

where $E[f_t(1 + r)^x]$ is equal to $D[f_t(1 + r)^x]$ when $f_t(1 + r)^x < \bar{f}$ and is equal to zero when $f_t(1 + r)^x \geq \bar{f}$; A and B determine the initial price if a ceiling is announced as an implicit function of the private stock and replace eq. (3) in the model of Secs. II and III.

[25] It is assumed in the text that the stock the government has on hand initially to peg the gold price exceeds the cumulative demand along a price path beginning at the specified peg and rising to the choke price at the rate of interest. Suppose, instead, that government reserves were smaller:

$$\bar{G} \leq \sum_{x=0}^{\infty} D[\bar{f}(1 + r)^x].$$

Two situations might arise. First, it is possible that

$$\bar{G} + I \leq \sum_{x=0}^{\infty} D[\bar{f}(1 + r)^x].$$

several periods, and the price remains at f as shown by LM. After a time, private market participants realize that the remaining government stock can be exhausted along MN, a path which begins at f and rises at the rate of interest to the choke price. Then the remaining government gold is purchased by market participants in a speculative attack. Consumption demand is satisfied from the newly acquired private stock.

If the private stock at the time of the announcement is positive, the post-announcement price path is a path like LOP. Private market participants realize that the government can sustain f for a time and that they will receive no capital gains during this time. Since both speculators and zero-cost extractors are unwilling to hold gold when they earn no capital gains, they immediately sell their entire stocks to the government at f.[26] The government alone then supplies gold to consumers at f for some time as shown by LO. Eventually, however, the augmented government stock is depleted to the point that it can be exhausted along OP, which is a lateral translation of MN, and the rest of the government gold is purchased in a

---

In this situation, if a pegging policy is announced the speculators attack immediately. The initial price on the post-announcement price path in each period is the same as if the government had announced an auction of its stock. The price path in anticipation of a pegging announcement is therefore *identical* with the path in anticipation of an auction. Second, it is possible that

$$\bar{G} + \bar{I} > \sum_{x=0}^{\infty} D[\bar{f}(1 + r)^x].$$

In this situation, the price path in anticipation of a pegging announcement will have two phases. In the last phase, depletion will have reduced the private stock below a critical level, $\bar{I}^*$, where

$$\bar{I}^* = \sum_{x=0}^{\infty} D[\bar{f}(1 + r)^x] - \bar{G}.$$

During this last phase, the pegging model is indistinguishable from the auction model of Sec. II for the reason given in the preceding paragraph. Now, consider the first phase, during which the private stock is strictly greater than $\bar{I}^*$. At the end of this phase (T') the private stock is $\bar{I}^*$; the price if a pegging policy is announced is $f_{T'} = \bar{f}$; and the price in the absence of such an announcement is $P_{T'}$. Since the end of this phase is also the beginning of the phase known to be identical with the model of Sec. II, $P_{T'} > \bar{f}$. The price path in anticipation of a pegging announcement prior to T' can be computed by working backward from these conditions and noting that $f_t = \bar{f}$, $t \leq T'$. For private stocks larger than $\bar{I}^*$ the path in anticipation of a pegging announcement differs from the path in anticipation of an auction. It has each of the properties discussed in Sec. IV between the designation for n. 27 and the end of the section. To verify this claim it is sufficient merely to replace the terminal condition used there ($P_T > \bar{f}$) with the condition mentioned above ($P_{T'} > \bar{f}$ when $S_{T'} = \bar{I}^*$) and then to repeat the relevant arguments.

[26] With increasing marginal extraction costs, each mine extracts more gradually and sells to the government over time. Initially, extraction proceeds at a declining rate so that marginal profit (the fixed government buying price less marginal cost) rises at the rate of interest. During this phase, consumers buy gold either directly from mines or else from the government. Eventually, however, the remaining government gold stock begins to be worth more than the price charged by the government. At that moment, the entire government stock is purchased in a speculative attack. It can be shown that speculators and extractors then coexist in the market for some period of time with both supplying bullion to consumers. Finally, however, the speculators exhaust their supplies, and the mines alone supply consumers until demand is choked off.

speculative attack. The larger the private stock, the longer the post-announcement price path remains at $\hat{f}$ and the longer the time between the announcement and the attack. The first price on the post-announcement price path is always $\hat{f}$ no matter what the size of the private stock, that is, $f_t = \hat{f}$ for all t.[27] The final segment of the post-announcement price path always begins at $\hat{f}$ and rises to P_c at the rate of interest.

Since the first price on the post-announcement price path is the same, regardless of the private stock, it is not difficult to establish the properties of the price path which emerges in anticipation of the announcement. The arbitrage condition (eq. [4]) can be rearranged to yield

$$P_{t+1} = \frac{1 + r}{1 - \alpha} P_t - \frac{\alpha}{1 - \alpha} \hat{f}. \tag{9}$$

From this difference equation it follows that unless the initial price, P_0, strictly exceeds $[\alpha/(r + \alpha)]\hat{f}$ (which is less than $\hat{f}$), price will subsequently remain at this value or fall below it. However, at termination, the price must reach the choke which is strictly greater than $\hat{f}$. Hence, the initial price must strictly exceed $[\alpha/(r + \alpha)]\hat{f}$, and the price path in anticipation of a pegging announcement must rise monotonically. Equation (9) can be rearranged to yield

$$R_t = \frac{P_{t+1} - P_t}{P_t} = r + \frac{\alpha}{1 - \alpha}\left[(1 + r) - \frac{\hat{f}}{P_t}\right]. \tag{10}$$

The price path may have an initial phase in which the rate of increase in the price is smaller than the rate of interest since $[\alpha/(r + \alpha)]\hat{f} < P_t < [\hat{f}/(1 + r)]$ implies $0 < R_t < r$. The potential peg may be so high that if the policy were announced before private stocks were substantially depleted gold holders would experience a capital gain in anticipation of which they would willingly hold gold earning less than the rate of interest. But since the price must reach the choke level, it must eventually exceed $[\hat{f}/(1 + r)]$. Hence, there will always be a final phase in which the percentage rate of increase in price exceeds the rate of interest. Equation (10) also implies that the percentage rate of increase in price always increases over time when an announcement of a pegging policy is anticipated.

V. Concluding Remarks

This paper has focused on the gold market. But, in concluding, we would like to note its pertinence to other problems of current concern. The analysis of the previous section, for example, indicates that attempts to restrict the price of any exhaustible resource by means of a buffer stock will in-

[27] This is the equation determining the potential price if it is announced that the gold price will be pegged at $\hat{f}$ and replaces eq. (3) in the model of Secs. II and III.

evitably result in a speculative attack. In this sense, recent proposals for the international stabilization of the prices of certain metals seem destined to fail. The auction model of Sections II and III may be viewed as the market solution to the social problem of how best to deplete existing reserves when additional supplies are anticipated to arrive at an unknown time. From this vantage point, the model applies equally to the optimal utilization of a reservoir when rain is anticipated to relieve a drought and to the utilization of proved reserves when exploration is anticipated to result in new discoveries.

Finally, to put our analysis in perspective, it should be noted that anticipations can affect capital formation as well as resource depletion. As we have seen, anticipations of government sales at an unknown time do not merely depress the gold price but also—because that reduced price stimulates more rapid depletion—have other effects which our paper has examined. Symmetrically, anticipations that at some unknown time the government will sharply increase its demand for, say, housing services or for the skills of nuclear physicists do not merely raise the current worth of owning such assets but also—because that increased value stimulates more rapid *expansion* of their stocks—have additional consequences, among which are depressed rents or wages, prior to the anticipated increase in demand.

Appendix

Anticipations of a Government Auction: A Continuous Time Treatment

The anticipations model of Sections II and III may be recast in continuous time by retaining equations (1) and (2) and modifying (3)–(5):

$$\int_{x=0}^{\infty} D[f(t)e^{\hat{r}x}]dx = \bar{G} + S(t) \tag{3'}$$

$$\frac{\dot{P}(t)}{P(t)} = r + \hat{\alpha}\left[1 - \frac{f(t)}{P(t)}\right] \tag{4'}$$

$$\dot{S}(t) = -D[P(t)] \tag{5'}$$

where $\hat{\alpha}$ and $\hat{r}$ are the continuous time analogues of α and r and

$$\hat{\alpha} = -\ln(1-\alpha),$$
$$\hat{r} = \ln(1+r).$$

Equation (4') may be derived in the following way. Holders of gold will force the current price to equal the discounted price now expected to prevail t moments in the future. This expected price is equal to the probability weighted average of the prices which would prevail at t if the auction occurred at different moments before t or if no auction occurred through t:

$$P(0)e^{\hat{r}t} = P(t)e^{-\hat{\alpha}t} + \int_{x=0}^{t} f(x)e^{\hat{r}(t-x)} \cdot \hat{\alpha}e^{-\hat{\alpha}x}\, dx.$$

Equation (4′) is obtained by differentiating this equation and simplifying the result.

The model can be solved most easily by utilizing the terminal conditions for P and S, working backward using the equations of motion (4′) and (5′), and stopping when S builds up to the initial inventory ($\bar{I}$). Alternatively, the initial price (P) can be determined by trial and error. For each initial price, the paths implied for P, f, and S can be deduced from equations (1) and (3′)–(5). Only one initial assignment of P will permit the terminal conditions (Z) to be satisfied.[28]

The properties of the model may be easily established. To prove that $f < P$ at every instant, assume the contrary ($f \geq P$, for some instant). From (4′), $\dot{P}/P \leq \hat{r}$. As will be shown below, (3′) implies that $\dot{f}/f = \{[\hat{r}D(P)]/[D(f)]\}$. Under the hypothesis that $f \geq P$, this would imply that $\dot{f}/f \geq \hat{r} \geq \dot{P}/P$. Hence, $f \geq P$ for all subsequent t. But since $f(T) < P(T)$, the consequence that $f \geq P$ for all subsequent t is inconsistent with the terminal conditions of the model. Hence the hypothesis ($f \geq P$ for some t), which generates that consequence, must be false.

Having established that $f < P$ for all t, we can infer immediately from (4′) that $\dot{P}/P > \hat{r}$. We will establish below that $\dot{f}/f < \hat{r}$. These two results and equation (4′) imply that $d/dt\{\dot{P}/P\} > 0$.

To establish that $\dot{f}/f = \hat{r}[D(P)/D(f)] < \hat{r}$, differentiate (3′) to obtain

$$\frac{df}{dS} = \frac{1}{\displaystyle\int_{x=0}^{\infty} e^{\hat{r}x} D'(fe^{\hat{r}x})\, dx} = -\frac{\hat{r}f}{D(f)},$$

use the chain rule to obtain $\dot{f}/f = 1/f \cdot (df/dS) \cdot \dot{S}$, and substitute the first result into the second equation.

To show conditions sufficient for the percentage increase in the potential auction price to decline over time, note that

$$\operatorname{sgn}\frac{d}{dt}\{\dot{f}/f\} = \operatorname{sgn}\frac{d}{dt}\{\ln \dot{f}/f\} = \operatorname{sgn}\frac{d}{dt}\{\ln D(P) - \ln D(f)\}$$

$$= \operatorname{sgn}\left\{\frac{\dot{f}}{f}\eta(f) - \frac{\dot{P}}{P}\eta(P)\right\},$$

where $\eta\,(\cdot)$ is absolute value of the point elasticity of demand. For all linear or concave demand curves and some convex demand curves, the magnitude of the demand elasticity rises with price. This is sufficient for the percentage increase in the auction price to decline over time as is illustrated in figures 2 and 4.

In this circumstance, a lower bound to the loss which the government would incur by postponing the auction can be derived. In figure 4, CC indicates the actual revenue per unit which the government would receive if it held the auction in x periods. On the other hand, CA indicates the revenue the government would receive if it sold its stock immediately and then let the proceeds earn interest for x periods. The difference represents the true loss from postponement. It is convenient to approximate the average revenue the government would receive from

---

[28] This latter approach can be used to verify that our results do not depend on the assumption that the demand curve has a choke price. If the demand curve were assumed to have no choke price, the terminal conditions (Z) would be replaced by $\lim_{t \to \infty} S_t = 0$. In this case, the trial and error procedure must be used to solve the model. Using this approach, it can again be shown (by contradiction) that $P_{(t)} > f_{(t)}$, for all t. Since all of the qualitative properties follow once this inequality is established, they continue to hold even if the demand curve is assumed to have no choke price.

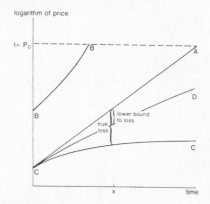

Fig. 4.—Lower bound on loss in government revenue from postponement of auction x periods.

an auction in x periods by assuming the potential auction price continues to grow in percentage terms at a constant rather than a declining rate. The approximation, which is represented by CD—the tangent to CC at C—overestimates the proceeds of the government and, therefore, underestimates its loss from postponing the auction for x periods.

A formula for this underestimate of the true loss can be computed as follows. If an auction occurred at t, the government would receive $f(t)$ per unit sold. If the auction occurred x years later, its discounted average revenue would be only $f(t + x)e^{-rx}$. Since $\dot{f}/f = D(P)/D(f) \cdot \hat{r}$, while, under the circumstances described above,

$$\frac{d}{dt}(\dot{f}/f) < 0, f(t + x)e^{-\hat{r}x} < f(t)e\{D[P(t)]/D[f(t)] - 1\}\hat{r}x,$$

the real discounted loss for a delay of length x is, therefore, equal to

$$\frac{f(t) - f(t + x)e^{-\hat{r}x}}{f(t)} > 1 - e\{D[P(t)]/D[f(t)] - 1\}\hat{r}x.$$

If, for example, demand at the current high price were 60 percent of the rate which would prevail if the auction were announced today and if the real rate of interest were 5 percent per year, then the postponement of the auction of a given amount for 10 years would cause a loss in real discounted revenue in excess of 18 percent.

References

Dasgupta, Partha, and Stiglitz, Joseph E. "Uncertainty and the Rate of Extraction under Alternative Institutional Arrangements." Technical Report no. 179, Inst. Math. Studies Soc. Sci., Stanford Univ., 1976.

Hotelling, Harold. "The Economics of Exhaustible Resources." *J.P.E.* 39, no. 2 (April 1931): 137–75.

International Monetary Fund. *International Financial Statistics*. Washington: International Monetary Fund, November 1977.

Lewis, Tracy R. "Monopoly Exploitation of an Exhaustible Resource." *J. Environmental Econ. and Management* 3 (October 1976): 198–204.

London Financial Times (August 4, 1972; July 21, 1973).

Long, Ngo V. "Resource Extraction under the Uncertainty about Possible Nationalization." *J. Econ. Theory* 10, no. 1 (February 1975): 42–53.

Machlup, Fritz. "Speculation on Gold Speculation." *A.E.R.* 59, no. 2 (May 1969): 332–43.

New York Times (August 2, August 7, 1972; May 24, 1974).

Paish, F. W. "Causes of Changes in the Gold Supply." *Economica*, n.s. 5 (November 1938): 379–409.

Salant, Stephen W. "Exhaustible Resources and Industrial Structure: A Nash-Cournot Approach to the World Oil Market." *J.P.E.* 84, no. 5 (October 1976): 1079–93.

———. "Staving Off the Backstop: Dynamic Limit Pricing with a Kinked Demand Curve." In *The Production and Pricing of Energy Resources*. Advances in the Economics of Energy Resources, vol. 2, edited by Robert S. Pindyck. Greenwich, Conn.: J.A.I. Press, 1978.

Salant, Stephen W., and Henderson, Dale W. "An Analysis of the Gold Market." Mimeographed. Washington: International Finance Division, Board of Governors of the Federal Reserve System, 1974.

Samuel Montagu & Co., Ltd. *Annual Bullion Review* 1972, 1973, and 1976. London: Montagu, 1973, 1974, and 1977.

Smithies, Arthur. "Monopolistic Price Policy in a Spatial Market." *Econometrica* 9 (January 1941): 63–73.

Solow, Robert M. "The Economics of Resources or the Resources of Economics." *A.E.R.* 64, no. 2 (May 1974): 1–14.

Stiglitz, Joseph E. "Monopoly and the Rate of Extraction of Exhaustible Resources." *A.E.R.* 66, no. 4 (September 1976): 655–61.

Washington Star-News (July 14, 1973).

Weinstein, Milton C., and Zeckhauser, Richard J. "The Optimal Consumption of Depletable Natural Resources." *Q.J.E.* 89, no. 3 (August 1975): 371–92.

Wolfe, Thomas A. "A Proposal for the Economic Use of Government Gold Stocks." *Mining Magazine* (January 1977), pp. 33–37.

discussion | **Theories of Speculation**

Jean Tirole

Massachusetts Institute of Technolgy

I. INTRODUCTION

The concept of "speculation" has always fascinated academics and members of the economic and financial community. Part of this fascination certainly comes from the fact that there is no well-accepted use of the word.[1] Various definitions have been offered to cover some of the many important facets of asset markets. The purpose of this comment is to briefly review and discuss these definitions.

II. FORECASTING FUTURE RETURNS

To start the review, we briefly come back to the economic setup behind the theory of asset markets. As is well known, in an (Arrow-Debreu) economy with complete markets all transactions occur initially, and only trades that are contracted for at date zero are implemented in the future. Markets need not reopen. This implies that agents do not have to forecast future prices. They, at most, form beliefs about the exogenous parameters of the economy.

When markets are incomplete and reopen over time, forecasting future returns becomes important. This is true even if markets are "essentially complete"—that is, if the set of existing assets spans the set of possible returns. Indeed, a necessary condition for essentially complete markets to perform the role of complete markets (and allow the economy to reach Pareto efficiency) is that traders perfectly foresee future prices (be they spot prices as in Arrow 1964 or asset prices as in Guesnerie and Jaffray 1974).

Giving a nontrivial role to asset markets implies that the traders forecast future prices (endogenous variables) and act on these forecasts. This forecasting activity may well correspond to the most frequent use of the word "speculation" in the nonacademic world.[2]

Let us next review the motives that lead agents to trade on asset markets. To

---

Research support from the Sloan Foundation and the National Science Foundation is gratefully acknowledged. The author is grateful to Sudipto Bhattacharya, Olivier Blanchard, and David Kreps for helpful comments.

simplify the taxonomy, let us consider an asset that represents a claim to some exogenously given (but possibly random) amount of real consumption tomorrow. Thus, we ensure that we focus on the trading of paper claims to consumption rather than on the creation or transformation of a real good.

Under rational expectations, traders will trade only if there exist gains from trade.

The first, and simplest, way to obtain trade gains is to introduce insurance motives. Asset markets are then seen as (generally imperfect) substitutes for Arrow-Debreu contingent markets. This is a well-developed theme in finance theory (starting with Keynes and Hicks). For instance, futures markets are means for producers with a risky output to hedge (for recent papers using this approach, see Danthine 1978 and Bray 1981). "Speculators" (a more appropriate name might be insurers) are often defined as those traders with a riskless initial position who are willing to share some of the producers' risk for a risk premium.

Second, some papers posit the existence of an exogenous (and possibly random) supply of (or demand for) the asset, or, more generally, this supply component does not explicitly come from an optimizing behavior (see Admati 1988 for a clear review of this approach). The existence of such supplies gives rise to gains from trade for the set of "rational" traders.

A third way of obtaining gains from trade considers the life-cycle aspect of savings. We will come back to this in detail in Section IV.

Fourth, traders may have "different beliefs" about the dividend (number of units of real good) attached to the asset. The word "beliefs" must be made precise. As a starting point, consider a simple Bayesian context in which the traders have the same priors about the dividend, and in which they obtain private information before trading (the structure of information is also common knowledge). Then if traders are risk neutral[3] and have rational expectations, they have no reason to trade.[4] This simple result is natural, because we know that in such a context only different priors can give rise to "gains from trade." So "different beliefs" should be taken to mean "different priors" rather than "different information," if we want to create a motive for trade (see Harrison and Kreps 1978 and Hirshleifer 1975, 1977 for studies of the implications of the existence of different priors). In this view speculators are traders who bet on opposite sides of the market because of their intrinsically divergent views of the world.

Lastly, I should mention the related literature on sequential trading with complete or incomplete markets (on whether agents trade again when markets reopen); for a review of this literature, see Hirshleifer and Riley (1979, section 2.2).

Remark. Interesting features of asset markets (e.g., price dynamics) can be obtained even in the absence of gains from trade. For instance, in a one-consumer economy, implicit asset prices can be computed that would clear asset markets if these were introduced (see, e.g., Lucas 1978).

III. ENDOGENOUS SUPPLY OF GOODS

In this section we focus not on the reallocation of exogenous claims to real consumption between traders as we did in the previous taxonomy, but on the supply of a given commodity. To some extent this is part of production theory. For instance, the Henderson-Salant (1978) gold suppliers decide on when to put ore on the market for consumption, in the tradition of Hotelling (1931). To do so, they forecast the influence of exogenous shocks to the supply of gold on the market price. "Speculators," in this sense, are suppliers of a commodity who choose the date of supply. No trading of paper claims to the good need be involved.

This definition of speculation is adopted in a number of contributions that followed Friedman's (1953) discussion of "stabilizing speculation" (e.g., Samuelson 1971, Schechtman and Scheinkman 1983, Salant 1983, 1984, Hart and Kreps 1986, Townsend 1977, Newbery and Stiglitz 1981, and references therein). Most of these contributions focus on storage, a special case of a production technology. Speculators buy the good on the spot market to resell it later on the spot market. Friedman argued that storage has a stabilizing influence—roughly, speculators buy the commodity on the spot market when the price is low and resell it when the price is high. So storage activity ought to be "stabilizing." There are lots of definitions that can be given to stabilization; see Hart and Kreps for a very lucid discussion of this. Unfortunately, the Friedman proposition does not always hold. Hart and Kreps and Salant offer examples in which a storage activity is destabilizing. Let us give the flavor of the Hart-Kreps example in which speculation, by all possible definitions, is destabilizing. In this example, demand is i.i.d. (independent identically distributed) and can be "high" or "low." It is inelastic when high, so the market price is not affected by past storage. When demand is low, traders get a "signal." If the signal is pessimistic, they do not store, and thus the current spot price is again unaffected by speculation if there has been no storage before. If the signal is optimistic, traders do store. This leaves the current price unaffected, because the low-state demand is inelastic for "normal" consumption. However, the low-state demand curve is downward sloping for higher consumptions; if next period's state of demand is low again, but next period's signal is pessimistic, there will be an increase in supply due to current speculation and a decrease in the spot price relative to the speculation-free case. So, most of the time, speculation does not affect the price, and the rest of the time, it reduces it when it was already low.

The word "stabilization" (like "speculation") has always exercised much fascination. However, it is not clear why we should care about this concept at all, as many authors have recognized (e.g., Hart and Kreps, Newbery and Stiglitz, and Salant). Salant even argues that "the Friedman proposition is not merely wrong.... It is also uninteresting." Indeed, the standard criterion for evaluating the desirability of economic activities is welfare or Pareto efficiency. "Stabilization," despite its seeming intuitive appeal, has no clear connection to Pareto optimality.

We know that a competitive equilibrium of an economy with production and complete markets is Pareto optimal. This applies in particular to economies with storage, which, as we said, is a special instance of production. Next, consider an economy with risk-neutral traders, which is done in most contributions. The absence of complete markets then need not prevent the competitive economy from reaching Pareto optimality. Indeed, the equilibria of the storage economies considered in Samuelson, Newbery and Stiglitz, and Schechtman and Scheinkman are Pareto optimal.

The effect of expectations on the supply of commodities has a lot of important facets, as shown by the above-mentioned contributions and by many others. I would formulate a slight (and unimportant) criticism of the use of the word "speculation" here. Giving content to this use generally consists of studying the economy with and without speculators. This explains why most contributions create a dichotomy between an exogenous intertemporal supply of the good and the activity that reallocates this supply of the good over time (storage). The equilibria with and without storage are then compared. However, in general, the initial supply is hardly exogenous. Investment and the choice of technology change the date of availability of commodities. Most forms of production thus have a speculative aspect to them, in the sense that they adapt the intertemporal supply of goods to expected market prices.[5] Thus this definition of speculation may be too broad.

IV. ASSET BUBBLES

Let us come back to the financial side of the economy, considered in Section II. To this purpose, we ignore the production process (Section III) to simply consider a claim that entitles its owner(s) to a flow of exogenously given dividends (i.e., units of real consumption): $\{d_t\}_{t=0,1,...}$. For simplicity, let d_t be deterministic for the moment.

In the rest of the chapter we focus on a definition of speculation due to Keynes (1936), which was more recently used by Harrison and Kreps (1978). This definition links speculation with the prospect of capital gains. To this purpose, let us consider the following thought experiment: suppose that there exists an infinitely lived agent (or family with strong bequest motives), and that, at date t, she is asked the following question: "Assuming that reselling the asset is prohibited, how much are you willing to pay for the asset?" If the capital market is perfect and r_t denotes the real rate of interest at time t, the agent answers

$$(1) \qquad F_t = \sum_{s=1}^{\infty} \frac{d_{t+s}}{(1 + r_{t+1})\cdots(1 + r_{t+s})}$$

in terms of real consumption. F_t, the real value of the asset, is called its *market fundamental*.

In a certain, perfect-foresight world, any asset is priced by arbitrage; the asset's price p_t (in terms of real consumption) must satisfy

(2) $$(1 + r_{t+1})p_t = p_{t+1} + d_{t+1}.$$

This first-order difference equation has a priori a family of solutions of the type

(3) $$p_t = F_t + B_t \text{ where } B_{t+1} = (1 + r_{t+1})B_t.$$

The family of solutions is indexed by the initial value of the B_t sequence (B_0). Furthermore, it is easily shown that if the asset can be freely disposed of, B_t must be nonnegative. See Tirole (1985, p. 1075).

B_t, the excess of the price over the market fundamental, is called the asset bubble. In an economy with infinitely lived agents, it is a measure of how much traders are willing to pay for the right to resell the asset.

A. Conditions of Existence of a Bubble

We already mentioned that a bubble must be nonnegative. Can it be strictly positive? An obvious requirement for a bubble to exist is that the asset be infinitely lived: if it is known that the asset stops being traded at time T, then at time T, $p_T = F_T$ ($= 0$ if dividends also stop being distributed after T). Thus, at $T - 1$, from the arbitrage equation, $p_{T-1} = (d_T + p_T)/(1 + r_T) = F_{T-1}$. So, $B_{T-1} = 0$. By backward induction, $B_0 = 0$.

Even if the asset is infinitely lived, an analysis of the economic environment surrounding the asset market is required to determine whether a bubble can exist. Although this is not crucial for finance theory, it is worth mentioning the existence conditions.

Consider first an economy with a finite number of infinitely lived traders. It can be shown that no bubble can exist in such an environment (see Tirole 1982). This proposition, which is very general (one could, for instance, introduce asymmetric information or short-sales constraints), rests on a simple intuition. From an aggregate point of view the asset is worth exactly its market fundamental; any trading is bound to be a zero-sum game. Suppose there exists a bubble on the asset. A possible trading strategy for an asset holder at date zero consists of selling the asset and leaving the market. This trader would then obtain more than the real value of her initial holdings. The set of remaining traders would then be stuck with an asset for which they would have paid more than what it will collectively be worth to them. More generally, the asset holder(s) might want to leave the market later on, but with a finite number of traders, not everyone can quit the market in finite time without someone being stuck with the asset (the "hot potato").

This suggests that we look at economies in which there is a constant inflow of new traders so that everyone can realize her capital gains without anyone being stuck with the asset. Samuelson (1958) built the first example of such an economy: the overlapping-generations model. He showed that in a model in which traders have finite lives, an asset that does not distribute dividends ($d_t = F_t = 0$) can have a strictly positive price (such an asset is called a *pure bubble*). The Samuelson model has later been worked thoroughly in too many contributions to be quoted here. Let us mention that the issue of bubbles is, in general, distinct from the issue of indeterminacy of equilibria in overlapping-generations economies, although, in the original Samuelson model, the indeterminacy is entirely due to bubbles. (Burmeister et al. 1973 show that in an economy with k capital goods, there can exist a continuum of equilibria converging to a given steady state. Kehoe and Levine 1985 show that the same phenomenon can occur in overlapping-generations exchange economies, and they study the dimensionality of the equilibrium set. Both results do not rely on the existence of bubbles.) However, even in overlapping-generations economies, bubbles may not exist. The general equilibrium setup may introduce "wealth constraints" that eliminate bubbles. The possibility of existence of bubbles roughly hinges on the comparison between the rate of interest of the "bubbleless" economy and the rate of growth of the economy. If the rate of interest exceeds the rate of growth, the bubble, which by arbitrage grows at the rate of interest, grows faster than the economy, so that at some point in time the savers cannot afford buying the asset from the dissavers. Let us simply mention that bubbles affect the interest rate by crowding out other assets such as capital and rents, and that only a study of underlying preferences, technology, and alternative assets can determine the conditions of their existence.[6]

Remark: Stochastic bubbles. The exposition has up to now assumed that bubbles are deterministic. But, just as the market fundamental of an asset can be stochastic (as in Henderson-Salant),[7] its bubble can also be stochastic. In particular, the bubble, and thus the asset price, can be contingent on "irrelevant" variables such as sunspots. Blanchard (1979a) gives an example of a bubble that bursts with positive probability at each period; it must then grow at a rate exceeding the rate of interest to offset the probability of bursting. Weil (1987) demonstrates the conditions under which such a phenomenon is consistent with general equilibrium. Similarly, Azariadis (1981) and Azariadis and Guesnerie (1983) construct economies in which a bubble follows a stationary process.

The latter general equilibrium approaches construct stochastic *aggregate* bubbles. But even if the aggregate bubble (that is, the sum of bubbles on all assets) is deterministic, the bubble on a particular asset need not be. If there exist several bubbly assets in the economy, there can be stochastic bubble substitution between these assets. The bubble on asset A can grow at the expense of that on asset B if there is a sunspot, and the reverse if there is no sunspot.

The possibility of the existence of a stochastic bubble naturally matters for tests of asset pricing, since many of these tests rely on the absence of a bubble (see, e.g., Shiller 1981, LeRoy and Porter 1981, and, for an econometric estimation with bubbles, Blanchard and Watson 1982).

B. Criticism of the Market Fundamental/Bubble Distinction

The price of an asset can always be decomposed into a market fundamental and a bubble, but this decomposition is not satisfactory for some assets. We mention here two main reasons for this.[8]

1. The Dividend May Not Be Independent of the Market Price. The previous assumption that d_t does not depend on p_t may be violated for some assets. To illustrate this, consider a diamond. Its dividend normally represents the enjoyment corresponding to looking at the diamond. It is then expressed in real terms, independently of the diamond's price.[9] However, in an economy in which snobbism effects exist, consumers may "enjoy" a diamond more if its price is higher (note that "enjoying more" refers to the dividend and is distinct from "being willing to pay more than for an artificial diamond," which can come from a bubble). This clearly creates problems with the dichotomy. Indeed, one can show that if, at each period, the dividend is proportional to the asset price, and if the coefficient of proportionality does not go to zero, then there cannot exist a bubble on the asset (for most assets, a bubble is feasible as long as the economic environment satisfies the conditions in IV.A). But there can then exist a multiplicity of market fundamentals. This reasoning also matters for an asset like money, whose liquidity value depends on its price in terms of a real good.

2. "Backed Assets." The second caveat in the dichotomy lies in the fact that some assets are backed, in the sense that their price cannot fall below some lower bound under which the asset would be used differently.

Consider the following metaphor. The produced good of Schmooland, the schmoo, is white. However, by a fluke, firms at date zero produce a few black schmoos. Everyone agrees that this productive miracle will never occur again. Also, it turns out that black schmoos and white schmoos are perfect substitutes in the consumers' utility function and that black schmoos are costlessly storable. At date zero everyone feels that, due to their scarcity, the black schmoos ought to be priced above the white schmoos; their price is equal to two, say, in terms of white schmoos. Assume that the rate of interest is zero. The price of black schmoos is then two forever. Thus, black schmoos are never consumed. They yield no dividend. Their market fundamental is equal to zero, and the bubble is equal to two.

Although there is no difficulty here, few people would say that the real value of black schmoos is zero. To give content to this objection, notice that, were their price to fall below one, the black schmoos would be consumed (i.e., destroyed as assets). Thus, the market fundamental does not necessarily represent the lower bound on the asset price. Along these lines, one can notice that, were the price of gold to fall considerably, the consumption of gold (dentistry, jewelry, engineering, etc.) would soar. Again, the real lower bound on the gold price (see Henderson-Salant for the computation of such a lower bound) exceeds the market fundamental of gold (zero, since gold ingots do not distribute dividends). Similarly, the lower bound on the stocks of the firm that does not distribute dividends exceeds its (zero) market fundamental (for instance, in a perfect-foresight frictionless economy, the lower bound equals the present discounted value of profits, rather than dividends).

3. Linear Models. The word "bubble" is also commonly used in linear models.[10,11] These models often start from a first-order difference equation. For instance, Flood and Garber (1980) use a Cagan money demand equation

$$(4) \qquad m_t - p_t = -\alpha(p_{t+1} - p_t),$$

where m_t = log of money stock, p_t = log of price of real consumption in terms of money (note that the notation differs from the previous one, which considered the price of an asset in terms of real consumption). Stochastic elements are usually added but are irrelevant to our discussion. Integrating (4), one obtains a family of solutions that are the sum of a "particular solution" or "forward solution" p_t^F and a "general solution" A_t of the homogeneous equation (indexed by its initial value A_0)

$$(5) \qquad p_t = p_t^F + A_t,$$

where

$$p_t^F = \sum_{s=0}^{\infty} \frac{\alpha^s}{(1+\alpha)^{s+1}} m_{t+s} \quad \text{and} \quad A_{t+1} = \frac{1+\alpha}{\alpha} A_t.$$

The particular solution p_t^T and the general solution A_t are often called *market fundamental* and *speculative bubble*, respectively. An analogy with the concepts defined earlier is that the first-order difference equation (4) without terminal condition also generally admits a one-parameter family of solutions. However, the two definitions differ. For instance, bubbles in the linear sense need not grow at the rate of interest (and the market fundamental need not represent the present discounted value of dividends).[12,13]

NOTES

[1] The *Oxford Universal Dictionary* gives several meanings to the word "speculation." Those of interest for our discussion are (a) "the faculty or power of seeing"; (b) "the exercise of the faculty of sight"; (c) "the action or practice of buying and selling goods, stocks and shares, etc., in order to profit by the rise or fall in the market value, as distinct from regular trading or investment."

[2] Sometimes speculation is even used to describe the forecast of exogenous variables such as the stock of oil in a field.

[3] This feature is not crucial, but, by ruling out insurance motives, allows a strong characterization.

[4] See Kreps (1977, section 6) for the original statement and proof of this result, Milgrom and Stokey (1982) for a generalization to more complex exchange economies and risk aversion, and Tirole (1982) for an extension of Kreps to a T-period model, in which traders receive private information over time.

[5] The Henderson-Salant gold owners example is also somewhat damaging for the dichotomy. If the fixed stock of gold is costlessly extracted and stored, it can either be entirely extracted and sold at date zero, in which case storage plays an important role, or it can be extracted to face demand at each period, in which case there is no storage. The two possibilities give rise to the same price path and owners' profits.

See also Benabou (1985), who looks at the strategic behavior of a monopolist who faces consumers who can store, has a cost of changing his price, and lives in an inflationary world.

[6] For a description of the crowding out, see Tirole (1985).

[7] The papers reviewed in Sections II and III rule out bubbles either explicitly or implicitly by positing a finite life for the asset.

[8] This discussion partly follows Tirole (1985, sections 7 and 8), to which the reader is referred for further details.

[9] The fact that artificial diamonds that cannot be distinguished with the naked eye from real ones command much lower prices does not contradict this statement. The difference may correspond to a bubble. If this hypothesis is correct, the price of an artificial diamond is a measure of the market fundamental.

[10] These have been thoroughly developed by, among others, Blanchard (1979b), Blanchard and Kahn (1980), Burmeister, Flood, and Garber (1983), Flood and Garber (1980), Gourieroux et al. (1982), Diba and Grossman (1985), and Taylor (1977).

[11] Note that equation (2) is linear only to the extent that the asset is small relative to the economy (p_t has no influence on r_t). But even if the asset is big relative to the economy, (2) can be integrated to obtain the dichotomy equation (3).

[12] Money is often the only asset in these economies. The rate of interest must then be obtained from the intertemporal marginal rate of substitution, or else one can introduce other assets, such as capital in the economy.

[13] A nonsemantic issue has to do with the use of linear models. Some (including myself) feel somewhat uncomfortable using such models to study solutions that may explode. Even if (4) can be derived as a one-period approximation of an optimizing model, it seems safer to use the nonlinear version of the model the way Brock (1975) and Obstfeld and Rogoff (1983) do for this model, for instance. Let us note in passing that these authors derive conditions under which a multiplicity of market fundamentals for money (in the sense of III.A and III.B) can exist.

REFERENCES

Admati, A. 1988. "Information in Financial Markets: The Rational Expectations Approach." Discussion, Chapter 14, this volume.

Arrow, K. 1964. "The Role of Securities in the Optimal Allocation of Risk Bearing." *The Review of Economic Studies* 31: 91–96.

Azariadis, C. 1981. "Self-Fulfilling Prophecies." *Journal of Economic Theory* 25: 380–96.

Azariadis, C., and Guesnerie, R. 1983. "The Persistence of Self-Fulfilling Theories" University of Pennsylvania (mimeo).

Benabou, R. 1985. "Optimal Price Dynamics and Speculation with a Storable Good." M.I.T. (mimeo).

Blanchard, O. 1979a. "Speculative Bubbles, Crashes and Rational Expectations." *Economics Letters* 3: 387–89.

———. 1979b. "Backward and Forward Solutions for Economies with Rational Expectations." *American Economic Review* 69: 114–18.

Blanchard, O., and Kahn, C. 1980. "The Solution of Linear Difference Models under Rational Expectations." *Econometrica* 48: 1305–12.

Blanchard, O., and Watson, M. 1982. "Bubbles, Rational Expectations and Financial Markets." In P. Wachtel, ed., *Crises in the Economic and Financial Structure.* Lexington, Mass.: Lexington Books.

Bray, M. 1981. "Futures Trading, Rational Expectations and the Efficient Market Hypothesis." *Econometrica* 49: 575–96.

Brock, W. 1975. "A Simple Perfect Foresight Monetary Model." *Journal of Monetary Economics* 1: 133–50.

Burmeister, E.; Caton, C.; Dobell, A.; and Ross, S. 1973. "The 'Saddlepoint Property' and the Structure of Dynamic Heterogeneous Capital Goods Models." *Econometrica* 41: 79–95.

Burmeister, E.; Flood, R.; and Garber, P. 1983. "On the Equivalence of Solutions in Rational Expectations Models." *Journal of Economic Dynamics and Control* 5: 311–21.

Danthine, J. P. 1978. "Information, Futures Prices and Stabilizing Speculation." *Journal of Economic Theory* 17: 79–98.

Diba, B., and Grossman, H. 1985. "The Impossibility of Rational Bubbles" (mimeo).

Flood, R., and Garber, P. 1980. "Market Fundamentals versus Price Level Bubbles: The First Tests." *Journal of Political Economy* 88: 745–70.

Friedman, M. 1953. *Essays in Positive Economics.* Chicago: University of Chicago Press.

Gourieroux, C.; Laffont, J.-J.; and Monfort, A. 1982. "Rational Expectations in Dynamic Linear Models: Analysis of the Solutions." *Econometrica* 50: 409–26.

Guesnerie, R., and Jaffray, J.-Y. 1974. "Optimality of Equilibrium of Plans, Prices and Price Expectations." In J. Dreze, ed., *Allocation under Uncertainty: Equilibrium and Optimality.* New York: Halsted Press.

Harrison, M., and Kreps, D. 1978. "Speculative Investor Behavior in a Stock Market with Heterogeneous Expectations." *Quarterly Journal of Economics* 92: 323–36.

Hart, O., and Kreps, D. 1986. "Price Destabilizing Speculation." *Journal of Political Economy* 94: 927–53.

Hirshleifer, J. 1975. "Speculation and Equilibrium: Information, Risks and Markets." *Quarterly Journal of Economics* 89: 519–42.

———. 1977. "The Theory of Speculation under Alternative Regimes of Markets." *Journal of Finance* 32: 975–1000.

Hirshleifer, J., and Riley, J. 1979. "The Analytics of Uncertainty and Information: An Expository Survey." *Journal of Economic Literature* 17: 1375–1421.

Hotelling, H. 1931. "The Economics of Exhaustible Resources." *Journal of Political Economy* 39: 131–75.

Kehoe, T., and Levine, D. 1985. "Comparative Statics and Perfect Foresight in Infinite Horizon Economies." *Econometrica* 53: 433–54.

Keynes, J. M. 1936. *The General Theory.* New York: Harcourt, Brace and World.

Kreps, D. 1977. "A Note on 'Fulfilled Expectations' Equilibria." *Journal of Economic Theory* 14: 32–43.

LeRoy, S., and Porter, R. 1981. "The Present-Value Relation: Tests Based on Implied Variance Bounds." *Econometrica* 49: 555–74.

Lucas, R. 1978. "Asset Prices in an Exchange Economy." *Econometrica* 46: 1429–45.

Milgrom, P., and Stokey, N. 1982. "Information, Trade and Common Knowledge." *Journal of Economic Theory* 26: 17–27.

Newbery, D., and Stiglitz, J. 1981. *The Theory of Commodity Price Stabilization: A Study in the Economics of Risk.* London: Oxford University Press.

Obstfeld, M., and Rogoff, K. 1983. "Speculative Hyperinflations in Maximizing Models: Can We Rule Them Out?" *Journal of Political Economy* 91: 675–87.

Salant, S. 1983. "The Vulnerability of Price Stabilization Schemes to Speculative Attack." *Journal of Political Economy* 91: 1–38.

———. 1984. "Profitable Speculation, Price Stability and Welfare" (mimeo).

Salant, S., and Henderson, D. 1978. "Market Anticipations of Government Policies and the Price of Gold." *Journal of Political Economy* 86: 627–48. Reprinted Chapter 10, this volume.

Samuelson, P. 1958. "An Exact Consumption-Loan Model of Interest with or without the Social Contrivance of Money." *Journal of Political Economy* 66: 467–82.

———. 1971. "Stochastic Speculative Prices." *Proceedings of the National Academy of Sciences.*

Schechtman, J., and Scheinkman, J. 1983. "A Simple Competitive Model with Production and Storage." *Review of Economic Studies* 50: 427–41.

Shiller, R. 1981. "Do Stock Prices Move too Much to Be Justified by Subsequent Changes in Dividends?" *American Economic Review* 71: 421–36.

Taylor, J. 1977. "On the Conditions for Unique Solutions in Stochastic Macroeconomic Models with Rational Expectations." *Econometrica* 45: 1377–85.

Tirole, J. 1982. "On the Possibility of Speculation under Rational Expectations." *Econometrica* 50: 1163–81.

———. 1985. "Asset Bubbles and Overlapping Generations." *Econometrica* 53: 1071–1100.

Townsend, R. 1977. "The Eventual Failure of Price Fixing Schemes." *Journal of Economic Theory* 14: 190–99.

Weil, P. 1987. "Confidence and the Real Value of Money in an Overlapping Generations Economy." *Quarterly Journal of Economics* 102: 1–22.